D1032404

TREE NUTS:
PRODUCTION
PROCESSING
PRODUCTS

SECOND EDITION

TREE NUTS

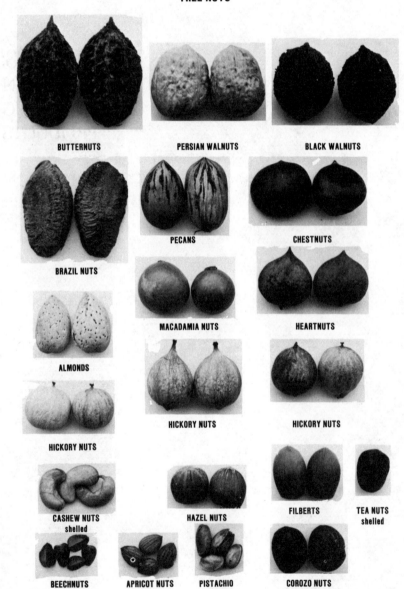

BUTTERNUTS

PERSIAN WALNUTS

BLACK WALNUTS

BRAZIL NUTS

PECANS

CHESTNUTS

ALMONDS

MACADAMIA NUTS

HEARTNUTS

HICKORY NUTS

HICKORY NUTS

HICKORY NUTS

CASHEW NUTS
shelled

HAZEL NUTS

FILBERTS

TEA NUTS
shelled

BEECHNUTS

APRICOT NUTS
shelled

PISTACHIO
NUTS

COROZO NUTS
shelled

TREE NUTS:
PRODUCTION
PROCESSING
PRODUCTS
SECOND EDITION

Jasper Guy Woodroof
University of Georgia

AVI PUBLISHING COMPANY, INC.
Westport, Connecticut

Library of Congress Cataloging in Publication Data

Woodroof, Jasper Guy, 1900-
    Tree nuts.

    Includes index.
    1. Nuts.   2. Nut products.   3. Cookery (Nuts)
I. Title.
SB401.A4W6   1979   641.3'4'5   78-24259
ISBN 0-87055-254-6

Printed in the United States of America

Preface To
The Second Edition

Tree nuts are the edible kernels of seeds of trees. They were one of man's important sources of food from prehistoric times. Through the centuries many tree nuts have been improved and domesticated. Among the cultivated tree nuts are almonds, apricot nuts, Brazil nuts, butternuts, cashew nuts, chestnuts, filberts, heartnuts, hickory nuts, pecans, black walnuts and Persian (English) walnuts. Among the important wild nuts in commerce are: apricot nuts, beechnuts, chestnuts, chinquapins, heartnuts, hickory nuts, pecans, pine nuts and black walnuts.

An average of 281,000 metric tons of tree nuts enter the channels of world trade, with an estimated 2000 tons being harvested and consumed, but not reported. Tree nuts are grown, processed and consumed in temperate climates around the world, and are being continuously improved by horticulturists, plant breeders, engineers, entomologists, plant pathologists, food scientists, nutritionists and food manufacturers.

The purpose of this book is to update the technical science and statistical data on production, processing and products of tree nuts, to increase the profit and to enhance the pleasure of growing and eating more than 20 kinds of tree nuts.

Tree nuts are among the most nutritionally concentrated human foods. They are high in oil, protein, certain vitamins and minerals, as well as high in energy, flavor, desirable texture, stability and distinctiveness.

Grateful acknowledgement is made to the same companies and corporations that contributed data and illustrative material to the First Edition for doing the same for the Second Edition. Changes in contributions of individuals are shown in the individual chapters.

Important changes characterizing the Second Edition include the following:

Volumes I and II have been combined under one cover, with some changes in chapter headings. Chapters 13 through 18 of Volume II have been reorganized into one major unit on pecans—see Chapter 12.

Data on tree nut production, exports, imports and processing have been updated in many tables, and several new figures used.

Tables for metric conversion are included in the Appendix. Metric equivalents for temperatures are used in the text. Formulas for spraying, fertilizing and product manufacture have been retained in English units (with reference to metric conversion tables).

"Cultivar" is used for "variety" of tree nuts throughout.

Chapter 4 has been enlarged to cover "Nutmeats in Candy Plants, Restaurants and Homes." In Chapter 12 the sections on "Irrigation of Pecans," "Controlling Weeds in Pecan Orchards," "Alternate Bearing in Pecans" and "Pecan Orchard Diseases and Insects" have been rewritten by new contributors. Chapter 14 on "Pistachio Nuts" has been rewritten by a new contributor, as has Chapter 16 on "Persian Walnuts."

Two additional nuts are included in Chapter 17, raising the number of nuts discussed in this edition to 20 kinds, 25 species and about 300 cultivars.

It is a pleasure to acknowledge the assistance of Karen Klivington, AVI Editorial Department, in bringing out this new edition. Thanks are extended also to Naomi C. Woodroof (my wife), Ann Autry and Jeanne Britt for assistance in copying and editing the manuscript.

JASPER GUY WOODROOF
Griffin, Georgia

November 1978

Preface To
The First Edition

Tree nuts are one of the oldest sources of food for man, birds and wild animals. Production and per capita consumption have continued to increase, especially during the past century. Methods of processing have been steadily improved, and formulas for using them approach 2,000. There is need for *Tree Nuts: Production, Processing and Products* to be brought up to date.

The book was prepared for those who grow, harvest, store, import, export, process, or manufacture products from nuts. It should be useful for teachers, researchers, and Cooperative Extension workers. The information is applicable to horticulturists, food scientists, human nutritionists, and to those in related fields.

The quality and quantity of tree nuts are influenced by many factors. These are discussed for each kind of nuts under varieties, soils, climate, culture, pest control, harvesting methods, storage facilities, methods of shelling and grading, containers and manufacturing procedures. Recipes for using nuts in the home and public eating places are included.

The information was prepared by more than a dozen specialists in their field. Sources of information were from personal experience; visits to many foreign countries by one or more of the contributors; trade associations which were most cooperative; proceedings of meetings recorded in journals on nut growing, food technology, food processing, horticulture, botany, chemistry, nutrition and others; and bulletins from numerous state, federal and commercial agencies.

Eleven kinds of tree nuts given major attention are: almonds, Brazil nuts, cashew nuts, chestnuts, filberts, Macadamia nuts, pecans, pine nuts, pistachio nuts, black walnuts and English walnuts. Six discussed, but given less attention, are: apricot nuts, beechnuts, butternuts, chinquapins, heartnuts and hickory nuts.

Sections prepared by specialists in their respective fields were:

Protection of Nuts from Insect Damage, H. Laudani, Entomologist, U.S. Department of Agriculture, Savannah, Georgia.

Candy Plant Sanitation with Particular Reference to Insects, Gerald S. Doolin, Director of Research and Sanitation, National Confectioners Association, Chicago.

Using Nutmeats in Restaurants, Jo Marie Powers, Holiday Inn, Atlanta,Georgia; and Frank L. Landergren, John Sexton & Company, Atlanta, Georgia.

Imitation Nut Flavors, Victor G. Fourman, Florasynth, Inc., New York.

Growing Pecan Nursery Trees, Richard H. Simpson, Nurseryman, Monticello, Florida.

Pecan Diseases, John R. Large, Pathologist, Big Bend Laboratory, Monticello, Florida.

Pecan Insects, John R. Large and Arthur M. Phillips, Entomologist, Florida Agricultural Experiment Station, Monticello, Florida.

Chestnut Production, J.W. McKay, U.S. Department of Agriculture, Washington, D.C.

Antioxidation of Nuts, Clyde Young, Chemist, Georgia Experiment Station, Experiment, Georgia.

Illustrative material and historical data were supplied by: The Atlantic Company, Atlanta, Ga.; American Cyanamid Co., Atlanta, Ga.; Air Products & Chemicals, Inc., Allentown, Pa.; Blaw-Knox Company, Buffalo, N.Y.; Benson's, Inc., Athens, Ga.; Bass Pecan Co., Lumberton, Miss.; California Almond Growers Exchange, Sacramento, Calif.; Claxton Bakery, Inc., Claxton, Ga.; Collins Street Bakery, Corsicana, Texas; Continental Moss-Gordin Gin Co., Prattville, Ala.; W.H. Curtin & Co., Atlanta, Ga.; Diamond Crystal Salt Co., St. Claire, Mich.; Clarence Davidson Co., Lakeport, Calif.; Diamond Walnut Kitchen, San Francisco, Calif.; Exact Weight Scale Co., Columbus, Ohio; R.E. Funsten Pecan Co., St. Louis, Mo.; Forestry Suppliers, Inc., Jackson, Miss.; Fry-O-Matic Co., Atlanta, Ga.; Foodco Appliance Corp., Waterloo, Ind.; Food Producers, Inc., Minneapolis, Minn.; Gormax, Inc., San Leandro, Calif.; Griffith Laboratories, Chicago, Ill.; Gold Kist Pecan Co., Atlanta, Ga.; Guidry's Nursery, St. Martinville, La.; Gould Bros., Inc., Milpilas, Calif.; Hardy Salt Co., St. Louis, Mo.; Hershey Chocolate Corp., Hershey, Pa.; Hammons Products Co., Stockton, Mo.; Karstrom Co., Milwaukee, Wis.; Kitchens of Sara Lee, Chicago, Ill.; The Mave Co., Newbery, Ore.; May Industries, Atlanta, Ga.; Microwave Instruments Co., Corona del Mar, Calif.; D.F. Milikan, Univ. of Missouri, Columbia, Mo.; Magnuson Engineers, Inc., San Jose, Calif.; F.E. Myers & Bros. Co., Ashland, Ohio; Morton Salt Co., Chicago, Ill.; Myer Machine Co., San Antonio, Texas; L.H. MacDaniels, Ithaca, N. Y.; National Pecan Shellers & Processors Association, Chicago,

Ill.; National Starch & Chemical Corp., N.Y.; National Equipment Corp., Bronx, N.Y.; Ohaus Scale Corp., Union, N.Y.; Oregon Filbert Commission, Portland, Ore.; Potts Mist Blower, Crawford, Miss.; Phelps Fan Manufacturing Co., Little Rock, Arkansas; Reed-Joseph Co., Greenville, Miss.; Ramacher Manufacturing Co., Linden, Calif.; Seedburo Equipment Co., Chicago, Ill.; Sortex Company, Lowell, Mich.; Stuckey's, Inc., Eastman, Ga.; Simpson Nurseries, Monticello, Fla.; Stahmann Farms, Las Cruces, N.M.; Spraying Systems Co., Bellwood, Ill.; Sonic Engineering Corp., Norwalk, Conn.; Speed Sprayer Plant, Orlando, Fla.; Spee-dee Packaging Machinery, Menomonee Falls, Wis.; Specialties Appliance Corp., Chicago, Ill.; Tennessee-Eastman Co., Kingsport, Tenn.; Tracy-Luckey Pecan Co., Harlem, Ga.; United States Department of Agriculture, Washington, D.C.; U.S. Cold Storage, Dallas, Texas; Wyandotte Chemical Co., Wyandotte, Mich.; Woodman Co., Inc., Decatur, Ga.; and D.K. Young, U.S. Dept. Agr. (Retired), Moultrie, Ga.

Thanks are extended to Naomi C. Woodroof (my wife) for assistance with the manuscript; and to Ann Autry and Geraldine Coates for copying and editing it.

The author has 46 years experience in growing pecans, chestnuts, walnuts and hickories; and more than 30 years research experience in storing and processing these nuts. This is a companion volume to *Peanuts—Production, Processing, Products,* by the same author and publisher.

JASPER GUY WOODROOF
Griffin, Georgia

July 1967

Contents

Tree Nuts of the World

There are ten major tree nuts of the world, the production of which is reported through the U. S. Foreign Agricultural Service and the Crop Reporting Board of the U. S. Department of Agriculture. Since production varies from year to year, the average figures for the six most recent years (1971-76) are given in metric tons[1], in-shell basis.

Almonds	205,183
Cashew nuts	116,666
Chestnuts	58,191
Filberts (hazelnuts)	35,345
Macadamia nuts	9,000
Pecans	16,566
Pignolias (pine nuts)	678.5
Pistachios	26,416
Walnuts, Persian	211,180
Total	679,225.5

There are at least eight minor tree nuts, the production of which is reported on a limited basis, and is often calculated from indirect sources. Recent figures in tons, in-shell basis, are:

Apricot nuts	more than 5
Beechnuts	less than 1
Betel nuts	more than 1
Butternuts	more than 5
Chinquapins	less than 1
Heart nuts	more than 1

---

[1]All tons are metric.

Hickory nuts	more than 1
Walnuts, black	1000

The consumption of tree nuts in the United States far exceeds the production by about one-third to one-fourth. Nuts imported include practically all of those listed above except chinquapins, hickory nuts and black walnuts. Data on production, imports and exports of tree nuts are given in chapters under specific nuts.

Tree nuts have been grown and consumed in the United States since colonial times, but the production of almonds, filberts, pecans and walnuts on a commercial basis dates back probably less than 75 years. During the period 1960-73, total production of tree nuts nearly doubled while the value of production more than tripled. Before the 1930s, the United States imported more tree nuts than were produced domestically, but in recent years imports of types of nuts produced domestically have been a minor part of our total supplies (with the exception of filberts).

The rapid expansion of the tree nut industries has been marked by wide fluctuations in the quantities of the various kinds of nuts produced, resulting in marketing problems for growers and marketing organizations.

Commercial production of the four major tree nuts in the United States has trended upward during the past three decades. In 1973 a record crop of approximately 449,300 tons of tree nuts (including 5500 tons of macadamia nuts) was produced. The 1960-64 average production was 277,563 tons, and this included the previous record crop of 340,000 tons in 1963.

Traditionally pecans and walnuts have been the largest domestic tree nut crops, but during the 1960s there was a rapid increase in bearing acres and production of almonds, which now account for about one-third of the total production. This compares with 15% of the total crop in the 1930s and 20% in the 1950s.

Commercial acreages of almonds and walnuts are located in California; filberts and a few walnuts are located in Oregon; and pecans are produced commercially in 15 southeastern, southcentral and southwestern states, ranging from North Carolina in the East to Arizona in the West and northward into southern portions of Missouri and Illinois. When Hawaii became a state, macadamia nuts were added to our domestic tree nuts and since 1970 pistachio nuts have been planted extensively in California and Arizona. These will be important domestic tree nuts in the years ahead (Powell 1975).

In recent years total commercial output of most major tree nut items has steadily increased, reflecting fair to good weather and improved technology. Producers of the major tree nuts—almonds, filberts and walnuts—include France, India, Spain, Turkey and the United States.

In 1974-75 the United States was the world's leader in the production and export of almonds and walnuts, with Spain a distant second in almond output and shipments, while France ranked as the second largest in walnut production and overseas sales. Turkey remains the largest producer of filberts, followed by Italy and Spain.

Cashew nut production and exports have also been on the increase in recent years. This is due primarily to increasing world demand for tree nut products. Mozambique and Tanzania still remain the world's largest producers of raw nuts. In 1974 these two countries combined to produce 350,000 tons or 73% of the world's total of 481,000 tons.

India continues as the major exporter of processed cashew nuts. In 1971 (the latest year with most complete data) India accounted for 68% of the world's exports, with Mozambique, exporting about 23%, ranking a distant second. However, with the changing political atmosphere in Africa, the prominence of Mozambique and Tanzania in cashew nut marketing is on the increase, as they move in the direction of processing and exporting their own cashew nuts. This would undoubtedly have an adverse effect on India's position as the world's leader in cashew exports.

In 1974 the world's output of almonds totaled 183,800 tons, up to 38% over that of 1973. The United States accounted for 54% of the total compared to 51% in 1973. The U. S. lead was followed by Spain with 30% and 29%, and Italy with 8% and 6%, respectively. World walnut output totaled 195,400 tons in 1974, down 16% from the 1973 level of 232,200 tons. However, filbert output in 1974 was 382,100 tons, over 36,000 tons above the 1973 level. Turkey and Italy accounted for 90% of the total in 1974 and 92% in 1973.

Exports of the other major nuts are also increasing. World almond exports totaled 65,318 tons in 1973-74 with the United States accounting for slightly over 49% and Spain for about 27%. In 1974-75, the year of the record U. S. crop, shipments from this country amounted to 45,000 tons, or 58% of total world almond exports. This was 13,000 tons more than the combined foreign total of 32,000 tons. However, with expected substantial increases in almond output in Spain, the United States will face keener competition on the export front. Western Europe and Japan continue as the primary outlets.

Total walnut exports amounted to 70,866 tons in 1973-74, up 8% over those of 1972-73. The U. S. share was 37%, while that of its nearest competitor, the People's Republic of China, was 19%, followed by France with 17%, India with 10%, and Italy with 9%. Major markets for walnuts were western Europe and Canada.

Filbert shipments for the same year totaled 306,410 tons, 21% more than 1972-73. Turkey accounted for over 81%, with Italy's share 15%, and the remainder shared by Spain (3%) and the United States. The principal markets were western Europe and the Soviet Union (Anon. 1976).

USES OF TREE NUTS

Of more than 2000 available recipes for serving nuts, representative ones are given in this book. Methods of processing and products that may be made from each kind of nut are given, but the list is incomplete because this would have involved a great deal of repetition. More formulas for using any one kind of nut may be obtained by: (a) referring to formulas for using a similar nut discussed in this volume; (b) requesting a list of recipes from the trade association which promotes the use of the particular kind of nut; (c) referring to cookbooks and gourmet magazines; and (d) contacting the local State Experiment Station, Cooperative Extension Service, or the U. S. Department of Agriculture.

Many of the choice nuts from the standpoint of eating quality are available only in limited quantity. The shagbark hickory nut, chinquapins, butternuts, black walnuts and native American chestnuts are examples. Hickory nuts are considered by some to be the best flavored of all nuts.

Except for roasting and salting, nuts are practically never used as a separate dish, but rather to add desirable aroma, flavor, crispness, mealiness, tenderness, a rich color or garnish to servings. They are used extensively as before-meal or between-meal snacks, and are usually "diluted" with drinks or less rich foods. A rapidly expanding outlet for nuts is through vending machines.

Variety in ways that nuts are used is provided not only by different formulas, but by varying the manner of serving. For example, salted pecans may be served many ways, including pieces, halves, in mixed nuts, and mixed with other snack items.

Nuts go well with nationality dishes—Chinese, Italian, German, Japanese, French, Spanish, Indian and American. Almonds, walnuts, chestnuts or Brazil nuts may be used in similar dishes to produce different qualities. In this way the number of variations in serving nuts is almost unlimited.

CONSUMPTION OF NUTS

Americans are eating more nuts today than ever before. The demand for both domestic and imported nuts is on the increase. The greatest actual and potential use of tree nuts will continue to be in confectionery and salting trades, which now use the bulk of them. The availability of most nuts in-shell, shelled, in pieces of many sizes, and as "paste" suggests new recipes for the home, small food shops and large commercial enterprises.

HISTORY OF TREE NUTS

Tree nuts have been used for food, and the trees, branches and flowers have been used on religious occasions since antiquity. Several tree nuts were mentioned in the Bible. Walnuts *(Juglans regia)* were cultivated in King Solomon's garden; pistachio nuts *(Pistacia vera)* were carried down to Egypt by Joseph's brothers; and almonds *(Amygdalus communis)* were used as models for ornamentation of the candlesticks in the temple. All three of these nuts have been eaten extensively in Biblical lands since very ancient times. It is believed that the name of the village Betonim, mentioned by Joshua, was derived from the abundance of pistachio trees in that locality at the time, and Luz, in Genesis, refers to the abundance of almond trees (Moldenke and Moldenke 1952).

The history, romance and folklore of nuts have been written in most countries and by many races. A more detailed history is given under chapters discussing individual nuts. Nuts were associated with the foods of the early Egyptians, Romans, Canaanites, Italians, Chinese, Japanese, Hawaiians, American Indians, Latin Americans, Mexicans, Africans, Asiatic Indians and others.

The gathering and processing (roasting, parching, drying and grinding into meal, boiling, pressing out the oil, distilling essential oils, use in breads, or with meats, mixing with honey or sugar, or use of the oil for curing human ailments) of tree nuts has been practiced since Moses led the children of Israel into the wilderness. Much was also known about harvesting, storing, keeping out insects, and formulating for eating many centuries ago.

Of the tree nuts native to North America, the pecan unquestionably ranks first in economic importance. Even among imported and native nuts it is the "queen of nuts." This is true both because of the quality and quantity of the wild nuts and because of its cultural promise. The acceptability of the quality of the meats, the relative thinness of the shells, and ease of cracking, in contrast to hickories and native walnuts, have won favor among consumers since white men reached the continent. This is why the wild crop from Texas to the Mississippi River assumed commercial importance in early American agriculture. The relatively wide climatic range of the species and the extent of variation in form, size, and quality of nut have stimulated efforts to develop methods of evaluating worthy seedlings and nursery propagation in widely scattered plantings, as well as commercial propagation of pecans.

ROMANCE OF NUTS

There is romance in growing tree nuts. Many who grew up on farms and in villages in America have nostalgic memories of gathering nuts in the autumn. The farm or village boy was aware of the kinds of nuts in his locality and usually had his favorite trees spotted well in advance of harvest.

Annual pilgrimages would be made to the woods before Thanksgiving, with baskets, buckets and bags, to gather wild chestnuts, chinquapins, black walnuts, butternuts, pecans, hazelnuts, shagbark or white hickory nuts. The nuts varied with the locality, but the occasions were similar. The harvests were carried home, shelled by some simple device and constituted basic ingredients for "goodies" for Thanksgiving, Christmas and New Year's holidays.

When the melancholy days of autumn arrived, it was nut gathering time to the early settlers of America. The nut hunter had a spirit kindred to the one who wrote the famous lines: "Woodsman spare that nut tree, touch not a single bough; In youth it sheltered me, and I'll protect it now."

Tree nuts are second only to turkeys as a delicacy for meals at Thanksgiving. Like turkeys, these are characteristically American, and were obtained from the wild for many decades. As the wild cultivars gradually disappeared, domesticated kinds have been used. Furthermore, tree nuts have become so popular and useful for specialty "sweets," that they are widely used throughout the year, especially for Valentine's Day, Easter and Independence Day.

Doubtless, the oldest method of cooking nuts is roasting in hot sand or ashes, and is still used by campers. The nuts were roasted in the hull and shell and eaten while hot. Roasted nuts are the cornerstone of between-meal snacks of today, in as much as: (a) roasting (chestnuts, pecans, almonds and others) brings out the natural flavor more completely than any other form of cooking; (b) roasted nuts have been eaten and relished from antiquity, even before the development of ovens or the discovery of electricity; (c) they can be eaten from the hand with a minimum of formality and table equipment; (d) the aroma of freshly roasted nuts is so fragrant and the flavor is so delectable that one can seldom eat one nut and quit; (e) roasted nuts go well with a wide variety of drinks and other snacks, and are equally compatible with sweets.

Wherever hardwoods are grown, one is likely to find edible nuts. Collecting wild nuts has been popular for hundreds of years. Unfortunately, however, this situation has changed, since most of the old trees have been cut for logs or to clear the land for mechanization. Also, modern farmers do not generally favor trespassing by the vastly increased population. The result is that if one is to have the benefit of harvesting and enjoying nuts, they must be grown on the home grounds, where they serve admirably for shade and ornament as well (MacDaniels 1965).

EXPANSION IN GROWING NUTS

Expansion and improvement in nut growing is active. Fortunately, through the efforts of the Northern Nut Growers Association, trade associations concerned with almonds, Brazil nuts, cashew nuts, chestnuts, filberts, pecans and walnuts, and various associations of horticulturists, nurserymen and research workers, superior cultivars of nut trees have been located, propagated and given cultivar names. Cultivars of most nuts have been developed by breeding, and cultivars of almonds, chestnuts, filberts, walnuts and pistachio nuts have been imported.

Growing tree nuts for pleasure can be engaged in almost anywhere in the United States. Practically every year a tree with more resistance to insects, disease, drought, winter injury or summer temperatures is "located." Those with superior productivity, bearing nuts of good size, quality and salability are propagated. Thus, superior cultivars are continuously replacing those with weaknesses. The new and superior seedling may bear the name of the man who found or propagated it, the location of the parent tree, or an outstanding characteristic of tree or nut.

The sciences of horticulture, chemistry, biology, nutrition and engineering have been applied to: (a) increase the productivity per tree and per acre; (b) distribute superior kinds for growing in all parts of the world; (c) extend the keeping quality of the nuts for shipment, all over the world; (d) vastly increase the number of ways nuts may be used; (e) develop means of controlling temperatures, moisture, pressures and mechanical handling of nuts and nut products; and (f) develop packages for protecting nuts and their products from the ravages of insects, molds, rancidity and damage from mechanical handling.

However, it is doubtful whether modern technologies have improved the basic qualities—color, texture, flavor, aroma—of the nuts themselves or many of the products made from them. For example, (a) the small native American chestnuts are superior in flavor to the large

FIG. 1.1.   THE AUTHOR STANDS BENEATH A 90–YEAR–OLD
SEEDLING PECAN TREE AT MILNER, GEORGIA

Chinese or Japanese introductions into America; (b) the small, wild
pecan seedlings from Texas and Oklahoma have texture and flavor
equal to or superior to the large "improved" cultivars grown in southeastern United States; (c) the wild black walnuts obtained from fields
and woodlots are equal or superior to nuts from planted groves; and
(d) the flavor of wild hickory nuts, beechnuts, pine nuts and others are
so good that they are still harvested from wild trees.

In some countries, the almond, chestnut, hazelnut, walnut and pecan
have been selected, bred, asexually propagated and grown in orchards
for generations. While seedling nuts may be processed and made into
delectable products, due to heterogenous sizes, flavors, colors and textures, the processing and products are difficult to standardize. For this
reason, mechanical and commercial processing and standardization of
products are dependent on the production of nuts by cultivars, with
emphasis on uniform size, grade and chemical composition.

Nuts grown in their native habitat as a source of pleasure, income and a diet supplement will continue to increase. Some of the highest yielding trees of nuts of superior eating qualities are grown singly or in small orchards around homes. These have contributed tremendously to the supply of nuts and nut technology.

Furthermore, most of the methods of harvesting, storing and preparation for eating were developed and tested with "home grown" nuts. Gradually these techniques were refined, mechanized, enlarged and improved to commercial proportions.

In recent years all steps in production, processing and marketing have been more mechanized, and exporting and importing have become well developed, so that today any country can enjoy tree nuts grown in any other country.

SUMMARY STATUS OF INDIVIDUAL KINDS OF NUTS

The name, approximate production, and leading producing countries of 19 kinds and 25 species of nuts described in this book are given in Table 1.1. Detailed discussion of production, processing and products of the nuts are given in chapters that follow.

Almonds are probably the oldest, most widely grown, and most extensively used nuts in the world. They are grown in much of the fruit-growing areas of the temperate zone on several continents. Handling almonds is easily mechanized, and they are one of the most stable nuts, either alone or in products.

The 1976 California almond crop was the largest in history. It totaled 138,000 shelled tons. Prices were attractive and sales were brisk, leaving limited inventories unsold (Kuzio 1977).

The number of ways to prepare and serve almonds exceeds that of any other kind of nut. They are used extensively in chocolate bars. Unique ways of using them are for stuffing olives and garnishing vegetable dishes. (See Chapter 6.)

Apricot nuts are of little importance in the nut trade, due to limited supply. They are similar to almonds, morphologically, chemically and in uses. The nuts are more "bitter" than sweet, and are used more for oil extraction than for eating whole nuts. (See Chapter 17.)

Beechnut trees have not been fully domesticated, and are grown more for shade, the wood and beauty of the trees, than for the small burs containing nuts. The harvested nuts are highly esteemed for the flavor of both the nuts and extracted oil. They are eaten extensively by wildlife. (See Chapter 17.)

Brazil nuts are imported from Brazil in large quantities in the shell. As methods of harvesting and shelling are improved, more of them are graded and imported shelled. Methods of processing, storing and hand-

TABLE 1.1
TREE NUTS OVER THE WORLD

Common Name	Scientific Name	Leading Producing Countries
Almond	*Prunus amygdalus*	Italy, United States, Iran, Spain, Morocco, Portugal
Apricot nut	*Prunus armeniaca*	Europe, United States, China
Beechnut	*Fagus*	Denmark, Germany, United States
Betel nut	*Areca catechu*	South Sea Islands, Palau and Yap Islands in the Carolines
Brazil nut	*Bertholletia excelsa*	Brazil, Bolivia, Peru
Butternut	*Juglans cinerea*	United States, Japan
Cashew nut	*Anacardium occidentale*	India, Kenya, Mozambique, Tanzania, Brazil
Chestnut		Italy, Portugal, Japan, France
American	*Castanea dentata*	Eastern United States
Chinese	*Castanea mollissima*	China
European	*Castanea sativa*	Europe
Japanese	*Castanea crenata*	Japan
Chinquapin	*Castanea pumila*	Eastern United States
Corozo nut	*Scheela macrocarpa*	Brazil, Central America
Filbert	*Corylus avellana* *Corylus americana*	West Germany, Switzerland, United Kingdom, France, United States, Czechoslovakia
Heartnut	*Juglans sieboldiana*	Japan, United States
Hickory nut	*Carya ovata* *Carya alba* *Carya laciniosa*	United States
Macadamia nut	*Macadamia ternifolia*	Hawaii, Kauai, Maui, Oahu, Australia
Pecan	*Carya pecan*	United States, Mexico
Pine nut	*Pinus*	Italy, Spain, Portugal, Iran, United States
Pistachio nut	*Pistacia vera*	Iran, Syria, Turkey, India, Afghanistan, United States
Walnut, Black	*Juglans nigra*	Central eastern and southwestern United States
Walnut, Persian	*Juglans regia*	United States, France, Italy, India, Turkey, Iran, Yugoslavia

ling these nuts have not kept pace with those for other imported nuts. (See Chapter 7.)

In 1976, 5280 tons of shelled Brazil nuts were used by confectioners, bakers and salters. The outlook for 1977 is for considerably less (Kuzio 1977).

Butternuts are grown in a limited way in the eastern United States and Japan. They are less favored than black walnuts, to which they are very similar. Both the trees and nuts have had insufficient research to greatly influence the nut trade.

Cashew nuts have made a tremendous impact on the salt nut trade.

Though they cannot be grown in the United States, they are one of the leading nuts of the world. They are among the lowest in cost and are extensively used salted, either alone or in mixed nuts. Cashew nuts are imported shelled and raw.

Present demand far exceeds the supply. New developments in processing methods and machinery, and new uses for by-products, particularly cashew shell oil, are stimulating production in East Africa and Brazil. (See Chapter 8.)

In 1976, 45,000 tons of cashews were used by confectioners, bakers and salters. The outlook for 1977 was pegged much lower due to a smaller crop and political influences. A range of 35,000 to 40,000 tons is forecast with prices practically doubled (Kuzio 1977).

Chestnuts are not considered nuts in the culinary sense, due to high starch content and practically no oil. Since most American chestnut trees died of blight about 1920, large quantities of the nuts are imported from Europe. The future for expansion of production in the United States depends upon when and if blight-resistant cultivars can be developed from Chinese or Japanese cultivars. No real progress has been made in chestnut production, processing and products anywhere in the world during the last half century.

Chinquapins are very high quality "small chestnuts" that have followed practically the same course as American chestnuts. They are too small in quantity to affect the nut trade. (See Chapter 17.)

Filberts are about third in importance world-wide. One reason is the broad area over which they are grown. However, production in the United States is confined to a relatively small area of Washington and Oregon. According to the Oregon Filbert Commission the production is fairly stable at 12,000 to 14,000 tons (Kuzio 1977).

Processing is easily mechanized and storage is rather simple. The nuts are roasted and salted, and used in confections and a wide variety of bakery products. While many of the filberts used in the United States are imported, the supply will doubtless continue to be more stable than most nuts. (See Chapter 10.)

Heartnuts and hickory nuts are grown almost entirely in the northern and eastern United States, and the supply is too limited for world distribution. Most of the limited supply is used for flavoring specialty products such as candies, cookies or ice cream.

Macadamia nuts are relatively new in the United States, though they cannot be grown on the American Continent. It was only in 1960 that accurate records of imports in this country from Hawaii were begun. Growing of this nut is changing the cropping pattern of Hawaiian farmers. Once the excellent qualities of the nuts are known, and processing is more mechanized, they will become more important in food processing. At present, few formulas for using them have been worked out, and most of them are salted. A unique method of promoting macadamia nuts is that of providing free samples to airplane passengers to and from Hawaii. They are imported to the United States fully processed.

The 1977 crop of macadamias is estimated at 9000 tons, in-shell, with annual increases for the next 15 years as more trees come into production (Kuzio 1977). (See Chapter 11.)

Pecans are one of the native hickories that has been improved to become the fifth leading tree nut in the world. Production is shifting westward into the desert areas of the United States and Mexico, and the supply for domestic and foreign use will probably slowly increase. Pecan production, processing and products are discussed more fully under specific chapter headings. (See Chapter 12.)

Pignolias (pine nuts) have been harvested from native pines in the drier southern European countries and southwestern desert section of the United States from prehistoric times. The nuts are very small, and harvesting and processing have been largely by hand. The crop is uncertain and uncontrollable, thereby limiting the supply and usefulness. Pine nuts are in demand for salting, confections and bakery products, and the demand far exceeds the supply.

Pistachio nuts have been grown around the eastern Mediterranean shores for 5000 years. A few are grown in the southwest United States. They are imported both in-shell and shelled. Pistachios are frequently salted, colored red, green, blue or white, and roasted in the shell. Others are used in specialty products such as cookies, candies and ice cream.

The Persian walnut is one of the leading nuts of the world, being grown throughout most of Europe, western Asia, California and Oregon. It does not grow well in the central and eastern United States.

Black walnuts compose a subdivision of the walnuts found over much of the continents of North America, Asia and Europe. Of several species only the eastern black walnut (*J. nigra*) is of commercial importance. It is extensively grown in the eastern and central United States.

The bulk of the crop is from native trees where mechanical harvesting cannot be practiced. The cracking percentage is low and the quality of the meats is high. They are almost entirely used raw for flavoring ice cream, bakery products and confections, and are seldom salted. There is little likelihood that production will expand.

REFERENCES

ANON. 1965. Tree nuts, world production and statistics. U.S. Dep. Agric. Foreign Agric. Serv.

ANON. 1976. Tree Nuts, World Production. U.S. Dep. Agric., Circ. *FN 1-76.*

BEARD, E. 1962. Hardy nuts for northern United States. Hortic. *40*(10) 514-515.

BRUCE, C.M. 1965. Fruits and nuts of the South. Hortic. *43* (2) 38-39, 50.

CENSUS, U.S. 1964. Agriculture. U.S. Dep. Commer., Washington, D.C.

KUZIO, W. 1977. Nutmeat roundup. Candy Ind. *142* (6) 25-42.

MACDANIELS, L.H. 1965. Walnuts, filberts, chestnuts, and hickories in your garden. Hortic. *43* (9) 22-23, 40.

MOLDENKE, H.N., and MOLDENKE, A.L. 1952. Plants in the Bible. Chronica Botanica Co., Waltham, Mass.

POWELL, J.V. 1975. Changing marketing patterns for domestic tree nuts. Fruit Situation. U.S. Dep. Agric., Circ. *TFS-194.*

PURCELL, J.G., and ELROD, J. C. 1966. The supply, price, and utilization of pecans. Ga. Exp. Stn. Mimeo Ser. *N.S. 182.*

Production and Marketing of Tree Nuts

Tree nuts have been grown and consumed in the United States since colonial times, but the production of almonds, filberts, pecans, and walnuts on a commercial basis is a relatively new agricultural enterprise. Aided by favorable growing conditions and a ready market, the tree nut industries have expanded rapidly. During the past 40 years total production has tripled. Since the early 1930s, the United States has produced more tree nuts than it has imported.

The rapid expansion of the tree nut industries has been marked by wide fluctuations in the quantities of the various kinds of nuts produced, with resulting marketing problems for growers and marketing organizations.

FIG. 2.1. TOP, HULLED AND UNHULLED BLACK WALNUTS;
LOWER, POLISHED AND UNPOLISHED PECANS

SUPPLY

Total supplies of tree nuts for domestic consumption are comprised of U.S. production plus imports. In recent years, domestic production has accounted for approximately 60% and imports about 40% of domestic supplies.

FIG. 2.2. L. TO R. (UPPER) MAHAN, SEEDLING, STUART PECANS; (LOWER) SCALYBARK HICKORIES, WHITE HICKORIES, BLACK WALNUT

Domestic Production

Commercial production of edible tree nuts in the United States has increased steadily since 1960 (Table 2.1).

Pecans and walnuts are the largest domestic tree nut crops. In the late 1940s and 1950s more walnuts were produced than pecans, but more pecans have been produced since the mid-1950s. Almonds have become increasingly important also, and now comprise nearly 20% of total domestic tree nut supplies, compared with about 15% in the 1930s (Table 2.2).

Commercial acreages of almonds, filberts and walnuts are located in California, Oregon and Washington. Pecans are grown in 14 southeastern and southcentral states, ranging from North Carolina on the east to New Mexico on the west and northward into southern portions of Missouri and Illinois.

Practically all of the commercial acreage of almonds is in California, principally in a central belt about 700 miles long. Between 1929 and 1976

TABLE 2.1

PRODUCTION OF LEADING DOMESTIC NUTS: ALMONDS, BRAZIL NUTS, CHESTNUTS, FILBERTS, PECANS, PISTACHIO NUTS, MACADAMIA NUTS AND MISCELLANEOUS NUTS

Year	In-Shell (Million lb)	Shelled
1960	957	–
1961	1,020	–
1962	918	–
1963	1,195	–
1964	1,178	–
1965	1,235	–
1966	1,154	–
1967	1,220	–
1968	1,258	–
1969	1,352	–
1970	1,384	–
1971	1,568	–
1972	–	274
1973	–	609
1974	–	635
1975	–	746

Source: Econ. Res. Serv., U.S. Dep. Agric. (1977).
Agricultural Economic Report No. 138, Supplement; Food Consumption, prices and expenditures. Economic Research Service. Jan. 1977. U.S.D.A.

TABLE 2.2

DOMESTIC PRODUCTION OF ALMONDS, FILBERTS, WALNUTS AND PECANS IN TONS

Name	In-Shell 1974	1975	1976	Shelled 1974	1975	1976
Almonds Calif.	–	–	–	189,000	160,000	230,000
Filberts Ore.	4,900	7,600	–	1,500	4,200	–
Wash.	242	283	–	48	37	–
Total	5,152	7,883	–	1,548	4,236	
Walnuts Calif.	48,720	71,300	–	106,280	126,700	–
Ore.	400	650	–	1,100	650	–
Total	849,120	71,950	–	107,380	127,350	–
Pecans U.S. (11 states)	23,430	34,550	–	113,670	212,249	–

Source: Econ. Res. Serv., U.S. Dep. Agric. (1977).

total commercial acreage of almonds increased approximately 50%. An output increase of about 350% was accompanied by an increase in *bearing* acreage of only about 35%. Because of annual fluctuations in yields, comparisons of years may be misleading. However, when 1929-33 average production is compared with 1976 production, the results are startling.

U.S. PRODUCTION OF FOUR MAJOR TREE NUTS

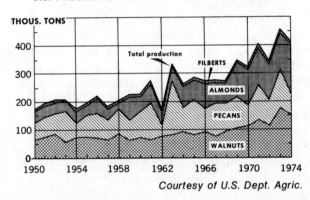

Courtesy of U.S. Dept. Agric.

FIG. 2.3.   U.S. PRODUCTION OF FOUR MAJOR TREE NUTS

Almost 90% of the acreage used for producing filberts is in Oregon, with most of the plantings in the Willamette Valley. The remaining acreage is located in the southwestern section of Washington. Commercial production of filberts is the newest domestic nut crop enterprise, and percentage increases in acreage and production have been larger than for other nuts. Production of filberts is still a relatively small portion of the total. Acreages of filberts rose from 2000 acres in Oregon and 300 acres in Washington in 1929 to 23,000 and 3000 acres, respectively, in the mid-1950s and declined to 17,734 and 813 acres. Total acreage has been reduced in recent years, due partially to a severe windstorm in 1962 which uprooted thousands of trees.

More than 90% of the domestic walnut acreage is in California. In recent years, the center of walnut production has moved from southern California north to the San Joaquin and Sacramento Valleys and to the coastal valleys both north and south of San Francisco. Most of the remaining domestic walnut acreage is found in the Willamette Valley of Oregon, but some walnuts are produced commercially in southwestern Washington.

Pecans are grown in widely scattered areas of the southern United States. There are no accurate data on total acres of pecan trees because many pecan trees are wild or seedlings, and have volunteered along streams and on broad alluvial plains throughout the South. Total production of pecans has shown a steady upward trend, with sharp year-to-year variations. During the 1969-73 period, cultivated cultivars comprised 55% of the total pecan crop. Georgia, Alabama, Mississippi and production of improved cultivars; while Texas, Oklahoma and Louisiana produce most of the seedling pecans. Average total production of all pecans increased 47% between the 1950-54 and 1969-73 periods. It is estimated that 100 tons of pecans were not harvested in 1974 due to weather and labor conditions.

Seedling production has increased over the years, although not as greatly as production of improved cultivars. Improved cultivars out-produce seedling trees by about two to one. During the decade ending 1939, seedling production averaged a little over 54 million pounds. Since then most seedling crops have ranged from about 70 to 80 million pounds, with sharp changes from year to year.

From one year to another, improved cultivars increase or decrease together. Consequently when these fluctuations are large they give rise to "feast or famine" supplies which accentuate the difficulty of merchandising the crop in an orderly manner and which have serious impact on the prices received by pecan producers.

The number of firms involved in the accumulation, shelling, and processing of pecans declined from 136 in 1961 to 124 in 1974, and the number of pecan shellers declined from 77 to 44. The number of firms declined most in Georgia and Texas, but Georgia continued to have the largest number of shellers (13), followed by Texas and Alabama with 6 each.

The trend is toward fewer plants that shell a half million pounds and less, and more plants that handle more than five million pounds. If this continues, probably less than 20 multishelling plants will shell all of the pecans by 1985.

Federal Marketing Programs

The marketing of domestically produced almonds, filberts, walnuts, and pecans is now regulated under Federal marketing agreement and order programs, as authorized under the Agricultural Marketing Agreement Act of 1937 (as amended). These programs are designed to improve grower returns through the establishment of minimum quality standards and/or volume restrictions, which provide adequate supplies to domestic markets, and for the diversion of the surplus portion of the crop to noncompetitive outlets.

Federal marketing agreement and order programs were adopted by producers of nuts as a means of improving prices. One of the problems among tree nut growers is that yields vary widely while acreage tends to

ciation; Northern Nut Growers Association; and Western Irrigated Pecan Growers Association.

In addition to Federal marketing agreement and order programs, the Department of Agriculture has the authority under Section 32 of Public Law 320, 74th Congress, as amended, to assist in the removal of surpluses by purchases and diversion payments.

World Production

The foreign production of almonds, filberts and walnuts is concentrated in countries with mild, dry climates bordering the Mediterranean Sea. In some of these countries, only part of the total production is on a commercial basis. In addition to orchards or groves, nut-bearing trees are found growing in scattered plantings amidst field crops or other tree crops, along roads and in yards. For this reason and inadequacies in crop-reporting methods, data on acreages used for growing these nuts are of limited usefulness. Estimates of production are more meaningful.

Almonds.—Led by the expected record harvests in the United States and Spain, the 1976 world almond crop set a record of 236,000 tons (shelled basis). A similar development also existed in the world filbert market with Turkey and Italy as the leaders. With the record almond crop of 127,000 tons in the United States and 65,000 tons in Spain, the commercial 1976 world almond forecast was set at 236,000 tons (shelled basis). This total represents a 45% gain over the 1975 crop of 162,300 tons and a substantial 27% jump from the previous record of 185,200 tons produced in 1974.

This was the fourth consecutive year that California produced more almonds than the rest of the world combined. This trend benefits the United States by further establishing California as a reliable supplier to the world of high-quality almonds—a definite plus at a time when traditional and potential purchasers are concerned about both quality and consistency in supply. On the other hand, these continued large increases in almond supplies (both domestic and foreign), fueled by rapidly expanding acreage and coupled with big jumps in the availability of competing tree nuts such as filberts and walnuts, can combine to have a dampening effect on world prices.

Foreign almond production at 109,000 tons in 1976 was the largest crop of record, followed by the previous high of 94,400 tons produced in 1968. Spain, the leader among foreign producers, had a bumper crop of 65,000 tons in 1976, up 49% over the output of 43,500 tons harvested in 1975 and about one-fifth more than the previous record achieved in 1974. The substantial gain in 1977 was directly attributable to additional acreage coming into bearing, excellent pollination conditions, and frost-free weather throughout the country's almond producing areas.

Italy, the second largest foreign producer, had a crop of 25,000 tons in 1976. This volume compared with the 20,000 tons produced in 1975 marked the sixth consecutive year of below-average (1964-73 average: 29,000 tons) production for the Italians. Reports from Italy indicate that because of the bad crops—attributed primarily to adverse weather conditions—many farmers lost interest in almond production and actually cut down a significant number of their trees. These growers have replaced almond area with grapes and other crops. In addition, many of the remaining trees are old and not pruned or fertilized. Therefore, it seems unlikely that the traditional crop yields of 35,000 to 38,000 tons that prevailed during the 1960s will be reached again soon.

In Iran, where the government has been encouraging producers to expand their output, production for 1976 was 8000 tons, slightly less than the 8300 tons in 1975. However, weather was excellent and quality good. The almond crop in Portugal was 6000 tons, 71% more than the level achieved the year before. Excellent weather conditions were primarily responsible for the expected large crop.

The crop in Morocco was 5000 tons, 2000 tons more than 1975.

Production in the United States was up 51% over the large crop of last year and 29% more than the previous record harvest of 98,700 tons in 1974. The gain in 1976 was attributable to additional bearing acreage coupled with increased tree vigor after a slight crop letdown the year before.

Exports.—Exports from the six major producing countries (Iran, Italy, Morocco, Portugal, Spain and the United States) during the 1975-76 season were 86,100 tons, up 15% over the 74,800-ton volume shipped the previous year. Exports during the 1973-74 season totaled 71,000 tons.

Foreign almond exports for the 1975-76 season were up, recovering from the previous season's low level. However, the 40,100-ton level was still considerably below the 46,000-ton average of the late 1960s and early 1970s.

The anticipated rise in 1977 foreign almond exports was attributed to the expected 64% increase in the Italian total and the 25% jump in Spain's exports. These increases are expected to be enough to offset the slight drop in shipments from the other major foreign exporters.

Almond exports from the United States for the 1975-76 marketing year were 46,000 tons, only 1000 tons more than were shipped during the previous season, but 42% more than the 1973-74 total of 32,200 tons. It should be noted that the U.S.'s share of world exports has been on the increase. During the current season, its share is expected to be 53% of the total, down 7 percentage points from the level of last season's but substantially above the 45% and 32% totals of the 1973-74 and 1972-73 seasons.

Brazil Nuts.—The 1976 output of Brazil nuts was 32,000 tons, green weight, down about 43% from the 1975 production of 56,000 tons. The drop is attributed primarily to tree strain after the large crop of the previous year.

Trade reports indicate that Brazil nut production as a commercial crop is on the decline. Sources state that the development of other economic activities in the Amazon Basin means a greater number of other opportunities for the available labor force, and the formation of pastures for large cattle-raising operations has resulted in the destruction of many of the country's Brazil nut groves. If these reports prove to be accurate, the large consumers of these nuts, such as West Germany, the United Kingdom, and the United States, can expect to see even higher prices in future years. Additionally, a large decline in Brazil's nut industry could also benefit the U.S. tree nut family. As fewer Brazil nuts are produced and exported, traditional consumers could substitute almonds, walnuts or pecans, which are plentiful in the United States.

Brazil nut exports during the 1975-76 year (April-March) amounted to 55,000 tons, green weight, up 60% over the preceding year's shipments of 34,300 tons. Exports for the 1976-77 season were 30,500 tons, reflecting the reduced output for 1976. The primary markets include West Germany, the United Kingdom, and the United States.

Domestic Brazilian consumption of Brazil nuts is usually considered insignificant, as Brazil exports the majority of its nuts. Industry officials place the annual domestic usage at about 1500 tons. Stocks are usually nonexistent, as the nuts are highly suceptible to spoilage. However, during years in which there are substantial stocks and therefore a high incidence of spoilage, the spoiled nuts are usually crushed for oil.

The Government of Brazil maintains a program of minimum prices for producers and processors of Brazil nuts.

Cashews.—Despite some unfavorable weather, 1976 production of raw cashews in India was 115,000 tons, up 5000 tons from the 1974-75 level. Rain in the heavy producing areas of the Malabar coast and south Kerala delayed flowering of the cashew plants, which ordinarily starts during late December-early January, and there were reports of some damage to the crop in Karnataka by the tea mosquito. Nevertheless, the crop was relatively large, mainly because of production from new plantations and decreasing imports, which are likely to induce a larger collection of raw nuts.

Exports of raw nuts during the 1976 marketing year were 217,000 tons, down 12% from those of the previous season. Exports during the 1975 marketing year reached a fairly high level (247,000 tons, raw-nut basis), sparked by heavy buying from Japan—a new large purchaser—and the United States.

The cashew trade has become more unpredictable of late, chiefly because of uncertainty over cashew imports from Africa and the relatively high prices demanded by African shippers. These developments have contributed to a slowdown in cashew processing in India; many plants are closed and are not expected to begin operation until the flow of indigenous crops begins in March. The processors, therefore, are very cautious concerning their new export commitments, and have apparently booked only very limited shipments so far this season.

In spite of all the difficulties confronting the industry, exports are expected to pick up. One reason for the optimism is that despite adverse factors, the industry does very well, indicating a solid world demand for cashews.

Imports of raw nuts during the 1976 marketing season were 130,000 tons, raw-nut basis, down 10% from the previous season's level of 145,000 tons and the lowest level in 11 years. Of the expected total imports in 1976, 60,000 tons came from Tanzania, 50,000 tons from Mozambique, and 20,000 tons from Kenya. Higher prices demanded by African shippers and the expanding African cashew processing industry are major reasons for the expected downturn. India also faces stiff competition for African cashews from Chinese and Brazilian importers.

Domestic consumption of cashews is rising yearly and is placed at 30,000 tons, raw-nut basis, for the 1976 marketing year, 5000 tons above that of 1975. Carryover stocks at the end of this year are estimated at 8000 tons, raw-nut basis, 20% below 1975's level, primarily because of anticipated lower imports in 1976.

The average export price for cashew kernels during 1975 was $1.12 per pound for 320 count, c/f New York, compared with $1.18 during 1974. Export prices declined during October-December 1975, mainly because of the availability of large stocks of packed kernels and consumer resistance in the overseas markets to steadily increasing prices during the past few years.

In efforts to increase output of raw cashews, the Government of India is encouraging the Cashew Corporation of India to budget funds for the promotion of cashew cultivation. The State Governments also have announced plans to boost cashew output by offering various incentives and subsidies. Research and development of higher yielding cashew strains are continuing at the Cashew Research Station of Kerala Agricultural University.

Filberts.—Foreign commercial filbert production during 1976 was at a record 415,000 tons (in-shell basis), up 2% from the 1975 estimated total of 406,500 tons. The slight rise in output is attributed to the anticipated substantial increases in production in Italy and Spain.

Turkey, the largest producer, had a slight drop in its 1976 harvest, which still was the second largest on record. Production in the United States in 1975 was 9500 tons, up 56% over the previous crop of 6100 tons. However, if the U.S. production cycle follows traditional trends, the filbert harvest can be expected to be down.

Even assuming a decline in the U.S. filbert crop, 1976 production was sufficient to bring the overall world total well in excess of the record 1975 harvest, thereby setting another unprecedented world output. Prices for 1976 continued their downward trend from year-earlier levels, reflecting the large quantity of filberts on the international market.

Production.—The 1976 Turkish harvest was 300,000 tons, down 6% from the record 1975 crop of 320,000 tons. This marks the fifth consecutive year that Turkish production has been sustained at a high level. This reflects the combined effects of technological and cultural improvements and favorable weather.

These continued substantial surges in output could make an already dim situation worse—i.e., in the form of depressed world prices, and adverse ramifications in the world nut market for competing tree nuts. Recognizing the impact of nut surpluses on the international markets, the Government of Turkey for the first time is in a position of having to keep support price for filberts at a minimum. The idea of support prices was inconsistent, since Turkish export prices are above world prices.

In Italy, filbert production was 90,000 tons in 1976, about one-fourth more than the 1975 output. This gain in production was attributed to satisfactory climatic conditions coupled with new acreage coming into bearing. However, the 1976 crop was about 13% less than the record harvest in 1974. Similarly, filbert production in Spain—the third largest foreign producer—for 1976 was 25,000 tons, a 72% jump from the low crop of 14,500 tons produced during 1975 but 24% less than record 1974 harvest of 33,000 tons.

Exports.—Filbert exports from the major producers (Turkey, Italy, Spain and the United States) during 1976 were 274,000 tons (in-shell), about 7500 tons more than previous and 6% over the total shipments during 1975. However, this was 12% down from the record shipments reported in 1973-74, when Turkey exported over 250,000 tons of filberts. Turkey's principal buyer continues to be West Germany, with France, the United Kingdom, and Switzerland as distant seconds.

For Spain, filbert exports during 1976 dropped to 8000 tons, compared with 20,000 tons in 1975. West Germany and France were major outlets for both Italian and Spanish filberts.

U.S. exports of filberts are generally negligible, totaling less than 1000 tons.

Imports.—U.S. imports of filberts during 1975 totaled 3700 tons, 68% below the 11,717 tons purchased during 1974. The decline was a result of expectations of the U.S. crop. Virtually all U.S. filbert imports originate from Turkey. U.S. importers purchased 6640 tons during the first 8 months of 1976, compared with 1701 tons during the same period a year earlier. In keeping with tradition, U.S. importers purchase larger quantities of filberts in years when U.S. production is expected to be on the downward cycle, as in the case of 1976.

Walnuts.—Spurred by a dramatic rise in U.S. output, world walnut production for 1975 was 242,000 tons (in-shell basis). Output in 1975 was 23% above the 1974 level of 196,500 tons and a record for countries for which data are available. (Such data are not available from the People's Republic of China—a known major producer.)

Foreign production in 1975, buoyed by higher output in India and Italy, reached 64,000 tons, 17% above previous year's level but still below the 1970-74 average of 67,180 tons. France, the largest foreign walnut producer for which data are available, had a 1975 harvest of 18,400 tons, down marginally from 19,700 tons in 1974. Hot, dry weather during the summer was the primary cause of the shortfall. Nut quality was reportedly good, with sizes average. Italy recorded an estimated 1975 crop of 17,000 tons, an increase of 31% compared with the harvest of a year earlier. Italian walnuts are much below normal in size because of the large tree yield and dry summer.

India's 1975 walnut production showed the greatest improvement among reporting foreign producers, rising 63% over last year's crop to 15,500 tons. Increased production was largely a result of timely precipitation during the blossoming stage (February-April) in the principal producing areas. The crop quality is reportedly very good, manifested by larger and lighter colored kernels, compared with the small, dark, lower quality kernels of last year.

Iran's output was down in 1975, following a generally downward trend in recent years. The main reason for lower Iranian production is the continuing illegal practice of cutting walnut trees in national forests for lumber. Turkey's 1975 commercial walnut production was 10,000 tons, up 1000 tons from that of 1974. Most of Turkey's production is noncommercial and is consumed mostly on the farm.

U.S. production in 1975, officially estimated at 178,000 tons, is the largest crop on record and a 25% increase over the 1974 level.

Exports.—Exports of foreign producers during 1976 were up slightly— 22,000 tons, compared with 21,100 tons in 1975. France, traditionally the largest foreign producer-exporter for which data are available, had a significantly reduced export level during 1976—6000 tons compared with 11,100 in 1975. The smaller crop is the main factor influencing the reduced export level. France's imports were up 74% to 4000 tons in 1976, and the U.S. walnut industry, with its record population in 1975, had a significant portion of the increased import requirements.

India will be a significant exporter, as well, on the strength of its much-improved harvests. Exports during the 1976 marketing season were 9000 tons, compared with only 3400 tons in 1975. There has been a sharp increase in overseas demand for Indian walnuts, primarily because of the inability of China to meet fully some of its export commitments.

FIG. 2.4.   UNSHELLED TREE NUTS
L. to R. (upper) pecans, Brazil nuts, Persian walnuts; (lower) chestnuts, filberts, almonds.

U.S. Imports

With the exception of World War II period, when imports of tree nuts dropped to approximately 10% of the 1935-39 average, the trend of tree nut imports has been upward since 1929. However, total imports have not risen as much as domestic production, and the United States now produces more tree nuts than are imported, which is the reverse of the situation prior to 1931. In addition, the increase in total imports has resulted from increased use of nuts which are not produced in this country. Imports of domestic-type tree nuts have actually declined.

Tree nuts are imported into the United States both in-shell and shelled. Increases in the volume of imports of shelled tree nuts are due to the growth in popularity of the cashew nut, which has never been imported in-shell. An increasing portion of imports of domestic-type tree nuts are also on a shelled basis. Imports of in-shell tree nuts totaled only 12,935 tons in 1962, compared with the 1959-62 average of nearly 21,000 tons

FIG. 2.5.   LEFT, BLACK WALNUT MEATS; MIDDLE (UPPER),
APRICOT NUTS, (LOWER) CASHEW NUTS; RIGHT, PISTACHIO
NUTS

and a high of 28,960 tons in 1932. Brazil nuts comprised 36% of the 1959-62 imports of in-shell tree nuts. Chestnuts were 35% of the total, and pistachios, 27%. The remaining 2% consisted of small quantities of almonds, filberts, pecans, pignolias and walnuts.

While imports of shelled tree nuts increased from 1929 to 1962, imports of domestic-type tree nuts—with the exception of filberts, and minor

FIG. 2.6.   NUTMEATS

Upper (l. to r.) Persian walnuts, Brazil nuts, pecans, pine nuts;
Lower, almond slivers, almond slices, cashew nuts, macadamia
nuts.

FIG. 2.7.   IMPORTED PINE NUTS, PISTACHIO NUTS
AND MACADAMIA NUTS

quantities of pecans—have declined. The rise in total imports of shelled tree nuts has been due entirely to the increasing popularity of cashew nuts, and the great increase in their importation. Between the two 5-year (average) periods, 1929-33 and 1959-62, total imports of shelled tree nuts increased from 19,709 tons to 38,218 tons. During the same interval, imports of cashews rose from 4600 tons to 29,133 tons. During 1959-62, cashews comprised 74% of the total imports of shelled tree nuts. Shelled Brazil nuts accounted for 12%, walnuts, 6%, and filberts, 5%. Small quantities of almonds, pecans, pignolias and pistachios comprised the remaining 3% of the total.

Practically all of the almonds imported into the United States come from Spain or Italy. Since 1951, the majority have come from Spain, but before that Italy was the chief supplier. Almonds are imported both in-shell and shelled, depending on the domestic crop and prices, but most of the imports are shelled. The imported shelled almonds are used primarily by candy manufacturers and nut salters; in-shell almonds are sold in the in-shell nut mixtures through retail outlets.

Filberts are imported into the United States from Turkey, Spain and Italy. Turkey is, by far, our major supplier. Since World War II, there has been a steady decline in the amount of filberts imported in-shell, and only 23 tons were imported on this basis from the 1962-63 crop. Italy was the sole supplier of in-shell filberts. Imports of shelled filberts have fluctuated from year to year, but the trend has been upward. Practically all of the shelled filberts come from Turkey, but small quantities are imported from Italy and some trans-shipped from West Germany. The nut-salting trade is the largest user of imported shelled filberts.

Walnuts may be imported from many foreign countries, both in-shell and shelled. Since 1960-61, only minor quantities have been imported in-shell, and all of these have come from Italy and France. France, Italy, and China were the major sources of supply for shelled walnuts, but since 1959-61 most of the shelled walnuts have been imported from Turkey and India. Other important suppliers of shelled walnuts are Iran, Italy, and Rumania. Most of the imported walnuts are smaller than domestic walnuts, and are used by the confectionery and baking industries.

The United States imports over half of the world exports of cashews. Most of these originate in India, as cashews produced in Africa are exported to India for processing. Practically all of the cashews are used by the nut-salting trade, but they are becoming increasingly popular in the confectionery trade.

Exports of cashew kernels from India reached a new high in 1963 according to the Cashew Trade Association at Quilon. Total exports were 2,325,000 50-pound cases in 1963, and 2,047,000 cases in 1962. The United States continues to be the leading buyer of Indian cashews, taking 55% of the 1963 crop; the Soviet Union took 17% and East Germany took 6%. The United Kingdom, Australia and Canada also purchase substantial quantities.

Production of raw cashew nuts continues to expand in Tanganyika and Kenya. Recent plantings in Kenya are expected to boost yields from 8400 short tons in 1963 to 13,000 tons in 1968; and in Tanganyika from 64,000 tons to 95,000 tons. The crops from these countries are expected to be even larger by 1970.

Cashews in these countries are exported in-shell to India for processing, but each country expects to set up shelling plants to handle from 1000 to 1300 tons. Until 1961, practically all Tanzania's cashews were sold through Asian traders, who either resold them to exporters or acted as exporter's agents.

Brazil nuts are imported, both in-shell and shelled, almost exclusively from Brazil. Small quantities of shelled Brazil nuts are also imported from Bolivia, Peru, and other South American countries. In-shell Brazil nuts are sold in in-shell nut mixtures through grocery stores primarily during the holiday season. Shelled Brazil nuts are used by nut salters and candy manufacturers (Powell 1964).

Tariffs

The commercial production of edible tree nuts in the United States has been fostered partially by tariffs[2] on imports of all tree nuts from other

---

[2]Tariff schedules of the United States under Section 102 of the Tariff Classifications Act of 1962, as amended.

countries. Tariffs on domestic-type tree nuts are higher than on other kinds of nuts, such as Brazil nuts and cashews. In addition, under Section 22 of the Agricultural Marketing Act of 1937, as amended, the President is authorized to impose quotas or fees on imports if it appears that nuts are being, or are likely to be, imported in such quantities as to render ineffective, or to interfere with, any program under the Act—i.e., the Federal marketing orders. This procedure has been used for almonds on a number of occasions, and has been requested by walnut marketers but never granted.

Expansion of the domestic tree nut industries in California and Oregon was partially fostered by tariffs on foreign tree nuts. Thus, a significant change in those tariffs would have a substantial impact.

Outlook For Supplies

Domestic Supplies.—Like most of the other tree crops, the current supply of tree nuts is relatively unaffected by current economic forces. The current demand for and prices of tree nuts, however, have a great deal to do with supplies that can be expected in the 1970s, just as increased production in the 1930s resulted from plantings made during 1921-28 when prices were favorable to nut growers. The increased average production in the early 1950s resulted from plantings made during the high price period of World War II.

The greatly expanded acreage of almond trees has been accompanied by higher yields of nuts per tree and per acre. New plantings of almonds have been made on new, fertile, irrigated land. The new plantings have also benefited from improved cultural practices, more efficient insect and disease control, and better protection from frost. Growers now report yields as high as 2000 lb of nuts per acre.

The total acreage of walnuts in California has also increased at a steady rate since the 1920s, the increases in northern and central California more than offsetting the decreases in southern California. In 1962, there were over 165,000 acres of walnuts in California. The total consisted of 126,200 acres of bearing trees and more than 39,000 acres of nonbearing trees. The bearing acreage was the largest since 1947, when the population explosion in southern California began to envelop the walnut land, and, in the early 1950s, reduced bearing acreage to 113,000 acres. The nonbearing acreage was the largest since the early 1930s. New plantings were less in 1963 than in any year since 1950, but the huge plantings made in the late 1950s in central and northern California indicate increased walnut production in the years ahead.

Although data are not available concerning the acreage of pecan trees, indications are that increased plantings of pecan trees have been made.

Large acreages of pecans have been planted in Georgia, Arkansas, Texas and New Mexico. Pecan production of New Mexico was not included in the national pecan production data in the mid-1950s, but now, that state is one of the leading producers of improved cultivars of pecans.

The tremendous increase in the number of pecan trees propagated and the larger number of trees planted in large groves assure increased pecan production in the years ahead. It is also indicated that an increasing portion of the total pecan crop will consist of improved cultivars.

Between 1949 and 1959, the number of filbert trees in Oregon and Washington declined from 2.4 million to 1.5 million. Tree numbers were reduced further by the severe windstorm in 1962. Nearly 87,000 trees were uprooted by the storm. An additional 84,000 were blown over but were reset. It is estimated that there were about 1.5 million filbert trees of all ages in Oregon and Washington in 1963. The acreage was estimated to be 18,547 acres, the lowest since the mid-1940s.

There is some evidence that growers are optimistic about the future of the filbert industry and wish to expand production. However, there is a severe shortage of nursery stock and the shortage will not be alleviated soon. Grower's intentions to plant additional trees will be strongly influenced by world production of filberts, the impact on domestic prices, and alternative land-use opportunities. Present production trends in foreign countries are upward, but so are population trends. Thus the filbert industry will probably be confronted with supply-demand relationships similar to those that now exist. These relationships are not conducive to rapid industry growth.

Foreign Supplies.—The trend of production of all domestic-type tree nuts is upward in countries that are important world suppliers. However, the rate of production increase is less than the rate of population growth. Hence per capita supplies of tree nuts should remain at or slightly below present levels in the years ahead. Further increases in production can be expected in those countries that appear to have comparative advantage in tree nut production. The share of world production supplied by countries that are now minor suppliers can be expected to decrease.

DOMESTIC MARKETING FIRMS

There are more than 150 firms in the United States that are directly engaged in procuring nuts, shelling them (or otherwise preparing them for market), and selling them to retail, wholesale, or industrial outlets. Approximately 80 of these firms are primarily engaged in marketing pecans. The remaining firms are located in California and Oregon, and are engaged in marketing almonds, filberts and walnuts.

Almonds

The entire crop of almonds is marketed by eight major firms and seven smaller firms, some of which are in the market only occasionally. The leading marketing firm in the almond industry is the California Almond Growers Exchange, a cooperative, which markets approximately 70% of the California almond crop. The Exchange handles almonds exclusively, while most of the other major firms handle other nuts as well. At least two of the firms are, or are subsidiaries of, large food corporations that market other food products as well as other kinds of domestic and imported tree nuts.

Of the six major firms, three are corporations, two are cooperatives, and one is a partnership. Four of the firms have been in business more than 20 years.

Led by the Exchange, the marketing of almonds has been more aggressive than the marketing of any other domestic nut. The seemingly endless array of almondine main-course dishes and desserts, and new candy products which advertise the natural complimentarity of chocolate and almonds have not happened by chance. The concerted effort and planning by almond growers and marketers to supply almonds of the kind and in the form that food manufacturers want is epic of the cooperative movement in the United States.

Filberts

Interviews were obtained with nine Oregon and two California firms that market filberts. Approximately four-fifths of the sales of in-shell filberts are made by the four largest Oregon handlers. Over half of the total sales of shelled filberts are made by two of the Oregon shellers.

Five of the Oregon firms are corporations and three are cooperatives. One is a proprietorship. In 1963, one of the corporations marketed filberts for a cooperative until this arrangement was discontinued in July. The marketing of filberts has been marked by rivalrous competition among the marketing agencies and particularly among the cooperatives, none of which has enough volume for significant market influence. Partially because there is no cohesive force in the filbert industry, marketing patterns within the industry have been slow to change, and the shift from in-shell to shelled sales has been slower than in most of the other tree nut industries. Part of the reason for this is the sharp competition from imported shelled filberts. Handlers believe the demand for in-shell filberts is inelastic, for shelled filberts very elastic. Thus a nearly constant quantity of in-shell filberts is sold each year, and the amount shelled varies directly with the size of the crop and prices of imported filberts. In most years, grower returns for in-shell filberts have exceeded the returns from shelled filberts.

Pecans

Pecans are marketed by approximately 80 firms located throughout the pecan belt from North Carolina to New Mexico and in St. Louis, Chicago, and Pittsburgh. The concentration of pecan shellers is greatest in those areas where pecan production is heaviest—Georgia and Texas. The concentration of pecan shellers in St. Louis and Chicago stems from the early 1900s when in-shell pecans were loaded in bags and sent up the Mississippi River to be sold for whatever price they would bring. The shelling industries were started as a salvage operation for the pecans that remained unsold after the holiday season.

Eight large firms market nearly 50% of the shelled pecans, and 37 firms market approximately 90% of all pecans that enter commercial channels. The remaining firms are small, may not be actively engaged in handling pecans every year, and are never in business more than two or three months during the peak marketing season. Most of their sales are made to local bakeries, confectioners, and gift packers. Of the large firms, one is a cooperative and the others are corporations.

There was no cohesive marketing force in the pecan industry, until the early 1950s. In 1950, the Gold Kist Pecan Growers Association, a cooperative, entered the pecan field and, with ample backing from its parent organization, Gold Kist Inc. of Atlanta, rapidly became a leading marketer of pecans with international as well as national marketing affiliations.

About 1965, the Nut Tree Pecan Company, a cooperative in Albany, Georgia, began large-scale production, harvesting, shelling, processing, storing, wholesaling and exporting of pecans. They handle more pecans from the orchard to end-users than any other firm in the world.

At about the same time, the independent pecan shellers, who had been until then highly competitive individualists, formed the National Pecan Shellers and Processors Association. Through the Association, the shellers are able to keep more fully apprised of supplies and prices. Also they began aggressive advertising and promotion campaigns to encourage the use of pecans. These campaigns have been notably successful.

The pecan industry is still in a state of flux, however, and many changes are taking place which will alter the competitive position of pecans in the years ahead. The pecan industry is inherently speculative because of the biennial production habit of pecan trees and the usual, but not always, wide fluctuations in supplies from year to year. Much of the speculation is being taken out of the industry, however, by increased knowledge concerning supplies and prices, and by the cooperative, which by its nature acts as a market stabilizer.

An additional stabilizing force is the entry of large multi-product food corporations into the pecan business. Within the past six years, three of the largest pecan-shelling establishments have been purchased by large food corporations. In order to assure themselves of adequate and regular supplies of pecans for their products, which must be planned months in advance, these corporations have found it desirable to purchase their own pecan shelling (and storage) facilities.

Another entry into the pecan marketing field is the large grower-sheller. These highly integrated organizations produce, shell and market their own pecans. Spurred by the success of such a firm in New Mexico, other firms have been started in Texas and Arkansas.

Although the pecan is native to North America, the pecan industry, from an organizational point of view, is the youngest domestic tree nut industry. The rapid and dramatic changes that are taking place in the industry portend vastly different supply-demand relationships for pecans in the future.

Walnuts

Walnuts are marketed by approximately 40 firms in California and 20 in Oregon. Six of the largest firms in California and six in Oregon were interviewed. The Diamond Walnut Growers, a cooperative, is by far the largest marketer of walnuts. It markets a vast majority of all the in-shell walnuts, and also handles more shelled walnuts than any other handler. About seven other California walnut handlers are large. Most of the rest are small and sell mostly shelled nuts. Only one of the Oregon walnut handlers is a real factor in the walnut industry. Although Oregon produces a walnut of good quality, the crop is harvested much later than in California; yields per acre and kernel percentages are lower, and processing costs are higher, thus putting Oregon walnuts at a competitive disadvantage with California walnuts.

Domestic Consumption

The consumption of individual kinds of nuts varies from year to year depending on the relative supplies and prices of each kind. For example, if walnuts are plentiful relative to almonds, filberts and pecans, a larger proportion of walnuts is included in the in-shell mixtures sold primarily through retail food stores. Similarly, if filberts or almonds are plentiful relative to other tree nuts, more of them will be included in the in-shell mixtures as well as in the shelled, salted mixtures.

While the total consumption and per capita consumption of all tree nuts has trended upward since the 1920s, the per capita consumption of domestic-type tree nuts has remained about steady and that of other nuts has increased. Most of the increase in total consumption of tree nuts has been due to the increased use of the cashew nut, which, as previously noted, comprises approximately 74% of our total imports of shelled nuts. Because "carry-in" and "carry-out" data are not available for pecans, per capita production can be estimated much more accurately than per capita consumption. Therefore, the per capita consumption of pecans is probably less than 0.51 lb per person and greater than 0.14 lb per person.

Channels of Distribution

Domestic tree nuts are sold either shelled or in-shell but the proportion of the crop sold on a shelled basis has been increasing steadily in recent years. In-shell nuts are sold almost exclusively for home consumption in straight-packs or mixtures, principally during the holiday season in November and December. Shelled nuts are sold to candy manufacturers, the salting trade, bakers, households, ice cream manufacturers and manufacturers of nut syrups and pastes (Table 2.4).

TABLE 2.4

SHELLED TREE NUTS—SALES OF MAJOR SUPPLIERS BY OUTLET, UNITED STATES

Outlet	Almonds	Filberts	Pecans %	Walnuts	Total
Grocery wholesalers	3.7	12.2	9.0	29.3	11.0
Retailers (direct)	7.3	7.0	11.0	30.0	13.4
Salters	15.1	62.7	6.0	1.6	9.4
Confectioners	47.6	3.4	20.1	10.0	28.2
Bakeries	10.0	12.2	38.0	14.2	22.4
Ice cream manufacturers	8.1	—	7.0	4.8	6.7
Gift packers	0.1	—	1.0	—	0.7
Other	8.1	2.5	8.0	10.1	8.2
Total	100.0	100.0	100.0	100.0	100.0

Candy manufacturers are the main outlet for shelled almonds; salters use most of the shelled filberts; and most of the shelled pecans and walnuts are used by bakers and for home consumption. As a whole, confectioners are the most important outlet for shelled domestic tree nuts, using approximately 28% of the total. The baking industry uses about 22%, households use 24%, and the salted nut trade uses about 9%. Ice cream manufacturers and manufacturers of nut pastes and syrups use approximately 7 and 8%, respectively.

Almonds.—Approximately 93% of the almonds are marketed on a shelled basis. Confectioners are the largest users of shelled almonds. In 1962-63, approximately 44% of the entire almond crop was sold to confectioners. Salters used about 15% of the crop, and about 11% was sold for household use through grocery wholesalers and retailers. Ice cream manufacturers used approximately 8% of the crop. An increasingly important use of almonds is for prepared food mixes and frozen foods. Noodles almondine, green beans almondine, various cake and frosting mixes using almonds, and other prepared foods are items which are having an impact on the dietary habits of consumers and on the marketing pattern for almonds. The cultivars of almonds are diced, sliced, slivered, blanched, roasted and salted so that there is a form of almond to meet almost every food need.

Filberts.—Most of the filberts are sold in-shell to wholesale and retail grocery firms for sale directly to consumers in packages of straight-packs or mixed nuts. The peak marketing season is in October, November and December. About 5% are exported. Salters use almost 63% of the shelled filberts. Sales to households through wholesale and retail grocers account for 19% of shelled filbert sales, and sales to bakeries, 12%. Confectioners bought 3% of the shelled filberts in 1962-63, and other users, 2.5%.

Courtesy of DuPont Magazine

FIG. 2.8. SALTED NUTS PACKED UNDER VACUUM IN FOIL
LAMINATED FLEXIBLE BAGS

The filbert industry has been slower to change from the in-shell to the shelled market than other tree nut industries. The U.S. filbert industry is small and accounts for a minor portion of the world production. Production costs are higher in the United States than in other parts of the world. Practically all of the imports of filberts are shelled, and the price of these imports determines the price of the shelled domestic filberts.

Oregon filberts dominate the domestic in-shell market, however, because Oregon marketers regularly supply large, well-graded filberts that are preferred in the United States. The growing European market has become increasingly lucrative for Turkish filberts, both shelled and in-shell. This expanded market has alleviated, somewhat, the pressure of imports on prices for domestic filberts.

Pecans.—The trend to marketing nuts on a shelled basis has been as pronounced for pecans as it has been for almonds. According to recent surveys, approximately 94% of the pecans that entered commercial channels were shelled. Most of the larger firms that sell both in-shell and shelled nuts have discontinued sales of in-shell pecans. The in-shell pecans that are sold go almost exclusively into straight-packs and mixtures of nuts for home use.

The primary user of shelled pecans is the baking industry. Bakeries use about 38% of the total supply. Sales to households through grocery wholesalers and chains accounted for 20% of the sales. Candy manufacturers used an additional 20%. Nut salters used 6% of the shelled pecans and ice cream manufacturers, 7%. Syrupers, repackers, and cello packers used an additional 8% of the total.

Walnuts.—The walnut industry has been slow to shift from the in-shell to the shelled market, but there is evidence that this shift is taking place. Approximately 58% of the walnuts are marketed shelled, compared with 47% in 1950-52. Grocery wholesalers, chainstores, and mixers are the largest purchasers of in-shell walnuts, accounting for nearly all of the total. These outlets are also the principal users of shelled walnuts. There has been a rapid growth in popularity of vacuum-packed cans and cellophane packages of shelled walnuts sold in grocery stores for use by housewives in home food preparation. Other users of shelled walnuts are bakeries or bakery suppliers, 8%; confectioners, 6%; and ice cream manufacturers, 3%.

Exports

U.S. exports of domestic tree nuts usually are less than 10% of total production, and the amount varies from year to year depending on domestic supplies, world supplies, and prices. Since the mid-1950s most of our exports have been shelled nuts. Only small amounts of filberts and pecans are exported, either shelled or in-shell.

TABLE 2.5

U.S. EXPORTS OF IN-SHELL AND SHELLED TREE NUTS, IN TONS, 1940-1974

Year Beginning October 1	In-shell[1]					Shelled				
	Almonds	Filberts	Pecans	Walnuts	Total	Almonds	Filberts	Pecans	Walnuts	Total
1940	[2]	[2]	102	1,422	1,524	[2]	[2]	[3]93	[3]22	115
1941	[2]	[2]	26	1,208	1,234	[2]	[2]	16	81	97
1942	[3]38	[3]12	8	182	240	0	0	8	36	44
1943	80	222	1,394	1,216	2,912	0	0	281	13	294
1944	173	254	616	1,805	2,848	0	0	272	69	341
1945	160	146	1,239	3,327	4,872	0	0	474	135	609
1946	540	331	232	2,492	3,595	0	0	96	114	210
1947	143	425	102	1,769	2,439	0	0	217	428	645
1948	113	194	313	1,320	1,940	0	0	586	172	758
1949	225	239	83	1,659	2,206	0	0	332	24	356
1950	88	338	135	1,642	2,203	0	[3]5	292	30	322
1951	148	346	347	1,521	2,362	[4]509	0	326	35	361
1952	345	482	355	1,837	3,019	1,992	0	370	42	412
1953	341	222	273	1,553	2,389	3,986	10	467	56	4,519
1954	359	934	174	4,664	6,132	2,417	6	293	61	2,777
1955	208	513	215	1,686	2,622	4,459	22	373	83	4,937
1956	642	249	187	1,993	3,071	7,641	5	444	37	8,127
1957	510	975	228	4,748	6,461	1,697	14	473	53	2,237
1958	152	701	253	2,321	3,427	2,052	3	450	543	3,048
1959	920	241	168	978	2,307	8,814	22	431	84	9,351
1960	574	130	315	1,147	2,166	4,410	39	574	97	5,120
1961	236	417	525	1,012	2,190	6,178	70	659	103	7,010
1962[5]	133	259	164	882	1,438	2,709	69	339	93	3,210
1969	867	209	351	2,009	3,436	7,508	55	694	357	8,614
1970	1,490	143	555	2,903	5,091	24,997	78	662	1,390	27,127
1971	1,416	330	269	6,451	8,466	25,196	74	672	1,170	27,112
1972	988	332	455	12,038	13,813	34,374	136	737	1,965	37,212
1973	2,424	328	316	10,754	13,822	24,817	193	919	1,720	27,749
1974	2,488	571	676	20,207	23,942	30,905	121	864	2,362	34,252

[1]Separated into in-shell and shelled as follows: Pecans and walnuts, January 1, 1941 (considered to be in-shell prior to that date); Almonds, January 1, 1952 (considered in-shell through November 1951, shelled in December of 1951); Filberts, January 1, 1952 (considered to be in-shell prior to that date).
[2]Not available.
[3]January to September only.
[4]December to September only.
[5]October to May only.

Almonds are exported both shelled and in-shell. Our principal customer for in-shell almonds is Canada. West Germany is by far the largest consumer of our shelled almonds, but Japan, Canada, and the Scandinavian countries are also important. A few shelled almonds are also exported to Mexico and to South America.

From 1955 to 1961, the American almond industry changed the United States from primarily an almond importing nation to one of the world's leading exporters. This came as a result of a general upswing in production together with an intensive marketing program which stresses high quality and uniformity of product.

United States almonds are generally larger than Mediterranean almonds. This factor alone opened up new markets for certain customers. Exporters stress quality and uniformity of size and shape, along with cleanliness and reliability. They are also separated by cultivars. Exports in good crop years reach 21,000,000 lb of meats.

Even though the United States has become a major almond exporter, some nuts are still imported for specialized uses. Considerable quantities are imported when the domestic crop is short. Imports vary from 2 to 13 million pounds of shelled almonds.

In 1961 Portugal produced 5000 tons of almond meats according to Anon. (1965).

Most of the exports of filberts are in-shell. Canada is by far the largest importer of our in-shell filberts. Other important customers are West Germany, the Scandinavian countries, and various countries in South America. Canada and the Scandinavian countries are our most important customers for shelled filberts. The filbert industry lost an important customer for in-shell filberts when the United States placed an embargo on trade with Cuba. During the 1950s, Cuba was our chief customer for in-shell filberts and often took as much as half of our total exports.

Although Turkey tops the world in filbert production, domestic consumption is rather low and the important part is allocated for export. Turkey has been exporting filberts for 560 years. These nuts reportedly contain more oil and better flavor than any others in the world. Turkish filberts are classified as follows: (1) plump, or oily filberts; (2) pointed filberts with tall pointed shell; (3) almond filbert—crude almond and special almond; (4) black filbert with dark color and thick shell; (5) black filbert with thin shell (55 to 60% of crop); (6) coarse filbert with striped shell; (7) blood filbert with red inside, output high; (8) fosha filbert, bright color, extremely large; (9) bird filbert, grows in Piraziz, Giresun; and (10) crude filbert, hard thick shell, wild.

In 1936 the National Pecan Association, consisting of growers from Texas to Florida, was organized to promote orderly marketing of pecans abroad. The necessity to export has become a vital factor in the overall economy of marketing pecans. Exporting is more complicated than selling domestically, but may be more profitable. It must be maintained on a fairly constant level on a year-round basis, rather than a market to be used only on surpluses from the domestic market following bumper crops.

The U.S. Department of Agriculture's Foreign Agricultural Service attaches overseas can help in locating the export markets showing the product, testing new markets, making contacts with potential customers, and handling deliveries. The U.S. Department of Commerce has field offices in many parts of the world. Offices of Chambers of Commerce, American shipping companies, and main air carriers are eager to help. All of these services are free.

Pointers for exporters:

(1) Exactly what do you have to sell?
(2) Are prices and quality "exportable?"
(3) Where are the overseas markets?
(4) Have you made certain, through market surveys, that you can compete in price?
(5) Is your production geared to sustain overseas deliveries?
(6) Who will best take care of overseas sales?
(7) Do overseas markets require special packaging?
(8) Have you tested foreign markets through U.S. trade fairs or trade centers?
(9) Have you arranged for overseas financing?
(10) Do you have the confidence, determination and salesmanship needed to build a profitable export business?

In 1965 the U.S. Department of Agriculture's Foreign Agricultural Service authorized the National Pecan Council of America, a non-profit corporation operating under the direction of The Federated Pecan Growers Association of the United States, to participate and cooperate in a full-year study of this overseas sales potential.

American representatives met with agricultural specialists in England, Germany, Sweden, Belgium and the Netherlands. Ray Bass, president of the National Pecan Council, Lumberton, Mississippi, reported to the group that in the United States production of pecans had grown from about a million pounds in 1900 to a peak of 350,000,000 lb in 1965, and even greater yields are predicted in the future.

In 1963, 1,172,398 lb of in-shell and 1,226,164 lb of shelled pecans were exported to 43 countries.

Walnuts are exported both shelled and in-shell but most are in-shell. In 1961-62, Canada purchased 800 of the 1008 tons of in-shell walnuts exported. Canada also purchased a third of the exports of shelled walnuts. Other customers for walnuts are Mexico and some of the South American countries.

Outlook for Demand

Long range supplies of domestic tree nuts depend a great deal upon producer's appraisals of future economic conditions. The consumption of tree nuts is closely associated with population growth, the general price level, and the amount of consumer disposable income.

Assuming that per capita consumption of all tree nuts remains at approximately the same level, the supplies of tree nuts that will be needed to satisfy demand in 1985 have been computed (Table 2.6). The Bureau of the Census estimates that the population of the United States will increase approximately 37% between 1965 and 1985. Assuming that per capita disappearance of domestic tree nuts remains at the 1955-59 level of 1 lb, more than 266,000,000 lb of the 4 major domestic tree nuts will be needed to satisfy the expected demand in 1985.

TABLE 2.6

POPULATION PROJECTION AND RESULTING PER CAPITA TREE NUT CONSUMPTION (SHELLED BASIS) BY KINDS

Year	Population Mils	Almonds Lb	Mil Lb	Filberts Lb	Mil Lb	Pecans Lb	Mil Lb	Walnuts Lb	Mil Lb	Total Lb	Mil Lb
1965	194.7	.25	48.7	.06	11.7	.35	68.1	.34	66.2	1.0	194.7
1970	209.0	.25	52.2	.06	12.5	.35	73.2	.34	71.1	1.0	209.0
1975	225.9	.25	56.5	.06	13.6	.35	79.1	.34	76.8	1.0	225.9
1980	245.3	.25	61.3	.06	14.7	.35	85.9	.34	83.4	1.0	245.3
1985	266.3	.25	66.6	.06	16.0	.35	93.2	.34	90.5	1.0	266.3

Assuming no changes in the general price level, population increases alone should result in much greater quantities of tree nuts being demanded.[3] However, if the general price level and personal disposable income increase, the per capita consumption of so-called luxury products, including tree nuts, would be expected to rise also.

At the present time, the bulk of the tree nuts is consumed in manufactured products such as candy, baked goods and ice cream. Trends in consumption of these products that incorporate tree nuts are not available, but it is estimated that the consumption of confectionery items has remained about stable at 17 lb per person (U.S. Dep. Commerce 1963) since World War II, and the per capita consumption of baked goods has followed the same general pattern. However, in 1963 per capita consumption of confectionery items rose to 17.7 lb. If average family incomes have risen to the point where additional income has no effect on per capita consumption, then any increase in total consumption of tree nuts must come from an increase in population and changes in consumer's tastes.

In the past few years, however, there has been a change in the pattern of foods purchased as well as a change in the forms in which they are purchased. More services are now incorporated in the products offered for sale in retail stores. In keeping with this trend, more tree nuts are now offered for sale shelled for use in the home either for out-of-hand eating or for use in preparation of other foods. The tree nut industry probably lagged behind other food industries in responding to the packaged convenience trend, partly because of the technical difficulties in keeping the nut kernels fresh and attractive when displayed in retail outlets. Many problems have been overcome, and some increased consumption of nuts can be expected from improved merchandising methods and increased consumer education concerning the use of nuts in main course dishes as well as in desserts and confections. The increased use of almonds in prepared mixes and frozen foods augurs expanding uses of almonds and perhaps the entrance of other tree nuts into these food fields.

Wholesale Prices

New York City is the leading market for both domestic and imported tree nuts and the largest port of entry. Limited information concerning wholesale prices for typical grades of tree nuts in New York is available. Some quotations appear in the New York Journal of Commerce and publications of private price-collecting agencies. Although these quotations are incomplete, and, in some instances, may not be the actual prices at which individual shipments of the nuts are bought and sold, they do indicate the trend of wholesale prices for domestic nuts. Roughly, the trend of wholesale prices for both shelled and in-shell nuts is comparable to the trend of grower prices.

Average prices for typical sizes and cultivars of in-shell tree nuts have tended to move together. Almonds are usually priced slightly higher than walnuts and pecans. Filberts are usually several cents lower. From year to year, however, prices for each of the tree nuts fluctuate widely, depending on production, carryover stocks, and supplies of competing tree nuts. Average price relationships among the tree nuts might not hold true for specified years.

Prices for shelled tree nuts should be a more important indicator of price trends to the producer since an ever increasing portion of the total nut crop is being marketed in the form of shelled meats. However, such is not the case. Since most of the shelled tree nuts are sold by large sellers to very large buyers, the bulk of the tree nuts do not enter a market for which prices are quoted.

It is a common practice among tree nut suppliers to contact their larger customers early in the season and consummate the sale for the customers' annual supplies of nuts. After the large accounts have been sold and prices determined, price lists are published. After the large suppliers have published their price lists, the smaller suppliers announce their prices, which are usually a cent or two per pound lower for each cultivar or kernel cut than prices of the industry leaders. In large crop years, however, these published prices mean little, and buyers canvass various sellers to determine where nuts can be purchased at the lowest cost. This often leads to sharp competition among the nut sellers.

In past years, the sharp price competition among tree nut sellers has often resulted in bankruptcy for smaller and less well-financed firms in the pecan industry. Due partially to marketing orders, the other three tree nuts industries have been more stable. To reduce the speculative nature of tree nut marketing, some firms have recently begun to sell nuts on the 18-month or 2-year contracts. This of course necessitates increased storage of nuts from year to year, so that contracts can be protected. While these marketing techniques increase the capital requirements of small operators, they also bring increased price stability to the industry. These techniques have also resulted in increased sales of tree nuts. In the past, large food manufacturers have been hesitant to include tree nut products in their long-range advertising and promotion plans because they were not sure whether sufficient quantities of tree nuts would be available at reasonable prices. The long-term contracts, which guarantee both quantity and price, restored confidence in tree nuts and have resulted in increased tree nut sales.

While the consumption of all nuts is expected to increase, consumption of the individual nuts is dependent upon the demand for products in which they are used and the degree of competition among nuts for these end uses. The competition may be among the kinds of tree nuts or between tree nuts as a group and peanuts.

At the present time, the consumption of tree nuts (shelled basis) is small compared with the consumption of peanuts. There are some 400,000,000 lb of peanuts used by the confectionery and salting trades, compared with less than 60,000,000 lb of domestic tree nuts. In all uses, nearly 850,000,000 lb of peanuts are used, compared with less than 150,000,000 lb of domestic tree nuts.

Peanuts compete with tree nuts to a limited extent in the baking trade, comprising approximately 12% of the total nuts used, compared with pecans, 43%, and walnuts, 26%. Few, if any, peanuts are used in ice cream manufacturing or are sold to households in an unsalted form. Almonds, pecans and walnuts predominate in these uses in approximately that order.

TABLE 2.7

TREE NUT PRODUCTION, PRICE AND VALUE

Crop and State	Utilized Production[1]			Price per Unit			Value of Utilized Production		
	1974	1975	1976	1974	1975	1976	1974	1975	1976
	(Tons, In-shell Basis)			(Dollars per Ton)			(1,000 Dollars)		
Almonds Calif.	189,000	160,000	233,000	900.00	800.00	790.00	170,100	128,000	184,070
Filberts									
Oreg.	6,400	11,800	6,950	560.00	610.00	640.00	3,584	7,198	4,448
Wash.	300	320	220	565.00	595.00	635.00	170	190	140
Total	6,700	12,120	7,170	560.00	610.00	640.00	3,754	7,388	4,588
Walnuts (Persian)									
Calif.	155,000	199,300	183,700	419.00	469.00	633.00	64,945	93,060	115,839
Oreg.	1,500	1,300	700	380.00	388.00	605.00	570	504	424
Total	156,500	199,300	183,700	419.00	469.00	633.00	65,515	93,564	116,263
	(1,000 lb, In-shell Basis)			(Cents per Pound)					
Macadamia Nuts Haw.	16,370	18,210	18,990	32.0	31.6	36.9	5,238	5,754	7,007

Source: Econ. Res. Serv., U.S. Dep. Agric.
[1]Excludes unharvested production and excess cullages, (tons): Oregon filberts, 1974—500; Oregon walnuts, 1975—200.

TABLE 2.8

UTILIZATION OF TREE NUTS

Crop and State	Utilization of Production						Meat Production of Nuts Sold Shelled (1,000 lb)		
	Sold In-shell			Sold Shelled					
	1974	1975	1976	1974	1975	1976	1974	1975	1976
Almonds¹				(Tons, In-shell Basis)					
Calif.				189,000	160,000	233,000	230,000	186,000	284,000
Filberts									
Oreg.	4,900	7,600	5,930	1,500	4,200	1,020	1,020	3,200	800
Wash.	252	283	185	48	237	35	33	28	27
Total	5,152	7,883	6,115	1,548	4,237	1,055	1,053	3,228	827
Walnuts (Persian)									
Calif.	48,720	71,300	65,000	106,280	126,700	118,000	71,846	90,000	84,800
Oreg.	400	650	410	1,100	650	290	800	400	190
Total	49,120	71,950	65,410	107,380	127,350	118,290	72,646	90,400	
	(1,000 lb In-shell Basis)								
Pecans									
U.S.	23,430	34,552	22,995	113,670	212,248	80,105			

Source: Econ. Res. Serv., U.S. Dep. Agric.
¹California almonds sold in-shell are included in sold shelled.

In the in-shell tree nut mixtures there is considerable direct competition between the kinds of tree nuts. If almonds are low priced relative to pecans or filberts, more almonds and fewer pecans and filberts are included in the mixture. If walnuts are expensive relative to other nuts, the percentage of walnuts is decreased and the percentage of the other nuts increased depending on the price of each, relative to the others. Standards for size, quality and quantity of each nut contained in in-shell mixed nut packs have recently been developed. Adoption of these standards should result in more uniformity in mixed-nut packs.

A typical in-shell mixture of tree nuts contains 30% (by weight) of walnuts, 20% each of almonds, filberts and Brazil nuts, and 10% of pecans. Large nuts are usually used, but in low-priced mixtures smaller sizes are used. The packer of in-shell nut mixtures usually charges 14 to 18% markup over costs; the retailer usually takes a 25% markup.

A recent development in marketing in-shell nuts at the retail level has been a return to an old merchandising method. In this method, tree nuts are displayed side-by-side in bulk bins and all are sold for the same price per pound. It has been found that housewives tend to take a scoopful of each kind, and they usually buy more than if nuts are displayed in one-pound packages. Some stores have reported sales increases of 1000% over prepackaged sales. Since the high-priced nuts (usually, but not always, pecans) are only slightly underpriced and the lower priced nuts are over-priced, the retailer makes a greater profit per pound and realizes a greatly increased total revenue from in-shell nut sales. The effectiveness of this merchandising method can be nullified, however, if the retailer uses lower grades of the expensive or high-priced nut.

The dominance of peanuts in those areas where they compete with tree nuts is due to price. Peanuts are much lower-priced than tree nuts. In 1960-63, the season average grower price for peanuts was $211 per ton compared with $583 for almonds, $428 for filberts, $514 for pecans, and $482 for walnuts. Converting these to a shelled basis and disregarding costs of shelling and any value of shells or other byproducts, peanuts cost the primary purchaser 15.1 cents per pound on a shelled basis, compared with 49.2 cents for almonds, 43.2 cents for filberts, 61.7 cents for walnuts, and 69.6 cents for pecans.

The present price differential between peanuts and tree nuts is expected to continue. The production of tree nuts is a long-range enterprise in which the bulk of the costs are fixed while the acreage of peanuts is decided on annually, and the costs of production are variable.

To increase the consumption of tree nuts at a rate greater than that expected through normal population growth, the tree nut industry should first enhance the competitive position of tree nuts in those outlets where they already have a competitive advantage, i.e., the baking industry, households (unsalted for home cooking use), and ice cream manufacturers. Effective advertising, product promotion, and merchandising plus research on new products, forms and uses of tree nuts should help to accomplish this. Secondly, increased use of tree nuts by the confectionery and salting trades should be encouraged through assuring adequate supplies at competitive prices over a period of years.

REFERENCES

ANON. 1948-1959. Statistical Reports. Tree nuts. U.S. Dep. Agric. Bureau Agric. Econ.

ANON. 1920-1963. Statistical Reports. U.S. Dep. Agric. Crop Reporting Serv.

ANON. 1965-1966. Statistical Report. World Agricultural Production and Trade. U.S. Dep. Agric., Foreign Agric. Serv. Stn. Repts. July, March.

ANON. 1976. Feb. Tree Nuts, World Production. U.S. Dep. Foreign Agric. Serv., Cir. *FN 1-76*.

JONES, S.A., and CHILDS, V.C. 1932. An economic study of the pecan industry. U.S. Dep. Agric. Tech. Bull. *324*.

MCELROY, R.C., and POWELL, J.V. 1963. Pecan production and marketing. U.S. Dep. Agric., Agric. Econ. Rept. *41*.

POWELL, J.V. 1963. The pecan nursery industry. U.S. Dep. Agric., Agric. Econ. Rept. *44*.

POWELL, J.V. 1964. The domestic tree nut industries. U.S. Dep. Agric., Agric. Econ. Rept. *62*.

POWELL, J.V. 1976. Changing marketing patterns for domestic tree nuts. Fruit Situation. U.S. Dep. Agric. Econ. Res. Serv., *TFS-194*.

POWELL, J.V., and REIMUND, D.A. 1962. The pecan shelling and processing industry. U.S. Dep. Agric., Agric. Econ. Rept. *15*.

PURCELL, J.C., and ELROD, J.C. 1963. The supply, price and utilization of pecans. Ga. Agric. Exp. Stn. Mimeo Series N.S. *182*, Rev. to 1966.

SEALS, A.D., JR. 1964. Costs and returns for a pecan enterprise. Miss. Agric. Exp. Stn. Bull. *686*.

U.S. DEP. COMMERCE. 1929-1963. Bureau of Census Repts.

U.S. DEP. COMMERCE. 1963. Confectionery Sales and Distribution. Business and Defense Administration. May.

WOODROOF, J.G., and HEATON, E.K. 1961. Pecans for processing. Ga. Agric. Exp. Stn. Bull., N.S. *80*.

3

Composition and Nutritive Value of Nuts

There is historical evidence that nuts played a prominent part in the feeding of man and beast in many civilizations and in quite different parts of the globe. The accessibility of nut nutrients is increased by processing, such as blanching, slicing, chopping, grinding into paste and butter, emulsifying, making into milk, and combining with other foods, especially carbohydrates.

Nuts have traditionally been regarded as tidbits, a special treat to be added to candy, cakes, cookies and salted specialties, or to be served at special parties or dinners. But they are also significant nutritionally. Many of the ideas regarding nuts are due to the fact that they are so frequently added to an already adequate meal. Nuts, served as a substantial part of the main dish, are a valuable addition to the meal.

Buying nutmeats, either as slices, slivers or sized pieces, saves time, labor and storage space, but nuts in the shells are cheaper and stay fresh longer. Unless special shelling equipment is on hand, it is cheaper to buy nutmeats graded and presized.

The flavor of nuts is largely dependent upon the oils and essential oils which they contain, although in some nuts there are specific flavoring substances. In most nut kernels the oil readily becomes rancid, and gives the disagreeable flavor found in so-called stale nuts. Since it is easier to prevent the nut kernels from becoming rancid than it is to remove the rancid flavor, nuts should be kept dry, cold, and away from light, air and other products from which they may absorb off-flavors. The containers should protect the nuts from excess moisture, heat, insects, rodents and molds.

Homemakers, as well as manufacturers of nut products, are seasonally oriented in their use of tree nuts. Until a few years ago, quality nuts were only available in the late fall and winter. Tree nuts have been traditionally used for gifts and entertaining at Thanksgiving, Christmas and New

Year's holidays—to dress up foods or for the fun of cracking nuts for the family or friends.

The frequency of use varies with the nuts, location and family income. The price is a determining factor as to whether one or another nut will be used in many products. Throughout the country Persian walnuts are most popular, followed by pecans, almonds and cashews. Of the domestic tree nuts served as snacks, filberts are more popular than Persian walnuts. Pecans and Persian walnuts are used more than other nuts in food preparation, more frequently in baking than in candy and salads.

There is a tendency for higher income, better educated homemakers living in metropolitan areas to use more tree nuts. The higher the income the more likely the homemaker is to use nuts in food preparation and the less likely she is to use them in snacks. Homemakers without children use them less frequently in baking and candy. With family incomes rising, and higher income families using more nuts, there should be expanding markets for packaged shelled nuts.

Total per capita consumption of commercially produced tree nuts is about the same as 50 years ago (1.3 lb per person per year). The use of walnuts, almonds and filberts has changed very little, while pecan consumption has more than tripled.

The increased availability of nuts, not only in the shell but shelled and in recipe-size packages, is stimulating a greater use of nuts. When nuts are for "dusting," a small package of chips, slivers or meal may save valuable time and be less expensive in the long run.

Nuts add many qualities to food besides fat. The movement to improve the flavor and texture of bland foods with nuts is in its infancy in the United States, and considerably behind many European countries. Nuts have a greater contribution to make to our diets than their present popular usage in desserts and nibbling foods after meals and for snacks. They give crunchiness to main dishes of meats, chicken and fish; to toppings for many vegetables, such as snap beans, broccoli, peas and beans; to both fruit and vegetable salads; and to desserts of many descriptions, including ice cream, pies and cakes. In fact, nuts may well add to meals three times a day, all seasons of the year.

A critical problem in the utilization of most nuts is the sporadic contamination by toxin-producing strains of common molds. The possibility of toxins entering foods intended for human consumption, as well as feedstuffs, is of utmost concern.

More information is needed as to the physical and chemical characteristics of those constituents in nuts which affect flavor, aroma, texture and other important properties of the raw and processed products.

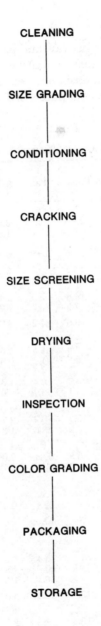

FIG. 3.1. TWELVE STEPS IN PROCESSING SHELLED NUTS

COMPOSITION OF NUTS

Proximate composition of most raw and processed tree nuts is given in Table 3.1 (Chatfield and Adams 1940; Adams 1975). The data given are averages on the as-purchased basis, and relate only to the edible portion; they are calculated on the basis of purchased weight, but have no bearing

TABLE 3.1

PROXIMATE COMPOSITION OF TREE NUTS

Nut	Refuse %	Water %	Protein %	Fat %	Ash %	Total Carbohydrates Fiber %	Sugars %	Starch %	Cal per Lb
Almonds, dried									
unblanched kernels	—	4.7	18.6	54.1	3.0	2.7	4.4	—	2,900
in-shells	49	2.4	9.5	27.6	1.5	1.4	—	—	1,480
meal, partially defatted	—	7.2	39.5	18.3	6.1	2.3	—	—	1,990
Beechnuts, in-shells	39	2.4	12.2	35.0	2.2	—	—	—	1,815
kernels	—	4.0	20.0	57.4	3.6	—	—	—	2,980
Brazil nuts, kernels	—	5.3	14.4	65.9	3.4	2.1	1.5	2.2	3,150
in-shells	50	2.6	7.2	33.0	1.7	1.0	—	—	—
Cashew nuts, roasted	—	4.1	19.6	47.2	2.7	1.0	6.8	10.7	2,760
Chestnuts									
fresh, kernels	—	53.2	2.8	1.5	1.0	1.1	6.4	14.8	865
in-shells	19	43.1	2.3	1.2	0.8	0.9	—	—	700
dried, kernels	—	8.4	6.7	4.1	2.2	2.5	14.4	41.1	1,715
in-shells	18	6.9	5.5	3.4	1.8	2.0	—	—	1,405
flour	—	11.7	6.1	3.7	2.6	2.0	—	—	1,640
Hazelnuts (filberts)									
kernels	—	6.0	12.7	60.9	2.7	3.4	3.2	1.6	3,040
in-shells	53	2.8	6.0	28.6	1.3	1.6	—	—	1,430
Hickory nuts									
kernels	—	3.5	13.9	67.4	2.0	2.2	—	—	3,245
in-shells	65	1.2	4.9	26.6	0.7	0.8	—	—	1,135
Macadamia nuts									
kernels	—	3.1	8.7	71.4	1.7	2.5	2.7	—	3,345
in-shells	69	1.0	2.7	22.1	0.5	0.8	—	—	1,035
Pecans, kernels	—	3.0	9.4	73.0	1.6	2.2	3.9	0	3,385
in-shells	48	1.6	4.9	38.0	0.8	1.1	—	—	1,760
Pine nuts									
kernels, pignolias	—	4.9	31.2	48.4	4.3	1.0	4.3	0	2,745
kernels, pinon	—	3.1	12.5	60.6	2.8	—	—	—	3,080
in-shells	42	1.8	7.2	35.1	1.6	—	—	—	1,790
Pistachio, kernels	—	5.6	19.6	53.2	3.0	2.2	6.1	—	2,865
Walnuts									
black, kernels	—	2.7	18.3	58.2	2.1	1.9	—	—	3,045
in-shells	78	0.6	4.0	12.8	0.5	0.4	—	—	670
Persian									
kernels	—	3.3	15.0	64.4	1.7	2.1	—	—	3,185
in-shells	55	1.5	6.8	29.0	0.8	0.9	—	—	1,435

Source: Chatfield and Adams (1940); Adams (1975).

TABLE 3.2

COMPOSITION OF TREE NUTS, 100-GRAM PORTIONS

Nut	Water %	Protein g	Fat g	Carbohydrate Total g	Carbohydrate Fiber g	Ash g	Calcium mg	Phosphorus mg	Iron mg	Sodium mg	Potassium mg	Vitamin A Value I.U.	Magnesium mg	Thiamin mg	Riboflavin mg	Niacin mg	Ascorbic Acid mg	Fuel Value cal
Almonds, dried	4.7	18.6	54.2	19.5	2.6	3.0	234	504	4.7	4	773	0	270	0.24	0.92	3.5	trace	598
roasted, salted	0.7	18.6	57.7	19.5	2.6	3.5	235	504	4.7	198	773	0	—	0.05	0.92	3.5	0	627
choc. coated	2.0	12.3	43.7	39.6	1.5	2.3	203	343	2.8	59	546	trace	—	0.12	0.53	1.7	trace	569
sugar coated	2.3	7.8	18.6	70.2	0.9	1.1	100	166	1.9	20	255	0	—	0.05	0.27	1.0	0	456
meal, partially defatted	7.2	39.5	18.3	28.9	2.3	6.1	424	914	8.5	7	400	0	—	0.32	1.68	6.3	trace	408
Beechnuts	6.6	19.4	50.0	20.3	3.7	3.7	—	—	—	—	—	—	—	—	—	—	—	568
Brazil nuts	4.6	14.3	66.9	10.9	3.1	3.3	186	693	3.4	1	715	trace	225	0.96	0.12	1.6	—	654
Chestnuts, fresh	52.5	2.9	1.5	42.1	1.1	1.0	27	88	1.7	6	454	—	41	0.22	0.22	0.6	—	194
dried	8.4	6.7	4.1	78.6	2.5	2.2	52	162	3.3	12	875	—	—	0.32	0.38	1.2	—	377
flour	11.4	6.1	3.7	76.2	2.0	2.6	50	164	3.2	11	847	—	—	0.23	0.37	1.0	—	362
Hazelnuts (filberts)	5.8	12.6	62.4	16.7	3.0	2.5	209	337	3.4	2	704	—	184	0.46	—	0.9	trace	634
Hickory nuts	3.3	13.2	68.7	12.6	1.9	2.0	trace	360	2.4	—	—	—	160	—	—	—	—	673
Macadamia nuts	3.0	7.8	71.6	15.9	2.5	1.7	48	161	2.0	—	264	0	—	0.34	0.11	1.3	0	691
Pecans	3.4	9.2	71.2	14.6	2.3	1.6	73	289	2.4	trace	603	130	142	0.86	0.13	0.9	2	687
Pine nuts, pignolias	5.6	31.1	47.4	11.6	0.9	4.3	—	604	5.2	—	—	30	—	0.62	0.23	—	trace	552
pinon	3.1	13.0	60.5	20.5	1.1	2.9	12	—	—	—	—	—	—	1.28	—	4.5	0	635
Pistachio nuts	5.3	19.3	53.7	19.0	1.9	2.7	131	500	7.3	—	972	230	158	0.67	—	1.4	30	594
Walnuts, black	3.1	20.5	59.3	14.8	1.7	2.3	trace	570	6.0	3	460	300	190	0.22	0.11	0.7	—	628
Persian	3.5	14.8	64.0	15.8	2.1	1.9	99	380	3.1	2	450	30	131	0.33	0.13	0.9	2	651

Source: Watt and Merrill (1963).

on the composition of inedible parts. For example, Brazil nuts contain, in the edible portion, about 14% protein and 66% fat. Since the purchased weight is 50% refuse, this reduces the percentages of protein and fat to about 7% and 33%, respectively.

Nuts are a very concentrated food and are better used as an integral part of the menu rather than as supplement to an already adequate meal.

Data in Table 3.2 show the organic, mineral and vitamin content of 100-g portions of raw and prepared tree nuts (Watt and Merrill 1963).

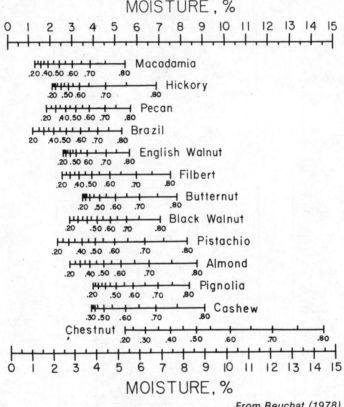

From Beuchat (1978)

FIG. 3.2. RELATIONSHIP BETWEEN WATER ACTIVITY (a$_w$) AND MOISTURE CONTENT OF TREE MEATS AT 21°C

By placing a ruler vertically in such a way as to line up identical moisture contents (%) indicated on the top and bottom scales, a$_w$ values from 0.20 to 0.80 for the 13 nutmeats can be readily estimated.

WATER

While green, tree nuts contain about 50% water, but when dried the moisture may be as low as 3%, as with hickory nuts, macadamia nuts, pecans, pine nuts and walnuts. The low moisture content is very important in the initial preservation, storage and processing of these nuts. As long as the moisture is low, molding will not occur and the fats, proteins and carbohydrates will be more stable. But in order for the moisture content to remain low the relative humidity in the storage environment has to be maintained at about 55%.

FATS AND OILS

The fats in most tree nuts are high, reaching more than 70% in macadamia nuts and pecans; and more than 60% in Brazil nuts, hazelnuts, pine nuts and walnuts. The high fat content is very important in curing, storing and processing nuts. For optimum stability of the fats, drying should be done with much air circulation, but without heat; storage should be at the lowest practical temperature; and processing should utilize heat for the shortest time possible and cooling should follow quickly.

Due to the high fat content nuts are very high in fuel value (calories). Few foods are as high in calories as macadamia nuts, pecans and hickory nuts. With the exception of chestnuts, all the other nuts contain from 5 to 6 cal per gram.

Chestnuts stand alone in having a very low fat content. Consequently they may be processed by boiling, drying and storing at moderate temperatures without a problem of rancidity.

Selected fatty acids in seven tree nuts are shown in Table 3.3. Almonds, beechnuts, cashew nuts, hazelnuts, hickory nuts, pecans, pistachio nuts and walnuts contain 5% or less saturated fatty acids, while Brazil nuts contain 13%. Hickory nuts and pecans are very high in the oleic acid group of unsaturated fatty acids, followed by almonds, walnuts, pistachio nuts and hazelnuts. Those highest in the linoleic acid group of unsaturated fatty acids are Persian walnuts, followed by Brazil nuts and beechnuts.

Oils used for cooking, cosmetics, pharmaceuticals and lubricants are pressed, extracted, distilled or centrifuged from many nuts such as almonds, pecans, walnuts, beechnuts and others.

PROTEINS

Tree nuts are moderately high in protein, and the percentage is increased by drying or defatting.

In protein value, the different nuts range from less than 5% to over 30%. Although nut protein is of good quality, the high fat content of most

TABLE 3.3

FATTY ACID ANALYSIS OF SEVERAL NUTS

	Myristic	Palmitic	Stearic	Oleic	Linoleic	Linolenic	Lignoceric
Almond (Subranamanyam 1957)	0.2	12.6	4.0	62.5	24.4	–	–
Beechnuts (Jacobs 1951)	–	–	–	48.4	33.2	2.8	–
Black walnuts (Osborne and Harris 1903)	0.4	3.4	1.8	35.6	48.6	7.4	0.04
Brazil nuts (Schnette and Enz 1930, 1931)							
Residual oil	1.79	13.55	2.58	55.64	21.65	–	–
Virgin oil	0.48	13.74	5.45	42.79	26.54	–	–
Cashew nuts (Jacobs 1951)	–	6.4	–	73.77	7.67	–	0.5
Pine nut (Jacobs 1951)							
Solid acids	–	92.2	8	–	–	–	–
Liquid acids	–	–	–	51-57	43-49	–	–
Pistachio nut (Jacobs 1951)	0.6	8.2	1.6	69.0	1.98	–	–

Source: Anon (1967), and others as indicated.

nuts makes them unsatisfactory as a substitute for meat or other sources of animal protein. While nuts make a useful contribution to the protein of the diet, under most circumstances it is better to consider them as a source of fat rather than of protein.

Pine nuts, beechnuts, pistachio nuts, black walnuts and almonds contain about 20% protein, while those very high in oil are lower in protein.

TOTAL CARBOHYDRATES

Carbohydrate content in tree nuts is moderate to low (with the exception of chestnuts). However, carbohydrates are added in the form of sugars, syrups, starch and pectin to many nuts during processing. Total natural carbohydrates run about 20% in pine nuts, pistachio nuts, beechnuts and almonds, and about 15% in walnuts, pecans, macadamia nuts, hazelnuts and cashew nuts.

ASH

Ash in nuts is below 3% in all those listed except pine nuts, Brazil nuts, beechnuts and almonds. It is less than 2% in fresh chestnuts, macadamia nuts, pecans and Persian walnuts. Fiber is also low in all nuts.

SUGAR

Sugars are low, but are high enough in some nuts to make them taste quite sweet. Among these are chestnuts, cashew nuts, pistachio nuts and pine nuts. Starch is very low in all nuts except chestnuts.

MINERALS

Most tree nuts contain large amounts of, but are considered a poor source of, calcium. They also contain phosphorus and potassium, a moderate amount of magnesium, and limited amounts of iron and sodium.

VITAMINS

In general, tree nuts are low in most vitamins. Black walnuts, pistachio nuts and pecans contain moderate amounts of vitamin A, while other nuts contain only traces. Pine nuts are the only kind of nuts with more than 1% thiamin; pecans and Brazil nuts contain slightly less; and almonds, chestnuts, Macadamia nuts and walnuts contain about 0.25% thiamin. Hazelnuts, chestnuts, Brazil nuts, walnuts, almonds and pecans are good sources of vitamin B-1. Almonds contain about 1% riboflavin and the others contain much less. Pine nuts and almonds contain 3 to 4.5% niacin, while the others contain less than 2%. With the exception of pistachio nuts, with 30% ascorbic acid, all of the nuts listed contain only traces of ascorbic acid.

Vitamin B-6 occurs naturally in nuts as pyridoxine, pyridoxal and pyridoxamine. It occurs either free or combined with other substances, such as phosphates, in amounts ranging from 1 to 6.5 mcg per gram. Filberts and Persian walnuts contain over 60% pyridoxal, while almonds, Brazil nuts, chestnuts and pecans contain a higher proportion of vitamin B-6 as pyridoxine (Table 3.4).

TABLE   3.4

VITAMIN B-6   OF   NUTS

Nut	Vitamin B-6 Chromatographed			
	Pyridoxine	Pyridoxal	Pyridoxamine	Total
		(μg/g)		
Almond (Calif.)				
with skins unblanched	0.65	0.32	0.17	1.14
without skins,				
blanched	0.56	0.30	0.21	1.07
skins, blanched	0.31	0.38	0.11	0.80
blanching liquid	0.02	0.01	0	0.03
Brazil nuts	1.84	0.25	0.43	2.52
Chestnuts (Italy)	2.61	0.51	0.18	3.30
Filberts (Ore. or Wash.)	0.08	0.06	0.25	0.39
Pecans (Ga.)	1.30	0.22	0.31	1.83
Walnuts, Persian (Calif.)	1.79	4.17	0.28	6.42

Source: Polansky and Murphy (1966).

OTHER   CHEMICAL   CONSTITUENTS

Phytin and Lipids

Important organic phosphorus compounds are phytin and lipids (q.v.), lecithin (q.v.), and cephalin. Phytin in foods occurs mainly as a mixed calcium, magnesium, and potassium salt of inositolphosphoric acid and supplies phosphorus and calcium in a readily available form. The percentages of total phosphorus in various nut kernels occurring as phytic acid phosphorus are for almond 82, Brazil nut 86, American chestnut 18, hazelnut 74, filbert 83, peanut 57, and Persian walnut 42. The phytin phosphorus content, calculated as $C_6H_{18}O_{24}P_6$, was found to be for almond 2.57%, Brazil nut 2.96%, filbert 1.66%, hickory nut 1.57%, peanut 1.67%, pecan 1.46%, Persian walnut 1.43%, and eastern black walnut 2.03% (Averill and King 1926). Lipids containing nitrogen and phosphorus are the phosphatides lecithin and cephalin, while alcohols devoid of nitrogen and phosphorus are cholesterol and its isomer phytosterol. Peanuts contain 0.5% lecithin and cephalin and piñon contains 1.0% lecithin (containing 3.6% P). In pecan there was found to be 0.53 mg per gram of choline, while in the peanut there was 1.70 mg and in peanut meal 2.52 mg per gram. Phytosterol occurs in the oil of beechnut to the extent of 0.18%, hazelnut 0.50%, and piñon 0.40%, while pecan oil contains 0.28% cholesterol.

Glycosides (q.v.) and Alkaloids

Saponins (q.v.) are glycosides that are mainly amorphous, soluble in water, and form colloidal solutions which foam readily and reduce surface tension. A saponin occurs in the pulp of soapnut to the extent of some 30%, while horse chestnut contains as bitter principles 10 to 14% of two saponins, esculin and argyrin. Esculin, $C_{15}H_{16}O_9$, is hydrolyzed by the action of an enzyme to glucose and esculetin, $C_9H_6O_2$. Amygdalin, $C_{20}H_{27}NO_{11}$, is the most important of the cyanogenetic glycosides, yielding hydrocyanic acid on hydrolysis. It is found in all seeds of the rose family and occurs more abundantly in the seed of the bitter almond (2.5 to 3.5%). On hydrolysis it is split by the enzymes amygdalase and prunase into glucose and benzaldehyde in addition to hydrocyanic acid:

$$C_{20}H_{27}NO_{11} + 2H_2O \rightarrow 2C_6H_{12}O_6 + C_6H_5CHO + HCN$$

Intermediary products are mandelonitrile glucoside (prunasin) and benzaldehyde cyanohydrin (mandelonitrile). Strychnus nux-vomica, poison nut, has as its chief constituent the alkaloids strychnine (0.4%) and brucine (90.2%). It also contains strychnic or igasuric acids, the glycoside loganin, sugar and fat.

Tannins

Tannins (see Tanning materials) are amorphous astringent substances that give colors (ink) with ferric salts and precipitate gelatin from solution (tanning). They are hydrolyzed by acids into various products such as sugar (d-glucose) and hydroxy acids. The process of tanning is the conversion of a hydrophilic gel into a relatively nonhydrophilic gel (leather), with both physical and chemical processes entering into the reaction. Tannins occur abundantly in some nuts and nut tree parts. The wood and bark of chestnuts are especially rich sources of commercial tannin. The integument of the pecan contains up to 25% tannin, while the outer shell has 6 to 8%; the almond hull contains 4.5%. Both pecan shell waste and almond hulls from processing plants are a source of commercial vegetable tannin (Cruess *et al.* 1947; Flemming 1947).

Some nut trees have been found to be accumulators of certain mineral elements. Hickory is notable as an accumulator of aluminum (Robinson and Edgington 1945), the ash of its leaves containing up to 37.5% Al_2O_3. Walnut, unlike hickory, does not accumulate aluminum; the ash of autumnal leaves of Persian walnut was found to contain only 0.032% Al. Hickory was found to be an accumulator of rare earth elements, greatly exceeding all other plants; the leaves showed up to 2296 ppm rare earths (scandium, yttrium, lanthanum, dysprosium, holmium, erbium, thulium, ytterbium and lutetium). The amounts of rare earth found in parts of the hickory nut were: kernels 5, shells 7, and shucks 17 ppm. Large amounts of barium accumulate in the kernel of the Brazil nut in an insoluble form; but when the nut is eaten barium dissolves in the hydrochloric acid of the stomach.

The main deficiencies in minor mineral elements which have shown up in the growing of nut crops are zinc deficiency in pecan, Persian walnut and almond, and boron deficiency in Persian walnut. The disorder of pecan called "rosette" was a threat to the growing of the crop for some time, until scientists in the U.S. Department of Agriculture found the cause to be a deficiency in zinc, which was corrected by application of zinc salts to the tree by various means. "Little leaf" of almond is also corrected by zinc treatment (Wood 1947). Symptoms of a deficiency of several elements in pecan trees grown in sand cultures were studied. It was noted that no single abnormality was sufficiently characteristic of an element to identify it as deficient in the tree (Alben *et al.* 1942). Boron deficiency in Persian walnuts is indicated by the shoots dying back ("snakeheads") and by nuts failing to set on the trees. Such a condition is corrected by application of 4 to 6 lb of borax per tree. Response to boron application in a walnut orchard noted for poor production was shown by the setting of so many nuts after boron treatment that many of the trees were broken down by the weight of the nuts (5000 lb green nuts per acre) (Stephenson 1947). Filberts, on the other hand, have never shown any deficiency symptoms or response to boron treatment. In an intensive study of the boron content of almond, olive, and Persian walnut tree parts, made to see whether there were deficiencies, the kernels of the almond were found to have 15.6 to 57.7, shells 21.8 to 102.5, husks 36.4 to 440.5, and leaves 30.4 to 53.6 ppm total boron (Haas 1945); while in the walnut there were 7.5 to 16.3 ppm boron in the kernels, 13.6 to 15.4 in shells, 21.7 to 79.0 in husks, and 35.9 to 516.0 in leaves. Much of the boron in the husk of the almond was water-soluble, while that in the husk of the walnut was water-insoluble.

TABLE 3.5

NUTRITIVE VALUE OF ALMONDS
TYPICAL CHEMICAL ANALYSIS

Content	Amount
Moisture	3.54%
Protein	21.66%
Vitamins	
Carotene (Provitamin A)	0.0078 mg/g
Vitamin B-1 (Thiamin)	0.0020 mg/g
Vitamin G (Riboflavin)	0.0033 mg/g
Vitamin E (Tocopherol)	2.00 mg/g
Nicotinic acid (Niacin)	0.07 mg/g
Pyridoxin (Vitamin B-6)	20.00 mg/g
Biotin	.000180 mg/g
Choline	0.8 mg/g
Minerals	
Sodium (Na)	0.267%
Potassium (K)	0.576%
Calcium (Ca)	0.240%
Magnesium (Mg)	0.285%
Silicon (Si)	0.003%
Iron (Fe)	0.0056%
Sulphur (S)	0.037%
Phosphorus (P)	0.511%
Chloride (Cl)	0.011%
Manganese (Mn)	0.0025%
Strontium (Sr)	0.0003%
Copper (Cu)	0.0003%
Aluminum (Al)	0.00003%
Chromium (Cr)	0.00003%
Amino Compounds	
Glycine or glycocoli	0.113%
Alanine	0.319%
Serine	trace
Valine	0.042%
Leucine, iso-leucine, and non-leucine	0.988%
Tyrosine	0.247%
Cystine	0.140%
Tryptophan	0.304%
Proline and hydroxy-proline	0.615%
Aspartic acid	1.205%
Glutamic acid and hydroxyglutamic acid	4.583%
Histidine	0.351%
Arginine	2.633%
Lysine	1.568%

Source: Kuzio (1977).

ALMONDS

Jacobs (1951) stated that the water content of the kernels of sweet almonds decreases from 79.6 to 82.8% to 25.8 to 28.2% during ripening, while the oil increases considerably. The iodine number and refractive index of almond oil remain nearly constant during ripening. No starch was observed during any phase of ripening. The absolute content of carbohydrates in the kernel either increases or remains unchanged during maturation; and the absolute amount of protein material increases, but the percentages of both decrease because of the greater increase in oil content. Benzaldehyde increases 15- to 18-fold; and no hydrocyanic acid was detected during ripening.

Almond oil is the fixed oil expressed from bitter (or sweet) almonds. The oil is straw-colored, nearly odorless, and nondrying, and is used chiefly in pharmacy. The essential oil of almonds is obtained only from bitter almonds (by decomposition of amygdalin) and is often called bitter almond oil or oil of bitter almonds, with a specific gravity of 1.04. It is colorless when pure and owes its characteristic odor and flavor to benzaldehyde. It contains also hydrocyanic (prussic) acid, which is removed when the oil is used in flavoring, the resulting oil being called oil of bitter almonds, without prussic acid, having a specific gravity of 0.91 to 0.92. The toxic nitrobenzene has been used to adulterate it. Both peach and apricot kernels yield fixed and essential oils so similar to almond oils that they are used as adulterants of, and as substitutes for, almond oils.

Other properties of almond oil are: refractive index, 1.4695; iodine number, 99.4; saponification number, 188.8; and acid number, 1.24 (Jacobs 1951).

In nutritive value 1 lb of almonds is equal to 8.55 lb of milk; 5.2 lb of eggs; 3.78 lb of mutton; and 9.18 lb of chicken, and contains 3030 calories. The refuse on shelling is 65% (Gouy 1960).

BEECHNUT

Beechnuts are collected in the eastern United States and Europe as a source of edible oil and seed cake. They are occasionally used for human food.

Dried beechnuts yield about 42% oil. The composition is calculated to be unsaponifiable matter 0.27%, oleic acid 48.4%, linoleic acid 33.2%, linolenic acid 2.8%, glycerol 4.5%, and saturated acids 11.5% (Jacobs 1951).

Properties of beechnut oil are: specific gravity at 24°C (75.2°F), 0.9124; refractive index, 15°, 0.9202; iodine number, 110.9; thiocyanogen value, 77.7; saponification number, 187.4; hehner number, 94.8; melting point, −17.8°C (0°F).

The nutritive value is the same as that of almonds. The refuse on shelling is 40% (Gouy 1960).

BRAZIL NUTS

All Brazil nuts consumed in the United States are imported. A nitrogenous material of Brazil nuts, excelsin, has the following composition: carbon, 52.18%; hydrogen, 6.92%; nitrogen, 18.12%; sulfur, 1.06% and oxygen, 21.72%. The total nitrogen is about as follows: ammonia, 1.48%; basic nitrogen (diamino), 5.76%; nonbasic nitrogen (monoamino), 10.97%; and nitrogen in magnesium oxide precipitate (humin), 0.17%. The hydrolytic products of excelsin are shown in Table 3.6.

TABLE 3.6

HYDROLYSIS OF EXCELSIN OF BRAZIL NUTS

Component	%	Component	%
Glycocol	0.60	Glutamic acid	12.94
Alanine	2.33	Tyrosine	3.03
Aminovaleric acid	1.51	Arginine	16.02
Leucine	8.70	Histidine	1.47
Proline	3.65	Lysine	1.64
Phenylalanine	3.55	Ammonia	1.80
Aspartic acid	3.85	Total	61.09

Source: Osborne and Harris (1903).

TABLE 3.7

NUTRITIVE VALUE OF BRAZIL NUTS
28.37 g, SHELLED

Content	Amount
Moisture	4.6%
Food energy	185.0 cal
Protein	4.1 g
Fat	19.0 g
Carbohydrate	3.1 g
Calcium	53.0 mg
Phosphorus	196.0 mg
Iron	1.0 mg
Sodium	trace
Potassium	203.0 mg
Vitamins	
Vitamin A value	trace
Thiamin	0.27 mg
Riboflavin	0.03 mg
Niacin	0.5 mg
Ascorbic acid	—

Source: Kuzio (1977).

Brazil nut oil is produced in quantity in Brazil, Bolivia, Guinea and Venezuela. It belongs to the semidrying group. The percentage composition of the residual oil (nuts first pressed and then the residual oil obtained by extraction of the residual pulp with low boiling petroleum ether, the final portions of which are removed from the oil in the presence of carbon dioxide) is: myristin, 1.79%; palmitin, 13.55%; stearin, 2.58%; olein, 55.64%; linolein, 21.65%; unsaponifiable matter, 0.68%; residue and undetermined, 4.11%. Free fatty acids were absent (Schnette and Enz 1930).

The approximate percentage composition of virgin Brazil oil is: myristin, 0.48%; palmitin, 13.74%; stearin, 5.45%; olein, 42.79%; and linolein, 26.54%. The solidification point is higher than that of oil recovered from residual pulp (Schnette and Enz 1931). Properties of Brazil nut oil are: specific gravity at 25°C (77°F), 0.9150; refractive index at 20°C (68°F), 1.4678; saponification number, 194; and acid number, 0.006. They have about 50% shells, with 46 to 48 kernels per pound (Gouy 1960).

BUTTERNUTS

Butternuts (white walnuts or oil nuts) are grown wild and cultivated in the eastern United States. They are purchased whole, salted, toasted or as paste, and are used as almonds. Refuse in cracking runs 86%.

CASHEW NUTS

The presence of starch distinguishes cashew nuts from almonds and most other nuts. These nuts yield a sweet oil of excellent quality.

A globulin, for which the name aracardein was suggested, may be isolated from cashew nuts in yields amounting to 17 to 18% of the fat-free seed. The ultimate approximate composition of aracardein is: carbon, 50.41%; hydrogen, 7.32%; nitrogen, 19.30%; sulfur, 0.78%; and oxygen, 22.19%. The nitrogen distribution of cashew nut globulin is reported to be: humin N, 1.40%; amide N, 11.91%; dicarboxylic acid N, 18.79%; arginine N, 21.57%; histidine N, 4.78%; lysine N, 1.54%; monoaminomonocarboxylic acid N, 29.50%; and nonamino N, 10.09%—totaling 99.58%.

Cashew nut kernels yield about 42.2% fixed oil by ether extraction. The glyceride acids are oleic, 73.77%; linoleic, 7.67%; palmitic, 6.4%; stearic, 11.24%; lignoceric, 0.5%; and unsaponifiable matter, 0.42%. Saturated acids comprise about 18.2% and the unsaturated acids 81.8%.

Properties of cashew nut oil are: specific gravity at 26°C (78.8°F), 0.9105; refractive index at 30°C (86°F), 1.4665; iodine number, 85.2; and acid number, 1.45 (Jacobs 1951).

TABLE 3.8

NUTRITIVE VALUE OF CASHEW NUTS
28.37 g, ROASTED IN OIL

Content	Amount
Moisture	5.2%
Food energy	159.0 cal
Protein	4.9 g
Fat	13.0 g
Carbohydrate	8.3 g
Calcium	11.0 mg
Phosphorus	106.0 mg
Iron	1.1 mg
Sodium	4.0 mg
Potassium	132.0 mg
Vitamins	
Vitamin A value	30 I.U.
Thiamin	0.12 mg
Riboflavin	0.07 mg
Ascorbic acid	—

Source: Kuzio (1977).

CHESTNUTS

Chestnuts and chinquapins are exceptions to all other tree nuts in that they contain little oil and are very high in carbohydrates, particularly in starch. This affects the way they are used in foods.

The chemical composition of chestnuts fits them for larger uses as food than most of our common (high oil) nuts. The large amount of oil in most nuts makes pulverizing difficult and tends to cause them to turn rancid. On the other hand, chestnuts, particularly the cultivated cultivars, contain comparatively little oil and are easily made digestible by roasting or boiling, in which process the starch grains are burst open and become less resistant to the attack of the digestive fluids. They contain relatively little astringent substances whose dietetic effects interfere with their use.

The composition of chestnuts includes: 21 to 25% shells, 4.5 to 6.5% moisture, and 69 to 72% dry matter.

Data in Table 3.9 show differences in fat, protein and nitrogen-free extract in Spanish, "paragon" and native chestnuts. The fat content of native chestnuts is about twice that of the Spanish cultivars. It was observed that when European cultivars are grown in America they tend to increase in fat, decrease in nitrogen-free extract, and become less albuminous. Fear (1891) concluded that chestnuts are starchy rather than oily. The European chestnuts closely resemble wheat in composition, but contain less starch and more dextrose and other water-

TABLE 3.9

COMPOSITION OF CHESTNUTS

Constituents	Cultivars				
	Spanish 1 %	Spanish 2 %	Paragon %	Native %	Native %
Ash	3.03	2.87	3.12	2.66	2.72
Albuminoids	8.38	9.28	10.91	11.84	10.53
Amids, etc.	1.23	1.68	1.23	0.39	1.67
Total protein	9.61	10.96	12.14	12.23	12.20
Fiber	2.55	2.84	2.86	3.63	2.84
Glucose	5.17	12.63	9.13	14.06	3.50
Dextrin	17.45	8.23	10.05	7.63	12.01
Starch	24.24	23.87	32.15	16.81	—
Other nitrogen-free extract	30.84	29.02	19.97	26.53	50.65
Total nitrogen-free extract	77.70	73.75	72.30	65.03	66.16
Fat	7.11	9.58	9.76	16.42	16.08

Source: Fear (1891).

soluble carbohydrates. The small, uncultivated American chestnuts are more oily than the nuts grown in Europe, and contain less starch, though they differ little from the other cultivars in their content in sugars, protein, fiber and other constituents.

McKay (1956) found an orange-kernel chestnut at Albany, Georgia, that contained 4.56 mg of total carotenoids and 3.1 mg of carotene per 100 g of fresh weight of kernel, whereas normal light-colored kernels had 0.83 mg of total carotenoid and 0.9 mg of carotene per 100 g of kernels. Thus the orange-kernel nuts contained 5½ times as much total carotenoids and 3½ times as much carotene, or vitamin A, as normal kernels.

FILBERTS

Usually considered starch-free, filberts contain corylin (globulin) with a composition of carbon, 50.72%; hydrogen, 6.86%; nitrogen, 19.17%; sulfur, 0.83%; and oxygen, 22.42%. Filbert oil has a mild agreeable taste and is edible. Properties of the expressed oil are: specific gravity at 20°C (68°F), 0.9144; refractive index at 20°C (68°F), 1.4698; iodine number, 84.7; saponification number, 191.1; saturated acids, 4.87%; and unsaturated acids, 90.96% (Jacobs 1951).

HICKORY NUTS

Hickory nut oil is suitable for salad oil, but the difficulty of extraction

TABLE 3.10

NUTRITIVE VALUE OF FILBERTS
1 CUP, WHOLE

Content	Amount
Moisture	5.8%
Food energy	856.0 cal
Protein	17.0 g
Fat	84.2 g
Carbohydrate	22.5 g
Calcium	282.0 mg
Phosphorous	455.0 mg
Iron	4.6 mg
Sodium	3.0 mg
Potassium	950.0 mg
Vitamins	
Vitamin A value	—
Thiamin	0.62 mg
Riboflavin	—
Niacin	1.2 mg
Ascorbic acid	trace

Source: Kuzio (1977).

makes commercial production improbable. Properties of the oil are: refractive index at 20°C (68°F), 1.4699; iodine number, 106.8; and saponification number, 189.8 (Jacobs 1951).

Bullnuts (mockernuts, white-heart hickory nuts) are purchased shelled or unshelled, separately or mixed with other nuts.

Pignuts have small, rather sweet kernels usually bought shelled. They are slightly bitter and are used in the same way as bitter almonds.

MACADAMIA NUTS

About 90 days after the macadamia flowers, embryo enlargement and accumulation of oil is very rapid. About 70% of the oil is formed in 44% of the total growing period of the fruit. Oil and protein synthesis occur simultaneously. In the early stages of oil synthesis, short-chain saturated fatty acids are formed first, from hexose sugars, and accumulate. Later, long-chain unsaturated fatty acids are formed as synthesis proceeds. No starch has been found in the embryo during development. Composition of macadamia nuts during development is shown in Table 3.11 by Jones and Shaw (1943).

Maturity of macadamia nuts more greatly affects the quality than do differences in climate, soil or seedling variation. Immature nuts turn dark rapidly when cooked in oil and develop a strong, rather unpleasant flavor and a hard, tough texture. Under similar cooking conditions the mature nuts are light brown, mild in flavor, and of crisp texture. The approximate dividing line between the desirable and undesirable nuts

TABLE 3.11

CARBOHYDRATES, NITROGEN, AND OIL CHANGES IN THE MACADAMIA
EMBRYO, EXPRESSED AS PERCENTAGE OF DRY WEIGHT IN RELATION TO AGE

Component	Days After Flowering				
	90	111	136	185	215
Reducing sugar	1.47	3.21	1.07	0.41	0.30
Sucrose	6.07	24.07	21.91	9.19	5.50
Total sugar	7.54	27.28	22.98	9.60	5.80
Soluble nitrogen	2.92	1.13	0.61	0.33	0.27
Insoluble nitrogen	1.96	1.91	1.58	1.39	1.43
Total nitrogen	4.88	3.04	2.19	1.72	1.70
Acid-hydrolyzable matter	4.54	4.88	3.85	2.56	2.16
Soluble solids in 80% alcohol	60.10	39.92	28.36	14.82	9.88
Ether- and alcohol-insoluble matter	36.43	28.88	23.69	17.89	16.68
Petroleum-ether extract	3.46	31.19	47.94	67.28	73.44

Source: Jones and Shaw (1943).

is in the specific gravity of 1.0, which is equivalent to an oil content of
about 70%. Specific gravity varies from 0.96 to 1.05, with those greater
than 1.0 being unsatisfactory.

TABLE 3.12

NUTRITIVE VALUE OF MACADAMIA NUTS
142 g, SHELLED

Content	Amount
Moisture	2.5 g
Food energy	204.0 cal/28.3 g
Protein	11.4 g
Fat	103.0 g
Carbohydrate	19.3 g
Calcium	1.8 g
Phosphorus	1.8 g
Iron	1.8 g
Potassium	1.8 g
Magnesium	1.8 g

Source: Kuzio (1977).

Cultivars

Two distinct cultivars of macadamia nuts are produced in Hawaii—
the rough-shelled and smooth-shelled. The rough-shelled contain an
average of 67% oil and 8% sugar, are less crisp, and have a more
pronounced sweet flavor; while the smooth-shelled nuts contain about
70% oil and 4% sugar, and after roasting have a crisp texture and nutty
flavor. The roasting qualities of the rough-shelled cultivars are similar
to those of the somewhat immature nuts of the smooth-shelled cultivar
(Jacobs 1951).

PECANS

Pecans contain the following percentages of carbohydrates on a moisture-free basis: sucrose 1.18, invert sugars 2.88, araban 1.95, methylpentosans 0.22, cellulose 1.76, amyloid 0.59, starch 0, tannins 0.33, and hemicellulose 4.09—a total of 13.00% (Friedermann 1920).

Pecans contain the following percentages of amino acids in the globulin: amide 9.8, humin 3.6, arginine 22.9, histidine 3.7, cystine 0.8, lysine 6.2, monoamino 51.7, nonamino 0.8—a total of 99.5%.

Properties of pecan oil are: specific gravity at 15°C (59°F), 0.9184; refractive index at 20°C (68°F), 1.4708; iodine number, 106.0; and saponification number, 198.0 (Jacobs 1951).

Data in Table 3.13 show the composition of the oil of 12 cultivars of pecans arranged in the order of increasing oleic acid content. The oleic acid ranged from 51 to 77%. The wide variation in unsaturated acid content of cultivars which were grown in the same area and under identical environmental conditions, suggests that genetic factors may be as important as cultural practices. These data were obtained by gas-liquid chromatography which showed close agreement with data from ultraviolet analysis (French 1962).

TABLE 3.13

COMPOSITION OF PECAN OILS

Cultivar	Palmitic Acid %	Stearic Acid %	Oleic Acid %	Linoleic Acid %	Linolenic Acid %	Arachidonic Acid %	Iodine Value
Moneymaker	6.3	2.6	51.0	37.8	1.7	0.4	118.0
Mobile	7.1	2.7	56.8	31.4	1.8	0.2	111.2
Big Z	5.9	2.9	59.7	30.3	1.6	0.4	110.0
Randall	6.0	2.9	61.3	28.2	1.5	0.1	107.2
Tesche	6.1	3.0	63.4	25.7	1.3	0.5	105.3
Frotcher	6.5	2.5	63.9	25.5	1.3	0.2	105.9
Stuart	6.6	2.2	68.8	21.0	1.1	0.2	101.3
Seedling 1	4.3	3.9	69.2	21.2	1.3	0.3	100.8
Seedling 2	6.3	3.2	71.0	18.5	0.9	trace	97.6
Curtis	6.1	3.1	71.8	18.1	0.8	0.1	98.3
Van Deman	5.1	2.9	74.6	16.0	0.9	trace	96.2
Success	5.4	2.9	76.5	13.5	1.3	0.4	94.5

Source: French (1962).

PINE NUTS

Pine nuts are used in confections for roasting, in bakery products, and for expressing the oil. The oil contains minute quantities of volatile fatty acids. The triglycerides are 5.5% solid and 94.5% liquid. The solid acids are 8% stearic and 92% palmitic; the liquid consists of 51 to 57% oleic and about 43 to 49% linoleic acids (Jacobs 1951).

Properties of pine nut oil are: specific gravity at 15°C (59°F), 0.9213; refractive index at 25°C (77°F), 1.4698; iodine number, 108.0; unsaturated acids, 1.98% (Jacobs 1951).

BLACK WALNUTS

In a study of the development of fat in black walnuts, it was found that starch, sugar and tannin were absent from the kernels at all periods of its development. Tannin was markedly present in the hull and tissue of the kernel capsule (future seed coat). When the kernel was entirely liquid (June 15) there was a pronounced fluid pressure. The first formation of the jelly-like kernel was on the interior surface of the capsule tissue. This gradually changed to a white solid, while the jelly-like formation retreated toward the center of the chamber of the capsule, replacing in turn the liquid and finally being itself replaced by the solid kernel. The fats increase out of proportion to the increase or decrease of other components (Table 3.14).

TABLE 3.14

CHANGE IN COMPOSITION OF THE KERNEL OF BLACK WALNUT
(IN PERCENT)

Component	June 15	July 15	July 29	August 12	August 26
Total solids	3.510	4.128	20.487	38.325	68.110
Ether extract	0.123	0.556	8.043	19.592	42.176
Total N	0.182	0.290	0.818	0.892	1.044
Amino N	0.111	0.145	0.290	0.312	0.466
Protein N	0.071	0.145	0.528	0.580	0.578
Pentosans	—	present	0.775	0.758	0.940
Ash	—	0.502	1.336	1.321	1.570
Potassium	0.312	0.253	0.485	0.675	—
Calcium	0.266	0.048	0.072	0.071	0.044
Phosphorus	0.127	0.086	0.055	0.091	0.051
Magnesium	—	0.011	0.079	0.098	—
Acidity	Acid	Acid	Neutral	Neutral	Neutral

Source: McClenahan (1909).

The nature of the fat in black walnuts changes during development. Before August 14, the fat becomes waxy on continued exposure to air; after that date it tends to remain liquid permanently. The early history of the ovule indicates a great preponderance of phosphatides over fats. The phosphatides linger in the developing ovules until about August 15, but their relative importance is insignificant after the material has changed from a limpid liquid to a jelly. This is also the case with the seedcoat except that their importance is insignificant after about June 28. The early life of the ovule is conditioned by the presence of a relatively large content of potassium, which becomes less important as the nut advances toward maturity. The nature of the tissue of the seedcoat is such that it is either not penetrable by tannin or contains substances that disrupt the tannin molecules into fragments that are able to penetrate the tissue (Jacobs 1951).

Plump black walnut kernels are as much as 7% higher in fat than shriveled kernels, but lower in moisture, ash, protein and carbohydrates (Table 3.15).

TABLE   3.15

COMPOSITION OF PLUMP AND SHRIVELED BLACK WALNUT KERNELS
(IN PERCENT)

Component	Shriveled, Immature Kernels	Plump Kernels
Moisture	4.7	4.27
Fat	48.53	55.20
Crude fiber	1.5	1.56
Ash	3.4	2.86
Protein	29.79	29.58
Carbohydrates	12.08	6.53
Protein/carbohydrate ratio	2.47	4.53

Source: Stokes (1941).

The percentage composition of nitrogen in the groups of nitrogenous decomposition products was found to be: nitrogen as ammonia, 1.80%; basic nitrogen (diamino), 5.77%; nonbasic nitrogen (monoamino), 11.14%; nitrogen in magnesium oxide precipitate (humin), 0.25%; total nitrogen, 18.96%.

The oil of black walnuts contains the following: saturated acids, 5.39%; unsaturated, 88.55%. The composition of the oil in terms of the percentage of fatty acids was: oleic, 35.6%; linoleic, 48.6%; linolenic, 7.4%; myristic, 0.4%; palmitic, 3.4%; stearic, 1.8%; and lignoceric, 0.04% (Osborne and Harris 1903).

The properties of black walnut oil are: refractive index at 25°C (77°F), 1.4730; iodine number, 135.1; saponification number, 193.5; and unsaturated acids, 88.14%.

Walnuts (black) are purchased shelled or unshelled and processed as salted, glazed, roasted, butter, meal or pickled (immature). They are used with almost any kind of cooked, baked or roasted foods, salads, breads, cakes, cookies, pies, fillings, frostings, candies, as a snack or a garnish.

PERSIAN WALNUTS

The very light-colored walnuts found on most markets were bleached in regular commercial practice. The shells are easily cracked and the kernels may be extracted whole.

The shriveling of walnut kernels takes place after they have passed from the liquid condition, have jelled, and are approaching the solid stage. The fresh weight, dry weight, and amount of ash per kernel decrease as the shriveling increases. The amount of each inorganic component of the ash per kernel shows an increase with the increased age of the kernel. The degree of shriveling is not related to the total phosphorus content of the mature kernels. There is a progressive increase in total phosphorus of walnut kernels as they increase in age (Haas and Batchelor 1928).

TABLE 3.16

NUTRITIVE VALUE OF WALNUTS
28.37g, SHELLED HALVES

Content	Amount
Moisture	3.5%
Food energy	185.0 cal
Protein	4.2 g
Fat	18.1 g
Carbohydrate	4.5 g
Calcium	28.0 mg
Phosphorus	108.0 mg
Iron	0.9 mg
Sodium	1.0 mg
Potassium	128.0 mg
Vitamins	
Vitamin A value	10.0 I.U.
Thiamin	0.09 mg
Riboflavin	0.04 mg
Niacin	0.3 mg
Ascorbic acid	1.0 mg

Source: Kuzio (1977).

Persian walnut oil is not on the market generally, but it has the following properties: specific gravity at 25°C (77°F), 0.9235; refractive index at 25°C (77°F), 1.4751; iodine number, 158.5; saponification number, 194.5; acid number, 5.11; saturated acids, 5.34%; and unsaturated acids, 89.74% (Jacobs 1951). Persian walnuts have the same general characteristics and uses as black walnuts.

Walnut oil is similar to hempseed oil in many properties and dries like soybean oil. Hot pressed walnut oil has been used in paints and artists' colors from early times. It reacts with styrene in the presence of a catalyst to produce excellent styrenated oils. It has been used in varnish and alkyd resin. Its use would become general if an adequate supply were available at a price less than that of linseed oil (Carrick 1950).

Walnuts contain 66.8% fat, of which 5.6% of the fatty acids are saturated—C_{14} 0.29%, C_{16} 3.49%, C_{18} 1.86%; 58.1% of the fatty acids are unsaturated—10.63% monoene, 38.9% diene, 8.66% triene, and 0.03% tetraene (Willard et al. 1954).

PISTACHIO NUTS

Pistachio nuts contain 53.7% oil, the fatty acids of which are: myristic acid, 0.6%; palmitic acid, 8.2%; stearic acid, 1.6%; oleic acid, 69.0%; linoleic acid, 19.8%; and unsaponifiable matter, 0.8%. The oil has a dark green color and an agreeable odor like the nut. The oil has the following properties: specific gravity at 24°C (75.2°F), 0.9134; refractive index at 20°C (68°F), 1.4687; iodine number, 83.8; saponification number, 194.5; acid number, 0.6 (Jacobs 1951).

HARMFUL COMPOUNDS IN NUTS

Toxic Constituents

The seed coat of European beechnut contains a toxic substance, which makes feeding of beechnut cake to certain farm animals hazardous (Eekelen and Laan 1945). A toxic concentration of barium (up to 4000 ppm) has been found in some Brazil nut kernels (Robinson and Edgington 1945; Seaber 1933); it has been reported to cause illness of children eating the nuts. Cashew nutshell contains a liquid containing anacardic acid, $C_{22}H_{32}O_3$, a brown crystalline substance (Guthrie et al. 1949), and cardol, $C_{21}H_{32}O_2$, a dark brown phenolic oil. Both are very toxic and irritating, producing blisters on the skin similar to those caused by poison ivy. Juglone (5-hydroxy-1,4-napthoquinone), yellow-brown crystals which stain the skin, occurs chiefly as its colorless reduction product (hydrojuglone, 1,4,5-napthalenetriol) in all green and growing parts of walnut trees and the unripe hulls of the nut.

Several nuts have unique compounds which have undesirable side effects. Some nuts carry specific glucosides which are disagreeable or toxic to some people. Bitter almonds, for instance, contain cyanogenetic glucoside which releases hydrocyanic acid, a potent toxic agent. Other nuts are strongly allergenic and may induce shocks. The presence of allergens has been demonstrated for Brazil nuts, filberts, pecans, peanuts, almonds, coconuts and walnuts. The nut allergens are composed of amino acids and in general are characterized by relatively high proportions of arginine and glutamic acid.

A third group of undesirable components of some nuts are tannin compounds which give a very unpleasant taste when eaten. Unripe nuts have a high degree of astringency which generally is reduced to minimal proportions in the ripe product. These tannins are injurious when ingested in nontolerable amounts.

A number of cardiac compounds and other pharmacodynamic agents have been encountered in small quantities in nuts. Serotonin is reported in sweet almonds, and tryptamine in various other nuts.

Fortunately many of the undesirable compounds in nuts decrease or are lost in ripening and processing. Among these are thorough maturity, complete curing, toasting, fermentation and grinding. Likewise, these compounds are present in such small quantities that much larger than normal quantities of nuts would have to be eaten to be detrimental to health (Borgstrom 1964).

NUTRITIVE VALUE OF NUTS

Nuts are essentially rich in protein and fat, and most of our important nuts (Table 3.17) supply about 3000 calories fuel value per pound of kernel, more than most other foods. Cereals supply some 1650, meats 810, and fresh fruits less than 300 calories per pound. Calories per pound of food is calculated by the formula:

$$18.6 \ (\% \ \text{protein} + \% \ \text{total carbohydrates (N-free extract + fiber))} + 42.2 \ (\% \ \text{fat})$$

One pound of nut kernels is equivalent in energy value to 2.3 lb of bread, 3.7 lb of steak, 12.3 lb of white potatoes, or 15 lb of oranges. A man at ordinary work requires 3000 calories per day for energy production; 75 g protein, 85 g fat, 0.67 g calcium, 1.44 g phosphorus, and 0.0015 g iron. Thus 1 lb of oily nuts supplies all the calories needed each day, approximately 40% of the protein, 60% of the phosphorus, 30% of the calcium and iron, and 4 times the requirement of fat. Nuts as a rule contain a good amount of vitamin A and vitamin B complex and are also a good source of iron, copper, manganese, and sulfur, but they are usually lacking in vitamin C and calcium. The peanut is an especially rich source of vitamins A, B-1, C and niacin. A 2-oz portion of peanuts supplies ⅛ of the total daily needs of riboflavin, since 2 mg is a fair daily allowance of this vitamin for an adult. Processing peanuts and other nuts by roasting or cooking in oil causes an appreciable loss in the vitamin content. Cooking macadamia nuts in hot oil at 135°C (275°F) for 12 to 15 min caused a loss of 16% of the original thiamin content (Miller and Louis 1941), while modern commercial methods of roasting or processing pea-

TABLE 3.17

SELECTED FATTY ACIDS

	Amount in 100-g Edible Portion			
Nut	Total Fat (g)	Total Saturated Fatty Acids (g)	Unsaturated Oleic $C_{18}(-2H)$ (g)	Fatty Acids Linoleic $C_{18}(-4H)$ (g)
Almonds				
Dried, in-shells	54.2	4	36	11
shelled	54.2	4	36	11
Roasted, salted	57.7	5	39	12
Sugar coated	18.6	1	12	4
Meal, partially defatted	18.3	1	12	4
Beechnuts				
In-shells	50.0	4	27	16
Shelled	50.0	4	27	16
Brazil nuts				
In-shells	66.9	13	32	17
Shelled	66.9	13	32	17
Cashew nuts	45.7	8	32	3
Hazelnuts (filberts)				
In-shells	62.4	3	34	10
Shelled	62.4	3	34	10
Hickory nuts				
In-shells	68.7	6	47	12
Shelled	68.7	6	47	12
Pecans				
In-shells	71.2	5	45	14
Shelled	71.2	5	45	14
Pistachio				
In-shells	53.7	5	35	10
Shelled	53.7	5	35	10
Walnuts				
Black, in-shells	59.3	4	21	28
shelled	59.3	4	21	28
Persian (English)				
in-shells	64.0	4	10	40
shelled	64.0	4	10	40

Source: Watt and Merrill (1963).

nuts in hot oils cause a destruction of about 70 to 80% of the thiamin value (Booher 1941). Nuts contain the essential amino acids tryptophan, phenylalanine, lysine, valine and leucine.

The reaction of edible nuts in the diet is mainly basic, though some nuts give an acid reaction. The alkaline (+) or acid (−) effect (ml 1 N reagent per 100 g, approx.) is as follows for nut kernels: almond, + 12.0; coconut

TABLE 3.18

OIL AND PROTEIN CONTENTS OF TREE NUTS AT 0.40 a_w

Nut	Botanical name	Oil (%)	Protein (%)
Almond	*Prunus amygdalus*	52.7	23.1
Butternut	*Juglans cinerea*	60.0	27.8
Brazil	*Berthrolletia myrtaceae*	68.7	16.9
Cashew	*Anacardium occidentale*	47.7	18.9
Chestnut	*Castanea mollisima*	2.5	7.3
Filbert	*Corylus* sp.	62.3	16.8
Hickory	*Caryaovata* sp.	70.4	12.1
Macadamia	*Macadamia* sp.	73.2	9.6
Pecan	*Carya illioensis*	70.3	11.7
Pignolia	*Pinus* sp.	48.1	35.5
Pistachio	*Pistachio vera*	57.0	20.8
Walnut, Black	*Juglans nigra*	59.0	28.1
Walnut, Persian	*Juglans regia*	67.4	17.4

Source: Beuchat (1978).

(dried), +8.3; American chestnut (fresh), +5.0; filbert, +4.8; Brazil nut, +4.5; peanut, −3.9 ; pecan, −5.6; and Persian walnut, −7.8.

Digestibility of nuts is high if the nuts are finely ground. Young white rats were fed several nuts *ad libitum* to obtain digestion coefficients of the protein and fat. Digestion coefficients for protein were pine nuts 95.12%, almonds 90.17%, peanuts 89.43%, hazelnuts 82.91%, and walnuts 79.49%. For fat the results were almonds 96.13%, peanuts 95.50%, hazelnuts 87.22%, pine nuts 82.93%, and walnuts 67.77%.

Nuts are a very concentrated food and may cause discomfort if they are not well masticated. The advantages of nuts over meats are that they are free from putrefactive bacteria and parasites, do not have to be prepared for eating, and are free from waste products such as uric acid formed from purines as in meats. Their chief disadvantage is that they do not supply the bulk for propulsion in the digestive system that meat and other foods do.

FRYING OIL

The amount of non-addict-forming fatty acid fraction (NAF) and molecular weights of frying oils increases with the time and temperature of heating (Sahasrabudhe and Bhalerao 1963).

There is no reason to believe that fats are nutritionally damaged when handled by normally accepted practice in present-day food preparation.

INEDIBLE COMPONENTS, SHELLS AND HULLS

Nutshell waste from shelling and processing plants is extensively used for a variety of purposes. Pecan and Persian walnut shells reduced to flour of various mesh sizes have wide usage as soft grit in blasting metals; as ingredient in plastic fillers, battery cases, molding resin forms, and industrial tile; as insecticide diluent; and for fur cleaning. Radio horns made from walnut shell flour seem to filter out vibrations more effectively than loud speakers made from other materials. Walnut shell flour has been produced on a commercial scale for some time as a diluent or spreader for agricultural insecticides, the product having a high lignin content; the presence of 5% cutin is responsible for its capacity to absorb and retain toxic agents. The cutin content in the shell flour reduces resin absorption when used in molding resins, and the lignin helps bind the molded product; the two in conjunction tend to reduce materially the proportion of resin necessary for making the molding compound (Baron 1948). A practical floor covering has been developed from a mixture of water-insoluble aluminum, nutshell flour pigment, and resinous materials. It is applied to a flexible base and the whole is covered with a coloring and binding material to fill any pores. About 4 million pounds of walnut shell flour is used annually in the plastics industry alone, and this amount represents about half the present production of the flour. Special machinery is required for grinding and transmission of the ground material since the dust is subject to spontaneous explosion. However, this hazard has been largely overcome by applying a very fine spray to the shell flour as it leaves the grinder.

Waste material from the pecan shelling industry has shown commercial possibilities for the recovery and production of oil, tannin, shell flour and activated charcoal, and a processing plant has been established at Weatherford, Texas (Flemming 1947). This plant is designed to utilize 25 to 30 tons of pecan shells per day for the extraction of tannin and 160,000 lb of 33% tannin per month. Tannic acid produced from pecan shells at this plant is used by the tanning industry and by the oil industry to control the viscosity of drilling muds. The United States has to import ⅔ of the tannin used in the leather industry; hence the extraction of this material from nutshells is of vital importance. The spent shells after extraction of tannin are used by two plants in Texas for making activated charcoal. Pecan shell is an excellent material for use in the production of activated charcoal (McElhenney et al. 1942), proving more effective for odor removal than the commercial carbons tested, while charcoal produced from pecans is comparable in decolorizing power with other vegetable charcoals when tested with dye or caramel solutions (Whitehead and Warshaw 1938). Activated charcoal, made by treating the pecan shell charcoal with concentrated hydrochloric acid, washing it free of acid, and heating it in an electric furnace for 4 hours at 674.6° to 985.7°C (1472° to 1832°F) in an atmosphere of carbon dioxide, had the same decolorizing effect on water solutions of azo dyes as had commercial activated charcoal. Much of the walnut shell charcoal produced is sold to poultry producers, and it is used to some extent as a filtrant for high-grade vinegar.

Attempts have been made to make yellow and brown dyes from filbert shells on a commercial scale by treating them with different chemicals; copper sulfate and concentrated nitric acid produce a yellow color, ferrous sulfate an olive-green, and ammonia a ruby-red color (Wiegand 1943). Methods of home-dyeing cotton and wool materials with natural dyes made from hulls of butternut, hickory, pecan, eastern black walnut and Persian walnut have been described (Furry and Viemont 1935). As a matter of historical interest, butternut hulls furnished the yellow dye for uniforms of the Confederate troops during the Civil War.

The peanut has been a subject of extensive chemurgic investigation for the development of numerous products, from dyes and ink to artificial wool. Dr. George W. Carver, of Tuskegee Institute, alone created 202 different products from the nut and its by-products (Woodroof 1966). Peanut shells or hulls may be used in the manufacture of lacquers, linoleum, dynamite, guncotton, celluloid, artificial leather, photographic film, cellophane and rayon. Peanut shells are also used as a stock feed by mixing ground hulls and molasses in the proportion of 80% hulls and 20% molasses, the product having a protein content of 6 to 7%. Insulation block is also made from the shells with an asphalt binder, and attempts have been made to use the ground shells in the preparation of magnesia tiles and plaster (Clay 1941). An artificial vegetable fiber, Ardil, which resembles wool and may be used for making clothing and other fabrics by weaving it with 50% wool, is produced from peanut protein.

REFERENCES

ADAMS, C.F. 1975. Nutritive value of American foods. Agric. Res. Serv., U.S. Dep. Agric. Handbook *456*.

ALBEN, A.O., HAMMER, H.E., and SITTON, B.G. 1942. Mineral deficiencies in pecans. Proc. Am. Soc. Hort. Sci. *41*, 53-60.

ANON. 1967. Encyclopedia of Chemical Technology. John Wiley & Sons, New York.

AVERILL, H.P., and KING, C.G. 1926. Chemical constituents of nuts. J. Am. Chem. Soc. *48*, 724-728.

BARON, L.C. 1948. Uses of nut shells. Peanut J. and Nut World *28* (1) 77-80.

BEUCHAT, L.R. 1978. Water activity as affected by moisture content of tree nuts. J. Food Sci. *43*.

BOOHER, L.E. 1941. Composition of peanuts. National Peanut Council Proc. *1*, 27-28.

BORGSTROM, G. 1964. Nuts in human food. Northern Nut Growers Assoc. Ann. Rept. *55*, 60-64.

CARRICK, L.L. 1950. Vegetable oil paints. J. Am. Oil Chem. Soc. *27*, 513-522.

CHATFIELD, D., and ADAMS, G. 1940. Proximate composition of American food materials. U.S. Dep. Agric. Circ. *549*.

CLAY, H.J. 1941. Uses of peanut shells. U.S. Dep. Agric. Misc. Pub. *416*.

CRUESS, W.V., KILBUCK, J.H., and HAHL, E. 1947. Utilization of almond hulls. Chemurgic Dig. *6* (13) 197-201.

FEAR, W. 1891. Analysis of several varieties of chestnuts. Penn. State Col. Ann. Rept. *17*, 173-178.

FLEMMING, J.R. 1947. Tannins in pecans. Peanut J. and Nut World *26* (11) 24-25.

FRENCH, R.B. 1962. Analyses of pecan oils by gas-liquid chromatography and ultraviolet spectrophotometry. J. Am. Oil Chem. *39*, 176-178.

FRIEDERMANN, W.G. 1920. Carbohydrates of the pecan. J. Am. Chem. Soc. *42*, 2286.

FURRY, M.S., and VIEMONT, B.M. 1935. Home dyeing and natural dyes. U.S. Dep. Agric. Misc. Pub. *230*, 28-33.

GOUY, L.P. 1960. The Gold Cook Book. Chilton Co., Philadelphia, Pa.

GUTHRIE, J.C., HOFFPAUIR, C.L., STANSBURY, M.F., and REEVES, W.A. 1949. Chemistry of cashew nuts. U.S. Dep. Agric., Bur. Agric. Ind. Chem. Mimeo Circ. *A1C-61*.

HAAS, A.R.C. 1945. Boron content in almond, olive and walnut trees. Proc. Am. Soc. Hort. Sci. *46*, 69-80.

HAAS, A.R.C., and BATCHELOR, L. 1928. Composition of walnuts. Bot. Gaz. *86*, 448.

JACOBS, M.B. 1951. The Chemistry and Technology of Food and Food Products, Vol. II. Interscience Publishers, New York.

JONES, W., and SHAW, L. 1943. The process of oil formation and accumulation in the macadamia. Plant Physiol. *18* (1) 1-7.

JUSTIN, M.M., RUST, L.O., and VAIL, G.E. 1940. Foods. Houghton Mifflin Co., Boston.

KUZIO, W. 1977. Nutmeat roundup. Candy Ind. *142* (6) 25-42.

MCCLENAHAN, F.M. 1909. Changes in composition of black walnut during growth. J. Am. Chem. Soc. *31*, 1093.

MCELHENNEY, T.R., BECKER, B.M., and JACOBS, P.B. 1942. Carbon from pecan shells. Iowa State Col. J. Sci. *16*, 227-239.

MCKAY, J.W. 1956. Orange-kernel chestnut. Northern Nut Growers Assoc. Ann. Rept. *47*, 45-47.

MILLER, C.D., and LOUIS, L. 1941. Thiamine in macadamia nuts. Food Res. *6*, 547-552.

MOREIRAS, O., and PUJOL, A. 1961. Digestibility of some dried nuts. Anales Biomatol. *13*, 21-27.

OSBORNE, T.B., and HARRIS, I.F. 1903. Composition of black walnuts. Oil & Soap *13*, 202.

OSBORNE, T.B., and HARRIS, I.F. 1903. Nitrogen materials in Brazil nuts. J. Am. Chem. Soc. *25*, 323, 842.

POLANSKY, M., and MURPHY, E.W. 1966. Vitamin B-6 components in fruits and nuts. J. Am. Diet. Assoc. *48*, 109-111.

ROBINSON, W.O., and EDGINGTON, G. 1945. Tree nut accumulate minerals. Soil Sci. *60*, 15-28.

ROSSI, L., DE CELSI, M.A., VIGNAU, S.L.P., and VIAN, N. 1947. Reagent for the detection of 1-ascorbic acid (vitamin C). Rev. Assoc. Bioquim. Argentina *14*, 30-34.

SAHASRABUDHE, M.R., and BHALERAO, V.R. 1963. A method for determination of the extent of polymerization in frying fat. J. Am. Oil Chem. Soc. *40*, 711-712.

SCHNETTE, H. A., and ENZ, W.W.F. 1930. Composition of residual Brazil nut oil. J. Am. Chem. Soc. *52*, 4114.

SCHNETTE, H.A., and ENZ, W.W.F. 1931. Composition of virgin Brazil nut oil. J. Am. Chem. Soc. *53*, 2756.

SEABER, W. 1933. Barium as a normal constituent of Brazil nuts. Analyst *58*, 575-580.

STEPHENSON, R.E. 1947. Boron deficiencies. Better Fruit *41* (11) 20, 24.

STOKES, H.F. 1941. Composition of black walnut kernels. Northern Nut Growers Assoc. Rept. *32*, 37.

SUBRAHMANYAM, V.V.R., and ACHAYA, K.T. 1957. Lesser-known Indian vegetable fats. I. Oleic-rich fats. J. Sci. Food Agr. *8*, 657-662.

U.S. DEP. AGRIC. 1955. Food consumption of households in the South. Household Food Consumption Survey Rept. *4*.

VAN EEKELEN, M., and VAN DER LAAN, P.J. 1945. The toxicity of beechnuts and beechnut flour. Voeding *4*, 11 (Chem. Abstr. *40*, 6179).

WATT, B.K., and MERRILL, A.L. 1963. Composition of foods. Agric. Res. Serv., U.S. Dep. Agric. Handbook *8*.

WHITEHEAD, T.H., and WARSHAW, H. 1938. Pecan charcoal. Ga. State Eng. Exp. Stn. Bull. *4*.

WIEGAND, E.H. 1943. The future of the filbert. Chemurgic Dig. *2* (17) 143-145.

WILLARD, E., ENGLERT, R.D., and RICHARDS, L.M. 1954. Fatty acid contents of several food products. J. Am. Oil Chem. Soc. *31*, 35.

WOOD, M. 1947. Almond littleleaf. Calif. Agric. Ext. Circ. *103*, 65-66.

WOODROOF, J.G. 1966. Peanuts: Production, Processing, Products. AVI Publishing Co., Westport, Conn.

4

Using Nutmeats in Candy Plants, Restaurants and Homes

NUTMEATS IN CONFECTIONS

Nutmeats have a unique place in confections. According to Kuzio (1977) nutmeats enhance confectionery and cookies by adding a crisp texture, a crunch, and a compatible flavor. By themselves when consumed raw, roasted and salted or combined with a smoked flavor, or ground into peanut butter, there is a distinctive flavor. But when combined in a confection there is a multiplying effect.

Nuts can be used in candies in many ways, and the primary deciding factors would be taste and size. Generally speaking, most nuts are classified as wholes, halves (sometimes halves and brokens), and brokens. In another series of classifications they may be referred to as large, medium and small, almost paralleling the size descriptions. Or they may have traditional names for each size or grade. Almonds, for example, include Nonpareils, IXL, Jordanola, Mission and Drake. Peanuts are classified by strain, such as Virginia, Spanish, etc.

The size of the nutmeat used is relative to the size of the piece of finished candy. Whole nuts can be incorporated into candies which are thick enough to encompass them without protrusions, such as solid molded chocolate bars, chocolate squares, chocolate bark, caramels, nougats, fudges, nut rolls, and chocolate or candy panned goods. Whole nutmeats such as almonds can also be used to top or decorate individual candies, such as chocolate pieces. Halves can also serve such purposes, as in the case of pecans, walnuts, hazelnuts and small Brazil nuts.

If a whole nut is too large for incorporation into a batch, it may be used as halves at less cost. Physical size is reduced, which permits the nutmeat to fit into candies easier, without protuberances which might affect wrapping machine operations. The halves settle within the confines of the slim bar with less difficulty. One example is the solid nut bar made of a solidified syrup and peanut halves. It is flat and even on all sides.

The brokens, or bits, can be worked into batches for candy centers more readily because of their smaller sizes. They can be mixed into chocolate coatings to make clusters. Smallness also permits them to be mechanically sprinkled onto nut rolls, caramels and slabs of fudge.

Several types of nutmeats are available in ground or paste form. These include peanut butter, hazelnut paste, and marzipan (almond paste). These moist and spreadable forms are used as material for centers, which are usually chocolate coated. The peanut butter cup is the most popular example.

Almonds

In the early confectionery manufacturing business, almonds were imported from Europe. Nowadays, most almonds are grown domestically in California. They come in six basic types — Nonpareil, IXL, Ne Plus Ultra, Jordanola, Mission and Drake. Whole nut sizes range from 16 to 18 per oz to the smallest at 40 to 50 per oz. Generally, the largest and smallest types are scarce. For production where uniformity of size is not a factor, the ungraded type known as "sheller run" can be used. The lowest grade is called "whole and broken," which is still of good flavor quality, but it can serve wherever chopped nuts or broken bits are permissible. The industry has even gone further in processing besides grading, and can supply blanched nuts, slivered, diced, chopped or ground nuts, either raw or roasted. In fact, the latest form announced recently is almond powder.

For chocolate dipping the candy maker could choose an 18/20 Nonpareil almond, which is large, fairly flat, and oval shaped. For an almond cluster, the Drake almond or Mission type would do. Candy-coated Jordan almonds are made with 27/30 Jordanette or Jordanola, which is medium size, long and narrow in shape. See Chapter 6 for more uses of almonds and Chapter 12 on Pecans.

Brazil Nuts

Brazil nuts come from the country of the same name. They have a delicate flavor and are rather high in oil content, although they will remain resistant to infestation if held under good storage conditions. They are not normally roasted before use, and appear in such confections as fudges, nougats and butterscotches, in the broken and chipped grades. The small (midget), medium and large sizes are used for coating, either with chocolate or sugar. See Chapter 7 for more uses of Brazil nuts and Chapter 12 on Pecans.

Cashew Nuts

Cashews are native to Brazil and South America, where they are still grown in large quantities. Africa also produced abundant crops when the cashew was introduced there. India became a factor with its own crops, and also a source of labor for processing the crops exported by Africa. Other sources are Tanzania and Mozambique.

Cashews have an outer shell and pulp which should not be consumed, and therefore must be very carefully processed to eliminate any traces of them. Roasting is essential before they are ready to eat.

Because cashews are fragile, the shelling process leaves the nutmeat in many other forms besides whole pieces. The small pieces can be used for clusters and brittles, fancy pieces adapt to clusters and patties, splits are used for panning and patties, butts serve in patties, the whole 250 grade is for dipping and patties, and the wholes 270 and 320 can also be used for dipping. Granules go well into brittles.

Cashew Praline Pattie

10 lb granulated cane sugar	5 lb medium brown sugar
1 oz salt	2 qt butterfat cream
Maple flavoring (if desired)	2½ lb cashew halves or pieces

Cook sugar, cream, salt and flavoring to 111°C (232°F), stirring constantly. Make sure all sugar crystals are washed down the sides of kettle before batch comes to a boil. Add cashews and cook to 114°C (237°F). Remove kettle from fire and carefully ladle some of the mixture into a container such as a 1 qt measure (about half full). Using tablespoon, stir this mixture, rubbing against sides of measure, etc., until grain appears. Then spoon out in patties of desired size on oiled or silicone-treated paper. When cup or measure is empty, repeat process, only this time it will not be necessary to initiate a grain. The residual material in the container will act as a seed. Care should be taken not to get any of this grain or seed back into the kettle.

Filberts

The hazelnut (also known as the filbert) is grown domestically in the states of Washington and Oregon where the combination of rich soil and mild climate is responsible for an abundant crop. When harvested the hazelnuts are certified by the Federal-State Inspection Service to meet all requirements established by the Filbert Marketing Order. The Oregon Filbert Commission plays an important role in marketing the product.

The crop, mainly from Oregon, produces a large, meaty and clean type of nut used for dipping into chocolate, panning and salting. Some hazelnuts are imported from the Mediterranean countries, and are of smaller size for use in making filbert paste, and occasionally for dipping in chocolate to make filbert clusters.

In-shell domestic varieties come in four sizes. The largest is the Giant, averaging 58/64 in., making 15 pieces per oz, unshelled. Jumbo is over 56/64 in. and averages 16 to 19 pieces per oz, unshelled. Large ranges from 49/64 to 56/64 in. and comes 20 to 24 pieces per oz, unshelled. The Medium has a size of 45/64 to 49/64 in. and yields 25 to 29 nuts per oz, unshelled. Small runs 30 to 40 per oz, unshelled.

Hazelnuts are commercially available as whole and broken (meaning roughly half kernels), chopped (pieces), sliced, and even flour form.

Roasting brings out the natural flavor. The nuts should be rubbed after cooling to loosen and eliminate the very thin brown inner skin.

Filbert Praline Patties

> 5 lb white sugar
> 5 lb warm (29°C) blanched, roasted filberts

Carefully melt the sugar in a gas-fired pan, with constant stirring. When sugar is completely melted, turn off the gas, and add the pre-warmed filberts and mix in. As soon as the hazelnuts are mixed in evenly, pour batch out onto a cool slab and spread out thinly. When batch is cool, break up into pieces and grind into a paste by passing through refining rollers. Stiffen this praline paste by mixing in approximately (depending upon the fluidity of the paste):

> Powdered sugar   2 lb

Then add:

> Salt   2 oz
> Rum flavor   ½ fl oz

Shape batch by hand into patties, pre-bottom and coat with milk chocolate.

Macadamia Nuts

The macadamia tree is native to Australia, but Hawaii has been its adopted home since it was introduced in 1870. Most of the current acreage in Hawaii has been planted since 1950, and the island is said to be the major source of macadamia nuts, with about 90% of the world's current supplies grown there.

Only about 20% of the nut is edible meat, making the product a prestige commodity with gourmet appeal.

Macadamia nuts, available as wholes, halves, diced and fines, can generally be substituted on a weight-for-weight basis with any other nuts in candy formulas. When used in candies, they must be completely enrobed to help protect their high oil content. The nuts blend well with either dark or milk chocolate, and also the colorful Confectioners Coatings. They can be used in cookies and biscuits.

Macadamia Nut Brittle

White sugar	4½ lb
Brown sugar	1 lb
Corn syrup	2¼ lb
Water to dissolve	
Macadamia nuts, large pieces such as halves	4½ lb
Butter	1 lb
Salt	1 tbsp (heaping)
Imitation vanilla	1 oz
Baking soda	2 tbsp

Put sugar and corn syrup into a kettle and wash down sides with enough water to dissolve ingredients. Cook to 137.8°C (280°F). Add the macadamia nuts, butter, salt and continue to cook to 145°C (295°F). Shut off fire. Add vanilla and baking soda and stir in thoroughly. When the mixture has fluffed up well, pour onto an oiled and floured slab. Spread with spatula; when firm, turn over and stretch thin. The batch must be stirred constantly after nuts are added and vigorously after soda is added.

Walnuts

Walnuts go back in history to ancient Persia, where it is said they were even used as a means for barter. They were transplanted from Carthage, the growing area, into Egypt, Constantinople, Rome and eventually to European countries and the New World.

About 95% of the domestic walnut crops comes from the central and northern sections of the San Joaquin and Sacramento valleys of California.

The walnut crop has been trending upward, although not at a consistent rate, according to figures supplied by Diamond/Sunsweet, Inc., Stockton, California, walnut growers. In the 1970-76 period, there was a 57% increase in total supply, which includes the carry-ins, as shown in Table 16.3.

Another version of this nut is the American black walnut which differs in size, shape, color and flavor.

An interesting development arising out of the pecan shortage was the growth of walnut sales, riding the tail of the pecan prices, as many users switched over looking for a replacement. Walnuts went up to $1.50 per lb (Kuzio 1977).

Walnut Old-Fashioned Fudge

Cream (20% butterfat)	1 gal.
Granulated sugar	15 lb
Brown sugar	5 lb
Corn syrup	5 lb
Salted dairy butter	1 lb
Fine crystal or powdered salt	1½ oz
Short fondant (wafer or pattie fondant)	3 lb
Vanilla, rum or maple flavor	to suit
Walnuts (broken or chopped)	5 lb

Place into a copper cooking pan half of the cream, the granulated and brown sugars, the corn syrup, butter and salt, and heat, stirring occasionally until it boils.

Stir the batch continuously, and gradually add the remainder of the cream (adding about a pint at a time, keeping the batch constantly boiling), and cook to 117° to 118°C (242.6° to 244.4°F) at sea level.

Pour the cooked batch onto an open-type cream beater, then drop the short fondant (cut into small pieces) on top of the cooked batch. When it has cooled to approximately 51° to 54°C (124° to 129°F), start the beater, add the desired flavor and the broken or chopped walnuts, and continue to beat until the fudge becomes plastic. The plastic fudge may be pressed into wax paper lined wooden or metal trays, or bread pans, or formed into mounds, and cut later.

The fudge batch may also be melted in a double boiler to 57° to 60°C (134.6° to 140°F), then deposited into wax paper lined trays or pans, or deposited into metal foil pie plates, or paper cups, placing the broken or chopped walnuts over the surface, and pressing the nuts into the fudge while it is warm. If the fudge is formed into sheets, it may be scored into squares, placing large walnut pieces in each square. To make a less expensive fudge, replace half of the cream with unsweetened evaporated milk (Kuzio 1977).

THE SALES APPEAL OF NUTMEATS

The merchandising advantage of using the variety of nutmeats on the market is often overlooked. For example, how many unimaginative dishes can be enhanced and sold for much more with a sprinkling of nutmeats on top? Take a simple chicken croquette and roll it in almonds, call it "Plantation Chicken Log Rolled in Almonds," and feature it on the menu. It sells so much better than "chicken croquettes" and tastes so much better.

Today, when many restaurants are drastically reducing their labor force in the kitchen, the kitchen manager is constantly looking for ways to make a specialty dish—as simply as possible. With the use of the excellent frozen prepared entrees becoming popular in many restaurants, nutmeats can be the answer for individualizing frozen prepared foods. For example, chicken a la king served in a patty shell with toasted pecans, almonds or macadamia nuts over the top becomes a gourmet luncheon. A curry surrounded with a ring of crushed pineapple and sprinkled with pecans or macadamia nuts becomes an "exotic Hawaiian dish." Any bland creamed dish is definitely improved by the crunchiness of nutmeats. If a restaurant is using prepared frozen foods, it should experiment with nutmeats as a garnish. Included in the recipes are three ideas for frozen prepared entrees—Ham and Chicken Shortcake Supreme, Turkey Curry Hawaiian Style, and Turkey and Almonds in a Pineapple Shell.

ENHANCING RECIPES WITH NUTMEATS

There is not one cake in general use that would not be made more saleable by decorating with big pecan halves, walnut halves or other nutmeats. When a pineapple upside down cake is baked, arrange lots of pecans with the pineapple. If desserts are displayed, put the nutmeats where they will show. Sprinkle them on top of the cream pie meringue; sprinkle toasted pecans on top of the best cake. Breakfast rolls have much more sales appeal to the customer when he sees nutmeats popping out of a cinnamon twist. Hot muffins (made from a prepared mix) are enhanced when nuts are added.

A "pancake house" favorite is pecan pancakes in which chopped pecans are sprinkled liberally in the batter and over the cooked pancakes. A delicious combination for a sandwich spread is pickled black walnuts and cream cheese.

SUBSTITUTING ONE NUTMEAT FOR ANOTHER

Each nutmeat does have its own distinctive flavor. If a recipe calls for one nutmeat, you can substitute any other nutmeat, in the same quantity. However, there will definitely be a change in flavor. This change in flavor sometimes makes a better dish—or, sometimes instead of one recipe you can have two or perhaps three distinctly different recipes, by using different nutmeats. For example, a wonderful hazelnut torte—the Viennese favorite (recipe p. 99)—becomes a pecan torte by substituting ground pecans. In the South, the pecan torte would be more readily purchased by restaurant clientele than the hazelnut torte because Southerners love pecans in any form.

An interesting folktale illustrates this. The praline, a famous New Orleans candy made from brown sugar, cream and pecans, is said to be the Creole substitute for a French candy. The French chefs make a delicious confection with almonds and granulated sugar. In New Orleans, the cooks had neither refined sugar nor almonds, so they substituted the

Courtesy of Foodco Appliance Corp.

FIG. 4.1. FOOD CHOPPER FOR CUTTING OR SHREDDING NUTS

By changing cones, nuts may be chopped to any desired size. It
is especially for use in public eating places.

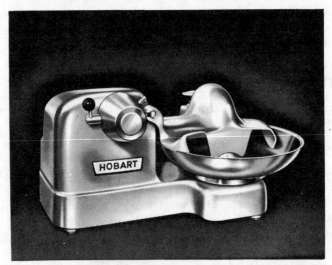

Courtesy of Hobart Mfg. Co.

FIG. 4.2. FOOD AND NUT CHOPPER FOR RESTAURANTS

It is ruggedly built for heavy duty action. The stainless steel
bowl and aluminum cover are light in weight and easy to handle.
It has several attachments.

unrefined brown sugar and pecans and, as a result, created one of the most delicious confections in the world.

On p. 94 the heirloom recipe for fruitcake is given. If a very nutty cake is desired, nutmeats can be substituted, weight for weight, for some of the fruit. If one particular nutmeat such as pecans is preferred, pecans can be substituted for almonds. Also, Brazil nuts are a delicious addition to this cake and can be substituted for some of the other nutmeats.

Substitutions can be made in many recipes. For example, nutmeats can be used instead of raisins in cookies. Finely chopped nutmeats can be substituted for coconut in macaroon recipes. Nutmeats can be substituted for a like quantity of bread in a poultry dressing, chestnuts being the most popular nutmeat to use for dressings.

USING NUTMEATS IN MAIN DISHES

Chicken, turkey, duckling, veal and fish are especially enhanced by nutmeats because of their bland flavor and soft texture. A nut-butter

Courtesy of Hobart Mfg. Co.

FIG. 4.3. BENCH MODEL 19-LITER MIXER FOR RESTAURANTS

It is food-acid resistant, easy to clean with deluxe finish, and sturdy for mixing nuts into batter. It has several attachments.

sauce adds texture, flavor contrast, and a pleasing garnish to dishes containing these meats. An amandine sauce is as simple as can be. This sauce may be molded into a roll which can then be cut off to order. What is not used can be stored in the refrigerator.

Ham is usually served with a raisin or fruit sauce. Adding sliced almonds to a sauce does wonders for it.

SERVING NUTS WITH BEVERAGES

The traditional accompaniment to beverages is roasted, salted pecans or peanuts. From dances to wedding receptions a bowl of roasted nuts next to the punch bowl or cokes is a must. Nuts are filling, however. Instead of putting out salted peanuts, put out the dry roasted or partially defatted peanuts (many other nutmeats are dry roasted too). Because they have less oil, they are not as filling. Some excellent restaurants serve dry roasted nuts in their lounges because they are tasty, but not filling.

BUYING NUTMEATS IN LARGE QUANTITIES

While broken nutmeats may be cheaper than the whole nuts, the whole nutmeats may have a better flavor. Wherever the broken piece has been exposed to air, it will have lost flavor.

Pecans, Persian walnuts and almonds are the three nutmeats commonly purchased for most cooking and baking. Since in many recipes one may be substituted for another, it might be wise to choose the cheapest of the three. This could prove to save much money in a bake shop or restaurant that uses lots of nutmeats. The price for these three nuts is established in the fall of the year after the nut harvest and remains about the same until the harvest the following fall. In the autumn the buyer can compare, pound for pound, the price of the three. The crop does vary greatly from year to year. The U.S. Department of Agriculture's "Plentiful Food Reports" lists the nutmeats in best supply every fall.

STORING NUTMEATS

After a can of nutmeats has been opened, it should be stored in the refrigerator, tightly covered. A glass mayonnaise jar is a good storage container because the amount remaining can easily be seen. Letting a container sit on a stockroom shelf, uncovered, greatly hastens deterioration in flavor.

PREPARING NUTMEATS FOR USE

Nutmeats taste much better immediately after they are roasted and salted. For salads, sandwiches, garnishing and "munching" the flavor is greatly improved by roasting.

Blanching Nuts

Nuts with heavy skins such as almonds are blanched first to remove this skin. To blanch, cover with boiling water. When the skins are loosened and puffy, pour hot water off and remove skins. Slip off skin of nut by pressing at large end and forcing kernel out at pointed end. Dry blanched nuts thoroughly.

Cooking Nutmeats on the Range

Heat two cups of oil in a large skillet for every quart of nuts. Add nuts and cook over low heat, stirring constantly until browned. Spread on absorbent paper to drain. Sprinkle with salt. Use about 3 g of salt for every quart.

Roasting Nutmeats in Oven

Spread nutmeats in a shallow pan. Dot with ¼ cup of butter for each quart of nuts. Brown in a hot oven 204°C (400°F), stirring every 5 min. Do not overcook—nuts darken as they cool. (Remove pecans from oven as soon as the butter sizzles.) The total time of roasting will be from 5 to 10 min.

USING NUTMEATS[1]

In Soup

One of the earliest nut soups prepared in America was an acorn soup made by Indian Pomo squaws in California. Other American nut soups are southern cream of pecan soup and purée of peanuts. Nut soups of other lands include Spanish almond soup, Turkish almond soup, almond buttermilk soup, Mexican walnut soup, South American almond soup, San Juan cashew soup, Polish chestnut soup, Brazilian coconut soup, American hazelnut soup, Virginia peanut soup, and pistachio soup of the Gay Nineties (Marett 1963).

---

[1]See Appendix for converting to metric measurements.

There are a few steps common to all nut soups: (a) the dried nutmeats are rolled or ground into paste or butter; (b) a portion of the paste (the amount depending upon the intensity of flavor desired) is added to a broth of chicken, beef, veal, ham hock or fish; (c) it is thickened with rice, hard-cooked egg yolks, starch, flour or corn grits; (d) vegetables such as asparagus, pimientos, celery, parsley, spinach or arrowroot are added for color and flavor; and (e) finally a "bouquet" is added with mace, nutmeg, bay leaf, basil, cinnamon, paprika and salt. Many cooks add sherry to nut soups.

Courtesy of McGraw-Edison Co.

FIG. 4.4. COMPACT NUT FRYING KETTLE FOR RESTAURANTS

It is 17 in. wide with storage space beneath, or it can be converted into table model. It has control switch and fire guard.

Frying in Deep Fat

Heat fat to 182° to 187°C (360° to 370°F). Spread nuts on bottom of fryer basket. Lower basket into heated fat and fry 4 to 5 min until browned. Drain well and sprinkle with salt.

Nut and Fruitcakes

Nutmeats are almost as important to fruitcakes as fruits themselves. They add assorted flavors as well as texture and color. While all tree nuts may be used in fruitcakes, those that are rich in flavor, high in oil, and of a brown color are most suitable. Pecans, Persian walnuts and black walnuts are most common; but hickories, Brazil nuts, macadamia and pistachio nuts are good. Pine nuts are suitable for very light-colored cakes.

Courtesy of Collin Street Bakery

FIG. 4.5. FAMOUS "CORSICANA FRUIT CAKE" TOPPED WITH PECAN HALVES

This cake has been made since 1900 and was shipped into 130 foreign lands in 1965 alone. Two-, three-, or five–pound cakes are shipped in beautifully decorated tins.

Snowy white fruitcake with jewel bright pieces of candied fruits, golden raisins and large chunky pieces of nuts have a colorful stained glass window effect when the cake is cut. Deep-toned mosaic fruitcakes are dark, moist, spicy and nutty. The in-between golden cakes may have only a suggestion of spice to enhance their mellowness.

Most fruitcakes reach the peak of flavor perfection after aging a few weeks. The cakes should be wrapped carefully and stored in a cool place. From time to time they should be sprinkled with spirits during this period. Decorations and fancy frostings are optional and go on for last-minute glamour.

California Fruitcake

1 cup butter	½ cup currant jelly
2 cups light brown sugar	1 tsp vanilla
4 eggs	2 cups dark seedless raisins
3 cups sifted flour	1 cup seeded muscat raisins
1 tsp baking powder	1 cup golden seedless raisins
1 tsp salt	1 cup halved candied cherries
½ tsp cinnamon	1 cup cut-up candied pineapple
½ tsp nutmeg	2 cups whole nutmeats
½ cup light rum	

Beat butter, sugar and eggs until very light and fluffy. Resift flour with baking powder, salt and spices. Add to egg mixture alternately with rum blended with jelly and vanilla. Stir in raisins, candied fruits and nuts. Spoon batter into two greased 9 × 5 × 3-in. loaf pans. Bake in slow oven 148°C (300°F) about 2½ hours, or until cake tests done. When thoroughly cold, sprinkle liberally with additional rum; wrap tightly in foil and store several weeks. Sprinkle with rum every week or so during aging. Makes two 9-in. loaves.

Elegant White Fruitcake

1 15-oz pkg golden seedless raisins	4½ cups sifted flour
2 cups mixed candied citrus peels, cut in chunks	1 cup shortening
	¼ cup butter
1 cup halved red candied cherries	1¾ cups sugar
	½ tsp almond extract
½ cup halved green candied cherries	1½ tsp baking powder
	1½ tsp salt
1 (6¾ oz) can mixed salted nuts	¾ cup pineapple juice
	8 egg whites
	½ tsp cream of tartar

Toss together raisins, peels, candied fruits and nuts with ½ cup flour. Beat shortening and butter together; add sugar gradually, continuing beating until very light and fluffy. Add almond extract. Resift remaining 4 cups flour with baking powder and salt. Add alternately with pineapple juice, beating well after each addition. Stir in fruit mixture. Sprinkle cream of tartar over egg whites; beat until stiff enough to hold peaks, but not dry. Fold into batter. Spoon batter evenly into 10-in. tube pan lined with well-greased and floured brown paper. Bake in slow oven 148°C (300°F) 3 hours. Place shallow pan of water on bottom of oven during baking. When baked remove cake from pan; cool on rack, pulling paper down from sides but leaving attached. When cooled, pull up paper around sides. Overwrap in foil or plastic wrap and store in cool place. If desired, sprinkle cake with brandy before wrapping and during aging period. Makes one 10-in. tube cake (5 lb).

Dark Fruitcake

2 lb raisins or currants
½ lb candied cherries
½ lb candied pineapple
½ lb citron
1 lb figs
1 lb butter or margarine
1 lb dark brown sugar, or
light brown or granulated
may be used
1 cup molasses

4 cups flour
6 eggs
⅓ cup sherry, brandy or
fruit juice
1½ tsp nutmeg
3 tsp cloves
3 tsp cinnamon
3 tsp baking powder
1½ lb nutmeats

Cream butter and sugar. Add beaten eggs. Sift flour and measure, then take out one cup of flour for dusting the cut-up fruit. Sift remainder of flour with the other ingredients and spices. Add the flour mixture, and the fruits and nuts alternately with the molasses and wine to the egg and butter or margarine mixture. Mix well. Use a large pan (the hands do the best job of greasing) and grease and paper line tube cake pan. (See section p. 97 on lining pans.) Bake in a slow oven, 135°C (275°F) for approximately 3½ to 4 hours, or until done. Makes about a 6½ lb cake.

White Fruitcake

2 cups sugar
4½ cups cake flour
½ lb butter (2 sticks)
1 cup water (scant)
Whites of 8 eggs, beaten
2 tsp baking powder
1 tsp lemon extract
1 tsp vanilla

2 lb white raisins
1 lb almonds, blanched and
chopped
½ lb light color citron, sliced
fine
½ lb red crystallized cherries,
cut in half
½ lb crystallized pineapple, cut up

Cream butter and sugar. Sift flour and use ½ cup for dusting fruit and nuts. Sift baking powder with remaining flour. Add water and flour alternately to the creamed mixture. Fold in beaten egg whites, add flavoring and then the floured fruit and nuts. Bake in a greased brown paper lined and greased-again pan. Bake at 135°C (275°F) for 2½ to 3 hours or until done.

Japanese Fruitcake

1 cup butter or margarine
2 cups sugar
4 eggs
1 cup buttermilk
1 cup chopped raisins
1 cup chopped nutmeats
3 cups flour

½ tsp salt
1 tsp cinnamon
1 tsp allspice
1 tsp cloves
1 tsp nutmeg
1 tsp soda

Cream butter and sugar together, add eggs one at a time, beating well after each addition. Sift dry ingredients together and combine the two mixtures. Flour raisins and nutmeats and add to above mixture. Pour into layer pans and bake in slow oven, 148°C (300°F), about 1 hour or until cake leaves sides of pan.

Japanese Fruitcake Filling

2 boxes of coconut

2 tbsp flour

2 lemons, grated rind and juice

2½ cups sugar

1½ cups hot water

Combine all ingredients, cook until thick. Cool slightly, put between layers.

Christmas Fruitcake

1½ cups sugar

2 cups flour

½ tsp salt

1 tsp baking powder

1 small jar maraschino
  cherries

1 lb pitted dates

½ cup cherry juice

4 well-beaten eggs

3 tbsp butter

1 lb Brazil nuts

1 lb walnuts

Sift together sugar, flour, salt and baking powder. Add cherries and dates; blend in cherry juice, eggs and butter. Add nuts; mix with hands and pack into two loaf pans. Bake 1½ hours in 162°C (325°F) oven.

Bakeless Fruitcake

½ lb graham crackers, crushed

½ lb dates, cut fine

1 cup thin cream

½ lb marshmallows, cut fine

½ cup chopped pecans

10 maraschino cherries, chopped

Mix thoroughly all the ingredients. Press firmly into a tube pan which has been lined with oiled heavy wax paper. Let stand overnight or longer in the refrigerator, as it will keep moist if well covered. May be served with whipped cream.

The dark fruitcake is best made about four weeks before Christmas so that it can mellow. The white fruitcake is best made and set aside about two weeks before Christmas. The Japanese fruitcake and bakeless fruitcake are made as needed.

In baking more than one fruitcake at a time, place them on the oven rack so the air can circulate between them. A shallow pan of water in the bottom of the oven during baking will give the cakes a soft crust. As soon as fruit cakes are baked remove them from their baking pans to a rack but do not remove the pan-lining papers. After the cakes cool, wrap them and store as directed.

The question often arises about storing a fruitcake in a freezer. In order to develop its rich flavor and texture it should be aged four weeks and then frozen.

When filling greased paper-lined containers with the fruitcake batter be sure not to fill them more than 1 in. from the top. This prevents a heavy crust from forming on top and allows for some expansion in baking.

Fruitcakes do not need special pans for baking. Tube pans or loaf pans are most often used for large cakes, whereas empty 1-lb coffee cans or fruit and vegetable cans may be used equally as well for small cakes.

General directions for fruitcake are . . . bake the fruitcakes in a slow oven 121° to 135°C (250° to 275°F) allowing about 2½ hours for 1-lb cakes or 3 to 4½ hours for larger ones. Cake is done if—when touched with fingertip—no imprint is left. Testing may also be done with a wooden pick.

Lining Fruitcake Pans.—Fruitcake pans should be lined with two thicknesses of greased brown paper and one thickness of greased waxed paper. The paper acts as insulation during the baking process and helps prevent a heavy crust. Before greasing, cut paper to fit size of pan, allowing it to extend an inch above top of pan. Make slashes, not folds, in paper so the corners will fit. Grease each layer of paper separately.

Storing Fruitcakes.—Wrap cake in cloth soaked in fruit juice. Wrap in waxed paper. Place in tightly covered can with a slice of apple for each cake. Do not place fruit directly on cake. Store in dry cool place. Redip cloth if it becomes dry, and change apple slices to keep them from molding. A large stone crock with a light cover is ideal for storing fruitcakes.

LARGE QUANTITY RECIPES[2]

The following quantity recipes use almonds, pecans and Persian walnuts. In addition, there are uses for black walnuts, cashews, macadamia nuts, pine nuts and Brazil nuts.

Meat

Fruit and Nut Sauce for Baked Ham

2 cups brown sugar, packed

---

[2]For recipes throughout—see Appendix for converting to metric measurements.

3 oz butter
2 tbsp prepared mustard
2 cups crushed pineapple (do not drain)
½ cup sliced maraschino cherries
½ cup chopped pecans

Melt butter; add brown sugar, mustard, pineapple, cherries and pecans. Boil together 5 min. Use 1½ oz over serving of baked ham. Serves 20.

Vegetables

Sweet Potatoes With Orange

9 lb cooked, peeled sweet potatoes (canned work fine)
⅓ cup grated orange rind
1½ cups melted butter
1½ cups brown sugar
1½ cups white sugar
1½ tsp nutmeg
1½ tsp salt
12 oz salad marshmallows
½ cup chopped pecans

Put potatoes into mixer and beat until fluffy with melted margarine and orange rind. Beat in sugars, nutmeg and salt. Pour into baking pan. Sprinkle with marshmallows and pecans. Bake at 176°C (350°F) for 20 min. Serves 30.

Salad

Lime Ring Mold Salad Filled With Chicken Salad

6 oz lime flavored gelatin
2 cups hot water
2 cups fruit juice
1 3-oz package cream cheese
1 8-oz can spiced white grapes
⅓ cup whole pecans

Add hot water to lime gelatin and stir until dissolved; add fruit juice. Let stand until partially set and pour into individual ring molds. Cut cream cheese into small cubes. Drain white grapes. Just before gelatin sets, place a few grapes, cubes of cream cheese, and pecans in each ring mold. Let stand until set. When ready to serve, turn out on crisp lettuce leaf or curly endive and fill the center with your favorite chicken salad. Sprinkle pecans over the top. Makes 12 servings.

Sandwiches

Cream Cheese, Olive and Nut Spread
on Whole Wheat Bread

1 lb cream cheese

1 cup stuffed olives, chopped
½ cup chopped pecans
2 tbsp mayonnaise

Soften cream cheese with mayonnaise. Blend in olives and nuts. Use one #116 scoop, 2 tsp butter and lettuce on 2 slices of whole wheat bread. Makes 12 servings.

Baked Goods

English Toffee Pie

3 lb (3 qt) finely crushed vanilla wafers
1 lb (1 qt) chopped nutmeats
2 lb (4 cups) butter
3 lb (7 cups) sifted powdered sugar
8 oz nonfat dry milk
2 lb (4 cups) eggs, separated
8 oz melted bitter chocolate
3 tbsp vanilla

Mix crushed vanilla wafers and finely chopped nutmeats with ¾ lb butter. Put two cups of this mixture into each pie pan. There will be some left over which is sprinkled on top of pies. Press crumbs firmly along bottom and sides. Cream remaining butter (1¼ lb). Add all ingredients except egg whites. Beat until smooth and fluffy. Fold in stiffly beaten egg whites. Divide among pies, spreading evenly over crust. Cover with remaining crumbs. Refrigerate for several hours. Spread each pie with ½ cup heavy cream, whipped and sweetened with 1 tbsp confectioners' sugar and 1 tsp vanilla. Cut each pie into 8 pieces. Makes 48 pieces.

Torte

Pecan or Hazelnut Torte

Ingredients for cake:
12 whole eggs
1 cup granulated sugar
1 lb ground hazelnuts or pecans

Ingredients for buttercream filling:
1 lb softened butter
1½ lb powdered sugar
3 egg yolks
½ cup sherry
1 square melted chocolate (1 oz)

Directions for making cake.—Beat eggs until fluffy. Add sugar a little at a time. Beat until it holds a peak (20 to 30 min). Fold in ground nuts. Grease and wax paper line 4 cake pans. Bake 1 hour at 176°C (350°F). Cool. Makes 16 servings.

Directions for making buttercream icing.—Cream butter and sugar. Beat in yolks and sherry (which have been beaten together). Beat in melted chocolate. Frost layers and refrigerate for several hours or until icing is firm and torte cuts easily. This will keep several days in refrigerator.

SUGARED AND SPICED NUTS

Spiced nuts (pecans) are popular as confections or toasted snacks. Pan-coated, sugared and spiced nuts prepared according to the following formula contain about 5.7% moisture. If hermetically sealed in glass, tin or plastic containers, without drying, they become moist, syrupy and musty within a week. Packing under vacuum is of no advantage in preventing dampness but prevents rapid staling.

The prepared nuts may be stabilized by (a) packing in moisture permeable containers and holding at 55% relative humidity to allow some of the moisture to evaporate, or (b) drying the nuts to about 4.0% moisture, by holding at 48° to 60°C (120° to 140°F) for 1 hour. Predried sugared and spiced nutmeats retain very good flavor at 21°C (70°F) for months without vacuum and for 6 months when packed under vacuum. The shelf-life may be doubled at −3° to 0°C (25° to 32°F).

A modified protein-starch (Cozeen) coating on the raw nuts retards sogginess due to the absorption of moisture, and rancidity caused by absorption of oxygen. The coating should be applied to the nuts and allowed to dry for 12 to 24 hours before the meats are mixed with the sugar and spices. Cozeen coated nuts require less sugar coating than do plain nuts. The coated nuts also have more desirable appearance, more gloss and uniform color, and are slightly more firm. The Cozeen coating contains an antioxidant and its use improves most of the desirable qualities of nut confections (Woodroof and Heaton 1961).

Sugared and Spiced Nuts (Pecans)

Nuts (whole, halves or large pieces)	12 lb
Sugar	12 lb
Water	1½ cups
Cinnamon	2 tbsp
Nutmeg	1 tbsp
Cloves	1 tbsp
Antioxidant (Tenox II)	½ oz

Heat sugar and water to 116°C (240°F) in revolving pan, add nuts and spices, and revolve until nuts are coated. Dry for 1 hour at 48°C (120°F), or 2 hours at room temperature, in circulated air. Pack in hermetically sealed tin cans, glass jars or plastic containers, preferably under vacuum. Hold at room temperature if they are to be eaten within a month, otherwise store under refrigeration.

For small batches where revolving pans are not available, the sugar, water and spices may be heated, added to the nutmeats, and stirred or tumbled until the meats are uniformly coated. The product may then be dried by spreading on a table in front of a fan for 2 hours.

Nut Topping

Topping made from pecans, black walnuts, Persian walnuts, hickory nuts, pistachio or macadamia nuts, has many uses in restaurants. Nut toppings are excellent at fountains, for desserts, salads, pies, puddings, cakes, cookies, hotcakes, waffles and breads.

For ease of packing and convenience of using, nutmeats are cut into medium or small pieces, before mixing with the syrup in proportions shown in the formula. The use of heavy corn syrup produces high viscosity and increased sheen without excess sweetness. Sealed in glass or tin containers, the topping retains good quality at room temperature for 1 year, at 2.2° to 3.3°C (36° to 38°F) for 3 years.

Nut (Pecan) Topping

Nuts (medium or small pieces)	5 lb
Corn syrup, 70° Brix	4 lb
Maple syrup, 70° Brix	1 lb
Vanilla flavor	1 tsp
Salt	2 tsp
Baking soda	1 tsp

Heat syrup to 100°C (212°F), add ingredients, mix thoroughly and pack in jars while hot. Close, invert jars until cool. Store in cool place or freeze (Woodroof and Heaton 1961).

Nut (Pecan) Topping Concentrate

A buttered pecan topping is being marketed in 10-lb cans. Large pecan pieces are covered with about 83° Brix syrup containing synthetic pecan flavor. For use the full can is heated in hot water for 30 min and diluted with an equal volume of regular corn syrup.

The product (manufactured by Food Producers, Inc., Minneapolis) is for institutional use, and must be used shortly after dilution, or else the nut pieces will become soggy and rise to the surface. This may be prevented by holding under refrigeration.

Nut (Pecan) Paste

This is a sweet, highly flavored, plastic product made of nuts (pecans) which can be spread, molded into many shapes and used in many recipes. The paste can be formed into balls and coated with chocolate or hard cream; the balls may be used for decorations; or the paste may be thinned with syrup and used in ice cream, boiled custard, desserts or salads.

Nut (Pecan) Paste

Pecan meats	2 cups
Brown sugar	1 cup
Beaten egg, optional	2
Cinnamon	Pinch
Salt	¼ tsp

Grind nuts and sugar, mix egg and seasoning, and beat until smooth.

Green Nuts for Condiments and Ornaments

Several nuts are used before they are fully ripe, and esteemed a delicacy. In California and Europe the markets quite commonly offer green almonds—that is, almonds picked while the husk is green and easily separated from the soft and immature shell. The kernel, after the skin is peeled off, is eaten with or without salt.

Persian walnuts, butternuts and hazelnuts are also eaten in the green state. They are pickled or made into catsup (Jaffa 1908).

NUT FLAVORS[3]

A number of edible nuts are used in considerable quantities in confectionery, baked products, ice cream and other food products, such as peanut butter and specialty foods. Among the most popular nuts used for these purposes are coconuts, almonds, pistachio nuts, filberts, peanuts, pecans, walnuts, cashews, macadamias, etc.

With the exception of peanuts, no nuts are used as extensively for confectionery as coconuts. They contain fatty acids of low molecular weight as well as volatile fatty acids, soluble to some extent in water. Thus they simulate butter fat when used in confectionery and ice cream, in addition to contributing the flavor characteristic of coconuts, which has a wide popularity the world over.

Black walnuts have a pleasant, resinous flavor and are used in a number of types of confectionery. Persian walnuts (sometimes known as butternuts or white walnuts) have a milder flavor. They are also used in confectionery, ice cream, etc.

Pecans, as such, have probably the greatest commercial importance in

---

[3]By Victor G. Fourman, Chemist, Florasynth, Inc., New York.

Courtesy of Kitchens of Sara Lee

FIG. 4.6. ALL-BUTTER PECAN COFFEE CAKE IS GOOD THE
YEAR-ROUND

Courtesy of Keith Thomas Co.

FIG. 4.7. ALMOND BUTTERSCOTCH CAKE

the United States, more than any other native nuts. Filberts (also known as hazelnuts) and macadamias, grown in Hawaii, are also of possible interest in connection with various food products.

Among the most popular nuts used in confectionery, baked products and ice cream are almonds. Shelled almonds are used in sugared almonds, chocolate almonds and almond nougats. Bars of sweet and milk chocolate containing almonds are also very popular.

Almond paste used for macaroons is made from blanched kernels and sugar. The best almond paste is prepared with about 35% sugar, 55% ground, blanched almonds and 10% water; mix these ingredients thoroughly until a smooth paste is formed. To this paste sometimes is added a small amount of bitter almond oil, or a specially prepared almond flavor which contains suitable fixatives, and is therefore more lasting. Marzipan is an almond paste to which various flavors are added. This paste is widely used in the production of confections and macaroons.

Imitation nut flavors are often added by manufacturers of confectionery, baked products and ice cream to the various types of nuts. These imitation nut flavors are employed to enhance and fortify the flavors contributed by the nuts. Much of the natural flavor of the nuts may disappear during the processing of the confectionery, baked goods or ice cream. Hence, the added flavor aids in bringing out the nut-like character.

The food manufacturer may wish to make the nut-like character more interesting and more distinctive. The flavor from the nuts may be supplemented with various imitation nut flavors or with other flavors that blend well with nut flavors, such as imitation butter flavor, imitation butterscotch flavor, imitation vanilla flavor, imitation maple flavor, imitation honey flavor, and many others.

It is not possible to give the number of imitation nut flavors which are being offered on the market, as every manufacturer of food flavors has a long list of such flavors to meet almost every requirement and taste.

The various imitation nut flavors are generally made from nut extractives and other plant extractives, together with various essential oils or suitable aromatics or both. Nor is it possible to describe the physical and chemical properties of those imitation nut flavors as these vary widely, depending on the type and quality of the flavor. The great majority of them are liquids but some are powdered, such as Entrapped Imitation Black Walnut Flavor.[4]

Nutritive Value of Imitation Nut Flavors

This is insignificant, since only minute quantities of such flavors are

___
[4]Registered by Florasynth, Inc., New York.

used in the finished product. For example, when a given imitation nut flavor is used at the rate of 4 oz of flavor for 100 lb of finished product, the flavor content of added flavor is only 0.25%. The tolerances are self-limiting since using too much of a given flavor is objectionable and results in "over-flavoring."

Standards for Imitation Flavors

All flavors, natural and imitation, should conform with all the requirements of both federal and state authorities, and generally do, if made by reputable manufacturers.

While it is not possible to give the physical and chemical properties of imitation nut flavors because there are so many variations, these flavors can be examined with respect to such physical characteristics as: specific gravity, refractive index, optical rotation, etc.

In this way standards may be established in the laboratory of the candy, baked goods, and ice cream producer so that quality control methods are employed to ensure uniformity of the flavor from batch to batch. It must be kept in mind, however, that such specifications as refractive index, optical rotation and specific gravity must represent a wide range, since most of these imitation nut flavors contain natural ingredients that vary considerably from year to year as a result of variations in weather and other conditions beyond the control of the flavor manufacturer.

Trend in Uses of Imitation Nut Flavors

The use of imitation nut flavors is constantly increasing as more and better flavors of these types are being produced.

It is difficult to specify the amount of flavor to use for each 100 lb of finished product, be it confectionery, baked goods or ice cream, as so much depends on the strength of the flavor used and on the intensity of flavor desired in the finished product. However, a few examples are given by way of illustration.

When imitation nut flavors are used for syrups, generally the ratio is ¼ oz for each gallon of syrup, provided the nut flavor is of good quality and high concentration.

Flavors of this type, used for confections such as cream centers, are recommended in the ratio of 1 oz per 100 lb of cream centers. For ice cream, they are often employed at the rate of ¼ oz for every 5 gal. of ice cream mix, and for baked-goods, about 1½ to 2 oz for 100 lb of the finished product. It must be kept in mind that these are only general suggestions. Every manufacturer must decide whether he should maintain, increase or decrease these ratios, depending on his own needs and ideas as well as on the type of market to which his products are being offered.

Concentrated Imitation Coconut Flavor is used 2½ to 3 oz for 100 lb of baked goods, but here again the concentration can be varied widely depending on circumstances. Three ounces of Imitation Marzipan Flavor are recommended for 100 lb of finished product, but the amount of flavor may be increased or decreased to suit the needs of the user.

Most imitation nut flavors are used as purchased, but they are also offered in the form of highly concentrated oils so that the manufacturer of confections, baked goods and ice cream can make his own finished flavor. For example, for Syntharome Imitation Black Walnut Oil and Syntharome Imitation English Walnut Oil, 8 oz of the flavor oil are added to 96 oz of propylene glycol, and then water is added to make 1 gal. of finished flavor.

REFERENCES

HARTLEY, G. 1966. Fruitcakes. Atlanta J. and Constitution Magazine, November 27.

HESS, E.G. 1925. 800 Proved Pecan Recipes. Keystone Pecan Res. Lab. Lancaster, Pa.

JAFFA, M.E. 1908. Nuts and their use as food. U.S. Dep. Agric. Farmer's Bull. *332.*

KUZIO, W. 1977. Nutmeat roundup. Candy Ind. *142* (6) 25-42.

MARETT, L. 1963. From nuts to soup. Gourmet *28,* 72, 74-77.

WOODROOF, J.G., and HEATON, E.K. 1961. Pecans for processing. Ga. Agric. Exp. Stn. Bull. N.S. *80.*

5

Roasting and Salting Nuts

Salting is the largest outlet for tree nuts, because a major portion is eaten in this form, with the exception of chestnuts. Most imported nuts—cashews, pistachios, macadamias, as well as Brazil nuts and pine nuts—are roasted in the shell and eaten without salt. More pecans are used in bakery products than are salted, and more almonds go into confections.

Nuts are roasted for salting either dry or in oil. They are dry roasted by radiant heat or microwaves. Before roasting the meats should be graded for size, color and imperfections, separated from shells and other foreign material, and sometimes counted.

Nut salters are becoming fewer but larger. Because of better-than-average profits and relatively low initial outlay, the industry is dominated by regional companies. To compensate for high labor and material costs, nut salters have turned to automation and quantity production. Companies are consolidating and serving larger areas, even overseas markets.

SALTING PROCEDURE

The following are eight steps for salting nuts:

(1) Roast at 121° to 176°C (250° to 350°F). Use coconut or other low-melting oil. It should melt at about 21°C (70°F) and solidify at about 26.5°C (80°F). The time varies from 5 to 25 min, depending on the kind and size of nuts.
(2) Cool to 65°C (150°F). Use forced air through bottom of vat.
(3) Apply oil dressing with antioxidant. Make first application of low-melting coconut or other oil at 66° to 93°C (150° to 200°F) by spraying.
(4) Apply salt with antioxidant. Sprinkle with 2% fine flake salt and stir thoroughly.
(5) Cool to 43°C (110°F). Use forced air through bottom of vat.

(6) Apply "shine" oil. Spray on and stir gently to "seal on" salt.
(7) Allow to set. Hold 1 to 3 hours to allow volatiles to escape, the dressing to set, and the oil on surface to equalize.
(8) Package. This may be under vacuum, in glass or tin containers, in small flexible bags or in bulk.

EQUIPMENT

Bauer Brothers Co. is responsible for engineering and constructing much of the equipment now used in nut processing. The company started small in 1878, as the Foos Manufacturing Co. In 1904 it was bought by Bauer Brothers, and by 1918 was making seed cleaners, various types of hullers, separators, shakers and attrition mills.

Courtesy of Calif. Almond Growers Assoc.

FIG. 5.1.   OIL ROASTING NUTS FOR SALTING

One hundred pounds of selected nuts are loaded into the basket and lowered into boiling oil until a crisp texture and golden color are reached. Subsequently the nuts are drained, centrifuged to remove excess oil, and given a dressing of seasoned salt.

The company expanded in research and development and in 1933 the first peanut butter mill was designed. Following closely was the development of a complete line of roasters, coolers, blanchers, separators, picking tables, granulators and "accessory" items.

The Meyer Machine Co., San Antonio, Texas, is the world's largest producer of edible-nut processing equipment. The equipment includes automatic nut crackers, in-shell graders, dial-type shellers, cull and shrivel removers, washers and conditioners, floating machines, centrifugal extractors, vacuum pumps and tanks, nutmeat cutters and breakers, and antioxidant-treating machines.

Courtesy of Sortex Company

FIG. 5.2. POLYGRADER FOR NUTS

A British-made unit for separating nuts into four grades.

Some of the nut kernels processed for market and for various nut products are blanched (removal of skin or membrane covering the white meat). Almonds are soaked in hot water until the skin slips off readily; they are then dehydrated and may be immersed in hot peanut or coconut oil at 148°C (300°F) and salted. Hot-water treatment is not sufficient to loosen and remove the skins from the wrinkled surface of Persian walnuts, so the kernels of these nuts are blanched by immersion in hot lye solution followed by a dilute acid rinse; this process gives a white nonastringent product. Pecan meats are not blanched. An improved glycerin-alkali process for blanching almonds, filberts, Brazil nuts and other nuts, which preserves the flavor and texture of the nuts, consists of passing the kernels through a heated solution of 1 oz glycerin and 6 oz sodium carbonate per gallon of water, removing the skins with a stream of water, and dipping the kernels in a weak citric acid solution to neutralize any alkali retained by the kernels (Leffingwell and Lesser 1946).

Courtesy of Sortex Company

FIG. 5.3. FRONT VIEW OF AMERICAN–MADE POLYGRADER
FOR NUTS

Specific Gravity Separator

One of the unique and most widely used machines in the nut industry is a specific gravity separator. This unit combines mechanical and pneumatic action to separate and classify dry materials of different or varying densities, sizes, consistencies or weights. It removes alien objects, imperfections and impurities, thus guarding product quality and simultaneously protecting other equipment from possible damage by foreign materials (Anon. 1966D).

These separators are used for cleaning and/or separating such products as raw or roasted shelled or unshelled pistachio nuts, nutmeats and products containing nuts. Piñon nuts are separated from pine needles, stones, dirt and other debris in these separators.

Magnetic Cleaner

Permanent, nonelectric magnets are used for removing tramp metal, rust particles and similar foreign objects from nuts being processed. Included in the line-up are magnetic plates, grates, pulleys and traps as well as special magnets for picking tables or inspection tables. These versatile units are employed for wet, dry or liquid materials, and are incorporated in chutes, ducts, spouts, hoppers, pipe lines, conveyor lines and in other places.

Courtesy of Exact Weight Scale Co.

FIG. 5.4. AUTOMATIC WEIGHING MACHINE FOR NUTS AND CANDIES

The magnets are specially developed nonmetallic materials energized for intense concentration of holding power, for holding ferrous impurities before they can enter and damage machinery. The units are available in a wide range of sizes and types. Wing and drawer-type grate magnets are in 163 standard sizes in single and double bank models for use in hoppers and floor openings or closed chutes and ducts (Anon. 1962C).

Courtesy of Woodman Co.

FIG. 5.5. A FULLY AUTOMATIC IN-SHELL NUT PACKAGING
MACHINE

Transparent bags are formed, filled with a pre-weighed
quantity of nuts and sealed. There are four weighing stations
and two bag forming and sealing units.

Nut Counter

One of the tests to determine grade of nuts is the count per pound. A
unit has been developed for determining both an average seed weight
and weight variability. The counter eliminates manual counting. It
utilizes a highly accurate electronic unit that counts peanuts and similar
nuts at the rate of 250 to 750 seeds per min, depending upon size and
uniformity.

The weighed sample is poured into the open top of the unit. Vibration
causes the nuts to travel in single file along a spiral track. This track
discharges into a chute where the seeds break a beam of light as they go
downward. Interruption of the light beam is detected by a photocell

Courtesy of Wyandotte Chemicals

FIG. 5.6. RIGID SANITATION IS NECESSARY IN THE BAKERY

Much of the cleaning requires hand brushing and a good
detergent. Here kettles are being cleaned and polished between
shifts.

which produces an electric pulse. The pulse is amplified by transistorized
amplifier to operate high speed count register. The counter registers total
count for each sample by convenient push button (Anon. 1962A).

New Moisture Determination Balance

Figure 5.7 shows a balance that provides automatic moisture determination with a full capacity, direct reading optical scale calibrated in both
grams and percentage of moisture loss. Solid or liquid material can be
tested easily and moisture loss or weight of drying sample can be read
directly throughout the entire drying cycle. No manual rebalancing is
required. The heating unit is a standard tungsten filament infrared lamp.
An automatic shut-off timer permits settings up to 60 min in 1 min
intervals. The heat is shut off at any preset time. The balance uses
disposable aluminum foil pan liners.

Electronic Sorters

After nuts are shelled and all foreign material is removed from the
meats, they are graded for color electronically by use of an "electric eye."

FIG. 5.7. AUTOMATIC MOISTURE DETERMINATION BALANCE

The sample of solid or liquid is dried with infrared heat, and moisture loss can be read at any time either in grams or percent.

This unit can be adjusted to separate the "wanted" from the "reject" nutmeats wherever there is a difference in color. Photocells accurately and speedily identify and separate individual particles passing before them at the rate of more than 100 per sec per cell.

The selector is compact, simple to operate, and easy to maintain. There are only two moving parts, two counter-rotating rollers, which feed material particles single-file into the scanning head.

Material is fed into a hopper from a holding bin and a vibratory feeder moves it in the desired volume onto the top end of the counter-rotating rollers. The nutmeats are scanned from two sides by two photocells. If the product is darker or lighter than the "set norm" a signal is given that is transmitted to the air valve which, in turn, ejects and pushes the bad particle out of its free flight path and down into the reject chutes (Anon. 1966D).

Through changes in optical filters in front of the photocells, and changes of background plates (at which the photocells "look"), it is possible to adjust for whatever level of sort is desired. Smaller deviations from the set norm can be accomplished by panel controls.

Capacities vary in accordance with the percentage of damage in the feed, quality required, value of product, and nature of the product. For example, medium size pecan pieces vary from 200 to 500 lb per hour. The

Courtesy of Microwave Instrument Co.

FIG. 5.8. MICROWAVE MOISTURE METER FOR NUTS AND
SIMILAR PRODUCTS, WITH INSET SHOWING SAMPLE BEING
TESTED

selector is equipped with unit circuits, which can be removed and re-placed in about 2 min in case of malfunction. Standard tubes and resistors are used throughout. The unit is mounted on casters and weighs about 300 lb.

The operator can change from one product to another in about 1 min. One attendant can supervise 50 or more machines and can be trained by in-plant instruction during the installation period (Anon. 1964).

Vertical Cooler

A recently developed vertical cooler reflects the nut industry's need for technological advancement, because it eliminates heavy manual labor, dangerous openings and rails in the floor, and requires only one-fourth the floor space needed for the usual type of cooling equipment. The vertical cooler is totally enclosed and incorporates many production and sanitation innovations.

HIGH FREQUENCY ROASTING

Nuts can be heated, roasted or "refreshed" by high frequency waves. In

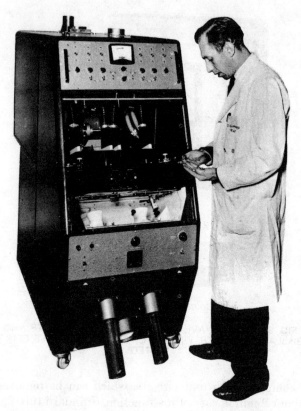

Courtesy of Sortex Co.

FIG. 5.9. ELECTRONIC COLOR SORTING MACHINE

(1) Fiberglass airleg showing air outlet pipe on top for connection of dust extractor to remove lightweight foreign particles; dust and fine pieces; (2) compressed air filter and air reservoir which connect to air ejection; (3) optical box and ejector power supplies; (4) delayed ejection control; (5) compressed air input fitting; (6) electrical power input receptacle; (7) fed chassis which contains motor driven feed belt and motor; and (8) blowthrough air duct.

commercial applications the shelf-life of peanuts heated to 82°C (180°F) is doubled. The high frequency heat waves sterilize the nuts, improve the flavor, and extend the shelf-life, by heating all the way through without overheating. Because of the high heating cycle, nuts can be processed fresh as needed.

Dielectric heating takes place between a pair of plates charged with high frequency current. Polar molecules in the product change position every time the polarity of the plates changes, and this generates heat by agitating the molecules (Manwaring 1966).

Courtesy of Gromax Inc.

FIG. 5.10. ELECTRONIC PECAN SORTING MACHINE

This unit can handle sizes from midgets to halves, without making any mechanical changes on the machine. Changes can be made by emptying the hopper of the one product and dumping the other. The photograph shows two outlets for the sorted nuts and one on the left for collecting dust, meal and other fine particles before the sorting process. The light source is tungsten filament incandescent.

DRY ROASTING

Dry roasting of nuts is an outstanding example of the predominance of rule of thumb methods in the preparation of a food.

In general, as the internal temperature of the nuts increases, the processing changes occur more rapidly and become more complex. As compared with most fresh foods, nuts are low in moisture, usually varying from 4 to 7%; and when subjected to an internal temperature of 121° to 148°C (250° to 300°F), the moisture is reduced to about 1%. Other changes include destruction of a large portion of the thiamin, while niacin, choline and riboflavin are little affected by roasting (Higgins *et al.* 1941; Pickett 1941, 1944, 1945; Pickett and Holley 1952). Although the proteins are denatured, as shown by the change in peptization in water, apparently their nutritive value is unchanged by moderate heat treatment, such as is used for blanching. Such constants of the oil as iodine number, saponification number, acetyl number, and free fatty acids do not change appreciably during the roasting process. Total sugars in nuts decrease when subjected to a heavy roast, while the starch and sulfur content is not significantly altered.

Batch Dry Roasting

There are many advantages in batch roasted nuts. The equipment is large and expensive to operate at less than capacity. On the other hand batch roasters are compact, fast, with high capacity and can be automated to provide the advantages of continuous operation without personal supervision (Anon. 1966).

The color control unit in each batch roaster assures uniform roasting and uniform color of the nuts. It actuates the pilot light, flame failure safety devices and the high temperature safety cut-off. It automatically charges the roaster from bulk or conveyor, discharges the unit, controls the cooler, and simultaneously provides a permanent record of temperature and time cycle.

By eliminating the possibility of human error, a key role is played in upgrading quality in the nuts. Nuts roasted by radiant heat are uniform in color and flavor. Burners inside the roaster cylinder use natural, manufactured mixed, carbureted or compressed propane or butane gas.

The capacity of the automatic batch roaster is one ton or more per hour, depending on the kind of nuts and color desired. For "white" roast it is greater than dark roast; and for pecans it is greater than for peanuts or almonds.

OIL ROASTING

Modern continuous nut roasters are in use in America as well as in European countries. The Burns Fry-O-Matic continuous oil nut roaster and cooler is an example (Fig. 5.11). This machine automatically roasts, cools, salts and glazes the product. It is economical to operate, with low fuel and maintenance costs, and no direct labor is required from the point of automatic feed to discharge except occasional supervisory attention. The time of immersion and temperature are accurately controlled so that each nut is subjected to the same amount of heat, and is immersed in oil for the same length of time.

One "3-bag nut roaster" has an extremely great rate of heat input— 250,000 Btu/hour (Fig. 5.12). The temperature of the roasting oil is restored to the initial temperature before the nuts are completely roasted, making it possible to induce succeeding batches of nuts immediately after the preceding ones have been removed from the roasting oil.

Courtesy of Fry-O-Matic Co.

FIG. 5.11. INTAKE END OF FRY-O-MATIC OIL NUT ROASTER

The batch roaster has a single roasting basket with a cooling table; or has a two basket setup, which includes a loading stand, roaster, drain table and a cooling table. With the two basket setup, basket number one is placed on the loading stand and filled with nuts, and is immersed into the oil when it is up to temperature. Basket number two is immediately filled with nuts. When basket number one is roasted it is removed from the roaster and placed on the drain table, and basket number two is placed in the roaster. When the nuts in basket number one are drained they are poured on the cooling table and the basket is returned for reloading.

With the two-basket setup, the roaster produces the maximum capacity with the highest possible rate of turnover (Anon. 1962B).

CONTROL OF COLOR DURING ROASTING

Control of color quality in nut roasting is becoming increasingly important as a means of quality control. But attempts to control objectively the color of nonhomogeneous and parti-colored products have given problems. Parti-colored products are those colored with different tints. Since it is the color of the surface that is being measured, grinding or dissolving are not satisfactory, and reflectance measurement is needed.

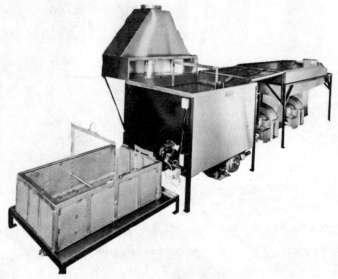

Courtesy of Specialities Appliance Corp.

FIG. 5.12. THREE-BAG NUT ROASTER

This is a two-basket operation, as there is a basket on the loading stand and one basket in the cooker. Between the cooker and the cooling table is a drain table.

Large samples are necessary to overcome variations when particles are rearranged; illumination is by diffuse light.

A wide area viewer is designed to operate with 400 Agtron, to measure the relative spectral characteristics of parti-colored nuts. The Agtron principle utilizes pure monochromatic (one color) light to illuminate the sample. The light is obtained from two concentric gaseous discharge tubes—one mercury vapor and one neon—which radiate light at specific lines or wavelengths which have zero bandwidth.

These tubes are ionized by a regular high voltage power supply such that the tubes produce bursts of luminous energy at a 120-cycle rate. The spectral lines of energy occur principally at 435.835 nm (nanometer=10^9 m), 546.074 nm, 640.225 nm, and 585.248 nm. Interference filters are used to "isolate" these lines and a phototube, which receives the reflected light, produces an output signal proportional to the luminous intensity.

Use of monochromatic light also permits shades-of-gray calibration standards. The meter reading is affected only by intensity without regard to spectral wavelength. Standardization consists simply of selecting the desired gray calibration disks and using two vernier controls to set the meter at zero and full scale span. Thus, standardization and sensitivity are set simultaneously without the use of a colored reference and without complicated calibration procedures (Simmons 1966).

DEEP FAT FRYING

It has been shown that maximum sensory scores resulted when potatoes were deep fat fried at 9½ min at 171°C (340°F), 8 min at 185°C (365°F), and 6½ min at 198°C (390°F). The absorption of fat was about the same for each of these conditions. The internal temperature of the potatoes rose to 102° to 104°C (216° to 220°F) in 2½ to 3 min and remained throughout the cooking period. The steam pressure from within and the surface coating hindered further oil pickup or change of internal temperature. Therefore, internal temperature could not be used as a criterion of doneness (Strock *et al.* 1966).

The following section was prepared by G. H. Scofield (1963) for the *Manufacturing Confectioner.*

The term "deep fat frying" is the processing of nuts by complete submersion in an edible fat heated to 121° to 176°C (250° to 350°F). The nuts are held in a basket or on a belt submerged in hot fat, which is in turn held in an open top holding tank. The nuts may be in a stationary position or conveyed through the heated fat until fried. They are removed from the fat, cooled, salted and dressed with oil.

Why Deep Fat Fry Nuts?

Deep fat frying alters and substantially improves the flavor, texture, color and appearance of nuts from the raw state. In the case of most nuts the flavor changes from a "green" raw taste to the roasted flavor so much enjoyed. In the case of cashew nuts the raw nut is largely devoid of flavor, whereas the deep fat fried product has a mildly sweet flavor.

The textural changes that nuts undergo after deep fat frying are almost as important as the flavor changes. The raw nuts are soft and pliable to an extent and may be termed "soggy." In contrast the fried nuts are crisp, a highly desirable characteristic. It is thought to be largely due to the decrease in moisture during deep fat frying. Thus, the lower the moisture, the more crisp the nut becomes.

Another term, perhaps more expressive than absorption or pickup, would be interfat transfer or exchange, for the evidence supports the view that fat transfer between nut fat and frying fat occurs.

All nuts appear to pick up about 5% of the frying medium. This is based on the frying fat lost relative to the weight of nuts fried. Pecans have a greater fat transfer or pickup of frying fat than this (10 to 15%). Why fat absorption should be larger for pecans, yet fairly constant for the other nuts, serves to illustrate the need for continuing the research effort in this area. Presumably the cellular structure of pecans accounts for these differences. It is known that nuts will absorb not only water vapor, but certain oily constituents other than frying fats to different extents and rates. Thus it is wholly believable that cellular constituents and structures vary among nuts.

Evidence for fat transfer may be shown by a simple experiment. Freshly refined coconut oil, cottonseed oil, or peanut oil does not foam when used separately as frying mediums. But if either of the latter two oils is added to the former, in ratios of 10 to 90%, foaming will occur upon deep fat frying.

Nut oils are similar in chemical composition to peanut oil and cottonseed oil, so it appears that when these constituents are added to coconut oil, the interaction of the fatty acids during frying causes foaming.

The high temperatures attained in frying are apparently sufficient to reduce both density and viscosity of the nut oil to such an extent that it is brought to the surface of the nut and is washed off, so to speak, into the frying medium. This nut oil is then diluted and mixed with the frying medium in a manner resembling the mixing of the fresh peanut oil with the fresh coconut oil. This explains the dilution of the frying oil with the nut oil. The absorption or pickup of the frying medium is evidenced by comparatively simple weight experiments in which all weights of oils lost and gained are carefully recorded. For some frying mediums, fresh fat is absorbed to a greater extent than used fat.

Changes Occurring in Heated Fats

It has been generally recognized that three types of degradative changes can occur in an oil. These are: (a) autoxidative oxidation which occurs at temperatures up to 100°C (212°F); (b) thermal polymerization which occurs in the absence of oxygen, between 198° and 260°C (390° and 500°F), and (c) thermal oxidation which occurs in the presence of air at about 100°C (212°F) (Perkins 1960).

Autoxidation.—Investigations have shown that in corn, cottonseed and other oils the essential fatty acids, carotene, vitamin A and biotin, are destroyed during autoxidation. When fed to animals in high percentages autoxidized (rancid) oils are toxic, producing diarrhea, loss of weight and even death. Riboflavin exerts some protective effect when rancid fat is consumed.

The chemistry of autoxidation of ethyl linoleate with oxygen leads to the formation of conjugated ethyl linolate hydroperoxides which can in turn cyclize and form higher perioxidic polymers or combine in other ways to form noncyclic branched chain products. Such peroxides may also decompose by addition of a carbon carbon double bond with the formation of other hydroxyl and epoxy compounds. Hydroperoxides may, if formed during the course of autoxidation, decompose to ketones, hydroxy epoxy, and keto hydroxy products. If unsaturated peroxides are present, both saturated and unsaturated aldehydic and ketonic products may arise.

Thermal Polymerization.—Oils subjected to heat 6 to 24 hours while frying nuts, potato chips and doughnuts become viscous and ropy due to polymerization. There may be slight decrease in caloric availability, but no significant changes in iodine value, melting point, settling point, fatty acids composition, free fatty acid content, isomerized acids content and solids content index.

In extreme cases such oils may be toxic, especially when taken in larger quantities than usually occurs when eating fat fried nuts.

The chemical changes taking place are primarily those of a normal Diels-Alder reaction. Polyunsaturated acids such as linoleic, linolenic and oleostearic acids undergo thermal polymerization after conjugation to form polymeric products. Thermal polymerization of an unsaturated oil results in the formation of cyclic monomers, diners, trimers and even higher polymers. Several other compounds are formed in small amounts as a result of the interaction of shorter chain compounds with normal fatty acids.

Thermal Oxidation.—The chemistry of oils oxidized at high temperatures is more complex than that of thermal or oxidative polymerization since both heat and oxygen are involved. During thermal oxidation unsaturation decreases, conjugation decreases, and nonconjugated acids increase. As the polymer content increases the Rast Molecular weight also increases while the iodine values decrease. Cyclic compounds do not form and Diels-Alder reactions occur only slightly. Thermal oxidation in some oils produces various types of polymeric materials of higher molecular weight and high oxygen content.

All of the above three types of reactions vary with the kind of frying oil used, the temperature, the amount of exposure to air, and the length of time it is used.

Fat Fryer Design

Today we have available large continuous fryers capable of frying 15,000 lb of nuts in a single shift. These machines are completely automatic and need only be set for each type of nut.

Batch deep fat fryers may be small, such as the 2-lb capacity unit, or large, such as the 800-lb capacity unit. These are semi-automatic, for an operator must direct the nuts into the baskets and must remove the nuts from the fat when frying is complete. The nuts are then cooled on a stationary table or continuous belt with air passing through the nuts.

One of the most important characteristics of a deep fat fryer, batch or continuous, is the ratio of nuts to fat. Its importance stems from its effect on the condition of the frying medium. This ratio refers to the number of pounds of nuts in the fryer at any time and not to the total pounds of nuts fried per shift.

An example may illustrate the point. If the amount of fat in a fryer is relatively large and the pounds of nuts relatively small, the turnover of frying fat in the deep fat fryer will be small. Suppose we had a continuous fryer which holds 1600 lb of fat. Secondly, suppose 15,000 lb of peanuts are to be fried on one shift. Assume the nuts absorb 5% of the frying fat and that this is replaced with fresh fat periodically throughout the frying of these nuts. Thus, after the first day's frying, 800 lb of the original fat has been absorbed, 800 lb remains and 800 lb of fresh fat has been added back. If we continue these assumptions for five days, we find that after this time 6¼%, or about 100 lb of the original fat remains; 12½% of the fat added on the second day remains; etc. Thus, turnover of the frying fat is slow if the ratio of nuts to fat is small.

Even if these same assumptions were maintained except for reducing the amount of frying fat to 1000 lb from 1600 lb, the situation, though improved, is not completely desirable, for on the third day there is still 7.5% of the original fat in the fryer.

In the batch fryers this ratio can very nearly approach "1"; that is, there can be about the same number of pounds of nuts as number of pounds of fat. This usually means that the turnover of frying fat is greater in a batch fryer and less heat degradation will take place. Equilibrium will be attained earlier and the equilibrium point will be lower, in properly designed batch fryers.

An equally important consideration is the method of heating the fat. The flame tube method is quite commonly used. However, equally satisfactory results should be attained by either remote heating (such as with heat exchangers) or by heating the fryer from underneath. The only difficulty that we might note that arises with flame tube heating or remote heating of the fats is the extra volume of fat that is required for the tubes or exchanger.

This rather large requirement of frying fat seems to be an inherent disadvantage of a continuous deep fat fryer. Ideally a continuous nut fryer should incorporate a minimum amount of fat relative to the pounds of nuts in the fryer at any one time.

The continuous deep fat fryer, unlike the batch fryer, maintains relatively constant temperatures throughout the period of frying. These temperatures must be maintained between 135°C (275°F) and 168°C (335°F) depending on the nuts to be fried. The Btu requirements to heat the fat to these temperatures and to maintain these temperatures while nuts are continuously conveyed through the fat are sizeable. It is not surprising that some chemical changes take place in the fat due to the intensity of the heat and the length of time the fat is subjected to it.

The advantages of the continuous fryer over the batch fryer are the number of pounds that can be processed, subjecting the nuts to a more uniform and consistent process, and a completely automatic operation, to name a few.

Some further considerations that must be taken into account in deep fat fryers are the conveying systems, continuous filtration and circulation of the frying fats, exhausting the steam volatiles, and accessibility and ease of cleaning of all parts of the machine, to mention some of the more important.

The primary concern of the continuous fryer is to convey nuts rapidly through the hot fat. The conveyor must be designed to carry the load at variable speeds, for different nuts require different lengths of time in the fat. The load, that is, the number of pounds of nuts on the belt at any one time, is generally quite small. Pecans and filberts may float on the frying fat and, therefore, devices to keep them immersed in the frying oil may have to be installed on continuous fryers.

A fryer should be equipped to continuously filter and circulate the frying fat. Filtration will remove some of the polymers and, of course, it does remove fines and other debris from the fats.

An efficient exhaust system is especially important for a continuous fryer because removal of the volatiles with the steam is important in order that these are not returned to the fat.

The fryer should be constructed of materials that are easily cleaned and will not induce rancidity or oxidative problems. All parts of it should be easily accessible, and in the case of a continuous fryer, the conveyor should be easily removable. It appears that this fact is largely true; but, since nuts are complex and little is known about the changes that take place in them during deep fat frying, other reactions—such as protein denaturation or oil expansion to disrupt the cellular structure—may occur and contribute to the crisp quality in some unknown way.

The color or appearance of either shelled or blanched nuts changes noticeably during the deep fat frying process. Blanched nuts develop a light golden brown color upon deep fat frying. Shelled nuts, those with the skins, develop a considerably darker skin color upon deep fat frying. The raw almond skin is a light red, whereas after deep fat frying the color becomes deeper reddish brown. This change is apparently due to a heat induced reaction affecting the tannins natural to the skin.

Salt is generally added to deep fat fried nuts after cooling to enhance the flavor. The addition of salt in a manner so that it will adhere to the surface of the nut is difficult to accomplish on a dry roasted peanut. Salt is easily added and it adheres to a deep fat fried nut especially well if a small amount of dressing oil is added. The granulation of the salt also affects the adherence to the deep fat fried nut, the rule being: the finer the salt the better the adherence.

Another point to consider is the small losses or gains of weight observed after deep fat frying. In contrast, when the nuts are dry roasted, considerable losses in weight from the raw product are encountered.

The situation is actually more complex, for weight losses or gains depend on at least four factors: (1) the kind of frying fat; (2) condition and type of nut; (3) length of time the nuts are immersed in the fat; and (4) the temperature of the frying fat.

The gain or loss in weight of the nut after frying is directly related to the absorption of frying fat by the nut. This also depends on the same four factors: fat, nuts, time and temperature. An example of this dependence is that both peanut oil and cottonseed oil are absorbed or picked up by nuts to a greater extent than coconut oil when these fats are used as frying mediums. Likewise at high temperatures of frying, comparing results from studies at 176°C (350°F) to those at 135°C (275°F), less frying fat will be picked up at 176°C (350°F).

There are some indications that the flavor of the deep fat fried nut is preferred to that of the dry roasted nut. This observation has not been noted with pecans, but is of special interest with cashews where the milk sweetness may be masked by dry roasting.

Thus, deep fat frying alters and improves the flavor, texture and appearance of nuts and is economically sound. Deep fat frying of nuts makes them much more pleasantly edible than they are in the raw state.

Changes After Frying

Changes that take place in nuts after being deep fat fried include both long-term and short-term flavor alterations. The major flavor development of decided economic importance to salters is staleness or rancidity. This flavor development makes the nuts unsalable and may lower their nutritional value if they are sufficiently oxidized.

The commonly known factors that affect or induce the development of rancidity and staleness are heat, certain light radiations, oxygen, certain heavy metals such as iron and copper, certain enzymes, and moisture. As mentioned earlier, the latter also affects the texture of nuts.

Other factors that affect the off-flavor development of nuts are the kind, type and condition of frying fat and dressing oil. These factors will be developed further in our discussion of frying mediums.

Less direct factors affecting off-flavor development are the handling, packaging and storage of the nuts after frying until they are consumed.

Nuts are packaged in vacuum cans or flexible plastic films and are merchandised either in these or in bulk in display cases. While the nuts packaged under vacuum are protected excellently, those in the plastic films, though protected very adequately, do have limited shelf-life. The nuts merchandised in display cases are subject to the least protection.

The nut which causes the greatest problem insofar as off-flavor development is concerned is the peanut. It has the shortest shelf-life of all nuts we fry, with the possible exception of shelled sunflower seeds.

Rapid flavor change does take place within a few days after frying for all nuts. That is to say, the freshly fried nuts may score "9" on the 9-point hedonic scale, but within a relatively short period, a matter of days, that freshly fried flavor is lost and the peanuts may then score only "8" or "7." The scores then stabilize for a period of time where apparently little flavor deterioration takes place. The transition from fresh flavor to rancidity or staleness is progressive and slow.

Courtesy of Rose Confections

FIG. 5.13.   SALTED NUT MIX IN METAL CONTAINER

A choice of flavors and textures are provided for many occasions.

The rapidity with which peanuts may develop staleness, of course, depends upon storage conditions. However, the slow but progressive deterioration just described takes place under room temperature conditions of about 24°C (75°F) and with nuts packaged in flexible films. The characteristic rancid or stale note will begin to be detected on the surface of the nut or skin at first. Later it will gradually permeate the entire nut.

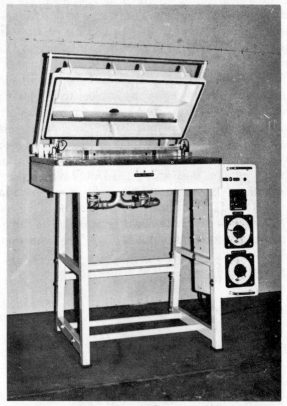

Courtesy of May Industries

FIG. 5.14. VACUUM SEALER FOR BAGS OF NUTS

The unit requires manual positioning of the filled pouches in the sealing chamber and manual closing of the cover. The vacuum, which is always on, locks the cover in place and evacuates the air from the chamber. At a predetermined point the sealing bar makes contact and the pouch is sealed and held under pressure until the seal has had time to cool. When the cycle is completed air is automatically fed into the chamber and the cover raises slightly. This unit can seal 20 4-inch pouches per minute, with a sealing cycle of 15 seconds.

Cashews and almonds may be characterized as similar; both take considerably longer to develop a rancid or stale flavor such as in the case with pecans, and in fact many never do. Cashews, however, have a flavor deterioration, presumably an oxidative change also, that is characteristic of this nut. It is difficult to describe the flavor changes that take place in cashews except to note the loss of sweetness, and this generally occurs rapidly. The cashew is still highly acceptable for a long period of time after this, but this delicate sweetness has lessened in intensity.

The cashew, incidentally, of all nuts, is the only one with an appreciable amount of natural sugar—about 5 to 7%.

Changes in Frying Medium

Changes often take place in a deep fat frying medium which affect the nuts. A simple test illustrating these changes may be outlined. In this experiment nuts which have been fried in a fresh medium are compared with those fried in a used medium. The used medium may represent the fat commonly employed as the frying fat in the plant. If taste tests and shelf-life studies are designed to compare the nuts fried in these two media, it will be found that the nuts fried in the fresh fat will have a longer shelf-life than the nuts fried in the used fat.

Courtesy of Karstrom Company

FIG. 5.15. ROTARY CAN UNSCRAMBLER TABLE AND
AUTOMATIC NUT FILLER

The unit is equipped with a "no container—no filler" device which automatically shuts the filler head off when flow is stopped.
Quickly interchangeable parts allow a wide range of products and weights, as well as containers, to be run.

Used fat is a frying medium to which freshly refined fat is added periodically to maintain a certain volume and which has achieved by this addition a type of equilibrium. The approach to this equilibrium may be by measuring any number or combination of analytical values such as color, viscosity, free fatty acids, iodine number, etc., to name some of the simplest. Once this quasi-equilibrium is attained, the analytical values chosen to measure it will vary between rather wide limits, depending upon the conditions of frying.

In some cases the quasi-equilibrium will, apparently, never be reached. This is because the frying conditions are such that the analytical values indicate progressive deterioration of the fat to such an extent that replacement of this fat is recommended before equilibrium is effected.

Thus, the used fats have undergone changes, since the nuts fried in the fresh fats are more stable than those fried in the used fats. This decrease is not large, but it is a present and an important consideration for deep fat fryers.

Courtesy of Karstrom Company

FIG. 5.16. DOUBLE DISCHARGE FILLER FOR NUTS AND CANDIES

It can be adjusted to automatically discharge weights of from 200 to 1000 g.

This phenomenon has been observed in all cases investigated. The patterns repeat themselves. Some fats show greater differences than others between the fresh and the used condition. But in all cases, the nuts fried in the fresh fat are more stable than those nuts fried in the used fats.

Another problem that may be encountered with frying mediums is off-flavor development in the nuts, apparently due to some constituent in the frying fat, either natural to the fat or picked up by the fat in improper processing, or perhaps due to something added to the fat inadvertently. In this case, the fat may be re-refined, rebleached, re-deodorized, or simply filtered continuously in the plant. In addition to this, when a new or modified frying fat is used, every effort to test the material for possible off-flavor development in the nuts in both fresh and used form should be used. This usually involves deep fat frying studies along with long-term shelf-life and taste panel studies on at least two kinds of nuts under two or three sets of storage conditions. Our criterion of judgment in this particular work is based on what cashews, etc., should taste like under standard conditions.

Courtesy of National Equipment Co.

FIG. 5.17. BAGGING MACHINE FOR NUTMEATS

This is a fully automatic machine using pre–made polyethylene bags. In operation, the hopper of the scale is filled with the product to be bagged. The vibrator accurately fills bucket. When the correct weight is in the bucket, bucket automatically discharges into the polyethylene bag. The next bag is opened, ready for filling while the bucket is being filled. The filled bag can be discharged automatically onto a tying machine or heat sealer.

One most important phenomenon that takes place in deep fat frying is the fat absorbed or picked up by the nut during frying. It appears to be a physical mechanism and is recognizable by the disappearance of frying fat and the need for replacement. It is also the reason why equilibrium of the frying fat exists. It is apparently the major factor which contributes to the decrease in the shelf-life of nuts fried in used fat.

Chemical Compounds Formed.—Chemical compounds formed in fats as a result of three types of degradative changes are autoxidation, thermal polymerization, and thermal oxidation. The compounds formed as a result of thermal oxidation are the most important in deep fat frying. Experiments to determine the effect of heating, turnover rate, and steam on the deterioration of cottonseed oil and tallow showed that the amount of polymeric material increased regularly as heating time increased. Heating, alternated with cooling cycles, increased the deterioration of cottonseed oil. The act of frying a food product or of simple addition of water exerted a strong deteriorative effect on heated cottonseed oil. Highly unsaturated oils form a multiplicity of compounds when they are heated as in deep frying. Twenty compounds, ranging in molecular weight from 446 to 970, have been isolated from thermally oxidized corn oil. One of these has been completely characterized and appears to be a mixture of four positional isomers of a branched long-chain dicarboxylic acid. To simplify problems in working with a highly oxidized mixture containing many components, synthetic triglycerides prepared from palmitic, stearic and oleic acids were prepared and oxidized. 2-Oleyl-1,3-distearin was oxidized for 24 hours in the presence of air. The major component of the oxidized material was isolated. Results obtained from chemical degradation and infrared and mass spectroscopic examination indicated that this compound was the branched-chain dicarboxylic acid, 10-propyl heptadecandioic acid (Anon. 1966A).

Kettle Composition.—Copper or copper-containing metals are to be avoided in any deep fat frying system, since copper has a highly pro-oxidant effect on the fat. Even one brass valve in the system or one bronze pump part can be a source of trouble. Since detergents are constantly used for cleaning, aluminum is not suitable for oil vats, and nickel is too expensive. Stainless steel is by far the most satisfactory.

Effect of Air.—The effect of air on hot fat is perhaps the major factor adversely affecting the deep fat system. Some contact with air cannot be avoided using presently available equipment. Such aeration occurs chiefly on the surface of the kettle fat as heating and frying proceeds, but air is inevitably drawn into the body of the fat owing to currents set up by normal convection or by circulation or agitation. However, excessive aeration due, for example, to cascading or spraying of hot fat anywhere in the system, is unnecessary and must be eliminated. So, also, must the use of pumps in the system which "suck" air, or "chum in" air. Because the steam given off in the frying process is helpful in purging the frying fat of volatile by-products, adequate exhaust of this by-product laden steam from the kettle surface must be provided. The exhaust system should be baffled so as to prevent flow-back and/or drip-back of the condensate into the bath. Direct draft must be avoided lest it cool the kettle fat too much and result in production of finished product quality problems (Robertson 1976).

SALT FOR NUTS

Salt varies in the amount of impurities, the size and shape of particles, solubility, uniformity, caking properties, density, additives and specific usefulness. Since nuts are low in moisture, the salt should be highly soluble and should contain 5 ppm yellow prussiate of soda to prevent caking, 1.0 to 1.5% tricalcium phosphate, and an antioxidant.

Improved fine flake salt incorporates the humectant ingredient, polyethylene glycol, which keeps salt free-flowing without caking or lumping. Physical properties include a solubility rate of 7.6 sec, caking resistance for 6 to 8 months, and apparent density of 0.833. The product has 54 million crystals per pound and insolubles of less than 20 ppm.

A typical analysis for a good nut salt follows.

Composition[1]

Sodium chloride	99.9%
Calcium sulfate	0.08%
Calcium chloride	0.006%
Total Insoluble Solids	10 ppm

Ions
Calcium	0.029%
Magnesium	0.002%
Sulfate	0.056%
Copper, less than	1.5 ppm
Iron, less than	0.2 ppm

Screen analysis (U.S. fine series)
Total over No. 40	trace
Through No. 40 over No. 50	18%
Through No. 50 over No. 70	48%
Through No. 70 over No. 100	27%
Through No. 100	7%

[1]Hardy Salt Company.

Moisture	0.05%
Density	61 lb/ft^3
Solubility	8 sec when fully dispersed
Additives, tricalcium phosphate	1.0%
Antioxidant	0

At times nut salters are bothered somewhat because the salt falls off the surface of the salted nuts and into the bottom of the bag or can, principally because of rough handling in shipping. This difficulty is more likely to be encountered where nuts are fried in liquid oils rather than solid shortenings. Where nuts are fried in solid shortening, the salt is applied before the nuts have cooled down to room temperature. At this point the frying fat is still in a melted condition on the surface of the nuts. When the nuts cool down to room temperature, the shortening on the surface sets up as a solid fat. The salt is thus held firmly to the surface of the nuts and will stay there in spite of considerable handling. This is also true in cases where nuts are fried in coconut oil, since coconut oil sets up at approximately 24.4°C (76°F). Below this temperature coconut oil is a fairly firm fat. Where nuts are fried in cottonseed oil, peanut oil, olive oil, or other oils that are liquid at room temperature, there is very little binding action to hold the salt on the surface of the nuts.

Some nut salters roast the nuts rather than fry them. Consequently, there is no solid fat to help bind the salt on the surface of the nut. In this case, the little binding action observed is caused by the trace of natural nut oil which comes to the surface during the roasting period.

If the salt falls off the nuts and drops to the bottom of the bag, the following suggestion will correct the difficulty. When the warm nuts are removed from the kettle and drained, or when they are removed from the ovens after roasting, they should be spread on a table to cool slightly. Then about 2 lb of warm coconut oil should be "atomized" on each 100 lb of nuts. Because the nuts are considerably warmer than the coconut oil, it will be noted that the oil does not seem to penetrate the nuts but remains on the surface. After the coconut oil is uniformly distributed on the nuts by mixing, the salt is added and the nuts are then allowed to cool to room temperature. It will be found that after this treatment the salt will adhere to the nuts very well, thus overcoming the difficulty.

The proper product to use is regular coconut oil which is often referred to as "76° coconut oil." It is not necessary to use plasticized coconut oil since the straightforward product will be entirely satisfactory.

This difficulty is quite likely to be encountered with new crop nuts. For some reason, freshly harvested nuts do not hold the salt as well as nuts that have been cured for a considerable period of time. It may be that the high moisture content is responsible, but this is not definitely known.

Naturally, the type of salt plays an important part in clearing up this difficulty. It is much more difficult to hold fine granulated salt on the surface of the nuts than is the case with a flake salt. The little cubes have much less surface and the binding action requires a high amount of surface. Crystal fine prepared salt is composed practically 100% of flasher flakes. Under a magnifying glass, it can be seen that these flakes are composed of minute cubes fastened together in odd shapes. There are little crevices and indentations on the surfaces of the tiny flakes that permit the fat on the surface of the nut to "catch hold" on the salt particles, binding the salt firmly to the surface of the nut. It is generally recognized in the trade that when nuts are salted with fine flake salt, because of its instant solubility, uniform granulation and high purity, the lips are not irritated by the salt.

Courtesy of Morton Salt Co.

FIG. 5.18. A GRAIN OF FLAKE SALT THAT ADHERES TO ROASTED NUTS

Nuts are by their very nature rich in oils. It is common knowledge that copper and iron accelerate rancidity of fats and oils and therefore shorten the shelf-life. It is essential to use a salt with the minimum amount of copper and iron impurities.

A companion salt product used by many nut salters is Diamond Crystal Fine Prepared Antioxidant or Fine Flake Prepared Antioxidant Salt. The shelf-life of salted nuts is increased up to 137% when using a 0.02% concentration in the cooking oil and salting with an antioxidant salt as shown in a Georgia Experiment Station test (Cecil and Woodroof 1951).

Antioxidand salts combine the right salt—the best nut coverage, solubility, grain size and shape—with the right amount of antioxidan ingredients to protect the delicate nut flavor the maximum length of time.

EDIBLE NUT COATINGS

An edible coating process is reported to add 12 months to the storage life of nutmeats when held at room temperature. The coating "Myvacet" is a patented product containing actylated monoglyceride, butylated hydroxyanisole and butylated hydroxytoluene. It is applied up to 5% to the nutmeats. The antioxidant level is 100 to 150 ppm. The process is applicable to pecans, almonds, filberts, walnuts and other nuts (Shea 1965).

Tapioca dextrin is used as a nut coating. This is a unique low viscosity, extremely clean starch product with an unusually bland flavor. The crystal gum is a white powder with about 7% moisture and a pH of about 4. It is easily dispersed in cold water but requires heating to achieve optimum solubility and application characteristics. The gum has little or no tendency to foam during heating or "shrink" on cooling (National Starch and Chemical Co. 1966).

Make a coating solution by blending the first four ingredients at 87.8°C (190°F), and allowing it to cool. Add the nutmeats and "pan coat" in revolving kettle at about 143.5°C (290°F) for 1½ to 3 min.

Formula

Crystal gum	992.9 g (3.5 oz)
Monosodium glutamate	14.3 g (0.5 oz)
Water	1844.9 g (6.5 oz)
Antioxidant	5.6 g (0.2 oz)
Nutmeats	4540.0 g (10 lb)

Zein is another nut coating. For nut coating zein provides an oil barrier, acetylated monoglycerides provide a moisture barrier, and a combination antioxidant (butylated hydroxyanisole, nordihydroguaiaretic acid and citric acid) extends the shelf-life of the product.

Treating nutmeats (pecans, black walnuts, Persian walnuts and others) with about 1% of the antioxidant (in alcohol solution) extends the shelf-life up to four times (Cosler 1958).

SYNTHETIC NUTS

Synthetic nuts that simulate particular varieties of nutmeats can be made under a patented new process. A film-former, such as dried egg albumen, and a filler, such as dried ground wheat germ, are blended with an oil, such as cottonseed oil, to form a smooth slurry. This is then agitated at high speed, during which sufficient water is added to hydrate the film-former. After all the water has been introduced the high speed is continued until a viscous dispersion results.

At this point, the product is a continuous hydrated film throughout which the oil component is dispersed. The jelly-like dispersion is then extruded into sheets, molds or other forming devices and dried. Since the moisture is in the cellular film portion and is partially insulated by fat globules, drying is slow.

REFERENCES

ANON. 1962A. Fast, accurate counter for peanuts. Peanut J. Nut World *42* (2) 9.

ANON. 1962B. Improved method of processing nutmeats. Peanut J. Nut World *41* (3) 16.

ANON. 1962C. Magnets for processing operations. Peanut J. Nut World *41* (12) 18-19.

ANON. 1964. New efficiency in peanut butter processing by Burns. Peanut J. Nut World *43* (3) 11.

ANON. 1966A. Chemistry and technology of deep-fat frying. Food Technol. *20* (7) 70-73.

ANON. 1966B. Diversification in action portrayed by Bauer Bros. Peanut J. Nut World *45* (5) 17-20.

ANON. 1966C. Summary of IFT symposia at 26th annual meeting. Food Technol. *20* (7) 72.

ANON. 1966D. Sortex sorters, electronic color sorting machines. Sorter Co. Circ. *512.*

CECIL, S.R., and WOODROOF, J.G. 1951. Butylated hydroxy anisole antioxidant for salted peanuts, salted pecans and peanut butter. Ga. Exp. Stn. Bul. *265.*

COSLER, H.B. 1958. Preventing staleness, rancidity in nutmeats. Peanut J. Nut World *37* (11) 10-11,15.

DUGAN, L.R., JR. 1961. Development and inhibition of oxidative rancidity in food. Food Technol. *15* (7) 10, 12, 14, 16, 18.

DURST, J.R. 1964. Nut-like food product and process. U.S. Pat. No. 2,952,544.

HIGGINS, B.B. *et al.* 1941. Thiamine chloride and nicotinic acid content of peanuts and peanut products. Ga. Exp. Stn. Bull. *213.*

LEA, C.H. 1961. Some biological aspects of fat deterioration. Food Technol. *15* (7) 33-34, 37-38, 40.

LEFFINGWELL, G., and LESSER, M.A. 1946. Glycerin in nut products. Peanut J. Nut World *25* (10) 25-30.

MANWARING, J. 1966. H-F heat challenges ovens. Food Eng. *38* (2) 48-50.

NATIONAL STARCH AND CHEMICAL CORP. 1966. Tech. Serv. Bull. *247.*

PERKINS, E.G. 1960. The nutritional and chemical changes occurring in heated fats: a review. Food Technol. *14*, 508-514.

PICKETT, T.A. 1941. Vitamins in peanuts. Ga. Exp. Stn. Circ. *128*.

PICKETT, T.A. 1944. Thiamine content of peanut butter. Ga. Exp. Stn. Circ. *146*.

PICKETT, T.A. 1945. Choline content of peanuts and peanut products. Ga. Exp. Stn. J.S. *145*.

PICKETT, T.A., and HOLLEY, K.T. 1952. Peanut roasting studies. Ga. Exp. Stn. Bull. *1*.

ROBERTSON, C.J. 1967. The practice of deep fat frying. Food Technol. *21* (1) 34-36.

ROCKLAND, L.B., SWARTHOUT, D.M., and JOHNSON, R.A. 1961. Studies in (Persian) walnuts, *Juglans regia* III. Food Technol. *15*, 112-116.

SCOFIELD, G.H. 1963. Deep-fat frying. Manufacturing Confectioner *43* (11) 32-37.

SHEA, R. 1965. Edible coating keeps nuts fresh. Food Processing *26*(5) 148-150.

SIMMONS, P.M. 1966. Measure color objectively. Food Eng. *38* (4) 52-53.

STROCK, H., BALL, C.O., CHANG, S.S., and STIER, E.F. 1966. Determination of frying end-point. Food Technol. *20*, 545-549.

6

Almonds

The almond (*Amygdalus communis* or *Prunus amygdalus*) is thought by some to be the origin of the peach, but this is evidently untenable. There are two species of almonds—the bitter and the sweet. The former has a bitter kernel, which is used in the manufacture of flavoring extracts and prussic acid. It is grown mostly in Mediterranean countries. Of the sweet or edible almonds, there are two classes—the hard shell and the soft shell. The soft-shell type produces commercial almonds.

Almonds are mentioned throughout history. The almond is supposed to have spread from India and Persia through southern and middle Europe, reaching England about 1600. It is commonly cultivated there and is quite hardy, attaining a height of 12 to 14 ft, blooming in very early spring (even as early as January) with a great abundance of light pink, peach-like blossoms, usually borne in pairs. Its leaves are long and ovate, with a serrate margin, and an acute apex. Its fruit is like that of the peach, but is oval in shape, with a downy succulent covering enclosing a hard shell in which is borne the edible kernel. It was much valued in the Orient because it furnished a very pleasant oil. It is cultivated in Syria where it grows wild on the northern and eastern hills. The commercial cultivation of almonds in the United States is confined to the west and even here it has yielded more firewood than any other fruit tree planted in California.

The two chief causes of failure in cultivation are the sterility of many cultivars without cross pollination, and the extreme propensity of the tree for early blooming, with the consequent destruction of the bloom or young fruit by temperatures below freezing. The almond is the earliest bloomer of our common fruits. It puts forth flowers sometime in January, but the usual date is February 10 for the earliest bloomers in the warm part of California, and April 1 for late bloomers (Bailey 1935).

ALMONDS IN CALIFORNIA

The earliest almond trees in the United States were those grown from seed introduced from Mexico and Spain when the missions were established in California. Apparently, these trees died after the missions were abandoned. No further attempts at almond growing in the United States were made until 1840, when some trees imported from Europe were planted in the New England States. The climate was too severe there and the attempt was not successful. In time, plantings were made down the length of the Atlantic seaboard and into the Gulf States. But everywhere the almond's exacting climatic requirements ruled it out of profitable production.

FIG. 6.1. LIMBS WITH HEAVY SET OF MATURE ALMONDS

The present industry in California developed from almond trees brought from the east coast in 1843. California is now the only important almond-producing state in this country. Almond orchards in California provide a living for more than 6000 growers and their families.

For the most part, the trees are grown in the central valleys and watered by the Sacramento and San Joaquin Rivers and their tributaries. Orchardists, notably A.T. Hatch of Suisun, undertook to improve the production by scientific cross-pollination. Three leading cultivars grown in California, the Nonpareil, Ne Plus Ultra and IXL, are Hatch cultivars. It took many years to get orchards from the hillsides—originally favored to escape frosts— into the valleys where they could be irrigated.

Through trial and error, much has been learned about the sensitiveness of almonds to frost, blight, insect pests, moisture control, harvesting methods, procedures for getting the nuts to market, and more recently about processing and products.

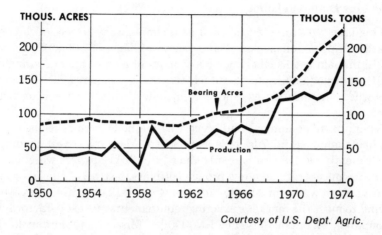

Courtesy of U.S. Dept. Agric.

FIG. 6.2. ACREAGE AND PRODUCTION OF ALMONDS,
CALIFORNIA

California Almond Growers Exchange

Marketing became the major problem, and many growers were lost trying to find a way of marketing through individual initiative, pools and cooperatives. In 1910 a group of growers representing nine small pools with a total of 230 members met at Sacramento and formed a federation under the name of California Almond Growers Exchange. J.P. Dargitz was the first manager when the total production of unshelled nuts was 2000 tons.

At the time of this combining of local cooperatives, almonds were sold in the shell almost entirely. Shelled almonds were supplied to the American market by foreign growers, themselves at the mercy of speculators and exporters.

Twelve years later, when the U.S. tariff on imported shelled almonds was increased, the Exchange went into the shelling of almonds. With chaotic conditions eliminated and almond prices stabilized, the development of a strong domestic almond industry became a reality. The existence of such a program became of great value to the end-user, the manufacturer and suppliers. The Exchange increased the popularity and versatility of almonds through its continuous efforts and specific steps to encourage consumption to develop a $150 million industry. Almonds are one of the fastest expanding tree crops in California, having several times shown phenomenal spurts in planting. It has expanded nearly three-fold in 15 years.

In 1962 the California Almond Growers Exchange built a three-story cold storage and manufacturing warehouse with a capacity of refrigerating 4000 tons of shelled almonds.

The Blue Diamond Label

This label was adopted in 1910 as a simple, easy-to-recognize trademark to appear on packages and bags. Millions of dollars have been spent in making this label known as a mark of highest almond standards and unexcelled quality to manufacturers and consumers alike. The grower-owned organization expanded to include both shelled and unshelled almonds.

As improved equipment and processing methods were developed, ever-higher quality standards were established. Mechanical test-grading of each member's delivery was introduced in 1931. Growers were encouraged to concentrate on a few proven cultivars, instead of the 70 or more cultivars grown commercially for many years. Seven that have been found to meet the market's exacting requirements most satisfactorily are Nonpareil, IXL, Ne Plus, Peerless, Drake, Mission and Jordanolo. The Exchange increased about 20 times its original size to a membership of 4500 grower-owners, which produce about 70% of the nation's commercial almond crop.

CULTIVARS

Over the years hundreds of cultivars of almonds have been grown. European cultivars were used exclusively in the earliest California orchards. Nearly all of these imports produced inferior quality nuts in California. The Jordan almond, considered the best nut produced in Europe, always fails here. It is a shy bearer, susceptible to brown rot, blooms early, and the nut is difficult to crack. All of the present commercial cultivars have been developed from seedlings grown in California.

Requirements for a cultivar are that (a) it be interfertile with all commercial cultivars; (b) the nuts should ripen all at the same time and not be blown off by the wind; (c) the tree should be vigorous and hardy; and (d) blooming should be over a long frost-free season. In addition to the seven cultivars listed on p. 149–150 recently introduced cultivars are Davey, Thompson, Merced and Kapareil. Others will be introduced from hundreds being tested.

ESTABLISHING THE ORCHARD

All almond cultivars require cross-pollination by another variety, and a planting should therefore be made up of a minimum of two cultivars. Because blooming dates of the different cultivars vary from year to year, at least two cultivars of pollinizers are frequently used. There are numerous possible planting arrangements.

Almond rootstock has been preferred for almond trees. On deep, well-drained soils, it is the best available rootstock because it is the most vigorous, and over a long period of time makes the most productive tree. Bitter almond is considered by some to be better, but there is no real proof that it is better than sweet almond root. Texas seedlings make good rootstocks and appear to do as well as bitter almond. Almond rootstock is affected by nematodes, crown gall, and oak root fungus. In almond areas of the state where excess boron is a problem, almond root has been more satisfactory than peach.

Rootstocks resistant to oak root fungus, nematodes, wet soil, etc., are most useful in replanting in an orchard where trees have been killed by these conditions. Before planting a new orchard where problems like these exist, growers should give serious consideration to growing some other crop that is not affected. Growers should not consider special rootstocks to be the solution to all of the problems arising from poor growing conditions.

It is usually best to receive the trees as whips, just as they grew in the nursery, and to head them back after they are planted. Plant the tree very high because it will settle a good deal after planting. When a tractor-mounted digger is used, it is easy to dig too deep. Then it is necessary to fill the hole back before the tree is planted. The tree should be planted so that the bud is on the southwest side of the tree. This helps to reduce sunburn on the stock.

The first pruning is done at the time the trees are planted. At this time the trees are cut back, or headed, to the height at which it is desired to have the permanent branches arise. The tendency now is to head trees higher than in the past to avoid damage from orchard equipment. Mechanical pickup machines require more space below the scaffold limbs, and all farm equipment is becoming larger and heavier. Many growers now head their trees at a height of from 24 to 30 in.

On trees that have grown vigorously in the nursery, there will be a number of small side branches when the trees are received. In addition to heading the tree, cut back these small side shoots but do not cut them off entirely. At least one base bud should be left on each shoot. When these side shoots are cut off entirely, the grower may not find new shoots properly placed for permanent scaffold branches later.

During the first summer, growers should devote some time to training the tree. It seems like a time-consuming operation, but is a money-making proposition both in value to the tree and in the amount of time saved at the first dormant pruning.

A tree requires energy to grow branches. When unwanted branches are not pruned off until after the first season's growth, the energy that went into growing this wood is largely wasted. If unwanted branches are pinched back when they are only a few inches long, the tree's energy can be directed toward more growth of the permanent branches.

Each tree should be examined when the new growth is 3 to 4 in. long. The shoots that are selected for main scaffold branches are left alone. All other shoots, which will not be wanted, are pinched back to only a few leaves to shade the trunk. Normally, after 4 to 6 weeks, it is advisable to check the trees again to make sure that no new undesirable shoots are growing.

If the shoots that are selected for future scaffolds grow very vigorously, their ends can be pinched off at about 30 in. from the trunk in order to make them branch. Summer training if properly done will greatly reduce the problem of selecting scaffold branches and the rest of the framework the following winter.

Some training may be done during the second summer's growth for the same reason as during the first summer—to eliminate unwanted wood before it makes too much growth at the expense of the rest of the tree.

Care of the Orchard

Irrigation.—Irrigation is the most important cultural operation that the grower has under his control. Its purpose is to keep the soil supplied with readily available moisture at all times.

At one time, most of the almonds in the state were not irrigated, even in the interior valleys. However, growers found that almonds responded so markedly to irrigation in terms of tree vigor and tremendously increased production, that a nonirrigated orchard is relatively uncommon now.

Water has many functions in the tree. It permits the root to absorb nutrients from the soil, it moves nutrients in the tree, it helps to cool the tree, and it supplies water as a raw material for making sugars, starches, cellulose, etc. Water maintains pressure in the cells so that growth can occur. When the supply of water is short, practically all functions in the tree stop. This results in smaller trees and lower production.

In deep soils, it has been found that mature almonds take about 50% of their moisture from the top 3 ft of soil. Another 25% is taken from the 3- to 6-ft level. Seventeen percent is taken from the 6- to 9-ft level. This gives a good indication of root distribution in the soil.

More and more of the soil tends to become dry as summer progresses. During the long, hot harvest period, no water can be applied. The trees soon wilt and remain wilted until the first rains come or a postharvest irrigation is applied. This situation can be avoided if the trees are irrigated near the start of harvest.

Irrigation water can be applied rapidly on level soil by the use of basins, furrows, or a combination of furrows and basins, if a good head of water is available. This method is an advantage in extremely hot weather if an extra irrigation is necessary.

Sprinklers have the advantage of applying water relatively evenly over the surface. This makes it possible to have a smooth surface for a mechanical harvester. Water costs will be higher because of increased pumping costs, but the total costs may be lower because of reduced labor costs. A disadvantage is that sprinklers have to be moved, generally twice a day, every day of the irrigating season.

Soil Management.—Soil compaction is a serious problem in many almond orchards. The amount of discing, cultipacking and rolling done in many orchards to achieve a flat surface for mechanical harvesting is responsible for this compaction.

There are several good reasons for cultivating the soil. These include preparing a seedbed for a cover crop, preparing the land for irrigation or harvest, and turning under late nuts to clean up the orchard and cut down the worm population.

What can be done to overcome damage to the soil structure resulting from cultivation? First, cultivation must not be done when soil is wet. Second, cultivate only when necessary. Third, a cover crop should be grown every year. These are the means of maintaining and developing good soil structure. A volunteer cover crop can be adequate if there are enough plants for a good stand.

A grassy cover crop makes it possible to get into the orchard with equipment much sooner after a rain than is possible where no cover crop or a broad-leaved cover crop is grown. Since so much pest control work must be done to almonds in winter, this can be a real advantage.

Fertilization.—It is necessary to replenish yearly the supply of nitrogen in the soil. One and one-half to two pounds of actual nitrogen per tree per year seems to be sufficient for almonds in most areas. They may grow more luxuriantly as a result of receiving larger amounts, but the crop sometimes actually decreases as a result of the shading of fruiting wood.

Potassium is the only other major element that is apt to be deficient for almond production. When a deficiency is found by leaf analysis or leaf symptoms, 25 lb of potassium sulfate per mature tree (applied in a ring) is recommended for orchards on deep soils. No followup is necessary until the trees show a deficiency again, which may be 10 to 15 years later.

In a foothill area, 5 lb of potash per tree is sufficient to correct a deficiency. An additional application of 1 lb per tree per year is enough to keep the soil at an adequate level.

The question of using mixed fertilizers for almonds often arises. Tree response from applications of phosphorus has not been observed in California almond orchards. Therefore, it is more economical to buy and apply needed elements, such as nitrogen and potash, as separate materials. As a rule, apply only those elements needed and apply them only in amounts sufficient to take care of the needs of the trees. Excessive use of any element is a waste of money. Fertilizers are not cure-alls. When trees look weak, extra fertilizer is often the first thing a grower considers. But, if the tree has been receiving a regular yearly application of those elements known to be needed, then a lack of some other element will probably not be a cause of the poor appearance. Insects, diseases, too much or too little water, root problems, or old age is more likely to be causing the trouble.

Zinc has been found to be deficient in some of the almond-growing areas. The condition is most likely to occur in a sandy soil. The leaves on trees affected by zinc deficiency are usually small, pointed, and light yellow colored between the veins. In severe cases the shoot growth is greatly reduced and production eventually may be affected. Dormant sprays, containing 25 to 35 lb of zinc sulfate (approximately 23% metallic zinc or the equivalent) per 100 gal. of water, or foliage sprays, containing 6 lb of zinc oxide per 100 gal. of water, have corrected this condition.

Boron has been found to be present in both deficient and excessive amounts in some of the areas planted with almonds. Boron deficiency will cause gumming of the almonds. This will be noticeable on the outsides of hulls and also on the insides of shells. Almonds so affected will be blanks. There are, of course, other reasons for gumming. All gumming cannot be attributed to boron deficiency. The suckers or water sprouts on boron-deficient trees will die back at the ends during the growing season. Fifty to one hundred pounds of borax or borax equivalent per acre applied in the fall may be used as a corrective treatment.

Soil analysis is of little value in determining fertilizer needs. Leaf analysis is a more meaningful tool to determine the nutrient level in a plant. Even here, long experience in interpreting the results is necessary, because various factors can influence the leaf content of any particular element. Leaves vary markedly in their composition throughout the season. June and July are the best months to take leaf samples for analysis.

Pollination.—Almonds require cross-pollination with another cultivar, not just another tree of the same cultivar, in order to set a crop. This pollinizing requires the movement of insects from tree to tree. Bees are responsible for most of this work.

To ensure that enough bees are present in the orchard at the proper time, it's best to make arrangements with a beekeeper to place hives in the orchard during the winter and on through the blooming period. Growers aim at 1½ to 2 hives per acre of trees. In large orchards, the most satisfactory distribution is groups of 5 to 10 hives placed throughout the orchard. Where there are enough wild bees, additional domestic bees are not needed. However, there often is not enough wild bee activity to be effective, except in an occasional orchard near undeveloped river land.

Pruning.—Almonds begin bearing relatively young. If the trees are well cared for and healthy, they will continue to increase in size and production for many years. Almonds produce most of their fruit on short spurs. These spurs grow a little longer each year that they are productive. On the average, spurs are considered to be fruitful for only about five years. It is necessary, therefore, to prune in such a way that new wood with new spur growth is constantly replacing the spurs that are no longer fruitful. To accomplish this, pruning is confined to the removal of the older branches ½ to 1½ in. in diameter. Very little thinning out of smaller wood is done except to remove unwanted water sprouts or suckers.

If the pruning is done every year and if enough wood is removed, it should result in the growth of sufficient new wood to maintain spur growth without heavy cuts.

Whether a pruning program is adequate can be judged in part by the length of the new shoots that arise over the whole tree each year. Trees under 10 or 12 years of age can be expected to make 9 to 18 in. of new growth; trees older than this should make at least 6 in. of new shoot growth.

Old trees lacking in vigor often can be invigorated by rather severe pruning. Naturally, this does not apply if the tree is affected by a disease such as crowngall or if the roots have been injured. The tops should be cut back to large lateral limbs and smaller weak wood should be thinned out heavily. If the top is cut severely enough, the tree will usually respond by growing many suckers the following year. These suckers should be thinned to prevent crowding. Those left can be used to replace old, unproductive wood, and a new top can be established on the tree. In unfertile soils, vigorous sucker growth can be obtained on old trees if the top is cut back severely and an extra amount of nitrogen is given to the tree.

Replanting.—Whatever the reason for replanting trees in an established orchard, it is important to spot-fumigate before the new tree is planted. Spot fumigation serves several useful purposes. If properly done, it will give the new tree an area of nematode-free and disease-free soil in which to make a start. Fumigation also will kill roots of older trees that have grown into the area of the new planting location. By reducing competition from the older trees for nutrients and water, the young replant will have a much better chance of doing well.

It is important to supply water and nutrients carefully to any newly planted tree, but it is even more important in the case of a replant. This is because of the competition from the surrounding old trees. Give replants extra irrigations, at least during the first year. Very small applications of a nitrogen fertilizer once or twice during the summer will also help to overcome the competition. Weeds should not be allowed to grow around a replant because they can become severe competitors for water and nutrients (Meith and Rizzi 1962).

Disease and Pest Control.—Almonds are subject to similar diseases and pests as peaches—San Jose scale, brown rot, peach twig borer, shot hole borers, peach tree borer, scab, tent caterpillar, zinc deficiency, and others—and control measures are similar. Since new developments are occurring continuously, a spray schedule and pest control measures are not given here in detail. It is suggested that a copy of "Pest and Disease Control Program for Almonds" be requested without cost from the California Agricultural Experiment Station, Davis, California.

Harvesting.—Harvesting at the earliest possible date is necessary to avoid worm damage to nuts. The date will vary from year to year, but it should be about September 1. Mallet wounds are a source of considerable damage to trees and, if knocking is attempted too early, it will take harder blows to dislodge the nuts. On the other hand, if knocking is delayed, the infestation of such worms as the Navel orange worm will be increased.

Nonpareil and Peerless almonds will be ready for harvest about the same time. The Peerless is generally harvested first because its nuts drop so badly if left on the tree. Ne Plus Ultra, IXL and Mission follow in that order. IXL can be the latest, but generally Mission is the latest. The Drake is difficult to get off regardless of its state of maturity.

Keep each cultivar separate when harvested. Mixtures of cultivars always will bring lower returns than the same cultivars delivered separately.

Courtesy of Ramacher Manufacturing Co.

FIG. 6.3.   SWEEP-TYPE HARVESTER SWEEPING ALMONDS
INTO WINDROWS

In more and more orchards the nuts are knocked to the ground and picked up mechanically. This is more economical than the old method of knocking on sheets, but it does introduce other problems in connection with worm control, handling and hulling facilities.

When nuts are knocked on a sheet, they are sacked and moved out of the orchard at frequent intervals. Growers like to knock several rows of the same cultivar at one time. The nuts may then be windrowed or at least raked away from the trees. Then the pickup machine is brought in.

The difficulty is that all the operations take time, and the knocking is often several days ahead of the pickup machine. Every day that the nuts are left on the ground greatly increases the amount of worm damage, often to a serious degree. Mechanical harvesting is here to stay, but every effort should be made to pick up the nuts and get them out of the orchard as soon as possible after they are knocked.

After the nuts are harvested, they should be hulled as soon as possible to cut down worm damage. Small operators normally have this operation done by a custom huller. Larger operators usually do their own hulling. After hulling, the nuts are sacked or loaded into bulk bins and taken to the receiving station (Meith and Rizzi 1962).

Growers usually deliver their crops to the cooperative in the unshelled form through local receiving stations. The cooperative supplies its members, free of charge, burlap bags which have been vacuum-cleaned, repaired and fumigated. Where feasible, bulk handling of growers' deliveries is accomplished in pallet boxes of approximately one ton capacity. These are designed for completely mechanized handling and furnished to members at cost. From each delivery a sample for testing purposes is drawn with the aid of a mechanical sampling device which assures a representative specimen of the entire lot.

A 1 lb division (about 220 nuts) is cracked and the meats examined. The percentage of sound and inedible kernels is determined. This assures ear-marking the lot for processing so as to net the greatest returns.

GRADES OF ALMONDS

No other nut comes in so many useful sizes, shapes and forms as almonds, yet the cultivars are few. A breakdown as given by the California Almond Growers Exchange is as follows (see U.S. Grades for Standards of Almonds in Appendix).

In-shell Cultivars

Nonpareil.—Papershell. Accounts for approximately 50% of total California production. Shelled for grocers and confectioners. Natural or blanched kernels favored by salters and bakers. Basic raw material for Sliced Natural.

IXL.—Softshell. Generally sold in-shell due to its attractive appearance. Also shelled for the confectionery trade.

Ne Plus Ultra.—Softshell. Popular with the grocery trade for sale in-shell. Shelled Ne Plus are extensively used for sugar panning (Jordan Almonds) by confectioners.

Peerless.—Semi-hardshell. Attractive, plump appearance. Sold almost entirely in-shell. Widely used in nut mixtures (Fig. 6.4).

Courtesy of Walter Kuzio, Candy Industry, New York

FIG. 6.4. PEERLESS CULTIVAR OF ALMOND

Drake.—Semi-hardshell. Has steady demand in shelled form with confectioners and almond paste manufacturers.

Mission.—Semi-hardhsell. Shelled and sold as meats. Favored by confectioners (pronounced almond flavor blends well with chocolate) and is basic raw material for cocktail almonds.

Jordanolo.—Softshell. A superb almond of outstanding flavor and appearance. Largest kernels are blanched for nut salters. Smaller kernels are used in sugar panning.

Shelling Operations

Almonds which have been classified and assembled for shelling accumulate in huge storage bins. From here they pass to a battery of cracking machines with a capacity of 175 in-shell tons per day. The kernels are mechanically separated from the shells and represent more than half the almonds by weight. The cracking percentage varies with different cultivars. By passing through an ingenious electric eye device, kernels that are broken, chipped or discolored, along with foreign material, are separated and diverted to special uses.

Courtesy of Gromax Inc.

FIG. 6.5. ELECTRONIC ALMOND SORTING MACHINE

This unit is similar to Fig. 5.10 except ultraviolet light is used to accomodate the white nuts.

The whole, perfect meats are further inspected and segregated by graders into sizes with variations of two kernels per ounce. Certain types of manufacturing trade have a decided preference for specific sizes, which in turn has an important bearing on the price. For example, the more than 40 chocolate bar manufacturers favor small almond kernels, whereas nut salters prefer those which are medium to large size.

Shelled Almonds.—Shelled almonds are sold by cultivars, grades (whole, unblanched, select sheller run, and blanched), and sizes (kernels per ounce). Many products require almonds of specific sizes, which can be specified by referring to Table 6.1. From 10 to 20% of the shelled almonds produced are further processed by blanching, dicing, slicing, halving, roasting or spicing.

Courtesy of Calif. Almond Growers Assoc.

FIG. 6.6. SHELLED ALMONDS ARE ELECTRONICALLY
GRADED FOR DEFECTS AT HIGH SPEED

Almond Pieces.—The Exchange recognizes 12 grades of cut almonds
as follows:

Sliced natural, unblanched
Sliced, blanched
Slivered, blanched
Broken, blanched
Splits, Nonpareil, blanched
Halves, Nonpareil unblanched,
cut lengthwise

Cubed, unblanched, cut crosswise
Steel cut, medium, unblanched
Steel cut, small, unblanched
Steel cut, fine, unblanched
Meal, unblanched
Diced, roasted buttered, unblanched

Almond pieces may be cut into other forms for special purposes.

PACKAGING

In 1922 the Exchange offered three shelled and three unshelled packs.
Since then, however, the packs have been expanded and changed to
include 76 distinct shelled items offered in 8 different types of containers
from a 5-oz tin to 100-lb bags.

There are at least ten unshelled packs, including flexible bags and
cartons and more than a dozen consumer size packages of blanched,

TABLE 6.1

SIZES OF ALMOND KERNELS BY CULTIVAR AND GRADE

Cultivar	Grade	16/18	18/20	20/22	23/25	27/30	30/32	32/34	36/40	40/50
Nonpareil	Whole, unblanched	16/18	18/20	20/22	23/25	27/30	30/32	32/34	36/40	40/50
	Select sheller run				23/25					
	Blanched		18/20		23/25					
IXL	Whole, unblanched		18/20		23/25					
	Select sheller run			20/22						
Ne Plus	Whole, unblanched					27/30				
	Select run			20/22						
	Whole and broken									
Peerless	Whole, unblanched			20/22						
	Select sheller run			20/22						
Drake	Whole, unblanched							32/34		40/50
	Select sheller run				23/25	27/30				
Mission	Whole, unblanched						30/32		36/40	
	Select sheller run					27/30	30/32			
	Whole and broken									
Jordanolo	Whole, unblanched	16/18	18/20		23/25					
	Blanched	16/18								

sliced, diced, chopped and halved almonds.

ALMOND INDUSTRY IN SPAIN

This section was taken from Bryan (1965), Assistant U.S. Agricultural Attache in Karachi, Pakistan.

The historic pattern of trade in almonds between Spain and the United States is changing. Spain has long been a traditional supplier of almonds to the United States—in fact, the major one for a number of years. However, quite recently the United States, because of rapidly increasing domestic production, has been able not only to meet more of its own needs but to enter the almond export market, sometimes competing with the Spanish product. It continues also to receive some Spanish almonds, especially certain cultivars needed for specialized uses, though imports have been decreasing. Both countries continue to expand the production on which their export potential is based.

Spain, a long-established almond producer and exporter, is one of six countries accounting for nearly all the world's commercial production of sweet almonds. With three other of these, Italy, Portugal and Morocco, it is located in the Mediterranean area, generally considered the center of world almond production. Aside from the United States, now one of the world's major producers, the remaining major commercial producer is Iran; minor ones are Turkey, Cyprus, Greece, Algeria, Afghanistan and Tunisia.

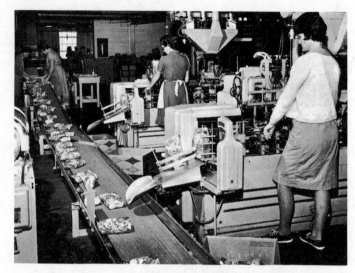

Courtesy of Calif. Almond Growers Assoc.

FIG. 6.7.   WHOLE ALMONDS ARE AUTOMATICALLY FILLED, CHECK/WEIGHED AND SEALED INTO ATTRACTIVE RETAIL TRANSPARENT BAGS

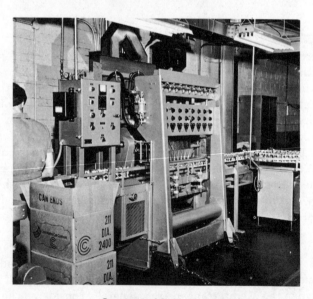

Courtesy of Calif. Almond Growers Assoc.

FIG. 6.8.   DICED, ROASTED AND BLANCHED SLIVERED ALMONDS ARE PACKED IN RETAIL TINS

TABLE 6.2

ALMOND EXPORTS FROM UNITED STATES
IN-SHELL

Country of Destination	1968-69	1969-70	1970-71	1971-72	1972-73	1973-74
			(metric tons)			
Europe						
Belgium-Luxembourg	–	–	–	13	–	48
Czechoslovakia	–	–	–	–	–	50
France	–	–	–	–	2	79
Germany, West	15	–	56	–	–	19
Italy	–	–	–	–	10	2
Netherlands	2	–	–	–	2	21
Norway	3	2	3	–	1	9
Sweden	–	7	27	–	–	–
United Kingdom	–	–	81	23	12	424
Other	3	1	6	2	2	1
Total	23	10	173	38	29	653
Latin America						
Argentina	89	100	382	173	127	100
Mexico	493	697	349	146	302	178
Venezuela	11	20	13	10	12	14
Other	15	15	10	9	40	21
Total	608	832	754	338	481	313
Bermuda and Caribbean	2	1	25	2	6	4
Other Countries						
Australia	–	1	12	–	–	345
Canada	188	211	308	427	501	674
Japan	17	62	136	170	1398	251
New Zealand	–	–	–	–	–	122
Other	29	23	8	13	9	126
Total	234	297	464	610	1908	1518
Grand Total	867	1140	1416	988	2424	2488

Source: Foreign Agric. Serv., FN 1-76.

For the most part, Spanish cultural practices have not changed greatly from those of 20 to 30 years ago; however, the more progressive farmers are beginning to adopt modern cultural practices. Where the terrain permits, some efforts also are being made toward mechanical or semi-mechanical harvesting.

Perhaps the most dramatic changes have taken place in marketing and processing of almonds. Exporters that used to hold considerable stocks during the year now prefer to buy from speculators or accumulators as

TABLE 6.3

COMMERCIAL ALMOND PRODUCTION IN SELECTED COUNTRIES, 1972-76
SHELLED BASIS

Region and Country	1972	1973	1974	1975	1976
			(1000 metric tons)		
Foreign					
Iran	9.0	8.1	8.5	8.3	8.0
Italy	15.0	8.0	14.0	20.0	25.0
Morocco	4.8	5.5	3.0	3.0	5.0
Portugal	5.5	8.0	5.0	3.5	6.0
Spain	50.0	37.0	55.0	43.5	65.0
Total	84.3	66.6	86.5	78.3	109.0
United States[1]	64.4	67.7	98.7	84.0	127.0
World Total	148.7	134.3	185.2	162.3	236.0

Source: Foreign Agric. Serv. FN6-76.
[1]Source: Almond Control Board.

need arises. In addition, the number of almond exporters is dwindling, and export trade is handled by a small number of large firms.

In processing, an increasing proportion of the crop is being handled by mechanical equipment. Innovations in packaging are taking place, with almonds now being packed in consumer-size packages. Increasing numbers are now being blanched, and more sold and shipped as selected sized cultivars.

• Much of the improvement in quality has come about through the exporters, who developed individual standards. However, the government also established in 1961, and amended in 1963, compulsory export standards and export inspection. Compulsory export packaging standards were also put into effect.

Domestic consumption has shown some increase, particularly in the candy industry.

Producing Areas

Almonds are grown throughout most of Spain. However, because of mountains inland and Mediterranean weather along the coast, the commercial producing area is concentrated in the provinces bordering the Mediterranean Sea, in a narrow strip of land, stretching from the base of the Pyrenees Mountains in the northeast some 750 miles along the coast to the Portuguese border in the southwest. The Balearic Islands, off the east coast, are included in the area. On the east and south coasts, the commercial almond plantings run, in general, inland from the coastal plain some 25 to 50 miles up the valleys, which run into the sea. Almond plantings also extend up the slopes and hills adjoining the valleys, and are planted inland of the valleys, on higher ground. In the northeast, the producing area extends further inland following the Ebro River and adjacent river valleys. Here, almond plantings are found mostly from the shoreline to an elevation of about 1500 ft. At higher elevations, less frequent plantings are made in such a way as to take advantage of exposure, using terrain to block off cold winds.

Of the six islands of the Balearics, only two, Majorca and Iviza, are important almond producers. Mountains along the western and northern sides of these islands protect the trees from cold northern winds. Majorca is almost entirely one almond grove, as trees are grown from the seashore in the south up through a fairly level-to-rolling plateau that rises from 600 to 1500 ft. Almonds, however, are not grown to a considerable extent in the mountainous areas.

Spain's almond producing area is usually considered divided into four "zones": Reus, Majorca, Alicante and Malaga. These are not precisely demarcated but are based on traditional almond trade patterns and similarities in climate, cultivars, and production problems. Areas producing almonds within a zone are not necessarily contiguous. Each zone is named after the city which is the major almond trade center.

Production

World production of almonds was off 8% in 1977 in spite of a record crop in the United States. Efforts to bring new areas into production and to improve the quality by introduction of new cultivars have had little effect on production in recent years.

Almond production in Spain was 30,000 metric tons in 1977, shelled basis, a 54% drop from the 1976 output. Principal exports included France, West Germany, Switzerland and Soviet Union. Exports for 1976 were 26,000 tons.

Italy's commercial almond crop in 1977 was 23,000 tons, 39% more than in 1976, and the largest since 1970. Italy's exports for 1977 totaled 7214 tons, 94% more than a year earlier, and, for 1978, 8000 tons. Major destinations were West Germany, the Netherlands and France.

Portugal's output for 1977 was 1560 tons, a 70% decline from 1976. Exports during 1976-77 were about 3000 tons, 67% above 1975-76. Domestic consumption was up.

Morocco's export market for 1976-77 was 110 tons, about the same as for the 2 previous years. Almond production in Iran in 1977 was 7600 tons, 9% larger than 1976, and three-fourths the size of the 1970 crop (Anon. 1977).

Climate

Spain's climate is well suited to almond culture. Individual areas vary somewhat, however. The northeast coastal and interior regions are generally cooler and more humid than the southeast. Nevertheless, because of the influence of the Mediterranean Sea, the climate throughout is generally free from extremely hot or cold weather.

The almond producing areas, as they are planted, range so widely over Spain that the entire crop is unlikely to be damaged by a single frost. Damage by frost to the production in each area is also limited, except in the case of a severe freeze, by variations in altitude and the fact that among the many cultivars there are different flowering periods. The presence of a multitude of almond cultivars is actually a hedge against complete crop failure, either in an area or even on an individual farm, because of frost hazards.

Spanish almonds generally blossom during the three-month period January through March, beginning in the south and gradually moving northward. Danger from frost exists in the south until early March, and in the north until the latter part of April.

In the southern areas, if frost damage should occur, it is not uncommon, in spite of this, for the trees to bear a limited crop from some later blooms, the so-called second blossom. High winds during flowering are sometimes also a hazard.

Annual rainfall in the almond producing areas averages 8 to 10 in. in the southeastern districts, and about 15 in. along the eastern coast. It ranges from 20 to 30 in. in the northeastern region and in the Balearic Island. Little rain falls in spring and summer months, although scattered showers—sometimes quite heavy—occur occasionally in summer. The rainy season—if it could be called that—is from late September through April. Growth and fruiting therefore take place during the dry season; this helps reduce disease.

Cultivars

Spain has a multitude of almond cultivars; the Island of Majorca alone is said to have over 100. Because of this large number, many have been grouped into a few main types of classes. Out of two classes and seven cultivars of commercial importance, seven are hard or semi-hard shell, and only two soft-shell. The main hard or semi-hard shell almonds are the Valencia and Majorca classes, and the cultivars Esperanza, Jordana, Longuette, Marcona and Planeta. Mollar and Fita are the better known soft-shell types.

Perhaps the best known of the Spanish almond classes is the Valencia. This is a commercial category into which unspecified cultivars, grown in any region except Majorca, are placed. Possibly 50 to 70% of Spain's total almond production falls into this grouping. The Valencia class thus consists of quite heterogeneous cultivars, except that the nuts tend to have a rather low shell-out or yield of kernel from whole nuts, estimated between 18 and 24%.

The Majorca, better known as the Farmer Majorca class is composed of the many cultivars grown on the Island of Majorca which are usually purchased on an orchard-run basis, hence the name Farmer Majorcas. Farmer Majorcas account for most of the almonds grown on the Balearic Islands and for about 15 to 20% of the total Spanish crop. One unique aspect of Farmer Majorcas is that all of the many cultivars are sweet, making this class a favorite among the candy manufacturers. The kernel yield is estimated in the 20 to 60% range.

The Jordana is one of Spain's better known almonds. Some consider it a cultivar; others claim that it is a group of fairly similar cultivars that produce a large, long, highly flavored almond with a smooth skin. The sugar-glazed almond confection, universally known, is made from the Jordana. About 5 to 10% of Spain's almond production is comprised of the Jordana. Production is almost entirely concentrated in the Malaga area. Shelling yield is estimated from 20 to 23%.

The Longuette cultivar is best known for its use in candy bars. Candy bars require small flat almonds, designated because of this use as "bar types." The Longuette cultivar accounts for possibly 8 to 20% of Spain's production. This cultivar is grown in both the Reus and Alicante zones. The Longuette's shelling yield, estimated at 22 to 26%, is one of the highest of the hard-shell types.

The Marcona cultivar is perhaps best known for its extremely sweet flavor, and is utilized by the candy trades, particularly for "turron" or nougat, which is basically made of almonds and honey. It is also suitable for salting and blanching. The kernel is round and thin. It is grown in the Reus and Alicante zones and accounts for approximately 3 to 7% of total production. Its kernel yield of 23 to 25% is one of the highest among the hard-shell cultivars.

Spanish soft-shell almonds sold in-shell are largely limited to two cultivars—the Mollar and Fita. Perhaps better known is the Mollar or Tarragona Mollar, indicating that it is grown in the Reus-Tarragona area. In recent years there has been some production of the Mollar cultivar in the Alicante zone. The kernel yield in this area is a little less than the 35 to 40% for the Mollar grown around Reus. The Fita cultivar is grown mainly on the Island of Iviza—one of the Balearic Islands. The kernel yield for the Fita is lower than for the Mollar with estimates of about 28 to 30%.

For Spain as a whole, the average shell-out is estimated at about 25%. In comparison with the 50% kernel yield, and even higher in some years, obtained from the chief California cultivar (Nonpareil), this is quite low. However, by far the majority of Spain's almond cultivars are hard or semi-hard shell cultivars while most of California's production is from soft-shell cultivars. Also, the average Spanish shell-out is comparable with that of other Mediterranean countries' almonds, such as Italy's and Portugal's. As indicated, the hard or semi-hard shell cultivars of Spain have a shell-out which is estimated to be in the 18 to 26% range, while the soft-shell cultivars probably average 30 to 35% with some cultivars even higher. However, as these soft-shell cultivars comprise only a small proportion of total production, the average shell-out for all the Spanish cultivars is low.

Even in converting in-shell exports to a shelled basis, a relatively low shell-out would apply because these in-shell exports include about equal quantities of soft and hard-shell cultivars.

Tree Spacing and Yields

Differing rainfall levels that characterize the various almond producing areas have resulted in considerable variation in tree spacing; variation exists also among plantings within an area. However, in all zones, orchard plantings are made on the diamond or square. In the case of scattered plantings, trees are located to take advantage of best available soil, topography, exposure and moisture. In the Alicante and Malaga zones, for instance, many such plantings are made on terraced mountain sides. Also, in the extremely dry valleys in these zones, trees are grown on the borders of dryland crop fields, spaced 40 ft apart within the borders and the borders considerably farther apart.

It is apparent that there is a considerable range in number of trees planted to the acre. Approximations of average number of trees per acre in the various zones are: Majorca 20; Malaga 24; Alicante 26; and Reus 28.

Though data on yields are very limited, it is obvious that production per tree is small. Main causes are: lack of adequate moisture (resulting in relatively small open trees); the nature of the cultural practices used; and the advanced age of most trees.

The areas that have been described as the commercial almond zones are also Spain's fruit and vegetable-producing areas. Instead of almonds, fruits and vegetables producing higher yields and more profits are grown on the superior land there, as well as on land with access to irrigation water. Coupled with the almond's hardiness and ability to produce crops even under driest and most adverse conditions, this situation has resulted in the almond being grown in the least desirable locations in terms of topography, soil and water, as well as with a minimum of labor.

Harvesting and Processing

Harvesting extends over approximately three months—August through October. In the earliest-blooming areas, Malaga and Alicante, harvest begins in early August and extends into October. In the later-blooming areas, Majorca and Reus, harvesting does not usually commence until early September.

Because of the nature of the almond plantings—the roughness of the terrain and the wide tree spacings—and the relative abundance of labor in most areas, the most common method of harvesting is for the almonds to be knocked off the trees with a pole. There are several variations of this practice. Usually a crew of men go through the plantings knocking the almonds off the trees, followed by a crew of women and children who gather the almonds off the ground. If the trees are heavy-bearing, sometimes a ground cloth is used.

In some areas a semi-mechanical harvesting method is being used. Carts with cloth frames on three sides are drawn under the trees; the almonds are then knocked into the cart.

Labor for harvesting is usually provided by the farm operator and his family. There is some exchange of labor, but very little is hired. Some of the larger operators, however, contract for harvesting; generally, however, they too have enough of their own labor. Also, although contract-harvesting is faster, damage to trees is greater.

Most growers have their own hulling machines. For those who do not, nearly every village has machines for custom use. The hulls are used quite extensively. Usually, they are burned and the ash is used for making soap or put into mixture with manure for fertilizer.

After the almonds are hulled, they are allowed to dry for several days in the sun; during this time they are turned frequently. When dry, they are stored in the shell on the farm until sold.

The Spanish almond packer-exporter has two means of obtaining almonds: (1) from his agents located throughout the producing areas or (2) from speculators located in the major trade centers (who have their own agents or buy from small speculators in the producing areas). Often agents also speculate for their own account.

Agents and speculators obtain their supplies of almonds in the same manner. The usual method is to purchase in-shell almonds from growers and shell the nuts at the semi-processor's own plants or send them directly to the packer-exporter for shelling.

There is a wide range in the size, amount and type of equipment among Spanish almond processing plants, as well as the number of employees. Typical, however, is a downward trend in the total number of processing plants accompanied by an increase in size of operations and amount of mechanical equipment in remaining plants. Machinery is, for the most part, of Spanish manufacture, often designed or modified by the individual almond processing firm. Some Italian machinery is used also.

Only a very small proportion of the crop is marketed unshelled. Shelling is done entirely by mechanical means. Small cracking plants in local producing areas process an estimated 30 to 40% of the crop. The remainder is shelled by packer-exporters in their relatively larger and more modern plants.

At many small plants the process consists merely of cracking the almonds and separating the kernels from the shells. The latter may be done either by hand or, in some plants, by shakers and screens. Often, all operations are performed by hand except for the cracking. In some cases, mechanical equipment moves the almonds through the different processes.

Exporting

Plants of the large packer-exporters are, for the most part, highly mechanized in their handling of almonds from the time of their arrival, throughout processing, until shipment.

In 1960, a total of 160 firms were listed as almond and filbert exporters. It is likely, however, that no more than 30 firms are active in the export market year-in and year-out. Possibly ten of these firms handle 90 to 95% of Spain's almond export trade.

Almonds in the shell normally arrive at the packer-exporter plants by truck, usually packed in 100-kg (220-lb) burlap sacks; sometimes, however, they arrive in bulk loads. Separation into cultivars and classes is maintained during all stages. Storage is done in burlap bags for small quantities of a cultivar, or in bulk in large underground concrete bins. When the nuts are to be processed they are lifted mechanically, often for several floors, to the cracking area. There they are put through cracking machines, screened and separated from the shell; they may be sized at this time also. (Almonds purchased already shelled may be rescreened and then sized.) Kernels are then stored by cultivar and size.

The shelled and sized almonds are usually given a final grading and sorting, as needed to fill specific contracts. During this process, a crew of women grade and sort the nuts as they pass along on a continuous belt. Often several selections are made at the same time. During this step, several inspections by the management are made to ensure that specified grades are being selected. Afterwards, the almonds are either blanched or immediately packed (either for export or domestic use). In the former operation, the almonds go through a blanching bath, for the prescribed time, are brought out mechanically on roller belts which remove skins and excess moisture, and are then placed on trays and put into small ovens to complete the process. Some Spanish packers believe that the ovens could be improved by controlling the timing and temperature uniformity. After removal and cooling, the blanched almonds are packed.

For export, almonds are packed in wooden boxes containing up to 50 kg (110 lb), in cardboard boxes holding up to 12.5 kg (27.5 lb), or in 50 kg burlap sacks. Increasingly, almonds are packed in individual consumer-size packages, usually of cellophane, in weights of 100 and 250 g; these are shipped in wooden or cardboard boxes.

Estimates of almond stocks in Spain are hardly better than "educated guesses." Many are held by individual growers, accumulators (speculators) both large and small, and exporters. Exporters, though, reportedly do not hold large stocks as in the past, but buy mainly on order.

Spain is usually the world's second largest exporter of almonds—after Italy—but some years Spain leads Italy in shipments. Only 15 to 20% of the crop is consumed domestically.

Spain's almonds are exported almost entirely in the form of kernels, which have averaged about 97% of the total in recent years. Exports of unshelled almonds have increased slightly in absolute terms but per-centagewise have remained about the same. They have ranged between 1400 and 3600 tons (unshelled basis) annually in recent years. Leading markets for unshelled almonds have been France, Egypt, Brazil, the United Kingdom and West Germany.

Among individual countries, France or the United Kingdom is usually the largest single customer. West Germany is generally third most important, followed by Sweden and Switzerland. Other smaller but important European markets are Norway, Denmark and the Netherlands. In North America, Canada has displaced the United States as the leading non-European market for Spanish almonds. Canadian purchases have increased moderately from the prewar level.

On the other hand, sales to the United States (where Spain has been the traditional supplier) have declined sharply because of the considerable expansion of almond production in California; the United States is now on a net export basis.

U.S. Imports.—Though Spain's exports of almonds to the United States are much smaller than in earlier years, Spain has become virtually the sole supplier of foreign almonds for the U.S. market. This is true for all three types of imports: unshelled, shelled and shelled blanched almonds. The limited U.S. imports are for specialized uses. Jordanas, Longuettes, Marconas and Valencias are the main Spanish almonds imported by the United States. The United States may also import heavily in years of short domestic crops.

Almond Export Standards.—Spain in 1961 established compulsory export standards for shelled almonds and for unshelled. A resolution of the office of the Director General of Foreign Trade—published in the *Official Bulletin* of March 23, 1961—established these standards which were amended in 1963. The Inspection Service of the Ministry of Commerce (SOIVRE) is responsible for the enforcement of export standards.

Spain's almond export standards seem to be patterned after U.S. standards, except for one major difference. Spanish standards for shelled almonds generally specify only two grades—either selected or unselected—for each cultivar or class. However, for Valencias and Majorcas there are three grades and for Esperanzas and Planetas only one. This contrasts with the U.S. standards, which provide seven grades for all cultivars.

Spanish standards take into consideration special characteristics of their cultivars in processing, handling, and use in determining tolerances allowed to meet their grade requirements. Considerable similarity with U.S. standards exists in the description of types of defects. However, in some groupings and separations of defects, the Spanish standards differ from the U.S. standards.

With some exceptions, the Spanish standards for the selected cultivars would come closest to meeting U.S. standards for grade No. 1. The Spanish standards for unselected cultivars, also with some exceptions, would come closest to meeting U.S. standards for Select Sheller Run.

Main differences between Spanish and U.S. standards for shelled almonds include:

(1) The Spanish standards permit an admixture of 5 to 20% of "other sweet cultivars," depending upon cultivar (or class) and grade (selected or unselected). The U.S. standards allow only 5% mixture of "other cultivars" (including bitters) regardless of cultivar or grade.

(2) The Spanish standards have various tolerances for admixture of bitter almonds (depending upon the cultivar or class of sweet almond) up to a 6% maximum. Tolerance of bitter almonds is usually lower in selected than unselected. By contrast, the U.S. standards permit only 1% bitter almonds, regardless of cultivar or grade.

(3) For all cultivars of Spanish selected almonds, except Esperanza, tolerance for doubles is equal to the 3% tolerance for U.S. fancy, or less.

For the most common Spanish almonds, unselected Valencias and Farmer Majorcas, there are high double tolerances of 20 and 40%, respectively, and for unselected in specified cultivars, 7 to 15%.

(4) Spanish tolerance for "broken" and "splits," in both selected and unselected, is low—2 and 3% respectively—except for a special category of Majorcas. There is a greater range in U.S. standards.

(5) Selected Spanish almonds have an 8% tolerance for damage by chip and scratch (mainly from machine damage); U.S. grade No. 1, 10%. For unselected Spanish almonds the 20% tolerance is the same as for U.S. Select and Standard Sheller Run.

(6) U.S. standards have separate tolerances for foreign material and for particles and dust, allowing 0.2% for foreign material and 0.1% for particles and dust in the top five grades, 0.3 and 1.0% respectively for Whole and Broken, and 0.3 and 1.0% respectively for No. 1 Pieces. Spanish standards have grouped these tolerances, allowing a combined total of 0.25% for particles, dust, and other foreign matter for both selected and unselected.

Classification

Shelled almonds in Spain may be classified in terms of size, or by count of kernels per unit of weight. Spanish classification by size is based on the width of the kernel. Sizes are determined by passing kernels through sieves, with openings equal to the minimum axis (width) measurement.

Intermediate sizes are authorized on special request for certain markets.

	Shape of Kernel	
Classification	Long	Round
Large	Axis equal to or over 14 mm (0.546 in.)	Axis equal to or over 14 mm (0.546 in.)
Medium	Axis between 11 and 14 mm (0.429 and 0.546 in.)	Axis between 11 and 14 mm (0.429 and 0.546 in.)
Small	Axis under 11 mm (0.429 in.)	Axis under 12 mm (0.468 in.)

A tolerance by weight of 5% is allowed for deviations from the designated size.

Shelled almonds are classified by weight on the basis of the number of kernels to an English ounce (28.35 g to the oz) as follows:

Count	Number of Kernels per Oz
16	16 or less
16/18	16-18 inclusive
18/20	18-20 inclusive
20/22	20-22 inclusive
22/24	22-24 inclusive
23/25	23-25 inclusive
24/26	24-26 inclusive
26/28	26-28 inclusive
27/30	27-30 inclusive
30/34	30-34 inclusive
36/40	36-40 inclusive
40/50	40-50 inclusive
50	50

Intermediate counts are allowed on special requests for certain markets. No tolerance is allowed for deviation from the designated count.

Packing For Export

Spanish almonds, either shelled or unshelled, may be exported in bags, boxes, or tin cans.

Bags may be of jute, esparto grass, or a combination of these two fibers, or of any other fiber resistant to damage from handling and transportation. The bags may be one of two folds and may be with or without paper lining. If lined, the paper must be new, dry, clean and lacking unpleasant odor. Maximum capacity is 50 kg (110 lb).

Boxes may be made of wood, cardboard, or any other material strong enough to stand handling and transportation. All materials used in box manufacture or lining must be free from any odor which could be absorbed by almonds. If colored paper is used, it must not discolor the contents. The wood must be dry, clean, and free from large knots. Maximum capacity for wooden boxes is 50 kg (110 lb), and for cardboard boxes (cartons) 12.5 kg (31 lb).

Cans must be made of new, clean and odorless tin plate. They must have openings and lids and must be lithographed. The maximum capacity is 25 kg (55 lb).

As for other containers, the Inspection Service of the Ministry of Commerce (SOIVRE) may authorize their use.

Marking of Containers.—Aside from brand names, the Spanish Government requires that containers be marked with the following information: (1) type of nut; (2) exporter's registry number; (3) net weight (for boxes); (4) type or name (for classified almonds); (5) the inscription, "Produced in or imported from Spain." This may be in Spanish or in any other language in a visible place.

ALMOND INDUSTRY IN ITALY

This section was taken from Bryan (1966), assistant U.S. Attache in Karachi, Pakistan.

In most recent years, Italy has led the world in commercial production of almonds, and in their export. However, in Italy almond production is cyclical in nature and is characterized by especially sharp year-to-year fluctuations. While Italy's commercial production in the ten-year period of 1955-1964 averaged 32,400 tons, and overshadowed that of other producers, Italian crops in that same period ranged from 66,000 tons in 1961 to only 13,000 tons in 1956.

Production

Several aspects of Italian almond production are particularly worthy of note. These include concentration of plantings near the "heel" of southern Italy in the region of Puglia and in the two islands, Sicily and Sardinia; the small size of plantings and the high incidence of mixed plantings; and the use of traditional cultural practices which tend to restrict yields. For export purposes, the production of a very large number of cultivars tends to be a drawback, since it makes standardization difficult.

Cultural practices have had a profound influence on Italian almond production. Prominent are traditional beliefs that almond trees will yield some return from even a poor or dry piece of land where hardly any other crop would be worth raising. A companion attitude is that since almond trees yield something even under unfavorable conditions, relatively little care is required. There is little use of fertilizer or pesticides; systematic pruning is not practiced, and few efforts have been made to improve output by irrigation, planting of better cultivars, or use of other modern cultural practices. Thus, raising of almonds with a view to maximizing output and income is relatively uncommon, and the natural tendency of almonds toward alternate-bearing years is not mitigated by progressive cultural practices.

Climate is particularly favorable for almond-growing in parts of Puglia and the island of Sicily because of Mediterranean-type features. The island of Sardinia also possesses such a climate. In all these areas, winters are mild and short. As evidence of the brevity of winter in southern Italy, the growing season is approximately 300 days.

In these areas, the rainfall pattern, too, is favorable to almond culture. Precipitation is very light in June, July and August and particularly heavy in November, December and January. Dryness in summer inhibits development of almond diseases, and in addition provides ideal conditions for harvesting the nuts. Wetness in winter, conversely, provides much-needed moisture reserves and occurs at a time when there is minimum interference with field work.

Averages, of course, do not reveal deviations from the "normal." Rain during blossoming, for instance, has in some years seriously reduced crops, as have severe late winter freezes and March frosts. Also, occasional dry hot winds (the "sirocco") from the Sahara desert have adversely affected crops in Sicily.

Acreage and Tree Numbers

Almond acreage in Italy is of two categories: "specialized" and "mixed." Specialized acreage refers to orchards solidly planted with almond trees. Mixed refers to almond trees interplanted with other types, such as olives, or with vines. Italian technicians have estimated that there are 150 almond trees per hectare in specialized plantings (60.73 trees per acre) and only 30 trees per hectare (12.15 trees per acre) in mixed plantings, or five times as many trees per acre in a specialized planting as in a mixed planting. In the most intensive almond-growing communities of Sicily (such as Avola) about 40 trees per hectare (100 trees per acre) serves as "rule-of-thumb" for specialized plantings. Of Italy's entire commercial production, roughly three-fifths of the crop is from trees in specialized plantings.

Italy is the world's leader in number of almond trees. There were an estimated 36.6 million almond trees in the commercial area of Italy in 1964 (based on the assumed densities in the specialized and mixed plantings), compared with an estimated 30 million trees in Spain and 9 million trees in California.

Cultivars

There are multitudes of almond cultivars in Italy; supposedly some 1200 have been identified. They are mostly sweet cultivars, but some bitters also are produced. Hard and semi-hard shell cultivars are mostly of little merit; but a few—both in Sicily and on the mainland—possess excellent qualities. However, the "excessive" number of cultivars cultivated in any region of Italy is considered by the trade there to be "an important negative aspect" of Italian almond culture. The production of only a small tonnage for each of many cultivars results in great heterogeneity of Italian almonds, and it is both difficult and costly to pack a large quantity of homogeneous almonds conforming to well-defined standards.

The cultivars grown in Sicily and Puglia are different. Sweet Sicilian almonds, mainly hard-shelled, are classified as follows by the Italian trade:

(1) "Choice Avola" (*Avola scelta*) is the trade designation for kernels of the variety "Pizzuta d' Avola," which is grown chiefly in the provinces of Siracusa and Ragusa. It is grown for export, commands a high price, and is highly desired by confectionery manufacturers.

(2) "Common Avola" (*Avola corrente*) is the trade designation for kernels of the cultivar "Romano," also grown mainly in Siracusa and Ragusa. It is also for export but is priced as a common cultivar and often mixed with other common cultivars and exported under the trade name "Palma-Girgenti."

(3) "Fascionello" is the trade term for kernels of the cultivar "Fasciuneddu," grown, too, in Siracusa and Ragusa. (These two provinces are renowned for superior cultivars.) When sorted and graded by the same criteria as Choice Avola it may be marketed as a Choice Avola. It thus commands a higher price than common types. It may, however, be graded less rigorously and shipped under the Palma-Girgenti category.

(4) "Nostra contrada" (meaning "our region's almonds"), also known as Etna almonds, is grown in a limited area near Mount Etna and when mixed (in variable proportions) with other cultivars is exported under the classification Palma-Girgenti.

(5) "Cuore," or "heart," consists of the kernels of the "Cuva" cultivar and occurs mainly in some communities in Catania. It is marketed largely for export.

(6) "Similaria nostra contrada" (meaning "similar to our regions' almonds") is a broad category consisting of various cultivars cultivated in a large part of the province of Catania and in some communities of Enna and Messina. The kernels are less uniform than the Etna (Nostra contrada) type. They may be mixed in varying proportions with other types under the designation Palma-Girgenti and thus exported.

(7) "Palma-Girgenti" is the name of a very broad grouping under which a portion of some of the types described and the many other Sicilian almond cultivars—grown anywhere in Sicily—are traded. "Twins" of well-known cultivars are also included. Palma-Girgenti accounts for 60 to 65% of Sicily's kernel production.

A rough breakdown of Sicily's kernel cultivars (as % of value) is as follows:

Avola scelta, Avola corrente, and Fascionello   20%
Etna or nostre contrada and similar   18%
Cuore   2%
Palma-Girgenti   60%
                                                ─────
                                                 100%

The leading in-shell cultivars grown in Sicily are the "Mollese di Nis-cemi," which have a soft shell and are exported largely to France and Germany, and the "Fellamase," a semi-hard-shell cultivar which is exported to the United Kingdom. Other soft-shelled cultivars are the Cavalera and the Regina.

In Puglia, the most valued cultivars are the Santora, Fraguilia and Tuono, all with a semi-hard shell, and the Rachele and Montrone, with a hard shell. Santora and Fraguilia are highly regarded in the export trade.

Shelling Yields

Italian almonds, being predominantly hard-shelled, have a relatively low yield of kernels upon shelling. The trade in Italy believes that the average shell-out is slightly in excess of 20%. This, of course, refers to shelling cultivars; these account for the overwhelming share of Italy's production and trade. Soft-shell cultivars have a much higher shelling yield, approaching 50%. Yields of the main Sicilian cultivars have been estimated[3] as follows:

Hard-shell cultivars	% Shell-out
Pizzuta (Choice Avola)	21
Romano (Common Avola)	20
Fascinuneddu (Fascionello)	22-23
Cuore	20-26

Semi-hard-shell cultivars	% Shell-out
Fellamase	35-36
Bottara	35-36

Soft-shell cultivars	
Mollese di Niscemi	45-55
Cavalere (Mollese)	45-48
Regina (Mollese)	47-50

---

[3]Matarazzo, G. *Tecnica Agricola*, Anno X, No. 1-2, 1958. Catania, Sicily.

Harvesting

As is typical of almond production in the Mediterranean area, a minimum of labor is hired in Italy. The farm operator—either the owner-operator or share-cropper—and his family usually provide the labor required. Larger units may employ full-time workers and, during harvest season only, part-time labor as well.

Farm labor in southern Italy and Sicily has traditionally been abundant and cheap because of the chronic underemployment in those areas. The availability of farm labor rarely presents a problem and the cost is minimal.

The most common method of harvesting is for the almonds to be knocked off the trees with poles, either onto the ground or cloths laid on the ground. Intercropping, small orchards, and irregular terrain preclude widespread mechanization of harvest. However, the rapidly increasing labor costs are expected to provide an impetus to mechanical harvesting, particularly in larger orchards.

Marketing

The grower sells his almonds to agents of the packer-exporters or to accumulator-speculators. When sold to the latter the almonds may change hands a number of times, depending upon market conditions, before they ultimately find their way to the packer-exporter.

There are probably about 20 large firms that export almonds, about a half dozen of which account for the bulk of the export business. In addition, there are possibly 50 small exporters that export almonds occasionally.

Unlike their Spanish counterparts, Italian packer-exporters generally carry large supplies of uncommitted almonds rather than relying on accumulator-speculators for supplies as orders are received. Those not able to market their stocks at the desired prices may carry them over into the next season.

As the need arises, the packer-exporter may shell the almonds that he had purchased in the shell in his plants in the producing areas, or as stated earlier, buy shelled almonds from a local sheller. At this state, only a rough grading and selection, i.e., sorting by size, are made. The shelled, roughly sorted almonds are then brought to the packer-exporter's plant, where final grading and selecting are performed, and the almonds are then packed for export or domestic shipment.

Processing

While little has changed in the techniques of producing almonds in

Italy, there has been a radical change in the processing technology. In only a relatively few seasons, Italian industry has converted to mechanized shelling and selection operations.

Processing plants vary considerably in size, equipment, and number of employees. Much of the equipment is of new design; plants with older equipment are gradually making replacements or going out of business. Almost all of the machinery is of Italian design and manufacture, though there is some of Spanish origin.

It is estimated that there are about 25 large shellers which handle 2 to 10 tons per day and over 100 small shellers which handle ½ to 2 tons daily. The large plants perform the varied functions of cracking, separation of kernels from shell, and selecting. The small plants often perform only the cracking operation; some, though, also do some selecting. Blanching of almonds is much less important in Italy than in Spain.

Several of the large packer-exporters have automatic equipment which packs premium almonds in 100- and 200-g cellophane bags. Polyethylene bags of 250 and 500 g—packed in cardboard boxes containing a net weight of 50 kg (110 lb)—are also used for retail packages of premium almonds.

Packaging for export is generally in 50-kg (less frequently 100-kg) burlap bags and in wooden boxes containing up to 50 kg or cardboard boxes holding 12.5 kg (27.5 lb).

Exporting

As is the case in other Mediterranean countries, there are no reliable statistics on stocks. An estimate of stocks carried over from one season to the next is little more than a consensus of educated guesses made by members of the trade. Despite the fact that growers, accumulators, and speculators may hold stocks, the largest volume of stocks is probably held by the exporters. All hold these stocks in the shell. The almonds are not shelled until needed to fill a contract.

Like the estimates of stocks, figures on consumption of almonds in Italy are hardly more than guesses. Actually, the consumption figure is just a residual remaining after subtracting exports and estimated ending stocks from the supply.

Almonds are exported as either "unselected" or "selected." Unselected almonds are simply those that have not been as carefully culled, graded, or sized as selected almonds, the admixture with other cultivars or types may be greater; there may also be more bitters, doubles ("twins"), brokens, splits, and pieces as well as damaged kernels and other defects.

TABLE 6.4

ALMOND EXPORTS FROM SELECTED COUNTRIES, 1971-75
SHELLED BASIS

Country	1971-72	1972-73	1973-74	1974-75	1975-76
			1000 metric tons		
Foreign					
Iran	5.4	5.6	5.5	2.5	1.8
Italy	13.2	9.6	3.3	2.2	8.0
Morocco	1.5	3.6	4.3	1.6	0.8
Portugal	5.2	4.5	6.6	3.5	3.0
Spain	19.0	33.0	19.0	20.0	25.0
Total	44.3	56.3	38.7	29.8	40.1
United States	35.7	26.2	32.3	45.0	46.0
World Total	80.0	82.5	71.0	74.8	86.1

Source: Foreign Agric. Serv., FN 6-76.

Italian selected almonds may be designated as "clean," "hand-picked," "sieved," and "bar-type."

The almonds destined for export must be dry.

The following tolerances—to be calculated as the percentage of net weight—may not be exceeded:

For almonds to be exported in sacks, 1%, in aggregate, of kernels that have turned musty, have been attacked by worms, are completely shrivelled or empty, or shells, dust, siftings and other foreign substances; 5% of broken almonds; 3% admixture of bitter almonds in sweet almonds; 5% admixture of sweet almonds in bitter almonds.

For almonds to be exported in cases, 0.25%, in aggregate, of kernels that have turned musty, have been attacked by worms, are completely shrivelled or empty, of shells, dust, siftings and other foreign substances; 1% of broken almonds; 3% admixture of bitter almonds in sweet almonds; 5% admixture of sweet almonds in bitter almonds.

A category designated as "broken almonds" may be exported provided that the following tolerances in terms of net weight per case or sack are not exceeded: 10% of broken kernels—as a percentage of the weight of whole kernels; 1%, in aggregate, of shells, dust, shrivelled kernels, siftings and other foreign material.

These standards are not as detailed as those for Spanish or U.S. almonds. It is possible, however, to make rough comparisons with some Spanish and U.S. grades.

A firm intending to export almonds has to notify the nearest control office of the name and location of the plant where the nuts have been processed. Not less than 48 hours before the loading or shipping of the goods, the exporter has to present a "control application" to the control office. In exceptional cases, the application may be submitted on shorter notice, but at the exporter's risk. An application is to be presented for each shipment with various relevant information.

For the determination of the percentage of bitter almonds, a sample of 100 almonds is taken and each of the almonds is individually rubbed against a different place on a sheet of sandpaper. Then, distilled water as well as a 10% alcohol solution of guaiac resin and a 1% aqueous solution of copper sulphate are sprinkled on the sandpaper. The traces left by the bitter almonds turn a blue color. The number of blue spots, therefore, indicates the percentage of bitter almonds in a package. The Italian authorities point out that to be absolutely correct the percentage would have to be determined by weight; but in practice the numerical percentage is determined instead, since it is believed to coincide closely enough with the percentage by weight.

If the product subjected to the inspection meets the minimum quality standards, the official in charge of the control will issue the "Inspection Certificate" made out to the exporter. This certificate has to be turned over to the port or railroad authorities, as the case may be, in order for the export shipment to be permitted.

There has been a remarkable similarity in the export price movements of Italian and Spanish almonds. These parallel price movements do not imply identical prices for unselected Baris and Valencias. Actually, unselected Baris (and P.G.'s also) are usually 3 to 5 cents (per pound) cheaper than Valencias. At times this spread narrows appreciably, but it is rare for Valencias not to enjoy a premium over Baris and P.G.'s.

Foreign Trade.—Italy is normally the world's largest exporter of almonds, though in some years Spain leads. Exports are by far the main market outlet for Italian almonds. In the six-year period from 1968-73, an annual average of 15,565 metric tons were exported. There has been a rapid decline since 1968 when 31,922 tons were exported.

Italian exports are predominantly made in the form of kernels. Exports of unshelled almonds account for only 1 to 3% of the export volume. European countries, and in particular the United Kingdom, take the lion's share of the almonds exported in the shell. European markets account for an even larger share of Italy's kernel exports. Germany is traditionally Italy's best almond kernel customer.

Of the Soviet Bloc, only Czechoslovakia and East Germany are consistently large, and even expanding, markets. Among overseas outlets, Australia and Canada have been buying small and declining tonnages from Italy. The United States has now also become a very small—even insignificant—market for Italian almonds.

Outlook

While California and Spanish producers have reacted to indications of strengthening demand by increasing plantings of almonds, there has not been any expansion of almond acreage in Italy.

There may have been some slight increases in Italian production because of improved yields per tree. Despite the relatively backward state of Italian almond culture, there has been some improvement in technology and this improvement should take place at a faster rate in the future. There is no question but that Italian agriculture is modernizing and this change should spill over into the almond industry. Also, there have been reports that Italian growers have been more active in recent years in replacing old, unproductive trees with young stock.

The European trend of consolidation of uneconomically small farm units into larger enterprises able to afford more efficient practices may well extend into southern Italy, too. It, therefore, appears likely for a variety of reasons that almond production, even on the unchanged acreage base, will show some increase.

A modest increase in acreage coupled with a moderate improvement in yields could result in some expansion of production within the next few years.

USES OF ALMONDS

Modified Almond Powder

Finely ground blanched almond nutmeats are encapsulated in a light matrix of maltodextrins to improve flavor stability and isolate the problems created by excess moisture. Almond powder provides from 18 to 24% protein, 50 to 55% fat, 20 to 24% carbohydrate, and 3 to 4% ash. Moisture is controlled to 1%. This ingredient contains approximately 650 cal per 100 g, supplying 35% of the RDA for protein. Particle size is controlled at approximately 100 microns, the flavor is bland, and the powder is a pale cream color.

Among the numerous applications for almond powder are: beverages, beverage bases and mixes, soups, sauces, confections, toppings, fillings, bakery goods, snacks, dairy products, frozen confections, breading and stuffing mixes, icings, salad dressings, meat and fish specialties, glazes, dips and dip mixes, syrups and spreads. Because the ingredient is both a source of flavor and nutritional components of natural origin, it should find wide use.

As a result of the special processing, this ingredient will retain its typical flavor under storage for several months (Anon. 1976).

Almond Oil

Comparatively little almond oil is produced in the United States. Some companies combine almond oil with other specialty oils. When the shelled nuts, which contain about 50% of oil, are dried, coarsely ground, and cold pressed, about 75% of the oil is removed at 450 lb of pressure. The oil is low enough in free fatty acids to be refined as a high-grade salable product by the use of a bleaching agent alone. American almond oil has an iodine value of about 103, which is slightly higher than U.S.P. specifications; nevertheless it is commonly accepted by the trade. See Table 3.2 on Almond Composition.

Almond meal, containing about 20% oil, is edible but slightly bitter because of the skins. It is ground, sieved to various sizes, and sold to the cosmetic and baking trades.

High market prices make it difficult to devote first grade nuts to oil production. In shelling and grading plants, however, a noteworthy amount of shrivelled, resinous or otherwise inedible meats is rejected and could be used for oil recovery. There is also a considerable quantity of bitter almonds brought in by growers from trees planted as pollinizers to sweet almonds. Such almonds find little use except as seed for root stocks. The oil from bitter almonds can be rendered quite bland by deodorization (Kester 1949).

Manufacturers of confectionery and baked goods have found almonds to be the most versatile of the tree nuts, with the possible exception of pecans. This is due to both the qualities of the almond nuts, as well as the aggressiveness of the trade associations in developing extended uses.

Courtesy of Keith Thomas Co.

FIG. 6.9. ALMOND YEAST BUNS

The Exchange has published over 100 recipes,·using almonds in many categories: snacks and appetizers, main dishes, soups, vegetables, salads, desserts, cookies, breads and muffins, and candy. Many recipes which call for pecans and Brazil nuts are suitable for almonds.

Courtesy of Keith Thomas Co.

FIG. 6.10. ALMOND CRUNCH CAKE AND BRITTLE

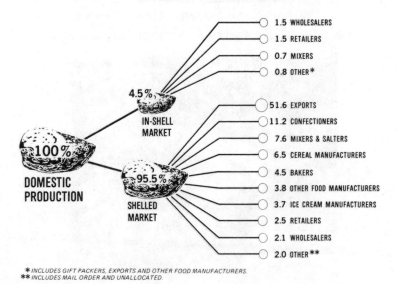

INCLUDES GIFT PACKERS, EXPORTS AND OTHER FOOD MANUFACTURERS.
**INCLUDES MAIL ORDER AND UNALLOCATED.*

Courtesy of U.S. Dept. Agric.

FIG. 6.11. DISTRIBUTION OF ALMONDS, 1973–1974

Among the confections that made almonds popular in the United States is the "Hershey Almond Bar," introduced in 1908. This was made along with a similar, flat milk chocolate bar without nuts. The bar with almonds quickly became, and remains, the most popular candy made by that company.

Almonds are preferred for this bar because they are flat, have a color and flavor that blends with that of chocolate, and are slower to turn rancid than pecans or walnuts.

Courtesy of Keith Thomas Co.

FIG. 6.12. SAUCY VEGETABLE CAROUSEL WITH ALMONDS

Courtesy of Keith Thomas Co.

FIG. 6.13. ALMOND FORTUNE COOKIES

Almond Formulas for Bakers, published by the Exchange, contains 26 formulas. In addition, the Exchange has formulas and colored photographs on separate 5 X 7 cards of the following dishes:

Maple Almond Griddle Cakes
Strawberry Almond Waffles
Almond Tuna Au Gratin with Egg Noodles
Plantation Ham Steak with Orange Almond Sauce
Almond Mushroom Sauce with Chuckwagon Beef Patties
Chicken Short Cake with Diced Roasted Almonds
Turkey Cutlet Supreme with Almond Mushroom Sauce
Almond Macaroons
Toppings for Vegetables and Soups
Toppings for Ice Cream, Sundaes, Pastries and Desserts
Chicken Salad Almondine
Chicken Croquettes Almondine
Fish Almondine
Baked Potato Almondine

REFERENCES

ANON. 1963A. Almond Recipes. Calif. Almond Grow. Exch., Sacramento, Calif.

ANON. 1963B. Almond Recipes, Blue Diamond. Calif. Almond Grow. Exch., Sacramento, Calif.

ANON. 1965A. Almonds in California. Calif. Almond Grow. Exch., Sacramento, Calif.

ANON. 1965B. Art of Almond Cookery. Calif. Almond Grow. Exch. Sacramento, Calif.

ANON. 1965C. California Almonds. Cultivars, Sizes and Products. Calif. Almond Grow. Exch., Sacramento, Calif.

ANON. 1966A. Formulas for Candy Makers. Calif. Almond Grow. Exch., Sacramento, Calif.

ANON. 1966B. Almond Gifts from California. Calif. Almond Grow. Exch., Sacramento, Calif.

ANON. 1966C. Statistical Report. World Agricultural Production and Trade. U.S. Dep. Agric., Foreign Agric. Serv. March Rept.

ANON. 1966D. Almond Formulas for Bakers. Calif. Almond Grow. Exch., Sacramento, Calif.

ANON. 1976. Natural almond powder modified to improve stability, flow, and dispersion. Food Prod. Dev. *10* (7) 40.

ANON. 1977. World almond crop dips. Foreign Agric. 12(26) 5. Foreign Agric. Serv., U.S. Dep. Agric.

BAILEY, L.H. 1935. The Standard Cyclopedia of Horticulture, Vol. I. The Macmillan Co., New York.

BARNES, M.M. *et al.* 1965. Almonds, pest and disease control. Calif. Agric. Exp. Stn. Serv. Leaf. *69.* Rev.

BLUMENTHAL, S. 1947. Food Products. Chem. Publ. Co., Brooklyn, N.Y.

BRYAN, H.C. 1965. The almond industry in Spain. FAS-M-165. U.S. Dep. Agric.

BRYAN, H.C. 1966. The almond industry in Italy. FAS-M-174. U.S. Dep. Agric.

FULLER, A.S. 1904. The Nut Culturist. Orange Judd Co., New York.

HASTINGS, J. 1937. Dictionary of the Bible. Chas. Scribner's Sons, New York.

KESTER, E.B. 1949. Minor oil-producing crops of the United States. J. Am. Oil Chem. Soc. *26,* 65-85.

KUZIO, W. 1977. Nutmeat roundup. Candy Ind. *142* (6) 25-42.

MEITH, C., and RIZZI, A.D. 1965. Almond Production, Part I. Establishing the orchard. Univ. Calif. Agric. Ext. Serv. AXT-83.

MEITH, C., and RIZZI, A.D. 1965. Almond Production, Part II. Care of the orchard. Univ. Calif. Agric. Ext. Serv. AXT-29.

MOLDENKE, H.N., and MOLDENKE, A.L. 1952. Plants of the Bible. Botanica Co., Waltham, Mass.

POWELL, J.V. 1964. Domestic tree nut industries. Agric. Econ. Rept. *62,* U.S. Dep. Agric.

VELASCO, M., SCHONER, C., JR., and LOFGREEN, G.P. 1965. Composition and feeding value of almond hulls and hull-shell meal. Calif. Agric. *19* (3) 12-14.

7

Brazil Nuts

The Brazil nut (*Bertholletia myrtaceae* or *B. excelsa*) is not grown anywhere in the United States due to the tenderness of the tree. It is indigenous to the Amazon region and attempts to produce it elsewhere have not been commercially successful. The Brazil nut is one of the principal products exported from the Amazon basin, and the industry is one of the most important in the economy of the area, and the most picturesque of the world's edible tree nut industries.

TABLE 7.1

BRAZIL NUT PRODUCTION, 1971-76

Year	1000 metric tons
1971	22.5
1972	50.0
1973	60.0
1974	42.3
1975	56.0
1976	32.0

Source: Foreign Agric. Serv., FN 1-76.

They form large forests on the banks of the Amazon and Rio Negro rivers in South America.

Large quantities of Brazil nuts are shipped from Para and received at New York, New Orleans and other ports, where they are placed in storage at 1.1° to 7.2°C (34° to 45°F) with a relative humidity of 65 to 70% (Lee 1946).

The 1976 output of Brazil nuts was 32,000 tons, down about 43% from the 1975 crop of 56,000 tons (Table 7.1). Trade reports indicate that Brazil nut production as a commercial crop is on the decline. Sources

181

state that development of other economic activities in the Amazon Basin means a greater number of other opportunities for the available labor force. In addition, the formation of pastures for large cattle-raising operations has resulted in destruction of many Brazil nut groves.

TABLE 7.2

BRAZIL NUT EXPORTS, 1971-76

Year	1000 metric tons
1971	35.0
1972	48.0
1973	55.6
1974	34.3
1975	55.0
1976	30.5

Source: Foreign Agric. Serv., FN 1-76.

The large consumers of these nuts, such as West Germany, the United Kingdom and the United States, can expect to see higher prices. Additionally, a large decline in Brazil's nut industry could also benefit the U.S. tree nut family. As fewer Brazil nuts are produced and exported, traditional consumers may begin to substitute almonds, walnuts or pecans.

Domestic consumption of Brazil nuts is usually considered insignificant, as Brazil exports the majority of its nuts. Industry officials place the annual domestic usage at about 1500 tons. Stocks are usually non-existent, as the nuts are highly susceptible to spoilage. Spoiled nuts are crushed for oil. The Government of Brazil maintains a program of minimum prices for producers and processors of Brazil nuts.

GROWING AREAS

The temperature in the Amazon Basin along and near the banks of rivers is relatively uniform and the humidity is high. Temperatures during the year vary from 17° to 38°C (64° to 101°F).

The rainfall in the Amazon Basin is heavy and typical of the tropics in this part of the world.

The Brazil nut tree is found scattered throughout the entire Amazon Basin. Its northern limit is southern Venezuela and Guyana, while its southern limit is the Beni Highland in northeastern Bolivia and northwestern Mato Grosso in Brazil. Its western limit is eastern Colombia and Peru near the Brazilian and Bolivian borders.

This report deals primarily with those cultivars found in Acre, Amapa, Amazonas, Guapore, Para, and Rio Branco, or, roughly speaking, in the Brazilian States and territories of the Amazon Basin. This area extends over approximately 42% of Brazil. Production in Bolivia, Guyana, Colombia, Peru, Venezuela, and Mato Grosso is relatively unimportant. Exports from these areas generally move to market via the Brazilian States of Amazonas or Para.

The inhabitants of the Amazon Basin are known as caboclos, meaning "copper colored ones." The term originally referred to Indians but now includes the whites, mestizos, mulattoes, Indians and Negroes who live in the interior. It is from the ranks of these caboclos that the castanheiros, or nut gatherers, are drawn.

There are two types of caboclos—the permanent residents of the Amazon Basin and the migratory workers who come into the area from other parts of Brazil. Whenever drought or other adverse weather or economic conditions prevail in northeastern Brazil, large numbers of laborers migrate to the Amazon Basin to work for a season or longer.

The Amazon Basin is larger than the combined area of the 11 western states of the United States, or more than eight times the size of California. It is nearly a hundred times as large as the Netherlands, whose citizens were said to have been the first foreigners to recognize the value of the Brazil nut. The wooded area alone is seven times the size of California. It is, for the most part, dense tropical jungle. There are as many as 150 cultivars of trees to an acre, and it is said that there are more than 2500 cultivars in the territory. The number of bearing castanha trees in Brazil is unknown, because of the nature of the region. A mathematical approach to the solution of this question might be made by dividing total average annual production by the estimated yield per tree. The average annual production for the 10 years 1933 to 1942 was 41,100 short tons, and the average yield per tree is said to be from 500 to 800 lb of nuts, not including weight of the outer shell. If the lower figure of 500 lb is used, it is indicated that some 165,000 trees are harvested during an average year. The yield, however, may average considerably less, and there are hundreds of thousands of trees from which the fruit is never harvested.

There are only three commercial plantings of Brazil nuts in the Brazilian portion of the Amazon Basin. The largest plantation is located near Boa Vista in the Federal Territory of Rio Branco in the north of the state of Amazonas. It contains about 14,000 trees and produces from 84 to 112 tons of unshelled nuts per year.

The second largest plantation is located near Parintins in Amazonas. This plantation, containing an estimated 12,000 trees, was planted by a Japanese agricultural firm but has since passed into the hands of a Brazil nut exporting firm in Manaus. The production from this plantation is still very limited as the trees are still young.

The third plantation is located near Manaus and contains about 4000 trees. This planting was made in conjunction with an attempt to start a rubber plantation. The rubber trees for various reasons died and the plantation was for some years abandoned. It has since been revived as a Brazil nut plantation and is producing on a commercial scale.

These three plantations are relatively young as far as Brazil nut trees go and do not supply an accurate guide as to the economic feasibility of plantations. The abundance of wild trees and the length of time and cost involved to bring a plantation into profitable bearing makes the venture somewhat doubtful from a profit point of view. There are a number of advantages to having such plantations but there are also disadvantages. A well-planned plantation would permit the use of wagons or other means of transportation of the pods from the base of the trees to some central point where they might be cut open with power saws or other type of equipment. Such a plantation also would offer the owner an opportunity to estimate the probable tonnage he would harvest and thus would permit him to sell at better advantage. It would also reduce the number of laborers required to harvest the nuts. The probable returns from such a plantation would generally not justify the expenditure during the lifetime of the person planting them. However, 30 years or more after planting, such a venture might be profitable. The planting of Brazil nuts in conjunction with other short-term jungle crops might be feasible economically.

BRAZIL NUT TREES AND FRUIT

The Brazil nut tree is one of the largest in the Amazon Basin, being from 75 to 150 ft high, and usually reaches well above the surrounding jungle. The height of the tree depends on its age, the soil, and other growing factors.

The trunk of the Brazil nut tree is generally smooth and is covered with a brown or ash-colored bark. It is very straight and devoid of lower branches. The crown of the tree spreads out like that of the American white oak and is often as much as 100 ft in diameter. It is covered with large oblong-shaped leaves that are dark green and deeply ribbed. The base of the tree is usually well buttressed, and at maturity the trunk is from 4 to 6 ft in diameter. A few trees were observed with trunks as much as 10 ft in diameter.

The wood is clear-grained and gray in color. The long, straight, thick trunk makes good saw timber, though relatively few trees are felled for lumber because the trees are more valuable for nut production. The bark of the Brazil nut is used in the manufacture of oakum and a coarse cloth used by natives. The bark is also pounded into flexibility for use as sleeping mats by the nut gatherers and as containers for other jungle products.

The fruit of the tree is a sort of large, woody, shelled capsule, closely resembling a coconut without its husk. The pod is dark brown and from 3 to 8 in. in diameter. It is known as an ourico, which in Portuguese means "rough prickly shell of chestnut covered with bristles or bristle-like attachments." This description is not altogether accurate because the pod's outer covering is rough but is not covered with bristles. The outer covering of the pod is composed of a brown vegetable substance about ¼ in. thick. This covering in some respects resembles the outer covering of the Persian walnut. Unlike that of the walnut, however, it becomes very hard, though somewhat brittle. After the pod falls to the ground the outer covering begins to break, the splits becoming larger the longer the pod remains on the ground. In the Spanish-speaking countries the pod is referred to as a coco.

Inside the outer shell is a very hard, fibrous, rough pod about ¼ in. thick. This pod resembles a huge black walnut after the husk is removed and contains from 12 to 20 nuts. The pod, when cut and polished, in some respects resembles the grain of bird's-eye maple. There appears to be no uniformity as to the number of nuts per pod on any given tree. Several pods from the same tree were cut open and found to contain different numbers of nuts. The experiment was repeated in several different areas with the same result. This divergence is probably due to incomplete pollination, which results in the development of only a part of the nuts.

The nuts are arranged in the pod similar to the segments of an orange and are held in place by a fibrous growth. This fibrous substance dries as the fruit matures. When the pod falls from the tree to the ground, the impact breaks the fiber into small pieces and loosens the nuts within the pod. If a pod is turned upside down and shaken, the small bits of broken fiber drop out of the stem end. The opening at the stem end of an average pod is about as large as a dime.

The tree grows wild and is propagated by the small nuts in the pods. A notion was prevalent in the Amazon Basin and elsewhere for many years that only the nuts in the pods would germinate, but nuts have been germinated at experiment stations after they were removed from the pod. It usually requires three months or more for the nuts to sprout. In prewar years (about 1940) the experimental plantation at Kuala Lumpur in the Malay Peninsula found that approximately 50% of the nuts planted germinated. Germination would require from 3 to 12 months after planting of the seed. The results obtained in Malaya may be due in part to conditions prevailing in that area. Experiment station records for

Brazil are not available. Under natural conditions, however, it was observed that the germination rate was high and the length of time was shorter than that reported for Malaya. Some nuts were found that were alleged to have germinated in about a month. The young tree reaches a height of about a foot the first year and thereafter grows with fair rapidity, reaching a height of 15 to 20 ft in a period of five years. The tree fights its way above the surrounding jungle but grows at a somewhat slower rate after the fifth or sixth year.

The Brazil nut tree is usually found growing on well-drained ground and seldom within the reach of high water. The tree prefers a clay or clay-loam soil, from 50 to 100 ft from streams or swamps. The trees are usually found in groups of six or more, often forming fair-sized groves. They also are found so far inland that the difficulty in transporting the nuts to the waterways precludes their being harvested.

The tree begins to flower in its fifth or sixth year but little fruit is produced until the twelfth to fifteenth year. Flowering takes place from October to March in most of the producing areas, though in some sections, such as Acre and Rio Negro, blossoming takes place slightly earlier. The flowers grow in cream or white clusters and resemble in some respects the ornamental hydrangea of the United States.

The flowers are borne on the small outer branches. There are generally several clusters of flowers on the same branch, but as a rule only 2 or 3 produce fruit. Pollination appears to be effected by insects flying from one tree to another.

It is usually at least a year from the blossom state to the time when the pods mature and drop to the ground. A point of particular interest is that blossoms and mature, or nearly mature, fruit are found on the Brazil nut tree at the same time. The quantity of blossoms on the tree in a current year, therefore, gives a preliminary indication of the potential yield a year hence. Such a preliminary indication on a commercial plantation of fruits or nuts would normally be of considerable help in forecasting production. In the case of Brazil nuts, however, it is only a partial indication as to what the harvested crop will be because of a great many unpredictable factors. These are chiefly the availability of labor, the amount of water in streams, the occurrence of severe windstorms and rainstorms before fruit is mature, causing it to fall prematurely, and the prices offered by trading posts to natives.

There is comparatively little loss from diseases or insect pests, according to the information available. There is a loss when pods crack and air and rain are admitted, causing the nuts to mold. This cracking may be brought about by disease or insects. However, since it is physically impossible to examine the pods on the tree, because of their great height, the cause must remain unknown, for the time being at least. Another source of loss is a small jungle rodent, similar in some respects to a squirrel or wood rat, which carries off many nuts for food.

The trees bear about the same quantity of nuts each year, provided growing conditions are satisfactory. The effect of a heavy yield one year on that of the following year is considerably less noticeable than in the case of such cultivated nuts as almonds. Severe storms during the blossoming and pollination period, however, cause a light set for the following year. Since the Amazon Basin is in the tropics, no frost damage ever occurs. The vast area in which these trees are found naturally make losses due to the weather inevitable in some parts of the region each year. The total harvest is therefore not materially affected by weather conditions, and the economic factors mentioned are far more important in determining production.

HARVESTING BRAZIL NUTS

Harvesting Season

The pods, or ouricos, that contain the commercial Brazil nut begin to drop from the trees in late November and continue into early June. There is a slight variation in the season according to the section of the country. Those in Acre and Rio Negro are usually the first to ripen. Because of the immense size of the tree and the pod, the pods are never gathered by ascending the tree.

The action of the winds breaks the heavy pods loose and they drop to the ground. Laborers make it a point not to be under the trees on windy or rainy days; and even on calm days they are constantly on guard against falling ouricos. The pods weigh from 2 to 4 lb and fall at the rate of from 800 to 1000 ft per minute. If a laborer is unfortunate enough to be hit by a falling pod he may suffer serious injury, if not death.

The harvesting period in general is from November to June, and its activity is dependent upon the availability of labor, which in turn is more or less determined by prices received for the nuts at the barracao, or trading post. When prices of unshelled nuts go down to a level where returns to labor are no longer attractive, gathering stops or is greatly reduced. On the other hand, since the vast bulk of the annual production must be transported by water, a cessation of gathering operations during the rainy or high-water period makes it difficult to bring additional supplies to tidewater even should prices strengthen appreciably.

The dampness and heat of the region make it impossible to store one year's production of Brazil nuts in the jungle for disposal the following year. The nuts are almost certain to spoil, and, therefore, there can be no carry-over. When nuts are said to be "abandoned" in the jungle, the word is used literally.

Methods of Harvesting

The gathering or harvesting operations are comparatively simple. The caboclo and possibly the members of his family collect the pods in baskets or throw them out from under the trees and collect them later. The pods are then carried to the camp where they are cut open with a tercado, a long knife similar to a sugarcane knife and one of the prized possessions of all caboclos. The task of cutting open the pods is usually reserved for days on which it is dangerous to be under the trees because of the wind or rain. The pod, which is extremely hard and requires considerable effort to open, contains from 12 to 20 nuts. The nuts are put into a basket or on mats on the ground until a sufficient quantity has been collected to deliver to the local trading post.

The nuts are washed by the castanheiro and then sold in lots of approximately 1 hectoliter (about 112 lb). The empty pods are used for fuel in the caboclo's camp or are discarded, though a few are used for cups and other household utensils.

In the interior and at the trading post, Brazil nuts are stored in the open. Whether the land on which the trees are found is publicly or privately owned makes little difference to the caboclo. Where the land is privately owned, he is compelled by law to deliver the produce to the owner. If the land is publicly owned, the caboclo may collect nuts and other products without payment of taxes and may sell wherever he chooses. There is no control exercised by the State over harvesting on publicly owned land. During the past 30 years, however, most of the suitable Brazil nut areas have passed into private hands in one way or another.

TRADING POSTS

Trading posts are usually located a few miles apart on the banks of the larger streams in the Brazil nut area. There is little incentive for the caboclo to carry his produce any farther than the nearest post. He exchanges his produce, which in addition to Brazil nuts may include rubber, hides, cacao, tonka beans and other commodities, for such items as hardware, matches, cotton cloth, beans, mandioca, flour, dried beef and sugar.

The price received by the caboclo for his nuts indirectly affected by the F.O.B. price in Belem and Manaus; that is, the more difficult the transportation to the export centers, the higher the freight and, consequently, the smaller the amount paid the caboclo.

Each trader has from a few to perhaps as many as 200 or more caboclo customers in his trading area. He collects the various commodities received in trade until he has enough to ship to Belem or Manaus, where he disposes of them through brokers or exporters.

The combined collection of Brazil nuts by these traders runs into a substantial tonnage each year, and this tonnage, rather than the total yield of all the trees in the Amazon Basin, is the "production" given in Brazil nut statistics.

The production of nuts depends not so much on the yield of the trees as it does on foreign demand. If there were sufficient foreign demand at remunerative levels, production would be greatly expanded. Strong foreign demand would result in higher prices, which in turn would cause traders in the interior to make more effort to tap areas normally not harvested. As it is, only the most readily accessible stands are now being worked.

The trend of the Brazil nut industry is toward encouraging the exportation of shelled rather than unshelled nuts. The shelling industry gives employment in Brazil and, furthermore, shelled nuts bring more foreign exchange than the unshelled. The profits derived by the trade in Brazil from shelled nuts tend to be a little larger than on unshelled exports, and there is less worry about spoilage, shrinkage, and outturn weights at destination. Furthermore, shelling costs in Brazil are considerably lower than they are in the United States and other Northern Hemisphere countries.

THE BRAZIL NUT SHELLING INDUSTRY

The largest of the shelling plants in Belem has an annual production capacity in excess of 1300 tons of shelled Brazil nuts. It employs more than 1000 workers during the peak season and prepares both shelled and blanched nuts. The plant is one of the most modern and hygienic in Brazil. Great care is given to grade, quality and sanitation. The industry is justly proud of this shelling plant and its efforts toward bettering foreign demand by constantly striving to improve the quality of its product. This plant has inspired other shellers to modernize their plants and operations.

Shelling plants buy their unshelled nuts through brokers much the same as do exporters of unshelled nuts. Many shellers, in fact, are also exporters of unshelled nuts. The sheller, however, is in a slightly better position on purchases than is the exporter of unshelled nuts. He can buy odd and distressed lots and store them until needed. Many shelling-plant operators buy for future delivery, although this sometimes works out to their disadvantage. The sheller can buy at times when foreign demand is slack and he need not worry about the grading of the shelled nuts as to size. His average cost of unshelled, therefore, is usually slightly below that of the exporter of unshelled nuts. The shelling plant usually manages to keep sufficient unshelled nuts on hand to keep the plant running steadily all season.

The nuts to be shelled are placed in large cement vats and covered with water. They are permitted to soak about 24 hours and then are placed in boiling water for from 3 to 5 min to soften the shell. After the nuts are removed from the boiling water, they are taken into the cracking room.

The cracking machines are hand operated and in many respects resemble a home bottle capper, such as is used in the United States. The nuts are placed endwise in a small cup, and the handle of the machine is pressed down until the shell breaks. Care must be taken in this work not to exert too much pressure on the shell and so damage the kernel. In a few of the smaller plants a small piece of iron or a wooden club is used instead of a machine.

Several pounds of nuts are cracked and the kernels and shells are thrown to one side of the bench. The worker then sorts out the sound kernels and pieces and places them in a small wooden box. The shells and spoiled kernels are used as fuel in the furnaces to supply heat for the dryers and power for the shelling plant.

The dried nuts are passed to graders for sizing. For blanched nuts the brown skin is removed before the nuts go to the dryers.

The ratio of unshelled to shelled nuts varies somewhat. At the beginning of the season a loss of at least 1% must be figured for bad nuts and foreign matter, such as dirt, pebbles and sticks. This percentage increases as the season advances, sometimes reaching more than 5%. The average shellout from a hectoliter of 112 lb of good quality unshelled nuts is about 40 lb of kernels, though it varies from 35 to 44 lb. In actual practice a hectoliter of Brazil nuts at export centers may weigh as much as 120 lb and as little as 105. The weight depends on the moisture content and size of the nuts and on the variation of thickness of the shell, as well as on the spoilage, shrinkage, etc.

It should be noted that the estimated shelling ratio is somewhat higher than is normally used for these nuts in the United States. The unshelled nuts received in the United States have been cleaned of the foreign matter and most of the spoiled nuts, commonly found in the shipments from the interior, have also lost some of their moisture.

COMPOSITION OF BRAZIL NUTS

Brazil nuts have two important components which add to their nutritive value—protein and fat. The oil contains significant amounts of linoleic and oleic acids. Biological tests show that both the oil and nut press-cake may be suitable for both human and animal diets (Elias and Bressani 1961).

The kernel of the Brazil nut contains from 65 to 70% oil, which is of a pale yellow color. In normal times production of oil is limited, as it is extracted only as a by-product from spoiled, surplus, and sometimes broken or low-grade nuts. During World War II when exports were curtailed, surplus nuts on hand were crushed for oil; however, the venture was not profitable. The oil is generally used for soap and other industrial purposes.

TABLE 7.3

PROXIMATE COMPOSITION OF THE BRAZIL NUT

Nutrient	Decorticated Nut %	Flour %
Moisture	2.00	15.60
Protein (N x 6.25)	16.30	44.80
Ether extract	68.30	6.44
Crude fiber	6.60	7.80
Ash	3.61	7.36

TABLE 7.4

PROPERTIES OF CRUDE BRAZIL NUT OIL

	Solvent Extracted	Pressure Extracted
Iodine value (Wijs)	98.10	99.60
Unsaponifiable	0.61	0.54
Lovibond color	35 yellow/3.39 red	3 yellow/0.47 red
Fatty acids		
Myristic	0.01%	0.05%
Palmitic	16.60	13.85
Palmitoleic	0.30	0.45
Stearic	10.35	10.25
Oleic	31.00	30.50
Linoleic	41.65	44.90
Total	99.91	100.00

The relatively high cost of producing oil from Brazil nuts compared with oils from other oilseeds will probably prevent a major industrial development in this commodity.

The food value of Brazil nuts is high compared with that of fruits and other nuts. One ounce of Brazil nuts contains 197 calories. This figure is higher than that for all other nuts except pecans and walnuts. It is said that two Brazil nut kernels have the same caloric food value as an average-sized egg (Schrieber 1950).

EXPORTATION OF BRAZIL NUTS

Brazil nuts are sold to exporters through brokers by private negotiation, and the auction market, as such, no longer exists. Sales through brokers are much the same as auction sales, for brokers offer the merchandise to several exporters, the highest bidder receiving the nuts. The number of exporting firms, however, is relatively small, and the prices offered or asked are generally only a fraction apart. At times the prices offered by all the exporters and quoted by the brokers on a given day are identical.

The broker bases his offers to sell to exporters on what he thinks the New York and other foreign markets will pay. If there is a strong demand from abroad, he advances his prices to exporters. Conversely, if there is little demand, prices go down.

The selling and buying procedure for Brazil nuts varies somewhat, but, in general, follows the usual pattern of international trade. The Brazilian exporter usually is represented by a broker in New York, and in other American markets, who attempts to sell importers there and who cables offers to buy or requests firm offers for prospective customers. If offers from New York are not high enough, only sufficient nuts are sold to keep the American importers interested.

TABLE 7.5

BRAZIL NUT IMPORTS INTO UNITED STATES

Country of Origin	1968-69	1969-70	1970-71	1971-72	1972-73	1973-74
			(metric tons)			
In-Shell						
Brazil	9451	6786	7008	7868	9515	5704
Other	80	12	28	110	68	40
Total	9531	6798	7036	7978	9583	5744
Shelled						
Bolivia	1075	1258	696	801	319	578
Brazil	5694	3955	5454	5295	6507	4877
Chile	52	153	28	1	33	33
India	180	31	12	48	30	–
Peru	435	113	382	244	237	106
United Kingdom	79	91	93	41	177	105
Other	16	171	134	68	50	43
Total	7531	5772	6799	6498	7353	5742

Source: Foreign Agric. Serv., FN 1-76.

Export of Shelled Nuts

Shelled nuts purchased in the United States or elsewhere at much below the prevailing price are generally of inferior quality. Some exporters of shelled nuts who consistently underbid the market price ship nuts of the lowest possible quality that will be accepted. The whole industry is injured by such trading, and every effort should be made to prevent it.

Data on production and export of Brazil nuts are shown in Tables 7.1 and 7.2. Brazil nut production statistics are at best only estimates, but by repeated checking from month to month they represent rather closely both production and exports. The condition of the rivers influences the production (quantity of nuts harvested).

There appears to be little information to indicate any material change in the pattern and volume of Brazilian exports of this nut to the United States. There will, of course, be seasonal fluctuations resulting from the size of the harvest and the level of consumer demand. Any nut regardless of its high food value is generally considered a luxury or semiluxury item. It follows that when the consuming public is well supplied with funds consumption goes up and when funds are short consumption declines.

USING BRAZIL NUTS

Brazil nuts require precaution in handling. They are subject to bruising, molding and insect infestation. Since they are high in protein and fat, they are subject to staleness, rancidity, loss of natural flavor and absorption of foreign flavors. Like pecans, they respond to low humidity and low temperature storage.

Shelling, blanching, slicing, chopping and grinding tend to stimulate the rancidity because of multiplying the amount of surface exposed to light and air. Therefore, nuts so processed should be (a) vacuum packed, (b) held in a cold, dark environment, or (c) used within a limited time.

Brazil nuts are good when eaten raw from the shell. They are excellent for roasting and salting, for ice cream and for bakery products, but are used most extensively in confections.

The variety of formulas presented in this book indicates the wide range of uses for Brazils in confections. These formulas were especially developed for Brazil nuts by Applied Sugar Laboratories, Inc., of New York under the personal supervision of A. King, director, of the Nulomoline Company, and the Brazil Nut Association (discontinued). These formulas are offered merely as suggestions. The addition of Brazils to formulas will add variety and result in the production of new, delicious pieces and bars.

Some of the formulas are designed primarily for wholesale manufacturers and some are designed primarily for retailers. The letter "W" after the formula indicates a wholesale formula, and "R," a retail formula.

BRITTLES AND CRUNCHES

Brazil Nut Caramel Chips (R)

7 lb sugar	2½ lb sliced Brazil nuts
3 lb corn syrup	Flavor as desired
2 qt cream	Salt to taste
(20% butter fat)	

Place one quart of cream into a clean pan, add the sugar and corn syrup and stir the batch until it boils. Then gradually add the balance of the cream and cook the batch to a hard crack, 150° to 155°C (310° to 315°F). Then add the sliced Brazil nuts, salt and flavoring as desired. (Suggested flavoring: vanilla, maple, chocolate, rum.) Turn the batch out on a greased slab and as it cools fold it together and when sufficiently firm pass it through drop rolls in the form of chips. The chips may be wrapped in paper or if properly protected from moisture they may be sold "as is."

Brazil Nut Butter Snaps (R)

6 lb sugar	1½ lb hard coconut butter
1 lb corn syrup	3 lb sliced Brazil nuts
1½ lb dairy butter	½ tsp bicarbonate soda

Place the sugar and corn syrup into a kettle with sufficient water to dissolve the sugar. Mix well, then bring the batch to the boiling point. Add the dairy butter and coconut butter and cook the batch to a good crack, 148° to 150°C (300° to 310°F). Remove the batch from the fire, add the nuts, then the soda, mix thoroughly and spread on an oiled slab. When the batch is partially cooled turn it upside down and cut with roller knife or break it into rough pieces. This piece may be sold "as is" or it may be coated with milk or vanilla chocolate. It is also practical to grind or break this candy into small pieces and use it in ice cream.

CARAMEL TYPE CANDIES

Brazil Nut Caramel for Casting (W)

50 lb corn syrup	6 oz powdered salt
50 lb condensed milk (sweetened)	Flavor as desired
5 lb coconut oil	Ground Brazil nuts as
50 lb casting fondant	needed

Place the corn syrup, condensed milk, coconut oil into a caramel cooking kettle and boil the batch to a medium firm ball, then add the fondant and salt and mix well. Add the flavoring and deposit the batch into starch impressions to form bulk shapes or bars. Coat the caramels with icing, either by hand or by machine, and roll in ground Brazil nuts.

Chocolate Icing for Brazil Nut Caramels (W)

10 lb coconut oil
20 lb powdered sugar
Flavor as desired
10 lb cocoa
3 lb powdered milk
35 lb powdered sugar

7½ lb water
1½ oz salt
8 oz gelatin
10 lb invert sugar
5 lb coconut oil

Cream the first portion of the sugar (20 lb), flavoring and coconut oil until light. In the meantime, separately blend the cocoa, milk and the remainder of the sugar. Also, add the salt and gelatin to the water. Heat the soaked gelatin until fluid, and then dissolve the invert sugar in the gelatin solution. To the dissolved invert sugar, add the 5 lb of coconut oil, preferably coconut butter, and then heat the whole mixture until the coconut butter is melted. (By adjusting the temperature of this mixture, the final temperature of the batch may be regulated. Working conditions determine final batch temperatures; however, about 82°C (180°F) usually gives good results.) Add the blended cocoa, milk and powdered sugar, along with the warm mixture to the creamed mass. Beat the whole batch until it is smooth. Ground Brazil nuts may be mixed in the icing.

Brazil Nut Stand-Up Caramels (W)

60 lb corn syrup
12 lb hard coconut butter
(or part dairy butter)
10 lb invert sugar
100 lb condensed milk
(sweetened)

30 lb fine granulated sugar
6 oz powdered salt
15 lb raisins
20 lb broken Brazil nuts
Vanilla and butter flavorings

Place the coconut butter or butter, corn syrup, invert sugar, condensed milk and sugar into a kettle equipped with stirrers, turn the steam on partly and mix until the batch becomes fluid, then boil the batch rapidly to a soft ball, then add the Brazil nuts and raisins and cook to a firm ball. Add the salt and flavorings, mix thoroughly, then turn the batch out on an oiled slab and when cold, cut and size and wrap in waxed paper or transparent cellulose.

NOTE: It is also practical to sprinkle broken Brazil nuts over the caramel, pressing them into the batch before the batch is cold.

Brazil Nut Toffee Squares (W)

20 lb corn syrup
5 lb invert sugar

5 lb dairy butter
5 lb hard coconut butter

25 lb condensed milk
(sweetened)
10 lb fine granulated sugar
10 lb light brown sugar

4 oz salt (powdered)
Trace of vanilla flavoring
Trace of almond flavoring
7 lb sliced Brazil nuts

Heat the dairy butter, coconut butter, corn syrup, condensed milk and invert sugar together until the fats are dissolved, then add the fine granulated sugar and brown sugar, mix well and boil the batch to a soft ball, then add the sliced Brazil nuts and cook the batch to a firm ball. Now add the powdered salt and flavorings, mix well and spread the batch out ⅜ in. high and immediately cut with a toffee square frame or marker. A roller knife may also be used to cut the batch into squares or slabs weighing ⅛, ¼, or ½ lb. It is also practical to sprinkle broken Brazil nuts over the surface of the toffee while warm. Wrap the toffee in transparent cellulose or waxed paper.

Brazil Nut Caramel Kisses (W)

40 lb corn syrup
30 lb fine granulated sugar
15 lb invert sugar
2 lb hard coconut butter
4 lb dairy butter
8 lb water

20 lb condensed milk (sweetened)
5 oz powdered salt
10 lb frappe or nougat creme
Egg nog flavoring
Apple flavoring
12 lb sliced or broken Brazil nuts

Place into a kettle the corn syrup, sugar, invert sugar, coconut butter, dairy butter and water and stir until the batch boils. Wash down all grains of sugar from the inside of the kettle and boil the batch rapidly to 135°C (275°F); then add the condensed milk, stirring rapidly, and cook the batch to 135° to 137°C (275° to 280°F). Now add the frappe, salt and flavoring and turn the batch out on an oiled slab and when partially cooled, pull it well on the hook, then knead in the Brazil nuts and roll it down into sheet. Then cut into oblongs or strips. The batch may be cut into kiss shapes and wrapped in transparent cellulose or waxed paper.

Brazil Nut Caramel Taffy (R)

4 lb sugar
4 lb corn syrup
2 qt cream (20% butter fat)

Lemon flavoring
Powdered salt to taste
2½ lb sliced Brazil nuts

Place into a kettle 1 qt of the cream, the sugar, and the corn syrup. Place the batch on the fire, stir constantly until it boils, then gradually add the remainder of the cream and boil the batch to a medium firm ball. Add the Brazil nuts, lemon flavoring and salt and spread the batch on an oiled slab about ¼ in. high. When cold cut into strips 1 × 3 in. and wrap in transparent cellulose or wax paper. Suggested flavorings: vanilla, raspberry, orange, coffee and chocolate. For chocolate flavor add ¾ lb of unsweetened chocolate shortly after the batch has boiled.

Brazil Nut Amazon Toffee (W)
Part 1

1 lb albumen
2 lb water
4 lb standardized invert sugar

Dissolve the albumen in the water, add the standardized invert sugar and beat until light.

Part 2

45 lb corn syrup	3 lb coconut oil—76°
10 lb standardized invert	melting point
sugar	6 lb sweetened condensed
20 lb granulated sugar	milk
Water to dissolve the sugar	4 oz powdered salt
	8 lb sliced Brazil nuts

Cook the corn syrup, invert sugar, granulated sugar and water to 140° to 143°C (285° to 290°F) (sea level), add the coconut oil, condensed milk and salt and mix well, then gradually pour this into the whipped batch (Part 1) beating continuously until well mixed. Then add coloring, flavoring and 8 lb of sliced or broken Brazil nuts. Spread the batch on an oiled slab to form a sheet ¼ in. thick and when cool, cut into bars, strips, squares or into sheets to fit into pans. Wrap in waxed paper or coat in chocolate. Suggested flavorings: strawberry, chocolate, vanilla, orange, lemon, etc.

Brazil Nut Grained Caramel (R)

8 lb corn syrup	1½ oz salt (powdered)
2 lb invert sugar	5 lb raisins
5 lb granulated sugar	6 lb broken Brazil nuts
2 qt cream (20% butter fat)	Orange and vanilla flavorings
1 lb hard coconut butter	to taste
3 qt evaporated milk (unsweetened)	8 lb short fondant

Place into a kettle 1½ qt of the cream, add the sugar, invert sugar, corn syrup and coconut butter and bring to the boiling point, stirring constantly. Add the remainder of the cream and the evaporated milk, about a pint at a time, and boil the batch to a firm ball. Add the Brazil nuts, raisins, salt and 8 lb of short fondant, flavoring. Mix thoroughly and spread the batch out between bars on an oiled slab. When cold cut into oblongs about ¾ × ¾ × 1 ⅓ in. long. Place into paper cups or coat with chocolate.

Caramel Coating for Brazil Nuts (R)

5 lb corn syrup	3 lb sugar
1 lb hard coconut butter	Salt to taste
4 lb condensed whole milk	Vanilla flavoring
(sweetened)	Brazil nuts for dipping

Place the coconut butter and corn syrup into a kettle and heat to dissolve the butter. Then add the condensed milk and sugar, mix well, boil the batch, stirring constantly, and cook to a medium soft ball. Add the salt and flavoring, mix well. This caramel coating may be used for coating Brazil nuts. Dip the Brazil nuts into the caramel and drop the coated nuts on top of finely ground Brazil nuts, colored green. (For chocolate flavored caramel coating use ½ lb of coconut butter and ¾ lb of unsweetened chocolate along with the coconut butter.)

CHEWING CANDIES

Brazil Fruit Slices (W)

20 lb granulated sugar	3 oz salt (powdered)
Water to dissolve sugar	10 lb short fondant
15 lb corn syrup	5 lb frappe
5 lb standardized invert sugar	10 lb whole Brazil nuts
	Vanilla flavoring, white coloring
15 lb medium desiccated coconut	Pineapple flavoring, yellow coloring
8 lb diced assorted preserved fruits	Roman punch, pink coloring

Boil the sugar, corn syrup, invert sugar and water to 118° to 121°C (245° to 250°F), add the coconut, diced fruit, salt and fondant and mix until the fondant is melted, then add the frappe and Brazil nuts and mix well. Divide the batch into three parts. Add vanilla flavoring to one part; pineapple flavoring and yellow coloring to the second portion; and Roman punch and pink coloring to the third portion. Spread the batch out in layers on waxed paper. When they have set, they may be cut into slices, blocks, bars or small pieces.

Brazil Nut Chewing Coconut Bar (W)
Part 1

3 lb water
25 lb medium or long shred desiccated
   unsweetened coconut
20 lb invert sugar
4 oz powdered salt
15 lb sliced Brazil nuts

Heat the invert sugar until dissolved, add the water and mix this with the desiccated coconut and salt. Set this aside for 15 min.

Part 2

50 lb corn syrup
3 lb hard coconut butter

Raspberry flavoring
Red coloring

Boil the corn syrup to 118° to 121°C (245° to 250°F), pour this into the coconut batch, adding the coconut butter, coloring and flavoring and mix well. Now add the 15 lb of sliced Brazil nuts, mix thoroughly and spread the batch out on an oiled and well-dusted slab. Roll the batch down to the required height. When cold, cut into squares, strips or bars and wrap in waxed paper, transparent cellulose or coat with chocolate.

Brazil Nut Butterscotch for Wrapping (W)

10 lb condensed milk	10 lb invert sugar
(sweetened)	1 qt good grade
7 lb hard coconut	molasses
butter	6 oz salt
5 lb dairy butter	Lemon, mace, bergamot
30 lb corn syrup	and rum flavorings
35 lb granulated sugar	12 lb sliced Brazil nuts
2 qt water	

Place the coconut butter, dairy butter and condensed milk into a kettle and heat all together until the fats are dissolved, then add the sugar, corn syrup, invert sugar, molasses and 2 qt of water and boil the batch to a firm ball. Add the flavorings, Brazil nuts and salt, mix well, then spread the batch out on an oiled slab to cool. Size and cut into squares, oblongs, or bars.

Brazil Nut Malt Coconut Bars (W)

10 lb malt syrup	10 lb water
25 lb corn syrup	10 lb Brazil nuts
15 lb invert sugar	20 lb condensed milk
5 lb cocoa powder	(sweetened)
4 oz salt	40 lb desiccated coconut
Sufficient vanilla flavoring	(medium shred unsweetened)

Mix the desiccated coconut with the 10 lb of water, then add the malt syrup, corn syrup, invert sugar, condensed milk and cocoa powder and stir and cook the batch to a medium firm ball. Add the sliced Brazil nuts, flavoring and salt, mix thoroughly and spread the batch out on an oiled and well-dusted slab. When cold, the batch may be sized and cut into squares, oblongs, strips, or bars and wrapped in waxed paper, transparent cellulose or coated in chocolate or icing.

CREAM CENTERS

Spiced Brazil Nut Cast Cream Centers (W)
Part 1, Fondant

80 lb sugar	10 lb invert sugar

20 lb corn syrup   Water to dissolve the sugar

Boil all ingredients to 118°C (244°F). Then cool this syrup to 46° to 52°C (115° to 125°F) and beat into fondant.

Part 2, Bob Syrup

30 lb sugar   1½ oz Convertit
10 lb good grade molasses   Oil of cassia
10 lb corn syrup   Oil of cloves
Water to dissolve sugar   8 lb ground Brazil nuts

Boil together sugar, molasses, syrup and water to 113°C (236°F), then pour this into 100 lb of the fondant, mix well, then add 20 lb of frappe (formula below) and 1½ oz of Convertit and mix well. Flavor lightly with oil of cassia and oil of cloves, mix well, then add 8 lb of ground Brazil nuts and deposit into starch impressions suitable for bulk or bar goods.

Frappe

50 lb corn syrup   1 lb albumen dissolved in
50 lb invert sugar   2 lb water

Boil the corn syrup to 119°C (245°F), shut off the steam, add the invert sugar and stir until melted. Place the batch into a beater, start the beater, then gradually add the dissolved albumen and beat until light.

Brazil Nut Caramel Creams (W)
Part 1, Fondant

80 lb sugar   10 lb invert sugar
20 lb corn syrup   Water to dissolve the sugar

Boil all ingredients together to 117°C (242°F), cool 49° to 43°C (120° to 110°F), then cream.

Part 2, Bob

20 lb sugar   1½ oz Convertit
20 lb corn syrup   Salt
5 lb water   Butterscotch flavoring
20 lb condensed milk   Broken or whole Brazil
  (sweetened)   nuts
3 lb coconut oil

Boil together sugar, corn syrup, water, condensed milk and coconut oil to 115°C (240°F), then pour this into 100 lb of the fondant, mix well, then add 1½ oz of Convertit, mix well. Now add 15 lb of frappe, salt and butterscotch flavoring and mix. Cast the batch into starch impressions on top of a broken or whole Brazil nut. When cold, remove the centers from the starch and coat them with chocolate.

Frappe for Brazil Nut Caramel Creams

50 lb corn syrup	1 lb albumen dissolved in
50 lb invert sugar	2 lb of cold water

Boil the corn syrup to approximately 118°C (245°F). Shut off the steam and add the invert sugar and stir until melted. Place the batch into a marshmallow beater, start the beater, then gradually add the albumen solution and beat until light.

Brazil Nut Lemon Cast Creams (W)
Part 1, Fondant

80 lb sugar	10 lb invert sugar
20 lb corn syrup	Water to dissolve sugar

Boil all ingredients together to 117°C (242°F), cool to 48° to 43°C (120° to 110°F), then beat into a fondant.

Part 2, Bob

40 lb sugar	20 lb frappe
10 lb corn syrup	Yellow coloring
10 lb ground preserved	Citric acid to taste
lemon peel	1½ oz Convertit
Water to dissolve sugar	Broken or whole Brazil nuts

Boil the sugar, corn syrup and sufficient water to 113°C (236°F). Pour this into 100 lb of the fondant, mix well, then add the frappe, lemon peel and citric acid, color and mix well, then add 1½ oz of Convertit, mix thoroughly and cast the batch into starch impressions in which have been placed a broken or whole Brazil nut. When cold, remove from the starch and coat with chocolate.

Frappe for Brazil Nut Lemon Cast Creams

50 lb corn syrup	1 lb albumen dissolved in
50 lb invert sugar	2 lb of cold water

Boil the corn syrup to approximately 118°C (245°F). Shut off the steam, add the invert sugar and stir until melted. Place the batch into a marshmallow beater, start the beater, then gradually add the albumen solution and beat until light.

Brazil Nut Cast Whipped Creams (W)
Part 1, Fondant

80 lb sugar
20 lb corn syrup

10 lb invert sugar
Water to dissolve sugar

Boil all ingredients together to 117°C (242°F), then cool to 49° to 43°C (120° to 110°F) and cream.

Part 2, Bob

25 lb sugar
25 lb corn syrup
Water to dissolve sugar
Yellow coloring

Vanilla and pineapple flavorings
1½ oz Convertit
Whole or half Brazil nuts

Boil together sugar, corn syrup, water to 115°C (240°F). Pour this into 100 lb of the fondant, mix thoroughly, then add 30 lb of Whipped Cream Frappe (formula below), and mix well. Add vanilla and pineapple flavorings, yellow coloring and 1½ oz of Convertit, mix thoroughly and deposit the batch into starch impressions containing one whole or half a Brazil nut. When the creams have set, remove them from the starch and coat with chocolate.

Frappe for Brazil Nut Cast Whipped Creams

25 lb corn syrup
25 lb invert sugar
1 lb albumen dissolved in
2 lb cold water

½ lb low grade gelatin
dissolved in 1 lb hot water

Boil the corn syrup to 115°C (240°F), add the invert sugar and mix well. Place this into a beater, start the beater, then gradually add the dissolved albumen and beat. Now add the gelatin solution and beat until light.

Frappe for Cast Creams

50 lb corn syrup
50 lb invert sugar

1 lb albumen dissolved in
2 lb cold water

Boil the corn syrup to approximately 118°C (245°F). Shut off the steam, add the invert sugar and stir until melted, then place the batch into a marshmallow beater, start the beater, and gradually add the albumen solution and beat until light.

Brazil Nut Cream Centers (R)

16 lb sugar
1 lb corn syrup

1 teaspoonful Convertit
2 lb Brazil nuts, finely ground

1 lb invert sugar
2½ pints water

1½ lb frappe or nougat cream
Flavor as desired
Color as desired

Boil the water, sugar, corn syrup and invert sugar to 114° to 117°C (238° to 242°F). Then pour it into a cream beater and immediately sprinkle the surface of the batch with not more than 1 oz of water. When the syrup has cooled to approximately room temperature, beat it into fondant. Melt 15 lb of the fondant to 57° to 63°C (35° to 145°F). Then add 1 tsp of Convertit, flavoring and coloring as desired, and 2 lb of finely ground Brazil nuts. Mix well, then add 1½ lb of frappe or nougat cream and cast the batch into starch impressions. It is also practical to drop Brazil nuts cut in half into starch impressions and deposit the cream on top. This fondant may also be used to dip or cover whole Brazil nuts.

Cream Dipped Brazil Nuts

Boil the Brazil nuts in water for 1 min, then drain and permit them to dry. Melt a portion of the fondant, add flavoring and coloring, then dip the Brazil nuts in the fondant, placing the coated nuts on waxed paper. When cold they may be coated in milk or vanilla chocolate.

Frappe for Cast Cream Centers

Boil 10 lb of corn syrup to 118°C (245°F). Add 10 lb of invert sugar and mix until melted. Turn off the heat. Place this syrup into a beater. Start the beater, then add 4 oz of egg albumen which has been dissolved in 8 oz of cold water and beat until light. Set aside for future use.

Brazil Nut Roller Cream Centers (R)

18 lb sugar
2 lb invert sugar
3 qt water
¼ oz Convertit
(2 tsp)

3 lb light frappe or
nougat cream
Flavor and color as desired
2 lb sliced or ground
Brazil nuts

Boil the water, sugar and invert sugar to 116° to 118°C (242° to 244°F). Then pour the batch in a clean fondant beater and immediately sprinkle the surface of the batch with not more than 1 oz of cold water. When the batch cools to room temperature, add the Convertit and beat the batch until it becomes white. Then add the frappe, coloring and flavoring and when the frappe has been blended with the batch, add the Brazil nuts and beat the batch until it sets up into a moderately firm mass. When the batch is cold it may be formed into pieces of the desired size or passed through a rolled cream center machine. Coat the centers in milk or vanilla chocolate.

Note: If more than 2 oz of flavoring is used to a batch of the above weight, it may be necessary to boil the fondant batch 2 degrees higher. For larger pieces, the batch should be boiled to 119° to 121°C (248° to 250°F). If preferred, omit the addition of the sliced Brazil nuts and when rolling the cream, imbed ½ of a Brazil nut in the center and coat with chocolate.

Frappe for Rolled Cream Centers

10 lb sugar	10 lb invert sugar
3 lb water	12 oz egg albumen dissolved in
10 lb corn syrup	1½ pints water

Boil the sugar, water and corn syrup to 118°C (245°F). Then add 10 lb of invert sugar and mix until melted. Place this syrup into a marshmallow beater, start the beater, then gradually add 12 oz of egg albumen, which has been dissolved in 1½ pints of water. Beat the batch until light and set aside for future use.

Brazil Nut Butter Creams

18 lb sugar	3 lb sliced or ground Brazil nuts
2 lb invert sugar	3 pints water
1½ lb frappe or nougat	2 lb dairy butter
cream	1 tsp Convertit
Vanilla, rum, or other flavoring	

Boil the water, sugar and invert sugar to 118° to 121°C (244° to 246°F). Then pour the batch into a cold clean beater and immediately sprinkle the surface of the batch with not more than 1 oz of water.

When the batch has cooled to room temperature, add the Convertit and the dairy butter. Start the beater. When the batch becomes opaque, add the frappe and later the flavoring and Brazil nuts. Continue to work the batch until it sets up into a moderately firm mass and when cold form it into pieces of the desired size and coat with milk or vanilla chocolate.

Brazil Nut Rolled Cream Eggs (W)

40 lb granulated sugar	5 lb whole or broken Brazil nuts
10 lb standardized invert sugar	1½ lb diced preserved orange
Water to dissolve sugar	peel
½ oz invertase	1½ lb diced preserved glacé cherries
5 lb frappe, No. 1	1½ lb diced preserved grapefruit
Vanilla flavoring	peel
	1½ lb sliced Brazil nuts, colored green

Boil the sugar, standardized invert sugar and water to 121°C (250°F). Pour the batch into an open-type cream beater, and when the syrup has cooled to approximately 51°C (125°F), start beating, then add the invertase and flavoring. When the batch becomes moderately firm, add the Brazil nuts, orange peel, cherries and grapefruit peel and mix the batch no more than is necessary to distribute the nuts and fruits. When the batch is cold, form it into egg shapes or bars, dust well with powdered sugar and later coat with milk or dark chocolate.

Variation: Flavor part of the fondant with maple extract. Add burnt sugar coloring and form the batch into rolls, inserting a whole Brazil nut in the center of each egg or roll, then dust well with powdered sugar and when the rolls or eggs have set or formed a crust, coat with chocolate.

FONDANT KISSES

Spiced Brazil Nut Fondant Croquettes (R)

10 lb short bonbon cream
½ lb dairy butter
½ lb hard coconut butter
1 lb frappe or nougat cream
2 drops oil of anise

1 level tsp ground cinnamon
½ tsp ground cloves
Pink coloring
1 oz powdered salt
3 lb sliced Brazil nuts

Melt the dairy butter and bonbon cream together and heat to 49°C (120°F). Then add the coconut butter, anise oil, ground spices, salt and frappe and mix thoroughly. Now color the batch a light pink. Then work in the sliced Brazil nuts and set aside to permit the batch to cool for about 10 min. Then spoon the batch onto waxed paper or into parchment paper cups.

FUDGE TYPE CANDIES

Brazil Nut Fudge Kisses (W)

25 lb corn syrup
35 lb fine granulated sugar
8 lb hard coconut butter
45 lb condensed milk
  (sweetened)
15 lb invert sugar

10 oz salt
40 lb long shred desiccated
  coconut
Sufficient vanilla flavoring
20 lb sliced Brazil nuts
250 lb fondant (formula
  below)

Place the fondant into a warm mixing kettle but do not heat the fondant to more than 52° to 54°C (125° to 130°F), add the coconut, flavoring, salt and Brazil nuts and mix well. Meanwhile, place the corn syrup, coconut butter, invert sugar, sugar and condensed milk into a kettle and boil the batch, stirring constantly, to a firm ball. Pour this batch into the fondant-coconut-Brazil nut mixture. Mix for about 10 min or until the batch is sufficiently firm to be spooned into kisses or deposited in rough pieces onto heavy waxed paper. This batch may be spread onto oiled or waxed paper and marked and cut like fudge.

Fondant for Brazil Nut Fudge Kisses

240 lb sugar
60 lb corn syrup

30 lb invert sugar
60 lb water

Boil all ingredients together to 119°C (240°F), cool the syrup to 52°C (125°F) and beat into fondant.

Summer Time Caramel Cuts (W)

16 lb corn syrup	2 lb hard coconut butter
4 lb standardized invert sugar	16 lb short fondant
12 lb granulated sugar	4 oz salt
20 lb condensed milk (40% sugar)	Vanilla flavoring (Chocolate liquor, or cocoa powder)
2 lb dairy butter	5 lb whole Brazil nuts

Place the corn syrup, standardized invert sugar, condensed milk, butter and coconut butter into a kettle. Heat all together, then add the sugar, mixing well, and boil the batch to a firm ball. Turn off the heat, add the salt, fondant and vanilla flavoring, mixing well. Add the chocolate liquor or cocoa powder to color and flavor ⅓ of the batch and spread this on an oiled slab. Add 5 lb of whole Brazil nuts to the vanilla flavored portion of the batch. Turn out on a slab and as it cools form it into a loaf. Roll the chocolate flavored portion of the batch into a sheet and form it around vanilla flavored portion and form it into a loaf about 2 × 5 in. in section. Place the batch between bars so as to prevent it from losing its shape, and when cool cut into slices and wrap in transparent cellulose. The batch may also be formed into sheets or slabs and cut into squares.

Brazil Nut Malted Milk Fudge (W)

4 oz salt	30 lb corn syrup
30 lb condensed milk (sweetened)	3 lb hard coconut butter
50 lb fine granulated sugar	15 lb frappe or nougat creme
10 lb invert sugar	15 lb broken Brazil nuts
	Vanilla and butter flavorings

Place the corn syrup, invert sugar, condensed milk, sugar, water to dissolve the sugar, malt syrup and coconut butter into a kettle and stir constantly until it reaches a temperature of 118°C (244°F), then cool the batch to 93°C (200°F). Now add the salt and fondant, mix well, then add the flavorings and frappe, and the Brazil nuts. Spread the batch out on waxed paper to set and when cold, mark and cut into squares or oblongs.

Brazil Nut Cast Fudge

40 lb corn syrup	35 lb cast cream center fondant
20 lb condensed whole milk	10 lb frappe or nougat creme
5 lb invert sugar	

45 lb fine granulated
sugar
3 lb coconut oil

5 oz salt
Butter and vanilla flavorings
Brazil nuts, ground or sliced as
needed for rolling

Place the sugar, with sufficient water to dissolve the sugar, into a caramel cooking kettle, add the corn syrup, condensed milk, invert sugar and coconut oil and boil the batch to 115.5°C (240°F), then add the fondant, salt, frappe and flavorings, mix well and deposit the fudge into starch impressions suitable for penny pieces, bulk items or as a center for rolls. When the batch is cool, coat the centers with caramel and roll in ground or sliced Brazil nuts and later coat with chocolate.

Brazil Nut Fruit Bar (W)

90 lb sugar
50 lb corn syrup
40 lb condensed milk
(sweetened)
10 lb hard coconut butter
50 lb short fondant
30 lb frappe or nougat
creme
10 lb invert sugar

12 lb water
5 lb preserved cherry
pieces
5 lb preserved fruits
15 lb broken Brazil fruits
5 lb raisins
10 lb cocoa powder
6 oz salt
Vanilla flavoring

Boil the sugar, corn syrup, condensed milk, coconut butter, water and cocoa powder to 118°C (244°F), then add the invert sugar, fondant and frappe and mix well. Add the fruits, Brazil nuts, salt and flavoring, mix thoroughly and spread the batch out on oiled or heavily waxed paper and when cold, mark and cut into squares or bars.

Brazil Nut White Layer for Fudge (W)

40 lb sugar
10 lb water
15 lb corn syrup
5 lb invert sugar
4 lb hard coconut
butter

20 lb firm fondant
5 lb frappe or nougat
creme
6 lb sliced or broken
Brazil nuts
Color and flavor as desired

Boil the sugar, corn syrup, water and invert sugar to 121° to 124°C (250° to 256°F), then add the fondant, coconut butter, frappe, flavoring and coloring as desired, mix well, then work in the Brazil nuts and spread the batch over a sheet of chocolate or vanilla fudge.

HARD CANDIES

Brazil Nut Filled Clumps and Chips (W)
Part 1, Center

8 lb corn syrup

6 lb sliced Brazil nuts

4 lb sweetened condensed milk	Nutmeg flavoring
1 oz powdered salt	Yellow coloring

Cook the corn syrup and condensed milk to 110°C (230°F). Add the salt, flavoring and coloring and sliced Brazil nuts, mix well and keep warm 71° to 78°C (160° to 170°F).

Part 2, Hard Candy Jacket
(Open Fire Forced Draught Gas)

30 lb granulated sugar	Water to dissolve sugar
5 lb corn syrup	Maple flavoring
	Brown coloring

Boil the sugar, water and corn syrup to 160°C (320°F). Pour the batch on an oiled slab and when partly cool, add the coloring and flavoring and pull well on the hook. Spread the batch out and place the center into position, fold the jacket around the center and spin out into strips of various sizes and cut into clumps or chips.

JELLY FORMULAS

Brazil Nut Jelly Cordials (W)

35 lb fine granulated sugar	12 lb water
10 lb corn syrup	Rose flavoring
5 lb invert sugar	Red coloring
6 oz agar-agar	Finely ground Brazil nuts as required

Soak the agar-agar in the 12 lb of water for at least an hour (preferably overnight), then gradually heat and stir until it boils. Add the sugar, corn syrup and invert sugar and boil the batch to 113° to 115°C (236° to 238°F). Add the coloring and flavoring and deposit the jelly into starch which has been heated to 43° to 46°C (110° to 115°F). Immediately sprinkle the surface of the candies with dry warm starch. Place the starch trays containing the jellies into a hot room where the temperature is between 51° to 57°C (125° to 135°F) for approximately 12 to 15 hours. When a crust has formed on the jellies, take them out of the dry room and when cold, remove them from the starch and coat in icing and roll in finely ground Brazil nuts.

Icing for Brazil Nut Jelly Cordials

80 lb powdered sugar	10 lb water (hot)
10 lb invert sugar	Color and flavor, as desired

Mix together all of the ingredients until smooth, and then beat the whole mass until it is of the proper consistency. For greater opaqueness and more gloss, use from 3 to 8 lb of fat. For more body and quicker setting, dissolve in each pound of water used, ½ to 1½ oz either of egg albumen or gelatin; or, replace all of the water with egg whites.

Brazil Apricot Jelly Cuts

25 lb granulated sugar	55 lb water (cold)
15 lb corn syrup	2 oz cream of tartar
10 lb standardized invert	10 lb dried apricots
sugar	8 lb whole Brazil nuts
6 lb thin boiling starch	

Soak the dried apricots in enough water to cover for an hour or two, then drain off the water and pass the apricots through a meat grinder. Place the sugar, corn syrup, invert sugar, starch and cold water into a kettle and stir the batch constantly until it boils, then add the cream of tartar. Continue to stir and cook the batch to a jelly string, then add the ground apricots, and cook the batch to a heavy jelly or paste. Add the Brazil nuts and mix well. Spread the batch out on heavy wrapping paper, sprinkling the surface with fine granulated sugar. Allow the jelly to set for a day or so, after which it may be cut into squares, oblongs, or bars and rolled in fine granulated sugar.

MARSHMALLOW CANDIES

Brazil Nut Moco-Mallo (R)
(Cocoa flavored cut marshmallow)

11 lb water	2½ lb cocoa powder (Dutched)
1½ lb gelatin (#200)	5 lb standardized invert
15 lb granulated sugar	sugar
25 lb corn syrup	1 oz salt
10 lb standardized invert	Vanilla, rum or coffee flavorings
sugar	

First heat the 5 lb of invert sugar to approximately 80° to 88°C (175° to 190°F). Add the cocoa powder and mix until smooth, then add the flavoring and salt. Set this aside while preparing the following: Mix ½ of the water with the gelatin and set aside for at least 15 min.

Place the remainder of the water into a kettle, add the sugar, apply heat, and when the sugar is dissolved turn off the heat. Add the soaked gelatin, mixing until the gelatin is dissolved, then add the invert sugar and corn syrup, mixing well. Place the batch into a marshmallow beater and beat until the temperature of the batch is not in excess of 28°C (82°F). Then add the cocoa, invert sugar and flavoring, mixing it at slow speed for no longer than is necessary to distribute the flavor. The batch may now be spread out and handled in much the same manner as standard cut marshmallow work or the batch may be placed into a Friend machine and extruded into pieces of the desired size and shape.

When the batch has been spread or extruded, it is immediately sprinkled well with ground Brazil nuts, which may be either finely or coarsely ground. Permit the marshmallow to set until it is dry on the surface, after which it is ready to pack.

Gelatin Marshmallow (W)
(For Cutting)

35 lb corn syrup	40 lb water
35 lb fine granulated sugar	Rum and lime flavorings to taste
10 lb invert sugar	6 lb sliced Brazil nuts
2¾-3 lb best grade gelatin	13 lb Brazil nuts, finely ground
	Brown and green colorings

Mix the gelatin with half of the water and set aside for at least 15 min. Meanwhile place the sugar and the remaining half of the water into a kettle and heat until the sugar is entirely dissolved (do not boil). Add the soaked gelatin and mix until the gelatin is completely dissolved. Then add the invert sugar and corn syrup and beat the batch until quite cold. Add the flavorings, mix well, stir in the sliced Brazil nuts and spread the batch out on heavy wrapping paper. Level the batch to the required height, and immediately sprinkle over the surface finely ground Brazil nuts, which have been colored brown and green (suggested proportions of colored nuts—10 lb brown colored Brazils to 3 lb green colored Brazils). When the marshmallow has set, turn the sheets of marshmallow upside down, moisten the wrapping paper, then remove it and sprinkle the colored nuts on the moist sheet of marshmallow. Then cut into bars, squares or oblongs and roll in colored nuts.

MISCELLANEOUS FORMULAS

Brazil Nut Chocolate Blocks and Bars (W)
(For Slab Work)

35 lb dark or milk chocolate
15 lb whole or broken Brazil nuts

Melt the chocolate and temper it to 30° to 32°C (86° to 90°F). Add the Brazil nuts, mix well and mold the chocolate in large or small pans and transfer the batch to a chocolate cooling room where the temperature may vary from 10° to 18.3°C (50° to 65°F). When the chocolate has set, remove it from the pans.

Sliced Brazil Nut Chocolate Cakes

30 lb dark or milk chocolate
13 lb sliced Brazil nuts

Melt the chocolate and temper it to 30° to 32°C (86° to 90°F). Add the sliced Brazil nuts, mix well, then mold in the form of cakes, bars, etc. Transfer the molds to a chocolate cooling room where the temperature may vary from 10° to 18°C (50° to 65°F). When the chocolate has set, remove the cakes from the molds.

Sliced Toasted Green Brazil Nut Cakes and Bars

30 lb dark or milk chocolate
7 lb toasted sliced Brazil nuts
5 lb toasted sliced Brazil nuts, colored green

Melt the chocolate and temper it to 30° to 32°C (86° to 90°F). Add the toasted and green colored Brazil nuts, mix well, then mold in the form of cakes, bars, etc. Transfer the molds to a chocolate cooling room where the temperature may vary from 10° to 18°C (50° to 65°F). When the chocolate has set, remove the cakes or bars from the molds.

Creamed Milk Brazil Nuts (R)

10 lb whole or broken Brazil nuts
30 lb granulated sugar
1 lb corn syrup
5 lb condensed milk (40% sugar)
Rum flavoring

First make a gum arabic solution by dissolving 1 part of gum arabic in 3 parts of water. Add enough of the gum arabic solution to the whole or broken Brazil nuts to make them sticky and immediately roll the nuts in fruit or berry sugar. Permit the nuts to dry, then place them into a revolving pan or hand kettle. Boil the sugar, corn syrup and water to 118°C (244°F), gradually add the condensed milk, mixing well. Add the rum flavoring. Then apply a small amount of the cooked batch to the nuts, stirring vigorously. When a coating of the grained batch has adhered to the nuts continue to apply the balance of the batch, adding a little at a time until all of the batch has been used. Sift off the loose sugar and place the candies into crystallizing pans, cover them with cold crystallizing syrup of 34° Baume. Allow the candies to remain in the syrup for a minimum of 6 hours, after which the surplus is drained off and the candies are permitted to dry and later are packed.

Brazil Nut Bonbons (R)

25 lb granulated sugar   ½ oz gelatin dissolved in
8 lb water   1 oz hot water

Place the sugar and water into a kettle and stir the batch occasionally until it boils. Carefully wash down all grains of sugar that adhere to the kettle and boil the batch to 117° to 118°C (242° to 244°F). Turn off the heat. Meanwhile have the gelatin dissolved in a little hot water; add the dissolved gelatin to the cooking batch, mixing gently. Pour the batch at once into a clean beater. Immediately sprinkle the batch with 1½ oz of cold water. Permit the batch to cool to approximately 32° to 26°C (90° to 80°F) then beat into fondant. Allow the fondant to set until cool, then place it into covered crocks or metal containers free of iron rust. Place a small amount of the bonbon cream into a double boiler, mixing occasionally until the fondant is partly melted, and continue to mix until completely melted, adding portions of additional fondant from time to time. The fondant should be heated to approximately 54° to 63°C (130° to 145°F), after which coloring and flavoring may be added. Following are suggestions for use:

(1) The fondant may be used for center work; simply take a portion of the fondant, adding pistachio flavoring and a quantity of ground or sliced Brazil nuts which have been colored green. Knead the colored Brazil nuts into the fondant using a little powdered sugar to produce a firm mass, after which roll into the form of balls or ovals, then coat with fondant, placing a green colored Brazil nut piece on top.

(2) Follow the same procedure as above, with the exception that toasted sliced Brazils may be used instead of colored Brazils. Top each coated bonbon center with a toasted Brazil nut slice.

(3) Add coloring and flavoring, as desired, to the melted bonbon cream and coat medium size or large whole Brazils which may be topped with a preserved cherry piece, preserved pineapple piece, black currant, icing decorations, tiny chocolate wafers or chocolate decorettes.

(4) Coat the pointed half of a medium or large size Brazil nut in white or colored bonbon cream, then set it up on the coated end, simulating the form of a penguin.

(5) Dip medium size Brazil nuts in cinnamon or rum flavored bonbon cream, colored pink, and immediately roll in fine ground colored or toasted Brazil nuts.

(6) Dip medium or large size Brazil nuts into maple flavored bonbon cream, just coating the pointed half of the nut. Plunge the bonbon coated portion into extra fine Brazil nut siftings, thus giving it the shape of a mushroom. The extra fine Brazil nut siftings should be spread level in a pan or tray about an inch deep.

Brazil Nut Fluff Chocolate Bar (R)

10 lb hard coconut butter	15 lb frappe, No. 1
(94° melting point)	1 oz powdered salt
20 lb milk chocolate coating	Rum flavoring

Melt the coconut butter and milk chocolate together, then cool to 32°C (90°F). Add the frappe, salt and flavoring, mixing rapidly until a thorough mixture is obtained. Then add 6 lb of whole or broken Brazil nuts and spread out on waxed paper to form a sheet 1 in. high—or add 4 lb of sliced toasted Brazil nuts and 2 lb of sliced Brazil nuts colored green. Spread the batch on waxed paper to form a sheet ½ in. high and when the batch has set, cut into oblongs, squares or bars and coat with chocolate, sprinkling the surface with green colored sliced Brazils.

NOUGATS

Brazil Nut Spiced Chewing Nougat (W)

30 lb sugar	15 lb roughly broken
30 lb corn syrup	Brazil nuts

10 lb medium grade molasses
5 lb invert sugar
2 lb hard coconut butter
10 lb condensed milk
   (sweetened)

6 oz salt
Oil of cassia
Oil of nutmeg
Oil of cloves to taste
6 lb water

Place into a kettle the sugar, 6 lb of water, the corn syrup, invert sugar, molasses and coconut butter and boil together to 135°C (275°F). Gradually add the condensed milk, stirring constantly and cook the batch to 141°C (285°F). Pour this at once into 25 lb of the following frappe, beating well. Then add the spiced flavorings, salt, and the Brazil nuts, mix thoroughly and spread the batch out on an oiled slab to cool. When cold this may be cut into bars, penny pieces, or into pieces suitable for wrapping in waxed paper, transparent cellulose or coating with chocolate.

Frappe for Brazil Nut Spiced Chewing Nougat

Boil 25 lb of corn syrup to 118°C (245°F). Add 25 lb of invert sugar and stir until melted. Place this into a beater. Start the beater and gradually add 2 lb of egg albumen, dissolved in 4 lb of cold water, and beat until quite light.

Brazil Malt Short Nougat (W)

15 lb malt syrup
15 lb invert sugar

2 lb egg albumen dissolved in
4 lb cold water

Heat the invert sugar until melted. Add the malt syrup—mix well, then place this into a beater. Start the beater. Gradually add the dissolved albumen and beat until quite light. Place this into a nougat beating kettle and prepare the following:

60 lb sugar
40 lb corn syrup
Water to dissolve sugar
1½ lb hard coconut butter

4 oz powdered salt
15 lb roughly broken Brazil
   nuts
Vanilla flavoring

Boil the sugar, corn syrup and water to 132° to 134°C (270° to 275°F). Then break up the coconut butter and place it into the mixing kettle with the beaten batch. Gradually add the cooked batch to the whipped batch, beating constantly until it begins to shorten. Then add the salt, flavoring and Brazil nuts, mix well and spread the batch out on an oiled and well-dusted slab. Roll the batch down to the desired height and when it sets, cut it into penny pieces, bars, or strips, which may be iced, coated with chocolate or caramel, or wrapped in waxed paper, etc.

Brazil Nut Nougats for Casting into Starch
(For Penny Pieces, Bars and Bulk)

60 lb sugar

10 lb cream center fondant

40 lb corn syrup   10 lb Brazil nuts finely ground
Water to dissolve sugar   '   Pineapple flavoring
5 oz powdered salt   Yellow coloring

Boil the sugar, corn syrup and water together to 123° to 126°C (255° to 260°F). Meanwhile, place 35 lb of the following frappe into a clean cold kettle, equipped with mixer. Add 5 oz of powdered salt and gradually add the cooked batch, beating continuously at second speed. When the batch has been well mixed, add 10 lb of cream center fondant and beat at fast speed until grain develops. Then add 10 lb of finely ground Brazil nuts, pineapple flavoring and yellow coloring and cast the batch into starch impressions. When the centers have set firm, they may be removed from the starch and coated in icing, jelly, caramel or chocolate.

Frappe for the Above Batch

Boil 50 lb of corn syrup to 118°C (245°F). Add 50 lb of invert sugar and mix until melted. Place this syrup into a marshmallow beater. Start the beater, then gradually add 3 lb of egg albumen, which has been dissolved in 6 lb of cold water and beat the batch until light and set this aside until ready to use.

Brazil Nut Caramel Nougat (W)

35 lb corn syrup   2 oz powdered salt
20 lb sugar   Nutmeg
15 lb condensed milk   Maple flavoring
  (sweetened)   15 lb broken Brazil nuts
2 lb hard coconut butter

Boil the corn syrup and sugar, with water to dissolve the sugar, to 135°C (275°F). Then add the coconut butter and the condensed milk, mixing rapidly. Cook the batch to 137.8° to 140.5°C (280° to 285°F). Meanwhile, weigh off 15 lb of the frappe (formula below) and place it into a kettle equipped with stirrer and pour the boiled batch into the frappe, mixing constantly. Add a trace of nutmeg and maple flavoring, the salt and 15 lb of roughly broken Brazil nuts. Mix well and spread the batch out on an oiled slab to cool. When cold cut smaller pieces which may be wrapped in waxed paper, transparent cellulose or coated with chocolate.

Frappe for Brazil Nut Caramel Nougat

Boil 25 lb of corn syrup to 118°C (245°F). Then add 25 lb of invert sugar and stir until melted. Place this syrup into a beater. Start the beater and gradually add 2 lb of egg albumen dissolved in 4 lb of cold water and beat until light.

Brazil Nut Honey Chewing Nougat (R)

5 lb honey   ½ lb hard coconut butter
6 oz albumen dissolved in   5 lb chopped Brazil nuts
  12 oz cold water   1½ lb sliced Brazil nuts, colored green

10 lb sugar
Vanilla flavoring

10 lb corn syrup
3 pt water

Heat the honey until melted, then place this into a beater, start the beater in motion and gradually add the dissolved albumen and beat until quite light. Boil the sugar, corn syrup and water to 129° to 132°C (265° to 270°F), then pour this in a fine stream into the whipped honey batch, stirring constantly. Add the hard coconut butter, flavor and Brazil nuts, mix well and spread the batch out on an oiled slab. When cold it may be sized and cut into pieces of the desired size and then wrapped in wax paper, transparent cellulose or coated with chocolate.

Brazil Nut Grained Nougat (R)

4 lb corn syrup
4 lb invert sugar
1½ qt fresh or frozen egg
   whites
13 lb sugar
3 lb corn syrup
3 pt water

½ lb hard coconut butter
3 lb roughly ground Brazil
   nuts
1½ lb sliced Brazil nuts
   colored green
Orange flavor extract
Vanilla flavoring

Place the egg whites into a beater and beat until moderately stiff. Meanwhile boil the 4 lb of corn syrup and 4 lb of invert sugar to 121°C (250°F). Then pour this in a thin stream into the egg whites, beating constantly until quite light. Meanwhile boil the sugar and 3 lb of corn syrup with the 3 pt of water to 143°C (290°F). Pour this in a fine stream into the whipped batch and beat constantly, adding an ounce of icing sugar. Beat until the batch begins to grain, then add the flavorings, coconut butter and nutmeats, mix well and spread the batch out on heavy wax paper well dusted with powdered sugar. When the nougat has set it may be cut into squares, oblongs or bars and wrapped in wax paper, transparent cellulose or coated with chocolate.

Brazil Nut Nougat Chews (W)

Part 1
2 lb albumen
4 lb cold water
5 lb corn syrup

Dissolve the albumen in the water. Add the corn syrup and beat until light.

Part 2

30 lb corn syrup
10 lb standardized invert sugar

8 lb whole Brazil nuts
4 lb sliced Brazil nuts, colored green

30 lb granulated sugar	4 oz salt
Water to dissolve	Ceylon cinnamon, rum,
sugar	and pistachio flavorings

Boil the corn syrup, standardized sugar, granulated sugar and water to 121°C (250°F). Then add 1½ gal. of this syrup to the beaten batch (Part 1), and beat until light. Meanwhile boil the balance of the batch to 148° to 149°C (300° to 310°F). Then add this gradually to the beaten batch, mixing thoroughly. Add the salt, flavorings, whole Brazils and green colored Brazil nuts. Mix well and form the batch into slabs, slices, cakes, or place it into a lightly oiled deep chocolate pan so as to form a slab 6 in. or more deep. When cold the nougat chews may be broken and sold by weight or the batch may be cut into bars.

Brazil Nut Puffs (R)
Part 1

5 lb corn syrup
5 lb standardized invert sugar
1 lb egg albumen dissolved in
2½ lb water
1 lb corn starch

Part 2

40 lb granulated sugar	⅛ lb salt
10 lb corn syrup	20 lb casting fondant
10 lb water	Combination of maple and
8 lb sliced, ground or	almond flavorings
broken Brazil nuts	

Place the cold corn syrup and invert sugar into a bowl or an upright beater, add the starch and the albumen previously dissolved in the water and beat until light. Meanwhile prepare Part 2 as follows:

Boil the sugar, water and corn syrup at 121°C (250°F). Pour this into the whipped portion (Part 1), beating at second speed. After all of the syrup has been mixed well with the whipped portion, add the salt and casting fondant, mixing at slow speed until the fondant is melted. Then add the flavorings, beat well at high speed for 2 or 3 min, then add the Brazil nuts and the batch is ready to be spooned onto waxed paper to form kisses. If the batch is to be formed into sheets and later cut similar to fudge, it is suggested that Part 2 be boiled at 107°C (225°F).

TOPPINGS

Brazil Nut Topping for Candies,
Ice Cream, Cakes, Etc. (W)

25 lb sugar	Trace oil of cassia

2 lb invert sugar
½ lb dairy butter
Water to dissolve sugar
Red coloring

Vanilla flavoring
2 oz powdered salt
20 lb sliced or ground
    Brazil nuts

Boil the sugar, invert sugar and water to 140°C (285°F), add the butter, red coloring and mix well, then add the oil of cassia, vanilla, salt and Brazil nuts and stir the batch until it grains. Pass the topping through various sized sieves in order to secure a fine, medium or coarse topping. The fine topping may be used on cut marshmallow or plastic chocolate centers or for other centers coated with thin icing and later rolled in the topping. The medium or coarse topping may be used on the surface of chocolate coated bars, ice cream or by cake bakers.

Colored Brazil Nuts (Green) (W)

Place into a kettle 1 gal. of water, add 10 g of powdered green coloring, 6 g of powdered yellow coloring and then permit the colored water to boil for a minute or two. Then add the maximum amounts of sliced Brazil nuts and boil them for 5 min. Drain the colored water from the nuts, which should be placed on a screen and transferred to a drying room. When dry the nuts may be used as is or ground into finer particles.

Chocolate Fudge Meringues

¼ tsp cream of tartar
3 tsp butter
½ tsp salt
4 egg whites
4 egg yolks
1 cup sugar

½ tsp almond extract
½ tsp vanilla extract
2 tsp corn syrup
Chopped Brazil nuts
6 oz semi-sweet chocolate

Add cream of tartar and salt to egg whites and beat until almost stiff; gradually add sugar and beat until stiff. Add flavorings. Drop from teaspoon on sheets covered with heavy waxed paper. With a teaspoon, make a depression in center of each and fill with fudge mixture. Sprinkle with nuts. Bake in slow oven 148°C (300°F) about 25 min. Makes about 3½ dozen.

Chocolate Fudge: In the top of double boiler, melt 6 oz semi-sweet chocolate with 3 tsp butter. Add 4 egg yolks, slightly beaten with 2 tsp corn syrup. Cook, stirring 5 min. Remove from heat. Beat until spreading consistency.

REFERENCES

ANON. Undated. Parade of Commercial Formulas for Brazil Nut Candies. Brazil Nut Assoc., New York.

ANON. 1966. Foreign Agriculture. U.S. Dep. Agric., Foreign Agric. Serv. Rept., July 18.

ANON. 1976. Nuts. U.S. Dep. Agric., Foreign Agric. Serv. *FN 1-76.*

ANON. 1976. Tree Nuts. U.S. Dep. Agric., Foreign Agric. Serv. *FN 5-76.*

BAILEY, L.H.   1935.   The Standard Cyclopedia of Horticulture.   The Macmillan Co., New York.

ELIAS, L.G., and BRESSANI, R.   1961.   The nutritive value of Brazil nut oil.   J. Am. Oil. Chem. Soc. *38*, 450-452.

KUZIO, W.   1977.   Nutmeat roundup.   Candy Ind. *142* (6) 25-42.

LEE, J.P.   1946.   Brazil nuts.   Brazil *20*, 6, 2.

SCHREIBER, W.R.   1950.   The Amazon Basin Brazil nut industry.   U.S. Dep. Agric., Foreign Agric. Rept. *49*.

8

Cashew Nuts

The cashew nut (*Anarcadium occidentale* Linn) is native to Brazil. From there the tree spread to other parts of tropical South and Central America, Mexico and the West Indies. The generic name, *Anarcadium,* was bestowed upon it because it described the heart-like shape of the nut. The specific name, *occidentale,* was used because the nut came from the western Americas (Bailey 1935).

The only place in the United States where they are grown is the southern tip of Florida. The cashew plant is a jungle or semi-jungle tree by nature. The Portuguese introduced it into India and East Africa in the 16th century to help control erosion along the coastal regions of these countries.

The cashew tree grows with a minimum of attention and is easily cultivated. A three-year-old tree bears an average of 7 lb of nuts. By the fifteenth year trees average 70 lb of nuts per tree. Mature trees of exceptional quality have yielded as much as 200 lb. Many trees produce nuts for 15 to 20 years; others are known to be productive for as many as 45 years.

Because of their spreading branches cashew trees resemble large bushes. However, they are true trees and often attain a height of 30 to 40 ft. They are evergreen and are readily recognized by their light colored foliage. The yellow-green leaves, revealing distinct veins, are elliptical in shape and approximately 4 to 6 in. in length and 2 to 3 in. wide. They feel leathery to the touch.

Morton (1961) reported that the tree is very sensitive to cold when young, but becomes fairly hardy with age and is capable of withstanding short periods of light frost. It is extremely adaptable as to soil, flourishing even in the sand of open beaches, but it grows poorly in heavy clay or limestone. It is found from sea level to an altitude of 3000 ft and in regions with rainfall as high as 150 in. and as low as 20 in. However, for maximum productivity, good soil and adequate moisture are essential.

There are as yet very few cultivars named. Generally, a distinction is made only between those with yellow or red cashew apples. Tests have indicated that very large nuts usually have inferior kernels, are of low density, poor vitality and slow germination.

HARVESTING

The path of the cashew nut from harvesting to importation is an interesting one. Cashew trees bloom in India in mid-December and bear flowers until early February. In March and April the cashew "apples" are ripe and the main crop of nuts is ready for harvesting. Some trees yield an additional light crop in October and November. Harvesting periods differ seasonally in other cashew growing countries.

Ripe fruits are not plucked from the trees but fall to the ground and are picked up by the natives. The whole nuts are removed from the fruits by hand and a small percentage of the "apples" is shipped to market for local consumption. Most of the fruits are not utilized.

After the nuts are gathered they are sun-dried for two days. The moisture content is thus reduced from 16 to 7% so that the nuts can be safely stored. The nuts now may either be bagged and held for future processing or immediately processed, graded and packed for export.

Preparation of the cashew kernels for export is an intricate procedure compared to the preparation of other edible nuts. They are cleaned, processed to remove the oily shell liquid, "cracked" to liberate the kernel, dried to facilitate dehusking, "peeled" to remove the testa, graded and packed in compliance with the rules of the Indian Cashew Export Promotion Council. The United States used to import a major portion of its cashew nuts from India. In 1973-74, however, 43% of United States imports came from Mozambique and other African countries (due to new processing facilities) as opposed to 40% from India (Table 8.1). This increase in African cashew nuts first became a significant factor during the 1966 season, and has increased since that time. Another boost to the African operations is the sharply increased demand for shelled cashew nuts from the USSR.

PROCESSING

The first step in preparation is cleaning of the shell. Whole raw nuts are passed through rotary cleaners to remove any foreign substance that adheres to the outer surface. They are then washed in a water bath and stored in moist heaps or silos for 12 hours to make the shells brittle. Moisture is maintained at 7 to 10% at which range the cells within the shell readily rupture, liberate the oily shell liquid and retain it within the shell.

The nuts are now ready for processing to remove the shell liquid. Great advances have taken place in this process. Years ago this was performed by crude native methods. Whole raw nuts were roasted in shallow pans over open charcoal fires. Constant agitation was required during the roasting to reduce scorching of the nuts.

TABLE 8.1

CASHEW IMPORTS INTO UNITED STATES
SHELLED

Country of Origin	1968-69	1969-70	1970-71	1971-72	1972-73	1973-74
			(metric tons)			
Europe (total)	40	18	164	140	67	109
Latin America						
Brazil	2,771	5,335	4,608	4,011	5,677	5,110
Other	3	90	–	35	83	4
Total	2,774	5,425	4,608	4,046	5,760	5,114
Other Countries						
Canada	28	105	76	648	1,228	1,301
India	27,432	22,896	25,288	24,830	26,482	16,425
Kenya	121	111	116	184	67	95
Mozambique	9,076	9,913	11,095	15,775	16,996	16,898
South Africa	54	27	121	62	13	3
Tanzania	490	816	1,073	1,115	970	756
Other	131	128	95	69	122	79
Total	37,332	33,996	37,864	42,683	45,878	35,557
Grand Total	40,146	39,439	42,636	46,869	51,705	40,780

Source: Foreign Agric. Serv., FN 1-76.

Roasting by this method was dangerous and disagreeable. The shells burst, spurted the caustic liquid, and released clouds of acrid fumes which blistered the skin and irritated the workers. At the same time the valuable shell liquid was dissipated.

Methods were improvised to salvage the oil by roasting the nuts in perforated pans. Catch troughs were placed underneath to collect the liquid. About one half of it was recovered with this innovation, but the problem of irritation from the oil and its fumes still existed.

Processing equipment was improved to make roasting safe and to recover the shell liquid. Furnaces, fitted with chimneys which transfer and discharge the acrid fumes, are used as a controlled source of heat. The whole nuts are placed in large perforated cylinders which rotate at an angle above the source of heat. As the nuts travel down through the rotating cylinders the shell liquid flows through the holes in the cylinder and is captured in the catch troughs. When the roasted nuts emerge they are water sprayed and set aside to cool and dry.

Some of the larger factories are introducing still more advanced processing methods. Whole nuts are being treated in oil-bath tanks maintained at 187° to 193°C (370° to 380°F) to remove the shell liquid. Vents or flues, connected to the tanks, dispel the troublesome fumes and the equipment recovers 85 to 90% of the liquid.

A steam process for treating whole raw nuts has been patented, and if adopted, may have an added advantage, in that it claims to produce a better grade of cashew shell liquid.

Nut "cracking" is done manually by Indian women. Squatting on the floor with a small bowl of lime, ash, linseed or castor oil beside them they place the nut on a hard stone and "crack" the shell by hitting it with a wooden mallet. The kernel is then separated from the shell. During shelling the workers protect their hands by dipping them into the bowls to wash away any traces of the oily shell liquid (Morton 1961).

The hand "cracking" results in many broken kernels which bring a lower market price. A machine has recently been put into operation in Tanzania which removes the shell and keeps the kernel intact. The machine operator covers his hands with a coating of cream to protect them for the vesicating action of the shell liquid. He places the nut in a gripper which moves against a circular saw. This cuts a groove into the shell. A bladed implement inserted within the groove removes the kernel in a manner similar to the "shucking" process used to open an oyster. Machine "cracking" has increased production and a worker now opens from 600 to 1000 nuts per hour without breaking the kernels.

When raw kernels are shelled, they may be roasted in olive oil or peanut oil, using metal trays over a coal furnace. When roasting is half complete they are removed and mixed with a small amount of liquid paraffin, replaced on the tray, and given another 5 min roasting, sprinkled with a solution of salt, gum acacia and water, and finally reheated to remove excess moisture.

After "cracking" the nuts are dried and the resultant reduction in moisture causes shrinkage of the kernel. Removal of the reddish-brown testa surrounding each kernel now becomes a simple "peeling" operation and kernel "peelers" quickly and easily remove the loose, thin membrane-like pellicles. If the kernels are to be held in storage this "peeling" procedure may be deferred until they are graded to help retain the freshness of the nuts.

The testa is high in catechol-type tannin. During normal processing a small percentage of nuts develop bluish-black patches on the surface, which degrades them. This discoloration is due to the complex formation between polyphenol and iron. The discolored nuts show a higher iron content, which indicates either absorption of iron from external sources or a higher iron content in nuts susceptible to darkening. The formed pigment is easily washed away by dilute acid (Methew and Parpia 1970).

GRADING

"Garblers" grade the kernels according to size, shape, and characteristics described and defined in grading schedules. These schedules, drawn up by The Cashew Export Promotion Council in 1962 in India, are known as "The Cashew Products Export Grading and Marketing Rules." Under these grading rules, six schedules are established. Each schedule specifies the grade designation, trade name, number of kernels per pound for whole kernels, a description if necessary, and the general characteristics of the quality of kernels within the group. Tolerances are included for each schedule.

The schedules define and designate grades for whole cashews, scorched wholes, dessert wholes, white pieces, scorched pieces and dessert pieces.

There are no U.S. Standards for Grades for cashew nuts.

A new "Quality Control Scheme for Cashews" became effective in India on April 1, 1963. Under this plan qualified entomologists inspect cashew factories and advise management on necessary preventive and remedial measures to ensure proper plant sanitation. The entomologists also supervise special anti-infestation control measures such as insecticide spraying and fumigation with methyl bromide as a protective measure when necessary.

Only new, clean and dry leak-proof tins may be used for packing the kernels. The containers must be free from insect infestation, mold and rust. Four-gallon tins of 25-lb net weight capacity are used for bulk exports, except that white Baby Bits may be packed 28 lb to the tin.

Weevil infestation was a constant problem when the United States started importing quantities of cashew kernels shortly after World War I. Spoilage caused importers to sustain heavy losses and interest in the nut declined. Finally, a process was devised to hermetically seal the metal shipping container by replacing the air with carbon dioxide. From this point on imports to United States increased. Later the vacuum pack process was introduced, and shelf-life was further prolonged.

When kept under proper storage conditions cashew kernels show little or no deterioration in quality and may be safely warehoused throughout the year. Although the kernels are vacuum packed they require cold or "cool" storage at a temperature below $9°C$ ($48°F$). Below this point insect life remains dormant.

The Cashew Export Promotion Council of India has introduced a system of compulsory preshipment inspection and quality control. Under this system only packers having modern factories equipped with all processing facilities are certified as authorized packers. They have to follow strictly the rules relating to processing and packing and keep their factories in perfect sanitary condition. This vigilant quality control has been yielding good dividends in the form of increased reputation and demand for Indian cashew nuts in foreign countries.

TABLE 8.2

CASHEW EXPORTS FROM INDIA

Country of Destination	1969	1970	1971	1972	1973	1974
			(metric tons)			
United States	23,323	23,769	29,309	19,611	20,313	12,311
Europe						
Belgium-Luxembourg	101	49	116	221	123	188
Bulgaria	116	96	81	142	1	–
Czechoslovakia	328	347	674	952	743	533
France	510	255	198	401	157	160
Germany, East	2,156	2,501	1,793	1,889	957	614
Germany, West	616	394	428	1,065	1,124	811
Hungary	11	89	61	95	46	30
Italy	68	42	52	86	124	65
Netherlands	647	647	819	1,089	1,070	1,145
Poland	11	209	47	135	–	23
Romania	–	66	76	205	155	81
Spain	275	137	13	40	10	4
Sweden	53	8	11	18	18	13
Switzerland	46	20	18	98	98	109
United Kingdom	2,261	1,107	1,638	1,991	1,503	910
Yugoslavia	505	524	235	169	78	20
Other	29	21	63	46	–	–
Total	7,733	6,512	6,323	8,642	6,207	4,706
Other Countries						
Australia	1,910	1,073	1,079	1,332	1,120	1,900
Bahrain	46	66	70	102	83	74
Canada	1,776	2,297	3,788	5,486	3,978	3,615
Hong Kong	843	625	832	1,017	548	832
Iran	69	68	149	123	85	96
Japan	479	810	1,195	2,001	3,168	1,509
Kuwait	78	84	94	131	181	259
Lebanon	221	295	107	223	203	152
New Zealand	103	122	76	30	31	275
Singapore	253	314	375	389	390	342
U.S.S.R.	25,712	17,979	16,485	25,385	20,701	31,742
Other	134	57	112	120	54	163
Total	31,624	23,790	24,362	36,339	30,542	40,959
Grand Total	62,680	54,071	59,994	64,592	57,062	57,976

Grade designations for whole cashew kernels are:

W210   200-210 kernels/lb

W240	220-240 kernels/lb
W280	260-280 kernels/lb
W320	300-320 kernels/lb
W400	350-400 kernels/lb
W450	400-450 kernels/lb
W500	450-500 kernels/lb

Tolerance.—Broken kernels and kernels of the next lower grade, if any, shall not together exceed 5% at the time of packing (Anon. 1964). There are also grade designations for (a) whole scorched cashew kernels, (b) whole dessert cashew kernels, (c) white cashew kernel pieces, (d) scorched cashew kernel pieces, and (e) dessert cashew kernel pieces.

THE FRUIT AND SEED

The cashew has a fruit-like stalk called the cashew apple. The nuts are stripped from the plant and processed for their kernels and for the increasingly important oil from the shells. The deliciously juicy "apple" is little known outside the tropics. It is thin-skinned and spoils easily. Extraction and concentration of the juice would probably be a feasible method of marketing. If a market for the juice could be developed, the crop harvested for nuts is already available. Indian cashew apple wine and chutney are leading products, but the rest of the fruit is eaten locally, used for cattle feed, or simply wasted.

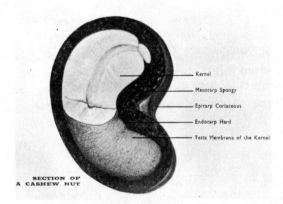

Courtesy Cashew Export Promotion Council, India

FIG. 8.1. SECTION OF A CASHEW NUT

Most fruits contain their seeds within the pulp or fleshy part of the fruit. This is not so with the cashew. The nut is on the outside of the pulp and is located at the distal end of the fruit, the point furthest away from its attachment to the stem. This unusual location of the nut gives the fruit an interesting and unique appearance.

The fruit varies in size from 2 to 4 in. in length and 1½ to 2 in. in width. It is yellowish-red in color and possesses a thin waxy skin. Broadly conical or pear-like in shape, it is called a cashew "pear" or cashew "apple."

The cashew "apples" or "pears" are displayed at local bazaars. They are succulent in taste with a sweet acid flavor. In the tropical Americas where they are grown, the native population is fond of them. Brazilians rate the fruit highly. In some parts of the West Indies and the tropical Americas, the nut is thrown away and the "apple" or "pear" is considered the delicacy. They are eaten raw or cooked and also prepared into a jam or preserve. The juice of the fruit is fermented and made into a wine by the people of Brazil, Portuguese East Africa and other countries. This wine, distilled into a spirit or liquor, is highly potent.

TABLE 8.3

COMPOSITION OF CASHEW APPLE

Moisture	87.8%
Proteins	.2%
Fat	.1%
Carbohydrates	11.6%
(90% fermentable sugars)	
Calcium	.01%
Phosphorus	.01%
Iron	.2 mg/100 g
Vitamin C	261.5 mg/100 g
Minerals	.2%
B. Caroline	.09%

Source: Indian Cashew (1966).

In India approximately 250,000 tons of apples are harvested annually. Eighty-five percent of this crop is wasted. Part of the remaining 15% is used as pig feed. Because it is highly perishable, even when held under cold storage temperatures, researchers are at work seeking new methods to extract and process the juice and testing new formulations in which it may be incorporated.

The fruit and wine, rich in vitamin C, possess antiscorbutic properties. Years ago the liquor was valued for its diuretic properties. It was claimed to have a healthful effect on the kidneys and was prescribed in advanced cases of cholera.

The shell of the nut is hard, about ⅛ in. thick, and is of honeycomb-like structure on the inside. It consists of two layers with an oily liquid between them. The outer layer, which is smooth surfaced, is thin and tough. The inner layer is hard. Between the two layers is the difficult-to-handle and troublesome cashew liquid which is marketed commercially and is growing in economic importance.

CASHEW SHELL LIQUID

Cashew shell liquid is extremely caustic and is a strong vesicating agent. Such blistering action to the skin precludes the importation and retail sale of unshelled cashew nuts.

Morton (1961) found that the raw juice is often prescribed for stomach disorders, is given to arrest vomiting, and is used as a gargle for sore throat. The juice, fresh or distilled, is said to be beneficial to patients with uterine complaints or dropsy.

The double shell that contains a toxic liquid comprises 70% of the cashew nut. The liquid contains aracardic acid, $C_{22}H_{32}O_3$, a brown crystalline substance, and cardol, $C_{21}H_{32}O_{21}$, a dark brown phenolic oil; both are very toxic and irritating, producing blisters on the skin similar to those caused by poison ivy. Before being shelled the nuts are heated in cashew nutshell liquid to make the shells brittle and to extract the toxic liquid. This liquid or oil is not to be confused with the fatty oil recovered from the kernel (Haagen-Smit 1931).

The principal constituents of the shell liquid are the chemicals cardol and anacardol. Both belong to the group of chemicals classified as higher phenols. It is believed that the cardol fraction, which comprises about 10% of the shell liquid, is responsible for the major irritant properties. The fumes from this liquid, which are liberated when the shells are heated for cracking, also possess this vesicating action.

Cardol, the principal irritant in cashew nut shell liquid, is a chemical relative of urushiol, which is the irritating factor in poison ivy. Both produce similar types of irritating skin reactions and thus the cashew tree is classified in the same family as poison ivy and poison sumac.

Cashew shell liquid is used to make several types of resins and these resins are used in the manufacture of varnishes. Frequent dermatitis conditions are reported in the case histories of workers who had contact with either the resins or varnishes.

CASHEW PRODUCTS[1]

Cashews are today one of the most popular nuts used by the confectionery industry. The largest percentage is utilized in nut salting. Confections, cakes and cookies are formulated with new and improved recipes which incorporate whole kernels and pieces. Their use will continue to grow. Modern techniques of processing and shelling will increase production. Better factory sanitation, quality control and grading procedures will improve quality. Reduction in tariffs will stimulate trade. And this will result in increased demand for the cashew nut.

---

[1]For information on salting cashew nuts, see Chapter 5; for recipes on use of cashews in confections, see p. 83; for their use in bakery items, see p. 97 and for substituting cashews for other nuts in restaurants, see p. 97.

Tuna-Cashew Casserole

¾ cup elbow macaroni,
  cooked and drained
1 cup sour cream
¼ tsp ground oregano
2 cans (14 oz) tuna, drained
½ cup sliced ripe olives

1 can (4 oz) sliced mushrooms,
  drained
¼ cup chopped green pepper
½ cup chopped cashew nuts
1½ tsp seasoned salt
¼ tsp pepper
1 cup grated, sharp cheddar cheese

Mix well all ingredients, except cheese. Put in shallow 1½-qt baking dish. Sprinkle with cheese. Bake in moderate oven 175°C (350°F) about 25 min. Serves 4 to 6.

Coffee Nut Macaroons

2 egg whites
1½ cups sugar
2 tsp instant coffee

⅔ cup chopped cashews
1 tsp vanilla extract

Beat egg whites until stiff, but not dry. Mix sugar and coffee; gradually add to egg whites, beating constantly until blended. Fold in nuts and vanilla. Drop by teaspoons onto greased sheets. Bake at 160°C (325°F) oven about 15 min. Makes 4 dozen.

Indian Cashew Drop Cookies

1 tbsp vanilla extract
1 cup (2 sticks) butter
  or margarine
1 cup sugar

½ cup salted cashew crumbs
4 dozen cashew nuts
1 egg
2 cups all-purpose flour

Blend together the first two ingredients, gradually add sugar. Stir in cashew nut crumbs and beat in egg. Gradually stir in flour. Drop from tablespoon onto ungreased cookie sheets 2 in. apart. Top each with a cashew nut. Bake in preheated 185°C (375°F) oven 7 min or until brown on edges. Cool on wire racks and store airtight.

Honey Cashew Pudding

2 tbsp butter or margarine
6 tbsp honey
½ cup cashew crumbs
½ cup rolled graham
  crackers
1½ tsp plain gelatin

1 tbsp water
1 cup milk
Salt
1 egg
½ tsp vanilla
½ cup whipping cream

Cream butter with 4 tbsp honey. Blend in cashew crumbs and cracker crumbs. Soften gelatin in water. Scald milk with remaining 2 tbsp honey and salt. Pour over lightly beaten egg, place over hot water, and cook and stir until mixture thickens slightly, 15 to 20 min. Remove from heat and blend in vanilla and softened gelatin. Cool until slightly thickened. Fold in whipped cream. Add cashew mixture and blend lightly, leaving it in small lumps. Chill thoroughly. Serves 6.

Cashew Juice Drink

To obtain juice for beverage purposes the steamed and washed fruit is put through a mechanical extractor or press. Casein, gelatin, pectin or lime juice is added to the juice, which is then strained. Thereafter sugar and citric acid are added to achieve 15° Brix and acidity of 0.4%. The juice is then boiled for a minute and pasteurized in bottles or cans. Variations that may be achieved are nectar, or "cloudy juice," spiced juice, concentrate, and blends with the juice of other fruits, such as pineapple, orange or grape.

Other By-products

Other by-products of the cashew also are economically important. In South America and India the amber-like cashew gum, which exudes from the bark of the tree, is used in book-binding as a retardant against insects, and as an adhesive where it serves as a substitute for gum arabic. It, too, is used to protect wood carvings and floors from wood-eating insects such as ants and termites.

The milky tree sap within the bark of the tree oxidizes on exposure to air and turns black in color. Native populations quickly realized the advantage of this property and applied it as an indelible ink marker for cottons and linens. They utilize the sap as a varnish, as a preservative for fishnets, and as a flux to solder metals.

The wood of the tree is soft to moderately hard and has limited value as timber. It is gray to reddish-brown in color, and is used mostly to make packing cases and frequently for building boats and wheel hubs. It also serves as a firewood and as charcoal.

A sweet tasting salad oil is expressed from the cashew kernels after which it is processed by clarification. Compared to other culinary oils it is expensive and therefore not marketed to any degree.

The semi-wild, jungle cashew tree can be cultivated. Although native to the Americas, eastern tropical countries supply the world with the bulk of its valuable by-products and luscious nuts. The leaves, gum, sap and wood merit increasing attention. With advances in technology, shell liquid continues to grow in economic importance. Successful research in methods to capture, preserve and more fully utilize the fruit juice can reap an added harvest. Man's ingenuity has accomplished new feats with the cashew tree.

CASHEW IMPORTS

India is the world's chief source and biggest exporter of cashews. India also imports from East Africa cashew nuts in the shell, then shells, packs and exports the nuts. About 90% of African raw cashews is imported by India. Difficulties encountered by East Africa in operating processing facilities make this necessary. The cashew has reached such importance today that among the tree nuts in world trade it ranks second only to the almond.

TABLE 8.4

CASHEW IMPORTS INTO INDIA

Country of Origin	1969	1970	1971	1972	1973	1974
			(metric tons)			
Dahomey	409	601	–	–	–	–
Ivory Coast	127	2,302	–	–	976	–
Kenya	7,592	15,007	16,313	17,453	8,338	20,642
Madagascar	–	–	–	–	–	7,755
Malagasy	901	815	851	508	937	–
Other E. Africa	103,308	81,840	58,427	65,981	33,577	61,879
Singapore	30	–	–	–	–	–
Tanzania	78,418	70,220	91,868	108,937	128,282	78,967
Total	190,785	170,785	167,459	192,879	172,110	169,243

Source: Foreign Agric. Serv., FN 1-76.

When the cashew nut was first introduced, it was promoted as a substitute for the more costly almond. It did not take long before the confectionery and baking industries learned the merits inherent in the bland tasting kernels and incorporated them in numerous kinds of candies, chocolates, mixed nutmeats, cakes and biscuits. Roasted and salted cashews proved a favorite of the American palate.

Of all tree nuts imported by the United States, cashews are exceeded in poundage only by the coconut. In dollar value, however, cashews exceed coconut imports.

REFERENCES

ANON. 1964. Exotic-delicious Indian cashews. Indian Cashew J. *3*, 3-6.

ANON. 1965. Cashew and cocktails. Indian Cashew J. *1*, 10-15.

ANON. 1966A. The cashew tree. Indian Cashew J. *1*, 2-9.

ANON. 1966B. Foreign Agricultural Service, U.S. Dep. of Agric., September 19.

ANON. 1976. Tree Nuts. Foreign Agricultural Service. U.S. Dep. Agric., *FN 3-76.*

BAILEY, L.H. 1935. The Standard Cyclopedia of Horticulture, Vol. 1. The Macmillan Co., New York.

HAAGEN-SMIT. 1931. Toxins in cashew shells. Proc. Acad. Sci., Amsterdam *34*, 165-168.

KUZIO, W. 1977. Nutmeat roundup. Candy Ind. *42* (6) 25-42.

MATHEW, A.G., and PARPIA, A.B. 1970. Polyphenols of cashew kernel testa. J. Food Sci. *35* (2) 140-143.

MORTON, J.F. 1961. The cashew's brighter future. Econ. Bot. *15*, 57-78.

RAPHAEL, M.H. 1963. The cashew nut. Manufacturing Confectioner *43* (9) 37-39; (10) 32-35.

RICHARDS, S.I. 1964. Trends in India agricultural trade, F.S.E. U.S. Dep. Agric., Econ. Res. Ser. Reg. and Div. Rept. *15.*

9

Chestnuts

The chestnut (*Castanea*) is a cousin of the oak (*Quercus*), both belonging to the *Fagaceae* family of cup-bearing trees. The nut of the chestnut is similar morphologically to the acorn of the oak. The chestnut bur is a vegetative structure comparable to the acorn cup. The beech (*Fagus*) is also in the same family as chestnut and oak.

While chestnut trees have been grown in most temperate climates of the world for more than 4000 years for beauty, fuel and shelter, the food value of the nuts has always been of prime importance. Productivity, ease of harvesting, simplicity of preparation for eating, and diversity of uses for high and low income people, have been the impelling urge for the growing of chestnuts.

Fear (1891) thought that the chemical composition of chestnuts fit them for larger uses as food than most of our common (high oil) nuts. The large amount of oil in most nuts makes pulverizing difficult and tends to cause them to turn rancid. Chestnuts, and particularly the cultivated cultivars, on the other hand, contain comparatively little oil, are easily made digestible by roasting or boiling, in which process the starch grams are burst open and made less resistant to the attack of the digestive fluids, and contain relatively little astringent substances whose dietetic effects interfere with their use.

He reported that chestnuts range from 21 to 25% shells, 4.5 to 6.5% moisture, and 69 to 72% dry matter. For chemical composition and nutritive value of chestnuts, see Table 3.9.

Composition of the dry matter in chestnuts is shown in Table 9.1. These data show differences in fat, protein, and nitrogen-free extract in Spanish, "paragon" and native chestnuts. The fat content of native chestnuts is about twice that of the Spanish cultivars. It was observed that when European cultivars are grown in America they tend to increase in fat, decrease in nitrogen-free extract, and become less albuminous. Fear (1891) concluded that chestnuts are starchy rather than oily. The European chestnuts closely resemble wheat in composition, but contain less starch and more dextrose and other water-soluble carbohydrates. The small, uncultivated American chestnuts are more oily than the nuts grown in Europe, and contain less starch, though they differ little from the other cultivars in their content in sugars, protein, fiber and other constituents.

TABLE 9.1

COMPOSITION OF CHESTNUTS

Constituents	Spanish 1 %	Spanish 2 %	Paragon %	Native %	Native %
Ash	3.03	2.87	3.12	2.66	2.72
Albuminoids	8.38	9.28	10.91	11.84	10.53
Amids etc.	1.23	1.68	1.23	0.39	1.67
Total protein	9.61	10.96	12.14	12.23	12.20
Fiber	2.55	2.84	2.86	3.63	2.84
Glucose	5.17	12.63	9.13	14.96	3.50
Dextrin	17.45	8.23	10.05	7.63	12.01
Starch	24.24	23.87	32.15	16.81	50.65
Other nitrogen-free extract	30.84	29.02	19.97	26.53	
Total nitrogen-free extract	77.70	73.75	72.30	65.03	66.16
Fat	7.11	9.58	9.76	16.42	16.08

Source: Fear (1891).

Most authors list 7 to 12 species of chestnut and chinquapin. Some of them are so similar they are hard to identify correctly. Natural hybrids occur when two species grow in the same area, which makes identification more difficult. The botanical name is composed of two Latin terms, the first being the genus, the second the species. For example, Chinese chestnut is *Castanea mollissima* L., the letter L referring to the Swedish botanist Linnaeus who first assigned the name. Latin names of plants are the same in all languages, and when properly recorded in the literature, do not change. Common names of a plant may differ from one area to another.

Chinese Chestnut (*Castanea mollissima* B1)

The Chinese chestnut is recognized by the dense hairs on the young leaves. The species name *mollissima* means hairy. In general, the mature leaves are broader in relation to length than those of other species. The margins of leaves are not as deeply serrated as those of the American chestnut, but are deeper than those of the Japanese.

The small seed scar or hilum of the Chinese nut separates it from the

Japanese, which has a large spreading hilum. The Chinese nut has a thin, membranous pellicle or "skin," which separates readily from the kernel.

One of the most important introductions of Chinese chestnut seed to the United States from China was that received by the U.S. Department of Agriculture (McKay and Berry 1960). Seeds were received from several provinces in central and south China, and each was given an alphabetical label such as MBA, MAY and MKE. The seeds were planted at Philema, Georgia, and seedling trees began to bear nuts in 1941. Outstanding trees in this planting were propagated and tested, and in 1949 the cultivars Nanking, Meiling and Kuling were named and introduced.

Another outstanding planting of seedling Chinese chestnut trees was made in 1930 by the Eastern Shore Nurseries, Easton, Maryland (Hemming 1954). This nursery received 25 trees from the U.S. Department of Agriculture that originated from Chinese chestnut seed imported from Nanking, China, under Plant Introduction No. 70314. For many years nuts from these trees were used by the nursery in producing seedlings for sale. A high proportion of these seedling trees produced annual crops of acceptable nuts, and became known as the Hemming strain after the name of the nursery owner.

Japanese Chestnut (*C. crenata* Sieb. & Zucc.)

The Japanese chestnut is a variable species characterized by small leaves with scaly glands on the under surface. The largest nuts of all the chestnut group are produced by members of this species. In stature the Japanese chestnut may vary from a large tree to a small bush. Plants of the Miracle type produce nuts at 2 to 3 years of age when they are 5 ft tall. At Manheim, Pennsylvania, 35 year-old trees have trunks more than 2 ft in diameter.

The Japanese chestnut is more susceptible to blight than the Chinese species. Many trees are killed by the fungus before reaching maturity. A high proportion of the trees of this species deteriorates slowly, gradually loses productivity, and finally is killed by the bark disease. The trees are also less hardy than the Chinese.

Nuts of the Japanese chestnut are poorer in quality as compared to the best Chinese. The pellicle or "nut skin" is fibrous and adheres to the kernel more than in nuts of the Chinese. Nuts generally have a larger seed scar or hilum than those of the Chinese, and frequently are light tan in color.

European Chestnut (*C. sativa* Mill.)

The European chestnut is highly susceptible to blight. The disease is spreading rapidly in the native chestnut forests of Italy, Sicily, Spain and other Mediterranean countries. In a few decades this species may be killed by blight as was the American chestnut. The European chestnut is native in Italy, Sicily, France, Spain and other Mediterranean areas.

The long leaves of the European chestnut resemble those of the American species, both having coarsely toothed margins. However, close examination shows that leaves of *C. dentata* lack hairs and are wedge-shaped at the base, a characteristic that separates this species from the others.

Nuts of the European chestnut are generally dark brown in color, and are more resistant to drying out than those of other species because of the heavy fibrous pellicle. The kernel may be deeply grooved, and the pellicle is frequently folded in the grooves which causes a cleaning problem.

Courtesy of U.S. Dept. Agric.

FIG. 9.1.   LEAVES, NUTS AND BUR OF JAPANESE CHESTNUTS

American Chestnut (*C. dentata* **Borkh.**)

This species is recognized by its long green leaves, lacking hairs. The nuts are small, and usually have a tuft of hairs at the apical end. The nuts average 120 to 150 per lb.

The American chestnut was a large forest tree distributed widely over the Appalachian area of the eastern United States. It was killed during the first quarter of this century by a fungus disease known as chestnut blight, *Endothia parasitica*. The loss of the American chestnut is one of the few cases on record of the complete annihilation of a tree species by a fungus disease.

Stump sprouts still appear on many of the old chestnut roots 40 to 60 years after the trees were killed by blight. This is a remarkable tribute to the rot-resistant nature of the large underground roots. The sprouts sometimes live for several years, developing into small trees before becoming reinfected and eventually dying from blight infection.

Courtesy of U.S. Dept. Agric.

FIG. 9.2. BLIGHT-KILLED AMERICAN CHESTNUT TREES IN
THE MOUNTAINS OF NORTH CAROLINA

In less than 50 years, birds, insects and wind spread the fungus
from infested to healthy trees in every part of the natural range
of the species. A tremendous supply of natural food was cut off
from man, animals and birds.

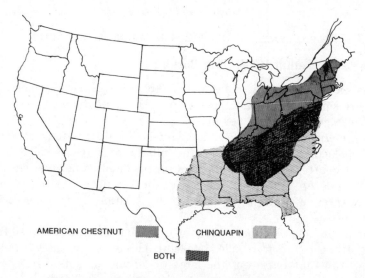

AMERICAN CHESTNUT   CHINQUAPIN

BOTH

FIG. 9.3. DISTRIBUTION OF AMERICAN CHESTNUT AND
CHINQUAPIN IN THE UNITED STATES

Courtesy of U.S. Dept. Agric.

FIG. 9.4. SLEEPING GIANT CULTIVAR OF CHESTNUTS

The prevailing opinion of foresters and pathologists is that the native American chestnut will come back on its own by natural selection. For reasons as yet unexplained, a few very large old American chestnut trees have survived the blight in different areas of the country. Diller (1952) collected scionwood from a number of these and conducted screening tests to determine if the trees showed resistance to blight. A total of 136 American chestnut trees were included in the test, and 4950 scions were distributed to field cooperators for grafting to suitable stocks. At the time of the report, most of the grafts had succumbed to the blight, yet a few were still alive. While the results indicated that most of the trees had simply escaped from the blight, there was some hope that a few of them represented by the living grafts might represent genetically resistant trees.

Chestnut Blight Poisoning.—In 1913, while thousands of acres of native chestnut trees were slowly dying of blight, reports appearing in newspapers and elsewhere of people and animals becoming sick or dying after eating chestnuts led to the suspicion the chestnut blight was a direct or indirect cause of poisoning.

A study revealed several possible causes of illness from eating chestnuts.

(1) Indigestibility of Chestnuts.—Since 13 of the 32 cases of illness reported were children that "ate freely of chestnuts," it was probable they ate more than they could digest at one time. One case reported was "of a woman who ate two quarts of chestnuts, and died from the effects of this overeating."

(2) Poisoning Due to Immaturity or Molding of Chestnuts.—Since no reference was found in literature that chestnuts were listed as poisonous plants, nor of the nuts possessing a poisonous principle, toxins must have developed in the nuts due to molds or other microorganisms. It was established that a period of unusually warm, dry weather in the fall, followed at the time of maturity by copious rains, tended to induce germination in the nuts while still on the trees, and after they fell to the ground. Such germinating chestnuts, though healthy, could not be considered free of toxins produced by enzymes in the nuts or by molds.

It was very probable that the chestnut burs, hulls and meats became contaminated with penicillium or other molds while lying on the damp ground. However, a mixture of rotten, wormy, moldy nuts was fed to white rats without harmful results. It may have been that the chestnuts picked up special toxin-producing fungi from the ground.

(3) Poisoning Due to Chestnut Blight.—The only chance of the blight playing a part would be either indirectly, by poisonous matter developed by the blight organism and carried in the sap to the nuts, which is highly improbable, or in a still more indirect manner, by its injurious action on the tree, causing imperfect ripening of the nuts. To check the toxicity of the fungus, pure cultures were fed to white rats without harmful effects.

(4) Chestnuts Contaminated with Bacteria.—Since some of the victims developed dysentery trouble induced by bacteria on chestnuts probably taken from a polluted stream, it may be that this type of contamination is general in some areas.

(5) Chestnuts with High Tannin.—It is well known that the bark and wood of the chestnut contains from 6 to 12% tannin, an astringent that would cause illness if taken in large enough quantities. It is also well known that some of the tannin is water soluble and may be dissolved and absorbed by meats. However, it is improbable that sufficient tannin was absorbed to produce the symptoms described.

CHARACTERISTICS OF THE CHINESE CHESTNUTS

The remainder of this chapter will be devoted to the Chinese chestnut because it is the most promising species from the standpoint of nut production. The other chestnut and chinquapin species are grown largely as specimen trees and for wildlife food. Moreover, much of the information for the Chinese chestnut applies also to other species.

The Chinese chestnut is suited to nut production in a wide range of climatic and soil conditions. It is as hardy as the peach and can withstand $-29°C$ ($-120°F$) when fully dormant. Trees apparently have a short cold requirement for breaking dormancy in the spring. Buds respond quickly to early warm temperatures and thus become subject to damage by late spring frosts. Chestnut orchards should be located on high or sloping ground to provide air drainage and protection against late spring frosts.

FIG. 9.5. A SEEDLING CHINESE CHESTNUT TREE THAT PRODUCED ONE BUSHEL OF NUTS IN ITS 12TH YEAR

Note the rounded and spreading form of the tree which provides a large number of terminal shoots for heavy nut production.

The cultivar Crane has been grown in Pennsylvania, Maryland, Georgia and Mississippi with equally good results. Orrin originated in northern Pennsylvania and may be suited to growing in northern areas. Chinese chestnut selection No. 7916 was propagated by grafting and the trees tested in a number of locations. The trees produced heavy crops of nuts and vegetative growth was reduced. As a result, weakened shoots were killed during the winter in northern areas, and the selection was a failure. In general, fully dormant trees of Chinese chestnut cultivars are hardy in all areas of the eastern United States.

Flowers and Fruit

The Chinese chestnut is one of the latest trees to blossom, the flowers appearing in early June in the vicinity of Washington, D.C. The flowers are produced in two kinds of catkins borne on current season shoots. The first to flower are the long, finger-like staminate, or male, catkins near the terminal portion of the shoot.

The sequence of bloom of the staminate and pistillate flowers is not always the same in all trees. The wholly staminate catkins on the lower portion of the shoot are the first to shed pollen. Several days later the staminate catkins near the tip of the shoot on the base of which the pistillate flowers are located shed pollen. However, the pistillate flowers may be ready for pollination either before or after the beginning of pollen shed in the first-flowering catkins. Each tree or cultivar has a distinctive pattern of flower maturity that is constant each season. Vilkomerson (1940) reported a number of variations of dichogamy in Chinese chestnut.

Courtesy of U.S. Dept. Agric.

FIG. 9.6. LEAVES, NUTS AND BUR OF CHINESE CHESTNUTS

The fruit of the Chinese chestnut is borne in a spiny involucre known as the "bur." Three nuts are usually produced in each bur (Fig. 9.6, upper left and right). The bur is a vegetative structure that encloses the fruits or nuts. Botanically, each nut is a complete fruit. The shell or the nut develops from the ovary wall. The kernel of the nut is a young embryo plant that develops from the fertilized egg of the ovule. The edible portion of the kernel is made up of two fleshy cotyledons plus minute internal growing points of shoot and root. Enclosing the kernel is a membranous covering called the "pellicle," which originates as the integument of the ovule.

An outstanding feature of the Chinese chestnut is the easily removed pellicle which simplifies preparation of the nuts for eating. The thin

Courtesy of U.S. Dept. Agric.

FIG. 9.7. LEAVES, NUTS AND BUR OF A FIRST–GENERATION
HYBRID BETWEEN THE CHINESE AND AMERICAN CHESTNUT

pellicle of the Chinese nut contrasts with the thick, difficult to remove, fibrous pellicle of Japanese and Italian nuts.

Pollination

So far as known, all cultivars and species of chestnut are self-sterile. Two or more cultivars or seedlings must be planted together to ensure cross-pollination. Young orchard trees may not set nuts when the first flowers are formed because of lack of pollination. When young trees start flowering the few staminate catkins apparently do not produce enough pollen to fertilize the pistillate flowers. Hence, the trees may not produce nuts the first year they blossom.

Clapper (1954) reported that chestnut is wind-pollinated, while others believe that it is pollinated by insects. Whether the agency of pollination is wind or insects, two trees should not be more than a city block apart in order to ensure nut production.

The planting of twin trees is a method of ensuring pollination of a single tree. McKay (1964) reported the discovery of an isolated Chinese chestnut that was unusually productive. Two seedlings grew in the same location, forming a dual trunk, each tree pollinating the other. This suggested the production of twin trees by grafting. In small yard plantings with room for only one tree, a grafted twin tree would be desirable.

Tree Habit

Many low branches are characteristic of the Chinese chestnut. A few low branches should be removed each year to permit freedom of movement under the tree.

Two cultivars, Meiling and Orrin, produce trees with upright growth. Low branches are formed at ground level, as in the cultivar Nanking, but they grow upward. Trees of Meiling and Orrin can be planted closer together in the orchard, and they also make excellent specimen trees in areas where little space is available.

Seedling trees show all intergrading differences between upright and spreading tree habit.

The Chinese chestnut is a long-lived tree that may reach very large size under good growing conditions. Single isolated specimens with a trunk diameter of more than 2 ft and a branch spread of 60 ft or more are known. The tree is slow to start, but once established it grows rapidly. A ten-year-old tree on good soil may be as large as a mature apple tree.

Cultivars

Before discussing cultivars, it should be pointed out that most growers plant seedlings because they cost less than grafted trees. The nurseryman can grow a seedling at less expense than a grafted tree, therefore he can sell the seedling at a lower price. Several growers have planted orchards of improved cultivars and state that grafted trees are superior to seedlings in nut production (Weaver 1957; Wilson 1958). The chestnut industry is young, and growers are not yet aware of the advantage of growing improved cultivars. Other fruit and nut industries passed through the "seedling" stage, and chestnut is likely to advance to "cultivar" status in the future. Other commercial nut industries, such as pecan and Persian walnut now based on horticultural cultivars, began with the planting of seedlings.

Abundance.—This cultivar was developed in the early 1930s from seed imported from China by Carroll D. Bush, Grapeview, Washington. This cultivar was propagated and distributed in the East by Fayette Etter of Lemesters, Pennsylvania.

Reed and Davidson (1954) gave the following description:

This variety is very attractive in appearance. The color of the nut is a rich brown, and its surface has very little down over it. The pellicle upon the kernel is very easily separated from the nut and the flavor is excellent. As a result of these qualities, the Abundance nut is attracting increasing attention among growers, many of whom are using it in topworking seedling trees of poorer qualities. It is likely to become more generally available through regular nursery channels.

Recent observations indicate that nuts of this cultivar are undersized when the tree becomes large. The importance of large size in the marketing of chestnuts pointed out by Wilson (1958) may mean that this cultivar will be superseded by others as the chestnut industry develops.

Crane.—The Crane cultivar originated as a seedling from nuts sent by Peter Liu to the Division of Plant Exploration and Introduction, Department of Agriculture in 1936 (McKay 1963). The nuts were planted at

Philema, Georgia, and the original tree was selected among other seedlings for testing. Scionwood of the cultivar was distributed as Selection No. 7932, and came from the same seed lot as did Nanking, Meiling and Kuling. Propagation was started in 1947 on Chinese chestnut seedling rootstocks and grafted trees were grown with Nanking and other selections at various locations in Louisiana, Mississippi and Maryland. The cultivar was selected by J. W. McKay and named in honor of Dr. H. L. Crane who for many years worked to improve nut tree crops.

The nuts are dark cherry red in color and almost completely glabrous, or without fuzz. The nuts average 32 per lb when well grown. Edibility is excellent when they are well cured, and their keeping quality is superior to all current cultivars.

The Crane cultivar flowers in midseason, concurrent with Nanking, and the two cultivars cross-pollinate. Grafted trees of Crane usually start to bear the second year after planting and may have some nuts the first year.

Kuling.—Seeds that produced the original Kuling cultivar were collected by Peter Liu at Hang Chow, China. One year-old seedlings were planted at Philema, Georgia, in 1936 by the U.S. Department of Agriculture. Seedling No. 7919 was selected for propagation and testing, and introduced commercially in 1949 as the cultivar Kuling. The nuts are dark brown in color and average 35 to 40 per lb. The tree is more upright in growth than most *C. molissima* trees.

Meiling.—This cultivar originated as Seedling No. 7880 at Philema, Georgia, from seed imported from Hsin Teng Sinting, China, under Plant Introduction No. 108,553. It was introduced by the U.S. Department of Agriculture, with cultivars Nanking and Kuling, in 1949. Nuts of Meiling are light tan in color and resemble Nanking so closely that the two cannot be distinguished from each other. The tree is distinctly upright in growth habit, which distinguishes it from most other cultivars and seedlings.

Nanking.—Nanking is perhaps the most widely planted of all Chinese chestnut cultivars. It originated as Seedling No. 7930 in the Philema planting and from Seed Lot No. 108,552, which also produced Kuling. Nanking is second only to Crane in precocity, grafted trees frequently bearing nuts in their second year. The tree continues to bear heavy crops of nuts annually, often producing 30 or more lb of nuts at 10 years of age. Nuts are dark tan in color and usually yield 30 to 35 per lb.

Orrin.—The Orrin cultivar originated on the farm of Mr. Orrin S. Good at Lockhaven, Pennsylvania. Mr. Good planted his orchard with seedlings obtained from Leeland Farms Nursery, Leesburg, Georgia. Since

Leeland Farms obtained seed from the orchard in which Nanking, Mei-ling and Kuling were grown, this cultivar has a similar origin to these cultivars. Mr. Good made these selections available to the Horticultural Crops Research Branch of the U.S. Department of Agriculture for prop-agation, evaluation and potential introduction. The cultivar, tested as Good C-7, was named Orrin in honor of Mr. Good.

The nuts are dark mahogany, almost black in color, with a slightly pubescent tip. The light-colored seed scar contrasting with the dark color gives the nuts of Orrin a distinctive appearance. The nuts usually aver-age 32 per lb, and are earlier maturing than Nanking. Keeping quality is superior to that of all other cultivars except Crane.

Colby.—Chinese-American hybrid (*C. mollissima sativa*) was devel-oped by Dr. A. S. Colby of the University of Illinois, Urbana, Illinois. The original tree died of blight in 1948, and it is doubtful that the cultivar exists today.

Conard.—Russell Smith, proprietor of Sunny Ridge Nursery, Round Hill, Virginia, first listed this cultivar in 1948. He stated that it is Chinese and bears reasonably well. The nursery has been abandoned for many years, and the cultivar is probably not propagated.

Hemming.—The Hemming cultivar was developed at Eastern Shore Nurseries, Easton, Maryland, from seeds sent by the U.S. Department of Agriculture (1944). H.F. Stoke of Roanoke, Virginia, grafted six scions on a Chinese chestnut seedling, all of which made good unions. It is a successful cultivar, except that nuts tend to vary in size and occasionally split open when ripe.

Other Cultivars.—Older cultivars that have been propagated to a limited extent include **Carr, Hobson, Reliable, Stoke, Yankee, Honna** and **Zimmerman**. Many of these are probably obsolete and not available from nurserymen. The cultivars **Alaling, Alamoore** and **Black Beauty** were released by the Alabama Agricultural Experiment Station but have not been widely distributed. According to Fisher (1965) the cultivars **Chinkapin A, Colby** and **Hartselle** were introduced by the University of Illinois but no information is given.

Nut Quality and Size

Chestnut size is determined by several factors, chiefly tree nutrition. Nuts from two Nanking trees growing in different soil in the same orchard are shown in Fig. 9.8. Tree No. 3-1 was located in an eroded area with an impervious hardpan near the surface. The larger nuts from Tree 3-8 were produced on deep, alluvial soil in another part of the orchard.

Both trees were planted at the same time and received similar applications of fertilizer. This illustration emphasizes the importance of planting orchards on good soil. Overproduction will also cause nut size to be smaller than normal.

Tree age is another factor that influences nut size. Young trees usually bear larger nuts than mature trees of the same cultivar. Young trees frequently produce fewer nuts per unit leaf area than mature trees. Trees in young orchards have not exhausted mineral nutrients from the soil in the same way as mature trees.

Nut size on an individual tree may vary widely. Branches with a heavy crop bear smaller nuts than those with only a few burs. Variability in size of nuts from a single tree is shown graphically in Fig. 9.8. In this illustration, distribution of Nanking nuts in weight classes of 3 to 13 g follows approximately the normal curve of distribution.

FIG. 9.8. NUTS FROM TWO NANKING CHINESE CHESTNUT
TREES GROWING IN THE SAME ORCHARD

The small nuts of tree No. 3-1 were produced in eroded soil
having a shallow hardpan. Tree No. 3-8 was located in deep,
alluvial soil of high fertility.

Nut quality is greatly affected by condition and curing. Kernels of freshly harvested nuts contain mostly starch and very little sugar. Nuts dried to a 15% moisture loss develop up to 5% sugar in the kernels. This is called curing. An easy way to determine if nuts are properly cured is to press one between the thumb and forefinger; if it feels slightly soft it is properly cured.

Little is known about the chemical changes that occur in the nut at the time of curing. The author once collected nuts from the ground in an orchard in December; the sugar content of these was 10%. This is twice the amount normally occurring in well-cured nuts. Subsequent attempts were made, both in the laboratory and orchard, to produce the high sugar content of the nuts mentioned above, without success.

Many tests have been made to determine if nuts of one cultivar are superior to those of another in keeping quality. In most cases the difference is small and difficult to determine, and if significant the nuts have not usually received the same treatment. Quality in chestnuts is without question greatly influenced by methods of handling and storage.

A new kind of chestnut with an orange kernel having five times as much carotene as the normal nut was reported by McKay (1956B). However, only 2 to 4% of the nuts produced by 3 seedling Chinese chestnut trees contained the orange kernels. In order to be of nutritional importance, cultivars would have to be developed that produced 100% orange kernels.

Potential Yield and Bearing Characteristics

Seedling Chinese chestnut trees usually require 5 to 8 years to start bearing, whereas grafted trees of improved cultivars frequently bear nuts the second year after planting. Bearing capacity appears to be an inherited characteristic, and many seedling trees never bear satisfactory crops. In seedling orchards, poor yielding trees should be topworked to improve cultivars. An exceptional seedling tree that yielded 65 lb of nuts at 12 years of age is illustrated in Fig. 9.5.

Seedlings from seed produced by certain parent trees are superior to those produced by other parents. Seedlings from the cultivar Nanking produced a higher proportion of productive, superior trees than those from several other cultivars. The 19 Chinese chestnut trees planted by the Eastern Shore Nurseries, Easton, Maryland, in 1930 have produced a high proportion of excellent seedlings. The Hemming trees were remarkably uniform in all characteristics, and interpollinated to produce remarkably homogenous offspring. Growers planting seedlings should be sure they obtain trees from a source that supplies a high proportion of superior offspring.

VALUE OF CHESTNUT TREES

Orchards

Nut production in chestnut orchards is not extensive enough to determine the value of an individual tree. Storey (1964) gives a formula for estimating the value of a pecan tree based upon known production practices. As long as the chestnut industry is based upon the variable performance of seedling orchards, the evaluation of trees will be difficult. Planting grafted trees of improved cultivars is the first step towards standardizing orchard production so that individual trees may be evaluated with more certainty. The cost of planting is no greater than that for pecan or other nut trees.

The marketing outlook is one of the chief considerations in evaluating a chestnut orchard. The American public's familiarity with the chestnut as a food item has almost disappeared since the American species was killed by blight more than four decades ago. Chase (1956) points out that programs of consumer education are necessary to familiarize our younger generation with the Chinese chestnut. Three basic aspects of a successful marketing program may be listed as follows: (1) development of early-maturing cultivars that allow marketing before the European chestnuts appear; (2) production of a quality product at a moderate price (this includes grading and storing the nuts to assure a uniform product); (3) marketing the shelled nuts as clean kernels in polyethylene bags, both as a fresh and frozen food product.

Food Production for Wildlife

Nuts of the American chestnut provide food for a number of wildlife species. Loss of the chestnut resulted in a great reduction of many species and complete disappearance of others, as in the case of the wild turkey. Recognizing the value of the chestnut as food for wildlife, officials in several states began planting Chinese chestnuts on game preserves three or more decades ago. Anthony and Sherman (1951) estimated more than 50,000 seedling Chinese and Japanese chestnuts in State game areas and private plantings in Pennsylvania. Suitability of the Chinese chestnut for planting as food for wildlife in Virginia was reported by McKay (1952).

Timber

For many years the U.S. Department of Agriculture and the Connecticut Agricultural Experiment Station conducted research to develop a timber-producing tree by crossing the Chinese chestnut, *Castanea molissima*, with the American species, *C. dentata*. The U.S. Department of Agriculture program was discontinued in 1960 but the Connecticut research is still in progress (Diller *et al.* 1964; Graves and Jaynes 1959). To develop a timber tree for reforestation purposes, it would be necessary to inbreed the first-generation hybrids until uniform progeny of the desired type resulted. Meanwhile, pine poles are now treated with chemicals to make them last as long as chestnut, thus making it no longer necessary or profitable to produce chestnut poles.

Diller (1952) has been the foremost proponent of reforestation with the Chinese chestnut, and for many years he planted Chinese chestnut seedlings in state and national forests in the East with a standard spacing of 8 and 10 ft on the square. The trees grew tall straight trunks since they were crowded, and the lower limbs were shaded and soon died. Nut production was confined to the tops of the trees, and nuts were usually small in size. Diller found that soil type, available moisture and site were important in producing maximum growth of forest type trees. He concluded that large plantings for timber are not in prospect because Chinese chestnut requires good land for maximum timber production with closely spaced trees.

SPECIAL CULTURAL PRACTICES

Site

As much attention should be given to selecting a site for Chinese chestnut trees as the soil in which they are planted. The trees should be located on high sloping ground in order to provide adequate air drainage to prevent damage from late spring frosts. The tree blossoms late in the spring, and young flowers are formed soon after the buds begin to swell. They are therefore subject to killing in the same manner as flowers of peach and other fruit trees. Trees located on low ground or in frost pockets are almost sure to be injured by freezes in late spring. In some cases whole limbs or even the entire tree may be killed if growth has proceeded far enough to make the tree susceptible to frost damage.

In choosing a site for planting Chinese chestnut trees, it is well to plant a few trees on a trial basis until it is determined that the site is suitable for the orchard. Until more information is available as to cultural practices for the production of this new crop, it is best not to devote high-priced land to an unproved crop.

Soil

Experience has shown that Chinese chestnuts grow best on a sandy or sandy loam soil that is well drained. As a rule, the soil should be moderately to slightly acid, but in a few instances well-fertilized and well-cared-for trees are known to grow well on a slightly alkaline soil. Trees will not grow on low ground that is poorly drained. There are some indications that chestnut trees will withstand a moderate amount of drought when well established. Near Oklahoma City, Oklahoma, one planting produces regular crops of nuts even though frequent droughts are commonplace (Hirschi 1946).

On sandy soils of low fertility, organic matter should be increased by the use of green manure cover crops. Crimson clover in the South and Hairy Vetch in the North are leguminous crops that can be plowed under during the growing season for increasing organic matter in the soil. In some soil of low fertility, trace element deficiencies may develop in the trees which may be identified by leaf analysis. Most State Experiment Stations provide this service in connection with soil analysis procedures.

Young orchards should receive clean cultivation until the trees are established. Weeds and briars choke out young trees during the first or second year of growth unless they are removed. Row crops, such as corn or soybeans, may be grown between the trees for the first few years. A long drought immediately following planting may be fatal to young trees; hence, irrigation facilities are desirable in case they are needed.

The sod mulch system of orchard management may be employed with established trees. The orchard may be sowed to orchard grass or clover mixtures, and mowed once or twice during the growing season. The hay is then placed around the trees to prevent moisture loss and weed development. In some areas it is necessary to rake away the mulch from underneath the trees periodically to discourage field mice. The sod mulch system is desirable in hilly areas to control soil erosion. More fertilizer must be applied to the trees than in the clean cultivation system because of competition with the ground cover.

Fertilization

When chestnut trees are planted on eroded upland soils, it is necessary to fertilize the trees regularly. A good rule to follow is to apply 1 lb of 5-10-5 mixed fertilizer per year of tree age. Another method is to apply 1 lb of 5-10-5 mixed fertilizer per inch of tree trunk diameter. One caution is not to mix fertilizer with the soil when the tree is planted, or apply fertilizer around a newly planted tree. It is best to start fertilizer application the second year in order to avoid fertilizer burn caused by the tree not having roots to absorb nutrients.

With large established trees the fertilizer may be spread underneath the branches and several feet beyond. Tree roots develop in the soil to a distance of twice the spread of the branches in established trees.

Transplanting

Transplanting may be done either in the fall or spring in the South, preferably only in the spring in northern areas. Nursery trees dug with a special U-shaped blade are best for planting because there is little damage to the roots.

Chinese chestnut trees should be spaced at least 40 ft apart. The trend at present is towards closer spacing of trees in all fruit crops to increase production in early years of the orchard. Hedgerow pruning and other drastic pruning practices are employed to keep the trees small. One practice is to plant the trees 25 ft apart and later remove half the trees to give a final spacing of 50 ft.

Pruning

The Chinese chestnut forms a low-headed tree if left unpruned (Fig. 9.5). Unpruned trees start bearing sooner than those severely pruned. Early pruning stimulates vegetative growth instead of flower-producing shoots. Hence, for early nut production orchard trees should not be pruned for a few years. An ideal practice is to allow the trees to come into bearing before any pruning is done, then remove only a few of the lowest branches each year until the tree is properly headed. Lower limbs were removed gradually from the tree shown in Fig. 9.5 and this practice will be continued.

Harvesting

Peterson and Monroe (1960) reported that surveys of chestnut growers ranked harvesting as one of the major problems facing the chestnut industry. Chestnuts are a very perishable crop that requires prompt harvesting every 1 to 2 days. Traditionally, they have been hand gathered from the ground after falling naturally. This task is time consuming and the supply of labor for such work is decreasing yearly. It has been suggested that chestnuts can be easily harvested mechanically by shaking the burs from the trees and using a mechanical pickup device to gather the nuts, but there are few data to support this claim. If chestnuts can be shaken from the trees, it might be better to catch and collect the crop before it reaches the ground to reduce trash and contamination in the harvested crop.

Tests were made at Byron, Georgia on seedling Chinese chestnut trees that were 10 years old, had average trunk diameter of 7 in., and measured 3 ft above the ground. A commercially available inertia shaker and a half-rollout catching frame were used to mechanically harvest chestnuts. The trees were shaken for only 6 sec since nut removal stopped near the end of this shaking interval. As the chestnuts with burs were collected on the half-rollout catching frame, leaves and small sticks were removed by cleaning equipment on the unit. All remaining nuts on the trees were hand picked.

A mechanical means for removing chestnut burs was developed. The device consisted of a 26-in. diameter rotating rubber tire and a feed-in belt. The tire, which was perpendicular to the feed-in belt, rotated at 1.5 revolutions per second toward the incoming burs and the feed-in belt. The feed-in belt was driven at $\frac{1}{14}$ the speed of the tire, and was spaced from ¼ to ¾ in. from the tire, depending on bur size. As the chestnuts and burs passed between the rotating tire and the feed-in belt they were subjected to a rolling and squeezing action that caused the chestnuts to separate from the burs. Both the chestnuts and burs were then dropped into an air stream. The burs were carried away by the air stream to a discard container, and the nuts dropped into another container. Any bur that still contained a chestnut fell into the nut container and was then run through the deburring device again. Deburring was 90% effective.

The chestnuts were then treated in a 20 ppm solution of Benlate and Botran (2,6-Dichloro-4-nitroaniline) to prevent spoilage. They were cured for 5 days at 21° (70°F).

For the conventional hand harvesting of chestnuts from the ground, the time between first harvest for the earliest seedling and the first harvest for the latest seedling is 16 days. The harvest period for each tree lasted from a minimum of 17 days to a maximum of 30 days and averaged 23 days. The inertia shaker and half-rollout catching frame were effective in harvesting an average 94% of the crop.

The conclusion of this test that, at the time of initial nut drop, most Chinese chestnut seedlings do not have the uniform maturity necessary for once-over mechanical harvesting, seems feasible. Selecting seedlings for uniform maturity would be worthwhile in any chestnut breeding program. Furthermore, the use of the shaker, catching frame and bur removal device was considered effective.

Storing

Fresh chestnuts contain 40 to 45% carbohydrates, mostly in the form of starch, about 5% oil and about 50% moisture. They are highly perishable because the nuts lose moisture rapidly at room temperature, causing the kernel to become hard and inedible.

Spoilage is almost always due to mold. To prevent molding: (a) the mold organisms must be destroyed; (b) the moisture content of the nutmeats must be 10% or lower; (c) the relative humidity of the storage atmosphere must be 70% or lower; or (d) the storage temperature must be 0°C (32°F) or lower.

Mold on chestnuts may be destroyed by hot water bath. Freshly harvested chestnuts with as high as 50% incipient fungus infection may be held for 2 months, in perforated polyethylene bags, at 4.4°C (40°F) after one hour in 51.7°C (125°F) water. A lower temperature or shorter time in the bath fails to destroy mold organisms, and a higher temperature of 60.0°C (140°F) causes severe injury to the chestnuts.

Spoilage may be prevented by proper drying. Freshly harvested chestnuts may be held for more than 1 year at 4.4°C (40°F) if they are reduced to 10% moisture over a period of about 4 days. Drying temperatures above 4.4°C (40°F) should be avoided and the moisture content should not go below 6%. To use these excessively dry and hard meats in cooking, they need moistening by soaking or steaming for about 30 min.

One of the best ways of drying chestnuts is to put them in mesh bags and hold at 4.4°C (40°F) with well-circulated air at 70% relative humidity. Under these conditions the nuts will "cure" and dry to the optimum moisture content without further attention.

A third method of preventing spoilage is to place the freshly harvested chestnuts at 1.1°C (34°F). At this temperature they will not mold, and will gradually dry to an optimum moisture content. Freezing will injure fresh chestnuts, but will not injure "cured" or hot water "blanched" chestnuts.

Chestnuts must be kept dry on the surface at all times to prevent slime and recontamination with mold. They should be held at 4.4°C (40°F) or lower to prevent infestation with insects. Rancidity, as with other nuts, is not a problem in storing chestnuts.

Courtesy of U.S. Dept. Agric.

FIG. 9.9. CHESTNUTS ARE AMONG THE EASIEST OF ALL NUTS TO HANDLE MECHANICALLY

This includes shaking from the trees, gathering, separating the hulls and trash, grading, storing, shelling and using in foods.

The storage problem has been partly solved through the selection of new cultivars having nuts resistant to storage organisms. The new horticultural cultivars Crane and Orrin were selected because of the excellent keeping qualities of the nuts. However, the chestnut industry is still based mostly upon the planting of seedling trees. Until growers plant improved cultivars with nuts resistant to spoilage the storage problem will remain.

It was formerly considered necessary to cure the nuts before storage. Tests have shown that the nuts may be placed in storage immediately after harvest as long as the containers are left partially open to allow condensation to escape. Curing, or drying, of the nuts is important to prepare them for eating. The nuts should remain in a dry room at normal temperature for at least four days, or until they become partially soft. Some of the starches are then changed to sugar, which improves the eating quality.

Propagation from Seed

Chestnut seeds planted immediately after harvest germinate poorly. A storage treatment of 1 to 2 months at 0° to 2.2°C (32° to 36°F) is necessary to break the dormancy of chestnut embryos and ensure uniform germination.

Chestnut seeds should be planted early in the spring as soon as the soil is slightly warm and can be worked. Late March and early April are suitable periods for most areas. The nuts are usually planted 6 in. apart in rows 3 ft wide to allow for intensive cultivation. Seeds are planted 2 to 3 in. deep, or 3 times the diameter of the nut. The rows are cultivated often during the first year of growth, and all weeds are removed to give the nut seedlings room to grow and to eliminate competition for moisture and nutrients. When the seedlings are 6 to 8 in. tall, fertilizer may be applied by adding one handful of 5-10-5 mixed fertilizer to each 4 ft of row. The fertilizer should be placed in a band on each side of the row at a distance of 6 in. from the seedlings and worked into the soil.

Grafting and Budding

The three main essentials to success in grafting are (1) good scionwood, (2) proper timing, and (3) suitable technique. In the judgment of the writer, these are listed in the order of importance. A great deal can be learned by reading and studying about the first and third essentials, but the second, which deals mostly with condition of the stock, is a matter of training and experience.

One of the main reasons why many people have difficulty in propagating nut trees is the use of too many techniques. Most bulletins and textbooks giving directions for nut tree propagation list a great many grafting and budding procedures. Each worker should limit his endeavors to one or two grafting techniques until he becomes skilled in these procedures.

Since good scionwood is the first essential in successful grafting, knowing how to select it is important. The first rule is to be sure the shoot has good buds with a small pith and a high proportion of wood. In general, only the basal part of the current year's growth has sufficient wood for desirable use. Food reserves are stored in the wood, which explains why scionwood should have very little pith.

If scionwood is cut from a mature bearing tree which does not have vigorous one-year-old wood, each piece cut should include part of the two-year-old portion of the shoot. The two-year-old portion is then used in making the cut for attaching the scion to the stock. In this kind of material, each piece of scionwood will yield only one scion.

The second rule in cutting scionwood is to be certain the buds are dormant when the shoots are collected. The month of March is considered safe for cutting dormant scionwood in most of the northern areas, whereas it should be cut somewhat earlier in more southern locations.

When it is possible to anticipate needs, the best scionwood is produced by cutting back portions of a tree to stimulate the production of large, vigorous shoots the following year. Shoots of 2 to 4 ft in length can usually be produced on trees of average vigor. The basal half of such shoots makes excellent scionwood.

The simplest and most efficient method of storing scionwood is to place the shoots in polyethylene bags and store at 0° to 2.2°C (32° to 36°F). Most workers cut scionwood in lengths of 8 to 10 in., which results in each piece yielding 2 scions.

Grafting is discussed under three headings: rootstocks, nursery practice, and topworking.

Rootstocks for cultivars of the Chinese chestnut should be seedlings of the same species, *Castanea mollisima*. Chestnut species hybridize freely when planted near each other, and seedlings from such mixed plantings are likely to show hybrid characteristics. Use of such seedlings as rootstocks is a possible explanation of graft union failure in propagation of Chinese chestnut cultivars. MacDaniels (1955) suggests that incompatible grafts between Chinese chestnut cultivars and supposedly Chinese chestnut stocks may be due to differences in strains of Chinese chestnut stocks. The "strains" of MacDaniels could be hybrid seedlings that have originated from mixed plantings where species hybridization has prevented the harvesting of pure Chinese chestnut seed. Nurserymen and others growing Chinese chestnut seedlings for rootstocks should be sure that Japanese chestnut, chinquapins and other chestnut species are not growing near the trees from which seeds are harvested.

Nursery grafting is the propagation of small trees for transplanting. Splice grafting, using scion and stock of the same diameter, is the most satisfactory technique. Whip grafting, a modified form of the splice technique, is used by some workers.

Two important considerations in nursery grafting are (1) to allow the rootstock to leaf out fully, and (2) to use dormant scionwood. Many workers graft early in the spring when buds of the rootstock begin to swell. Buds of grafts put on this early may start growth in time to be killed by a late spring frost. The chestnut has only one bud at each node and if it is killed by a late spring frost, no further growth occurs. The operator may thus lose the results of an entire season by grafting too early.

Buds of scionwood must be dormant so they will not dry out after grafting. Dormant buds are provided with protective bud scales to ensure against water loss. When buds become active and start to grow, this protective covering is lost.

Topworking a large chestnut tree has two objectives: (1) the quick fruitage of the new top, and (2) improving a poor producer. The inlay bark graft described by Romberg is the most satisfactory method of grafting limbs of a large tree (1945). As in nursery grafting, the stock tree should be allowed to leaf out before the grafting is done. This is usually late April or early May for northern areas, and earlier in southern locations. Dormant scionwood of ⅜ to ¾ in. diameter with good buds is essential for best results.

Budding of chestnut is not widely practiced because the wood is fluted or grooved, and the cambium of bud and stock do not join uniformly.

Special methods of propagating chestnuts include the buried-in-arch method of rooting cuttings, developed by Jaynes (1961). He (1964) also developed a method of rooting cuttings by use of sprouted seeds as nurse plants. At present these methods are largely used in research, but with further refinement they may find more extended use in general nursery and orchard practice.

USES OF CHESTNUTS OVER THE WORLD

Powell (1899) stated that before chestnut culture can become a prominent industry, there will need to be a larger appreciation of the uses of chestnuts. In many European countries, chestnuts are looked upon as a staple article of diet. He continued:

In France from the Bay of Biscay to Switzerland, there are large plantations, and almost forests, of chestnut trees. The nuts are large, broad, and resemble the American horse-chestnut or buckeye (*Esculus hippocastanum*) and are extensively eaten by human beings and animals ... The poor people, during fall and winter, often make two meals daily from chestnuts. The ordinary way of cooking them is is to remove the outside shell, blanch them, then a wet cloth is placed in an earthen pot, which is almost filled with raw chestnuts; they are covered with a second wet cloth and put on the fire to steam; they are eaten with salt and milk. Hot steamed chestnuts are carried around the city streets in baskets or pails; the majority of the working people, who usually have no fire in the morning, eat them for their first breakfast, with or without milk.... These nuts are often eaten as a vegetable, and are very popular, being found on the table of the well-to-do and wealthy. They are served not only boiled, but roasted, steamed, pureed, and as dressings for poultry and meats.

Chestnuts are made into bread by the mountain peasantry. After the nuts have been blanched, they are dried and ground. From this flour, a sweet, heavy, flat cake is made. It resembles the oaten cake so popular among the peasants.

In Italy, the chestnut forms a considerable part of the diet of people during the fall and winter, where they are generally eaten roasted. They are also much eaten in the cooked state; often prepared like a stew, with gravy. Also, the chestnuts are dried until they are hard as dried peas, then shelled, after horses have been driven over them to crack the shells. The dried nuts can be shipped anywhere, and are said to be as good for cooking purposes as the fresh ones. These are also sold on the streets and eaten like peanuts.

In Korea, by far the most common food nut is the chestnut, which the potato occupies with us. The chestnut is used raw, boiled, roasted, cooked with meat, made into confections, powdered and mixed with candy, and dried whole, in which latter condition it becomes quite sweet, but is apt to be affected by worms.

In Japan, great quantities of chestnuts are raised, but they are used less for human food than they are elsewhere. They are fed largely to swine. The latter practice may account for the poorer quality of the Japanese chestnut, quantity rather than quality, being the desideratum among the Japanese. However, large quantities are sold for human food in Tokyo.

FORMULAS FOR USING CHESTNUTS

Chestnuts have been used in food combinations in Asia, Europe and America since recorded history. Formulas have accumulated in history books and cookbooks in many languages so that it is impossible to give the usual credit to those who first used them. The following 32 old and new methods of using chestnuts provide a choice for serving them in the home, in public eating places and by manufacturers.

To Shell Chestnuts

Cut a ½ in. gash on flat side of nut and put in a skillet, allowing ½ tsp of butter to each cup of chestnuts. Shake over heat until butter is melted. Put in oven and let stand 5 min. Remove from oven and with a small knife take off shells. By this method shelling and blanching are accomplished at the same time, as skins adhere to the shells.

To Boil Chestnuts

Place in a sauce pan and half cover with water. Boil 20 min, empty water and leave chestnuts in the pan to dry off before shelling. By leaving on low heat and drying slightly, the chestnut kernels do not crumble on shelling. Chestnuts may be stored in jars in refrigerator for later use in other chestnut recipes.

To Bake Chestnuts

Remove shells from one pint of chestnuts, put in a baking dish, cover with stock, season with salt and pepper, bake until soft, keep tin covered until nearly done. There should be a small quantity of stock in pan to serve with chestnuts.

To Roast Chestnuts

After making a cut through the shell near the base to avoid bursting or exploding during roasting, place the prepared nuts in a pan and put in moderate oven 190°C (375°F). When chestnuts appear about three-quarters roasted, remove from oven and place them in the folds of a wool cloth, to keep them soft while cooling down. Chestnuts prepared this way are very tasty.

To Sand Roast Chestnuts

Half fill a frying pan with sand and heat over hot fire. Put in a handful of raw chestnuts. If sand is real hot, it will require about 12 min to cook the chestnuts.

Chestnut Stuffing #1

2 lb chestnuts	Salt and pepper to taste
1 egg	½ pint stock
1 tsp sugar	4 oz drippings
Pinch of dried herbs	2 oz bread crumbs

Slit and boil the chestnuts for 15 min. Skin them and put them into the stock. Simmer for 1 hour. Then rub them through sieve and add the egg and the drippings, mixed herbs and seasonings. Use as needed.

Chestnut Stuffing #2

3 cups chestnuts	⅓ tsp pepper
½ cup butter	¼ cup cream
1 tsp salt	1 cup cracker crumbs

Shell and blanch chestnuts. Cook in boiling salted water until soft. Drain and mash, adding one-half of butter, salt, pepper and cream. Melt remaining butter, mix with cracker crumbs.

Chestnut Stuffing #3

1½ cups finely chopped onion	1½ tsp salt
1½ cups finely chopped celery	⅛ tsp pepper
⅔ stick (⅓ cup) butter	½ tsp poultry seasoning
8 cups dry bread cubes	½ tsp sage
1 cup chopped cooked chestnuts	¼ cup water
	1 egg, well beaten

Cook onion and celery in butter in a skillet until tender. Add mixture to bread cubes which have been placed in a large pan. Add nuts and sprinkle with seasonings. Combine. Add water and egg. Toss together with forks. Stuff bird immediately and roast. Enough for a 12-lb bird.

Chestnut and Prune Stuffing

Simmer 18 large prunes in ⅓ cup red wine in a saucepan until tender, and allow to cool. Remove the seed, cut prunes into quarters, and return them to the pan. Cook one small bunch of celery, trimmed of leaves and thinly sliced, and one medium onion, coarsely chopped, in 3 tbsp butter for few minutes, or until they begin to soften. Remove from the heat, stir in 3 cups cooked chestnuts, broken into pieces. Add the grated rind of ½ large lemon, 1½ tsp salt, ¾ tsp summer savory, ½ tsp freshly ground pepper, and the prunes with the wine. Let the mixture cool completely. Mix one egg, beaten slightly. Makes enough stuffing for two large turkeys.

Sausage and Chestnut Stuffing

1 small onion chopped	¼ tsp pepper
¼ cup butter	¼ tsp thyme
½ lb of pork sausage	2 tbsp chopped parsley
2 lb chestnuts	1 cup soft stale bread cubes

Cook onion in the butter 3 min. Add sausage meat and cook 5 min longer. Cook, and shell chestnuts and mash them coarsely. Add onion mixture and remaining ingredients; mix well. Use as stuffing for chicken. Makes about 6 cups.

Chestnut Purée

1 lb chestnuts	½ tsp sugar
½ cup milk	½ cup butter
¼ tsp salt	

Peel chestnuts, boil in water 30 min, or until tender, remove from fire and peel off skin. Place chestnuts in saucepan with milk, mash with fork until smooth, add salt, sugar and butter and mix well over low fire. Serves 4.

Chestnut Soup

Roast lightly a pound of chestnuts. Shell, chop coarsely and heat in double boiler with a pint of milk and seasonings for half an hour. Rub through sieve. Add 3 pints of chicken stock, 1 tbsp each of butter and flour blended together and cook for 20 min. Just before serving, add 1 egg beaten in 3 tbsp sherry.
NOTE: To blend butter and flour, melt butter, add flour and stir until smooth.

Potato Salad with Chestnuts

Peel 24 small cooked potatoes and while still warm combine them with ¼ cup scallions and 2 tbsp parsley, both minced, ¼ cup melted butter, ¾ cup white wine mixed with 2 tbsp white wine vinegar and a scant ½ cup olive oil, 2 pimientos, cut in small pieces, and ¾ cup whole cooked chestnuts. Add salt and pepper to taste and let the salad stand in a cool place for several hours before serving.

Brussels Sprouts and Chestnuts

3 pkg (10 oz each) frozen	1 cup (4 oz) Bonbel cheese
Brussels sprouts	1 can (11 oz) whole chestnuts,
¼ cup (½ stick) butter	drained
¼ cup flour	Salt and white pepper
1 cup chicken broth	4 strips bacon, cubed and fried
1 cup (½ pint) light cream	until crisp

Cook Brussels sprouts in salted boiling water just to cover until they are tender. Drain. Melt butter and stir in flour. Gradually stir in chicken broth and cream. Cook over low heat, stirring constantly until mixture bubbles and thickens. Add Bonbel cheese and stir until cheese melts. Fold in Brussels sprouts and chestnuts. Reheat and season to taste with salt and pepper. Pour mixture into a serving dish and sprinkle with crumbled bacon. Serve hot. Makes 6 to 8 servings.

Chestnut-Turkey Chop Suey

1 can (4 oz) mushroom	1 can (16 oz) Chinese
pieces and stems, drained	vegetables
1 medium onion, sliced (about	1 can (5 oz) water chestnuts,
1 cup)	drained and sliced
2 tbsp butter or margarine	1 tbsp soy sauce

1 pkg (2 lb) giblet gravy   Cooked rice
and sliced turkey

Cook mushrooms and onion in butter until mushrooms are lightly browned. Remove frozen turkey slices in gravy from foil pan. Place in large skillet. Add remaining ingredients, except rice. Heat covered over medium heat 15 min or until turkey is hot. Stir occasionally to separate slices. Uncover. Simmer 8 min or until sauce is of desired consistency. Serve over rice. Serves 4 to 5.

Souffle of Chestnuts

1½ lb of chestnuts   2 egg whites, beaten
¼ tsp of salt   stiff
1½ cups stock   1 tsp butter

Shell chestnuts, boil 30 min, or until tender, remove from fire and remove second skin. Force through colander. Place in saucepan, add salt, butter and stock and cook, stirring well, until stock has evaporated. Cool. Fold in stiff egg whites and pour mixture into greased casserole. Bake in moderate oven 190°C (375°F) 20 min. Serves 4.

Chestnut Duck

Clean and chop a duck in pieces. Put in a kettle, cover with boiling water, and cook slowly for 1 hour. Add 6 cups of chestnuts and 2 cups mushrooms, salt, pepper, and 4 tbsp of Chinese sauce. Cook for 30 min and serve hot.

Deviled Chestnuts

Roast or boil desired amount of chestnuts and remove shells. Sprinkle with salt and cook in skillet in butter (enough to grease well) for about 5 min. If more seasoning is preferred sprinkle with pepper, Worchestershire sauce or Tabasco sauce.

Candied Yams with Chestnuts

Prepare potatoes as usual for your favorite candied yams recipe. Alternate layer of potatoes with layer of boiled shelled chestnuts, making the top layer potatoes to prevent drying of chestnuts. Makes a delicious casserole dish.

Waldorf Salad

3 cups diced apples   Mix with mayonnaise
2 tsp lemon juice   1 cup raisins
1 cup chopped celery   1 cup diced chestnuts

Mix ingredients as listed and serve on crisp lettuce leaf. Serves 10.

Chestnut Pie

¼ cup butter
⅔ cup brown sugar
¼ tsp salt
¾ cup dark corn syrup

3 eggs, beaten
1 tsp vanilla
½ recipe for plain pastry
2 cups grated or ground chestnuts
(after boiling and peeling)

Cream butter and sugar together until fluffy; add next 4 ingredients. Line pie pan with pastry and sprinkle with chestnuts. Bake in very hot oven, 232°C (450°F) 10 min; reduce temperature to moderate, 176°C (350°F) and bake 35 min longer or until knife inserted in center comes out clean. Makes one 8-in. pie.

Chestnuts in Syrup

Shell and blanch 2 lb of chestnuts. Simmer in water until nearly tender (about 30 min). Drain well. Make a syrup with ¾ lb sugar and 1 pint of water. Cook syrup 15 min, then add chestnuts and ½ tsp vanilla flavoring. Cook for 30 min more, then take out chestnuts and put into hot sterilized jars. Boil the syrup until very thick; pour boiling hot over the chestnuts, filling jars to top. Seal.

Chestnut Cakes

These may be served instead of potatoes. Mash a pound of chestnuts, previously cooked in the oven, with level teaspoonful of chopped, cooked onion, 1 oz of butter and a beaten egg. Shape into flat cakes, dip in flour, then beaten egg, then bread crumbs, and wet fry until golden brown. Drain well on paper.

Chestnut Pudding

Cook chestnuts in oven until very tender. Skin them and mash lightly. Grease a casserole dish. Make a layer of the mashed chestnuts, top with a layer of cooked dried fruit (apple or apricot). Top with mixture of ½ cup flour, ¼ cup butter, ½ cup brown sugar. Cook about 20 min at 163°C (325°F).

Italian Chestnut Chocolate Dessert

1 pkg (4 oz) sweet
cooking chocolate
1 cup sweet butter
1 tsp vanilla extract

1½ cups canned chestnut
cream
Whipped cream
Chocolate curls

Melt chocolate in the top of double boiler over hot water. Cream butter until fluffy. Stir in vanilla and chestnut cream. Beat in melted chocolate and beat until absolutely smooth. Line bottom of 8 in. layer pan or pie pan, or 8 × 8 × 2 in. square pan with waxed paper. Press mixture into pan and chill. Unmold and remove waxed paper. Decorate with whipped cream and chocolate curls. Serves 12.

Chestnut Mousse

½ cup dark brown sugar, firmly
  packed
½ cup granulated sugar
1 cup unsweetened chestnut pureé
3 tbsp water
2 unflavored gelatin envelopes

¼ cup white rum
4 eggs
3 egg yolks
½ tsp vanilla
Chocolate sauce to cover

Soften gelatin in cold water for 5 min; gently mix other ingredients except chocolate, and heat until it thickens; mix with gelatin, place in individual molds, cover with chocolate sauce. Chill until congealed and serve on lettuce leaf. Serves 10.

Chocolate Sauce for Chestnut Mousse

2 sweet chocolate, 4 oz bars
1 cup hot water
⅔ cup heavy cream, whipped

Salt, finely granulated as desired
½ tsp vanilla

Cut chocolate in small pieces, melt in hot water over low heat. Cool slightly, fold in cream and serve at room temperature.

REFERENCES

ANON. 1962-1966. Statistical Reports, Foreign Agric. Serv., U.S. Dep. Agric.

ANON. 1976. Tree nuts. Foreign Agric. Serv., U.S. Dep. Agric. *FN 1-76.*

ANTHONY, R.D., and SHERMAN, L.W. 1951. Opportunities for better chestnuts and walnuts in Pennsylvania. Am. Soc. Hort. Sci. *57,* 191-192.

CHASE, S.B. 1956. What are the problems limiting the development of the chestnut industry? Proc. Nor. Nut Grow. Assoc. *47,* 94-95.

CLAPPER, R.B. 1944. American and blight-resistant chestnuts. Flower Grower *31* (10) 488.

CLAPPER, R.B. 1954. Chestnut breeding, techniques and results. J. Hered. *45,* 107-114.

CLINTON, G.P. 1914. So-called chestnut blight poisoning. Conn. Agric. Exp. Stn. Ann. Rept. 30-42.

DILLER, J.D. 1952. Foresters evaluate experiment in growing Asiatic chestnut trees on the Morgan-Monroe State Forest. J. For. *50,* 318-319.

DILLER, J.D. 1960. The present status of screening the American chestnut for blight resistance. Proc. Nor. Nut Grow. Assoc. *51,* 47-50.

DILLER, J.D., CLAPPER, R.B., and JAYNES, R.A. 1964. Cooperative test plots produce some promising Chinese and hybrid chestnut trees. U.S. For. Serv. Res. Note *NE-25.*

FEAR, W. 1891. Analysis of several varieties of chestnuts. Penn. State Col. Ann. Rept. *17*, 173-178.

FISHER, H.H. 1964. A survey of pears, nuts, and other fruitclones in the United States. U.S. Dep. Agric., Agric. Res. Ser. ARS *34-37-3*, July.

GARNER, R.J. 1958. The Grafters Handbook. Faber & Faber, London.

GRAVATT, G.F., and FOWLER, M.E. 1940. Disease of chestnut trees and nuts. Proc. Nor. Nut Grow. Assoc. *31*, 110-113.

GRAVES, A.H. 1949. Key to chestnut species and notes on some hybrids. Proc. Nor. Nut Grow. Assoc. *40*, 95-107.

GRAVES, A.H. 1956. Chestnut breeding—report for 1955 and 1956. Nor. Nut Grow. Assoc. Ann. Rept., *47*, 99-110.

GRAVES, A.H. 1961. Keys to chestnut species. Proc. Nor. Nut Grow. Assoc. *52*, 78-90.

GRAVES, A.H., and JAYNES, R.A. 1959. Chestnut breeding—report for 1958 and 1959. Proc. Nor. Nut Grow. Assoc. *50*, 62-71.

HARDY, M.B. 1948. Chestnut growing in the Southeast. Proc. Nor. Nut Grow. Assoc. *39*, 41-50.

HEMMING, E.S. 1944. Chinese chestnuts in Maryland. Proc. Nor. Nut Grow. Assoc. *35*, 32-34.

HEMMING, E.S. 1954. Our experiences with the Chinese chestnut. Proc. Nor. Nut Grow. Assoc. *45*, 90-93.

HIRSCHI, A.G. 1946. Nut growing under semi-arid conditions. Proc. Nor. Nut Grow. Assoc. *37*, 32-37.

JAMES, R.A. 1964. Chestnuts. Horticulture *42* (9) 16-17, 39.

JAYNES, R.A. 1961. Buried-in-arch technique for rooting chestnut cuttings. Proc. Nor. Nut Grow. Assoc. *52*, 37-39.

JAYNES, R.A. 1964. Grafting chestnuts without stock plants. Proc. Nor. Nut Grow. Assoc. *55*, 16-20.

KAINS, M.G., and MCQUESTEN, L.M. 1952. Propagation of Plants. Orange Judd, New York.

MACDANIELS, L.H. 1955. Stock-scion incompatibility in nut trees. Proc. Nor. Nut Grow. Assoc. *46*, 92-97.

MCKAY, J.W. 1952. Chestnuts again. Va. Wildlife *14*, 16-18.

MCKAY, J.W. 1956A. Albino seedlings in chestnut. Records Genetics Soc. Amer. *25*, 653 (Abstract).

MCKAY, J.W. 1956B. Orange-kernel chestnut. Proc. Nor. Nut Grow. Assoc. *47*, 45-47.

MCKAY, J.W. 1956C. Variability in chestnut progenies as related to breeding and propagation. Proc. Nor. Nut Grow. Assoc. *47*, 90-91.

MCKAY, J.W. 1963. Crane and Orrin, two new Chinese chestnut varieties released by the United States Department of Agriculture. Fruit Var. Hortic. Dig. *17* (4) 73-74.

MCKAY, J.W. 1964. Twins in Chinese chestnut. Proc. Nor. Nut Grow. Assoc. *55*, 20-23.

MCKAY, J.W., and BERRY, F.H. 1960. Introduction and distribution of Chinese chestnuts in the United States. Proc. Nor. Nut Grow. Assoc. *51*, 31-36.

MCKAY, J.W., and CRANE, H.L. 1953. Chinese chestnut—a promising new orchard crop. Econ. Bot. *7*, 228-242.

MOLDENKE, H.N., and MOLDENKE, A.L. 1952. Plants of the Bible. Chronica Botanica Co., Waltham, Mass.

POWELL, G.H. 1899. European and Japanese chestnuts in the eastern United States. Del. Agric. Exp. Stn. Ann. Rept. *11*, 101-134.

REED, C.A. 1950. Chinese chestnut varieties. Am. Nurseryman *91*, 7-8, 66-69.

REED, C.A., and DAVIDSON, J. 1954. The Improved Nut Trees of North America. Devin Adair, New York.

REHDER, A. 1940. Manual of Cultivated Trees and Shrubs Hardy in North America, 2nd Edition. Macmillan Co., New York.

ROSBOROUGH, J.F., BRISON, F.R., SMITH, C.L., and ROMBERG, L.D. 1949. Propagation of pecans by budding and grafting. Texas Agric. Coll. Ext. Bull. *B-166*.

STOKES, H.F. 1962. Grafting nut trees. Nutshell. Nor. Nut Grow. Assoc. Ann. Rept. *53*, 37-38.

STOREY, J.B. 1964. Pecan orchard evaluation. Proc. Texas Pecan Grow. Assoc. *43*, 85-89.

THORNTON, J.E. 1966. Turkeys West. Va. Wildlife *27*(5). 4-6.

VILKOMERSON, H. 1960. Flowering habits of chestnut. Proc. Nor. Nut Grow. Assoc. *31*, 114-116.

WEAVER, W.S. 1957. My experience in growing Chinese chestnuts in Pennsylvania. Proc. Nor. Nut Grow. Assoc. *48*, 58-60.

WILSON, W.J. 1958. Experiences in growing and marketing Chinese chestnuts. Proc. Nor. Nut Grow. Assoc. *49*, 55-59.

10

Filberts

Filberts (*Corylus avellana* and *C. maxima*) grow wild in Europe, particularly in the Mediterranean region and the Balkans. By selection and hybridization of these, many improved cultivars have been secured which are the basis of the commercial filbert industry. This had spread through western Europe into England and east through Turkey.

The American hazel (*Corylus americana*) and the beaked hazel (*Corylus rostrata*) are native to the northeastern and middle western part of the United States. The plants are sprawling shrubs, and are scattered in the margin of woodlands and fence rows. The nuts from the wild plants, with few exceptions, are small and hardly worth gathering. The nuts are abundant and furnish food for wildlife. The American hazel has the valuable characteristic of being extremely hardy, its range extending into the far north of Canada (MacDaniels 1964).

Wild hazelnuts were used extensively by the Indians in the Pacific northwest. The nuts, while small and very hard-shelled, produced more edible food than chinquapins or beechnuts. The wild hazelnut trees are quite variable in size, and grow on dry rocky hillsides, never exceeding 8 ft in height. They are being replaced by the (cultivated) European filberts.

HISTORY OF FILBERTS

The terms filbert and hazelnut are apparently used interchangeably to include all plants in the genus *Corylus*. Groeschke (1887) in his monograph on *Corylus* used the term hazelnut. The L.H. Bailey (1949) and Rehder (1956) manuals of cultivated plants give hazelnuts as the preferred common name for the genus. In Great Britain a distinction is made between filberts, which have the husk longer than the nut, and cobnuts in which the husks are shorter than the nuts (Howes 1948). In the United States filbert is commonly used to designate nuts derived from European species while native American sorts are called hazelnuts (Slate 1930).

The most important sources of commercial cultivars are *C. avellana* and *C. maxima,* both of European origin. The American species *C. americana* has been hybridized with the European filberts to produce hardy cultivars of some commercial promise. The beaked hazel, *C. cornuta,* a very hardy species, is widespread in North America and its counterpart on the Pacific coast has apparently not been used. The Turkish hazel, *C. colurna,* native to southeastern Europe and western Asia, grows to be a tree 80 ft in height and, because of its non-suckering habit, has been used experimentally as a stock for filberts. Several other species in China, Japan and temperate parts of Asia have apparently not been used in commercial nut production though nuts undoubtedly find local use.

Courtesy of Oregon Filbert Commission

FIG. 10.1.   A BEARING FILBERT ORCHARD

Filberts date back to ancient times. Old Chinese manuscripts indicate that their use is as old as agricultural history, going back nearly 5000 years (Peker 1962). Filbert culture was known to the ancient Greeks and Romans and the nuts were supposed to have medicinal qualities in addition to their food value. Through centuries of selection, cultivated types and clones have been secured and propagated in various countries where the European hazels have been native, and the culture extended to areas beyond their natural range where climate and soil conditions are favorable.

The name filbert is supposed by some to have originated from "full beard," referring to the fact that in some cultivars the husk entirely covers the nut. By others, it is thought to have been derived from St. Philibert, as August 22 is dedicated to him, a date that corresponds in England to the ripening of the earliest filberts (Anon. 1963).

Fairchild (1939) reported that Istria was noted for its filberts, and he secured different leaf-spot resistant cultivars grown in that region for importing into America. None of the Istrian species fruited well in California, although C. tubulosa proved to be an excellent pollen-producing cultivar and was used for this purpose in Oregon and Washington.

COMPOSITION OF FILBERTS

Data on the composition of filbert kernels, shells and oil are shown in Tables 10.1 and 10.2. The Barcelona and DuChilly filberts are grown in Oregon (85%) and Washington (15%), and were introduced from Europe in 1885 by Felix Gillette. For comparison a few determinations of European filberts are shown (Fang and Bullis 1949). Additional data on composition and nutritive value of filberts are shown in Table 10.3.

TABLE 10.1

FATTY ACID COMPOSITION OF BARCELONA AND DUCHILLY FILBERT OIL
(IN PERCENT)

| | Barcelona | | DuChilly | |
| | Solid Acid Fraction | Liquid Acid Fraction | Solid Acid Fraction | Liquid Acid Fraction |
Content	35.61%	63.99%	63.03%	36.62%
Saturated				
Palmitic	0.49	1.80	0.04	0.46
Stearic	1.57	0	0.77	0
Arachidic	1.41	0	3.05	0
Unsaturated				
Oleic	24.42	31.78	47.38	17.45
Linoleic	2.77	14.05	5.29	9.94
C_{20} mono-ethenoid	4.97	15.98	6.49	8.76
C_{22} mono-ethenoid	0	0.40	0	0
Unsaponifiable	0	0.40	–	0.35

AREAS OF PRODUCTION

The areas where filberts are grown commercially are relatively small compared with the very large areas in which the plants grow wild. In parts of Yugoslavia, for example, there are thousands of acres of hazel scrub producing very small, thick-shelled nuts, but commercial culture in Yugoslavia is restricted to climatically favorable areas along the Adriatic coast. At the present time the greatest production of filberts is in Turkey along the south shore of the Black Sea (Schreiber 1947; Serr 1964). Other exporting areas are southern Italy and Spain. Considerable quantities are also produced in parts of Germany, France and Kent, England (Anon. 1916), but are consumed mostly in the countries where they are grown. During the past half century a commercial filbert industry has developed on the Pacific coast of the United States in Oregon and Washington, producing about 10,000 tons of unshelled filberts a year which is only about 6% of world production of filberts. Filberts account for about 20% of the world production of all tree nuts (Groder 1963).

TABLE 10.2

CHEMICAL COMPOSITION OF BARCELONA AND DUCHILLY FILBERT SHELLS AND KERNELS (IN PERCENT)

Content	Shells		Kernels	
	Barcelona	DuChilly	Barcelona	DuChilly
Moisture	7.08	7.81	3.43	3.58
Total ash	0.997	1.297	2.53	2.69
Hot water insoluble ash	0.416	0.645	1.09	1.50
Hot water soluble ash	0.581	0.652	1.44	1.19
Alkalinity of insoluble ash	0.87	1.36	2.02	1.90
Alkalinity of soluble ash	0.34	0.92	0.78	1.29
Crude protein N · 6.25	1.35	1.70	17.1	15.6
Ether extract	nil	nil	65.5	63.1
Reducing sugars	0.98	1.15	0.12	0.18
Sucrose	0.20	0.75	4.79	5.57
Starch	nil	nil	3.54	4.16
Pentosans	27.0	67.7	–	–
Crude fiber	–	–	2.09	1.94

Much of the world's filbert production comes from plants of local origin which are seedling types developed in the area rather than named clones. Thus there are groups of clones of Turkish, German or Spanish origin which have recognizable characteristics but are not definite clones. There is much confusion in cultivar names except where preference is given to some clone of proven value. In Oregon, the Barcelona is the one clone that is grown commercially in any quantity except for Daviana and DuChilly which are used as pollinizers (Zielinski 1959). In Turkey, the Tombul is reported as the leading cultivar with Sivri and Badem used as pollinizers. In Great Britain, Kentish Cob (Lambert's filbert) is the chief commercial cultivar with Cosford, Daviana and others as pollinizers. Extensive cultivar tests have been made and are now in progress at the Oregon State Experiment Station. The industry there is based on the cultivar Barcelona (85%) and its pollinizers and, though some other cultivars appear to have promise, there seems to be no move to replace this cultivar with anything else (Zielinski 1959).

Over the years 1968-74 the tonnage of filberts in-shell increased from 203,000 to 306,000 metric tons. The major portion of this is from Turkey which now ships approximately 82% of the world's tonnage.

TABLE 10.3

WORLD FILBERT IN-SHELL PRODUCTION

Country	1971	1972	1973	1974	1975	1976
			(1000 metric tons)			
Italy	95.0	75.0	80.0	103.0	80.0	95.0
Spain	20.0	20.0	15.5	33.0	14.5	25.0
Turkey	150.0	190.0	240.0	240.0	320.0	270.0
U.S.	10.3	−	11.1	6.1	10.8	7.0
Total	275.3	294.2	346.6	382.1	425.5	397.0

Source: Foreign Agric. Serv., FN 4-76.

TABLE 10.4

WORLD FILBERT IN-SHELL EXPORTS

Country	1972	1973	1974	1975	1976
			(1000 metric tons)		
Italy	62.8	50.7	47.0	75.0	55.0
Spain	18.5	15.6	8.4	22.1	8.0
Turkey	145.3	185.4	250.2	161.7	225.0
U.S.	0.7	0.8	0.9	0.8	0.9
Total	227.3	252.5	308.5	269.6	288.9

Source: Foreign Agric. Serv., FN 4-76.

The Willamette Valley of Oregon and corresponding territory in Washington have proved suitable for filbert growing. In the Willamette Valley filberts have been grown for about five decades, and results show that production on suitable sites and soils is a commercial success.

Tests made in various other sections of Oregon for the past few years indicate that filberts can be commercially grown, more or less profitably, in certain districts outside of the Willamette Valley.

The fact that filbert catkins when fully dormant are killed at a temperature of about 26.1°C (15°F) prohibits commercial production in most parts of eastern Oregon. In some areas of eastern Oregon, however, hardier cultivars survive and bear a few nuts. Along the coast the success of filbert growing has not yet been fully demonstrated, although in the Coast Range some orchards are doing very well.

In the Umpqua Valley a few orchards on good land are profitable. Near Scottsburg the oldest and largest filbert tree in the Pacific Northwest is located. It is more than 100 years old, with a spread of more than 50 ft. South of the Umpqua Valley filbert growing has not proved successful. Considerable experimental work and testing must still be done before the value of this fruit can be definitely determined for many sections of Oregon.

SUITABLE SOILS

The importance of good soils cannot be overemphasized. Too often the owner is encouraged by growth and production, so maintains the trees until the 8th or 12th year. At this time, having exhausted the productive capacity of the soil, tree growth and nut production become stationary instead of increasing as expected.

With trees on mediocre soils, production does not increase with increasing age, and size of trees and extreme fluctuations in crop yields occur. A good crop one year may be followed by several years of low production. In a year of heavy production, new shoot growth is very short and unproductive and it may require two or more years for the tree to develop the strong shoot growth that precedes heavy production. When orchards reach this condition, because of the soil on which filbert trees are growing, there is little that can be done to improve production. Natural physical conditions associated with fertility and moisture-holding capacity of the soil strictly limit its productive capacity.

The exact type of soil best suited to filberts varies in different districts, but in all cases it should be deep, fertile and well drained.

Good filbert soil should be 8 to 10 ft or more in depth. Recent investigations show that it is doubtful whether a soil 6 ft deep will maintain a mature orchard in regular, heavy production. Deep soils naturally afford a large supply of water and plant nutrients during the dry season. The effective depth of any soil is determined by the distribution of tree roots in it. If roots can grow to a depth of only 3 ft, effective soil is shallow regardless of what is below. The idea that filbert trees are shallow rooted has practically been discarded since investigations have shown that under favorable soil conditions roots readily grow to a depth of 8 to 11½ ft. Root penetration is stopped by rock, impervious hardpan, water table, sand or gravel, and lack of aeration in the soil. All of these conditions except lack of aeration can be located in the field by boring with a soil tube to a depth of 8 to 10 ft. Aeration of soil can be determined only by laboratory methods. Compact subsoils with a mottled color, indicating poor drainage, are often found. Besides affording few or no openings large enough for roots to enter, this kind of subsoil layer often supports a water layer that further restricts or inhibits root development.

Fertile soil is essential to proper development of filbert trees. As the fruit is largely borne laterally on one-year-old wood, plant food materials should be present in the soil in sufficient quantity so that, with a plentiful supply of moisture, good vegetative growth can be obtained each season. Attempts to obtain this growth by means other than high soil fertility usually meet with failure.

Filberts will not thrive in waterlogged soils. Trees will survive very adverse conditions, but tree growth and yields of nuts will be better in optimum conditions. In soils where the water table, lying on a heavy impervious subsoil, comes close to the surface for long periods of time during rainy seasons, filbert trees may survive for years. Some trees 25 years old are still growing on such soil, but they are little higher than a man's head and have produced few nuts.

Filbert orchard soils should be well drained during the entire year, yet should be capable of storing a large quantity of water for the trees during the dry season. Filbert roots make a very extensive growth during winter in western Oregon, but if the soil is waterlogged this growth is retarded or entirely inhibited. Growth of tree tops is dependent on the formation of new roots. As a result of lack of root growth, when the demand comes during the growing season for large amounts of plant food materials and moisture, the root system is not extensive enough to provide for a good, vigorous growth of the top (Anon. 1963).

FILBERT CULTIVARS

A number of filbert cultivars have been grown and tested in the Pacific Northwest. Some individual collections now contain more than 80 named cultivars. In addition, a large number of seedlings have been under observation, and a few have been recognized.

Barcelona and its pollinizing cultivars are grown in nearly all commercial orchards in Oregon. Brixnut has been planted to a limited extent. In Washington, the DuChilly cultivar has been planted commercially as a companion cultivar to Barcelona in some sections and as the sole commercial cultivar in others.

In the future new cultivars will undoubtedly be introduced to the public. Thousands of seedling trees are fruiting; from these, promising ones are being selected and named. Some of these seedlings have such qualities as large size, thin shell, and white kernels, which make the nuts appear attractive. Any new cultivar, however, before becoming established commercially, must be grown for years under orchard conditions. Growers may be justified in planting a few trees of a new cultivar as a test, but those wishing the safest investment will plant principally the

old standard cultivars. Since any list of new cultivars now being put on
the market will be out-of-date within a very short time because of the
elimination and addition of cultivars, no list of such cultivars is given.

Courtesy of L.H. MacDaniels

FIG. 10.2. THREE CULTIVARS OF FILBERTS, SHELLED
AND UNSHELLED

(A) Barcelona—thick shell; (B) hybrid with *C. americana*—
thin shell; and (C) hybrid with thick shell.

Cultivar tests have been made also at the New York State Experiment
Station at Geneva, New York, in an attempt to find cultivars that are
adapted to the eastern United States. Of 120 cultivars tried, none was
sufficiently promising to warrant commercial culture. Because of their
hardiness, Cosford and Medium Long were the most successful. Barcelona and Italian Red were the most productive, but were badly damaged by winter cold.

Attempts have been made to increase the hardiness of the filberts by
crossing them with the wild hazel (*C. americana*). Early hybrids produced were the Bixby and Buchannon made by Mr. J. F. Jones of Lancaster, Pennsylvania, who crossed the filbert Cosford with the wild hazel,
Rush. More recently the U.S. Department of Agriculture has released
two promising clones, the Reed and the Potomac (Reed and Davidson
1958). Also, at the Geneva, New York Station, several hybrids have been
produced by Slate (1930) and are under test. These are promising for
growing in the eastern United States at least on a non-commercial basis.

Although the Chinese and Turkish hazels are good sized trees with a
single trunk, the species from which the commercial filberts are derived
grow normally as bushes with many trunks coming from a common root

system. Left to itself the plant soon forms a thicket of many trunks which crowd each other and result in unfruitfulness. In orchard culture, one of the most difficult problems is to maintain a single trunked tree that can be properly managed.

Courtesy of Cornell Agric. Exp. Stn.

FIG. 10.3. FILBERT LEAVES, AND FRUIT OF DIFFERENT CULTIVARS, SHOWING DIFFERENT TYPES OF HUSKS

POLLINATION OF FILBERT TREES

Self-sterility of filbert cultivars makes interplanting a necessity in order to provide cross-pollination. An orchard of one single cultivar invariably produces a few scattering nuts; therefore self-sterility cannot be said to be absolute, but in a commercial sense it is so nearly complete that it may be considered so. This has been proved true by experiments and by the experience of growers.

Under normal conditions the blooming season of the filbert extends over a period of at least three months, counting the time from the beginning of pollen shedding by early cultivars to full bloom of pistillate flowers of late cultivars. Within this period there is (for many cultivars) a natural sequence of blooming. Considerable variation occurs in the sequence from season to season and in the length of time during which a cultivar may be in bloom. These variations are caused by climatic conditions. Seasons have been noted where late blooming cultivars have shed pollen at the same time as normally early blooming cultivars.

Proportionately, one pollinizer tree to eight trees of the main cultivar has been the regular practice. The use of one pollinizer to five trees is not out of proportion when orchards are young, or in unfavorable seasons after they are more fully grown; in favorable seasons and in older orchards, use a smaller number of pollinizers, in the ratio of 1 to 15 or 1 to 24. It is in unfavorable seasons, which occur frequently, that greater number of pollinizers will undoubtedly prove their worth.

If any change in pollinizers is considered, it is recommended that early and late blooming cultivars be included.

Grafting one limb in every tree to a pollinizing cultivar provides the best distribution of pollen but presents several difficulties unless nuts from these limbs are very similar to those of the commercial cultivar or so small they will not be picked up. If all nuts are harvested together, tolerance in grading rules may be exceeded. Grafting pollinizing cultivars in the trees will delay production as the blossoming of grafted limbs will be behind the main part of the tree. The difficulty of obtaining a good stand of scions often still further delays nut production. In some cases several years have been required to graft in the required number of pollinizers.

In an orchard lacking pollination, it can be provided by bringing in limbs with unopened catkins of the proper cultivar. If this is done just as the first pollen is being shed and the limbs are put in buckets of water suspended in the trees, considerable viable pollen will be shed that will aid in setting a number of nuts. This procedure is not practical on a large scale, but it can be used in a limited way until the trees planted or grafted for pollination purposes begin to produce pollen.

Many growers have attempted to pollinate their filbert trees by bringing native hazel branches into the orchard at the time pollen is being shed. This has failed in every case noted, since the pollen of native hazel is incompatible with filberts (Anon. 1963).

The pistillate flowers which develop into the nuts are borne within lateral and terminal buds on the previous season's growth. The staminate flowers which produce pollen are borne in naked catkins on short stalks either laterally on the previous season's growth or terminal on short spurs which may also bear leaf or fruit buds. In normal development, after a short chilling period in the fall, these catkins will respond to temperatures above freezing by elongating to twice their dormant length and shedding their pollen. In mild climates such as Oregon this may occur in January or perhaps earlier. In colder climates, without warm weather during the winter, pollen shedding may be delayed until late February or early March. At the same time the pollen is being shed, the pistillate flowers extend their red stigmas through the tips of the buds where they are exposed to the wind-borne pollen. After pollination the stigmas dry up and are not conspicuous. Fertilization takes place within the bud which remains apparently dormant until the warm weather of spring promotes bud break and leaf development. The fertilized pistillate flowers develop very slowly at first and do not become conspicuous until late spring. The shell of the nut then develops rapidly to full size and becomes filled with white endosperm. The embryo, which, up to this time, has remained small, now develops rapidly into the kernel of the nut which fills the shell cavity at harvest.

Courtesy of L.H. MacDaniels

FIG. 10.4. FILBERT FLOWERS THAT COME OUT IN WINTER

(A) Dormant catkins; (B) catkins shedding pollen;
and (C) buds containing pistillate flowers.

The limits of the commercial culture of the filbert are, for the most part, determined by the nature of the plant itself, particularly in relation to low winter temperatures, late spring freezes and drying winds. The naked staminate catkins are particularly susceptible to winter cold. Although killing temperatures will vary with cultivar and condition of the plant, 9.4°C (49°F) is critical for killing dormant catkins (Schuster 1944) and lower temperatures may damage trunks and crotches as well. Serious damage occurs when warm weather which causes pollen shedding is followed by freezing temperatures. Both pistillate and staminate flowers will withstand some frost but temperatures around 9.4°C (49°F) are critical. Cold damage may be greatly increased if there are drying winds. Filberts are temperate zone plants and their culture is limited in the south by lack of chilling and too early pollen shedding and probably other factors.

PROPAGATION OF FILBERTS

Although filberts are easily raised from seed, nuts from the resulting plants lack uniformity and the practice is little used commercially. A possible exception is the Turkish Hazel (*C. colurna*) which is raised experimentally for use as a non-suckering stock. Standard nursery procedure is to propagate cultivars by some form of layerage. In mound layering the parent plant or stool is cut to the ground. This forces many suckers into growth and after these are well started, earth is mounded up to a depth of 1 ft or more over their base. If this is done in late spring and the soil kept damp, roots will, in most cases, form at the base of each sucker and it may be removed from the parent plant in the fall. These rooted cuttings or suckers will not be good nursery trees and are usually planted out in the nursery row for another year when they are dug and sold (Schuster 1944).

In continuous layering, the stool plant is cut to the ground and the suckers allowed to grow for open season. The next spring these suckers are bent radially away from the stool and staked down in shallow trenches. As shoots grow upright from the buds on the layered sucker, the earth is filled in around their bases and kept moist. In the fall the new shoots will have rooted at their base and are cut with a part of the original sucker attached. These are grown in the nursery for a season and when dug the parts of the original sucker are trimmed off to reduce new sucker formation.

If only a small number of plants are wanted, tip layering is used. In this method vigorous suckers on the parent plant are bent in the form of a V and the point of the V is covered with about 8 in. of moist soil, leaving 1 ft or more of the tip of the sucker beyond the V exposed. After a season's growth under good conditions most of these tips will have rooted and may be dug and set in the nursery row for another season's growth. Basal suckering on the nursery tree can be reduced by cutting off the lower part of the rooted sucker.

FILBERT CULTURE

Filbert cultivation practices are essentially the same as for other kinds of fruit trees. Under conditions prevailing in filbert growing districts of the state, cultivation is primarily for the purpose of conserving moisture during the growing season. During the past few years the tendency has been for growers to reduce the frequency and depth of cultivation. This tendency is in line with results obtained in soil investigations, which show that cultivation that destroys all weed or cover-crop growth and maintains a shallow mulch is sufficient.

In maintaining soil fertility, a program that ensures the incorporation of large amounts of organic matter into the soil is of first importance. Growing cover crops is the cheapest and usually the most satisfactory method of supplying organic matter. Vetch such as hairy, Willamette, or common, with some grain such as wheat, oats, or rye is the most commonly grown cover crop and the one most generally suited to various soils. Vetch seed should be sown in early September at the rate of 40 to 50 lb per acre with an equal or variable amout of grain. In many cases the greatest growth occurs in late spring after the time that crops should be turned under to avoid loss of soil moisture. There is a tendency to delay turning vetch under in order to obtain a greater quantity of green manure.

Quickly available fertilizers like nitrate of soda are of little value applied in the fall as they leach out so quickly that plants obtain only a small part of the nutrient. Applied in late winter or early spring, they have been more successful. Ammoniated phosphate 16-20-0 and ammonium sulphate as sources of nitrogen applied either in the fall or in late winter have been most satisfactory, and when combined with the other necessary materials listed above have given the best returns. Regardless of the exact materials used, however, amounts have been adjusted so that approximately 100 lb of nitrogen have been applied per acre, with 135 lb of phosphorus as P_2O_5, 50 lb of sulfur, and 100 lb of potassium as K_2O—varying a few pounds according to the materials used.

Lime added to the soil is of value only for leguminous crops and only in a few districts having high soil acidity. As a soil amendment or fertilizer for filbert trees themselves, it is of questionable value (Anon. 1963).

For satisfactory commercial production filberts require deep, well-drained soils of good fertility and moisture holding capacity. It is true that wild hazels persist on poor soil and in some countries that produce filberts, they are planted on poor, rough land or in hedgerows and out of the way places where they receive little care. However, in situations like Oregon and Washington where land and labor costs are high, profitable production can be secured only on good soil. Neutral or slightly acid soils about pH 6 are favorable to filbert culture. The site chosen for filberts should also have good air drainage and some protection from drying winds.

Standard planting distances for filberts in Oregon has been 20 to 25 ft on the square or diagonal system. At these distances on good soil the trees, if lightly pruned, become crowded. With a better understanding of renewal pruning it is now considered possible and profitable to use the 20 ft distance or even less. Planting distances chosen depend on intention to grow intercrops or plant filler trees. In the filbert producing areas of Turkey the filberts are planted in clumps with centers 16 to 24 ft apart and little pruning is done (Serr 1964).

In Oregon, filberts are planted in early winter or spring. Holes are dug 18 in. across and 8 in. deep at the sides leaving a firm mound or cone of soil in the center about 4 in. below ground level. The tree is set on this mound with the root extending outwards and downwards toward the outside of the hole. Topsoil is firmed over the roots, and the area around the tree is mulched with sawdust or loose soil, making sure that the tree is well supplied with water. Shallow planting after this pattern is done to reduce the number of suckers and to make their removal easier (Sander 1963). Newly planted trees are headed at 20 to 30 in. and the trunks protected from sunscald by covering them with white paint or wrapping them with white paper.

In the mechanized orchards of the western United States, intercropping is rarely done. In the Mediterranean region and elsewhere where more intensive use is made of the land, various intercrops are used. In some places the filbert trees serve as posts to support wires in vineyards. Weeds are usually controlled by pasturing with sheep and goats.

The soil management problems in the orchards of the northwest are complicated by the practice of mechanized harvesting. In general, the cultural requirements of filberts are the same as with other tree crops, involving cultivation during the early growing season to release nitrogen and reduce competition with the ground cover.

Where mechanical harvesting is to be done, the ground surface must be kept free from weeds during the growing season so that at harvest this surface is smooth and relatively hard. Sowing the cover crop is delayed so that the seedlings will not interfere with the harvest. Obviously sod culture is not adapted to mechanical harvesting. However, limited experience in Oregon showed good growth and production of filberts in orchards with more or less permanent cover pastured by sheep. In other countries where labor is cheap and hand harvesting practiced, grazing is common practice.

In growing single trunk orchard trees, the removal of suckers which form at the base of the trunk is a very important practice. The filbert plant is basically a shrub or bush and left to itself will form a thick mass of trunks that is unmanageable in the orchard. Much can be done to reduce suckering by root pruning at time of planting, cutting off the basal part of the rooted nursery tree from which most of the suckers arise and leaving only the upper part of the root system. Covering the base of the tree with only 4 or 5 in. of soil in planting, as described above, will not only reduce the number of suckers formed but will also make it easier to remove the earth from the base of the tree in the suckering process. For effective sucker control it is essential to remove them 3 or 4 times a season for the first several years after the tree is planted. The buds or primordia from which the suckers grow are formed on the underground base of the nursery tree and on the bases of the suckers which grow from these. It is therefore important to remove the new suckers as close as possible to their point of origin. To do this the new suckers are removed as soon as they appear by digging the soil away from the base of the newly planted tree and pulling the suckers off before the wood has hardened. This should be done 3 or 4 times during the first 3 or 4 years after planting or until the suckers cease to appear. More recently, weed killers, 2-4,D, amine and several others, have been used with some success (Parker 1955). Pasturing with sheep also serves to control suckering.

Courtesy of L.H. MacDaniels

FIG. 10.5. FILBERT ORCHARD IN OREGON, WITH GROUND PREPARED FOR MECHANICAL HARVESTING

In common with other orchard trees filberts pass through several stages in pruning practice. At planting time, root pruning is done at the base of the nursery tree to reduce suckering and the tree is headed at the height of 20 to 30 in. During the next few years the purpose of pruning is to shape the tree and build a strong framework. The modified leader tree with three main branches is the pattern usually sought. Removal of suckers is also important at this stage.

In the eastern United States, so-called filbert blight is caused by a fungus which occurs frequently on the wild hazels and causes damage to filbert plantings. Control measures other than cutting out dead and diseased branches are not practiced (Anon. 1965).

The most important insect pest of filberts is the filbert worm or filbert moth. Sevin, 80% wettable powder 2 lb to 100 gal. water, has given good controls and replaces Arsenate of Lead and DDT. Sevin and Guthion were also effective in controlling filbert leaf roller and filbert aphids. There is growing concern for the filbert budmite, but to date no effective control has been worked out (Jones 1964).

Filbert yields vary greatly according to age and vigor of trees, planting distance, soil, cultural practice and many other factors. Exceptional yields may be up to 4000 lb per acre (Engler 1953), good yields 2000 lb (dry basis), and on the average about 1000 lb can be expected. Yields in mature orchards fluctuate greatly from year to year. Heavy production one year is usually followed by a light crop in the year following. Frost, rain and other factors may cause reduced crops or crop failure. It is thought that heavy renewal pruning may correct or modify the natural alternate bearing tendency (Painter 1962).

HARVESTING AND DRYING

Filberts are picked up after they are fully mature and have dropped to the ground. Cultivars that do not naturally free themselves from their husks must be husked out by hand or machinery.

Many different types of field harvesting machines are now in use and the cost of harvesting has been drastically reduced by the use of these machines. There are some machines that pick nuts up off the ground, hull them, remove blanks, dirt and stones, and pour them into sacks. The most commonly used machines, however, are really field cleaners. Nuts are hand raked into piles or windrowed by a side delivery type sweeper. Then nuts, leaves and litter are dumped by hand into a hopper on the machine and the cleaned nuts are run into the sacks. The blanks, leaves, twigs, dirt and stones are discarded by the machine.

Husking the nuts is also done mostly by hand although some simple huskers have been developed (Serr 1964). In the Pacific Northwest, where labor costs are high and mechanization possible, various machines have been devised to do all or part of the harvesting work. An essential part of mechanized harvesting is the preparation of the land to have a smooth, hard surface free from weeds at harvest time. Nuts fall naturally or are shaken from the trees, then hand raked or mechanically swept into windrows along with husks and leaves. From the windrow they may be picked up with a vacuum picker and taken to a processing shed where they are raked into piles from the windrow and then picked up mechanically or shoveled into containers. Although commercially built machines are available, some growers devise their own. A recent invention is a blower which separates the leaves from the nuts in the orchard before they are picked up (Anon. 1966). In the filbert country there are commercial firms and co-ops that will clean, husk, dry and sack nuts as they come from the orchard, and shell and sack the nuts after drying. The handling of filberts is apparently not standardized in the field or the processing plant and various types of field containers are used. In the move toward mechanization, bulk handling is increasing, replacing sacks and boxes both in the field and processing plant (Anon. 1958).

Prompt harvesting of the filbert crop is desirable. Nuts should be gathered 2 or 3 times during the season. Filberts lying on the damp ground for two weeks gradually darken. Rainy weather increases the discoloration of shells.

Damp or undried filberts should not be stored in sacks or large containers for more than two weeks, because kernels become moldy or off-flavored even if such a condition is not evident from the appearance of the shells. If nuts cannot be dried promptly, it is better to leave them in the field as they will not mold as easily when spread out on the ground. Delay in harvesting, however, does not produce the best product. Since present market requirements demand that nuts must be clean, washing is a general practice. Only under exceptional seasonal conditions will nuts be clean enough to market when brought in from the field without being washed. Various types of washing machines and equipment are used for this purpose.

Artificial drying at temperatures of 32.2° to 38°C (90° to 100°F) is used in practically all cases. It is only with small crops or in very dry seasons that filbert nuts can be dried without artificial heat by being spread out in a thin layer. As nearly all filberts are shipped to out-of-state markets, if too much moisture remains there will be loss in weight and spoilage before they are consumed. To avoid any possibility of this loss, nuts should be dried until their moisture content is reduced to 8 to 10%. Kernels containing 8 to 10% moisture snap if bitten when cold.

Driers of various types are in use—prune driers, hop driers, and bin driers. The amount of heat necessary to dry filberts to the required standard is so small that expensive equipment is not needed. Speed in drying is not essential except where large crops are to be handled.

Many inexpensive, fairly efficient driers have been made by remodeling old buildings already on the ranch. The heating unit should be placed 8 to 10 ft below the floor on which filberts are spread and sufficient openings made in the lower side walls to allow entrance of cold air. The drying floor is made of wire cloth laid on strips 1 × 2 in. or 2 × 3 in. so that at least 50% of the floor space is open, allowing air to pass upward. Outlets in the roof of sufficient size to allow free upward movement of air should be provided. Few growers maintain drying temperatures continuously for 24 hours a day. Aid in designing new driers or in remodeling old buildings for drying purposes can be obtained from the Oregon Agricultural Experiment Station, Corvallis.

Small lots of filberts can be dried by spreading them out only a few layers deep on the floor in a dry room. The nuts should be stirred frequently.

In small lots of nuts, those containing no kernels can be searated from the good ones by pouring all of them into water and then picking out the ones that float high. This is a slow process but with a little experience can be well done (Anon. 1963).

Courtesy of The Wave Company

FIG. 10.6. FILBERT GRADER AND FILBERT WINNOWER

The grader separates filberts and similar nuts into five grades by size, and additional screens with different size holes are available. The winnower separates nutmeats after cracking.

STORING FILBERTS

For export for year-round consumption, filberts must be stored for one year, and to tie-over a short crop it may be desirable to store them two years. It is well to estimate the probable storage period at harvest time, then grade and store the lots under conditions which would assure adequate storage at minimum cost.

After the filberts are dried to an in-shell moisture content of 7 to 8%, or a shelled moisture content of 3½ to 4½%, they should be closely graded, fumigated and sealed in plastic lined boxes, bags or bins. The purpose of the plastic is to stabilize the moisture and prevent the absorption of flavors from other products. They should not be allowed to change weight by substantial gain or loss in moisture. The storage life depends largely upon the temperature.

At 21°C (70°F), or lower, filberts will keep in good condition for 14 months. They should be inspected at intervals for insects, mold and other forms of deterioration. Redrying, refumigating or rebagging may be required.

At 0° to 1.7°C (32° to 35°F), with 60 to 65% relative humidity, filberts will keep for 2 years without insect or mold growth; also the bags or boxes need not be sealed.

At 3.9° to 2.8°C (25° to 27°F), with 60 to 65% relative humidity, filberts may be stored in bulk for 4 years. They should be removed to 1.7° to 4.4°C (35° to 40°F) for 24 hours before being brought to room temperature, to prevent moisture condensation.

MARKETING FILBERTS

In some of the producing countries of Europe, filberts are extensively used as food by the grower and his family and only the surplus gets into commercial channels. In areas of more intensive culture (for example, Turkey) small lots are carried to buyers in local collection centers, then to larger towns, and then to export centers in Istanbul, by boat. In this city there is a well-organized marketing organization that sells the crop mainly for export. The shelling and marketing situation in Italy and Spain is about the same as in Turkey (Schreiber 1947).

In the United States, marketing problems are of the greatest importance and are apparently more difficult to solve than those of production. The filbert exporting countries of Turkey, Italy and Spain have been growing filberts for centuries and have well organized export facilities. Exports from these countries to the United States were well entrenched before growing filberts commercially here was even begun. Because of low labor costs and generally favorable growing conditions the Mediterranean countries are able to sell filberts on the world market at a price below that which the U.S. growers consider necessary to maintain the industry. This has led to giving much attention to reducing production costs through mechanization and cultural efficiency and to formation of the Oregon Filbert Commission and the Filbert Control Board. The Filbert Commission is concerned with price protection through tariffs on filbert imports and the promotion of filbert sales through advertising, packaging and increased utilization in the new products (Ward 1965). The Filbert Control Board, working through a Federal Marketing order, is concerned with balancing supply with demand. The domestic in-shell demand for filberts appears to be stabilized at about 5000 tons yearly, and the Board works to divert yearly production in excess of this into carryover to the next year of limited quantities of in-shell nuts, to shelled nuts which may bring a smaller return to the grower or to export (Duncan 1965). The problems of marketing filberts appear to be about the same as with almonds and Persian walnuts. On a world basis, filberts compete with all other nuts including peanuts for the market.

TABLE 10.5

FILBERT IMPORTS INTO UNITED STATES

Country of Origin	1968-69	1969-70	1970-71	1971-72	1972-73	1974-75
			(metric tons)			
In-Shell						
India	–	–	–	–	–	5
Italy	2	–	–	–	–	–
Turkey	12	–	–	–	–	20
Total	34	–	–	–	–	25
Shelled						
Europe						
Greece	–	15	10	45	–	–
Italy	66	34	156	65	47	6
Turkey	3642	1865	3010	1809	3645	5769
West Germany	25	67	5	1	1	–
Other	–	2	2	3	3	3
Total	3744	1985	3183	1928	3696	5778
Other countries						
Brazil	12	31	23	15	–	–
Canada	–	–	–	–	58	20
India	5	–	–	–	5	28
Mozambique	5	–	–	–	–	33
Other	–	–	14	2	2	–
Total	22	31	37	17	65	81
Grand Total	3766	2016	3220	1945	3761	5859

Source: Foreign Agric. Serv., FN 1-76.

Filberts appear in the retail stores mostly in pound cellophane bags of whole nuts or smaller lots of kernels, either whole or chips. They also form a part, though a relatively small part, of the in-shell mixed nut packs and mixed salted nuts. An extensive federal survey in 1957 (Weidenhamer 1957) showed filberts to be in relatively less demand than other tree nuts. This is borne out by examination of nut offerings in local supermarkets.

Filberts are used in various ways in different countries depending on their availability and the local customs. In Turkey filberts are roasted and sold by street vendors in the cities and towns. They are the nuts used most in confections, Turkish delight or locoum, which is much used in Turkey and Greece.

In the United States, in addition to the use of filberts as nuts, in-shell, shelled and chips, much attention has been given to developing other products such as filbert butter, filbert oil, filbert meal and making use of by-products, particularly shells (Wiegand 1950). The techniques of processing have been adapted from those used with other nuts but apparently because of the cost of producing filberts, relative to peanuts or other tree nut crops, these filbert products are not economically feasible (Miller and Devlin 1948). The use of filberts in ice cream and confections has apparently not been developed as successfully as with other nuts.

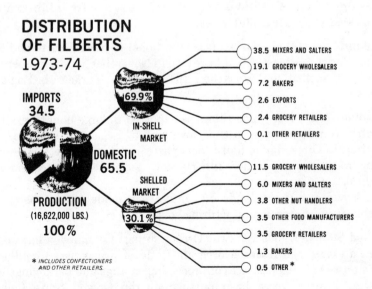

DISTRIBUTION OF FILBERTS 1973-74

IMPORTS 34.5

PRODUCTION (16,622,000 LBS.) 100%

DOMESTIC 65.5

IN-SHELL MARKET 69.9%

SHELLED MARKET 30.1%

* INCLUDES CONFECTIONERS AND OTHER RETAILERS.

38.5 MIXERS AND SALTERS
19.1 GROCERY WHOLESALERS
7.2 BAKERS
2.6 EXPORTS
2.4 GROCERY RETAILERS
0.1 OTHER RETAILERS

11.5 GROCERY WHOLESALERS
6.0 MIXERS AND SALTERS
3.8 OTHER NUT HANDLERS
3.5 OTHER FOOD MANUFACTURERS
3.5 GROCERY RETAILERS
1.3 BAKERS
0.5 OTHER *

FIG. 10.7. DISTRIBUTION OF FILBERTS

HUMAN HEALTH AND THE FILBERT

Filberts have been used for food and as a medicine since earliest writings (Peker 1962). According to a manuscript found in China dating back to 2838 B.C., filbert takes its place among the five sacred nourishments God bestowed to human beings. So it is understood that the cultivation of filbert is as old as agricultural history.

Uses of Filberts

Following are the ways in which filberts are eaten in various countries (Peker 1962).

China.—Fresh filberts are roasted on the fire, then they are pounded and drunk with tea. In Peking, confectioners in the bazaar make various kinds of filbert candies. The filbert is consumed also as a dried fruit. They are also preserved in chests with salt sprinkled on them.

Italy.—The Romans used to eat filberts in both the fresh and dried state. They also roasted them.

In Italy today, filberts are used in chocolate manufacture and in confectionery. In some regions they are ground into powder and mixed with wheat and rye flour in order to make bread and cake.

Germany.—Filberts are mostly used in pastry chocolates but are eaten also as dried fruit. A delicious sauce is prepared from fresh filbert after it is pickled in bay leaf and vinegar.

England.—For Anglo-Saxons it is traditional to have filberts and figs at their Christmas feast. For that reason in November and December the exports of shelled and unshelled filberts from Turkey to England increases.

Arabian Countries.—The filbert is exported in large quantities. The domestic consumption is rather low and it is mostly eaten as an appetizer. In Giresun a kind of filbert paste, called merdane, is made by mixing roasted and mashed filberts with sugar which is considered healthful.

In Akcakoca, various kinds of candies are made from filberts. In Istanbul it is used in manufacturing soaps.

United States.—Since 1952 the Oregon Filbert Commission has maintained a long-range research program to develop new uses for filberts and improve existing practices of processing, storage and packaging. The following projects have been pursued at the Oregon State College Experiment Station: (1) development of a method of removing the pellicle from the filbert kernels; (2) the use of filbert nuts in ice cream and related products; (3) the effect of added filbert extracts on the rate of ripening and market quality of cheese; (4) the use of filberts in cheese, cheese food and dairy spread; (5) development of uses of filberts in food products; and (6) effect of storage and handling procedures on the keeping quality of filberts.

Blanching Filberts

In 1953 a method of blanching (removal of pellicles from filbert kernels) on a continuous basis was developed at Oregon State College. The method consists of first treating the kernels with lye, then with an acid solution. This chemical treatment loosens the pellicle so that it can readily be removed in a high-pressure water spray in the next step in the procedure. If the kernels are to be roasted immediately the moisture picked up during the blanching is removed during roasting. If the kernels are to be stored they need to be dried to 4½% moisture.

Under optimum operating conditions 90% of the kernels are completely peeled and remain whole. Only 5% remain unpeeled and only 5% split. There is no apparent effect of the process on the flavor of peeled kernels and keeping quality. The new blanching method widened the use and popularity of filberts.

Filbert Flavor

The filbert flavor is apparently not present in the fat of the kernels (as in peanuts, pecans and other high fat nuts), and the pellicle seemingly imparts little else than brittleness to the flavor of unblanched kernels. Many consumers prefer the slightly bitter unblanched kernels to the more bland blanched kernels.

There is a qualitative similarity associated with heat-induced volatile flavors in most nuts. The interaction involves the carbohydrates, protein and lipids, which are responsible for development of the flavors. Forty flavor components were identified in roasted filberts, and 11 components were listed qualitatively in the oil from nuts roasted for different periods of time (Sheldon et al. 1972).

Roasting develops more flavor in filberts—a flavor that is basically very similar to that of the raw nuts. Chopping or grinding the kernels also appears to develop more flavor. A significant fact about filbert flavor is that it can be extracted and concentrated. This suggests a possibility that such a flavor concentrate might be made commercially and used widely in such food products as ice cream, cookies, other baked goods, and candies. Alcohol appeared to be the best solvent for extracting filbert flavor (Anon. 1954).

The occurrence of bitter flavor and shriveled nuts is serious among filberts; and this, connected with wormy and moldy nuts, constitutes a real problem in quality. It has been determined that much of the low quality is connected directly or indirectly with insect attacks, and can be controlled in part by spraying with insecticides (Gilpin and Dawson 1953).

Filberts in Ice Cream

New ways of preparing filberts for use in ice cream have been developed. The problem involves: (a) suitable roasting of the kernels to develop desirable flavors, (b) providing the most acceptable particle size, and (c) treating the particles to retain their crispness in the ice cream.

Correct end-point in roasting can be determined by measuring the temperature of the nuts, also observing the color of the cavity of the nuts. Cutting rather than grinding provides the best particle size and shape with the least "flouring." Coating the particles with sugar by the "panning" method appears to help prevent loss of crispness and enhance flavor. Best filbert flavor in ice cream is attained when about half of the roasted nuts are finely ground into butter (Anon. 1955).

Splitting of Filberts

This is a serious problem in some years. Splitting may be due to the particular cultivar and other causes, but is primarily due to too rapid drying. Nuts with low moisture content which dry slowly do not split.

FILBERT SHELLS

Filbert shells are used in making artificial wood, plywood and linoleum. The mixture with powdered coal and lignite is used for making cinder blocks. Their smoke is very dense, and it is used in making poisonous gases and for gas masks. Two of the common uses are for fuel and mulching. They contain 13.2% phosphorus, 14.8% calcium, 13% moisture and 1.75% ash. The nitrogen is very low (Peker 1962).

RECIPES FOR FILBERTS

Filbert Chocolate Taffy

½ cup filberts	2 squares chocolate
1 cup sugar	2 dashes cinnamon
½ cup molasses	½ tsp salt
½ cup corn syrup	1 tsp vanilla
½ cup water	

Chop filberts coarsely and set aside. Combine all other ingredients, except vanilla, in a saucepan. Mix thoroughly. Cook slowly, with occasional stirring, until in firm ball state, 124°C (256°F). Remove from heat and pour at once onto a well-buttered shallow pan. When the edges stiffen and mixture is cool enough to handle, pour the vanilla into the center. Fold the corners to the center, remove from the pan and pull. Pull into a long roll, using the thumb and fingers rather than the whole hand. Continue folding and pulling until candy begins to lose its gloss. Add nuts in the folds of the taffy and continue pulling. When hard to pull, twist into a rope and cut in pieces. Turn rope half over before cutting next piece. Drop pieces on a buttered plate or wrap each in waxed paper.

Viennese Filbert Coffee

½ cup filbert praline powder'
1 cup heavy cream, whipped
5 measuring cups strong hot coffee
Chopped toasted filberts

Fold filbert praline powder into whipped cream. Serve on top of hot coffee. Garnish top with chopped toasted filberts, if desired.

To Toast Filberts.—Spread whole filberts in shallow pan. Bake in 204.5°C (400°F) (hot) oven 10 to 15 min. Stir or shake nuts occasionally during baking.

To Grind Filberts.—Place nuts in electric blender jar. Run blender until nuts are finely ground. Or put nuts through food grinder, using medium-fine blade. One cup whole filberts yields about 1 ⅓ cups ground nuts.

Filbert-Stuffed Pork Chops

½ cup each chopped filberts
1 tbsp each chopped onion
  and green pepper
2 tbsp butter or margarine
1 tsp grated orange peel
1 cup diced orange

1 cup small bread cubes, cut
  from day old bread
2 tbsp raisins
Salt
Dash each pepper, ginger
4 double-bone center cut
  pork chops, with pocket

In large oven-proof skillet, saute filberts, celery, onion and green pepper in butter until filberts are toasted. Combine filbert mixture with orange peel,

---

'Filbert Praline Powder: In small saucepan combine ¾ cup granulated sugar, ¼ cup water and 1 tsp light corn syrup. Cook over medium heat, stirring constantly until sugar is dissolved and mixture boils. Stir in filberts. Cook over high heat without stirring until mixture is the coloring of molasses. Pour onto oiled cookie sheet. Cool. Break into pieces and whirl in electric blender until powdered, or place pieces of praline in a clean folded towel and crush with a rolling pin until powdered. Store in covered jar and use as needed as a topping or flavoring for desserts. Makes 8 servings.

orange, bread, raisins, 1 tsp salt and spices; toss lightly. Stuff into chop pockets; secure with toothpicks. Sprinkle chops with salt. In same skillet, brown chops on both sides. Add orange juice. Bake covered in 176°C (350°F) (moderate) oven 1 hour; uncover, bake 15 min longer or until fork-tender. Remove chops to serving platter. Skim off excess fat from pan juices; serve over chops. Makes 4 servings.

Filbert-Camembert Round

1 box (8 oz) Camembert cheese,
  or 6 individually wrapped pieces
  (1⅓ oz each)
1 cup dry white wine

½ cup butter or
  margarine
1 to 1½ cups toasted
  chopped filberts

Soak Camembert in wine overnight, turning occasionally. Drain; scrape any discolored parts off cheese but do not remove rind. In small bowl of electric mixer cream butter; gradually add drained Camembert and beat until smooth. Chill about 1 hour. Place Camembert mixture on waxed paper and shape into a ball. Cover with part of chopped filberts and shape into a flat round about 5 in. in diameter. Turn upside down onto serving plate, remove waxed paper and coat top with remaining chopped filberts. Chill. Remove from refrigerator about ½ hour before serving time. Serve with French bread or heated crackers as an hors d'oeuvre or with fruit as a dessert. Makes 8 to 10 servings.

Filbert Rice Cream

3½ cups cold cooked rice
1¾ cups sifted confectioners'
  sugar
2 tbsp vanilla
2 envelopes unflavored gelatin
⅔ cup cold water

2½ cups heavy cream,
  whipped
1 cup toasted finely
  chopped filberts
Fresh or frozen strawberries
  or raspberries

Mix rice with sugar and vanilla in large bowl. Soften gelatin in cold water in small saucepan, then stir over low heat until dissolved. Stir into rice mixture. Cool, stirring occasionally. (Mixture should be thickened slightly.) Fold in whipped cream and filberts. Spoon into a 2-qt mold; chill until firm. Unmold, garnish and serve with strawberries or raspberries. Makes 8 to 10 servings.

Filbert Creme Brulee

1 pint (2 cups) heavy cream
⅓ cup firmly packed brown
  sugar
⅛ tsp salt
7 egg yolks

1 tbsp sherry
½ cup sliced toasted
  filberts
Brown sugar

Scald cream with ⅓ cup brown sugar and salt in top of double boiler. Beat egg yolks with sherry. Gradually stir hot cream into egg yolks. Cook in double boiler, stirring constantly, until mixture thickens to the consistency of a medium cream sauce. Pour into 1 large or 6 individual oven-proof dishes. Chill at least 12 hours. About 2 hours before serving, sprinkle top of cream with filberts; sift enough brown sugar over top of cream to cover evenly about ¼-in. thick. Make sure the surface is smooth. Broil 2 to 3 min, or until sugar melts and begins to brown. Watch carefully so that sugar does not burn. Chill until serving tme. Makes 6 servings.

Kugilhoff Mit Haselnuss

½ cup milk	4 eggs
1 package activated dry yeast	2 tsp light rum
¼ cup warm water	¾ tsp salt
2⅔ cups sifted all-purpose	2 tsp grated lemon rind
flour	¼ cup graham cracker crumbs
1 cup seedless raisins	⅔ cup whole toasted filberts
1 cup boiling water	1 cup toasted chopped filberts
⅔ cup butter or margarine	Confectioners' sugar
½ cup sugar	

Scald milk, cool to lukewarm in bowl. Meanwhile, dissolve yeast in warm water. Add yeast mixture to milk; beat in 1 cup flour. Cover bowl with towel; let rise in warm place, about 1½ hours. Plump raisins in boiling water; drain. In mixing bowl, cream butter and sugar until light and fluffy; add eggs, one at a time, beating well after each addition. Stir in rum and salt. Stir in yeast mixture and remaining 1⅔ cups flour; beat until smooth. Stir in lemon peel and raisins. Beat batter until shiny and elastic, about 10 to 15 min. (Batter may be beaten in electric mixer.) Generously grease a 2-qt mold; coat with graham cracker crumbs and arrange the whole filberts on bottom of mold. Carefully pour in ½ of batter; sprinkle with half of the chopped filberts. Add other ½ of batter. Cover mold and let rise in warm place about 1 hour. Bake in 176.6°C (350°F) (moderate) oven 55 to 60 min, or until cake tests done. Let cool in pan 15 min. Remove from pan and sprinkle with confectioners' sugar, if desired. Serve warm or cool. Makes 1 cake.

Filbert-Stuffed Chicken

¾ cup chopped filberts	¾ tsp salt
⅓ cup chopped celery	½ tsp monosodium glutamate
3 tbsp chopped onion	⅛ to ¼ tsp crushed rosemary
3 tbsp butter or	⅛ tsp pepper
margarine	⅓ cup chicken broth
3 cups small bread cubes, cut	6 lb roasting chicken
from day-old bread	Melted butter or margarine
⅓ cup shredded peeled apple	

Sauté filberts, celery and onion in butter until filberts are lightly toasted. Toss lightly with bread, apple, giblets, seasonings and broth. Stuff chicken and truss. Roast on rack in shallow roasting pan 190°C (375°F) oven 2 hours or until chicken

tests done. Baste frequently with melted butter, then with pan drippings during roasting. Makes 4 to 6 servings.
NOTE: Double recipe for 12-lb turkey.

Filbert Meringue Crinkles

6 egg whites
⅛ tsp salt
2¾ cups firmly packed light
    brown sugar, sifted

1 lb toasted filberts
    ground
1 tsp vanilla
Granulated sugar

Beat eggs and salt together until soft peaks form. Gradually add brown sugar, about 3 tbsp at a time, beating well after each addition. Fold in filberts and vanilla. Drop by teaspoonfuls into bowl of granulated sugar. Lightly shape into 1-in. balls. Place on greased baking sheets and bake in 162°C (325°F) oven 20 to 30 min or until lightly browned. Makes about 5 dozen.

Vanilla Strips

4 egg whites
1 lb confectioners' sugar,
    sifted
1 lb toasted filberts, ground

1½ tsp vanilla
Additional confectioner's
    sugar

Beat egg whites until frothy; gradually beat in 1 lb confectioners' sugar; continue beating 15 min. Divide mixture in half. To one-half of mixture stir in filberts and vanilla. Roll filbert mixture to ¼-in. thickness on a board, using additional sifted confectioners' sugar to prevent mixture from sticking; cut into 3 × ¾-in. strips. Place strips on lightly greased baking sheets. Frost each strip with remaining half of egg white mixture. Bake in 163°C (325°F) oven 20 min, or until edges are very lightly browned. Makes 6 dozen.

Spiced Filberts

3 to 4 cups filberts
1 egg white, slightly
    beaten
2 tbsp cold water
½ cup sugar

2 tbsp cinnamon
¼ tsp cloves
⅛ tsp nutmeg
½ tsp salt

Toss nuts in bowl of egg white mixed with the water. Pour nuts into a sieve to drain off excess egg white. Place dry ingredients in paper bag and mix. Put nuts into bag containing spice mixture. Shake bag to coat nuts. Remove excess seasonings and place nuts on a baking sheet. Bake in slow oven 148°C (300°F) for about 20 min.

English Filbert Fruit Cake

The English Filbert Fruit Cake is dark and rich with fruit and nuts.

Make the cake well in advance and give it a chance to mellow and age in a cool place.

Wrap the cake in cheesecloth or some other porous cloth that's been soaked in brandy. Then every once in a while during the mellowing process, re-soak the cloth with brandy.

One of the things that's distinctively English about this cake, in addition to having about 90% fruit and nuts, is the filberts or, as they are known in England, hazelnuts.

The word hazel comes from the Anglo-Saxon "hasil," meaning hat or helmet, and refers to the husk of the nut.

English Filbert Fruit Cake

1 cup butter or margarine
2 cups firmly packed dark
   brown sugar
6 eggs
½ cup each currant jelly and
   molasses
Grated peel and juice of
   1 orange and 1 lemon
3 cups sifted all-purpose flour
1 tsp each baking powder,
   salt, cinnamon, nutmeg

½ tsp each mace, cloves, baking
   soda
¾ cup cognac
1 lb each dark seedless
   raisins, mixed candied fruits
½ lb each chopped dates,
   golden seedless raisins
½ lb toasted coarsely
   chopped filberts
Cognac glaze
Halved filberts

Cream together butter and sugar until fluffy; beat in eggs one at a time. Blend in jelly, molasses, the orange and lemon peel and juice. Sift together flour, baking powder, salt, spices and baking soda. Add to creamed mixture alternately with cognac. Combine fruits and chopped filberts; mix with batter. Turn into greased and foil-lined 10-in. tube pan or two 9 × 5 × 3-in. loaf pans. Bake in 148°C (300°F) oven about 2½ hours for 9-in. loaves and 3½ hours for 10-in. cake, or until cake tests done.

Filbert Chocolate Pudding

⅓ cup butter or margarine
⅓ cup granulated sugar
¼ cup light brown sugar
2 eggs
1 tsp vanilla
2 squares (1 oz each) unsweetened
   chocolate, melted and cooled
1½ cups sifted cake flour

2 tsp baking powder
½ tsp salt
¾ cup milk
1 jar (8 oz) red maraschino
   cherries, well drained and
   chopped (save juice)
⅓ cup chopped filberts
Creamy eggnog sauce

Cream together butter and sugars. Beat in eggs one at a time, beating well after each addition. Stir in vanilla and chocolate. Sift together flour, baking powder and salt. Stir in half of flour mixture; then milk. Toss fruits and nuts with remaining flour mixture; gently stir into batter. Turn into well-greased 1½-qt mold. Cover with foil and tie with string. Place on trivet in large kettle. Fill ¾ full with boiling water. Boil gently 3 hours. Serve with Creamy Eggnog Sauce. Makes one pudding.

Creamy Eggnog Sauce.—Beat one egg until thick and lemon colored. Gradually beat in ½ cup confectioners' sugar, 2 tbsp reserved cherry syrup and 1 tbsp cognac (optional). Whip 1 cup heavy cream; fold in egg mixture. Makes about 2½ cups.

Filbert Cherry Rum Pudding

1½ cups sifted all-purpose flour
½ cup firmly packed dark brown
   sugar
½ tsp each baking soda, salt,
   cinnamon, ground allspice
¼ tsp ground ginger
1½ cups fine soft bread crumbs
   (day-old bread)
¼ lb ground suet
1 cup quartered red glaze
   cherries

1 cup chopped dates
½ cup raisins
½ cup chopped filberts
¼ cup diced lemon peel
¼ cup marmalade
4 eggs
½ cup milk
⅓ cup rum or apple juice
Cherry hard sauce

Sift together flour, sugar, baking soda, salt and spices. Add bread crumbs, suet, cherries, dates, raisins, filberts and lemon peel; toss lightly until fruits are coated with flour mixture. Beat marmalade with eggs, stir in milk and rum. Stir egg mixture into flour mixture without beating. Turn into well greased 1½ qt mold. Cover with foil and tie with string. Place on trivet in large kettle. Fill ¾ full with boiling water. Boil gently 3 hours, adding extra boiling water if necessary. Pipe cherry hard sauce around pudding and garnish with stemmed red maraschino cherries and holly, as desired. Makes one pudding.

Filbert Drops

1 egg
1 egg white
½ cup sugar
½ cup chopped mixed
   candied fruits

¾ cup finely chopped
   filberts
⅓ cup sifted flour
Candied cherries

Beat egg, egg white and sugar with rotary beater until well blended. Add fruit and nuts. Stir in flour. Drop from a teaspoon onto greased cookie sheets. Top each cookie with a small piece of candied cherry. Bake at 160°C (325°F) for about 12 min or until lightly browned, about 10 min. Remove from cookie sheets and cool; put together in pairs with currant jelly. Makes about 4 dozen cookies.

Filbert Cookies

½ cup butter or margarine

1 cup sifted flour

¼ cup sugar   ¼ cup currant jelly
½ cup ground filberts

Cream butter and sugar together. Add nuts and flour. Shape into roll 1 in. diameter. Chill for several hours, wrapped in waxed paper. Slice thin and bake at 176°C (350°F) until lightly browned, about 10 min. Remove from cookie sheets and cool; put together in pairs with currant jelly. Makes about 4 dozen cookies.

Filbert Crescents

1 cup soft butter   1 cup filberts, ground
¼ cup sugar   (or finely chopped in
2 cups sifted flour   blender)
                                           1 tsp vanilla

Cream butter and sugar until light and fluffy; add remaining ingredients, and mix well. Chill until firm. With hands, shape small pieces of dough into tiny rolls. Twist on cookie sheets to form crescents. Bake in moderate oven, 176°C (350°F), about 10 min. Store in airtight container. Will not ship well. Makes 8 to 10 dozen.

REFERENCES

ANON. 1916. Sources of supply of hazelnuts. Imperial Institute of Great Britain *14*, 261-267.

ANON. 1952-1965. Annual Reports. Filbert Growers Commission.

ANON. 1958. A Panel. Bulk handling of filberts and walnuts. Proc. Nut Grow. Soc. Ore. Wash. *44*, 35-38.

ANON. 1961. Oregon sweets. Ore. State Univ. Coop. Ext. Circ. *688.*

ANON. 1963. Filberts in Oregon. Ore. State Univ. Coop. Ext. Bull. *628.*

ANON. 1965A. Filbert blight. Ore. State Univ. Coop. Ext. Circ. *645.*

ANON. 1965B. Filbert insect pests. Ore. State Univ. Coop. Ext. Circ. *728.*

ANON. 1966. New invention helps speed up harvest in filbert orchards. Better Fruit *61* (2) 6-7.

ANON. 1976. Tree Nuts. U.S. Dep. Agric., Foreign Agric. Serv. *FN 1-76.*

BAILEY, L.H. 1949. Manual of Cultivated Plants, Rev. Edition. Macmillan Co., New York.

DUNCAN, D. 1965. Your filbert control board. Proc. Nut Grow. Soc. Ore. Wash. *51*, 33-35.

ENGLER, H.F. 1953. Observations in the use of chemical fertilizers. Proc. Nut Grow. Soc. Ore. Wash. *39*, 182-183.

FAIRCHILD, D. 1939. The World Was My Garden. Charles Scribner's Sons, New York.

FANG, S.C., and BULLIS, D.E. 1949. Chemical study of Barcelona and Du Chilly filbert nuts and oil. J. Am. Oil Chem. Soc. *26*, 512-515.

GILPIN, G.L., and DAWSON, E.H. 1953. Quality and yield of filbert nut meats as affected by time of insect attack and insecticides. Food Technol. 7, 329-331.

GRODER, R.H. 1963. The worlds supply of nuts and import-export trends. Proc. Nut Grow. Soc. Ore. Wash. 49, 20-26.

GROESCHKE, F. 1887. Die Haselnuss, Ihre Arten und Ihre Kultur 1099, Berlin. (German)

HOWES, F.N. 1948. Nuts, Their Production and Everyday Uses. 1-264. Faber and Faber, London.

JONES, S.C. 1964. The big bud-mite problem on filberts. Proc. Nut Grow. Soc. Ore. Wash. 50, 27-28.

KINLIN, T.E. et al. 1972. Volatile components of roasted filberts. J. Agric. Food Chem. 20, 1021.

KUZIO, W. 1977. Nutmeat roundup. Candy Ind. 142 (6) 25-42.

MACDANIELS, L.H. 1964. Hazelnuts and filberts. Horticulture 42 (10) 44-45, 53.

MILLER, R.C., and DEVLIN, K. 1948. Processing filbert nuts. Ore. State Coll. Agric. Exp. Stn. Bull. 15, 1-16.

PAINTER, J.H. 1962. The role of potassium fertilization in filberts in Oregon. Proc. Nut Grow. Soc. Ore. Wash. 48, 20-23.

PARKER, W.B., WESSELER, P., and ROBERTS, W. 1955. A Panel—Filbert sprout sprays. Proc. Ore. State Hort. Soc. 47, 223-224.

PEKER, K. 1962. Human health and the filbert, a medical history. Peanut J. and Nut World 41 (5) 30-31, 38-40; (6) 38-39.

REED, C.A., and DAVIDSON, J. 1958. The Improved Nut Trees of North America and How to Grow Them. Devin Adair, New York.

REHDER, A. 1956. Manual of Cultivated Trees and Shrubs Hardy in North America, 2nd Edition. Macmillan Co., New York.

SANDER, E. 1963. The filbert tree and how to plant it. Nut Grow. Soc. Ore. Wash. 49, 43-44.

SCHREIBER, W.K. 1947. A discussion of the nut industry of the Mediterranean Basin. Proc. Nut Grow. Soc. Ore. Wash. 33, 101, 108.

SCHUSTER, C.E. 1944. Filberts. Ore. State Univ. Ext. Bull. 628.

SCHUSTER, C.E., and STEPHENSON, R.E. 1947. Summary of thirteen years work in soil and fertilizers in filbert and walnut orchards. Nut Grow. Soc. Ore. Wash. 33, 86-92.

SERR, E.F. 1964. The nut crops of Turkey. Proc. Nut Grow. Soc. Ore. Wash. 50, 11-20.

SHELDON, R.M., LINDSEY, R.L., and LIBBEY, L.M. 1972. Identification of volatile compounds in roasted filberts. J. Food Sci. 37 (2) 313-316.

SLATE, G.L. 1930. Filberts. N.Y. State Agric. Exp. Stn. Bull. (Geneva) 558.

WARD, R.A. 1965. Report of the Oregon Filbert Commission. Proc. Nut Grow. Soc. Ore. Wash. *351*, 30-33.

WEIDENHAMER, M.H. 1957. Homemakers' use of and opinion about peanuts and tree nuts. U.S. Dep. Agric. Res. Rept. *203*.

WIEGAND, E.H. 1950. Utilization of filberts in manufactured foods. Proc. Nut Grow. Soc. Ore. Wash. *36*, 148-149.

ZIELINSKI, Q.B. 1959. The search for new varieties of filberts for Oregon. Nut Grow. Soc. Ore. Wash. *45*, 2-4.

11

Macadamia Nuts

This is a relatively new nut to the United States, but it is rapidly gaining in popularity. Practically all of the domestic supply is either brought in from Hawaii or imported and will continue to be, due to the fact that optimum climatic requirements for growing them do not exist in this country.

The crops have never been sufficient to satisfy the demand on either the Hawaiian Islands or the mainland. Plantings are increasing but do not keep up with the market demand for this flavorsome nut with its excellent quality and texture.

The area suitable for macadamia growing in Hawaii is limited, so the expansion will probably never be great enough to seriously affect the potential culture and marketing of the crop in other regions and countries of similar climate. As more and more people become acquainted with macadamia nuts, the market potential will increase.

HISTORY AND ADAPTATION

The rain forests of Queensland and New South Wales are the original home of the macadamia, hence the sometimes used names of "Queensland Nut" and "Australian Nut." Some half-dozen species have been described. They belong to the *Proteaceae,* unrelated to other families containing nut trees. The macadamia is cultivated to some extent in Australia, but it is in Hawaii that the greatest development and improvements have been made. The superior cultivars selected in Hawaii and the investigations there pertaining to growth, culture, and fruitfulness have made macadamia growing the successful enterprise it is today.

Two species of macadamia are grown in Hawaii, *Macadamia integrifolia,* the smooth-shell type, and *M. tetraphylla,* the rough-shell type. Both of these were introduced in the decade between 1882 and 1892, and several of the original trees of each species are still existing in a vigorous condition. All of the named cultivars belong to the smooth-shell type. The rough-shell type is grown commercially to some extent, not only in Hawaii, but also in Australia. In addition, hybrids between the two species may be found occasionally and may prove of value.

The macadamia nut is being introduced into many parts of the tropical and subtropical world. Established seedling plantings are found in California, Florida, Central America, and southeast Asia. Since the macadamia nut is a broad-leafed evergreen plant that can stand only a few degrees of frost, it should be planted only in frost-free areas, somewhat under the same temperature conditions as for orange and lemon trees. It apparently produces its best crops where there is a more or less pronounced alternation of wet and dry seasons. A dry or cool season induces flowering and fruiting. However, wide variations among cultivars occur in this respect (O'Rourke 1959).

The smooth-shell macadamia nut is perhaps the most promising of various tree crops being considered for increased planting in the Hawaiian Islands at the present time. There are several reasons for this. The finished vacuum-packed product ranks among the finest confectionery nuts of the world in texture and flavor, it may be exported from the Islands, it commands a fairly high price, and it finds ready consumer acceptance in both local and mainland markets. The demand for macadamia nuts on the United States mainland presently exceeds local production. With only limited acreage in Hawaii available for planting macadamia orchards, there seems to be little prospect of overproduction in the foreseeable future.

MACADAMIA NUTS IN HAWAII

The macadamia nut, introduced into Hawaii from Australia almost a century ago, has developed into one of the major crops of the Hawaiian Islands. According to government statistics, 440 growers cultivated 10,400 acres of macadamia trees (including 3320 acres with trees of prebearing age) and produced 16,800,000 lb of in-shell nuts valued at $5,040,000 in 1975. Macadamia nut production is now spreading to many other countries, especially those in Latin America and Africa.

The relatively large increase in the area of macadamia nut orchards is one of the notable changes in Hawaii's cropping pattern since 1946. The macadamia nut industry in Hawaii is relatively new, and can be expanded without competition with sugarcane and pineapple, since these nuts can be grown on marginal soils not generally suited to other farm crops (Mollett 1962). In fact, most of the commercial macadamia trees in Hawaii are planted on lands which are too hilly or too rocky for other crops. Many of the trees are planted on very slightly weathered volcanic lava. Although a considerable number of acres planted in other crops were converted to macadamia, the bulk of the present plantings was made on virgin land including old lava flows where little evidence of weathering is discernable.

TABLE 11.1

PRODUCTION AND VALUE OF MACADAMIA NUTS (HAWAII)

Year	Production (1,000 lb)	Price per lb (cents)	Value (1,000 dollars)
1946	630	15.2	96
1947	680	16.9	115
1948	700	17.0	119
1949	680	16.9	115
1950	755	17.0	128
1951	850	16.9	144
1952	965	17.1	165
1953	970	17.0	165
1954	930	17.1	159
1955	902	17.9	162
1956	1,037	18.4	189
1957	1,343	18.7	248
1958	1,836	18.5	339
1959	2,114	18.2	384
1960	2,609	18.4	474
1961	3,771	18.5	695
1962	5,194	18.4	956
1963	6,015	17.7	1,062
1964	7,872	15.6	1,192
1965	8,649	19.4	1,654
1973	12,124	25.5	3,092
1974	16,370	32.0	5,238
1975	16,800	30.0	5,040

Source: U.S. Dep. Agric., Agricultural Handbook No. 186. 1975.

Since the macadamia is heterozygous (does not come true to seed), each seedling may be considered a separate cultivar. Hence it can be said that there are as many cultivars as there are seedlings. There were some 70,000 seedling trees in Hawaii during the 1930s. However, since seedlings vary greatly in productivity, nut characteristics (size, shape, shell thickness, quality, color, etc.), resistance to diseases and tree characteristics, the Hawaii Agricultural Experiment Station (of the University of Hawaii College of Tropical Agriculture) undertook the job of upgrading the industry by selecting high yielding cultivars with good nut characteristics from the 70,000 odd seedlings. This was begun in 1936 and the first preliminary cultivars were announced in 1948. Some cultivars selected in the 1930s are still being tested under different conditions. Seedlings were also planted closely spaced in the 1960s for developing new cultivars. Clonal cultivars being used by growers in Hawaii at present are: HAES #246 (Keauhou), #333 (Ikaika), #344 (Kau), #660 (Keaau), and #508 (Kakea).

The two earliest known importations of macadamia seed nuts of the smooth-shell type were by William Purvis of Kukuihaele, Hawaii, between 1882 and 1885, and E. W. Jordan and R. A. Jordan of Honolulu in 1892. One of the original seedling trees planted by Mr. Purvis is still alive and in good condition at Kukuihaele, and trees grown from nuts of the original importation made by the Jordan brothers are still growing in Honolulu. The success of early plantings was so encouraging that macadamia trees have been widely planted on all of the four major islands.

In 1922, the Hawaiian Macadamia Nut Company was organized to produce and process macadamia nuts. Two orchards were established by this company: one on the Tantalus slopes overlooking Honolulu at an elevation of about 900 ft, and the other at Keauhou in the Kona section at about 1800 ft elevation. By 1934 there were about 25 acres planted on Tantalus and about 100 acres at Keauhou.

In order to stimulate interest in macadamia culture, the 1927 Territorial Legislature passed an act exempting properties in the Territory used solely for the culture or production of macadamia nuts from taxation for a period of five years beginning January 1, 1927.

Production in commercial quantities began in the early 1930s and as processed nuts began to appear on the market, interest in macadamia growing increased. Planted acreage increased from about 423 acres in 1932 up to approximately 1086 acres in 1938.

From 1938 to 1941, the first orchards of grafted trees were planted in the Hawaiian Islands. These were the trial orchards of the Hawaii Agricultural Experiment Station established to test clonal selections in various locations on Hawaii, Maui, Oahu, and Kauai.

The following discussion on growing and harvesting macadamia nuts was taken from Scott (1958), O'Rourke (1959), Hamilton and Fukunaga (1959), Castle and Cook (1960) and Mollett (1962).

ORCHARDS

A new macadamia orchard represents a long-time investment. The profitable life of orchards in Hawaii has not been fully determined, but with good soil, favorable moisture conditions, and suitable climate, macadamia trees appear capable of producing satisfactory crops for 40 to 60 years and probably even longer. Older, larger trees present no difficulty when spaced far enough apart to prevent crowding. Since the nuts are harvested after they fall to the ground, it is no more difficult to pick them up under trees 50 ft high, than under younger, smaller trees. From limited records available, it appears that healthy, well-grown trees may continue to increase in productivity as they grow older and larger.

Macadamia orchards on good soils and with adequate care may begin to produce profitable crops in about 6 to 7 years from the time of transplanting. Up to about seven years, yields may be low and the expenses of transplanting and caring for the young trees relatively high. However, after that period, the income from well-managed orchards on good sites should increase rapidly.

Choosing the Site

Good sites are extremely important in growing macadamias. In the past, much of the land planted to macadamia trees was not suitable for producing nuts economically. The trees were often planted on poor land, known to be unsatisfactory for cane and pineapple. The fact that the trees were even able to exist on shallow soils and windswept locations is evidence of their hardiness and tolerance to adverse conditions.

Certain tracts of land possessing good natural wind protection, but not suited to commercial sugarcane or pineapple production because of location or topography, may prove well adapted to macadamia growing. Other lands which are being retired from sugarcane production because they do not fit into modern mechanized operations might well be planted to macadamia trees. However, the fairly widespread notion that the macadamias may be an ideal crop to plant on shallow, unproductive land not suitable for the cultivation of sugarcane, pineapple, or other crops, has no scientific or practical basis.

The cultivar and cultural test orchards of the Hawaii Agricultural Experiment Station, located at branch stations and with private cooperators, as well as seedling orchards set out by individuals and companies on various islands, have been a source of much valuable information. Some of the early seedling orchards were planted on soils so shallow, or locations so exposed to strong winds, that the trees failed to grow satisfactorily. Such orchards have largely been abandoned or operated at a loss. Obviously, it is best to caution against new plantings on these or similar locations. Other seedling orchards planted in more favorable locations have been more successful, and up to now have produced most of the macadamia nuts processed in Hawaii.

Soil and Climatic Requirements

Soil and climatic requirements for growing macadamias are very similar to those for common guava. Because of this, it is extremely valuable in selecting sites for macadamia orchards to examine the condition and size of guava trees growing in the area being considered. Where guava trees grow large and luxuriantly, one can be almost certain that the site is suitable for macadamias. Where guavas do not thrive, there is probably something wrong. Either the soil may be poor or the climatic conditions unsuitable. In such cases, expert advice and a careful analysis of the situation become necessary.

The areas suitable for coffee growing are also ideal for macadamia nuts. When they are planted in rows 35 to 40 ft apart, coffee or passion fruit vines on trellises may be grown as an intercrop during the first 10 years of the orchard. The coffee or other crop should be removed as the macadamia trees come into bearing. During the earlier years, these intercrops will not only produce an income, but will also tend to keep down weeds by close shading, and will serve as effective windbreaks, both to the macadamia trees and to the intercrop itself.

Both macadamia and coffee should be protected from winds. The orchard should be placed either on relatively windless sites or protected on the windward sides by rows of tall forest trees. In areas exposed to "trade winds" young trees are sometimes staked.

Important factors to be considered in deciding on a suitable location for a new orchard are (1) soil, (2) natural wind protection, (3) rainfall, and (4) accessibility for harvesting and cultural operations.

Soil.—There is certainly no factor of greater importance in an orchard than the soil. An ideal macadamia soil should be reasonably fertile, and loose and friable enough to permit good root growth to a depth of at least 2½ ft. Under-drainage should be good and, if possible, a fair amount of organic matter is desirable. Practically all soils in Hawaii suitable for orchards will need to be fertilized, the amount and type of fertilizer depending upon the character of the soil as well as the size and condition of the trees.

It is strongly recommended that prospective macadamia growers starting new orchards secure the best available technical advice and information from persons who have up-to-date information on the soil requirements of macadamia trees. A representative sample of soil, down to a depth of at least 3 ft, should be examined. A chemical analysis of the topsoil and subsoil is also desirable.

High manganese soils, commonly known as "red soils," have sometimes given unsatisfactory tree growth. Macadamia trees grown on red soil may develop characteristic "yellow-leaf" patterns and sometimes appear lacking in vigor and productivity. On the other hand, the growth of young trees in some high manganese soils has been reasonably satisfactory. Factors such as depth of topsoil and hardpans undoubtedly influence tree growth on red soils. It would be safest to have the soil examined by a qualified soils specialist before deciding to plant a macadamia orchard on red upland soils relatively high in manganese.

Courtesy Hawaiian Holiday Macadamia Nut Co.

FIG. 11.1. MACADAMIA NUT ORCHARD IN HAWAII, ON
STONE-LIKE LAVA "SOIL"

Although the soil acidity or pH range most favorable to the growth of
macadamia trees has not been definitely determined, a pH range between 4.5 and 6.5 appears to be favorable for this crop in Hawaii.

Wind Protection.—Natural wind protection for new macadamia orchards is essential. Many macadamia trees, grown on exposed locations,
have been lost or severely injured by winds. Even trees in relatively
sheltered areas are sometimes damaged by the occasional heavy windstorms usually referred to as "Kona" winds.

Trees exposed to steady trade winds frequently present a problem.
They may continue to grow, but usually lean away from the winds at an
angle and seldom produce satisfactory crops of nuts. One should take
advantage of hollows, sheltered slopes, and valleys in choosing an orchard
location. Windswept slopes and exposed areas should be avoided. Whenever trees are planted in areas exposed to steady winds, a well-planned
system of planted windbreaks should be provided.

Macadamias grow well in Hawaii at elevations ranging from near sea
level up to about 2500 ft. The shells of nuts of all cultivars tend to
become thicker at elevations above 2500 ft. Growth of the tree is also
slower and production is less.

Rainfall Requirements.—The annual rainfall in sections of Hawaii
where macadamia trees grow best ranges from about 50 to 120 in. The
average amount of rain per year may be less important than the distribution of rainfall, depth of rooting, and type of soil. Macadamia trees

have been known to thrive in areas where average yearly rainfall is only about 35 in., provided it is well distributed. However, it is probably best to avoid planting in areas with less than 45 in. of annual rainfall, unless adequate irrigation water is available if needed. Once the trees have become well established, they will survive considerable periods of drought. However, trees planted in dry areas cannot be depended upon to bear good crops consistently without irrigation, although they may survive for many years.

Accessibilities.—An important consideration in planning a new orchard is accessibility for harvesting and other cultural operations such as weeding and fertilizing. A satisfactory location should permit the construction of roads into the orchard at reasonable cost. Since macadamia nuts are picked up off the ground by hand, the space under the branches must be leveled and cleared of weed growth to facilitate gathering the nuts.

On excessively steep slopes, or extremely rough or rocky land, it is apparent that the cost of clearing and leveling or terracing the space under the trees might be prohibitive.

Propagation

The following discussion on propagating, culture, harvesting, husking and drying was taken largely from Hamilton and Fukunaga (1959).

By means of a testing program started in 1936, the Hawaii Agricultural Experiment Station has selected and named seven clones. Of these, Kakea, Ikaika and Keauhou seem most promising. Individual trees of these clones have produced between 150 and 200 lb of hulled nuts at 16 years of age, which is 3 to 5 times as much as seedling trees of the same age.

Propagation is by grafting on seedling rootstocks. The side wedge graft is used by making a slanting cut about 2 to 3 in. above a wedge-shaped scion in an upright position. The graft is firmly wrapped with raffia or tape and waxed with paraffin. After 4 to 6 months the stock is cut off cleanly.

In general, these field-run seedlings have been satisfactory for rootstocks, although there is some variation in size due to differences in the time required for seed of different varieties to germinate. In general, thin-shelled nuts germinate faster than thick-shelled nuts. Nuts used for seed should be mature and not more than 4 or 5 months old. Seed nuts should always be husked before planting, since it has been demonstrated that germination of unhusked nuts occurs only after the husks have been removed or have rotted.

Seedlings for rootstocks are produced by either of two alternative methods: direct seeding, or transplanting seedlings from a germinating box. Both methods have advantages as well as disadvantages and the method used depends somewhat on location and circumstances.

Direct seeding is commonly known as the "drop-seed" method. The main advantage of this method is that the seedlings grow to grafting size sooner than those of similar age transplanted from the sandbox.

Furrows about 4 in. deep and at least 3 ft apart are made in well-tilled soil in a nursery area kept free of weeds. To facilitate weed control, the entire nursery area can be sprayed with activated diesel oil emulsion before the macadamia seeds have germinated. The seed nuts are planted in the bottom of the furrow, approximately 2 in. apart, and covered with about 1 in. of soil. Three to four months later when the faster growing plants are about 5 in. tall, the seedlings are thinned to one plant every 6 to 8 in. All weak-growing, off-color, and chlorotic seedlings are eliminated during the thinning operation. Seedlings should be fertilized with 8-8-8 or 10-10-10 fertilizer after thinning and again a few weeks before grafting. Weeds should be controlled by hoeing when small, and by spraying with diesel oil emulsion after the macadamia seedlings are several inches high.

It is necessary to transplant seedlings whenever pests such as pheasants, rats, or cardinals, which destroy seed or young seedlings have access to the nursery area. When any of these pests becomes a problem, direct seeding in the nursery row is impractical.

Advantages of germinating seedlings in a sandbox before transplanting them to the nursery row are that (1) labor and expense of watering, weeding, and insect control are kept at a minimum; (2) transplanted seedlings characteristically develop better lateral root systems; (3) a more uniform stand of seedlings in the nursery row is assured; and (4) damage caused by rats, cardinals, or pheasants digging up and eating germinating seed and seedlings can be avoided.

Sandboxes or beds for germinating seed should be at least 12 in. deep. Other dimensions depend on convenience. Coral beach sand, black volcanic sand, or vermiculite may be used as germination media. Ordinary coral beach sand is a very satisfactory and economical medium.

The sandbox should be placed in full sun. In planting, the box is filled with sand to within about 3 in. of the top. A single layer of seed nuts is then spread evenly over the surface and covered with about 1 in. of sand. The sand should be kept moist at all times. Some of the seed nut will begin to germinate within 3 to 4 weeks. When the first 4 or 5 leaves become hardened, the seedlings are ready for transplanting into the nursery row. Plants may be kept in the germinating box longer, but it is best to transplant seedlings into the nursery row as soon as possible. Usually, there is very little fertility in the sand and seedlings may become stunted.

The seedlings are pulled up carefully one by one and transplanted into the nursery row. Excess sand adhering to the roots can be shaken off. Care should be taken not to break off the nut (*cotyledons*) attached to the young plant. Whenever this nut is broken off accidentally, the plant should be discarded because such plants develop very slowly. Weak and chlorotic plants are always discarded.

Plants should be spaced 6 to 8 in. apart in rows at least 3 ft apart. When the largest seedlings in the sandbox have attained transplanting size, many of the younger seedlings will be too small to transplant. Still other seeds may not have germinated. Therefore, in order to utilize all seedlings, each group of plants of about the same size should be planted when they attain transplanting size.

Culture

When the first plantings were made, very little was known about macadamia culture and growth habits. However, it has become clear that certain practices carried on in early orchard plantings were objectionable and should be changed. These practices include (1) pruning trees to a 4- to 6-ft trunk, which made them top-heavy, (2) failing to prune trees in such a way as to establish strong crotches, and (3) allowing young orchards to be pastured indiscriminately. Recommended cultural practices which include measures to remedy these mistakes will be discussed under the following headings: Training Stronger Trees, Cultivation and Weed Control, and Fertilization.

Training Stronger Trees

Selected cultivars of macadamia, when well grown without crowding or shading, develop into large, handsome, well-shaped trees. A certain amount of corrective pruning commonly referred to as "training" is highly desirable during the first two years after transplanting. The primary purpose in training young trees is to develop a strong, well-balanced framework for future growth. Macadamia trees developing naturally without training often produce several leaders. This necessitates pruning out extra leaders, leaving only the strongest, straightest one to develop into the trunk of the tree.

Training young trees to a desirable form should begin soon after the young transplanted tree begins to send out new growth. Corrective pruning and bracing in later years will not overcome the effects of weak, V-shaped crotches and crowded, poorly spaced main branches. The framework for a strong, well-balanced tree can only be established while the tree is young.

There are two main structural weaknesses commonly found in older trees which have developed without training or corrective pruning while young. One weakness of macadamia trees is a tendency for branches to be unevenly spaced along the trunk. Another serious defect which often develops is the formation of weak V-shaped crotches by main branches which tend to grow upward rather than outward. Fortunately, both faults can be eliminated by intelligent corrective pruning and training operations. In training young trees correctly, it is necessary to know something about the growth characteristics of the tree and have a suitable plan for establishing an adequate number of well-spaced main scaffold limbs on the trunk. The dominant idea should be to establish a strong durable framework of main branches that will not break off or split away from the trunk as the tree grows older and the limbs become heavier. It is well known that large trees often break and split because of the hard, brittle nature of the wood, especially when training has been neglected and V-shaped crotches are allowed to develop. The most satisfactory type of macadamia tree for orchard culture is a low-branching tree with only one trunk or leader, and several sets of main branches forming wide-angle crotches with the trunk. It is desirable to have a spacing of 1½ to 2 ft between sets of main branches.

In training young trees to a desirable form, a knowledge of macadamia growth characteristics is of considerable importance and value. The leaves of macadamia trees are arranged in groups of three at each node. The natural habit of growth is for three new shoots to come out simultaneously at the same height, at nodes where branching occurs. Since this is the natural growth habit of the tree, training practices differ from most other fruit and nut trees in which branching is either opposite or alternate.

The first operation in training is at the time of transplanting when the young tree is cut back to a single stem about 2½ ft high. When the young transplanted tree first begins to grow, usually the upper of the three buds in each of the leaf axils at the top node flushes. This results in three new shoots each about the same size. The strongest upright growing shoot is left as the "leader" which develops into the trunk of the tree. The other two shoots are removed by clipping them off, leaving a short stub about ½ in. long.

Macadamia buds occur in groups of three, crowded closely together one above the other in each leaf axil. When a small branch is removed, the second or middle bud located just below it often flushes, producing a new shoot which usually develops into a satisfactory main branch. Shoots from these second or middle buds develop with wider crotch angles than those produced by the upper buds and are therefore suitable for main scaffold branches. The bud located just below the shoot left as a leader may also flush, in which case it can be left to develop into a main branch.

The various buds mentioned often flush simultaneously, in which case training consists of merely saving those needed for the leader and scaffold limbs and removing all others.

At the beginning of new growth flushes, the first node is often formed with the usual number and arrangement of buds, but without leaves. Branches which arise from buds occurring at leafless nodes characteristically develop strong, L-shaped crotches. Whenever such branches are suitably spaced, they should be retained as scaffold limbs, because of their desirable crotch angles, and because they have a tendency to grow outward horizontally. This characteristic tendency of branches from leafless nodes to grow outward rather than upward makes them useful as scaffold branches, but undesirable for establishing an upright leader. Because of this, young trees should not be topped just above a leafless node. Whenever a young tree is topped to force branching, which also makes necessary the establishment of a new leader, the cut should be made just above the usual type of node with leaves.

It is important that each main scaffold branch has a strong, wide-angled crotch at the point of attachment to the trunk. Early in the cultivar selection program, the importance of strong crotches was recognized and the importance of desirable crotch angles was considered in the selection of all Hawaii Agricultural Experiment Station named cultivars. However, even with these cultivars, it may sometimes be desirable to establish main scaffold limbs with wider crotch angles. Whenever necessary, this may be done by forcing out new shoots from the middle or center buds. This is accomplished most conveniently after cutting back or capping the leader at the height branches are desired. When sufficient new shoots arise from middle buds, those needed for main branches can be retained. Whenever middle buds fail to flush after capping, they can usually be forced to grow by pruning out the branches from the top buds after they have grown 6 in. or more and begin to become woody.

The height of the first set of main branches is important. When the first grafted macadamia orchards were planted in Hawaii, the training of trees was patterned after that of pecan trees in mainland orchards. A main feature of this system of training was a tall, straight trunk with lower limbs 4 to 6 ft above the ground level. This training system was not satisfactory for growing macadamia trees, which often develop a large crown of heavy foliage during the first few years of growth. This heavy crown of branches and leaves on a tall trunk made many of the trees top-heavy. Trees trained to this form were often uprooted by winds, partly because they were top-heavy and partly because their root systems were shallow or not well balanced. In some cases, the trunks of trees with stronger root systems have also been snapped off by heavy winds. The heavy crown of these trees placed too great a strain on their relatively tall, slender trunks.

FIG. 11.2. BRANCHES AND CLUSTERS OF MACADAMIA NUTS

In foreground are macadamia nuts in–hull, in–shell and shelled.

It is recommended that the lowest branches be allowed to develop 2 to 3 ft above ground level. Successive groups of main branches should be spaced 1½ to 2 ft apart up and down the trunk, and arranged uniformly around the trunk. If possible, branches should not be permitted to develop directly above or below the next set of branches. This arrangement and spacing of main branches will establish trees of desirable form and maximum strength. As the leader grows, it will usually branch often enough so that groups of 2 or 3 branches at a node can be selected at desirable spacing intervals.

Some trees have a tendency to grow long and whiplike without branching. When this occurs, it may be neccessary to force out new branches by cutting back the leader, just above the node where branching is desired. This causes the three upper buds at the top node to flush, and a leader and main branches can then be selected at any desired height in the same way that the original leader and first set of branches were established. Cutting back the leader to force branching may be done as many times as necessary. However, it is usually not necessary to cut back the leader more than once or twice because natural branching ordinarily takes place often enough so that sufficient, well-spaced scaffold limbs can be selected and surplus branches removed. When sufficient natural branching occurs at intervals of less than 2 ft, suitable scaffold limbs can usually be selected without difficulty.

Weed and Pest Control

Weed control is usually a serious problem in young orchards. Shallow cultivation at frequent enough intervals to keep the weeds from going to seed can be used in controlling weeds in young orchards located on level tillable land. It will, however, be more economical in most instances to control weeds in young orchards by the use of herbicide sprays. Methods should follow the pattern described for use of herbicides in mature orchards, with even greater care exercised to avoid spraying herbicide on the bark or foliage of young trees.

Intercropping with cultivated crops will provide satisfactory weed control if well done. On rough, stony or sloping land, it may be advisable to leave part of the orchard in sod or weeds.

Weeds should be kept under control at all times. The area immediately surrounding each tree should be kept as free from weeds as possible. Macadamia trees have many shallow roots and their growth is handicapped by excessive competition from weeds. It has been demonstrated repeatedly that the best orchards are those in which the weeds are kept under control.

Since the fibrous roots of macadamia trees are relatively shallow, deep cultivation should be avoided in the root zone. Weeding near trees should be limited to hoeing or the careful use of herbicides. Perhaps the best contact herbicide to use in the orchard is activated oil emulsion. Aromatic oil herbicides such as Union Solvent 4276, Shell Weedkiller series and 55AR are among the more effective herbicides in use. Aromatic oils are very effective as weed killers.

Agitation is an operation of primary importance in using oil emulsions since the oil particles in the emulsion tend to separate out or "cream." Power sprayers equipped with mechanical agitators are best, although good emulsions can also be prepared by hand mixing. Activated oil emulsions may be prepared with aromatic oil or diesel oil. More emulsifying agent is necessary to emulsify aromatic oils than diesel oil. Aromatic oils are also stronger in action than diesel oil and should not be used for controlling weeds in the nursery.

When aromatic oils are used, either pentachlorophenol (PCP) or sodium PCP may be used as an activator. PCP will not dissolve in water and must be dissolved in the aromatic oil before making the emulsion. Similarly, PCP will not dissolve in diesel oil. The activator is prepared by adding 50 lb of PCP to 50 gal. of aromatic oil. The mixture should be warmed a little, since PCP dissolves very slowly in cold oil.

The emulsion is made in the same manner as in the diesel oil emulsion, except that no additional activator is added since it is already dissolved in the oil. The amount of aromatic oil-PCP mixture used is in inverse proportion to the concentration of PCP. Formerly 16 gal. of aromatic oil-PCP stock were used in making up to 100 gal. of emulsion when the stock contained only 18 lb of PCP in 50 gal. of aromatic oil. When the PCP concentration is raised to 50 lb in 50 gal., only about 6 gal. per 100 gal. of emulsion is necessary.

PCP has some advantages over sodium PCP. PCP is cheaper and since it is not soluble in water, it is not so easily washed off or carried below the soil surface by rain water. Since it is dissolved in the oil and not the water, it is carried into the leaves and stems of the weeds with the oil. When the emulsion is sprayed on, the water evaporates, leaving a thin film of oil. It is this oil-plus-activator which penetrates the weeds and kills them. If the activator is dissolved in the oil, it works better, because the oil carries the PCP with it as it penetrates the plant tissues.

2,4-D may be used in the orchard if special precautions are taken to control drift. Weeds like honohono (*Commelina diffusa*) and joee (*Stachytarpheta cayennensis*) can be most economically eradicated with 2,4-D. Only non-volatile forms—sodium salt, amine salt, or the so-called low volatile esters—should be used. A solution of 1 lb of 2,4-D per 100 gal. of water is sufficient for most 2,4-D susceptible weeds, although double this concentration is often used. Due care should be exercised to avoid spraying too close to the trees, and spraying should not be done when trees are flushing new growth.

To kill perennial grasses like kikuyu grass (*Pennisetum clandestinum*), panicum grass (*Panicum purpurescens*), Bermuda grass (*Cynodon dactylon*), etc., TCA is effective. These grasses are not controlled by contact herbicides such as activated oil emulsion because they have underground rootstalks. Two or three sprayings spaced about a month apart, of a solution containing 25 lb of TCA in 100 gal. of water sprayed over an acre of land, will usually completely eradicate these grasses.

Another very effective grass herbicide called Dalapon has recently appeared on the market. However, all new herbicides must be cleared by the U.S. Pure Food and Drug Administration. TCA and Dalapon cannot be used directly under macadamia trees as yet. Tests conducted at the Kona Branch Station showed the Dalapon sprayed in the orchard at the recommended rate of 10 lb per acre did not adversely affect macadamia trees. Even twice this rate of application did not damage the trees. One or two sprayings were sufficient to eradicate grasses. However, until clearance is obtained, Dalapon should be limited to spraying on field roads and along the edges of the orchard.

Herbicide spraying should not be done in the orchard when there are nuts on the ground. This is especially true when oil emulsions are used. Nuts will absorb the odor of the herbicide, even when sprayed on nuts still in the husk. Nuts sprayed with herbicides are unfit for human consumption.

Although certain insect and disease pests do some damage, direct control of these pests by active means such as spraying is not commonplace. Some insects such as the stink bug (*Nezara viridula*) and the native koa seed worm (*Cryptophlebia illepida*) are biologically controlled; hence the damage by these insects is minimal. Some fungus diseases are troublesome in certain regions.

Fertilization

Soils on which macadamias are grown vary widely in structure and chemical composition. Differences in fertility usually increase the longer the soil is under cultivation. Natural deficiencies and changes in amounts of nutrient elements in the soil have led to the adoption of fertilizer practices by which deficient elements are added. Macadamia trees in Hawaii are fertilized more heavily than most other tree crops except perhaps coffee. Mature trees on large plantings are fertilized by plane.

A critical time in the life of a young tree is when it is becoming established after being transplanted into the orchard. Too often, young grafted trees are transplanted into the orchard and then left to compete with weeds and grasses without adequate care or attention. Many trees handled in this manner die or, if they survive, make very little growth. Proper culture and fertilization should result in rapid vigorous growth by young trees during the first year after transplanting. Young transplanted trees must be kept growing vigorously. It is always false economy to attempt to economize on fertilizer or care given young trees. This is especially true of macadamias as it is well known that the faster the young tree grows, the sooner it will come into bearing.

Table 11.2 is based upon a suggested amount of about ¾ lb of fertilizer per in. of trunk diameter, plus additional nitrogen at the rate of ¼ lb per in. of trunk diameter shortly before the peak blossoming season. It is assumed that nitrogen applied at this time would probably increase fruit set and also encourage net growth. The amounts of fertilizer listed in Table 11.2 are suggested mainly as guide or point of departure in working out a satisfactory fertilizer practice in specific orchards. The amounts, formulas, and times of application of fertilizers may be expected to change as experience is gained and further knowledge of soil fertility and the response of trees to fertilizer becomes available.

Following Table 11.2 as a guide, about 12 lb of fertilizer per year would be used for a tree 1 ft in diameter. However, for heavily producing trees in areas of abundant sunlight and adequate rainfall, it would probably be profitable to increase the amount of fertilizer applied. The heavier bearing trees in an orchard should receive more fertilizer than those which produce light crops.

TABLE 11.2

SUGGESTED YEARLY FERTILIZER APPLICATIONS OF AMMONIUM SULFATE
FOR MACADAMIA TREES

Trunk Diameter (in.)	Before Peak Bloom (lb)	(oz)	Summer Application (lb)	(oz)	Formula	Fall Application (lb)	(oz)	Formula	Total Application Per Year (lb)
3		12	1	2	10–10–10	1	2	10–10–10	3
6	1	8	2	4	10–10–15	2	4	10–10–15	6
9	2	4	3	6	10–10–15	3	6	10–10–15	9
12	3		4	8	10–10–15	4	8	10–10–15	12
15	3	12	5	10	10–10–15	5	10	10–10–15	15

Productive macadamia nut trees will have high requirements for nitrogen and potassium as well as phosphorus. These requirements will be greater than the capacity of most soils to furnish them. Nitrogen facilitates growth of the tree as well as increasing the size of nuts. When the supply of potassium is low, increasing the supply will promote new growth and also tend to speed up development of the kernels and increase their oil content. Phosphorus is important in the transfer of energy produced by respiration processes within the plant. Organic compounds containing phosphorus are essential in energy transfer for all synthetic processes including those involved in growth and oil formation. Most growers apply a complete fertilizer containing all three of these elements. Older trees in heavy production utilize relatively large amounts of nitrogen and potassium, much of which is removed from the field when the crop is harvested.

In Table 11.2 a 10-10-15 formula is suggested for bearing trees over 6 in. in diameter. For small trees not yet in production, a complete fertilizer with high nitrogen and phosphorus to promote vegetative growth would probably be more appropriate. In Table 11.2 a 10-10-10 fertilizer formula is suggested for young trees which have not yet come into heavy bearing. An 8-8-8 formula would probably serve equally well.

Harvesting

The nuts are borne profusely in long grape-like open clusters. When mature, they fall to the ground. They must be gathered and hulled within 2 or 3 days to prevent deterioration from the decaying husks. Several types of hullers are used, including an automobile wheel in a trough. After hulling, the nuts are usually air-dried in screen-bottom trays, to about 3.5% moisture. They are then sold to local mills for about 30 cents per pound.

The hulled nuts are about 1 in. in diameter. They are often hard shell and about 60 are in a pound. For export, they are often cracked and the sound kernels packed in vacuum jars. Either way, directly from the shell or from the jars, the flavor is delicious.

The ripe nuts drop to the ground, and to provide a smooth surface some areas are coated with volcanic cinders for the nuts to fall on. Mechanical harvesters are being tested.

About 90% of the crop is harvested between mid-September and mid-December with the peak in October. The earlier harvested nuts are higher in quality, as determined by flotation tests for oil content of the cracked nuts.

It is practically impossible to distinguish mature nuts from immature nuts on the tree, and picking nuts from the tree is therefore impractical. In addition, nuts which are shaken off, knocked off, or picked from the tree are often immature and must be discarded as culls when processed.

Nuts should be picked up rather often, especially during rainy or humid weather when nuts left on the ground soon begin to rot, mold, or germinate. Rat damage may be a problem and rats sometimes eat considerable amounts of nuts if harvesting is not rather frequent.

During the main harvest season, nuts should be gathered at intervals of from 2 to 4 weeks, depending on the weather and amount of nuts falling. During the rest of the year, nuts are picked up at least once a month, and sometimes more often if sufficient nuts have fallen to make picking worthwhile. Nuts are usually picked into metal buckets or wire baskets and then sacked in burlap bags for transportation from the orchard. Mechanical picking methods are being investigated in some of the larger orchards, but at present, practically all of the crop is picked by hand.

PROCESSING

Husking

Mature nuts fall from the tree enclosed in a fleshy green husk of carpel. This husk must be removed by hand or with some sort of husking machine, preferably within 2 or 3 days after harvesting. Nuts stored in sacks, bins, or piles during humid weather soon begin to ferment and spoil, generating heat which causes rapid deterioration in quality and flavor of the kernels. If husking must be delayed more than three days for any reason, nuts should be spread out to dry in thin layers preferably on wire racks in a drying shed.

Hand husking is too inefficient and laborious, and a number of different types of home-made huskers have been improvised and used with varying degrees of success. Several larger, more expensive commercial models have also been devised and used. These husking machines all have strong points and weaknesses. They operate on different principles and all have been more or less successful. Large commercial walnut hullers and a high capacity plate type husker devised by the Agricultural Engineering Department of the University of Hawaii have been used with some degree of success for husking nuts. This machinery is rather expensive and is most suitable for large growers and processors.

It was found that macadamia nuts may be mechanically husked by giving the husk an impact tangential to the nut shell. This force may be applied by a plate, or cylinder or "rubber tire" which loosens or knocks off the entire husk or the greater part of it. Care needs to be taken to operate the husker so that the hull is removed while the shell and kernel remain undamaged (Kinch *et al.* 1961).

When nuts are green the moisture content is high and the shells fit tightly, protecting the kernel from damage. As the nuts dry, the kernels shrink and leave a space between the shell and kernel. Impact is then transferred to the kernel, possibly causing damage. It is, therefore, desirable to husk the nuts as soon after they drop to the ground as is possible.

In addition to mechanical damage to the kernels caused by husking, other quality variations, such as tendency toward rancidity, occur. Plate huskers with a capacity of 1400 lb per hour, cracked only 1% of the shells and did not reduce the storage-life of the nuts beyond that of hand husked nuts.

After husking, the nuts and husks are usually separated by hand. Mechanical husk separators have been constructed, but these are too complicated to be built on most farms and will not be discussed here.

Drying

Freshly husked nuts ordinarily contain up to about 20% water and should be dried down to about 3.5% moisture as soon as possible after husking. If freshly husked nuts are stored in sacks, bins or boxes without drying, molds and rots frequently cause considerable spoilage, especially to nuts which have cracks or openings in the shell. Because of this, husked nuts are usually dried on wire racks for 2 to 3 weeks before storing. The drying time may be less if nuts are delivered to the processing plant before storage. (See Figs. 3.1 and 3.2.)

Freshly husked nuts can be dried in the shade and, since showers are usually frequent during the main harvesting season, some sort of rain-proof shelter or drying shed is often needed to protect the trays or racks on which the nuts are placed for drying.

Satisfactory drying racks can be constructed from ½ in. or ¼ in. mesh hardware cloth stapled to light wooden frames. Such racks or trays may be stacked on top of the other, provided a few inches of space are allowed between racks to permit air circulation.

Nuts should be placed in the racks in a shallow even layer to permit rapid drying. After nuts have been air dried, they may be stored in sacks or bins where they will usually keep satisfactorily under dry, well-ventilated conditions for at least 4 to 5 months.

Husked nuts can also be dried in forced-air dryers at ambient temperatures or at temperatures below 43°C (110°F) for a few days and then at 57° to 60°C (135° to 140°F).

Cracking

Differences in size and shape of nut, and in thickness and texture of the shell, present many problems in developing a cracking machine adapted to macadamia nuts. The shells are extremely hard and vary from $\frac{1}{16}$ in. to $\frac{1}{4}$ in. in thickness, with the thicker shells predominating. The shell, therefore, presents an armor-like coat with about $\frac{1}{32}$ in. clearance between the kernel and shell. When the macadamia nut is struck a sharp blow, the tough shell tends to crack only partially, and a portion is often forced inward damaging the tender kernel. An iron vise, or a plunger that is permitted to extend a specified distance, is much preferred to a hammer or uncontrolled plunger.

Moltzau and Ripperton (1939) developed a cracker of simple design which employs the principle of a vise. The nut is held between two blunt movable wedges and the shell is cracked into clean halves by gently applying pressure. An efficiency of 96% whole, undamaged kernels was obtained.

The crackers are adjusted to various size nuts. A sizing machine sorts the nuts and feeds them into crackers adjusted to handle specified sizes. The cracking machines force open the shells and automatic separators shake out the loose kernels. Kernels which adhere to the shells are separated by hand. One unit handles 2 tons of air-cured nuts per 8-hour day.

Quality Grading

Dried macadamia kernels disclose marked differences in appearance which are reflected in the quality of the cooked product. Commercial grading is based on the fact that plump, smooth-surfaced, light colored kernels have a high oil content and low specific gravity. As the oil content decreases the kernels become heavier, darker and less mild in flavor.

These observations have led to a simple method of commercial grading by using specific gravity solutions. Grade 1 comprises all kernels so light as to float in tap water at room temperature, having a specific gravity of 1.0. Grade 2 kernels have a specific gravity between 1.0 and 1.025, and are usually sold to the confectionery and bakery trade. A convenient solution to use is made up of 5½ oz of sodium chloride (table salt) per gallon of water. Kernels which sink in this solution are Grade 3 and are discarded.

The procedure for grading is simple. Air-dried kernels are immersed in pure water at room temperature and stirred freely to rid them of air bubbles. The kernels which float (Grade 1) are skimmed off and dried, first by draining, then by centrifuging. The kernels which sink in the water are drained and immersed in the salt solution and the floating kernels are skimmed off as Grade 2. Those which sink are Grade 3. During grading, the kernels absorb up to 8 to 10% moisture; this is removed by dehydration before further processing (Moltzau and Ripperton 1939).

The shell of rough-shell cultivars is thinner than that of the smooth-shell type, and is therefore easier to crack. Moreover, the kernel of the former has a firmer texture and there is greater shrinkage during drying. Because of their ellipsoidal shape the rough-shell nuts are more easily cracked by hand.

The rough-shell nuts produce smaller percentages of Grade 1 kernels. With some trees, the entire crop may be Grades 2 and 3, while with the smooth-shell nuts, 90% Grade 1 is common. The rough-shell nuts are inferior in flavor, so much so that the two types should not be mixed. They also cook more rapidly, and an oil roasting temperature of 127°C (260°F) for 12 min is recommended.

All nuts with diameters less than ⅝ in. (1.6 cm) are eliminated in the sizing machines and discarded as culls. Shipments of nuts may lose up to 10% in weight when dried to the 3.5% moisture content desirable for cracking.

Cooking

Macadamia nuts are cooked before eating—either by immersion in hot oil or dry roasting. The unusually high oil content of 70 to 80% for Grade 1 nuts makes them adaptable to dry roasting. A heat of 135°C (275°F) for 40 to 50 min produces the most desirable rate for dry roasting; higher temperatures cause the surface of the kernels to brown rapidly while the center may remain uncooked. Frequent stirring or constant tumbling of the nuts is necessary to prevent scorching.

The color, texture, flavor and consumer-preference of dry-roasted and oil-roasted macadamia nuts are equal for Grade 1 nuts; but Grade 2 nuts dry out severely and become dull when dry roasted. Therefore, oil roasting at 135°C (275°F) for 12 to 15 min has been found most satisfactory for all grades of nuts. A higher temperature causes uneven cooking and a lower temperature produces oil-soaked nuts. The oil roasting is judged to be complete when the kernels have reached an established stage of brownness. Cooking continues for a few minutes after removal from the oil.

Stainless steel or glass vessels are recommended for oil roasting nuts. A refined coconut oil prepared especially for nuts is recommended for macadamia nuts. Care must be taken to remove particles of kernels which tend to darken the oil and reduce its effective life. It is estimated that 13 gal. of oil are required for 1000 lb of kernels. The heat is increased as each new charge is added, so that the cold kernels will not reduce the temperature of the oil below 135°C (275°F). When cooking is complete the kernels are removed from the oil, drained, centrifuged and cooled rapidly by air.

The salting technique is important and follows when the kernels are lukewarm to cool. An adhesive oil is applied before salting—for ovenroasted kernels a 15% water solution of gum arabic, or for oil-roasted kernels a special oil which melts at 32.2°C (90°F). The kernels are sprayed and stirred, and the salt is applied immediately. A special grade of flake salt, of medium grain and free from impurities, is used. The adhesive solidifies on the surface of the kernels at room temperature and holds the salt grains.

Because cooked kernels absorb moisture readily, packing should proceed as soon as the kernels are salted and cooled. Vacuum packing in glass jars has become almost universal. Except at unusually high temperatures, vacuum-packed kernels will keep without deterioration for several years. The use of various inert gases, such as nitrogen and carbon dioxide, appears to have little advantage over vacuum and cold storage.

STABILITY OF MACADAMIA NUTS

Fresh macadamia nuts stored without drying deteriorate rapidly due to respiratory, lipoytic, and proteolytic activity. Both temperature and moisture content are important to stability of raw kernels. Stability of the kernels decreases with increasing moisture and increasing storage temperature. At moisture of 1.4% only very small changes occur in flavor and chemical composition after 18 months even at room temperature. At higher moisture levels and storage temperatures, total sugars decrease and reducing sugars and free fatty acids increase as the moisture content increases to 2.5 or 4.5%. Temperatures as low as -17.8°C (0°F) are to maintain quality for 18 months. Light apparently has no effect on stability of raw or roasted macadamia kernels.

TABLE 11.3

COMPOSITION OF MACADAMIA NUTS AND OIL

Nuts	Raw %	Roasted %
Moisture	1.40	–
Ether	76.95	77.25
Total sugars	5.56	4.98
Reducing sugars	0.04	0.07
Iodine number	80.90	76.29
Free fatty acid mg KOH/g oil	0.44	0.38
Amino nitrogen	0.04	0.03
Oil	% of Total Fatty Acids	
Laurate	trace	0.62
Myristate	0.75	0.75
Palmitate	7.37	6.15
Palmitoleate	18.46	19.11
Stearate	2.78	1.64
Oleate	64.96	67.14
Linoleate	1.51	1.34
Arachidate	1.85	1.50
Eicosenate	2.33	1.74

Source: Cavaletto *et al.* (1966).

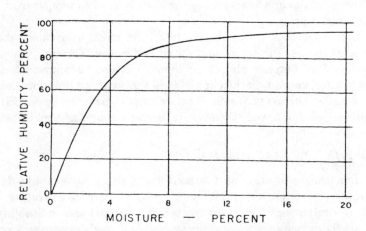

FIG. 11.3. PERCENT MOISTURE OF MACADAMIA KERNELS IN EQUILIBRIUM WITH AIR AT VARIOUS RELATIVE HUMIDITIES

To maintain good color and flavor in raw nuts for 18 months, room temperature is satisfactory for 1.4% moisture, 1.7°C (35°F) is required for 2.3% moisture, and 0°F is necessary for 4.3% moisture. Changes in chemical composition due to moisture content and storage temperature of raw kernels parallel changes in color and flavor.

Changes in total and reducing sugars in raw kernels are due to enzymatic activity. These enzymes are inactivated during roasting. However, the influence of moisture and temperature on the stability of roasted macadamia kernels is similar to that of raw kernels. For storage of three months or more the moisture content should be 1%. Moisture contents of 1.7% or 3.0% may be maintained only when the storage temperature is 1.7° and -17.8°C (35° and 0°F), respectively.

Research on the stability of fresh and roasted macadamia nuts at the University of Hawaii showed that there were (a) only minor differences in the quality and chemical characteristics of cultivars of nuts; (b) roasted kernels maintained quality better than raw kernels; (c) flavor deterioration closely paralleled darkening of kernels; (d) kernel stability increased with decreasing moisture content down to 1%; (e) kernel stability decreased with increasing storage temperature; and (f) quality changes were essentially identical for kernels stored in the light and dark (Cavaletto et al. 1966).

Macadamia nuts are being offered as a taste treat to passengers aboard many U.S. airlines at the rate of about 5,000,000 nuts per month. The nuts are packaged in an aluminum foil cup about 3 in. in diameter, with vegetable parchment on the bottom. Each cup contains ⅔ oz, or about a dozen finely salted macadamias. Printed on the circular cup liner is a brief description of the gourmet delicacy.

USES OF MACADAMIA NUTS

Processing has been improved recently. Equipment for removing the outer husk, for dehydrating, for size-grading, for cracking the shell, for oil roasting and automatic weighing and packaging is being developed. Even quality-grading has been mechanized with flotation units, leaving removal of the hulls as the only essentially hand operation.

By-products are being developed. Husks were first used as mulch, but are now being pulverized and mixed with molasses and pineapple bran for cattle feed. The hull powder is also being used as a filler for plastics.

Scott (1958) studied characteristics of consumer demand for macadamia nuts in Hawaii and found the chief uses of macadamia nuts to be salted, chocolate-coated nut candy and nut ice cream.

Eighty-seven percent of consumers preferred whole or halved, as compared with pea-size pieces. A majority of homemakers preferred macadamia nuts to all other nuts in so far as flavor and texture were concerned. The nearest competitor tastewise was cashew, and the least was the filbert. Some wanted them in tin cans, others in polyethylene or glass jars, and a few from bulk dispensers.

Nineteen percent of homemakers found fault with macadamia nuts. Major complaints were that they were too oily, too fattening, too rich, soggy, rancid or salty. Fifty percent bought the nuts year-round, while half bought them only in holiday seasons.

Sixty-three percent of consumers used macadamia nuts as a between-meal snack; 31% used them with cocktails or other beverages; 13% used them for baking or toppings; and 9% bought them for gifts only and did not use any themselves. All of the uses varied with the income. Forty-six percent thought macadamia nuts were too high in price for general use.

Courtesy of Hawaii's Brewer Orchards and Walter Kuzio,
Candy Industry, New York

FIG. 11.4. MACADAMIA NUT PRODUCTS

The largest producer of macadamia nuts, Hawaii's Brewer Orchards, also sells choice-grade cultivars of its Mauna Loa nut on a commercial pack basis to candy manufacturers, bakeries and other food processors. Finely ground pieces (right) are used primarily in cakes and pastries. Halves and wholes find their way into candies, primarily chocolate-covered confections. Diced nuts (center) are exceptional garnishes and are even made into ice cream. While unflavored nuts are sold to suppliers, the consumer may purchase them lightly salted and roasted, in coconut oil, or in brittle or chocolate-covered candy. A macadamia sprig with "nutlets" and loose, mature nuts in the shell is also pictured.

Macadamia nuts readily absorb odors from storage rooms and other products. They apparently do respond to refrigerated storage as readily as most other nuts of comparable oil content. A satisfactory method of storage is to dry the nuts to 2% moisture, close in tins or other suitable containers, and hold at 3.3°C (38°F).

Macadamia nuts are used as a dessert nut, and marketed mostly in the cooked, salted form, vacuum packed in glass jars. They are easily chopped into small cubes and used in candies, to which they impart a characteristic texture and flavor.

While either the unprocessed or roasted macadamia nuts have a long storage life as compared with other high oil content nuts, they do deteriorate slowly. Deterioration in flavor may be due to absorption of cold storage odors, development of rancidity, or merely to a gradual loss of the delicate nutty flavor.

Deterioration in texture appears first as a loss of crispness and slight mealiness. In time the kernel loses all resemblance to its original texture and becomes either tough or soggy. Deterioration in color is evident as an almost black color when affected nuts are cooked. Fresh kernels remain bright when cooked.

Salting is virtually the sole method of processing and exporting macadamia nuts from Hawaii. These are in turn used in many ways as a snack between meals, with cocktails, after meals, in confections, in bakery goods, on salads and desserts, and with meats, chicken or fish dishes. Macadamia nuts may be used as a substitute for almonds, cashews, filberts or pecans in many dishes where a nutty flavor and crisp texture are desired.

MACADAMIA NUT PRODUCTS

The roasted kernels of macadamia nuts are considered by many to be among the finest of confectionery nuts in flavor and texture. The kernels are generally roasted in coconut oil at about 135°C (275°F) to a light golden brown color. Since only a small amount of roasting oil is consumed or lost in the process, it is replenished only periodically with small quantities of fresh oil, and may be used for an entire season of 6 to 7 months.

Usually, antioxidants [approximately 76 ppm BHA (butylated hydroxyanisole) or BHT (butylated hydroxytoluene)] are added to the oil for protection of the oil itself against rancidity and carry-over to the kernels. The kernels are oil roasted in batches or continuously treated with adhesive oil, salted and vacuum packed. Packages are glass, tin, aluminum or film.

Usually free fatty acids, color (absorbance at 550 mm), refractive index and viscosity of the roasting oil increase with use. The iodine number of the oil shows wide change with use, from a value of about 9.75, typical of coconut oil, to a high value of 57.4, approaching that of macadamia nuts; indicating considerable exchange of fats between macadamia nuts and cooking oil. Further evidence of exchange is in the fatty acid composition of the roasting oil, which changes from a pattern typical for coconut oil to more like macadamia oil. The percentage of coconut oil and macadamia oil can be estimated by the laureate or palmitoleate content, since these fatty acids are characteristic of coconut and macadamia oil, respectively. In two weeks of use, the oil may change from 100% of coconut oil to 20% macadamia oil, and to 75% macadamia nut oil after 13 weeks. This high rate of exchange, which exceeds that reported by other deep-fat cooking processes, is probably due to the high oil content of macadamia nuts.

Cavaletto et al. (1966) found that the most important factor for raw macadamia stability was moisture. Macadamia nuts must be husked within 24 hours of harvest and dried rapidly to 3.5% moisture or lower to prevent quality deterioration. For maximum stability, kernels must be dried to 1% moisture and stored at low temperatures, preferably -17.8°C (0°F). At higher moistures and higher temperatures the flavor, texture and color deteriorate; total sugars decrease and reducing sugars and free fatty acids increase.

Cruz et al. (1966) found that roasted macadamia nuts with 1.1% moisture scored higher than 1.7% kernels which scored higher than 2.9% kernels after storage at -17.8°C (0°F) for all periods up to 14 months. The 1.1% moisture kernels were stable for 8 months at 1.7°C (35°F), with slight loss of flavor and texture at ambient temperature.

No significant differences were found between roasted macadamias stored in light and dark. At higher moisture levels and higher storage temperatures the kernels darkened. Roasted kernels picked up moisture quickly and became rancid.

Crain and Tang (1975) identified 41 flavor compounds in roasted macadamia nuts, and concluded that methyl sulfide plays a role in the characteristic macadamia flavor. The compound is highly volatile and is driven off by prolonged roasting.

Cavaletto and Yamamoto (1971) added 200 ppm each of BHT and BHA to fresh coconut oil and found that antioxidant loss was very rapid. After two weeks of use only 22 ppm of antioxidant remained and after four weeks there was only a trace.

They found the addition of antioxidants to the adhesive oil very effective, which was more beneficial than packing under vacuum or in inert gas.

The following macadamia nut products are on the market: raw in-shell macadamia nuts in 1-, 2-, and 5-lb bags; raw shelled macadamia in 1-, 2-, and 5-lb glasses or cans; roasted, salted and packed under vacuum in glass jars or in cans. In addition to salt, hydrogenated vegetable protein, sugar, hickory smoke and other flavors, monosodium glutamate and gums are sometimes added.

Macadamia nut brittle with sugar, corn syrup, baking soda, salt and imitation vanilla is the most common confection made from the nut. Other candies include chocolate covered whole nuts, nut halves, nut clusters, nut crunch, and nuts with coconut. The nuts are also covered with milk chocolate and with hard cream, and sometimes flavored with butter rum, pineapple or mint. Special candies with macadamia nuts include "bark," bars, corals, patties and toffee. Bakery products containing macadamia nuts include cakes, cookies, nut bread and fruit-cakes.

A booklet published by Hawaiian Holiday Macadamia Nut Company, Honokaa, Hawaii 96727, *My Macadamia Nut Recipes*, contains recipes for:

Baked bananas with macadamia nuts
Baked green beans with macadamia nuts
Banana macadamia cream pie
Bourbon balls with macadamia nuts
Cherry-macadamia nut bars
Dutch butter slices with macadamia nuts
Gourmet macadamia nut ice cream sauce
Macanut candied papaya
Macadamia candy logs
Macadamia nut bars
Macadamia nut cream pie
Macadamia nut ice cream
Macadamia nut pancakes
Macadamia nut stuffing
Mango nut chutney
Matrimonial cake with macadamia nuts

Mincemeat bread with macadamia nuts
Mocho cheesecake
Passion fruit chiffon pie with macadamia nuts
Pear crunch with macadamia nuts
Pie crust with macadamia nuts
Pineapple macadamia carrot cake
Pineapple macadamia nut ice cream sauce
Pineapple macadamia muffins
Ragged robins, macadamia nuts
Sour cream coffeecake with macadamia nuts
Thumbprints with macadamia nuts
Vegetable bake with macadamia nuts
Wild rice stuffing

REFERENCES

ANON. 1957. Statistics of Hawaiian Agriculture. Hawaii Coop. Crop and Livestock Reporting Service, Agric. Econ. Rept. *35.* Honolulu.

ANON. 1960A. Statistics of Hawaiian Agriculture. Ext. Serv. Agric. Econ. Rept. *53*. University of Hawaii, Honolulu.

ANON. 1960B. Macadamia gears for progress in Hawaii. Canner /Packer *129* (8) 32-33.

BAILEY, L.H. 1935. The Standard Cyclopedia of Horticulture, Vol. 2. Macmillan Co., New York.

CAVALETTO, C.G., CRUZ, A., ROSS, E., and YAMAMOTO, H.Y. 1966. Factors affecting macadamia nut stability. I. Raw Kernels. Food Technol. *20* (8) 1084-1087.

CAVALETTO, C.G., and YAMAMOTO, H.Y. 1971. Factors affecting macadamia nut stability. III. Roasting oil quality and antioxidants. J. Food Sci. *36* (1) 81-83.

CRAIN, W.P., and TANG, C.S. 1975. Volatile components of roasted macadamia nuts. J. Food Sci. *40* (1) 207-208.

CRUZ, A., CAVALETTO, C., YAMAMOTO, H.Y., and ROSS, E. 1966. Factors affecting macadamia nut stability. II. Roasted kernels. Food Technol. *20* (9) 1217-1218.

HAMILTON, R.A., and FUKUNAGA, E.T. 1959. Growing macadamia nuts in Hawaii. Hawaii Agric. Exp. Stn. Bull. *121*.

KINCH, D.M., WANG, J.K., and STROHMAN, R.E. 1961. Equipment for husking macadamia nuts. Hawaii Agric. Exp. Stn. Bull. *126*.

MOLLETT, J.A. 1962. Hawaii's future agriculture. Agric. Econ. Rept. *59*. Hawaii Agric. Exp. Stn., Honolulu.

MOLTZAU, R.A., and RIPPERTON, J.C. 1939. Processing of the macadamia. Hawaii Agric. Exp. Stn. Bull. *83*.

O'ROURKE, F.L.S. 1959. Macadamia, the nut crop of the 50th state. Northern Nut Grow. Assoc. *50*, 84-86.

SCOTT, F.S., JR. 1958. Macadamia nuts. Hawaii Agric. Exp. Stn., Agric. Econ. Bull. *16*.

12

Pecans

The history of pecans is closely related to the history of American Indians in the southern United States. Of all the horticultural products given by our continent to civilization, none are of more importance than the pecan, nor destined to play a more vital role in our pomological future. Indigenous over a large area of North America, it has taken four centuries for this plant to become a cultivated crop. Belonging as it does to the walnut family, the presumption is reasonable that it made its appearance during Cretaceous times, as walnuts are known to have had a place in the flora of that geological period. Whether the pecan originated in the northern area of its present range and was water borne to southern territory, or whether it appeared simultaneously over a wide section are merely matters of conjecture. A glance at the map of North America during the Cretaceous period will show a probability of northern origin and water distribution, as the tree is certainly more adapted and more common along water courses; this, however, does not explain the presence of native nuts in western Alabama unless ocean currents contributed to the dissemination or water-ways existed then, records of which have been obliterated.

There is no doubt that the Indian tribes inhabiting the Mississippi Valley and the tributaries thereto from Missouri and Illinois to the southward, as also in eastern and western Texas and southern Oklahoma, knew and used the pecan long before the advent of the white man, as the early Spanish explorers found it in use and have given us definite information on the subject.

The way in which the pecan species became scattered throughout the North American continent is a most fascinating study of the interaction between plant and animal species. Prior to the 1700s and to a certain extent even into the 18th Century, the American Indians were primarily responsible for the substantial increase in the growing range of the pecan.

In the south central areas of the United States, the pecan was a staple component of the Indian diet. The nuts were easy to collect and could be kept for an extended period of time. An ample store of pecans was good insurance against hard times during the months of the year when the other sources of food were scarce. Moreover the Indians traded the pecans for other goods such as furs, flint, tobacco or even a good pipe! It is believed that as the Indians traveled, they planted pecan nuts in the vicinity of their campsites—to provide "grubstakes" for their future descendants. Since the Mississippi and its dozens of tributaries were the canoe highways of the Indians, the Mighty River also provided the inroads for the spread of pecan growing over hundreds, possibly even thousands, of miles of waterway country.

When the Indians planted nuts in the vicinity of their campsites, they preferred to plant the biggest and the thinnest-shelled selections because in those days of rudimentary cracking tools a large, thin-shelled nut was a considerable attraction. Thus the Indian tribes not only increased the growing range of the pecan but also through their haphazard selection and planting activities greatly improved the quality of their favorite nut.

It is fascinating to observe that the Indians must have had some favorite stopover points in which they re-established campsites many times and consequently had more than just a few nut planting ceremonies. Nuts which were planted in the rich river-bottom shorelands or the many islands of the Mississippi system thrived magnificently and grew into astonishingly huge trees, often to heights of 200 ft. Now great natural groves of pecans exist in many scattered points along the Mississippi River system from the Gulf of Mexico to northern locations such as Dubuque, Iowa, and even a few scattered trees as far north as the Chicago area.

The early European settlers soon recognized the great potential wealth in the pecan for commercial purposes. The selection and distribution of improved cultivars for orchard plantings proceeded at an explosive rate. It has been estimated that as many as 500 selections of pecans have been advanced for "named" status.

Since the pecan has acclimatized itself to so many localities beyond the confines of its original birthplace, the question begs to be answered, Can the pecan adapt to Ontario conditions? Some serious studies have been made of the potential adaptability of the pecan to the Ontario climate. Although the pecan has made its reputation as a bit of a traveler to many different climates and latitudes, the species does tend to have a few hesitations about discarding all of its southern traditions.

There are some sacrifices which are made when pecans are grown in the north. The size of the northern pecans is not as great as that of their southern cousins. Also, the kernel percentage tends to be a few points lower on the average than the glamorous southern "papershells." However, nature has some marvelous compensations: the flavor of the true northern pecan is unbeatable (Campbell 1975).

CULTIVATION

First Plantings for Nut Production

There seems to be no definite record of the first planting of pecans with nut production in view. In 1911 Onderdonk reported trees set on irrigated land at Bustamente, Mexico, 100 miles from Laredo, Texas, that are thought to be 200 years old; this is certainly prior to any planting done in the colonies. Washington was planting pecans in 1775, calling them Mississippi nuts and saying they were something like a pignut but larger, thinner shelled and fuller of meat. Jefferson sowed seed in 1779, for he described a two-year-old tree in 1781. Nuttall brought back the nuts from Arkansas in 1819 and distributed them to interested individuals around the Chesapeake section and undoubtedly a search of that territory would bring to light some trees of considerable age.

Pecans First Propagated

Michaux suggested the grafting of the pecan in 1810, realizing that this must precede the establishment of orchards, but contented himself merely with the suggestion. Abner Landrum of Edgefield, South Carolina, stated in the American Farmer of 1822 that he had "This summer, budded some dozens of pecans on the common hickory nut, without a single failure as yet, and some of them are growing finely." Nothing seems to have come of this work; it certainly made no impression and was not followed up by others or further reported by Landrum. It remained for Antoine, a slave gardener on Oak Alley Plantation in Louisiana, to first work pecan scions on pecan stocks. Suffice it to say here that in the winter of 1846-47, he successfully grafted sixteen trees and later worked over more, so that by the end of the Civil War there were 126 trees of the cultivar which was later named Centennial, on the plantation bearing nuts that sold for from $50.00 to $75.00 per barrel. The slave Antoine had thus laid the foundation upon which was to be erected a great industry, as no pomological crop can depend upon seedlings. For almost a half century, however, the industry progressed through the planting of nuts and many of the oldest orchards are seedlings; but gradually asexually propagated trees were obtainable in quantities and at prices sufficiently reasonable to permit extended planting.

The Mexican War seems to have been at the bottom of the first planting in Florida. A seedling orchard was set at Bagdad by John Hunt sometime after his return from Mexico. In 1924 some of these trees were still standing, though they had been neglected and were covered with Spanish moss. Tradition has it that the first planting of seedlings in Georgia was about 1830, following a storm and shipwreck. A barrel of nuts was washed ashore near Saint Mary's, and the nuts were planted through the territory. This same tradition holds for a part of northern Florida.

All of the early plantings were of seedlings, as it was considered practically impossible to get the pecan to take when grafted. The work of Antoine had either never been known, or forgotten, and it remained for Emile Bourgeois of Saint James Parish, Louisiana, to revive the art in 1877. He set 22 top grafts that year and got 11 of them to take. When these began bearing he continued the work and supplied nearby plantations with grafted stock.

Seedling planting continued, however, as grafted stock was limited and hard to get, even at $2.50 per plant. During the nineties, E.E. Risien of San Saba, Texas, perfected ring budding and, as this was most successful, the supply of named and asexually propagated cultivars increased and prices came down. So from in the nineties, following the introduction of the Stuart, Van Deman, San Saba and other cultivars, the plantings were exclusively of named sorts. There followed, also, a great deal of top working in the seedling orchards and in the native range of the plant enormous numbers of the wild trees have been changed to known sorts. A great deal of this work has been done since 1920.

Reports of large yields and great profits from individual trees and early plantings spurred and stirred the American bent for speculation and about 1900 a large number of individuals began planting pecans, not for the profits they anticipated out of this crop, but for the money they could make through selling orchards.

Sizable orchards have not developed along the northern limit of the pecan area, though a large number of named cultivars have been brought to notice from that section. These northern cultivars are not comparable to those of the South in size and yield and therefore cannot compete with them commercially. There is always, however, the chance for sorts of worth to be found that may take their commercial place in competition with the southern cultivars.

DISTRIBUTION OF PECANS IN THE UNITED STATES

The tree does not grow north of the mouth of the Great Mackalsity River on the Mississippi at a latitude of 42° 51'. Generally, the northern range is placed at Davenport, Iowa. Clinton marks the extreme northern point at which pecans are known to be produced from native trees. This is latitude 41° 50 ', and quite closely harmonizes with the information Michaux (1819) obtained over 100 years ago. From this point the tree is found south in the valley of the Mississippi and ascending its tributaries both east and west. It is reported up the Ohio to Cincinnati, up the Wabash to Terre Haute, Indiana, and by some up the Tennessee as far east as Chattanooga; in this last there seems to be some chance of error. Large seedling trees have been observed in the neighborhood of this city, but they have always given unmistakable evidence of being planted. It extends well up the Arkansas into Oklahoma, is found along the Red River, the Brazos, the Colorado and other streams in Texas, and to some extent along the Rio Grande. The tree is also found in northern Mexico, out of which section from three to five million pounds of interior seedlings are shipped to the United States annually. The limits of its distribution have not been well delineated (Reed 1925).

The pecan is not found in any numbers below Natchez on the Mississippi, as it avoids lands subject to long overflow. The pecan has been experimentally planted from the Great Lakes to the Gulf, and from the Atlantic to the Pacific, but has only developed commercially in the South. The first, or southern, belt runs from Wilmington, N.C., to Atlanta, Ga.; Birmingham, Ala., drops to Jackson, Miss., thence to Pine Bluff, Ark., and to McAlester, Okla., thence south to the Gulf just west of Galveston. This region has an average of from 270 to 290 growing days and many cultivars require this number for maturity. It is in the territory south of this line that practically all of the large commercial plantings have been made.

The northern line of the middle belt starts at Newport, drops to Asheville, N.C., then turns north to Louisville, Ky., going from there to Vincennes, Ind., and to Hannibal, Mo.; turning to the southwest there, it runs south of the Ozark Mountains and thence west to Santa Fe, N. Mex. This region has from 180 to 200 growing days and is adapted to cultivars originating along the Ohio River and similar localities. In its southeastern section in Piedmont North Carolina, northern Alabama and Mississippi, some of the southern sorts are grown, but the nuts are smaller than in the southern region. No great development has taken place in this section, though it is capable of good production through the proper choice of cultivars. They, however, cannot compete with the larger nuts grown further south. Yields have declined in South Carolina, Florida, Arkansas, and Oklahoma since about 1950; North Carolina and Mississippi have shown small increases; and increases for other southern states have been good.

The northern belt is restricted to that portion of the United States east of the Rocky Mountains that has a growing season of from 170 to 190 days. Experimental plantings made in this area have been disappointing in fruit, but the tree grows well and is of ornamental value.

The fourth belt area added by Stuckey and Kyle (1925) is called the western belt and takes in western Texas. This has a semi-arid climate and the native groves are found in the valleys between the hills or mountains of the territory. The altitude best adapted to the trees is from 800 to 2500 ft, and the rainfall from 18 to 40 in. There are 81 pecan producing counties in this belt and the majority of the Texas pecans come from this area, in which are to be found some of the largest orchards in the country. In the higher altitudes with a decreasing rainfall the trees become more spreading and of less height, though more nearly annual producers. The best part of this west Texas area has an altitude of from 1000 to 1800 ft and a rainfall of from 20 to 30 in.

The fifth belt includes west Texas, lower New Mexico, Arizona and California, where most of the expansion has occurred since about 1950. Pecan growing in this area is characterized by the following: development of cultivars particularly adapted to irrigation; high-density plantings of 30 to 40 trees per acre; increased tree and acre (hectare) yields; younger bearing trees; minimal alternate bearing; more resistance to insects and diseases; and complete mechanical harvesting and processing.

Several new orchards of 2500 to 7500 acres, with potential yield of 1760 lb per acre, are being planted. A crop of 6,600,000 lb by 1985 is predicted.

There are numerous rivers in Oklahoma and the valleys are full of magnificent pecan groves. There are several centers of development, one of the most prominent being Ardmore. With the thousands of trees worked over to improved kinds, the production from this territory will increase annually for many years.

Georgia, though not within the native range of the pecan, has become the leading state in producing named and improved sorts. The largest plantings of budded trees are found around Albany and Thomasville, but numerous other localities have made the pecan a major crop. Some of the greatest advances in orchard management and handling have come out of Georgia. It must not be supposed that all the planting is in the southern section of the state, for many orchards are to be found in the Upper Piedmont, but the nuts produced here are not as large as those of the south.

Louisiana is a heavy producer both of seedlings and improved kinds. Practically the whole state is adapted to the production of this nut and it may be said that it is the cradle of improved pecan production, for the first successful grafting was done there during the winter of 1846 or 1847. The largest recorded pecan tree is found in Louisiana. This plant is

20 ft 3 in. in circumference, breast high, 107 ft tall with a spread of 135 ft, and has produced 25 barrels of nuts in one season estimated at 3000 lb. It stands on a plantation in Ascension Parish on the west bank of the Mississippi River, and was dedicated by the National Pecan Association in 1927 to the yet unborn and future pecan growers of America. The northwestern section around Shreveport is doing more with the improved cultivars than the area farther east, where the bulk of the crop is seedlings.

Mississippi is a larger producer of seedlings with budded sorts being extensively grown in the southeast near the Gulf. Some of the finest cultivars have come out of this state.

In Alabama, plantings are to be found from Mobile to north of Montgomery. The seedling production is practically nothing, the entire output being improved cultivars.

Florida, like Georgia, is out of the native range of the pecan, but in the northern part from Jacksonville west to the Alabama line trees have been planted with satisfactory yields. Monticello has long been the center of production and interest.

There has been considerable interest in both North Carolina and South Carolina, and the production has been mainly from grafted stock, though some early and large plantings of seedlings were made, especially in South Carolina, not far from Charleston. The orchards are mostly in the coastal sections though the Piedmont areas of both states are as well adapted as the similar sections of Georgia.

In Arkansas, many native trees are found along the streams; however, the growing of improved cultivars is really just beginning.

The far western pecan situation is of considerable interest. In the Pacific Northwest there seems to be little hope of the industry developing; the trees grow well but fail in fruit, probably because of a comparatively short summer with cool nights. In California, conditions do not seem to be much more promising. The high priced land gives better returns from other crops, and pecans do not appear to be able to compete with the walnut where that tree is adapted. In the interior valleys pecan culture seems more favorable. In Southern California, climatic conditions do not appear as adapted for trees, as in other parts of the state. The pecan does not have a definite period of harvest, but drops its nuts from October to January, failing to come in for the all important Thanksgiving and Christmas markets. Like many other plants native to the eastern section of America, it does not find congenial conditions on the Pacific coast.

In the Ohio River states of Illinois, Indiana and Kentucky, as well as in Tennessee, little interest has been shown. Southern cultivars are not adapted, therefore the industry must be based on local cultivars and these have been hard to obtain from the nurseries; besides, they are not equal in size to the southern nuts and consequently do not command the attention on the markets. Seedlings are gathered in these states, mainly in the western sections along the main streams, and put into the channels of trade, but the quantity is not impressive.

In northern Virginia, Maryland and Pennsylvania, there has been little planting of the pecan commercially. Along the eastern shore of Maryland there are many large trees known to be over a century old, the results of the work of the early botanists in that territory. In 1908, the Maryland Experiment Station distributed numerous pecan and walnut trees, but little came of the work. In the coastal section of Virginia the plant succeeds, but interest in setting it has been slow in developing.

DISTRIBUTION WORLDWIDE

Pecans are produced in seven countries—Australia, Canada, India, Israel, Mexico, West Africa, and in more than 20 states of the United States. They are consumed around the world, wherever domesticated nuts are traded.

Israel

The first pecan trees were introduced into Israel about 1930, and during the ten years following several dozen grafted trees were imported. For about 20 years only about ½ acre plantings were made, until 1955 when one 300-acre orchard was planted. Within 10 years 1750 acres were planted—one orchard with 500 acres, another with 125 acres and about 25 with 25 to 50 acres. Currently 1000 to 1250 acres are planted annually. By 1975 the acreage had reached 7500 acres. Production in long tons have been:

1966—160	1971—550
1967—120	1972—850
1968—150	1973—1000
1969—350	1974—1250
1970—170[1]	1975—1450

The main regions of growing pecans are the coastal area and the northern inland valley at elevations of 300 ft. The winters are mild and the rainfall averages about 25 in.

During the first 20 years 13 cultivars of U.S. origin were planted: Delmas, Burkett, Nelis, San Saba, Halbert, Garner, Big-Z, Desirable, Moneymaker, Western Schley, Govett, Eastern Schley, and Cherokee. In

[1]Crop failure due to heat wave of 46°C (115°F).

1966 many of the newer cultivars were introduced: Wichita, Choctaw, Apache, Comanche, Texhan, Hastings, Mohawk, Caddo, Sioux, Shawnee, Clark, Cheyenne, Royal, Ideal, and Bradley. Most of the plantings are 10 × 10 m (Homsky 1977).

Pecans in Africa

The Republic of South Africa has had a small but flourishing pecan nut industry for many years. Since about 1965 interest has been particularly high, and many new trees of U.S. Department of Agriculture cultivars have been planted—mainly in the Eastern and Northern Transvaal. With 500 acres of improved cultivars, and fairly close spacing, yields exceeding 880 lb per acre should be reached within 10 years. Fortunately the pecan in South Africa is remarkably free of serious diseases and pests. The relatively low rainfall of 26 in. is an advantage from the standpoint of scab disease. The soils appear to be eminently suitable for pecans, and irrigation water is available (Pearson 1977).

PECAN CULTIVARS

Pecan trees are very long-lived. Native trees are known to be 1000 years old, and some plantings are now 100 years old. Therefore, all available information from existing plantings, state experiment stations, state cooperative extension services and the U.S. Department of Agriculture, should be utilized in selecting cultivars and establishing commercial pecan orchards.

The majority of the more than 500 named cultivars of pecans that have been described and propagated were selections from wild seedlings. Many choice cultivars such as Stuart, Schley, Success, Pabst and others originated in Mississippi. Some of the cultivars bear the name of the place of origin, such as Mobile, Queen Lake, Kentucky, Illinois, or Ohio; but most of them are of the individual who found or propagated it, such as Curtis, Brooks, Barton, Mahan, Odom, or Tesche.

The Stuart cultivar originated from a pecan planted in a garden in Pascagoula, Mississippi, in 1870. A nut from the resulting Stuart tree, planted in 1881, became the Schley cultivar. The Stuart tree produced 350 lbs in 1892, and was felled by a tornado in 1893. The popularity of the Stuart grew rapidly and by 1920 was one of the "big four cultivars" —Stuart, Schley, Pabst and Alley. By about 1930 Stuart was the nation's most widely planted cultivar. Since about 1960 it has given way to more productive, earlier bearing, more weevil-resistant cultivars that are suitable for close planting. Since 1960, however, plantings west of Louisiana have been predominantly of cultivars developed for areas with less than 20 in. of annual rainfall.

In addition to the improved cultivars, there are many thousands of unnamed pecan seedlings bearing marketable nuts. Most of these are original trees in the native groves, while many were planted outside of the native range before commercial propagation was successful. Some nurseries still offer "vigorous seedlings" for sale at about half the price of budded or grafted trees.

Cultivar Groups

Pecans on the market are either seedlings or improved cultivars. Seedlings appear in hundreds of sizes and shapes. In fact, every tree bears nuts differing from every other tree. The trees must be productive and the quality of nuts must be good to justify their being harvested.

Improved pecan cultivars, in general, are divided into three groups, based on their origin and adaptability. They are (a) western, or those having their origin in Texas and other western and drier parts of the pecan belt with rainfall of 20 in. or less; (b) the southern, or those originating in Georgia and other areas with growing season of 200 days or more between bloom and harvest, and rainfall of 40 in. or more and with more fungus diseases; and (c) northern, or those originating in Illinois or other areas with hard winters and growing seasons of 165 days or less.

Throughout the pecan belt improved or cultivated cultivars are replacing seedlings. This is true in New Mexico and westward, in the southeastern states, and throughout the Mississippi Valley states. The continued movement toward better cultivars is for (a) increased productivity, (b) insect and disease resistance, and (c) better standardization of nuts and nut products.

Improved cultivars take precedence where uniformity and large size are important. These are favorites of the salters, the fancy nut counters, and retail trade where appearance is a primary factor. These are demanded for in-shell trade.

A more definite grouping for processing and product manufacturing is by placing them in three groups according to size of the nuts. They are (a) large, or those producing nuts of 50 or fewer nuts per pound, such as Mahan and Nelson; (b) medium, or those producing nuts from 50 to about 70 per pound, such as Stuart, Success, Desirable, Pabst, Frotcher, Farley and Schley; and (c) small, or those producing nuts requiring more than 70 per pound, of which San Saba, Curtis, Moore, Randall, Kennedy, and most seedlings are examples.

Quality Cultivars

A suitable cultivar must come into bearing early, and be a prolific and consistent producer. Nuts should be medium to large in size, and have shells that crack easily, with plump, straw-colored kernels of good flavor and quality. The cultivar should be highly resistant to diseases or at least sufficiently so that it can be sprayed economically. Insects and diseases attack most cultivars and may cause heavy losses. Therefore, a cultivar should be prolific, respond to good orchard management and produce profitable crops to justify a suitable spray program when necessary (see Table 12.1).

High Density Planting

High density planting is a concept of planting pecan trees close together to increase yields per acre (hectare). By intensive pruning the trees are "dwarfed"; and by improved culture and fertilization the trees are stimulated into early, heavy and regular bearing of higher quality nuts. Irrigation is used to provide the added water required.

Highly precocious and prolific cultivars which bear a commercial crop in 4 to 6 years, and with fine lateral branches suitable for pruning in a close-spaced tree, are recommended. Divergent cultivars are best for pollination and ensure against alternate bearing. Since about 1960 many orchards have been planted at 30 × 30 ft, 20 × 40 ft, 25 × 25 ft, 17 × 35 ft, and 15 × 30 ft, spacing with 48, 54, 70, 71, 97 trees per acre, respectively.

In Table 12.2, cultivars marked (*) are recommended for high density planting. Standard cultivars are planted about 50 ft apart, with 17 trees per acre (Madden 1972).

A new cultivar of pecans is judged not by the way it looks now, but how it looks after 25 years of growth under a wide range of conditions. In the unshelled trade where appearance is a primary factor, highest prices may be obtained for large, thin-shelled nuts with high quality kernels as Schley, Stuart and Desirable. Since the majority of pecans now go to commercial shelling plants where they are cracked and shelled automatically, size of nut is of less importance if they are to be sold as meats. Consequently, prolific cultivars which produce uniform small to medium sized nuts of good quality are in demand. Elliott, Farley, Curtis, Caddo, Moore and San Saba are examples. Low quality nuts, regardless of size, bring low prices, and during years of heavy production may not be easily sold. Tesche, Frotcher, Mobile, and sometimes Schley and Mahan are examples.

For the home or small orchard where spraying would be very difficult, cultivars should be selected that are notably scab-resistant over wide areas.

Highly productive cultivars such as Bradley, Mahan, Mobile, Moneymaker, Moore, Success and Tesche are attractive from the standpoint

TABLE 12.1

QUALITY OF 50 REPRESENTATIVE CULTIVARS OF PECANS

Cultivar	Nuts per lb	Kernel %	Oil in Kernel %	Quality of Kernel	Filling of Kernel	Resistance to Scab	Extent Grown	Adaptability	Productivity
Alley	92	50	73	excellent	very good	very susceptible	small	southern	good
Barton	89	53	78	excellent	excellent	resistant	moderate	southern	very good
Big Z	64	49	64	good	good	very resistant	small	central	poor
Bradley	70	44	67	good	good	very resistant	small	southern	good
Brooks	77	38	68	excellent	fair	moderate	small	southern	good
Caspiana	68	49	73	excellent	excellent	moderate	small	southern	good
Curtis	102	54	69	excellent	very good	very resistant	moderate	southern	very good
Delmas	86	36	64	poor	poor	very susceptible	very small	southern	medium
Dependable	52	42	71	excellent	very good	moderate	moderate	southern	medium
Desirable	52	46	70	excellent	good	resistant	small	southern	very good
Elliott	73	43	68	good	good	resistant	moderate	southern	very good
Evans	67	47	71	excellent	excellent	susceptible	small	western	good
Farley	57	47	71	excellent	very good	resistant	moderate	southern	very good
Frotcher	64	47	65	medium	medium	fair	moderate	central	medium
Green River	65	46	68	excellent	very good	susceptible	small	western	good
Halbert	55	38	63	good	fair	susceptible	moderate	western	good
Ideal	66	49	75	excellent	very good	susceptible	moderate	western	good
Jennings	60	47	65	medium	medium	fair	small	western	medium
Lewis	51	46	69	very good	good	moderate	small	western	very good
Love	65	46	60	good	very good	susceptible	small	southern	moderate
Magenta	65	27	53	poor	poor	susceptible	very small	western	poor
Mahan	40	40	66	poor	poor	susceptible	moderate	central	moderate
Mobile	75	39	61	poor	very poor	susceptible	small	central	excellent
Monarch	65	27	53	poor	poor	susceptible	very small	western	poor
Moneymaker	58	43	70	fair	fair	susceptible	moderate	central	excellent
Moore	84	44	67	very good	medium	very resistant	small	southern	excellent

Nelson	42	38	68	medium	poor	very resistant	very small	central	very poor
Odom	53	45	57	poor	poor	susceptible	very small	western	poor
Riverside	60	40	72	excellent	very good	susceptible	small	western	good
Sabine	45	49	77	excellent	excellent	—	small	southern	good
San Saba	95	57	68	excellent	excellent	moderate	moderate	western	excellent
Schley	80	55	72	excellent	very good	very susceptible	moderate	central	fair
Seminole	99	62	77	excellent	very good	moderate	small	southern	moderate
Shence	60	53	74	excellent	very good	moderate	small	southern	moderate
Stevens	90	44	62	excellent	excellent	susceptible	small	western	moderate
Stuart	56	45	72	good	excellent	very resistant	extensive	extensive	very good
Success	65	48	66	excellent	medium	resistant	moderate	central	good
Squirrels Delight	62	47	72	very good	very good	susceptible	small	western	excellent
Summer	84	44	71	medium	good	moderate	small	southern	good
Summers	69	40	65	excellent	good	moderate	small	southern	good
Tesche	70	45	68	excellent	poor	resistant	moderate	southern	very good
Texan	71	40	72	good	very good	susceptible	small	western	very good
Texas 60	80	52	71	excellent	excellent	susceptible	moderate	western	good
Texas Prolific	78	38	70	very good	good	susceptible	moderate	western	good
Van Deman	67	39	73	good	good	susceptible	small	central	medium
Wichita	53	60	78	excellent	excellent	moderate	small	western	medium
Williamson	55	43	70	very good	very good	susceptible	small	western	good
Western	63	50	70	excellent	excellent	susceptible	moderate	western	excellent
Western Schley	66	47	71	excellent	excellent	susceptible	moderate	western	excellent
Seedlings	75-200	30-52	50-72	excellent	very good	varies	extensive	very wide	poor

TABLE 12.2

CULTIVARS AND HYBRIDS PECANS CURRENTLY BEING
GROWN OR TESTED

Cultivar or Selection	Parentage	Nuts per lb	Kernel (%)	Comments
Apache	Burkett × Schley	51	60	U.S.D.A. 1940
Barton	Moore × Success	60	57	U.S.D.A. 1937
Burkett	–			Texas seedling 1900
Burton	Pecan × Hickory			Hican from Kentucky
*Caddo	Brooks × Alley	69	58	Georgia 1922
Candy (H)	–			Louisiana Experiment Station, about 1960
Cape Fear (H)	Seedling	51	52	North Carolina
*Cherokee (H,S)	Schley × Evers	63	57	U.S.D.A. 1948, early bearing, scab resistant
*Cheyenne (S)	Clark × Odom	63	57	U.S.D.A. 1943, scab resistant
Chickasaw	Brooks × Evers	55	55	U.S.D.A. 1944
*Cowley	Seedling			Perkins, Oklahoma 1960
Choctaw	Success × Mahan	45	60	U.S.D.A. 1946
Clark	–			
Comanche	Burkett × Success	49	57	U.S.D.A. 1937
*Desirable (H)	Success × Jewett	71	53	Central Texas, scab resistant, a good pollinizer
Elliott (H)	–	63	55	Milton, FL; small, easy to crack
Farley (H)	Seedling		51	Excellent quality, about 1925
Grabolis	Mahan × Odom	49	58	U.S.D.A.
Indiana	–			Indiana
Jack Doby		32	61	Travis County, TX 1964
Kiowa	Mahan × Odom	45	56	U.S.D.A. 1954
Kernold (S)	–			Highly scab resistant
Maramec	Mahan seedling			Oklahoma, 1963
Mohawk	Success × Mahan	41	58	U.S.D.A. 1946
Shawnee	Schley × Barron	54	58	U.S.D.A. 1949; good for inshell trade
*Shoshoni	Odom × Evers	37-56	54-60	U.S.D.A. 1944
Sioux	Schley × Carmichael	70	60	U.S.D.A. 1943, scab resistant
Stuart (H)	Seedling	23	45	Jackson County Mississippi; before 1920, good for inshell trade
Tejas	Mahan × Risien	70	56	U.S.D.A. 1944
*Western	Seedling × Texas	68	54	Central Texas
*Wichita	Halbert × Mahan	50	60	U.S.D.A. 1940, scab resistant
40-9-266	Halbert × Mahan	66	69	U.S.D.A.
41-19-20	San Saba × Mahan	96	58	U.S.D.A.
45-3-3	Brake × Ga. 104	76	56	
48-9-25	Mahan × Evers	52	59	
48-13-311	Moore × Schley	77	61	
53-9-1	Mahan × Odom	49	51	
53-11-139	Moore × Stuart	79	53	
61-6-67	Mohawk × Starking	47	53	
61-6-96	Mohawk × Starking	57	58	

NOTE: Cultivars marked (*) recommended for high density planting; those marked (H) recommended for home planting; and those marked (S) are highly resistant to scab; those designated by numbers will be given names or eliminated after being fully tested.

of yield. However, practically all of these have one or more defects, such as susceptibility to scab, alternate bearing, poor filling, low kernel content, or are unsatisfactory for cracking—the results being that returns are often reduced to the extent that they are, in many instances, less profitable than the moderately productive kinds such as Stuart, Curtis, Farley and Desirable.

Prolific cultivars have a tendency to produce crops biannually, or during alternate years. A heavy crop seems to throw the tree out of balance in so far as normal production is concerned. The results of a very heavy crop are that nuts of the current crop are poorly filled, and the tree becomes so devitalized that it does not produce fruit buds for the next crop. Mobile, Tesche and Frotcher are commonly alternate bearing.

Pecan Qualities

Size.—The Nelson is probably the largest cultivar with an average of 42 nuts per pound, with the Curtis or San Saba running as high as 102 per pound, and some seedlings averaging more than 200 nuts per lb. The same cultivar (Stuart, for example) varies with the location grown; in south Georgia, with a long growing season, 45 nuts make a pound while in more northern areas, with a shorter growing season, 63 or more are

FIG. 12.1. YOUNG PECAN TREES AT END OF FIRST YEAR
AFTER BUDDING

U.S. PECAN PRODUCTION

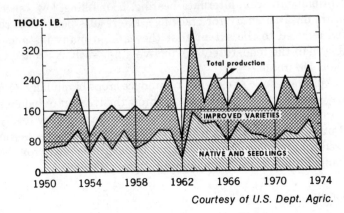

Courtesy of U.S. Dept. Agric.

FIG. 12.2. PECAN PRODUCTION, 1950–74.

required for a pound. The size of nuts is increased by good cultural practices such as fertilizers, spraying and control of leaf insects and diseases, adequate spacing of trees, irrigation, and removing weeds and intercrops that compete for moisture, nutrients and light. Drought, leaf spot diseases or certain insects (web worms) during mid-summer cause pecans to be small.

Filling.—Some of the cultivars with the highest filling percentages are Schley, Seminole, Wichita and Texas which run as high as 62% kernels. Poor filling cultivars may run less than 40% kernels and include Nelson, Tesche, Mobile, Monarch and Halbert. Nuts of lightly loaded trees of a single cultivar are better filled than nuts of lightly loaded trees of different cultivars. Drought, leaf spot diseases, insects or other unfavorable growing conditions during late summer cause nuts to be poorly filled.

FIG. 12.3. VARIATIONS IN PECAN SIZE

Left—Mahan; Center—Stuart; Right—seedling pecans.

Eating Quality.—There is no correlation between the quality (flavor, texture, color, aroma, oil content) of pecans and the size of the nuts. Some of the cultivars (Curtis, San Saba, Moore, Alley and seedlings) that produce very small nuts are very high in quality; while some of the largest nuts (Nelson, Mobile) are poor in quality. However, the best filled nuts of a particular cultivar, are the highest in quality. The same cultural conditions which produce the best filled nuts also produce nuts of the highest quality. Therefore, a processor might well ignore the size of nuts and emphasize the shelling percentage and oil content of the meats.

Cultivars Recommended for Leading Producing Areas

Florida.—Many apparently promising cultivars have been abandoned because of their susceptibility to scab or because of their poor nut development. In new plantings, only scab resistant cultivars should be used. These include Desirable, Curtis, Elliott and Stuart. Promising new cultivars for trial plantings are Barton, Mahan, Stuart, Pensacola, Cluster, Davis, Hastings and Harris Super. Pecan plantings in this state have not increased since about 1955.

Georgia and Alabama.—Productivity and scab resistance are most important. Scab-susceptible cultivars should be abandoned, topworked or sprayed regularly. Recommended cultivars in order of importance are: Stuart, Desirable, Elliott, Farley, Success, Schley, Hastings and Dependable.

The Stuart is the backbone of Georgia's commercial pecan crop. Due to improved programs of spraying, fertilization, irrigation, and harvesting, the "on" crop years about double the "off" crop years, and they are not as far apart as they were before about 1960. New plantings include Desirable, up to about 50%, with about 10% each of Cherokee, Wichita, Cape Fear, Chicksaw and Farley. For home planting Elliott, Harris and Curtis may be used (Livingston 1975).

Carolinas.—There are limited plantings of pecans in both North and South Carolina of Stuart, Farley, Mahan, Schley, Success, Hasting, and Desirable.

Mississippi.—There are possibly more cultivars of pecans grown in Mississippi than any other state. Cultivars include Stuart, Stevens, Monarch, Odom, Lewis, Tesche, Pabst, Van Deman, Moneymaker, Frotcher, Success, Moore, Schley, and Mahan.

Louisiana.—Louisiana cultivars include Stuart, Sabine, Caspiana, Magenta, Dependable, Elliott, Jennings, Desirable, Moore, Schley, Mahan, and Moneymaker.

Texas.—Texas cultivars for eastern Texas are similar to those for Louisiana, and those for western Texas are similar to those for New Mexico. Texas cultivars include Barton, Desirable, Sioux, Apache, Choctaw, Wichita, Western Schley, Eastern, Schley, San Saba, Ideal, Stuart, Burkett, Mahan, Squirrels Delight, Texan, Riverside and Evans.

The U.S. Department of Agriculture Pecan Breeding Station, Brownwood, Texas, has produced more than 120 promising selections from crosses of the following cultivars: Brake, Candy, Sioux, Odom, Barton, Evers, Brooks, Moore, Mahan, Schley, Curtis, Stuart, Desirable, Mohawk, Comanche, and Apache. (See Table 12.3.)

New Mexico.—There were about 600,000 acres of newly planted trees in 1967, with more than 100,000 trees being planted annually. The cultivars are Western Schley, Clark, Barton, Mahan, Desirable, Squirrel and several newly developed cultivars from the USDA Brownwood, Texas, Pecan Breeding Station.

Kansas.—Pecan production is on an increase in this state, with northern cultivars predominating. Leading cultivars include Illinois, Buice, Squirrel and Giles.

Northern Areas.—Cultivars for northern areas including Ohio should include those that are productive and of large size such as Stuart, Mahan, Farley and Elliott.

Oklahoma.—There is considerable planting of new orchards in this state. Cultivars include Squirrel, Barton, Western Schley, and Mahan.

Mexico.—While native pecans provide a large supply of excellent quality pecans in Mexico, improved cultivars of the type grown in western Texas are being planted.

Africa.—There are limited reports that pecans have been grown in Africa for about 100 years. The trees are apparently grown from nuts brought in from America and are never budded or grafted.

GROWING PECAN NURSERY TREES[1]

Deep, rich sandy soil is ideal for growing vigorous trees with a long taproot. The rows are straight and mechanical planters, cultivators and diggers are used. However, each tree that is budded or grafted must receive individual attention at least 12 times before it leaves the nursery. To provide vigorous scion wood of many cultivars of pecans, and to make

---

[1] This section was prepared by Richard H. Simpson, Monticello, Florida, whose family has specialized in growing pecan trees since 1902.

TABLE 12.3

PECAN PRODUCTION, PRICE AND VALUE

CULTIVAR AND STATE	UTILIZED PRODUCTION[1] (1000 lb)			PRICE PER POUND (CENTS)			VALUE OF UTILIZED PRODUCTION (1000 DOLLARS)		
	1974	1975	1976	1974	1975	1976	1974	1975	1976
Improved Cultivars									
Alabama	8,800	11,400	4,000	53.0	38.0	88.0	4,664	4,332	3,520
Arkansas	500	500	700	65.0	55.0	85.0	325	275	595
Florida	1,200	2,000	1,000	49.0	40.0	76.0	588	800	760
Georgia	47,000	60,000	43,000	52.0	45.0	85.0	24,440	27,000	36,550
Louisiana	1,000	5,000	700	64.0	36.0	95.0	640	1,800	665
Mississippi	1,200	2,000	1,000	51.2	46.0	88.5	614	920	885
New Mexico	13,200	13,100	11,500	51.0	57.0	100.0	6,732	7,467	11,500
North Carolina	1,500	1,000	1,900	50.0	45.0	72.0	750	450	1,368
Oklahoma	200	1,500	800	59.0	55.0	90.0	118	825	720
South Carolina	1,500	600	1,700	52.0	45.9	80.0	780	275	1,360
Texas	9,500	13,000	11,000	55.0	54.0	88.0	5,225	7,020	9,680
United States	85,600	110,100	77,300	52.4	46.5	87.5	44,876	51,164	67,603
Native & Seedling									
Alabama	2,200	8,600	1,000	38.0	32.0	65.5	836	2,752	655
Arkansas	700	3,000	300	40.0	34.0	61.0	280	1,020	183
Florida	1,300	3,000	1,500	38.5	33.0	60.0	501	990	900
Georgia	11,000	15,000	9,000	39.0	34.0	65.0	4,290	5,100	5,850
Louisiana	2,000	27,000	1,300	35.0	34.0	60.0	700	9,180	780
Mississippi	1,800	4,000	500	43.0	34.0	62.5	774	1,360	313
North Carolina	700	1,200	900	35.0	35.0	53.0	245	420	477
Oklahoma	2,300	18,500	1,500	36.0	32.0	60.0	828	5,920	900
South Carolina	1,000	1,400	800	39.9	35.3	59.0	399	494	472
Texas	28,500	55,000	9,000	38.0	36.0	65.0	10,830	19,800	5,850
United States	51,500	136,700	25,800	38.2	34.4	63.5	19,683	47,036	16,380

TABLE 12.3 (Continued)

PECAN PRODUCTION, PRICE AND VALUE

CULTIVAR AND STATE	UTILIZED PRODUCTION[1] (1000 lb)			PRICE PER POUND (CENTS)			VALUE OF UTILIZED PRODUCTION (1000 DOLLARS)		
	1974	1975	1976	1974	1975	1976	1974	1975	1976
All Pecans									
Alabama	11,000	20,000	5,000	50.0	35.4	83.5	5,500	7,084	4,175
Arkansas	1,200	3,500	1,000	50.4	37.0	77.8	605	1,295	778
Florida	2,500	5,000	2,500	43.6	35.8	66.4	1,089	1,790	1,660
Georgia	58,000	75,000	52,000	49.5	42.8	81.5	28,730	32,100	42,400
Louisiana	3,000	32,000	2,000	44.7	34.3	72.3	1,340	10,980	1,445
Mississippi	3,000	6,000	1,500	46.3	38.0	79.8	1,388	2,280	1,198
New Mexico	13,200	13,100	11,500	51.0	57.0	100.0	6,732	7,467	11,500
North Carolina	2,200	2,200	2,800	45.2	39.5	65.9	995	870	1,845
Oklahoma	2,500	20,000	2,300	37.8	33.7	70.4	946	6,745	1,620
South Carolina	2,500	2,000	2,500	47.2	38.5	73.3	1,179	769	1,832
Texas	38,000	68,000	20,000	42.3	39.4	77.7	16,055	26,820	15,530
United States	137,100	246,800	103,100	47.1	39.8	81.5	64,559	98,200	83,983

Source: U.S.Dep. Agric. (1977).

[1]Excludes unharvested production and excess cullage. (1000 pounds): Florida 1974 - improved cultivars 100, native and seedling cultivars 100; 1975 - improved cultivars 600, native and seedling cultivars 900.

sure of the trueness of cultivars and resistance to scab and other diseases, pecan nurserymen also maintain orchards of considerable size.

The tremendous increase in the number of pecan trees propagated, the increased number of trees planted in large groves and the increasing portion of the total crop of improved cultivars indicate the trend of the pecan industry. There is a shift in production to Texas, Arizona, and New Mexico and an increase in western cultivars.

Soils

Careful attention should be given to the selection of soils for pecan nursery stock. Of first importance is the selection of well-drained soils. Pecans will not stand wet feet. Soils with a high water table, even if well drained on the surface, will grow trees with very short taproots. Because the pecan trees grow to be very large, a good taproot is necessary to keep the trees from blowing over. It is generally felt that a long taproot in the nursery tree will grow into a long taproot on the mature tree. The taproot on the nursery tree should be 30 to 36 in. long at the time of digging.

Pecan trees will grow on a wide range of soils. Soils that will provide fast growth and ease of digging should be considered. Pecan nursery trees grow well on the heavy clay soils but it is almost impossible to dig enough taproot on these heavy hard soils.

The ideal soil is a fine sandy loam soil about 18 to 24 in. deep, with a sandy clay subsoil. The clay will help hold moisture. The topsoil is easily penetrated by the fine side roots. Soils of this type are not too hard to dig in with a spade or a mechanical tree digger.

Preparation of soils is very important. The best pecan nursery trees are often grown following two good summer cover crops and two good winter cover crops. Crotalaria is an excellent summer cover crop but it must be remembered that this crop is poisonous to livestock. Other good summer cover crops for the lower south are hairy indigo, cow peas, velvet beans, and soybeans. Use the crop that makes the best growth in your area. The various lupines and crimson clover are good winter cover crops. The common bitter lupine will make growth as high as an automobile when following summer leguminous crops or crops that have been highly fertilized.

Kind of Nuts to Plant

The selection of the pecan nuts to plant is important. Good, well-filled nuts should be selected so that the very young seedling will send its roots down rapidly and force its top up through the soil. Weak and poorly filled nuts will usually not germinate well and when they do germinate, their seedlings are often very weak.

Many people plant seedling nuts, which are usually well filled. Some seedling trees produce nuts from which excellent seedling trees are produced. Other seedling trees will produce nuts which in turn produce seedling trees which are shorter and slimmer. For these reasons, it is recommended that the nuts of a certain known cultivar be used. Nuts of the Waukeenah, Elliott, Curtis and well-filled nuts of the Moore cultivar have produced excellent seedlings. It is recommended that a scab resistant cultivar be selected. There is a distinct, but as yet unproved, possibility that seedlings from scab resistant cultivars may pass on some scab resistance to the mature trees.

How and When to Plant Nuts

The pecan nuts must be placed in the ground weeks and even months before they are expected to sprout and emerge as seedling plants. This is necessary in order that the soil moisture have ample time to penetrate the hard pecan shell. A good time to plant is between December 15 and January 15. Later plantings are often successful but a cold dry spring might cause a poor stand.

Good soil preparation will make it easier to plant the nuts and the seedlings will grow off better when they emerge. The rows should be laid out with a tractor so that the width is uniform. Some nurseries still plant in rows 4 ft apart while others are going to rows even as far apart as 6 ft, so a tractor disk harrow can be run down the middles. The width of the row is determined largely by the type of equipment which is to be used in cultivation and digging.

The row should be opened with some type of opener that will open a trench wide enough to receive the pecan nuts which of course are large compared to other seed. Most growers drop the nuts by hand. To get a stand of seedlings 1 ft apart in the row, it is suggested that the nuts be dropped about 4 in. apart.

Some of the larger nurseries use nut planters. Some of the planters are homemade, others are converted from other uses. A planter which will plant a peach seed can usually be used to plant pecans. If the planter is used, the rows should still be laid out with a tractor so that there will be a uniform spacing of the rows.

Immediately after the nuts are planted they should be covered with soil. It is recommended that the nuts be covered by throwing up a bed of soil at least 6 in. high. This high bed will keep the soil from drying out around the nuts. The beds should be dragged down when the sprout on the nuts is 1 to 2 in. long. The dragging will remove early spring weeds so that the nuts may emerge in clean soil.

Early Care

The newly emerged pecan seedling is very succulent, and is easy to break off. Because of this, the seedlings will have to be handled very carefully. As soon as the rows of seedlings are visible, they should be cultivated. Very narrow cultivator shovels should be used so they will not throw dirt on the seedling. A tractor which has cultivating equipment, placed where the driver can see what he is doing, should be used. The middles of the rows should be cultivated at the same time. Frequent cultivation, about once every two weeks, should be practiced until September 1.

Following the first cultivation, it is usually necessary to hand weed the rows. This hand weeding is tedious and very expensive.

The seedlings should be fertilized with the first or second cultivation. Put the fertilizer in bands on each side of the row and as close to the seedlings as possible. Use about 400 lb of 4-7-5 fertilizer per acre. Use a fertilizer containing 25 to 50% of organic material so that the fertilizer will become available over a longer period of time. A second application of the same fertilizer and amount should be made about June 1. Nitrate of soda and nitrate of potash are good for side dressing. It is often necessary to spray during the first year for nursery blight. This blight causes black spots to appear on the new growth. When this appears, spray with a good fungicide. Bordeaux mixture used to be used exclusively for this spray. Now newer and easier to apply sprays can be used. It is recommended that the grower ask his County Agent to get from the State Experiment Station the latest recommended fungicide and insecticide. An insecticide should be included in the spray if bud worms appear. The budworm will destroy the young bud in the top of the seedling. This will stop growth for a period of time.

Second Year Care

The second year care is much like the first year. Keep the seedlings well cultivated and the rows clean. Use two applications of at least 400 lb of 4-7-5 fertilizer. In addition to this fertilizer, sidedress with about 200 lb of nitrate of soda per acre. The spray schedule is the same as for the first year, except that the seedlings should be sprayed every two weeks, to cause rapid growth, so that budding may begin in the middle of July. Stop cultivating again on September 1 so that trees will have ample time to harden before cold weather.

Budding and Grafting

Pecan seedlings should be pencil size and larger to be budded or grafted.

They usually reach this size the second year. Some nurserymen prefer to bud and some to graft. It does not make a great deal of difference and there are some advantages to each method. The buds are put on a smooth part of the seedling trunk about 6 to 12 in. above the ground. In this way the budded tree will have a section of seedling stock between the bud and the ground. This section of seedling stock is usually more cold resistant than most of the pecan cultivars. So by budding, cold protection is obtained that is not available with grafts. Budded trees usually grow bigger than grafted nursery trees the first year. Grafted trees have a better appearance as they grow from the soil level and do not have the slight crook that is present on all buds. The grafted trees tend to grow straighter than the budded trees. Budding is done in the summer months when the bark on stock and scion will peel. Grafting is done in the winter or early spring when stocks and scions are dormant.

FIG. 12.4. PECAN GRAFTER AT WORK

Budding and grafting are highly skilled operations. Neither should be undertaken on a large scale by those with little or no experience. It is usually extremely difficult to hire men skilled in budding or grafting. The commercial nurseries usually teach this art to boys during their high school days. They learn rapidly at this age and of course the young men are available to replace the regular men should they leave the job for one reason or another. After the budder or grafter has had two or more years of experience, he is usually offered some form of incentive pay for the number of buds or grafts put in. This incentive pay system has been known to increase the percentage of live buds or grafts materially.

Budding can be done during the summer months when the bark on the scion trees and on the seedlings will slip or peel. The bark should also be reasonably mature. If it is possible to penetrate the bark easily with the fingernail, the bark is too green or too immature. The seedling bark will usually mature first and does not require as much attention as does the bark in the scion wood. If the bark on the scion wood is too green, it will bruise in handling and also will not live as well as the buds from the mature wood. The several cultivars mature their bark at different times. The nurseryman must constantly watch his scion trees so that buds of each cultivar will be put in at the proper time. This variation of maturity enables the nurseryman to do his budding over a longer period of time. There will usually be some cultivars ready to bud by July 15. Budding can be done until the first to the middle of September. This time will vary according to the rainfall, the fertilization and the cultivation of the scion wood and the seedlings.

The ring method of budding is commonly used on pecans. This is done with a knife having two parallel blades. The budder sits on a low stool in front of the seedling. Under the seat on this stool, the budder keeps his supply of needed materials. He should keep his scion wood wrapped in a damp cloth. His budding cloth and possibly a pruning knife to cut off limbs that the trimmers have left are also kept in this box under the seat. Boys are sent down the rows to prune low limbs off the seedlings ahead of the budder. This saves the budder time and makes a straight smooth area of the seedling available for the bud. The budder, sitting on the stool, places the two-bladed knife as far as he can reach on the back side of the seedling. He then pulls the knife around the seedling until he has completely circled it. He must apply enough pressure on the knife to go through the bark but the knife should not go into the wood of the seedling If the knife goes too deeply into the wood it may cause the top of the seedling to blow out later. After the budder has circled the seedling with his two-bladed knife he makes a vertical cut between the two cuts he has just made with the big two-bladed knife. This last cut will allow the budder to remove the ring of bark from the seedling. However, he should not do this until he is ready to take a ring of bark from the scion stick. This ring of bark will contain the bud he wants to place on the seedling. The ring of bark is taken off the scion wood by holding the scion in one hand and by ringing the scion stick with the two-bladed knife held in his other hand. Again he makes a cut in the bark on the back of the scion. He is now ready to take the ring of bark containing the bud and place it in the space on the seedling from which he now removes the ring of bark he has already cut. The bark will stick to the scion wood and the seedling so it is necessary for him to gently loosen it, using a brass or bone attachment that is fastened to the handle of the budding knife. The ring of bark with the bud should be placed on the seedling with the bud facing in the row so that it will not be damaged by a plow or cultivator. The bud ring should have been taken from scion wood that is about the same diameter as the seedling on which it is to be placed. For best results the bud ring should, when placed on the seedling, have an opening of about the thickness of a dime. If the bud ring is larger than the seedling, a piece should be taken from it so that the opening opposite the bud will be the thickness of a dime.

When budding on very large seedlings, it is often difficult to get scion wood as large as the seedling. In this case proceed as above but have a patch of bark on the seedling of such a size as to make the opening left when the scion bark is placed on the seedling about the thickness of a dime. This is called patch budding and is used quite often in topworking. Now the budder is ready to wrap the bud. This is a very important part of the procedure. A variety of wrapping material is available. Waxed cloth is still used by many. Rubber strips and plastic strips are also used. The strip of material should be 10 to 12 in. long and about ¾ in. wide. Wrapping should start about 1 in. below the bottom cut on the seedling. This anchors the wrapping material so that even pressure can be applied as the wrapping material is wound around the seedling. The wrapping material should be wound as close to the buds as possible to hold it tight against the seedling. The wrap should extend at least 1 in. above the top ring made by the budding knife. The wrap can be made secure if the leaf stem is cut as close to the bud as possible. The leaves are removed from the budsticks as soon as they are cut from the parent tree in this manner. The wrap is taken off when the space left in the back of the bud has healed over. This is usually about three weeks. Keep seedling suckers trimmed off below the buds for the rest of the growing season. Some of the buds will start to grow, but most of them will remain dormant until spring. Some nurserymen cut the tops of the seedling back by about one-half when the wraps are taken off. This will make more buds to start out. There is no real advantage in this and it is a general practice to leave the tops on the seedling until they are cut back to the upper ring of the bud before growth starts next spring. As stated, this budding is a highly skilled operation. An experienced budder can put in a bud per minute if the seedlings and scion wood are of average size and are in good condition.

Usually the top of a tree of known cultivar is cut back rather severely in the dormant season so that long healthy growth may occur in the spring and summer. This growth is longer and greater in diameter than it would have been if the trees had not been cut back. This lush growth makes good scion wood for buds and grafts. It is well to let these scion trees bear one or two crops of nuts before cutting back so that the nurseryman will be sure of the cultivar. Experienced men can tell the cultivar by the appearance of the wood. But it is good to verify this judgment by letting the tree bear nuts before it is used for scion wood.

In the Southeast, the grafting is done between December 15 and the middle of March. In places where the cold is more severe, the grafts are put in around March 1.

A number of different methods can be used in grafting pecans. The whip graft is used generally for nursery stock. The seedling row is barred off, usually with a small tractor so as to get up close to the rows. Dirt is then dug out of the rows to be grafted, to a depth of about six in. Then a man comes along with a piece of burlap to wipe each seedling, removing all dirt and moisture. The seedling is now ready for the grafter. He usually sits on a pad on the ground so that he will be close to his work. He has scions about six in. long in a box which he keeps close to him. The scions of known cultivar are taken from the scion orchard.

The grafter takes the top of the seedling in his left hand (if he is right handed). With a single-bladed grafting knife in his right hand he cuts the seedling off about 2 in. below the ground line. This cut is sloping and should be 1½ to 2½ in. long depending on the size of the seedling. He then makes a cut downward in the slope and at right angles to it. This cut should start at a point on the slope close to the top. The grafter now takes a scion of about the same size as the seedling. He cuts a slope on the lower end of the scion just as he did in the seedling. He also makes a second cut in the scion just like he did in the seedling. This second cut in the scion should start at a point about a third of the way from the top of the slope. The grafter then takes the scion in his right hand and fits the scion to the stock. The two vertical cuts make it possible to tightly fasten the scion to the seedling by exerting downward pressure with the right hand. As the grafter applies the scion to the stock he guides it with his right forefinger so that the cambian layer of one side of the scion is in contact with the cambian layer of the stock. A perfect graft would have the cambian line up on each side of the scion. This seldom happens with commercial grafting and the graft will live if the cambians are in contact on one side only. The grafter is now ready to go to the next seedling.

A person who ties the graft sits on a pad and follows the grafter down the row. The tier has a very important part to pla in this operation. The grafter has left him enough hand room so that he can begin his tie about 1 in. below the bottom of the graft cut. The tier uses waxed thread, rubber bands, cloth or plastic tape. His job is to fasten the scion tight to the stock by firmly wrapping from the starting point to about 1 in. above the top of the graft cut. The operation is now ready for the packer who comes along and packs, with his gloved hands, loose dirt around the section that has been tied. He then takes soil out of the middle on each side of the row, mounds the soil up on the graft so that only about ¼ in. of each scion is exposed.

Grafting is a highly skilled operation from beginning to end. It should not be attempted on a large scale, by untrained workers. Soon after the seedling row has been grafted it should be cultivated so as to level the soil and to help hold moisture. The mounded soil on the grafts should not be disturbed in this cultivation. Some nurserymen bud and graft in the same row. The budding is done first in the summer and the dead buds and seedlings too small to bud are grafted at the proper time.

First Year Care After Budding

The fields which have been budded or grafted must have intensive care during the growing season. Four hundred pounds per acre of 4-7-5 fertilizer are applied before growth starts. Another 400 lb of the same are applied around May 1. It is good to sidedress with 200 lb of nitrate of soda or nitrate of potash around July 1. The nurseryman should inspect his trees every day. He may want to use more fertilizer if the growth is not entirely satisfactory to him. The rows should be regularly cultivated until September 1.

FIG. 12.5. DIGGING PECAN TREES AT THE RATE OF 10,000 PER DAY

The trees are cut to a height of four feet and "pulled up" with taproots four feet long. The 500,000 tree nursery is in Las Cruces, New Mexico.

Digging

Digging can start as soon as the trees are completely dormant. Many trees are dug with spades. Again this is a highly skilled operation. It is customary to pay for this by the tree rather than by the hour or day. A highly skilled man can average 200 to 300 trees per day. He usually uses a No. 2 square point spade with a long handle. The roots on budded trees should be dug to a depth of at least 30 in. and the grafts to a depth of 36 in. Wide side roots are most desirable.

Several of the pecan nurseries use a mechanical tree digger of some kind. These diggers are very costly. If the grower has large numbers of trees to dig, he will save money by using a mechanical tree digger. The roots are better than the hand dug roots. For this reason the grower builds considerable customer good will by furnishing trees with long tap and side roots. Some of the mechanical tree diggers can dig 5000 to 10,000 trees per day.

Shipping

Pecan trees, if properly packed, can be shipped by any method of transportation. It is important to keep the tree roots moist until the packing process is complete.

Many buyers of pecan trees now come to the nursery with their own trucks to pick up the trees.

The nurseryman trims off any damaged roots and any excess sprouts on the trunk of the tree. The trees are then graded according to height above the ground mark. The trees are then usually tied in bundles of ten trees each. When the trees are to go on a customer's truck, little or no packing material is used. The trees are loaded on the truck and the roots are wet until water runs off. A good tarpaulin is then put over the trees and fastened down securely. If they do not reach their destination in 12 hours, the tarpaulin should be rolled back and the trees wet down again. The trees should be carefully heeled in the ground as soon as they reach their destination. The trees can stay in these heels, if they are watered regularly, until the grower is ready to plant them.

Trees that are to be shipped by express, parcel post (small trees only), rail freight, motor freight and by bus are usually packed in bales. They are trimmed and graded as described above before they are baled. Twenty-five to 100 trees are placed in a bale depending on the size of the trees. The bales are made by tying ropes securely around the roots and the tops of the pile of trees to go in the bale. Usually the bale is then wrapped with packing paper, and with burlap. The burlap can be tied or sewed in place. The trees are wet before they are put in the bales. Packing material is placed about the roots in the bale to hold moisture. Sphagnum moss is the best packing material.

PECAN ROOT CUTTINGS

Multiple identical, or clonal, seedlings for use as rootstocks can easily be produced by making cuttings of the taproot or main branch roots of seedling trees. Cuttings ¼ to 1 in. in diameter and 3 in. long are taken during the winter. They are held in wet sphagnum moss at 85° to 90°F. until one or more adventitious buds are developed on apical callus. The cuttings are then placed upright in moist sand and covered with glass to prevent drying.

After leafing has begun the cuttings are taken up, and if not well rooted, are treated with indolebutyric acid in lanolin on the basal callus; and planted in containers for a year. They are then transferred to the nursery and finally to the orchard.

PLANTING A PECAN ORCHARD

Pecan plantings range from a single tree for nuts and shade around the house, to a 600,000-acre orchard (in New Mexico). The trees will thrive wherever native hickories are found. On the other hand soils that are too wet, dry or poor for hickories or white oak, are unsuitable for pecans, unless drainage and a large amount of water and fertilizer are used.

The selection of soil is of major importance in commercial orchards. It should be level enough to permit the trees to be planted in rows for spraying, cultivation and harvesting. The soil should have at least three feet of well drained, porous and fairly fertile top soil; underlaid with a slightly porous clay subsoil. Soils with high water table or with hardpan, hard plastic or tight clay, or mottling at depths of less than 36 in. should be avoided. Pecans are not to be planted commercially on land that is submarginal for growing other row crops. A pecan grove may be expected to have a life of 100 years and the location, soil and climate are conditions that cannot be easily changed.

Soil Preparation and Tree Spacing

The soil should be put in good condition by plowing under all vegetation and thoroughly disking. The field should be staked off, spacing the trees as desired (see high density planting). The orchard is generally laid out by the square method, but where terracing is necessary it can be planted on the contour.

In West Texas and New Mexico, pecan trees are frequently spaced with the irrigation ditches which are 60 ft apart. A row of "temporary" pecan or other trees may be interplanted between these.

Transplanting

When ready to set, the bales or boxes of trees are taken to the field. When removed from the boxes the tree roots should not be permitted to dry out from exposure to sun and wind. Care should be exercised in setting and placing the roots and filling in the hole, for it is best to place the roots in as near a normal position as possible. Prune off broken and damaged roots by making a smooth cut with a knife or pruning shears. A shovelful or two of peat mixed into the hole at planting is suggested as good practice on lighter soils. The soil should be pressed firmly as the hole is filled, leaving it about as it was when the trees were growing in the nursery. A planting board, although not absolutely necessary, aids in setting trees at the proper depth and in lining them up in the row. Use two or three gallons of water around each tree when the hole is ¾ full of soil. If no water is used, the roots may be puddled in wet clay just before setting. In filling the holes the soil is made firm to the top, leaving a slight depression around the base of the tree. During the first year after trees are transplanted it will be necessary to water them several times if there is insufficient rainfall.

Remove ⅓ to ½ of the top of the tree when setting, to approach a balance between top and roots. This gives the tree a better opportunity to live and simplifies the problem of proper heading later. It is a good practice to wrap the trunks of newly set trees the first year. Special paper wraps are available from nurseries.

Care of Young Trees

Probably the highest percentage of young tree losses the first summer after transplanting to the field result from failure to water adequately or control weeds and grass. Some provision should be made to insure adequate water at all times during the first growing season. For an average year watering two or three times during the spring may be sufficient, but much more frequent watering may be required. After the first year the young pecans should be well enough established to withstand anything but the most severe drought. A heavy mulch of straw or other plant material placed in a circle 3 to 5 ft in diameter around the base of the tree for the first few years will help maintain the soil moisture and reduce weed competition.

Overfertilization can be a common fault in the management of young trees. No fertilizer should be used at the time of planting, but the young tree may be given an early summer fertilization, between June 1 and July 1, of no more than 1 lb of 8-8-8 spread evenly over the soil from the trunk out to a distance of 2 or 3 ft. The second year the trees may be fertilized with 1 lb of 8-8-8 in February and another pound of 8-8-8 in early July. Late summer fertilization of young trees should be avoided since it may stimulate flush of growth which could result in serious freeze damage. After the second year, fertilization of the young trees depends upon the cropping system followed.

TOPWORKING PECAN TREES[1]

Topworking is a means of replacing the top of an undesirable seedling or cultivar with a more desirable cultivar or cultivars. By this means many

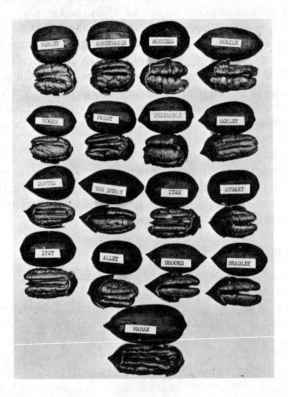

FIG. 12.6. CHARACTERISTICS OF 17 CULTIVARS OF WHOLE AND SHELLED PECANS

thousands of native seedlings have been made to produce nuts of improved cultivars; and many trees of nonproductive or disease susceptible cultivars have been converted to productive disease resistant cultivars.

Topworking is an important phase of pecan growing. Since pecan trees

---

[1]Source: M.B. Hardy (1938).

trees do not normally die of old age it is much more satisfactory to topwork existing trees than to plant young trees. Topworked old trees reach profitable bearing age much quicker than young newly planted trees. To insure proper pollination it may be advisable to topwork more than one cultivar on a single large tree.

Unfortunately, it is seldom possible for the orchard owner to do all of the work required in topworking a large number of trees and more or less expert help must be obtained. However, the owner of a pecan orchard can easily learn enough about the practice to prevent most of the common mistakes made by inexperienced help. It is hoped that the outline of the procedure to be followed in topworking pecan trees, with appropriate mention of the common mistakes, will be of material help in future topworking operations.

Cultivars which should be topworked to some other cultivar are those which are very susceptible to infection by pecan scab, or are not prolific, or produce nuts of low quality, or do not produce profitable crops because of soil, moisture, or climatic conditions. The individual grower must decide for himself which cultivars to eliminate from his orchard by topworking. Furthermore, topworking should not be resorted to as a cure-all for lack of production when some change in the cultural program such as thinning the stand of trees, spraying, increasing or altering the fertilizer applications, terracing, and growing cover crops may increase the production of good nuts to a profitable degree. Frequently, topworking should go hand in hand with an altered cultural program.

Cutting Back the Stock Cultivar

In order to produce sprouts as near the trunk of the tree as possible into which the buds can be inserted in July, August, and September, the limbs of the trees to be topworked must be cut back to stubs during the dormant season. Many of the difficulties attending the cutting back of trees for topworking are associated with too severe or careless cutting back. Not over two-thirds to three-fourths of the tops should be removed and the cuts should be made at points where the limbs are not over four inches in diameter. Care should be taken that the bark of the stub is not peeled off when the cut limb falls.

Care should also be taken to make the cuts so that the uncut "feeder" limbs are left well distributed and so that stubs not less than eight inches are left above every feeder limb. On the other hand, stubs longer than 2 to 3 ft above a feeder limb, are not desirable. In order to maintain the shape of the tree when the new top is produced the surfaces of the cut stubs should be of approximately the same conical contour as the original periphery of the tree.

All cut surfaces should be covered with some compound such as white lead, red lead, or some material commercially prepared for this use as an aid in preventing the entrance of wood rotting fungi.

Preparing for Budding

Often little or nothing needs to be done from the time of cutting back the tree in the dormant season until the time when budding is done. On relatively weak trees it may be necessary to fertilize heavily with nitrogen and to keep the sprouts which develop on the stubs thinned to 2 or 3 in order to force more vigorous growth. On vigorous trees this is usually not necessary. Just previous to inserting the buds, if not done previously, it is necessary to reduce the number of sprouts on each stub to two or three well placed sprouts which are from ½ to 1 in. in diameter. The top one-fourth to one-third of these remaining shoots should be cut off to reduce the possibility of wind breakage after the buds are inserted, and to reduce the loss of buds through the breakage of the tender union between bud and stock as a result of flexing of the shoot without breakage on windy days.

Budwood

Budwood should be a desired cultivar and should be contracted for or prepared for during the dormant season. It is usually necessary to severely prune the trees from which budwood is to be obtained and this must be done in late winter or very early spring. The budwood is best cut the same day the buds are inserted but delays of a few days are not serious if the wood is kept moist and cool.

Shoots to be cut for budwood must be sufficiently mature so that the ring of bark will not split readily when the bud is placed on the stock shoot and it must also "slip" readily. Furthermore, the type of budwood most desirable should be straight and smooth and of a size averaging just slightly smaller than the size of the shoots into which the buds are inserted. Proper attention to these details reduces the number of buds which are lost through splitting and poor fitting and also appears to produce better results because the bark of both the bud and stock are of more nearly the same thickness. As soon as the bud sticks are cut the leaves must be removed by cutting at a point even with the bud tips in order to reduce water loss to a minimum.

Inserting the Bud.—The technique of inserting the bud, applying the protection wax, and supporting the new shoot on topworked pecan trees is similar to that for nursery trees.

If, at the time of unwrapping, the bud is dead and there are not a sufficient number of live buds on other shoots from which to build the new top, another bud should be inserted below the previous point of insertion. This second budding seldom fails to provide the necessary number of live buds.

Care of the Budded Tree.—After unwrapping the buds no additional attention need be given the trees until the following dormant season. At that time the feeder limbs should be removed, the stubs above the points where the stock shoots grew should be cut off flush with the point of attachment of the most distal shoot and repainted, and the stock shoots should be cut back to a length of about 12 in. above the live ring bud to be used later as a support to which the tender shoots from the ring bud can be tied. If a stock shoot is located in a desirable position but does not have a live ring bud on it such a shoot should be cut back to a stub 3 to 5 in. long from which a new shoot will grow which can be budded in the second summer.

During the spring and summer following the budding all efforts must be concentrated on forcing the ring buds into growth and preventing loss of these new growths by breakage. The procedure is simple and consists of rubbing off all new shoot growth except that produced from the ring bud. When the new growth from the ring bud is from 6 to 8 in. long it should be tied loosely to the stub of the stock shoot, and as further growth takes place it should again be tied farther along its length. Later in the summer, if growth of the new shoots is excessive, a portion of the terminal of each shoot should be cut off to reduce the possibility of wind breakage.

SUMMARY OF TOPWORKING SCHEDULE

Time	*Operation*
(1) During any dormant season.	Cut back trees to be topworked. Remove not over ¾ of the old top and cut branches no larger than 4 in. in diameter. Leave well distributed "feeder" limbs. Paint pruning wounds.
(2) During same dormant season.	Locate source of budwood of the desired cultivar or heavily prune trees of the desired cultivar to stimulate vigorous growth of shoots for use as budwood.

(3) During spring or early summer of the first growing season following the cutting back of trees or just previous to budding.

Thin stock shoots produced on stubs of the cut back trees to two or three per stub and remove ¼ to ⅓ of the terminal end of the remaining shoots to reduce breakage by wind.

(4) Not over 2 or 3 days before use.

Cut budwood of a size approximately the same as the stock shoots. Budwood should be mature enough for the bark to slip well and not split too easily. Keep moist and cool.

(5) From the middle of July to the middle of September of the first growing season following the cutting back of the trees.

Insert ring buds on stock shoots, doing the work rapidly and carefully so as to prevent excessive oxidation and desiccation and so as to obtain a close fit of the cambium and cut surfaces. Wrap immediately with waxed cloth or some patented material to prevent any subsequent oxidation and desiccation and to hold the bud firmly in place.

(6) From 21 to 25 days after the buds were wrapped.

Unwrap buds and rebud if first bud inserted does not live.

(7) During the first dormant season following the insertion of the ring buds or the cutting back of the trees.

Cut off stubs of cut back tree flush with most distal stock shoot. Cut off the feeder limbs. Paint all wounds. Cut stock shoots to stubs approximately 12 in. long above ring bud. Cut back stock shoots with no live ring bud to a stub 3 to 5 in. in length.

(8) During spring and summer of the second growing season following cutting back of the trees.

Force growth from ring bud by rubbing off all other growth. Tie new shoots from ring buds to stubs of stock shoots to prevent wind breakage. Cut off terminal portion of too vigorous shoots from the ring buds to prevent wind breakage.

(9) From the middle of July to the middle of September during the second growing season following the cutting back of the trees.

Rebud stock shoots produced from the 3 to 5 in. stubs left for the purpose, if desired, and by the same methods previously used.

(10) During second and subsequent dormant seasons following the cutting back of the trees.

Shape tree and space branches by pruning. Repaint wounds. Remove stubs of the stock shoots left for support. Also see Item 7. Subsequently, keep all pruning wounds well painted until healed.

ORCHARDS

The production of nuts in a pecan orchard, aside from disease, insect injury, and cultivars, is dependent largely upon soil moisture and fertility. These in turn, are largely dependent upon the cover crops grown, the time, type, and number of cultivations, and the fertilizer applied. Many of the pecan orchards of the United States are planted on land that has a normally low level of soil fertility and during the years prior to planting the orchards little or no effort had been made to maintain or improve it. During the life of any pecan orchard there can probably be found periods when soil-improving cover crops were grown, fertilizers were applied, and cultivation was practiced but these efforts at soil improvement have had little or no permanent benefits and have been expensive orchard practices.

During almost every growing season there are one or more periods when rainfall is lacking and soil moisture becomes very low. Pecan trees draw heavily upon the soil moisture at all times during the summer but a lack of soil moisture during the periods when the nuts are enlarging rapidly and when filling is taking place has the most serious consequences, and it is of prime importance at these periods that the available soil moisture be conserved as much as possible for the use of the tree. This is best accomplished by clean cultivation, but such cultivation long continued hastens the decomposition of organic matter in the soil, and thereby decreases the water holding capacity. In many of the lighter soil types it is difficult to build up any great content of organic matter and it is all the more important, therefore, to practice the proper cultural program on these soils.

It is quite geneally thought that the greatest value of cultivation comes from the stirring of the soil, but as a factor in the conservation of soil moisture, the destruction of weeds which remove water from the soil and give it off into the air through the leaves is more effective in maintaining the soil moisture content than of evaporation of moisture from the surface of the soil. While many summer cover crops may be very valuable as soil building crops they make such strong growth that the soil moisture reserves are depleted much more rapidly than if only weeds and grasses are grown.

During the winter season the moisture content of the soil is usually at a maximum and yet the trees make but very little demand for moisture. At the same time temperatures may be sufficiently high to allow decomposition of the organic matter in the soil to progress at a fairly rapid rate. Since this decomposition forms soluble nutrients which may be lost completely by leaching or carried below the level of the soil containing the pecan roots it is important that some crop be grown during the winter which will take up the soluble materials as they are formed. When these cover crops are returned to the soil in the spring or summer by cultivation the products of their decomposition will be taken up by the pecan trees, and at the same time the water-holding capacity of the soil will be increased by the addition of the organic matter. Since decomposition of organic matter progresses even more rapidly in the summer than in the winter, and is further hastened by cultivation, it is essential that a consistent program of soil improvement be carried on continually if the soil fertility is to be maintained.

Irrigation[1]

Irrigation has been a means of extending pecan acreage into regions where rainfall is insufficient for meaningful production. In arid and semi-arid regions, irrigation is necessary as most or all of the water required for pecan production is supplied by irrigation. Although not essential, irrigation is beneficial in humid regions as droughts occur with sufficient duration to result in reduction in yields. Experiments in humid areas have shown that irrigation increased yield of pecans, increased size

---

[1]This section was prepared by J. W. Daniell, Dept. of Horticulture, University of Georgia, Georgia Station, Experiment, Georgia.

of pecans, and increased percentage of kernels (Alben 1958, Daniell, 1976C).

Yield increases from irrigation do not automatically result in increases in net farm income. In order to increase profits, the use of irrigation must result in an increase in yield or quality of pecans large enough to more than cover the cost of irrigation. Therefore, good horticultural practices must be used along with irrigation to maximize net income.

Irrigation may be accomplished in four different ways: (1) by flooding; (2) by means of furrows; (3) by applying water underneath the land surface through subirrigation or above the land through drip irrigation; or (4) by use of sprinklers. Most of the land available for flood irrigation has been utilized. Flood irrigation is suited where the land is fairly level and can be economically shaped for water applications and where water is relatively inexpensive. However, growers and irrigation workers have known for a long time that furrow and flood irrigation systems result in loss of water not used by trees. With these systems, exceptionally high loss of water may occur from evaporation in open ditches and in the flooded area. Also, high water loss may occur from deep percolation in soils and field tailwater losses.

Most irrigation procedures rely on completely refilling the root zone each irrigation. Recent research at Nebraska (Fischbach 1975) reveals a more efficient method of scheduling irrigation for subarid and humid areas. This procedure makes effective use of rainfall during the growing season by not completely refilling the root zone each irrigation. This allows room for rainfall to replenish the soil moisture. It also draws on the stored soil moisture in the root zone during the peak use period of the crop.

In many areas of the world, water available for irrigation is being depleted rapidly. To obtain the maximum effect and utilization of water, it is necessary to supply water with the highest possible efficiency. Two methods that offer an increase in efficiency of water in pecan orchards are undertree sprinklers and trickle irrigation. Undertree sprinklers and trickle emitters operate below the foliage of trees, and, therefore, eliminate the disease problems associated with wetting foliage during irrigation. Sprinkler and trickle irrigation, with their flexibility and efficient control of water application, permit a wide range of soils to come under irrigation and allow a much greater acreage of land to be placed under irrigation. Sprinkler irrigation systems in pecan orchards are usually solid set systems with low angle nozzles to operate under foliage.

The advent of trickle or drip irrigation has opened up new avenues for more effective water utilization and is gaining in popularity. Trickle irrigation is the application of water to crops at low pressure at slow rates to maintain a part of the soil at or near field capacity (Kenworth 1974).

The basic concept is to prevent moisture stress of trees by maintaining adequate soil moisture in approximately 25% of the root system. Under systems of comparable efficiency, trickle irrigation should save from 20 to 40% of the water used under the other systems. A definite advantage of trickle irrigation is that it does not interfere with cultural practices and harvest. To eliminate problems in mechanical harvesting, the black plastic in-row laterals should be placed underground with top of emitters at or near the ground line.

To establish an effective irrigation program some knowledge of soil moisture or atmospheric condition is necessary. An estimate of soil moisture conditions can be obtained using tensiometers. Tensiometers measure soil suction which is a property of soil water. As it measures the soil moisture conditions and not the quantity of water, the tensiometer operation is largely independent of soil type. Research suggests that water should be applied to maintain soil suction at the 45 cm soil depth below 75 centibars (tensiometer reading of 75) for optimum growth and production of trees. Tensiometers should be located at strategic points in an orchard to give representative readings.

Timing of water applications for trickle irrigation based solely on soil moisture readings is difficult to accomplish as there are dry areas and very wet soil areas (wet area at emitters). A system based on evaporation from a Class A pan has been developed as an index of the need to irrigate and an estimate of the amount of water to apply. Such a system should be reliable as the amount of pan evaporation is influenced by rainfall, temperature, relative humidity and wind velocity which are the primary environmental factors affecting moisture loss through soil evaporation and transpiration from trees.

The quantity of water required to irrigate pecans with trickle irrigation can be estimated using 70% of the net evaporation loss (evaporation minus rainfall) from a Class A pan. The percentage of canopy of trees in relation to ground area should also be used in determining the quantity of water to apply. The weekly water required (WWR) for pecans can be estimated as follows:

WWR = Total net evaporation for week in cm × 70%
      × 90% canopy × 99,927 [liters (1.06 quarts) of water in
      1 hectare (2.5 acres) - cm].

Dividing the WWR by the number of emitters per hectare will give the quantity of water per emitter per week. Dividing the quantity of water per emitter per week by the emitter delivery rate per hour will give the hours of irrigation needed for the next week.

For all the winter cover crops mentioned the most satisfactory date of seeding has been found by experimenters to be from September 15 to October 15. Later seedings make satisfactory growth in some years when moisture and temperature conditions are favorable but generally the yield in green weight per acre is materially less. Because oats are sometimes subject to winter killing it is usually advisable to select rye for use.

Legumes in Pecan Orchards

The days of cheap nitrogen fertilizers have passed and more attention is being devoted to ways of cutting fertilizer costs. Thus, interest in legumes is on the increase. If all management practices are followed legumes can be produced to great benefit. A legume for a pecan orchard should (a) fix large amounts of nitrogen; (b) reseed; and (c) not interfere with nut harvest.

There are two legumes that should be successful in the Southeast; they are arrowleaf and crimson clovers. Both are capable of fixing about 100 lb of nitrogen per acre. This amount is sufficient to meet all of the nitrogen needs of the pecan trees. Legumes do not fix atmospheric nitrogen and release into the soil in large quantities. It is only when the roots, leaves and stems decompose that large amounts of nitrogen are released to the soil. Thus, it is only the second year that the full benefits are realized.

Arrowleaf and crimson clovers have good reseeding capabilities since they produce 30 to 75% and 75 to 80% hard seed, respectively. The hard seeds germinate throughout the fall and winter, producing plants which ultimately result in a good stand of clover. There are several cultivars of these clovers, and farmers should check with their Cooperative Extension Agents to determine those best adapted to his area.

The first step in establishing a legume in the pecan orchard is to test the soil to make sure that the pH is 6.3 to 6.5, and that there is ample calcium and magnesium in the soil. The proper pH not only increases the availability of phosphorus and potassium in the soil but favors the activity of Rhizobium bacteria. Arrowleaf and crimson clovers should be planted in the fall as soon as possible after harvest, at the rate of 20 lb per acre for crimson clover and 5 to 10 lb per acre for arrowleaf clover. Both types of clovers may be grazed or cut for hay in the spring (Wesley 1975).

Summer Cover Crops

Summer cover crops generally cannot be recommended for use in bearing orchards because of the injury frequently sustained by the trees and the nut crop from excessive competition for soil nutrients and moisture. However, in young orchards and in bearing orchards with the trees widely spaced summer cover crops are of great value in improving the fertility and moisture holding capacity of the soil through the organic matter returned. As was true with the winter cover crops, the summer legumes are of more value than nonlegumes in which latter classification are to be found many of the weeds and all of the grasses which make up the native growth during the summer. When summer cover crops are recommended for use in an orchard those found most valuable are *Crotalaria spectabilis,* velvet beans, soybeans, and cowpeas. In bearing orchards, soybeans, cowpeas, and several of the species of Crotalaria should not be utilized because they harbor stink bugs which cause kernel spot on the pecan nuts. Some of the native weeds have this same objection.

In preference to growing some crop during the summer primarily for a green manure crop, some pecan growers are growing row crops such as corn, cotton, or runner peanuts in the middles between the tree rows. In addition to requiring cultivation during the growing season, the fertilizers which should be applied to these row crops and the residue from them which is returned to the soil are of material benefit to the trees. Where these crops are grown it is necessary that they be planted only in the middles, leaving an area on each side of the tree rows which should be kept fairly clean of weeds and grass during the summer by several shallow cultivations. Row crops cannot be recommended for use in those orchards, on land of rolling topography and neither can clean cultivation over the whole area be used without considerable damage being done to the soil by erosion. Under such conditions some other system of culture must be followed during the growing season, or the orchard must be terraced.

As a summer cover crop, weeds are frequently about as useful as any of the planted crops. Natural vegetation in most pecan orchards includes many plants which are legumes and as such are as valuable as the planted legumes. Further, if weeds are allowed to grow as the summer cover crop the average grower does not hesitate as long in deciding to cultivate the orchard during drought periods as if the summer cover crop was one that had been planted.

Winter Cover Crops

A number of winter cover crops such as vetch, Austrian winter peas, rye, oats, and the clovers can be grown to advantage in a pecan orchard. The first two and the last named are legumes and, where they can be grown satisfactorily, are preferable to the nonlegumes because they add nitrogen to the soil through the action of the bacteria which form nodules on their roots. Rye and oats, which are nonlegumes, merely conserve the soluble soil nutrients in their tissues as a consequence of their growth. Various combinations of the plants listed can be used to good advantage, or they can be grown alone. Vetch and peas, vetch and rye or oats, and peas and oats make the best combinations. A combination of peas and rye is not as satisfactory as these others because rye is such a strong feeder in comparison with the peas that both the stand and growth of the peas is seriously reduced. The seed of all the winter legumes mentioned must be inoculated with the correct strain of nodule bacteria, when planted for the first time, if best results are to be obtained. The seeding rate of the vetches varies according to the size of the seed, the recommended rate of seeding of hairy vetch being 20 to 30 lb per acre and of Augusta vetch 15 to 25 lb per acre.

Any of the cultivars of oats and rye which are adapted to the section make fairly satisfactory winter cover crops although the total growth made is not as great nor as valuable as that of the legumes. Either oats or rye is of greatest value when grown in combination with either peas or vetch by acting as a support which prevents lodging, and by increasing the yield of green weight per acre.

Fertilizing Pecan Orchards

Pecan trees are sluggish in responding to fertilizers. Hammar and Hunter (1948) found that the leaves of pecan trees receiving applications of phosphatic fertilizers contained more phosphorus two years after the applications had been suspended than did leaves from trees receiving no phosphorus fertilizers. Pecan yields are a reflection of fertilizers applied over a period of years rather than the result of fertilizers applied in any particular year.

Since pecans have a tendency to be biennial in their bearing habit, it is advantageous to growers to make the largest portion of their fertilizers in the years of largest crops. Nitrogen should be applied every year, but potassium, phosphorus, calcium and trace elements might be applied on alternate years. While pecan trees are slow to respond to mineral fertilizers, once the elements are absorbed they exert an influence on yields for at least two years.

Zinc, one of the minor elements, has played an important role in the progress made in pecan culture since the discovery (Alben et al. 1932) that rosette is caused by a deficiency of this element. During the search for the cause of this disease, salts of practically all elements suspected of being limiting factors in plant growth were used on pecan trees under one condition or another. Included in the studies were salts of aluminum, boron, copper, iron, manganese, magnesium and zinc. Zinc was the only one that was effective in tree or nut growth (Hunter 1952).

The nutrient condition of pecan trees is associated with size of crop and filling of nuts. During filling, pecan nuts accumulate fairly large quantities of nitrogen, phosphorus, potassium and magnesium at the expense of the leaves and shoots. Moreover, the accumulation of these elements in the nuts coincides with the period of nut development, at which time such organic constituents as oil, proteins, and acidhydrolyzable polysaccharides are accumulating in the nuts. The mineral elements are associated with the elaboration of organic constituents that make up a large part of pecan kernels.

The percentage of well-filled nuts decreases as the number of nuts on a tree increases. Thus, any fertilizer treatment that increases the number of nuts per tree would make the problem of filling more difficult. It is important that a fertilizer that increases the number of nuts per tree also maintain a favorable nutritional balance in the trees for good filling. Therefore a balanced, mixed fertilizer is best for pecans. Seriously devitalized trees result from severe depletion of phosphorus and potassium in trees that produce heavy crops of nuts. Additional fertilizers and time are required for bearing trees to recover and produce another crop (Hunter and Hammar 1948).

pH Requirements.—From foliar analyses it has been shown that nitrogen and calcium increase in the leaves as the average yield of nuts per tree increases. The potassium, magnesium, and phosphorus content of the foliage is not significantly related to the nut crop (Hagler and Johnson 1955).

The best growth of pecan trees occurs at a pH of about 6.4. Since most pecan soils in the southeastern United States are more acid than this figure, it is usually profitable to apply lime to raise the pH to about 6.5. The application of zinc with the lime increases yields of nuts as well as growth of leaves and stems as shown in Table 12.4 (Johnson and Hagler 1955).

TABLE 12.4

EFFECT OF pH LEVELS ON GROWTH OF PECAN SEEDLINGS

Soil pH Range	Dry Weight of Pecan Seedlings in Grams			
	Leaves	Stems	Roots	Total
7.5	26.2	13.1	72.6	111.9
6.1	21.7	14.7	71.2	107.6
5.6	14.3	7.9	34.4	56.6
4.9	5.4	4.6	25.1	35.1
4.5	3.2	2.3	17.3	22.8

General Fertilizer Requirements.—The fertilization of pecans may vary widely, depending upon the general system of management selected. For young trees a recommended fertilization is 1½ to 2 lb of 8-8-8 for each year of tree age. This fertilizer should be applied in the early spring and spread evenly from two feet of the trunk to just beyond the branch spread of the tree. As the trees develop in size individual fertilization of the trees, in some systems of management, may be gradually discarded in favor of a general fertilization of the entire area occupied by the grove.

Mature trees may also be fertilized with 8-8-8 or similar mixed fertilizers at rates of 1000 to 1200 lb per acre. However, experiments conducted in recent years indicate that the fertilizer needs of a mature tree would be better met by a fertilizer ratio such as 8-1-3. Such ratios are not commercially available at this time and other factors in the management of orchards influence their fertilizer requirements. Some growers may prefer to consider the requirements of the individual elements in planning their fertilization and management programs.

Because of the wide variation in management practices, the individual grower will have to determine for himself whether his current fertilization practices meet the minimum requirements for the trees and, if not, how best to alter his practices to meet them.

Nitrogen.—Deficiency of this element causes light green foliage, weak shoot growth and earlier fall defoliation. Work in Florida and Alabama indicates that nitrogen is the element most closely associated with yields. Many orchards are far below their potential yielding capacity because they are deficient in this element. As long as the trees do not compete heavily with grasses or non-leguminous weeds, an annual nitrogen supply of 100 lb of N per acre (approximately 300 lb of ammonium nitrate) will meet the requirements of the trees. When heavy grass sods are present, additional nitrogen will be needed to keep both the trees and grass adequately supplied with this nutrient. Nitrogen may be supplied to the trees through leguminous cover crops, indirectly by fertilization of grass or other intercrops and by direct application under the branch spread of the trees.

Potassium.—Annual applications of 25 to 50 kg per hectare (25 to 50 lb per acre) of K_2O (40 to 80 lb of 60% muriate of potash) will probably adequately provide the potassium requirements of the trees. Since more than this amount is required for a good legume cover crop, additional fertilization of the trees with potassium is usually considered unnecessary. Although never a problem under good management systems, severe potassium deficiency does occur in neglected trees. The deficiency rarely becomes so severe that typical leaf scorch symptoms appear, but it does weaken the trees so that severe winter killing may take place. Following a particularly severe winter, up to 50% of the tree may be killed back. Yields from trees suffering from winter killing can be reduced drastically.

Phosphorus.—Deficiency of this element has been described as causing unthrifty growth and chlorosis in pot cultures, but no characteristic deficiency has been observed in field plantings in Florida. In recent years no significant increases in yields have been obtained from phosphate applications in mature groves. Repeated fertilizations have resulted in a gradual build-up of phosphorus in these soils, so that phosphorus applied to the cover crop or intercrop is more than adequate to meet the requirements. The recommended 8-8-8 fertilizer for young trees should supply all the phosphorus required.

Lime, Calcium and Magnesium.—For many years pecan growers have avoided the use of lime because they feared an increase in pecan rosette, or zinc deficiency. Recent experiments have indicated that a general increase in soil fertility may stimulate tree growth and the development of rosette far more than the addition of lime. Proper precautions should be taken to guard against the development of rosette, but the lack of zinc should not be used as an excuse to permit general deterioration of other factors important to maintaining soil condition and fertility.

The proper use of lime in the orchard is the key to the best management practices, since it reduces the leaching of fertilizer phosphorus and potassium, and increases the soil pH to levels more suitable for maximum growth and nitrogen fixation by leguminous cover crops. Lime reduces the solubility of manganese, an essential element for growth, but that also is found in near toxic quantities in some soils. Calcium and magnesium are two essential plant nutrients found in limestone. Deficiency of calcium in pot culture has caused small terminal leaflets and weak growth. Calcium deficiency has not been identified in pecans but calcium can replace much of the potassium required in pecan leaves, especially in years of heavy cropping. Magnesium deficiency has been observed frequently in pecans growing on the sandier soils, and occasionally it becomes severe enough to cause defoliation with subsequent reduction in yield. Magnesium deficiency is characterized by marginal yellowing of leaves with interveinal chlorosis and necrosis becoming more severe in late summer.

High calcic lime is an excellent source of calcium while dolomitic lime contains both calcium and magnesium. When magnesium levels are adequate, high calcic lime may be used to correct the soil acidity in pecan orchards, but dolomitic lime should be used whenever magnesium levels are low. Dolomitic lime has an additional advantage of being less soluble in the soil once the pH reaches 6.0 or higher, and is therefore less likely to cause overliming injury when an excessive amount is used.

Orchard soils should be limed to the range of pH 5.5 to 6.0 if no leguminous cover crop is grown and from pH 6.0 to 6.5 when such a cover crop is used. In correcting the pH, the pecan grower should arrange through his county agricultural agent for a soil test so that the proper quantity of liming material is applied.

Zinc.—Rosette is a physiological disorder of pecan trees caused by a lack of sufficient zinc to produce normal growth. It is manifested by a bronzing and crinkling of the leaflets which may become greatly reduced in size; shortening of the internodes which gives the effect of multiple bud development; and thus causing the appearance of a rosette of leaves on the twigs. In severe cases it causes twigs, and eventually branches, to die back; growth and development of the trees are greatly retarded and the trees produce no nuts on the badly affected parts.

This condition is corrected by the application of zinc in some form that will become available to the tree. Zinc sulfate is used most extensively because it gives a quicker response than other forms. Zinc oxide can be used also in soil applications, but the response of the trees to this form may be slower than with zinc sulfate.

Zinc is mobile enough to reach pecan roots when applied directly to the soil surface. It can be applied conveniently as part of the regular fertilizer or by separate application. Time of application to the soil is relatively unimportant, but visual improvement of the tree usually will not be noted before the new growth starts in the spring following the application.

In correcting zinc deficiency symptoms in mature trees, 2 to 2½ lb of zinc sulfate per tree spread evenly under the branch spread is usually sufficient on the sandy soils. Sandy loams and heavier-textured soils may require 5 to 10 lb of zinc sulfate per tree to accomplish the same result. For very young trees 2 to 4 oz of zinc sulfate may be sufficient. Mature groves exhibiting only slight rosette may be protected by including 1 or 2% of zinc in the regular fertilizer application. Once the deficiency is corrected, additional zinc applications should not be made more often than once in 5 or 10 years, since high zinc levels are toxic to plants.

Rosette may also be corrected by direct sprays on the foliage. Since trees respond more rapidly to zinc when it is sprayed on the leaves than when it is applied to the soil, the use of a spray is particularly desirable in cases of severe rosette, in order to reduce the damage to the framework of the tree. Foliage sprays should contain 4 lb of zinc sulfate and

2 lb of lime per 100 gal. of water. Where the recommended bordeaux spray applications are being made, zinc sulfate can be added at the rate of 4 lb of zinc sulfate to each 100 gal. of bordeaux. Spray applications of zinc should be made between May 25 and June 15 for best results, although fair results can be obtained later in the season.

Manganese.—A leaf deformity known as "mouse ear" or "little leaf," observed primarily in dooryard plantings and in coastal areas, has been identified as manganese deficiency. It has little economic importance but may be of considerable concern to home owners whose trees occasionally are severely injured. It is usually found when leaf manganese levels are less than 100 ppm. The manganese levels in normal pecan leaves range from 300 to over 2000 ppm. Associated with very high soil pH values, "mouse-eared" trees are often found near limerock driveways, waste building materials or growing in soils that naturally contain shell or marl.

Correction of "mouse ear" can be obtained by application of manganese sulfate to the soil. Depending on tree size and severity of symptoms, application of 2 to 10 lb of manganese sulfate plus 3 to 15 lb of ammonium sulfate per tree should correct the symptoms. Sulfur can be used in place of the ammonium sulfate at the rate of 1 to 5 lb per tree in order to lower the soil pH and increase availability of the manganese. All of these materials should be broadcast evenly to the branch spread.

Boron.—Deficiency of boron on pecans has not bee recognized in Florida and no significant responses to boron have been obtained. Normal boron content of leaves seems to range from 10 to 90 ppm. It should be pointed out, however, that the legume cover crops have a relatively high boron requirement. Hence, it is often necessary to include boron in pecan fertilizer in order to insure a good cover crop. Fertilizers which contain sufficient boron to provide the equivalent of 10 to 15 lb per acre of borax will provide adequate boron in most areas where a deficiency is encountered (Sharpe and Gammon 1958).

Alternate Bearing in Pecans

While all tree nuts tend to produce a heavy crop on alternate years, pecans seem to consistently bear on "on" and "off" years. In the spring of the "off" crop year trees of a particular cultivar may fail to produce pistillate flowers or the nutlets may abort. Staminant flowers (catkins) do not appear to be a factor in alternate bearing.

The cycle of "on" and "off" crop years may follow individual trees, cultivars or an entire orchard. One reason for planting four or more cultivars is the hope that at least half of the trees and cultivars will produce "on" crops each year.

The cause of alternate bearing is that high yields one year tend to inhibit fruit the following year. The dry weight of the nuts is composed mostly of carbohydrates and substances (chiefly oil) derived from carbohydrates. During a heavy "on" crop year there may not be enough carbohydrates produced to mature the fruit and store sufficient carbohydrates for next season's growth and fruiting. Whether a tree is "on" or "off" depends on the level of carbohydrates that accumulates during the previous season. Vigorous early growth of shoots, leaves, pistillate flowers, and staminant flowers depends upon carbohydrates that come from reserves stored during the previous season.

The relationship of alternate bearing to stress of kernel development emphasizes the need for controlling leaf diseases and holding foliage on the trees until after nut harvest. Late sprays to continue leaf function serves to promote filling of the current crop of nuts, and store carbohydrates for differentiation of pistillate flowers for the next crop. Increasing the functioning leaf area per unit of fruit increases the tendency for an "on" crop year. If the leaf area is too low, kernel development is depressed; "pops" are high, even on "on" crop years, and the chances for an "off" crop year following are increased. A low leaf area is related to an "off" crop year also through decreased shoot growth, and low vigor of surviving shoots. Large shoot size and length is a good indication of heavy leaf area, and prospects for an "on" crop, irrespective of the current crop.

Recent experiments and commercial practices have shown that alternate bearing can be virtually eliminated by orchard management that includes (a) high fertilization with all essential elements; (b) optimum moisture by controlled irrigation and/or drainage; (c) rigid control of orchard insects and diseases, especially that would cause malfunction of leaves; (d) spacing trees so that no outside shoots are shaded by other trees; and (e) pruning to allow all bearing branches exposure to light (Sparks 1974).

Controlling Weeds In Pecan Orchard With Herbicides[1]

Control of unwanted vegetation in pecan orchards is necessary for maximum growth and yield of nuts. Until recently, vegetation control was by harrowing, mowing, or grazing. Herbicide or sod-herbicide systems used for effective weed control are now widely accepted, resulting from the advantages offered by these methods over other methods of vegetation control as follows: (1) a less likely spread of crown gall by eliminating mechanical cultivation or mowing close to trees, which has been shown to spread the bacteria through injury to trunks or roots of

[1]By J.W. Daniell, Dept. of Horticulture, University of Georgia, Georgia Station, Experiment, Georgia.

trees; (2) elimination of mechanical injury to trunks and feeder roots which are near the soil surface; (3) better maintenance of the orchard floor in a smoothed, settled condition which is necessary for effective mechanical harvesting of nuts; (4) no contamination of nuts by manure from grazing animals; (5) less soil erosion when compared to mechanical tillage; (6) reduced cost for weed control; (7) less soil compaction from equipment; (8) area free of weeds near sprinklers or drippers if irrigated; and (9) increased yields and grade of pecans through improved weed control and improved water infiltration into soil.

With use of mechanical harvesters, the sod-herbicide system has become popular. With this system, herbicides are used in tree rows to give a weed-free strip of around 6 ft on each side of row and a closed-mowed sod maintained in row middles. The sod-herbicide system produces a very effective floor for mechanical harvesting of pecans. Harvesters can work efficiently from either a close-mowed sod or a weed-free area as long as the soil surface is in a settled and smooth condition. A weed-free strip along tree rows facilitates easy removal of nuts in the vicinity of trunks during the mechanical harvesting process. Also, the weed-free strip eliminates cross-mowing and trunk injury from mowers. Data from research suggest that weeds in the immediate vicinity of the trunks compete more strongly with young trees for nutrients and water than weeds in row middles. Grasses can be particularly troublesome in orchards maintained in permanent sod. Even with tillage, it is difficult to manually control grasses close to tree trunks.

It is useful to group herbicide applications into preemergence or postemergence. Preemergence application is any treatment made prior to emergence of specified weed. The application is usually applied to the soil surface and the herbicide must be moved into the soil by rainfall or irrigation to be effective. Herbicides applied to the soil as preemergence treatments are directly affected by soil characteristics. Postemergence application is any treatment made after emergence of a specified weed. The application is usually made to the foliage of weeds, thus the herbicide effectiveness is not directly related to soil characteristics.

The age of a weed often determines its response to a particular postemergence herbicide treatment, with younger plants less tolerant than older plants. Preemergence treatments which kill germinating seeds or seedlings commonly have little or no effect on established weeds.

Rejuvenating Neglected Orchards

A number of orchards in the pecan belt have been neglected to such an extent that they are liabilities rather than assets. Some of them can be reclaimed and put into profitable production by proper fertilization and management. In selecting an orchard for rejuvenation the grower must first determine that there is a reasonable chance that it can be made productive. The soil must be examined to determine that there is ample light-textured soil above the clay and that no hardpans, claypans or high water tables are present. The trees should be checked to be certain that they are of prolific cultivars known to produce satisfactorily in the area. These two factors, cultivars and soil, are the most important in determining whether rejuvenation can be successful. The trees should be planted at a recommended spacing or planted in such a way that they can be readily thinned or interplanted to the recommended spacing. The condition of the trees must not have declined so far that they cannot be brought back into profitable production.

In rejuvenating the neglected orchard the undergrowth of briars, bushes and young forest trees must be removed. Then it should be thoroughly disked to a depth of 3 or 4 in. Orchards on rolling land, subject to erosion, will require a system of terraces or sod strips to prevent undue washing after cultivation has been started.

The trees can be brought back slowly by initiating a regular orchard management program, but it must be remembered that trees in a neglected state are far below a productive level of fertility. It may be desirable to use extra fertilizer to overcome the deficiency in fertility and re-establish rapid vigorous growth as quickly as possible. If this is the case, the trees should be fertilized heavily the first year, especially with nitrogen. Neglected trees with a trunk circumference of 2 to 3 ft should be fertilized with 8 to 10 lb of nitrogen (24 to 30 lb of ammonium nitrate) and 4 or 5 lb of potash (7 to 10 lb of muriate of potash) per tree. This should be broadcast under the branch spread of the tree. The best time for this initial fertilization is between December 15 and February 1. Since neglected orchards are often zinc deficient, it would be well to apply 2½ lb of zinc sulfate per tree at the same time. Trees of larger or smaller trunk circumference should be fertilized at proportionately heavier or lighter rates. Usually standard management and fertilization practices may be followed after the first year in an orchard undergoing rejuvenation. However, in some groves above average rates of fertilization may be continued through the second and possibly the third years.

Herbicides for Pecan Orchards

Diuron [3-(3,4-dichlorophenyl)-1, 1-dimethylurea] applied at 2.2 to 4.5 lb per acre before emergence will control most annual grass and broadleaf weeds. Annual use of Diuron may result in a buildup of buckhorn plantain (*Plantago Lanceolata* L.) and other perennial weeds. However, by adding a surfactant to the spray solution, a foliar burn-down is obtained on all weeds. In this way, a burn-down of perennial weeds and a control of emerged annual weeds, as well as germinating seedlings, may be obtained. Diuron should not be used until trees have been established for three years and in orchards with young trees growing on very sandy soil.

Simazine [2-chloro-4,6-bis (ethylamino)-s-triazine], 2.2 to 4.5 lb per acre, is widely used to control annual grass and broadleaf weeds as a preemergence treatment. Simazine can be used to control summer annual weeds when applied in the spring and control winter annuals and some winter perennial weeds, such as mouseear chickweed (*Cerastium vulgatum* L.) when applied in the fall. Simazine has little or no foliar activity and must be absorbed by plant roots. It should be used only in orchards established two years or more.

Dichlobenil (2,6-dichlorobenzonitrile) inhibits germination of seeds of both grass and broadleaf weeds and some shallow rooted perennials such as nutsedge (*Cyperus esculentus* L.) but it does not control emerged weeds. It is relatively volatile and therefore needs to be leached into the soil by rainfall or irrigation soon after application. Granular formulation is superior to the wettable powder in pecan orchards. Dichlobenil (5.6 to 6.7 lb per acre) is more effective when applied in the fall or when the weather is cool. This herbicide can be used to control weeds after a waiting period of six months from transplanting of the trees.

Trifluralin (α, α, α-trifluoro-2,6-dinitro-N-N,-dipropyl-p-toluidine) can be applied at 0.56 to 1.1 lb per acre in fall or spring to control many annual weeds. However, it must be incorporated 2 to 3 in. into the soil immediately after application and, therefore, its use has been for preplant applications or in orchards which are at times mechanically tilled.

Oryzalin (3,5-dinitro-N^4,N^4-dipropyl sulfanilamide) is a preemergence herbicide which at 2.2 to 4.5 lb per acre is effective for controlling most annual grass and broadleaf weeds. Application of Oryzalin should be made to the soil surface during the rainy season so that rainfall will leach it into the weed germinating zone. In tests, excessive rainfall or irrigation has not leached Oryzalin out of the weed-seed germination zone. It has shown excellent tolerance for one-year-old or older trees.

Dalapon (2,2-dichloropropionic acid) is used to control annual and perennial grasses. It should be applied at rates from 5.6 to 7.8 lb per acre as a postemergence spray to control perennial grasses such as bermudagrass (*Cynodon daclylon* [L.] Pers.). An application of Dalapon is most effective when weeds are actively growing and up to three to four weeks before leaves lose their green color. Repeat application should be made when new foliage develops on the grass. Injury can result on young trees if excessive rainfall immediately follows application. Therefore, the safety of Dalapon close to very young trees is questionable.

Paraquat (1,1'-dimethyl-4,4-bypyridinium ion) at rates of 0.56 to 1.1 lb per acre has emerged as very useful on all tree crops, particularly pecans. It is used as a postemergence spray to kill all annual grasses and broadleaf weeds. It is used to top kill perennial weeds but regrowth will occur. It is speedily inactivated in the soil and, therefore, has no residual control and is essentially nonphytotoxic to roots of plants in soils. Care must be taken to keep Paraquat sprays from contacting green stems or foliage of pecans.

Glyphosate [N-(phosphonomethyl) glycine] at rates of 1.1 to 3.4 lb per acre gives outstanding control of perennial grasses such as bermudagrass, johnsongrass (*Sorghum halepense* [L.] Pers.), and quackgrass (*Agropyron repens* [L.] Beauv.) Even at the low rate of 1.1 lb per acre, it is effective as a postemergence spray in the control of annual grasses and broadleaf weeds. Glyphosate, as a foliar spray, is also effective in controlling certain perennial broadleaf weeds and vines such as poison ivy (*Phus radicans*). Translocation throughout the plant occurs following absorption through foliage. The roots of perennial species are affected, resulting in failure of regrowth from meristematic tissue. Maximum translocation into roots occurs usually when weeds are flowering or heading. Glyphosate has no preemergence activity as it is rapidly degraded in the soil.

Weed oil and Dinoseb (2-sec-butyl-4,6-dinitrophenol) are contact herbicides applied to foliage of annual weeds. These herbicides have not been used extensively in orchards as only young weed seedlings are controlled by the sprays.

In pecan orchards, initially the primary weed problem is annual weeds. However, with continuous use of a single herbicide applied preemergence, tolerant weeds may invade the area. In the essentially noncompetitive environment, the tolerant weeds flourish. An effective, long-term program will prevent a buildup of tolerant weeds. The program would include a rotation of two or more herbicides and the use of mixtures of herbicides to broaden the spectrum of herbicidal action to kill a greater variety of weeds. Also, the program would include the use of contact herbicides such as Paraquat or Glyphosate when needed to retard or kill the tolerant weeds.

In conjunction with close mowing, management of the sod should include the use of low rates of Paraquat or Glyphosate at times to "chemical mow" or retard weeds. This would reduce the number of mechanical mowings during the season and further reduce competition of weeds with the trees at critical periods such as when nuts are filling.

Observe all directions, restrictions and precautions on herbicide labels.

Chemical Thinning of Pecans

Pecan trees of some cultivars set more nuts in "on" years than they can mature with well-developed kernels. If the nut crop could be thinned sufficiently in years of heavy set it should be possible for the trees to set a crop the next year as well as to mature the current crop normally.

According to Smith and Harris (1957), malic hydrazide (sodium salt of 1,2-trichlorophenoxyacetic-3,6-dione) was a promising spray for spray-thinning when applied in late May in aqueous solutions of 0.04 to 0.08%. Spraying should be applied in about three weeks past the receptive stage of the pistillate flowers, and thinning of from 10 to 40% may be expected, depending on the cultivar and timing of the application. Higher concentrations may cause twig injury to sensitive cultivars.

CIPC (isopropyl N-3-chlorophenyl carbamate) in 200 ppm concentration caused about 20% thinning; while 400 ppm concentrations caused 75% thinning and slight twig injury. A third chemical 2,4,5-T (2,4,5-trichlorophenoxyacetic) in concentration of 10 to 25 ppm caused dropping from 16 to 60%, and produced some twig injury (Smith and Harris 1957).

Dwarf Pecan Trees

Pecan trees continue to grow larger and taller for an indefinite period as shown in Fig. 12.7. As this occurs the trees become more crowded, more difficult to spray and almost impossible to prune; the nuts become more difficult to harvest; and the number of trees per acre may be reduced to as little as ten.

As mechanical pruning, spraying and harvesting becomes imperative in large orchards, it is very desirable that the trees remain a uniform and moderate size. This may be accomplished by breeding but will require many decades. In the meantime, fair success is being had by keeping the trees to a desired size by systematic annual pruning. Indications are that the yield per tree and yield per acre are increased by removing terminal shoots each year. In this way the size of the trees is held down and the number of fruiting shoots is increased. The shape of the trees is more uniform and there is less damage from wind to the trees.

Dropping of Pecan Nuts

Most discussions dealing with pecan production problems are primarily concerned with the factors which will increase the blossoming of the trees and only incidentally with the factors causing a loss of the crop during the period from blossoming to harvest. It is an accepted fact that trees must blossom heavily if a good crop is to be produced since it is to be expected that a certain percentage of the blossoms and immature nuts

Courtesy of John Large

FIG. 12.7. SPRAYING PECAN TREES WITH HELICOPTER, USING
LOW VOLUME CONCENTRATE AT THE RATE OF LESS
THAN TEN GALLONS PER ACRE

will be lost from one cause or another during the season. It is impossible to say which is the more important from the standpoint of profitable production of nuts, growing trees which will blossom heavily or protecting the nuts on the trees from injuries or conditions which will cause them to drop. Certainly neither would be profitable without attention to the other and for some factors the two phases cannot be considered separately. Proper cultural and fertilization practices must be applied in an orchard if the trees are to produce an abundance of pistillate blossoms and these same practices also influence the percentage of the blossoms which drop. Experimental studies have shown that moderately long shoots of large diameter not only blossom more heavily but also show a smaller percentage of drop than do shorter or more slender shoots.

The more vigorous shoot with its better developed vascular system and its larger leaf area is better able to obtain sufficient moisture in competition with weaker shoots, to obtain a larger amount of essential food supplies, and also to manufacture the amounts of carbohydrate materials necessary for protein synthesis, growth of the nuts, wood growth, and storage.

Undeveloped Flowers.—The first drop noted is that of undeveloped flowers. Early spring applications of quickly available nitrogenous fertilizers will tend to decrease this drop by increasing the number of pistillate flowers per cluster that attain full development. It is difficult to separate this blossom drop from the drop occurring during the six weeks following the period of receptivity. To a large extent the drop which takes place during the six weeks following pollination is due to lack of normal development of the ovule in flowers apparently normal from outward appearance, lack of pollination, or lack of fertilization of the ovule. The lack of normal development of the ovule and the failure of fertilization are closely allied with vigor and nutritional condition of the shoot on which they are borne. This factor probably operates to some extent in all blossoming shoots and, therefore, cannot be entirely eliminated. However, as shoot vigor increases the number of normal pistillate flowers will increase in proportion to the number of normal appearing flowers with undeveloped ovules. All nuts not fertilized, through lack of pollination, abnormal growth of the pollen tube, or because of an undeveloped ovule will drop within six weeks from the time the flowers are receptive.

During the period of rapid growth of the nuts following fertilization and up to the time the shells harden there is a more or less constant drop, the causes for which cannot be definitely identified in all instances. During this period insects and diseases, as well as abnormal moisture conditions, cause a large percentage of the drop but, again, the nutritional condition of the shoots, as distinct from moisture relationships, is partly responsible (see section on alternate bearing).

Diseases.—Except for scab, diseases are of relatively little direct importance. Pecan scab infections on the nuts, if present in sufficient number, will cause them to drop during the latter part of this period and this disease must be controlled by spraying if a profitable yield of nuts is to be obtained on trees of the scab susceptible cultivars. All the other diseases indirectly affect the nuts by injuring the foliage and causing premature defoliation. Therefore, the control of foliage diseases is important for the maintenance of proper food reserves in the trees but is of little direct benefit in reducing the drop of nuts.

Insects.—Insects do a great deal of direct damage to individual nuts and to whole clusters. The pecan leaf case-bearer may cause an indirect loss of nuts through the destruction of shoots which would blossom if the infestation is heavy and late, but if the infestation is light or early relatively little damage occurs because secondary buds may produce blossoming shoots in sufficient number to replace those destroyed.

The pecan nut case-bearer causes injury to the crop in some sections of the southeastern pecan belt each year. In most sections, however, the loss of nuts is usually small but at intervals of a few years the infestation of this insect becomes heavy enough to cause the loss of most or all of the crop. Early in the season one "worm" or larva of this insect may destroy the entire cluster of nuts but during the second and succeeding generations relatively few nuts are destroyed because one nut generally suffices as food for each larva. When the infestation is heavy spraying is very important if the crop is to be saved.

The hickory shuckworm causes heavy loss to nut crops in many orchards. With most cultivars one feeding tunnel of the larva of this insect before the shell hardening period will cause the nut to drop within a few days and because there may be as many as four generations of the insect per year the increase in population may cause a very serious loss of nuts. Unfortunately, it has not yet been possible to work out a satisfactory control. Sanitation is of some benefit, especially in an orchard situated at a distance from sources of infestation.

The black pecan aphid is apparently the direct cause of very little dropping of nuts. Ordinarily, this insect has a much greater injurious effect on the crop of nuts the year following a heavy infestation by causing serious defoliation, with the consequent effect on nutrition, and so should be controlled by spraying before much defoliation has occurred.

Several species of "stink bugs" may cause a heavy drop of nuts, if present in very large numbers, by puncturing the nuts while feeding in approximately the same time and manner as the pecan weevil. However, damage by these insects is easily prevented if proper cultural practices are applied in an orchard.

Malnutrition.—The drop of nuts caused by nutritional, drought, and other physiological factors cannot be as easily described and prevented as the drop caused by insects and diseases. There is experimental evidence showing that the drop of nuts during the period from about June 15 to August 30 is somewhat less on vigorous trees with the foliage maintained in good condition than on less vigorous trees. In event of drought, trees in well cared for orchards show much less drop than trees in poorly cared for orchards. From June 15 to August 1 the drop caused by conditions arising within the tree is generally quite light. Nuts which fall during this period show a decreased growth rate for 3 to 4 weeks prior to the time they drop indicating that they are losing out in the competition for nutrients and moisture. Just why this occurs is not known. Very serious droughts can and will cause the loss of most or all the nuts despite anything the grower can do other than apply irrigation water which may not be economical under present conditions in the southeastern pecan growing sections.

From all standpoints, the most critical period in the development of the pecan nut occurs during the month of August. At this time the nut is in the "water" stage, the shell hardens, and the embryo starts to develop. During this period insect injury and moisture conditions will cause the nuts to drop within three to five days after an injury occurs. Nuts dropping at this time show no decreased growth rate prior to dropping as they do earlier in the season. During the critical "water" stage of the nuts the seed coat is extending rapidly down into the packing material partially because of the internal pressure of the "water" or endosperm material filling it. This endosperm material is fairly high in sugars, and, if drought conditions develop, and then are followed by heavy rains, the internal or turgor pressure becomes so great that splitting of the hardening shell occurs. When this happens, oxidation takes place rapidly, food material for the growth of the embryo is lost, and the further development of the embryo is impossible. Sometimes the splitting does not extend through the shell and shuck and become visible on the surface of the nut, but, whenever the seed coat is ruptured, the nut will drop. Insect injury during this same stage of development may cause a similar splitting which may be almost as extensive as that caused by moisture relationship. As shell hardening develops almost to completion, splitting may occur without causing the nut to drop and these splits are sometimes visible at harvest.

WORLD'S LARGEST PECAN OPERATIONS

On the desert south of Tucson, Arizona, is the largest pecan orchard in the world. This totally irrigated pecan orchard encompasses 6000 acres of more than 300,000 trees winding 12 miles down the heart of the Santa Cruz Valley in Sahuarita, Arizona. Situated in the center of the orchard is the Santa Cruz Valley Pecan Shelling Plant that processes the entire production, and markets the meats both in bulk and consumer-size cello bags, under the Funsten name.

Highly mechanized harvesting and cleaning of the pecans is followed by processing with modern techniques and equipment designed to produce economical, high quality, bacteria-free products. Moving through the plant, pecans are sized, sanitized, cracked, sorted, and inspected as finished meats for ice cream makers, confectioners, bakery manufacturers, salters and snack food repackers.

Projected production will be 10 million tons by 1980 or $1/10$ of the U.S. production. The total irrigation concept allows for strictly controlled moisture and nutritional requirements in the orchard.

Funsten Nut, a division of Pet, Inc., since 1962, began in St. Louis in 1892 as the R.E. Funsten Dried Fruit and Nut Company with a nut processing operation. Since those early beginnings, Funsten has emerged as the world's largest sheller of pecans, the leading independent processor of California walnuts and noted processor of California almonds and eastern black walnuts with production plants in Andalusia, Alabama; Modesto, California; Bolivar, Missouri; and Muskogee, Oklahoma (Anon. 1976).

A major development in the southeastern United States is Plantation Services, Inc., of Albany, Georgia. It is a package program of growing, harvesting, storing and delivering pecans to their final destination with nothing left to chance. The objective is to hold production to 20% of the normal without sacrificing quality.

The complex covers 2000 acres under irrigation; about 2,000 acres of young trees of Wichita, Cherokee, Chickasaw, and Desirable cultivars; and other thousands of acres under "custom" management. A rigorous program of disease and insect control, irrigation, fertilization and soil conditioning is followed. Cultivation, harvesting, quick drying, grading and packaging are entirely mechanized. Nuts are immediately refrigerated, and held for year-round removal for shelling and delivery to end users. A substantial portion of the production is exported (Anon. 1973).

The Stahmann Farms, Inc., Santo Tomas, New Mexico, was (in 1970) the world's largest producing orchard, containing about 200,000 trees with an annual yield of 3000 to 4000 tons. Much of the pioneer work on irrigation was done on 4000 acres of bearing orchard.

Pecan growing in Australia became active about 1960. Stahmann Farms, Inc., Las Cruces, New Mexico, is developing the largest nut project at Biniguy in north New South Wales, Australia. The planting covers 1850 acres of densely planted Western Schley and Wichita cultivars, set 11 ft apart, with about 65 trees per acre. A yield of 7500 lb per acre is expected with an annual production of 2.7 million pounds. The entire orchard will be irrigated (Gillin 1973).

Other densely planted pecan orchards are underway in Australia (Gardner 1976).

Pecan growing is expanding in Israel. Present production area in Israel is 50,000 acres with 75,000 acres expected by 1980. Half of the expected production of 3000 tons is intended for export. In larger orchards heavy equipment is used for cultivation, fertilizing, irrigation and harvesting. For small plantations a massive harvesting machine is economically unfeasible and the need exists for a compact, portable nut harvester, relatively inexpensive and simple to operate (Sarig 1973).

The climate in Israel is similar to that of California, and plantings are being increased at the rate of 500 to 750 acres per year. Cultivars include Burkett, Schley, Mahan, Moneymaker, Wichita, Choctaw, Apache and Delmas (Croll 1973).

PECAN ORCHARD DISEASES AND INSECTS[1]

Control of pecan diseases and insect pests is seldom easy. In some situations and circumstances control is almost impossible, even with the highly effective pesticides now available.

The applications of sprays for the control of insects and diseases is a very important factor in pecan production. In many seasons it will be the difference between a short crop and a good crop. Even with the best chemicals and the most modern equipment, insect and disease control is not an easy job. Approximately seven months are required for growth and development of a pecan crop. At some time during this period, weather conditions are likely to be favorable for numerous pests.

A good nut crop may not be produced even with an ideal spray program unless good sanitary and cultural practices are followed. The following are important supplemental practices in the control of diseases and insects.

(1) Either turn under all leaves, leaf stems, and shucks, or rake up and burn during the winter. In sodded groves where raking and turning of shucks and leaves is impractical, keep weeds mowed close to the ground. Scab is much more difficult to control in groves where weeds are allowed to grow beneath the trees.

(2) Prune low-hanging limbs. This operation allows better air circulation and sunlight penetration close to the ground, thus shortening the infection period of scab and other foliage diseases.

(3) Keep trees in a vigorous growing condition by following recommended fertility practices (Harris and McGlohon 1966).

Spraying pecans for disease and insect control is a paying proposition. Some cultivars cannot be produced without a spray program. The effectiveness of any pecan spray program depends upon knowledge of the following factors influencing it.

The Control of Scab

Some cultivars are susceptible to scab, others are resistant. The type of spray program for susceptible cultivars may be altogether different from the program for resistant cultivars.

Scab-susceptible cultivars must be sprayed several times with Cyprex during each season to get adequate scab control. Some susceptible cultivars are Pabst, Brooks, Tesche, President, Frotcher, Mobile, Delmas, Alley, Nelson, Centennial, Moneymaker, Schley, Success, Mahan, and in certain areas, Stuart. Many seedling trees are also scab-suscep-

[1] Revised by N. E. McGlohon and E. D. Harris, Plant Pathologist and Entomologist, respectively, Cooperative Extension Service, University of Georgia, Athens.

tible. Some of the above cultivars are more scab-susceptible than others. Success and Moneymaker are only moderately susceptible, and a limited crop can be made some years without spraying. However, for maximum yields these cultivars should be treated as other susceptible cultivars.

It is not necessary to spray resistant cultivars, such as Curtis, Elliott and Farley. Certain seedling trees are also resistant to scab. Stuart is susceptible to scab in many areas, and should be sprayed in these areas the same as other susceptible cultivars. These scab-resistant cultivars are susceptible to other leafspot diseases and powdery mildew, and should be sprayed two or three times during the summer.

Where scab-resistant and susceptible cultivars are planted together, they should be separated in some manner. One procedure used to separate cultivars in a grove is to paint different colored rings around scab-susceptible and resistant cultivars. During the spray operation the fungicide can be omitted on all resistant cultivars for scab control. This can considerably reduce spray cost.

The Moore and Van Deman cultivars are susceptible to scab, but must be sprayed with Duter, since Cyprex may injure the foliage of these cultivars.

Spray Coverage.—Every leaf, twig, and nut must be wet thoroughly during each spray application. Adequate coverage cannot be obtained unless the spray equipment used will force the chemical to the top of the highest tree. It is extremely important that the sprayer operator take his time to cover each tree thoroughly with spray from top to bottom. Poor coverage during any spray period can result in severe disease and insect damage.

The amount of spray required to cover a tree adequately depends largely on the type of sprayer used. Therefore, the rates in the Spray Guide are based on the amount per acre or tree, rather than per 100 gal. of spray.

Spray Concentration.—This is expressed as the amount of pesticide formulation per 100 gal. of spray. The spray concentration used depends on (1) the amount of pesticide formulation recommended per tree, and (2) the amount of spray needed for equipment to thoroughly cover the tree. Table 12.5 gives the amount of pesticide formulation to make 100 gal. of spray.

Timing of Spray Applications.—To obtain adequate disease and insect control, proper timing of spray applications is essential. The first spray is probably one of the most important. It should be put on just as the young leaves unfold and before diseases have a chance to become established. If you wait until you see the disease, it is usually too late to

TABLE 12.5

AMOUNT OF PESTICIDE NEEDED PER TREE AND PER 100 GALLONS[1]

Pesticide Formulation	Amount Per Tree lb	Gallons of Spray per Medium-Sized Tree							
		20	15	10	7.5	5	4	3	2
		Lb of Wettable Powder per 100 Gal.							
Benlate 50% WP	0.08	0.4	0.5	0.8	1.1	1.6	2.0	2.7	4.0
Du-Ter 50% WP	0.08	0.4	0.5	0.8	1.1	1.6	2.0	2.7	4.0
Guthion 50% WP or Cyprex 65% WP	0.20	1	1.3	2	2.7	4	5	6.7	10
Parathion 15% WP or Zolone 25% WP or	0.40	2	2.7	4	5.3	8	10	13.3	20
Sevin 25% WP	0.30	1.5	2	3	4	6	7.5	10	15
Malathion 25% WP	0.60	3	4	6	8	12	15	20	30
Sevin 80% WP	0.50	2.5	3.3	5	6.7	10	12.5	16.7	25
Toxaphene 40% WP	1.20	6	8	12	16	24	30	40	60
		Pints of Emulsifiable Concentrate per 100 Gal[2]							
Parathion 4 lb/gal. EC	0.125	0.6	0.8	1.3	1.7	2.5	3.1	4.1	6.2
Systox 2 lb/gal. EC or Torak 4 lb/gal. EC	0.20	1	1.3	2	2.7	4	5	6.7	10
Parathion 2 lb/gal. EC or Malathion 5 lb/gal. EC or Zolone 3 lb/gal. EC	0.25	1.3	1.7	2.5	3.3	5	6.3	8.3	12.5
Guthion 2 lb/gal. EC or Supracide 2 lb/gal. EC	0.40	2	2.7	4	5.3	8	10	13.3	20
Sevimol 4	0.50	2.5	3.3	5	6.7	10	12.5	16.7	25
Toxaphene 6 lb/gal. EC	0.67	3.3	4.5	6.7	9	13.3	16.7	22.3	33.3

[1]These figures are for medium-sized (25-35 ft) trees. For small trees (under 25 ft) use three-fourths of either the indicated gallons per tree or amount of pesticide formulation per 100 gallons. For large trees (over 35 ft.) multiply either the gallons per tree or amount of pesticide formulation per 100 gallons by 1.25.

[2]Some emulsifiable concentrate forms of the above insecticides may not contain the same amount of actual toxicant per gallon as shown in this table. Be sure to use an equivalent amount of actual toxicant per 100 gallons.

start spraying. A disease such as scab must be prevented rather than cured. A fungicide must be applied to scab-susceptible cultivars at least every 21 days during normal weather and every 14 days during rainy weather. If one application is omitted, or is late in being applied, yields can be greatly reduced.

Tree Size.—The number of gallons of spray necessary for adequate coverage will depend upon the tree size. Large trees may require twice

as much spray material for adequate coverage as will small trees. Therefore, the cost of spraying will increase proportionally. The type of
equipment necessary for good coverage will also depend somewhat on
tree size. Table 12.6 gives approximate number of gallons necessary for
good coverage on various tree sizes with different types of equipment.

TABLE 12.6

APPROXIMATE NUMBER OF GALLONS NECESSARY FOR GOOD
COVERAGE ON VARIOUS TREE SIZES WITH DIFFERENT TYPES OF
EQUIPMENT

Type of Equipment	Gallons of Spray by Tree Size		
	Small (under 25 ft)	Medium (25–35 ft)	Large (over 35 ft)
Air-blast[1]	4–10	5–15	7½–30
Hydraulic	15	20	30
Mist-blower	3	4	5
Airplane	1	2	2½

[1]As little as 5 gal. of water per tree can be applied with the air-blast sprayer with certain nozzle sizes. The same amount of pesticide formulation per tree must be applied regardless of the amount of water used.

Spray Equipment.—Air-Blast or air-delivery sprayers should be used
for pecan orchards of more than 40 to 50 acres, especially if part of the
acreage is in scab-susceptible cultivars.

This type of sprayer gives excellent coverage on even the largest trees.
The operator manages the whole machine from his tractor seat. One
man with an air-blast sprayer can spray three times as many trees per
day as three men can with a high-pressure or hydraulic sprayer. The
higher cost for the air-blast sprayer is offset by the lower cost of
maintenance, low labor requirements, less time per application, and
better spray coverage.

To obtain adequate coverage, both sides of a tree should be sprayed.
In some cases large trees must be circled.

High-pressure or hydraulic sprayers are good for spraying trees of any
size, but should be used primarily for groves of 25 to 30 acres or less.
This sprayer takes at least two or three men to operate it efficiently.
They can spray only ⅓ to ½ as many acres per day as can be sprayed
with an air-blast sprayer. The hydraulic sprayer costs much less than
the air-blast sprayer, but it requires an experienced crew to get thorough coverage. This sprayer should deliver 25 to 35 gal. per minute and
maintain pressure of 400 to 600 lb per sq in. when spraying.

Mist-Blower Concentrate Sprayers.—This type sprayer is smaller
than hydraulic or air-blast sprayers. It applies from 3 to 5 gal of spray

Courtesy of F.E. Meyers and Bros. Co.

FIG. 12.8. PECAN AIR ORCHARD SPRAYER

The air discharge head has two 42-in. fans capable of developing 95,000 cu ft of air per min. The sprayer consists of two-stage centrifugal pump with 500 gal. tank.

per tree at a tractor speed of 3 miles per hour. Diseases and insects can be controlled with a mist-blower if it is equipped and powered to cover large trees thoroughly. Before buying this type of sprayer, make sure it will deliver spray material to the top of the highest trees. Also remember that this is a concentrate sprayer which requires 4 to 5 times as much spray material (chemical) per 100 gal. of water as hydraulic equipment.

Aerial Application of Fungicides and Insecticides.—Aerial applications of insecticides have been used since 1923 (Emery 1963). Pierce (1960, 1963) in Louisiana used aerial applications in 1959 and 1960 for control of pecan aphids, phyloxera and mites. Phillips (1963) sprayed a pecan nursery twice on May 23 and June 27, 1962, using a plane equipped with a micronair rotary atomizer and obtained excellent control of pecan bud moth. The spray consisted of 5 pints of 47% parathion emulsion and 2 lb of Zineb (Dithane Z 78) fungicide in 10 gal. of water applied at the rate of 2 gal. of spray per acre. Research workers thought that air application of fungicides would not control disease, and that this method of application would not be efficient or economical. This delayed the use of aeroplanes for scab control for many years.

Large (1953, 1954, 1956) started aeroplane spraying of fungicides on pecans in 1953 and repeated these experiments in 1954 and 1955, using each year one of the forms of Zineb; Parzate; Dithane Z 78; or Nabam plus zinc sulfate (3.6 lb Zineb plus ⅛ pint of oil per acre). The best commercial control was on Moore trees in 1955 using that strength of Nabam plus zinc sulfate plus oil. Large (1961) sprayed pecan trees from a helicopter in 1961, using Zineb (Dithane Z 78) plus Plyac 3.6% to 10 gal. of water per acre and obtained excellent control of scab on Moore trees. Cole (1964) in Georgia, and Graves (1961, 1962) in Mississippi, applied Dodine (Cyprex) from the air with fixed wing planes and obtained excellent control of scab.

Graves (1964) sprayed pecan trees from a helicopter in 1963, and stated, "the helicopter compared favorably with both fixed wing and hydraulic applications techniques in terms of disease control on pecans." His experiments with fixed wing aeroplanes indicated that excellent control of pecan scab *Fusicladium effusm* was obtained with Dodine (trade name Cyprex) at the rate of 4 lb per acre when applied in 20 gal. of water, using 5 or 6 applications per season. A practical degree of control was obtained when only 2 lb of Dodine was used per acre under the same conditions. A degree of control was also obtained with Zineb (Dithane Z 78) at 8 lb per acre and Maneb (Dithane M 22) at 8 lb per acre. Effectiveness was markedly reduced when the gallonage of water per acre was decreased. Dodine applied by aeroplane also gave excellent control of brown leaf spot (*Cercospore fusca*). None of the materials was particularly outstanding for control of powdery mildew (*Miscrosphaera alni*). He suggests that pecan growers organize in groups to make aerial application available to the smallest. In 1966, 15 or more communities in northeast and central Mississippi were controlling scab by spraying pecan trees from the air (Hines 1967).

Mist Blower.—A mist blower was developed by Potts (1962) for applying spray in concentrated form to increase speed of application and to reduce mixing time, water hauling, labor and cost of equipment. A concentrated spray has three necessary characteristics: (a) high concentration of pesticide in the mixture; (b) low gallonage per tree or per acre; and (c) fine atomization to obtain good coverage with low gallonage. The blower adds a fourth characteristic in the use of air velocity and air volume to atomize the mixture and to serve as a primary carrier for the spray instead of water.

Coverage rate for pecans is 1 to 2 acres per hour, or 1½ to 2½ min per tree, depending on size and height of trees. Normally, 50 to 55 ft trees require 30 to 35 gal. of conventional dilute spray per tree. In concentrated spray applications one uses ¹⁄₁₂ as much water per tree as for the conventional hydraulic sprayer. A tree that requires 30 gal. of conventional, fully diluted spray would receive 2½ gal. of concentrate spray mixture when applied by mist blowers.

Ultra Low Volume Ground Sprayer.—A new concept in aerial pest control was begun in 1962 with the introduction of the British Micronair rotary atomizer. Insect control was achieved at volumes as low as one pint per acre. In addition it was demonstrated that a conventional boom and nozzle system could be employed for dispensing very low volumes of liquid. In concentrate spraying the amount of water varies from 10 to 200 gal. per acre, while in dilute spraying approximately 400 gal. of water are required, although the amount of pesticide remains constant.

New equipment made it possible to introduce low-volume malathion concentrate in 1963. This material contains 95% active ingredient and has inherent chemical and physical properties that make it possible to

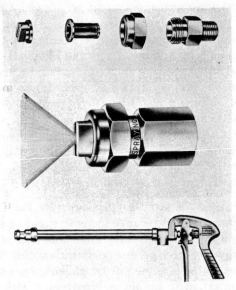

Courtesy of Spraying Systems Co.

FIG. 12.9. LOW VOLUME TEEJET NOZZLE

(a) Nozzle parts; (b) assembled nozzle; and (c) gunjet.

use it directly without additives. This material has been successfully used for ground or aerial applications. Because of drift problems, aerial applications are limited to low volume malathion since this pesticide has a low mammalian toxicity in addition to good settling properties, and a low evaporative rate. This development of ground sprayers modified for low volume work offered the most feasible method of reducing the hazard of drift.

A Buffalo Turbine "CHS" Model and a Hudson Peerless Economy Mist sprayer were modified for ultra low volume applications. A pressurized tank with a pressure regulator, a metering valve, and mini-spins were included in equipment modifications for the concentrate. Outstanding control of malathion-sensitive insects was obtained in Michigan by Howitt and Pshea (1965).

Ground spraying of undiluted malathion at low-volume rates looks highly promising for insect control of nut trees. The low-volume spray technique, first developed by U.S. Department of Agriculture-Agricultural Research Service for use with aircraft, is regarded as a milestone in safe and economical pesticide use (Anon. 1965). By applying less insecticide, farmers not only save time and money, but also minimize residue hazards.

When spraying with mist blowers, concentrated sprays in 10 Micron to 50 Micron-sized drops are carried in a high volume of air onto the pecan foliage. This method of application controls scab and other pecan diseases. Excellent control of pecan scab has been observed with 4 and 8 lb of Dodine (Cyprex) in 25 gal. of water. Good control was obtained with Dodine at the 2 lb per acre rate (Graves 1966; Potts 1962). With concentrated spray applications, trees 55 to 60 ft in height require 1 to 3 gal. of concentrated spray mixture when applied with mist blowers. One hundred gallons of concentrated spray will cover 50 pecan trees. The advantage of using the mist blower is that the orchard can be sprayed faster with only 7 to 10% as much water as is needed for dilute spray concentrations.

Systemics.—Systemic insecticides that can be applied to the soil or to the tree will not wash off with rain for it is picked up and carried throughout the tree and will control aphids. Twenty-five pounds of Disyston per acre applied the first week in April on two sides of the tree as a ground application has given good control of aphids. The use of 25 lb of 10% granules of Disyston per acre has been recommended and approved for use in New Mexico (Denman *et al.* 1966). Results with Disyston have been erratic in the Southeast.

---

*See Table in Appendix for converting to metric measurements

TABLE 12.7

SPRAY GUIDE FOR SCAB-SUSCEPTIBLE CULTIVARS

(Check precautions and restrictions before using any chemical listed in this spray guide.)

Spray Time Of Application	Pest To Control	Spray Materials Per Acre For Medium-Sized Trees[1]	Remarks
Prepollination Spray— when first buds begin to open	Leaf Casebearer Downy Spot	Malathion 25% WP 6 lb or Parathion 15% WP 4 lb plus either Cyprex 65% WP 2 lb or Benlate 50% WP 0.8 lb or Du-Ter 50% WP 0.8 lb	It is not necessary to add parathion or malathion to this spray in groves where the insect control program was followed the previous season if there is no current insect problem. If spittlebugs are a problem. apply 3 lb of 80% Sevin WP, 4 lb of 15% parathion WP, 2 lb of 50% Guthion WP, or 4 lb of Zolone 25% WP per acre when the leaves are half grown. Where downy spot has been a problem, apply Cyprex, Du-Ter, or Benlate when buds first break and again two weeks later.
First Prepollination Spray— when first buds have opened	Scab Leaf Casebearer	Cyprex 65% WP 2 lb or Du-Ter 50% WP 0.8 lb or Benlate 50% WP 0.5 lb plus Du-Ter 50% WP 0.5 lb plus either Parathion 15% WP 4 lb or Malathion 25% WP 6 lb	Do not use Benlate alone. Where downy spot has been a problem, make first fungicide application 7 to 10 days earlier than normal and apply first 3 applications at 2-week intervals. It is not necessary to add parathion or malathion to this spray in groves where the insect control program was followed the previous year and there is no current insect problem.

[1]The amounts shown are for medium-sized trees (25-35 ft) in rows 60 ft apart. On smaller trees use three-fourths of the indicated amount; on larger trees increase the indicated amount by one-fourth. Use twice as much spray material per acre on trees that are planted in rows that are 30 ft apart.

NOTE: Do not use Cyprex on Moore and Van Deman cultivars. Du-Ter may be substituted.

Second Prepollination Spray— two weeks after first pre- pollination spray	Scab	Cyprex 65% WP 2 lb or Du-Ter 50% WP 0.8 lb or Benlate 50% WP 0.5 lb plus Du-Ter 50% WP 0.5 lb	These first two spray applications are extremely important for scab control. Early sprays prevent scab from becoming established. If spittlebugs are a problem in your grove, apply 3 lb of 80% Sevin WP, 4 lb of 15% parathion WP, 2 lb of 50% Guthion WP, or 4 lb of Zolone 25% WP per acre to medium-sized trees when the leaves are half grown.
First Cover Spray— when young "nuts" first appear or two weeks after second prepollination spray	Scab Nut Casebearer Mites Aphids	Cyprex 65% WP 2 lb or Du-Ter 50% WP 0.8 lb or Benlate 50% WP 0.5 lb plus Du-Ter 50% WP 0.5 lb plus either Parathion 15% WP 4 lb or Malathion 25% WP 6 lb or Zolone 25% WP 4 lb	Do not use Benlate alone. To be effective against casebearers, parathion, malathion or Zolone must be applied when the young nuts are present. This insecticide application is very important, especially if an insecticide was not used in the first spray. Make a second application 1 week later if nut casebearer populations are heavy.
Second Cover Spray— three weeks after first cover spray	Scab Powdery Mildew	Cyprex 65% WP 2 lb or Du-Ter 50% WP 0.8 lb or Benlate 50% WP 0.5 lb plus Du-Ter 50% WP 0.5 lb	If powdery mildew becomes a problem use Benlate at 1 lb per acre. If aphids or mites require additional control at this time, apply Zolone as recommended in First Cover Spray or 2 pt of Systox 2 lb/gal EC per acre.

TABLE 12.7 (Continued)

Spray Time Of Application	Pest To Control	Spray Materials Per Acre For Medium-Sized Trees	REMARKS
Third Cover Spray— two to three weeks after Second Cover Spray	Scab Powdery Mildew Downy Spot Brown Leafspot	Cyprex 65% WP 2 lb or Du-Ter 50% WP 0.8 lb or Benlate 50% WP 0.5 lb plus Du-Ter 50% WP 0.5 lb	If powdery mildew becomes a problem, use Benlate at 1 lb per acre. More Benlate is required for mildew control than for scab control. Do not use Benlate alone. If extended wet periods occur, increase Benlate to 1 lb per acre for zonate leafspot control. If a grove has a history of a high incidence of nut drop caused by hickory shuckworms before shell hardening, 2 lb of Guthion 50% WP, 2 pt of Torak 4 lb/gal. EC, 4 pt of Supracide 2 lb/gal. EC, or 4 lb of Zolone 25% WP per acre should be applied during the first week of July in light crop years.
Fourth Cover Spray— two to three weeks after Third Cover Spray	Scab Powdery Mildew Downy Spot Brown Leafspot	Cyprex 65% WP 2 lb or Du-Ter 50% WP 0.8 lb or Benlate 50% WP 0.5 lb plus Du-Ter 50% WP 0.5 lb	If excessive nut drop results from pecan weevil adult feeding punctures before pecan shells begin to harden, apply a pecan weevil spray at once. When possible, use ground sprayers. But, aircraft can be used if it is otherwise impossible to apply pecan weevil sprays every 7 days. Use at least 10 gal. of water per acre. In areas where zonate leafspot has been a problem, use Benlate at 1 lb per acre along with Du-Ter at 0.5 lb per acre.
Fifth Cover Spray— two to three weeks after Fourth Cover Spray	Scab Powdery Mildew Downy Spot Brown Leafspot	Cyprex 65% WP 2 lb or Du-Ter 50% WP 0.8 lb or Benlate 50% WP 0.5 lb plus Du-Ter 50% WP 0.5 lb	If mites or aphids are a problem, apply 4 lb of Zolone 25% WP or 2 pt of Systox 2 lb/gal. EC per acre.

Sixth Cover Spray— two to three weeks after Fifth Cover Spray	Scab Black Aphid Shuckworm	Cyprex 65% WP 2 lb or Du-Ter 50% WP 0.8 lb or Benlate 50% WP 0.5 lb plus Du-Ter 50% WP 0.5 lb	If rainy weather conditions exist, it may be necessary to put on another scab spray 2 to 3 weeks after this spray. Additional insecticide applications may be necessary for black pecan aphid or mite control if dry weather prevails during this period.
Pecan Weevil Sprays— every 7 days from the time that pecan shells begin to harden (about August 10-15) until mid-September and even later if adult weevils are still present	Pecan Weevils Shuckworms	Sevin 80% WP 3 lb or Torak 4 lb/gal. EC 2 pt	If pecan weevils are not a problem in your grove, you can control shuckworms by applying Guthion, 2 pt of Torak 4 lb/gal. EC, 4 pt of Supracide 2 lb/gal. EC, or 4 lb of Zolone 25% WP per acre. For shuckworm control, make the first of three applications when the pecan shells begin to harden. Applications should be made at two-week intervals. Remember to apply Du-Ter or Cyprex every 2 to 3 weeks as recommended in the fourth, fifth and sixth cover sprays. Aphid or mite populations may build up where Sevin is used. If mites or aphids are a problem, apply 4 lb of 25% Zolone WP or 2 pt of Systox 2 lb/gal. EC per acre.

Spray Materials For Disease Control.—*Cyprex* (Dodine 65% WP) is the oldest fungicide being used on pecans for scab control. This chemical has given excellent control of scab for over 15 years. *Cyprex* will not control some of the minor leafspot diseases or powdery mildew. It is compatible with other fungicides and insecticides but cannot be used on the Moore and Van Deman cultivars. *Cyprex* must be used at 2 lb per acre on a full season schedule making applications every 2 to 3 weeks.

Duter (50% WP) ranks at the top of the list for scab control. *Duter*, when used at 1 lb per acre, gives excellent control of all pecan diseases except powdery mildew and scorch. *Duter* has a long residual action and will control scab even when applied at 4-week intervals.

Benlate(Benomyl 50% WP) started out as an excellent fungicide for scab and powdery mildew control, but scab resistance soon developed which handicapped its use. Littrell (1976) found scab resistance to *Benlate* in several groves in Dougherty County, Georgia. It is not recommended for scab control unless used in combination with *Duter*. *Benlate* gives good control of zonate leafspot and powdery mildew when used at 1 lb per acre.

Spray Materials for Insect Control.—*Parathion* (15% WP or 2 to 8 lb/gal. EC), an organic phosphate insecticide, will control leaf casebearers, nut casebearers, spittlebugs, webworms, stink bugs, May beetles, and twig girdlers.

Malathion (25% WP or 5 lb/gal. EC), an organic phosphate insecticide will control leaf casebearers and nut casebearers.

Guthion (50% WP or 2 lb/gal. EC), an organic phosphate insecticide, controls hickory shuckworms, spittlebugs, stink bugs, aphids, mites, fall webworms, May beetles, leaf casebearers, nut casebearers, and twig girdlers.

Systox (6 lb/gal. EC) is a systemic organic phosphate insecticide effective in aphid and mite control.

Zolone (25% WP and 3 lb/gal. EC), an organic phosphate insecticide, will control aphids, hickory shuckworms, pecan nut casebearers, spittlebugs, and mites.

Sevin (50% WP, 80% WP or Sevimol 4), a carbamate insecticide, is effective against pecan weevils, nut casebearers, and spittlebugs.

Torak (4 lb/gal. EC), an organic phosphate insecticide, will control pecan weevils, hickory shuckworms and aphids.

Supracide (2 lb/gal. EC), an organic phosphate insecticide, will control hickory shuckworms and aphids. It should not be mixed with fungicides because plant damage may result.

Pesticide Precautions.—Pesticide materials listed in this publication are toxic to man and other warm-blooded animals. Care should be exercised in their use. Follow these steps:

(1) Read the label.—Carefully read all pesticide labels to be certain you are using recommended chemicals and observing all precautions. Poor pest control, serious spray injury, and illegal residues may result if improper chemicals are used. It is illegal to apply any pesticide in a manner that is inconsistent with the label.

(2) Tolerances.—Tolerances given for pesticides in Table 12.7 have been established by the Food and Drug Administration. Failure to abide by dosages and time limitations given may result in the seizure of your crop due to excessive residues.

(3) Highly toxic materials.—Parathion, Torak, Guthion and Demeton (Systox) are highly toxic insecticides, and should be applied only by a trained operator. The precautions on the manufacturer's label should be followed carefully. All pesticides should be handled with respect, and used only in accordance with official recommendations or label directions.

(4) Storage and disposal.—Pesticides should be stored in the original containers with labels intact. The storage area should be locked so that children, irresponsible persons and animals will not have access to it. Surplus pesticides should be buried deeply in a remote area and where water will not become contaminated through drainage. Cartons, bags and cardboard drums should be burned. Metal containers should be crushed, glass containers broken, and buried deeply away from wells and streams.[1]

(5) Drift.—The drift of pesticides to pasture and forage crops may result in illegal residues in milk, eggs and meat. If vegetable or fruit crops are nearby, drift may result in illegal residues in the produce. Of course, drift into homes, barns, livestock pens, poultry houses and ponds is hazardous and must be avoided.

(6) Honeybees.—Honeybees may be killed by any of the insecticides recommended for control of pecan pests. Bees are vitally needed for pollination of clovers, many fruits, flowers, vegetables, and field crops. Therefore, efforts should be made to eliminate or reduce the killing of bees and other beneficial insects. Insecticidal applications, particularly by airplane, should be made in late afternoon or early morning when honeybees are not in the groves (Harris and McGlohon 1966).

Custom Application

Many pecan groves are too small to justify spray equipment, and must be sprayed by custom applicators. Individuals spraying pecan trees for a

[1]See U.S. Dept. Agric. Bull., "Safe Disposal of Empty Pesticide Containers and Surplus Pesticides" (1964).

fee should ask these questions before making binding agreements with growers.

(1) What is the pecan cultivar to be sprayed? The cost of spraying a cultivar susceptible to scab may be twice as much as spraying a scab-resistant cultivar.

(2) What is the condition of the grove? If briars and weeds cover the ground beneath the trees, it may take several more spray applications to get adequate disease control than if the grove is clean.

(3) How large are the trees? Large trees may require twice as much spray material for adequate coverage as smaller trees. The cost of spraying increases proportionally.

(4) Where are the trees located? Special care must be taken in spraying trees on lawns, near play grounds, around gardens, pastures and animal feed lots. The choice of chemicals to be used in such areas would be restricted.

(5) Where is the nearest source of water? If water must be transported over long distances, spray cost can increase considerably.

Blacklight For Insect Control.—Blacklight traps are used for collecting insects to determine insect population at a given time and place. This provides a means of timing applications for insecticides. They are also used as a means of suppressing or controlling certain pecan insects as hickory shuckworm, pecan nut casebearer, and pecan leaf casebearer.

Blacklight traps vary in size and construction, but all have lamps that emit their principal radiation in the near-ultraviolet region of the electromagnetic spectrum (3200 to 3800 angstroms), and are fitted with some kind of apparatus to trap or kill the insects attracted to the light. Blacklight traps are effective only at night against nocturnal flying insects (Tedders and Osburn 1966).

PECAN DISEASES[1]

Diseases of pecans may be due to specific organisms, fungi, or bacteria; to mineral deficiency; or to climatic conditions (Phillips *et al.* 1964).

Pecan Scab

Pecan scab (*Fusicladium effusum* Wint.) is the most serious disease of pecans. The following cultivars may be severely infected with scab: Alley, Brooks, Centennial, Curtis, Delmas, Elliott, Frotcher, Kennedy, Mobile,

---

[1]By John R. Large, Big Bend Horticultural Laboratory, Monticello, Florida.

Moneymaker, Moore, Nelson, Pabst, President, Schley, Success, Tesche, and in certain areas, Stuart. Scab can be controlled by spraying the trees with Duter or Cyprex.

The scab fungus attacks the rapidly growing tissues of the leaves, shoots, and nuts. When these tissues cease growing they become completely immune. On highly susceptible cultivars such as the Schley, partial defoliation sometimes occurs, especially when frequent infections occur in early spring, but most damage is to the nuts, where losses frequently range from 75 to 95%.

The scab fungus is carried over winter in the infected spots on old leaves and shucks and lesions on the shoots of the trees. Leaf and nut infection is correlated with rainfall during spring and early summer. Frequent rains and cloudy weather which keep the leaves wet overnight, or for 12 hours or more, favor infection. Initial leaf infections may occur prior to the middle of April and these develop rapidly. If no spraying is done, new crops of spores are produced by the last of April or first of May which cause numerous secondary infections, which may cause areas of the leaves to become almost black due to coalescing of the spots. The spots of infections are small, black, circular and slightly raised at first, but later may become sunken. With severe infection the whole surface appears black. These severely infected nuts may drop prematurely or stop growth and remain attached to the shoots indefinitely.

Control.—The amount and seasonal distribution of rainfall is an important factor in the development and control of pecan scab. Pecan scab can be controlled by 6 to 8 applications of fungicide made at about 3-week intervals starting about the middle of April. The most effective are the organic fungicides Cyprex, Duter, and Benlate. (See Table 12.7.)

Pecan Leaf Blotch

Pecan leaf blotch (*Mycosphaerella dendroides* [Cke.] Demaree and Cole) is a foliage disease of nursery and orchard trees. The fruiting bodies first appear on mature leaves in June or July as olive green velvety tufts of conidiophores on the under surface, while yellow spots appear later on the upper surface of the leaves. The perfect stage makes its appearance about midsummer, as black pimple-like structures which unite giving the leaves a black, shiny blotched appearance. Leaf blotch only attacks orchard trees which are lowered in vigor by neglect, overcrowding or injuries. Nursery trees are more susceptible to attack than mature trees. The disease is usually present where nursery blight disease is present.

Control.—Destroy or plow under old infected leaves. Fungicides used for control of scab or downy spot will control leaf blotch.

Brown Leaf Spot

Brown leaf spot (*Cercospora fusca* Rand.) is a disease of minor importance, especially on healthy vigorous trees. The disease occurs in June or July on mature leaflets and may cause serious defoliation in localities having high rainfall and where orchards lack vigor as a result of neglect. Primary diseased spots are circular, reddish brown and often develop greyish concentric rings. Later these spots become irregular in outline. The Stuart is very susceptible while other cultivars are more resistant.

Control.—Fungicides used for scab control will also control brown leaf spot. Adequate fertilizer program is also beneficial.

Gnomonia Leaf Spot

The Gnomonia leaf spot (*Gnomonia dispora* Demaree and Cole) is another pecan disease of minor importance, occasionally found in Florida and southern Georgia. The disease has not been serious enough to justify control measures. So far it has been found only on rosetted trees, which suggests that the fungus is a weak parasite.

Vein Spot

Vein spot (*Gnomonia nerviseda* Cole) is a fungus that attacks pecan leaves. It is present in the states of Arkansas, Louisiana, Mississippi, Oklahoma, and Texas. The lesions of vein spot on leaf stems (rachises) resemble those caused by scab, so that one disease may be mistaken for the other. On lateral veins, vein spot lesions are circular or oval, and about ¼ in. in diameter. On mid ribs, spots sometimes extend from the base to the apex of the leaflet. Vein spot does not attack shoots or nuts, and attacks tissues only a short distance on each side of the vein. Premature defoliation often follows moderate to severe infections. The fungus winters over on old leaves and infects young growing tissue in the spring.

Control.—To control vein spot, plow under old leaves before bud break, in the spring, and spray the trees with Cyprex, Duter or Benlate.

Zonate Leaf Spot

Zonate leaf spot first showed up in Dougherty County, Georgia, in the fall of 1966. Shortly thereafter Dr. Archie Latham at Auburn University identified the disease and found that it was caused by the fungus *Cristulariella pyramidalis*. Since then, the disease has been seen in isolated areas of Florida, Alabama and Georgia. The symptoms on pecans are similar to those on other hosts. Greyish-brown spots develop all over the mature leaflet surface but the most noticeable symptom is a concentric ring formation in the spots. Young, small lesions usually are circular. Under very moist conditions, fruiting structures can be seen on both upper and lower faces of the leaves. The structures are cone-shaped, tan fruiting bodies, shaped very much like a Christmas tree.

Severely infected leaves usually begin to drop from the tree by early August. This disease is severe during extended rainy periods but stops when relative humidity is 90% or lower. In Georgia the disease was noted during 1967 through 1969, but it seemed to cause very little damage. In 1970 there were isolated cases where trees were defoliated by the zonate leaf spot fungus. During the summer of 1971 after several weeks of rainy weather in July, this disease became a severe problem in many groves in southwest Georgia. It caused severe defoliation, especially on border rows or trees in low areas. The organism responsible for this disease seems to come from hedgerows and wild hosts into the pecan grove. Very little damage has been noted since 1971.

It is not known which fungicide is most effective against zonate leaf spot. Data from tests conducted in the Albany, Georgia area indicated that *Benlate* plus oil will give adequate control of zonate.

Liver Spot

Liver spot (*Gnomonia caryae* Var *Pecanae* Cole) occurs in the same states as vein spot. This disease first appears in May or June as dark brown circular spots on the lower surface of leaflets, mainly along each side of the midrib. Spots are about ⅛ to ⅜ in. in diameter. In September and October the color of the spots changes to a cinnamon brown and small, dark spore-bearing bodies appear in the center of the spots. Leaflets with many spots will fall in September or October. Spores from old leaves on the ground infect new growth in the spring. The first three scab applications will control liver spot. (See Table 12.7.)

Nursery Blight

In seasos of excessive rainfall, pecan nursery blight (*Elsinoe randi* Jenkins and Bitancourt) becomes one of the most important limiting factors in the production of budded pecan trees, especially in coastal areas. Seedling trees that are severely affected by nursery blight make little growth and are often too small for budding at the end of the second season. This disease is confined to nursery trees. The fungus invades both young and old leaflets and early infections in April result in reddish lesions on both surfaces of the leaflets. Later, the spots on the upper surface turn ash grey and drop out, leaving the leaves with a ragged shot hole appearance.

Control.—Nursery blight can be controlled by applying Cyprex or Benlate. Make first application about April 15 and follow with three additional applications at monthly intervals.

Thread Blight

Thread blight (*Pellicularia koleroga* Cke.) attacks pecans and numerous other woody plants in humid regions. The fungus overwinters in compact masses of red brown fungus tissue known as sclerotia. The fungus threads grow rapidly in May and June from the sclerotia on the twigs on new petioles and leaflets. The most common symptom of thread blight during summer is the matting together of dead leaves.

Control.—Following the regular scab spray schedule should control this disease.

Powdery Mildew

Powdery mildew (*Microsphaera alni* Wint.) usually is of minor importance on the pecan, although it occasionally causes serious damage to the nuts. This disease affects both the foliage and the nuts, forming a white superficial fungus growth usually in July. Occasionally premature defoliation occurs under conditions very favorable for the development of the fungus. When the nuts are infected early in the season, the shucks split prematurely, causing shriveled kernels.

Control.—Benlate is the only chemical registered for use on pecans for powdery mildew control. Use Benlate at 1 lb per acre beginning at first sign of the disease.

Pink Mold

Pink mold (*Cephalothecium roseum* Corde.) is frequently observed during late summer and early fall as a pinkish fungus growth on nuts that have been attacked by the scab disease, or where the shuck has been injured by mechanical means, especially insect punctures. The fungus will penetrate the shell and enter the kernel of thin-shelled cultivars, causing a decay that is known as "pink rot." Affected nuts leak oil, and their shells have an oiled appearance and often a strong rancid odor.

Control.—A spray program that controls scab will usually control pink rot.

Fungal Leaf Scorch

It has never been determined what actually causes the problem known as fungal leaf scorch. R.H. Littrell has studied this problem more than anyone else. He believes that several fungi are involved in the development of scorch symptoms. This condition, which seems to be more prevalent in Georgia than in other states, begins on the leaflet margin and tips and advances over the entire leaf. By late summer, infected leaflets turn tan, curl and drop from the tree. Scorch usually is isolated and does not occur in the same groves each year; but when it does occur, it can cause complete defoliation.

Littrell has reduced the amount of scorch by using fungicides. He pointed out that symptoms similar to fungal leaf scorch also can be caused by a nutritional imbalance of potassium as well as spider mites. Cultivars vary greatly in their susceptibility to scorch. Cape Fear and Van Deman are highly susceptible while Mahan seems to be resistant.

Control.—Several fungicides have been tested for their effectiveness against scorch but Difolatan and Benlate are the only ones which seem to be effective (Wells *et al.* 1976).

Research on leaf scorch is underway in Georgia and hopefully the basic causes can be identified which will bring about a more effective control.

Dieback

Dieback (*Botryosphaeria berengeriana* DeNot.), a twig and limb disease identified by sudden wilting and dying of the leaves on terminal twigs and limbs, may occur in heavily fertilized nursery and rarely in rapidly growing young trees in the orchard.

Control.—Pecan dieback may be controlled by pruning out all the dead wood and burning it. It is best to prune in the fall and again in the spring to remove any remaining diseased branches.

Crown Gall

Crown gall (*Agrobacterium tumefaciens* [E.F. Smith & Town] Conn.) is a bacterial disease of pecans which does extensive damage in the nursery and may even kill trees in mature pecan orchards. Wart-like growths develop at soil level on nursery trees, these growths often extend several inches above the surface soil and from a few inches to a foot or more in diameter on orchard trees. Early stages of growth may be easily confused with callus over-growths formed at the graft or bud unions.

Control.—All nursery trees infected with crown gall should be destroyed by burning, preferably at the time of digging. Only disease-free trees should be planted in new orchards. Do not cultivate the soil near the trunks of infected trees; the tools may spread the disease. There is no effective chemical treatment recommended for crown gall control at the present time.

Bunch Disease

The symptom of bunch disease is a bushy growth of slender, willowy shoots that result from an abnormal forcing of lateral buds into growth. Symptoms resemble those of some virus diseases of other woody plants such as peach yellow and bunch disease of walnuts. In trees lightly infected with bunch disease only portions of one branch or several scattered branches will show the characteristic symptoms. Bunch disease is conspicuous in early spring and summer, because the leaf growth is earlier and greater than that of normal branches. Seriously affected trees become mere skeletons of main lateral branches covered with thick broomy, sucker growth.

Control.—Kenknight (1965, 1967) reports that there is no definite control of bunch disease. Pruning out the diseased limbs and painting the wound with pruning compounds, destroying diseased trees, and planting only healthy nursery trees may eradicate the disease from the orchard. In a few instances growers have topworked bunch-diseased trees to Stuart and obtained apparently normal Stuart trees. At present it is not known whether or not Stuart trees topworked on bunch-diseased trunks are symptomless carriers of the virus. Probably such trees are susceptible to the strain of the virus that affects Stuart.

Cotton Root Rot

Cotton root rot (*Phymatotrichum omnivorum* [Shear] Dug.), a soil inhabiting fungus, is usually found on cotton, alfalfa and other plants in Texas and other western states. It has killed pecan trees in Arizona and Texas. The fungus kills the roots, reducing the moisture and mineral supply to the tops. Infected trees have yellow sparse leaves and die in one or two years after symptoms of the disease appear.

Control.—There is no practical control of cotton root rot. Do not plant trees in soil known to be infected with the fungus.

Wood Rot

Broken branches or other wounds on pecan trees provide possible points of entrance for wood rotting fungi. Wounds flush with the trunk or main branches heal more quickly than those that have broken stubs.

Control.—Wood rot can be controlled by painting the wounds once annually with commercial tree wound paint, or with 1 part of commercial creosote to 3 parts of coal tar.

Rosette

Rosette, prior to 1931 a limiting factor in pecan production, now of minor importance, is a nutritional disease caused by an inadequate a-mount of available zinc in the soil. Yellow mottling, or chlorosis, and crinkling of the leaves in the tops of trees are characteristic of rosette in the early stage of its development. As the disease progresses, the symptoms appear on the lower branches. In advanced stages the leaves become dwarfed, the internodes are shortened, and gradually the twigs and branches in the tops of the trees die. Several rosetted trees usually are nonproductive and may become so weakened that they die from attacks of borers or from other causes. However, rosette alone has never been known to kill pecan trees. The Stuart cultivar is most susceptible, while Moneymaker in most localities usually is quite resistant.

Control.—Rosette may be corrected by applying zinc sulfate in solution as a spray to the trees or applying the dry salt to the soil. Soil applications are not effective in orchards growing on neutral or alkaline soils. Spray application is effective regardless of the soil condition. On acid soil, 5 lb of 36% zinc sulfate per tree will cure mild rosette symptoms. Trees severely affected may require up to 10 lb annually for 2 or more years to overcome the disease.

Mouse Ear

Mouse ear (little leaf) is caused by a deficiency of manganese. The leaflets are often reduced to a length of only 1 to 2 inches exclusive of the petiole or leaf stem, and have blunt lobed tips. A slightly affected leaflet may be normal in size, the only visible sign being the blunt point. This disease is of minor importance. It may occur near houses where lime has been dumped on the ground under a tree.

Control.—Spraying the trees with 1 or 2% manganese sulfate, or applying 2 to 4 lb of manganese sulfate to the soil around mature trees resulted in about 50% recovery in 2 years.

Spanish Moss

Spanish Moss (*Tillandsia usneoides* L.) occasionally becomes noxious to pecan trees, particularly in neglected orchards near swamps and especially where the trees are growing in proximity to live oak trees.

Control.—Moss can be partially controlled by spraying the trees with 10 lb of copper sulfate plus 2 lb of hydrated lime to 100 gal. of water. Spray in February while trees are dormant. The moss is rarely observed in regularly sprayed trees.

Lichens

Lichens are low forms of plant life that grow in humid shaded localities. A common form is the greyish-green paper-like moss that occurs on the bark of pecan trees.

Control.—Since lichens are not considered to be injurious to pecan trees, no spray program has been worked out for their control. However, most fungicides will readily control lichens.

Injuries Due To Climatic Conditions

Winter injury is easily recognized. The affected tree usually leafs out and grows normally in the spring, but the leaves wither and the tree suddenly dies, as soon as hot weather begins. By cutting through the bark, it is easy to detect the "sour-sap" and discolored wood.

Control.—Handle young trees with extreme care to prevent winter injury. Fertilize young trees only in early spring and do not cultivate later than midsummer. Trees handled this way will prevent late growth and the trees' wood will be in mature condition in late fall.

Sunscald

Sunscald is indicated by dead areas of bark on the southwest side of a tree, and may be confused with winter injury. It occurs mostly on young trees but also on older ones that have been cut back for top working to some other cultivar.

Control.—Head the young trees as close to the ground as possible. Do not prune off lower limbs for several years, as the limbs shade the trunk of the tree. Wrap the trunk of the tree with aluminum foil, old newspaper, or burlap bags, or whitewash the trunk with lime paint.

Lightning Injury

When a pecan tree is struck by lightning, the visible injury may consist of a narrow split in the bark extending from a branch in the top down the trunk to the ground, or the bark may be completely peeled from the trunk especially near the ground. There is a yellowing of the leaves and partial or complete defoliation may occur 30 to 60 days after the tree has been struck.

Control.—There is no practical control of lightning, but limbs which are killed should be pruned out and the wounds painted with pruning compound or coal tar creosote as recommended under *Wood Rot.*

Leaf Scorch

The general ailment called "leaf scorch" comprises more than one type of scorch, based on appearance and cause. Hardy *et al.* (1939) described it as "a condition in which necrotic (or dead) areas develop on the basal edges of the leaflets." As the disease advanced defoliation started. Gossard (1961) stated that leaf scorch is most frequently associated with very wet or very dry soil. Imbalance of minerals translocated to the leaves may very likely be involved at times, but this is probably associated with too much or too little soil moisture. Because leaf scorch occurs in the summer or early fall, the first effect to be observed is poor filling of nuts, and can cause a complete crop failure in the year following the one in which the scorch occurs.

Control.—Moderate shading by covering small trees with cheesecloth to reduce transpiration, moderate summer cultivation, mowing or grazing of sod orchards reduce water loss through grass and weeds. Irrigation is helpful under extremely dry conditions. Thinning of badly crowded trees is also helpful.

PECAN INSECTS[1]

Phillips, Large and Cole (1964), and Osburn *et al.* (1963) give detailed life histories of 23 insects and 12 diseases which infest pecan nuts and foliage. Their damage is especially severe in planted and top worked orchards of one or possibly more cultivars, than in native or seedling groves in which every tree is different. It is a waste of money to fertilize pecan trees and omit spraying for insects and disease control. Orchards of good cultivars such as Schley, Farley, Curtis, Stuart, or Desirable, will amply repay a complete cultural and spray program.

Hickory Shuckworm

The hickory shuckworm (*Laspeyresia caryana* Fitch), also called the pecan shuckworm, is one of the most serious insect pests of the pecan.

[1]The author wishes to thank Mr. Watson and Mr. Hamilton of Monticello Florida Nursery for this information.

TABLE 12.8

SPRAY GUIDE FOR SCAB-RESISTANT CULTIVARS

Check precautions and restrictions before using any chemical listed in this spray guide.

Spray Time of Application	Pest to Control	Spray Materials Per Acre For Medium-Sized Trees	Remarks
Prepollination Spray— when first buds begin to open	Leaf Casebearer Downy Spot	Malathion 25% WP 6 lb or Parathion 15% WP 4 lb plus either Cyprex 65% WP 2 lb or Benlate 50% WP 0.8 lb or Du-Ter 50% WP 0.8 lb	It is not necessary to add parathion or malathion to this spray in groves where the insect control program was followed the previous season if there is no current insect problem. If spittlebugs are a problem, apply 3 lb of 80% Sevin WP, 4 lb of 15% parathion WP, 2 lb of 50% Guthion WP, or 4 lb of Zolone 25% WP per acre when the leaves are half grown. Where downy spot has been a problem, apply Cyprex, Du-Ter, or Benlate when buds first break and again two weeks later.
First Cover Spray— When young "nuts" first appear but no more than 5 weeks after prepollination spray	Nut Casebearer Aphids Mites	Cyprex 65% WP 2 lb or Du-Ter 50% WP 0.8 lb or Benlate 50% WP 0.8 lb plus either Parathion 15% WP 4 lb or Zolone 25% WP 4 lb or Malathion 25% WP 6 lb	This insecticide application is very important, especially if the Prepollination Spray was not applied. Make a second application 1 week later if nut casebearer populations are heavy.

Spray	Pest/Disease	Material and Rate	Remarks
Second Cover Spray—4 to 5 weeks after First Cover Spray	Brown Leafspot Downy Spot	Du-Ter 50% WP 0.8 lb or Cyprex 65% WP 2 lb or Benlate 50% WP 0.8 lb	If aphids, mites or casebearers require control at this time, apply Zolone as recommended in the First Cover Spray or 2 pt of Systox 2 lb/gal. EC per acre. If a grove has a history of a high incidence of nut drop caused by hickory shuckworms before shell hardening, 2 lb of Guthion 50% WP, 2 pt of Torak 4 lb/gal. EC, 4 pt of Supracide 2 lb/gal. EC, or 4 lb of Zolone 25% WP per acre should be applied during the first week of July in light crop years.
Third Cover Spray—3 weeks after Second Cover Spray	Brown Leafspot Downy Spot	Cyprex 65% WP 2 lb or Du-Ter 50% WP 0.8 lb or Benlate 50% WP 0.8 lb	If excessive nut drop results from pecan weevil adult feeding punctures before pecan shells begin to harden, apply a pecan weevil spray at once. When possible, use ground sprayers. But, aircraft can be used if it is otherwise impossible to apply pecan weevil sprays every 7 days. Use at least 10 gal. of water per acre.
Pecan Weevil Sprays—every 7 days from the time that pecan shells begin to harden (about August 10–15) until mid-September and even later if adult weevils are still present	Pecan Weevils Shuckworms	Sevin 80% WP 3 lb or Torak 4 lb/gal. EC 2 pt	If pecan weevils are not a problem in your grove, you can control shuckworms by applying Guthion, 2 pt of Torak 4 lb/gal. EC, 4 pt of Supracide 2 lb/gal. EC, or 4 lb of Zolone 25% WP per acre. For shuckworm control, make the first of three applications when the pecan shells begin to harden. Applications should be made at two-week intervals. Systox, parathion or malathion can be used for black pecan aphid or mite control during this period. Aphid or mite populations often build up on trees where Sevin is used. If mites or aphids are a problem, apply 4 lb of 25% Zolone WP or 2 pt of Systox 2 lb/gal. EC per acre.

This insect also feeds on various species of hickory. The moths are very inconspicuous and rarely noticed in the orchard. Eggs are deposited on the young nuts or leaves. Upon hatching, the small larvae attack the green nuts and cause them to drop. After the shells harden, the larvae tunnel in the shucks, preventing the kernels from developing properly, and cause the shucks to stick to the shell. Full grown larvae pass the winter in shucks on the ground or in the tree.

Control.—A high percentage of larvae that winter in old pecan shucks may be killed by gathering and destroying the shucks at harvest. Plowing them under about March 1, after the larvae have pupated, also will help reduce shuckworm infestation during the summer. A grower with only a few trees should pick up the drops during midsummer and burn them. For control with spray materials, see spray schedule.

Pecan Nut Casebearer

The pecan nut casebearer (*Acrobasis carya* Grote.) is one of the most serious insect pests attacking pecans. Its damage is especially serious during seasons when trees set a light crop of nuts or on cultivars which generally are not heavy bearers.

These insects pass the winter as partly grown larvae in inconspicuous small cases, or hibernacula, which generally are found where the buds join the stem. The adults, or moths, emerge from the hibernacula from the latter part of April until about May 20. Peak emergence of this generation usually coincides fairly well with the setting of the nuts. The moths lay their tiny greenish-white eggs singly on either end of the nut. This generation causes the greatest damage to the pecan crop in May and June.

Soon after hatching the young larvae usually descend and feed for a short period on the buds just below the cluster of nuts. Then they crawl back up and attack the newly set nuts, usually entering them at the stem end. Infested nuts are easily recognized by the characteristic masses of borings, held together by fine silken threads cast out by the larvae. A single larvae of this generation may destroy several nuts or an entire cluster. Usually there are only three generations of this insect a year, although sometimes there is a partial fourth in Florida. Larvae of the third generation that do not complete their life cycle the first year and larvae of the fourth generation (if there is one) form the hibernacula or cases about the buds.

Control.—Since larvae of the first generation cause the most damage, apply the insecticidal spray when small nuts begin to appear. For chemicals to control this insect, see spray schedule in Table 12.7.

Pecan Weevil

Pecan weevils (*Curculio caryae* Horn.), both as adults and grubs, destroy nuts. Only the adults damage nuts before the shells harden. Nuts drop a few days after they feed by inserting their long snouts through the husk and unhardened shell. Damaged nuts can be recognized by a dark circle about ¼ in. in diameter, centered by a pin-sized puncture that extends through the husk and unhardened shell. This damage is usually not as extensive as that caused by legless grubs that hatch from eggs laid in the nuts after the shells harden. Grub infested nuts are not only useless, but are hard to separate from undamaged nuts.

Prior to shell-hardening, the presence of an insect larva in the nut indicates that damage was caused by another species of insect. Pecan weevil grubs are not normally found in nuts with unhardened shells.

Overwintering adults usually leave the soil and move to the tree between August 1 and September 15 and occasionally as early as mid-July or as late as mid-October, but do not begin laying eggs until the pecan shells harden. Grubs that hatch from these eggs feed on the kernels.

Between late September and late December and sometimes later, the grub cuts a circular hole about ⅛ in. in diameter through the shell and leaves the nut to enter the soil. It remains there for one or two winters before pupating during September or October. Adults emerge from the pupae in about three weeks, but stay in the soil until the following summer. The complete life cycle requires 2 or 3 years.

Late-maturing cultivars such as Success and Van Deman, usually are not attacked if nearby early-maturing cultivars, such as Stuart, Schley, Mahan, and Moneymaker, contain enough nuts to supply the weevils with adequate food and egg-laying sites.

Pecan trees growing in low areas or near hickory trees are more likely to be infested by pecan weevils. Adult pecan weevils apparently return to the tree in which they fed as grubs if that tree contains nuts. Certain trees in a grove may be heavily infested year after year whereas nearby trees, even of the same cultivar, may be almost weevil-free. When looking for pecan weevils or their damage, you should check trees that were infested during previous years.

Control.—The first pecan weevil control spray should be applied when the pecan shells begin to harden on your earliest cultivars or earlier if excessive nut drop results from adult feeding. Shells will usually harden first on nuts near the top of the tree. Sevin or Torak should be applied every seven days until mid-September and even later if adult pecan weevils are still found in the grove. Additional information on the pecan weevil and its control can be found in Georgia Cooperative Extension Leaflet No. 26, "Pecan Weevil."

The Southern Green Stink Bug

The southern green stink bug (*Nezara viridula* L), other stink bugs, and plant bugs produce the trouble known as "black pit." Punctured young nuts drop prematurely. After the shells harden the stink bug puncture produces a condition known as kernel spot, instead of black pit.

Control.—The most effective control measure is to eliminate or reduce populations of the bugs' host plants within and near the pecan grove.

Lush vegetation in and near the grove should be discouraged by close mowing or herbicides. A special effort should be made to eliminate favored wild hosts such as beggarweed, thistle, jimsonweed, and maypop. Soybeans and southern peas are preferred hosts and should not be planted near the pecan grove.

Spittle Bug

The spittle bug (*Clastoptera achatina* Germ.) produces froth-like material about the buds of young pecans which contain one or more immature insects. Adult spittle bugs, "frog hoppers," are found wandering around on shrubs and trees.

Control.—Apply Zolone, Parathion, Guthion, or Sevin when you notice spittlebug masses.

Insects Attacking the Foliage and Shoots

There are 20 insects which attack the foliage and shoots. The black pecan aphid (*Melanocallis caryaefoliage* Davis) causes more or less rectangular, bright yellow spots which appear on the leaflets around the feeding punctures during August and September. These turn brown and the little leaflets may drop prematurely, defoliating the tree.

Control.—Spray with regular insecticides. (See Table 12.7.)

Three Species of Yellow Aphids

The yellow hickory aphid (*Monellia caryella* Fitch, *M. nigropuncta* Granovsky) and the black margined aphid (*M. costalis* Fitch) attack pecan leaves, often occurring in large numbers on the underside of the leaflets. They do not cause any observable direct injury to the trees. However, they excrete large quantities of honeydew on the leaves, which supports the growth of a black fungus that disfigures the foliage and may reduce photosynthesis. This honeydew also supports the growth of scab spores.

Control.—Predacious insects, parasites and fungus diseases kill numerous aphids. They increase in dry warm weather but cold wet weather reduces their numbers. The insecticides used for black aphids will also control yellow aphids.

Mites

The mite (*Tetranychus hicoriae* McGregor) may cause serious injury to pecan foliage, and premature defoliation in many southern states. The leaflets first show a light brown discoloration along the midrib, where the mites start to feed; as the injury increases the leaflet looks as if it had been scorched by fire. Severely injured leaflets drop off and excessive early defoliation may occur.

Control.—Use Zolone or Systox as recommended in the spray schedule (Tables 12.7 and 12.8).

Fall Webworm

The larvae of the fall webworm (*Hyphantria cunea* Drury) form unsightly webs over the twigs and foliage. The adult moth is about 1 in. across when the wings are spread, usually pure white but sometimes with brown or black spots on the wings. The eggs are deposited in masses on the leaves and hatch in about one week. The larvae feed in colonies on the leaves within the web. The webworm has two broods a year. Moths of the first brood appear in April and May, the second during the middle of summer. The larvae of the second brood feed during summer and fall. The webworm passes the winter in the pupal stage in cocoons under loose rubbish on the ground or just below the surface of the soil.

Control.—Spray with parathion or Guthion. See spray schedule (Tables 12.7 and 12.8).

Walnut Caterpillar

The walnut caterpillar (*Datana integerrima* G.&R.) is a major pest some seasons. The moths from the over wintering pupae emerge from the ground from the middle of April to the middle of July. The eggs are laid in masses on the undersides of leaflets and hatch in about one week. The larvae feed in colonies, but do not form a web. The larvae crawl to the trunk and molt. After molting, they return to the upper limbs and continue feeding. When full grown they crawl down to the soil to pupate.

Control.—Use the same sprays as for fall webworms or the colonies may be removed from the trees and destroyed by crushing or burning.

Pape (1960) reported excellent control of this insect in Guadalupe Valley, Texas, by airplane applications of 1½ qt of malathion in 10 gal. per acre applied with a helicopter.

Leaf Miners

Osborn (1962) reported that leaf miners caused foliage injury to pecans in some areas of Louisiana and Texas. The work of at least one of these species of leaf miners feeding between the lower and upper surfaces of leaflets results in characteristic figures and designs. Heavy infestations of these insects may cause defoliation during the summer and fall.

Pecan Bud Moth

The pecan bud moth (*Gretchena bolliana* Sling) often causes considerable damage to nursery stock by feeding on and in the terminal buds and foliage, causing excessive branching and stunted growth. Phillips (1945) reported that the larvae occasionally defoliate large pecan trees, feed on the tips of, and bore into young twigs in the spring, and infest the shucks in the fall.

This insect passes the winter as a moth, which is grey with blackish-brown patches and about ⅔ in. across the extended wings. When the buds begin to open, the overwintered moths lay eggs on the twigs near the buds. Moths of later generations lay eggs on the leaves. There are probably five or six generations each season.

Control.—Young nursery trees should be kept in a vigorous growing condition by proper cultivation and fertilization. Rapidly growing trees withstand attacks of the bud moth better than slow growing ones. Spraying with 2 lb malathion 25% wettable powder per 100 gal. of water will control the bud moth. Phillips (1965) obtained excellent control with airplane application of parathion from a Micronair Rotary Atomizer.

Pecan Leaf Casebearer

The pecan leaf casebearer (*Acrobasis juglandis* LeB.) is also considered to be serious in Georgia and Florida. These insects overwinter as larvae in hybernacula near the buds. When the larvae emerge from their overwintering cases in early spring, they feed on the unfolding buds and leaves. Sometimes mature trees are kept in a semi-defoliated condition for three or four weeks. The small greyish brown moths appear from the middle of May to the first of August. There is only one generation a year. The moths deposit their eggs on the lower surface of the leaves along a vein or midrib. The young larvae that hatch from these eggs feed sparingly from the middle of May until November. On reaching maturity, the larvae are about ½ in. long, dark green, and have shiny dark brownish heads; they transform to pupae in a case. Late in August or early September, they leave their cases on the leaves and migrate to the buds, where they construct their winter cocoons.

Control.—Parathion or malathion in the first prepollination spray will control these pests if they are present.

Pecan Nursery Casebearer

Pecan nursery casebearer (*Acrobasis carvivorella* Ragonot) is found chiefly on pecan nursery stock. In northern Florida it causes considerable damage in nurseries. Like the other casebearers, these insects pass the winter as partly grown larvae in hibernacula. After feeding on the leaves, the larvae pupate in cocoons on the leaves folded up in the top of the young nursery trees. There are probably three or four generations in one season.

Control.—The same nursery practices and control measures recommended for the bud moth should control this casebearer.

Pecan Cigar Casebearer

Pecan cigar casebearer (*Coleophora caryaefoliella* Clem.), usually a minor pest, may become serious in some areas. This insect passes the winter as a larvae in a light brown case resembling a miniature cigar, attached to twigs and limbs. Larvae feed in the spring on buds and foliage. The adults develop about the middle of May and lay their eggs on the leaves. There are several generations during the season.

Control.—Same as for the casebearer or leaf casebearer.

Phyloxera

Two pecan phyloxera, *Phyloxera devastatrix* Perg. and the leaf phyloxera *P. notabilis* Perg., are closely related to aphids; they cause conspicuous swellings or galls on leaves, shoots or nuts. They are more serious west of the Mississippi River. The insects pass the winter as eggs on the branches. The young appear as the buds unfold. They insert their beaks in the new growth and a gall forms which soon covers the insect. The insect matures within the gall, lays a large number of eggs; then dies. The young insects develop into winged adults and emerge from the split gall in May or June.

Control.—Spray trees thoroughly, when buds are beginning to burst, with 1⅔ qt of 1 lb/gal. BHC EC or 1 qt of 20% Lindane EC/100 gal.

The caterpillar *Datana integerruna* G.&R. is a major pest some seasons. The moth from the overwintered pupae emerge from the ground, from the middle of April to the middle of July. The eggs are laid in masses on the underside of leaflets and hatch in about a week. The larvae feed in colonies but do not form a web. The larvae crawl to the trunk of the tree and molt. After molting, they return to the upper limbs and continue feeding. When full grown, they crawl down to the soil and propupate.

Control.—The sprays used for fall webworm will control this pest or the colonies may be removed from the trees and destroyed by crushing or burning.

Pecan Catocala

The pecan catocala (*Catocala maestosa* Hist.), when abundant, may strip the leaves until only the petioles and stems remain. The caterpillar is dark grey and grows to be 3 in. in length. They hide under the bark during the daytime, and overwinter as eggs under the bark scales. The eggs hatch in the spring and the caterpillars feed on the foliage during spring and early summer. The moths appear as early as the last of June and continue to emerge until fall.

Control.—Insecticides applied for control of nut casebearer or the leaf casebearer will control the caterpillars of the pecan catocala.

May Beetle

May beetles or June bugs (*Phyllophaga spp.* and *Anomala spp.*) are leaf feeding insects that may cause serious defoliation of young pecan trees in early spring. The beetles feed at night; in the daytime they hide just beneath the soil surface. They lay eggs in the soil and the larvae, white grubs, feed on the roots of grasses and other plants.

Control.—Sevin sprays will control this pest.

Hickory Horned Devil

The hickory horned devil (*Citheronia regalis* F.) is a very minor pest. This large caterpillar can be recognized by the large spiny horns with which it is armed. It is the larvae of the regal moth. It can be controlled by picking from the plant, or spraying with parathion.

Hickory Shoot Curculio

The hickory shoot curculio (*Conotrachelus aratus* Germ.) attacks young pecan trees in the nursery and bearing trees. The larvae tunnel within the shoots and leaf stems. Growers have reported heavy damage to nut bearing shoots on pecan trees, resulting in a reduction in the nut crop.

Control.—BHC and Lindane have been effective against the hickory shoot curculio when applied as the buds are beginning to burst.

INSECTS INJURING THE TRUNK AND BRANCHES

Twig Girdler

The twig girdler (*Oncideres cingulata* Say) cuts off the twigs during the late summer and fall. It attacks nursery trees and mature trees in the orchard. Adult beetles appear in pecan orchards the latter part of August. Twigs are girdled to provide food for the larvae. The eggs are deposited in the severed portion of the twig. They hatch in about three weeks but grow very little during fall and winter. The larvae complete their transformation to adult beetles in the twigs by the last of August.

Control.—Pick up and destroy fallen twigs. This insect is usually not a problem in sprayed groves.

Obscure Scale

Obscure scale (*Chrysomphalus obscurus*) is a serious pest of pecans in Texas, Arkansas and Mississippi. It may occur in other parts of the pecan belt. The scale is dark grey, the color of the bark, so that the insect is difficult to detect until it becomes abundant. This insect sucks the sap from plant tissues. The greatest injury comes from the gradual killing of branches less than 3 in. in diameter. There is only one generation a year. The young, or crawlers, are present from the middle of May until early in August. Soon after they hatch, the crawlers settle on the bark, insert their beaks and begin to form their waxy coverings. Only the adult males are able to move around, but females remain under the waxy covering.

Control.—Spray infected trees thoroughly with a dormant oil emulsion before the buds begin to swell, in January or February. Commercial oil emulsions have directions for use on the container.

Flat-Headed Apple Tree Borer

Flat-headed apple tree borers (*Chrysobothris femorata* Oliv.) and shot hole borers (*Xylobiops basilaris* Say) attack pecan trees that are in a weakened condition. Apple tree borers are creamy white with a greatly enlarged flattened head. They bore tunnels beneath the bark in the cambium layer. These borers prefer unhealthy, dying or dead trees.

Control.—Remove borers with a knife. Paint exposed woody parts with pruning compound or a mixture of one part creosote and three parts coal tar. Keep tree fertilized and in a thrifty growing condition.

Termites

Termites (*Reticulitermes flavipes* Kollar), woodlice or white ants, live in dead wood. Pecan nursery stock and small trees are sometimes killed by termites feeding in the roots. They frequently feed on wood stakes for young trees.

Control.—Do not use recently cleared land for a pecan nursery or orchard. Remove all dead wood and stumps. Only termite-resistant wood or wood treated with creosote should be used near newly planted trees.

PECAN ORCHARD ANIMAL PESTS

There are several animal pests that may inflict losses in a pecan orchard. Control is necessary in most orchards and consists of killing or repelling.

Carlton (1975) reported that the greatest damage is caused by crows, bluejays and squirrels, with some damage done by deer, raccoon and rats. The crow eats approximately 1 oz of food per day (about 6% of its weight). If pecans yield 50% meat, a crow may eat 2 oz per day. The crow also pecks, contaminates and carries off an equal amount for a total loss of 8 oz.

A bluejay may eat, waste and lose about half as much as a squirrel, or about 12 oz per month. A squirrel will eat about 24 oz per week, and waste and bury another 2 lb, or 14 lbs during a harvest season.

All three predators take pecans from the tree or ground. They begin when the kernel forms and continue for a month, or until harvest is complete.

Crows

"Crow shoots" have been publicized as a means of reducing crow population. Killing crows with a shotgun or rifle is time-consuming and expensive. Firearms both kill and repel crows and thus reduce the damage. Crows prefer small, well-filled, thin-shelled nuts, and are therefore much worse in some orchards than others.

Automatic (scare-away machine) explosion devices are the most economical and efficient means of controlling crows. One of these is the acetylene gas machine which uses inexpensive calcium carbide to create frequent blasts similar to those made by a 12-gage shotgun. This "mechanical scarecrow" is a valuable repellent for each 20 acres of trees.

This is a portable unit that produces gun-like noises as fast as once every 10 sec or as slow as once every 10 min. There are approximately 5000 shots in 130 cu ft of acetylene gas. While the shots may be heard for a half mile, the effective range is much shorter. Normal speed is 20 detonations per hour, and the unit should be serviced daily. Suggestions for operation of scare-away are: (1) start scare-away early in the morning before the birds reach the field and settle down; (2) mount scare-away above the growing crop on a stand so the sound will not be obstructed or retarded by the growing crop; (3) change the location of the scare-away in the field at least every two days so the crows will not become accustomed to one location; (4) clean the carbide container daily with clean water; (5) thoroughly lubricate all moving parts daily; (6) use only 1¼ X⅜ in. nut carbide; and (7) check flint daily and add water as needed.

Crows may ignore the blasting device if it is employed for too long a time. It is well to kill a few crows with a shotgun occasionally so that shooting and killing will be associated. When well regulated, shooting will repel more than 90% of the crows. When a blast occurs the crows leave their perch and fly about in bewilderment. By the time they alight again, another blast occurs to start the cycle over again. Crow may change their route to avoid proximity of the blasts.

The "rope firecracker" repels crows by the same principle as the acetylene blast machine. This is a piece of 5/16 in. cotton rope, into the strands of which fuses of "cherry bomb" or "salute" firecrackers are inserted. The rope is suspended by one end from a tree or tall pole and the other is ignited. As the slow burning of the rope continues, the firecrackers explode. The effectiveness is the same as the acetylene gun but is more expensive. Both are sanctioned by the U.S. Fish and Wildlife Service.

Poisoned grain may be used to kill crows but is dangerous, and all precautions must be taken to prevent injury to oneself, other persons, pets and beneficial wildlife. The local game warden should be consulted before using poison bait. One formula is:

Mito maize	100 lb
Strychnine alkaloid	10 oz
Oil lecithin	10 oz
Borax	5 oz

Screen the borax to remove lumps, and mix with grain for 5 min. Mix strychnine and oil together, and then mix with the grain. All materials should be mixed for 30 min. Feed crows unpoisoned malo maze in large shallow pans for several days. Then overnight substitute the poisoned bait. Bury all uneaten poisoned bait.

Tree Squirrels

These may be very damaging if they are allowed to nest in hardwood trees near pecan orchards. Killing tree squirrels with firearms is one means of control where firearms are permitted and there is no danger to persons or property.

Trapping is often used in controlling squirrels. Wire or fasten securely No. 0 or No. 1 steel traps to the trunks of pecan trees, and bait with pecan meats or peanut butter. Live traps may be made or bought and set near pecan trees. Bait with corn or peanut butter. Poisoning may kill some squirrels, but it is less effective than either shooting or trapping.

Rodents

Ground squirrels, rats and mice are troublesome in pecan orchards if there is mulch for them to raise the young. Poisoning is the best control. A poison bait may be made as follows:

Steamed-rolled oats	98 lb
Amber petroleum jelly	10 oz
Mineral oil	10 oz
Zinc phosphide	1 lb

Warm the mineral oil and the petroleum jelly together until they are fluid but not hot. Add the zinc phosphide and stir briskly. Mix all ingredients thoroughly and sack immediately. Place 1 tsp in each mouse or rat runway or at the entrance of burrows. Regular warfarin rat poison may be used also (Kennemar 1959).

Jay Birds

Blue Jays carry off or eat on the spot hundreds of pounds of small, thin-shelled pecans. Control is the same as for crows.

Predators

From a survey of peach growers in Georgia, done by the Cooperative Extension Service, it was estimated that 10,000,000 lb of pecans would be lost to crows, squirrels, black birds and jay birds in Georgia annually. Estimated losses by a few growers were: "25,000 lb of Mahans and Schleys in a 425-acre orchard," "15,000 lb of Schleys lost in one orchard," "3,000 lb (half of the crop) of Frotchers in a 50-acre orchard," "an estimated 3,000 lb crop reduced to 300 lb," "10,000 lb (half of the crop) in a 350-acre orchard." One grower reported killing 425 squirrels in one year in a 100-acre orchard; others reported killing thousands of black birds and jay birds by poisoning. Seedlings were most severely attacked by predators because of the small size and thin shells. Cultivars worst attacked were Schley, Curtis, Moore, Alley and San Saba.

Predators attack pecan orchards early, and seriously damage the crop several weeks before the nuts are normally harvested. Each nut is picked from the tree as the hull cracks; in this way the choice nuts are taken first.

HARVESTING, DRYING AND GRADING PECANS

The time-honored method of gathering pecans has been to allow them to fall to the ground naturally, which was necessary with very large and tall trees; or to thrash the nuts from the trees with bamboo poles and to pick them from the ground by hand. This method results in high quality pecans but is slow, tedious, and expensive.

This is still the practice with home orchards, or with scattered trees where mechanical harvesting is not feasible. Hand shaking and gathering are practiced when an abundance of labor, mostly children, is available; or when trees of different cultivars are mixed in the orchard.

Harvesting, accumulating and marketing generally take place during October in the southernmost part of the pecan belt and extend well into February and March the following year. No matter where they are grown, pecans can be classified into seedlings and improved cultivars. The seedlings, or wild pecans, grow unattended in the pecan belt west of the Mississippi River. For the most part, they receive little care other than the cutting out of "weed" or undesirable trees. Therefore, whether the crop is large or small depends largely on the elements, and the size of the crop is unpredictable. Seedling pecans are smaller than the improved cultivars, but their flavor, sturdiness and full firm meat make them especially adapted, either in halves or pieces, for the confectioner, baker or ice cream maker.

Many orchards are managed in such a way that conversion to mechanical harvesting will be no problem. Mechanical harvesting consists of three operations. First, the trees are shaken after the nuts have ripened to the extent that all of the hulls have split. This may be a once-over or twice-over operation, depending on the cultivar. Second, the nuts are picked up directly or are swept into windrows. In either case a firm soil surface is very important. Third, the nuts are cleaned of sticks, clods, leaves and other trash in preparation for drying and grading for market. For a small producer, picking over the nuts on hardware cloth is satisfactory. Large quantities of nuts are cleaned by a series of blowers and screens.

In many cases mechanical equipment is so fast that a single shaker, picker or cleaner should meet the needs of several growers. The grower has a choice that ranges from a small "walk behind" harvester capable of harvesting about 1 acre per day, to large self-propelled machines that harvest 5 or more acres per day. With clean culture the soil should be leveled, cleaned, and firmed for harvest; with sod culture the soil should be firmed and the sod close-cut (Gammon 1976).

The Food Machinery Corporation has developed a new tree shaker for nut trees. The head features a scissor which clamps up to 26-in. trunks, is adjustable and has a long life. Shaker sprockets are positive driven by heavy duty chain. A dry-type air cleaner with precleaner is standard equipment (Anon. 1976). The percentage of the crop "stolen" is much higher in years of short crop (when the price is higher) as in 1966. Sometimes every nut on a tree is taken by predators in years of a short crop. Thus pecans in many areas of Georgia become borderline between a cash crop and wildlife feed.

MECHANICAL HARVESTING

An improvement was made when mechanical tree shakers, operated with tractor power, were introduced about 1950. With these, some growers used large sheets to spread under the trees to catch the pecans. Under favorable conditions these sheets enable the growers to harvest pecans in less time and at less cost. The sheets collected not only the good nuts but "pops," leaves, dead twigs and hulls as well. Special effort was needed not only to separate the good nuts from the trash, but to move the large sheets. Besides, many of the nuts often fell beyond the sheets.

Tree Shakers

There are several types of tree shakers. The most common shaker for pecans is shown in Fig. 12.10. The aluminum boom remains stationary while power is transmitted through a cable. This makes possible easily operated up and down control as well as "automatic shaking." Shaking action begins when the shaker boom is placed in contact with a tree or limb. On tractors where live power is not available the automatic feature does not come into effect.

This one-man shaker will shake limbs or trunks up to approximately 18 in. in diameter. Features are: (1) boom remains stationary while tree is shaking (lift cable will not be slackened); (2) two position (27 ft and 33½ ft) telescoping boom; (3) low maintenance, simple construction without hydraulic parts; (4) complete up and down easily operated boom control; (5) can be mounted on all except very small tractors; (6) boom may be raised and lowered while machine is stationary without shifting to neutral gear; (7) shaking starts automatically when boom is placed in contact with tree.

Courtesy of Phelps Mfg. Co.

FIG. 12.10.   TREE SHAKER FOR PECANS

Each large limb is shaken separately.

A second type of tree shaker is shown in Figs. 15.3, 15.4 and 15.5. There are two shaker heads, one for medium size and another for very large trees. "Bean bag" cushions are provided in the jaws of the "vibra shock" shaker for small trees or trees with tender bark. This type shaker is suitable for native pecan trees which may have very high branches and large trunks.

A third type of tree shaker is the helicopter (Fig. 12.7). In very large plantings the same unit can be used for low-volume spraying and for harvesting. One of the first demonstrations of harvesting pecans by helicopter was in Albany, Georgia, October 10, 1956, as a part of 100% mechanical harvesting. Pecans were blown from trees by air swirling into the trees at the rate of 70 mph. Only a few nuts on the lower limbs remained on the trees. Successful harvesting by helicopter was possible only after all of the nuts on the trees were mature.

After the nuts are blown to the ground, harvesting machines work the same as if the nuts were removed by shakers. The most common method is to suck up the nuts, separate the trash, and deposit the nuts into trailers that are pulled along behind.

Sweep-Type Harvesters

Since about 1945, nut growers and equipment manufacturers have concentrated efforts on development of completely mechanical harvesters.

The Ramacher Manufacturing Company, Linden, California, was founded in 1946 to provide mechanization for the back-breaking job of harvesting nuts. Its first five years were spent entirely in experimental work, but from this solid foundation came two machines and the first production models were introduced in 1951. Within 15 years, 750 machines were put into use.

This company manufactures two self-propelled machines. The first is a side-delivery nut sweeper, employing a short-coupled reel fitted with two

Courtesy of Ramacher Mfg Co.,

FIG. 12.11. THE RAMACHER HARVESTER NO. 348
OPERATING IN HEAVY LEAVES
This unit can handle with ease all of the problems involved in handling pecans, almonds, filberts and macadamia nuts.

sets of spiral mounted rubber sweeps to move the fallen nuts into neat windrows without digging into the prepared soil.

The second is an ingenious machine which gets the crop off the ground in two steps. The first step is accomplished by four rows of tough rubber flippers which gather the nuts from holes and depressions; the second step is accomplished by four rows of steel rakes (or combs) which scoop off the top of this constantly forming windrow, and transfer the nuts to a conveyor. The picking unit glides on shoes which closely follow the ground contour and permit instant lever control of the height of the picking reel (Anon. 1965).

Courtesy of Ramacher Mfg. Co.

FIG. 12.12. SWEEPER THAT HANDLES WITH EASE
THE WINDROWING OF PECANS, ALMONDS, FILBERTS,
WALNUTS AND MACADAMIA NUTS
This type of machine sweeps a 10-meter swath away from the tree row and at the same time blows the nuts away from the tree trunk into the next row.

The machines are assigned to work with walnuts, almonds, pecans, tiny nuts and others where the ground can be suitably prepared, and the nuts can be removed from the tree for a single harvest.

Vacuum–Type Pecan Harvester

The Phelps Harvester was developed in 1954 and has been successfully used for harvesting pecans since then. The suction of a powerful blower (mounted at the front of the tractor) picks up all loose material from the ground including pecans, hulls, leaves, twigs and sticks. A tank separator removes the pecans and heavier material from the air allowing leaves and other light materials to be pulverized as they pass out through the fan. The cleaning system removes most of the remaining sticks from the pecans and deposits the pecans in a trailer drawn behind the tractor. Even when pecans are scattered this harvester picks up an average of 1000 lb per hour.

In addition to harvesting this machine has the following advantages: (1) it gets pecans which hand pickers frequently miss; (2) leaves fewer pecans on the ground, thus reducing the problem of unwanted pecan sprouts; (3) pulverizes the leaves which reduces their ability to support tree diseases; and (4) pecans can be harvested rapidly and reduce "weathering" on the ground.

Courtesy of Phelps Fan Mfg. Co.

FIG. 12.13. PECAN HARVESTER

After being shaken from the trees the nuts (and leaves) are sucked from the ground. The trash is separated and the pecans are collected in the trailer.

Short-cut, permanent grass presents the best condition for vacuum pecan harvesting. In general, when the ground is solid so that the wheels which support and regulate the suction nozzle do not tend to sink into soft soil or sand, the harvester works best. In orchards where the land is

Courtesy of Phelps Fan Mfg. Co.

FIG. 12.14. FRONT VIEW OF NUT VACUUM-TYPE HARVESTER
IN PECAN ORCHARD

Three men are required to operate it continuously—one to
drive tractor, one to keep the harvester, and another to go
ahead and remove large rocks and sticks.

cultivated, ground conditions are not likely to be favorable for air vacuum harvesting. Often small clods are created which enter the machine's air stream and collect with the pecans. Also, cultivated sandy soil without grass allows the equipment to pick up dirt.

Dry weather is an important necessity for mechanical harvesting. The harvester will not function properly in wet weather. Cattle must be removed well before harvesting in order to give manure time to cake and dry.

During the first year of suction harvesting in an orchard, there is likely to be a considerable amount of "old wood" picked up with the pecans. There should be less of this in subsequent years.

While the land does not need to be flat, land smoothing is necessary. The smoothing operation consists of discing once, spike tooth harrowing and finally dragging the land, prior to planting grass. Irrigated land is suitable for mechanical harvesting of pecans.

Much experimental work is under way, both by state and federal experiment stations and by industry, to improve mechanical nut harvesters. They are still too expensive for small orchardists. There is need for a fairly light, compact harvester that picks up the nuts, with some trash, and loads them on light trucks that carry them to a nearby station for cleaning and grading the nuts.

FARM CLEANING PECANS

Small lots of farmers' stock pecans are picked up by hand and graded at the same time. In this case, removal of pops and shrivels and sizing is done at the collecting point. Many farmers harvest from 1000 to 50,000 lb of pecans by machine which should be cleaned and graded immediately. A typical operation where a mechanical harvester is used is to have the nuts come to processing equipment in bulk. The nuts may be processed directly from the harvester trailer or they may be held temporarily in holding bins.

In either case, a flight type elevator might be used. It should provide at least ¾ in. clearance between the end of the cleat and the side of the elevator trough to prevent crushing of the nuts. Most bucket type or augers are not satisfactory for nuts.

Stick Remover

The first cleaning operation is to remove the sticks with a "rodding" machine. This is a cylindrical cage with spaced rods for the outside and placed in a horizontal position. One end is slightly higher than the other. As the cage rotates, sticks are picked up by finger bars and dropped on a separate outlet from the pecans. Dirt and most leaves also fall through the rods.

Courtesy of (Davebilt) Clarance Davidson Co.

FIG. 12.15. "BLOWER" TO PILE PECAN (OR ALMOND, FILBERT, WALNUT) LEAVES SO THAT NUTS CAN BE GATHERED BY "PICKER" SHOWN BELOW

Pop and Shrivel Remover

The nuts go from the rodding machine onto an open chain link belt, and pass under an air vacuum nozzle, where the light nuts (pops) and any remaining leaves are removed. Vacuum is controlled by adjusting the height of the nozzle above the belt. Adjustments of the nozzle may be necessary when the cultivar of nuts being processed is changed.

A second vacuum nozzle may be used just past the first to remove the shrivels which have limited commercial value. Both vacuums may be operated from the same fan but separate collection for material removed must be provided.

Courtesy of (Davebilt) Clarance Davidson Co.

FIG. 12.16. "PICKER" FOR HARVESTING NUTS FROM THE GROUND FOLLOWING REMOVAL OF LEAVES BY "BLOWER" SHOWN ABOVE

Grading Table

Unhulled and broken nuts need to be removed prior to sizing. This is a hand operation performed by passing the nuts over a second flexible steel belt in front of the workers.

Sizing Machine

Nuts should now be sized. Some equipment will separate the nuts into three sizes—small, medium, and large. Larger equipment will separate the nuts in up to six sizes usually from $^{10}/_{16}$ in. to $^{15}/_{16}$ in. in $^{1}/_{16}$ in. increments. However, no equipment is available for separation according to cultivar.

POSTHARVEST CHANGES IN PECANS

The first changes that occur in pecans after harvest result in improvement of quality by curing; later changes result in degrading the quality by staling, discoloration and rancidification. Postharvest changes include: (1) decrease of moisture in the kernel volume by about 10%; (2) increase in peroxide values from 0 to 1.5 mM of oxygen per kg of oil, increase in free fatty acid values from 0 to 0.5% as oleic acid; (3) oxidation of tannins in the seed coat, causing a change in color from pale to medium tan; and (4) development of characteristics of pecan appearance, aroma, flavor and texture, resulting in optimum eating qualities.

Changes during curing differ among cultivars and at different temperatures and moisture levels, most of which enhance the marketability and eating qualities. However, when allowed to continue at room temperature for more than about three weeks, at 37.8°C (100°F) for more than one week, or at 10°C (50°F) for more than three months, there is a gradual development of staleness and rancidity in the nuts (Woodroof and Heaton 1961).

Optimum flavor develops in pecans when held under farmhouse conditions for about three weeks after harvest. After this time, storage at 4.4°C (40°F) or lower with 70 to 80% RH is necessary to hold the fresh color, aroma and flavor to more than three months.

Freshly harvested pecans are sensitive to moisture. The first evidence of this is in the orchard where pecans are subject to weathering, infection with mold, splitting and occasional sprouting. Pecans gathered as they fall from the trees are practically free of molds; whereas those which remain on the damp ground for a week or more are high in moisture and usually contain a high percentage of discolored and moldy kernels. (See Figs. 3.1 and 3.2.)

Pecan Kernel Color

The color of pecan kernels is considered to be a primary factor in ascertaining general nut quality. The importance of kernel color as a quality measure is due less to its effect on aesthetic appeal than to the general association between dark kernel color and rancidity. A number of pre- and postharvest factors can alter kernel color without necessarily decreasing other quality attributes.

Kernel color can be measured either subjectively or objectively for the separation of bulk samples of pecans into the various USDA color classes (light, light amber, amber, dark amber). Subjective or visual grading is typically done with small volumes by individuals on sorting lines. It is also used to complement electronic sorting. Objective techniques rely on electronic measurement of color through the reflectance or transmittance of the sample. The latter technique is used extensively now by the major pecan processors.

Time of harvest in relation to the physiological development of the kernel is also of critical importance with regard to kernel color. Early harvest, prior to normal development of pigmentation, often results in abnormally light or cream-colored kernels. Conversely, late harvest often produces dark kernels which decrease the product's color grade. The effect of late harvest appears to vary with season. It is especially critical during seasons with prolonged periods of rainy, humid weather during harvest.

Removal of excess kernel moisture to approximately 3.5 to 4.0% as readily as possible after harvest is of primary importance in the maintenance of optimum color. Storage of nuts in gas atmospheres with high moisture levels can result in a re-equilibration of the kernel moisture content leading to an acceleration of kernel darkening. It is important, therefore, to maintain the kernel moisture level at 3.5 to 4.0% throughout the storage period.

Storage of pecans at low temperatures greatly minimizes undesirable color and quality changes. Generally the lower the storage temperature, the greater the storage life of the nut. Temperatures above 4.4°C (40°F) result in rapid discoloration of the kernels, while temperatures of -6.7°C (20°F) or lower allow storage for several years.

Exposure to ammonia gas represents, for pecan processors, one of the most rapid and dramatic changes in color quality encountered. Within minutes shelled nuts may be transformed from a state of optimum color to a black unmarketable product. The degree of discoloration varies with the percentage moisture of the kernel, concentration of the gas, length of exposure, temperature and age of the nut. The adverse color change is isolated in the testa (outer skin) of the kernel, with the interior portion remaining normal. While the flavor of the exposed pecans is seldom adversely affected, the unattractiveness of the kernel renders it an unmarketable product. The frequency of occurrence of ammonia damage to pecans has decreased with the general shift away from ammonia as a cold storage refrigerant.

Exposure of shelled nuts to light, especially in the red wavelength of the visible spectrum, is detrimental to kernel color. Storage of pecan kernels in red cellophane containers results in higher color quality ratings after 15 weeks exposure to fluorescent light than does storage in clear, amber or green containers. Natural light is more detrimental than fluorescent lighting, with the rate of unfavorable color change increasing with increasing transmittance of the storage container. Also, a major contributor to the development of discoloration during storage is oxygen. The detrimental effect of oxygen is concentration and temperature dependent.

Prompt harvest and drying result in optimum kernel color. Changes that occur in these pigments after this period will depend on time and on the way the nuts are handled.

A group of pigments responsible for darkening of the testa during storage are pH sensitive. Under basic conditions, for example, exposure to ammonia gas, these pigments alter to a black form. Under acidic conditions they are bright yellow. Acidification of kernels prior to, after, and both before and after storage has established that this group is in part responsible for the normal darkening during storage.

Early frost, a common problem in the northern areas of the pecan belt, presents another distinct discoloration problem. The intensely dark pigmentation produced is quite bitter and appears to be chemically related to the phenols. The pigments are substantially soluble in water and are located in the testa of the kernel (Kays and Wilson 1976).

Kays and Wilson (1977) reported that the color of pecan meats can be significantly altered by treating with dilute solutions of acids or darkened with alkalis. Phosphoric acid was most effective in producing a substantial color change without a detectable effect on the flavor of the kernels. Treatments with citric acid or sulfur dioxide resulted in substantial change in both color and flavor. Hydrochloric acid also modified the flavor. It was deemed possible to raise pecan meats from one USDA grade to a higher grade by acidification, resulting in substantial increase in the product market value. Prior to acidification the pecan kernels were soaked in water for 30 min to raise the moisture content. Treatments were for 30 min at room temperature.

The effectiveness of the treatment depended upon the cultivar, degree of hydration of the kernels, age of the nutmeats, and nature of the pigments. Meats of some cultivars were found to be more sensitive to color alterations than others; the more moisture in the kernels the more sensitive they were to color change by altering the pH; acidification altered only the pH sensitive group(s) of pigments which comprise only a portion of the kernel's entire complement of pigments; colors associated with rancidity, staleness, or old age were not beneficially altered by change in pH; nor were nutmeats blackened by ammonia made more marketable by acidification.

The red-brown discoloration in the testa of pecan (*Carya illinoensis* [Wang] K. Koch) kernels appears to be caused by the oxidation of endogenous leucocyanidin and leucodelphinidin to phlobaphenes and to their respective anthocyanidin derivatives, cyanidin and delphinidin. Oxidation was progressive in kernels of the Stuart and Schley cultivars during storage for 16 weeks at 32°C (90°F) and 50% RH. Leucoanthocyanidin contents differed significantly between the two cultivars, but the rates of transformation did not differ. Correlations between weekly increases in the quantities of anthocyanidins or phlobaphenes and peroxides formed in the oils were low; therefore, neither type pigment would be useful as an index of kernel quality. Peroxide values and Hunter values, which indicate both red and yellow colorations of the kernels, correlated reasonably well. Thus, color measurement may enable the nondestructive evaluation of pecan kernel quality. The levels of phenolic compounds in the two cultivars of pecans analyzed differed significantly and appeared to affect the storage stabilities of the two cultivars (Center et al. 1977).

Experiments showed a direct relation between the time pecans laid on wet soil, the moisture content and molding of the kernels. Molding increased from 2 to 26% due to lying on the ground 3 days where a small amount of chicken manure had been spread, and from 44 to 66% due to 6 days exposure. Thus, nuts that fall on the ground in pastures are more likely to mold than those which fall on practically sterile soil (Woodroof and Heaton 1958).

Furthermore, pecans which lie on wet soil for an extended period or until they become fully wet, turn amber color slowly while in the shell and discolor immediately after shelling. This is due to absorption of soluble tannins from the hulls, or packing tissue of the shells, by the kernels. This discoloration is retarded by refrigeration but is resumed upon removal from refrigeration. When shelled and exposed to air at room temperature, the meats darken within a few minutes. Discoloration due to weathering affects the appearance and grade of the meats more than the flavor. Unless such nuts are dried promptly they mold or develop bitter pit. Schley and other thin shell cultivars are especially subject to post-harvest discoloration, if allowed to weather before storage.

On the other hand, pecans which were harvested without weathering or "moisture pick-up" neither discolored nor molded while in common storage through the winter, or at -17.8°C (0°F) for more than five years. There was also no change in color upon removal from 1.1°C (34°F) or -17.8°C (0°F) storage for shelling. These nuts had a bright tan color, crunchy texture, and very desirable flavor.

DRYING PECANS

Pecans need to be dried to a kernel moisture level of about 4.5% as soon as practical after harvesting. This is to prevent molding, discoloration, and breakdown of the oil. Drying is necessary also to properly shrink the kernels and prevent "stick-tight" shells during subsequent shelling. Controlling moisture is the most important factor in harvesting, storing or processing pecans, even for as short a time as one week.

Moisture Content

The first problem of harvesting is removal of sap moisture from the nuts to prevent molding and discoloration. Under fair weather conditions this moisture in the pecan kernel drops gradually from about 30 to 8% as the nuts mature on the trees and normally dehisce. Drying is accelerated as the nuts lay on dry soil or leaves, or are held for two to four weeks in dry storage. Under these conditions moisture content of the meats equalizes at about 4½% and that of the entire nuts at about 8.5 to 9%. It is also under these conditions that optimum color and maximum flavor develop.

Removal of sap moisture is first from the outershell, followed in order by removal from the inner shell, the middle partition and finally the kernel. Tests have shown that the most satisfactory color, texture, stability and flavor result when pecans are dried "naturally"—that is, by constant movement of dry air around the nuts for at least three days. Artificial or rapid drying methods with heat should not be used for normal drying of pecans which have not been rewet.

FIG. 12.17. PECANS THAT GERMINATED (SPLIT) WHILE ON THE TREE DURING WET WEATHER

They usually mold at the apex.

Should removal of sap moisture be interrupted by prolonged rain while the nuts are on the trees, molding, rotting or sprouting may occur. Splitting of shells or sprouting on the trees results in rupturing the seed coats and discoloration of the kernels, and if allowed to continue for a week or more, will destroy the sale value of the nuts.

Schley and other thin shell cultivars are especially subject to cracking or

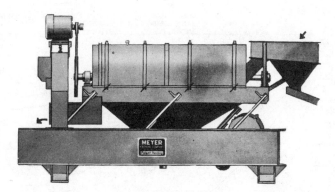

Courtesy of Meyer Machine Co.

FIG. 12.18. CONTINUOUS NUTMEAT MOISTURE EXTRACTOR

The unit is 4 ft high and about 8 ft long. Wet nuts enter on left
and are discharged at right, with moisture drain at the bottom.
It is a production line unit that dries nutmeats in minutes.

sprouting on the trees. They are also the cultivars that do not dehisce
readily. When prolonged rain occurs during the ripening period, these
should be harvested quickly and dried as rapidly as practical.

Rewetting, after the sap moisture has been reduced to about 5%, is
probably the cause of more discoloration, molding, rotting, souring and
otherwise degrading of pecans than of all other conditions combined.
This may occur from rain, prolonged high humidity before harvesting,
lying on wet soil, or from storing in air more than 70% RH.

Rewetting interrupts the normal drying process. The outer shell is the
first to be rewet and this becomes darker. The inner shell is the next
layer to become brown due to solubility of tannins. The tannins stain the
seed coat and kernels and impart a bitter flavor.

To prevent the growth of microorganisms rewet pecans must be dried
or refrigerated within a week. Rapidly circulated low moisture air, at
room temperature, is recommended for drying the surface and outer shell
of rewet pecans. The moisture from the kernels then migrates to the
surface and evaporates. A safe moisture equilibrium is then attained
after 24 hours. To accomplish this the nuts should be placed on racks at a
depth of not more than 2 in. and dried. The air should be warmed,
recirculated and dried, or partially replaced with outside air.

Drying in rapidly circulated, low moisture air at refrigerated temperatures is also recommended. This is what occurs in a refrigerated
warehouse when air of 65% RH or lower is circulated by unit coolers.
The pecans are improved by lowering the moisture content. The quality

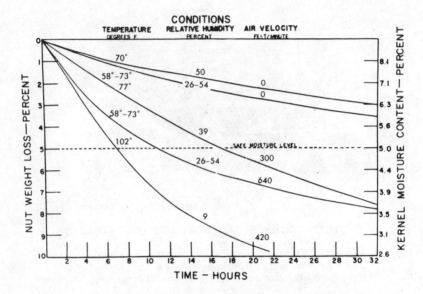

FIG. 12.19.   THE RELATION OF LOSS IN WEIGHT OF
UNSHELLED PECANS, AND CHANGE IN MOISTURE CONTENT
OF THE KERNELS, TO TIME OF DRYING, AT VARIOUS
CONDITIONS OF TEMPERATURE, RELATIVE HUMIDITY
AND AIR VELOCITY

is retained by lowering the temperature. Drying with refrigerated air is advantageous also in that the color and flavor are better maintained than when heated air is used.

Equalization of Moisture During Storage

Moisture in pecans stored at 23.3°C (73°F) and 55% RH for 4 months may increase or decrease, depending upon the moisture content when stored. Results showed the following:

(1) Very dry pecans (7.9% whole nut and 3.6% kernel moisture) gained in total moisture. This increase occurred in the shell while the meats remained unchanged.

(2) In normally dry pecans (8.7% whole nut and 4.4% kernel moisture) there was a shift in moisture from the meats to the shells, without a change in total moisture. Most of this moisture transfer was from meats to the inner shells.

(3) In slightly wet pecans (9.7% whole nut and 5.5% kernel moisture) there was a decrease in total and kernel moisture.

(4) Wet pecans (12.2% whole nut and 7.9% kernel moisture) decreased in moisture in the whole nuts, kernels and shells.

TABLE 12.9

MOISTURE IN PECANS

Region	Very Fresh Pecans (%)	Fully Dried Pecans (%)	Rewet Pecans (%)
Outer shell	20.9	11.3	15−16
Inner meats	50.5	17.9	20−24
Meats	24.3	3.8	8−12
Middle Partition	−	−	20−24

It was found that in normally dry pecans, 22 to 25% of the total moisture was in the kernels, 27 to 30% was in the inner shells, and 44 to 51% in the outer shells. Since pecans are, on the average, 40 to 50% kernels, and 50 to 55% shells, and 75 to 78% of moisture is found in the shells, gains or losses in weight during drying or storage would be greater in the shells. These data are summarized in Table 12.9.

TABLE 12.10

DISTRIBUTION OF MOISTURE IN THREE AREAS OF VERY DRY, NORMALLY DRY, SLIGHTLY WET PECANS, AND WET PECANS, BEFORE AND AFTER STORAGE AT 22.8° (73°F), WITH 55% RH

Parts of Nuts	Moisture Content (%)		Proportion of Total Moisture (%)	
	Initial	Stored	Initial	Stored
		Very Dry		
Whole nut	7.86	8.36		
Meats	3.63	3.61	22	21
Inner Shell	15.17	16.76	27	28
Outer Shell	10.83	11.18	51	51
		Normally Dry		
Whole nut	8.72	8.69		
Meats	4.36	4.19	23	22
Inner Shell	15.74	16.81	28	30
Outer Shell	10.97	11.04	49	48
		Slightly Wet		
Whole nut	9.69	9.19		
Meats	5.48	4.50	24	22
Inner Shell	17.17	17.26	27	29
Outer Shell	12.00	11.52	49	49
		Wet		
Whole nut	12.24	9.39		
Meats	7.87	4.55	25	22
Inner Shell	20.53	17.35	30	28
Outer Shell	14.26	11.85	45	50

Source: Heaton and Woodruff (1965).

Changes in moisture during drying and storage were similar for most cultivars, i.e., all lost moisture and weight, and decreased in percentage of total moisture in the kernels. They increased in shelling percentage and percentage of total moisture in the shells. During drying 6 samples of Schley, the kernel content increased from 50.9 to 51.5%; the kernel and whole nut moisture decreased from 4.9 to 4.1% and from 9.0 to 8.3%, respectively; and the percentage of the whole nut moisture found in the shells increased from 72.2 to 74.6%.

When 20 samples of mixed cultivars were dried in storage, the kernel content increased from 45.7 to 46.0%, the moisture content of the meats fell from 4.3 to 3.9%; the whole nut moisture remained unchanged; and the percentage of whole nut moisture in the shells rose from 77.1 to 78.9%.

TABLE 12.11

DISTRIBUTION OF MOISTURE IN THREE AREAS OF THREE LOTS OF PECANS
BEFORE AND AFTER STORAGE AT 23°C (73°F) WITH 55% RH

Parts of Nuts	Proportion of Total Nut (%)		Moisture Content (%)		Proportion of Total Moisture (%)	
	Initial	Stored	Initial	Stored	Initial	Stored
			Schley			
Whole nut			8.99	8.25		
Outer shell	36.4	36.2	11.83	11.26	47.9	49.3
Inner shell	12.8	12.5	17.11	16.70	24.3	25.3
Meats	50.9	51.4	4.92	4.06	27.8	25.3
			Mixed			
Whole nut			8.52	8.59		
Outer shell	40.5	39.7	10.42	11.21	51.8	51.9
Inner shell	13.9	14.2	15.39	16.42	25.2	27.1
Meats	45.7	46.0	4.28	3.92	22.9	21.0
			Stuart			
Whole nut			9.26	9.20		
Outer shell	39.4	38.7	11.30	11.26	48.0	47.4
Inner shell	16.1	16.7	16.94	17.47	29.5	31.6
Meats	43.3	44.6	4.80	4.33	22.5	21.0

Source: Heaton and Woodroof (1965).

Loss in Weight and Volume

There is sometimes a loss in weight during the storage of nuts. The cause of this was determined from moisture analysis of component parts of the nuts. Data showed that pecans, fresh from the orchard, might contain as high as 24.3% moisture in the meats, 20.9% in the outer shell, and 50.5% in the inner shell; corresponding figures for these nuts after being fully cured and dried were 3.8, 11.3 and 17.9%, respectively. It was found that during the adjustment of moisture in the shells after being stored, a loss in weight resulted in about as much as 10 to 15%, depending on the condition of the nuts when they were stored.

It was further found that in-shell pecans in storage may lose in volume as well as weight. There may be shrinkage in the length and diameter of the nuts that would cause slack pack.

Moisture determinations of 70 lots of pecans received at 2 refrigerated warehouses for storage showed that 38 of the lots were above optimum moisture and would be expected to lose weight while in storage; 13 of these were sufficiently high in moisture to produce molding upon removal from storage unless the moisture was reduced while in storage.

During storage, unshelled pecans in 85.3% of the warehouse samples shrank in length, diameter and volume, and 73.5% lost moisture from the meats. An example of shrinkage during storage is illustrated by one lot of pecans which weighed 32,488 lb when stored, and 31,132 lb when removed from storage 6 months later. This was a reduction in weight of 1356 lb or 3.5%, which should have occurred before storage.

It is important that warehousemen and clients understand that high moisture nuts will lose weight when stored properly, and in this way the quality of the nuts is superior to that when the nuts are dried by the use of heat outside of storage.

TABLE 12.12

THE INFLUENCE OF MOISTURE ON THE FREE OLEIC ACID OF 320 SAMPLES OF PECAN KERNELS

Moisture (%)	Free Oleic Acid (%)
2.0−2.9	0.34
3.0−3.9	0.40
4.0−4.9	0.42
5.0−5.9	0.49
6.0−6.9	0.69
7.0−7.9	1.22
8.0−8.9	1.25
9.0−10.9	1.38
11.0−12.9	3.80
13.0−14.9	12.55

Remoistening for Shelling

The moisture content of pecan kernels is raised to about 8.0% immediately prior to shelling. This is to reduce breaking of the meats during shelling. Following shelling and grading the meats, the added moisture should be removed as quickly as practical. This may be done by forcing warm dry air through the meats, held in bins, or on a belt; or by placing the meats in refrigerated rooms and circulating air at 65% RH (or lower) through them. In either case the moisture should be reduced to 4½% for storage.

The optimum moisture for pecan meats is about 3.5 to 4.0%. Below this point the meats are too brittle for handling without injury and above this point enzymatic and other activities are increased resulting in more rapid staling (Heaton and Woodroof 1965).

PECAN INSPECTION AND GRADES

The Federal Inspection Service originates and is maintained in the various states through the means of a cooperative agreement between the United States Department of Agriculture and some state agency, usually with the State Department of Agriculture. The cooperative agreement spells out the duties and responsibilities of both cooperating agencies. Federal-State inspection is available to all financially interested parties in practically all commercial producing areas.

Inspection and certification of pecans is invaluable to both growers, buyers and shippers, and in most cases they are willing to pay for the cost of inspection. It cuts down trading risks and can save them time, trouble and money (Scott 1960).

The following are reasons for official inspection:

(1) A clear definite interpretation and correct application of the official standards by an Inspection Service is indispensable as the first step in orderly marketing.

(2) An official inspection certificate furnishes a word picture of the commodity and provides a means of long distance dealings between seller and buyer.

(3) An inspection certificate provides a basis for fulfilments of contracts and satisfactory delivery of the product.

(4) The information given on the Inspection Certificate is accepted as prima facii evidence of the facts therein by State and Federal Courts.

(5) The inspector is trained as a professional in that field.

Quality

Standards for grades of pecans are shown in the appendix, and are a yardstick for measuring quality.

External qualities for grades of in-shell pecans are: finish of shells, color of shells, loose hulls and other foreign matter, shape, staining, and broken and punctured shells.

Internal qualities for grades are: curing, development of kernel, shriveling, leanness and hollowness, external discoloration, internal discoloration, dark kernel spots, reddish or brown dust, brownish or greyish material adhering from shell, decay, rancidness, mold, or insect injury.

Size

There is no size requirement in either U.S. No. 1 or the U.S. Commercial Grade. However, size is usually specified in connection with the grade as extra large, large or medium. The U.S. Standards provide size designations which may be used in specifying size and which are based upon a combination of count per pound and weight of the 10 smallest nuts in a representative 100-nut sample. Size also may be specified in accordance with the maximum number per pound or the range in number per pound without reference to the weight of the smallest nuts. The size may also be specified as an exact number per pound. In addition, size may be described in terms of the smallest nuts or the range in diameters, stated in sixteenths of an inch.

Pecans are covered by U.S. Standards. The two grades for pecans are the U.S. No. 1 Grade and U.S. Commercial Grade. Both permit certain tolerances for external and internal defects (see Appendix).

The packaging of pecans in accordance with Official Standards is the first step required for orderly marketing and efficient buying and selling. The Standards furnish the yardstick for measuring variations in quality, condition and size, and have provided a basis for satisfactory long-distance dealing.

Grades

In-shell pecans are graded as follows:

Size Designation	Number per Lb	Weight of 10 Smallest Nuts in 100 Representative Samples (oz)
Average	Not more than 52	2.50
Extra large	Not more than 60	2.25
Large	61-735	1.75
Medium	74-905	1.50
Small	91-115	1.25

Shelled pecans have four grades: U.S. No. 1 halves; U.S. Commercial halves; U.S. No. 1 pieces; U.S. Commercial pieces.

Quality factors for graded shelled pecans are: dryness, cleanliness, color, pieces of shell or foreign material, chipped halves, broken kernels and particles of dust, shriveling, leanness and hollowness, discoloration, rancidity, mold, decay or insect injury. In most cases there are specified tolerances, based on weight.

Shelled pecan halves are graded as follows:

	Per Lb
Mammoth	200-250
Junior Mammoth	251-300
Jumbo	301-350
Extra Large	351-450
Large	451-550
Medium	551-650
Topper	651-750
Large Amber	400 or less
Regular Amber	more than 400

Pecan pieces are graded as follows:

Size Designation	Will Pass Through Round Openings of the Following Diameters (In.)	Will Not Pass Through Round Openings of the Following Diameters (In.)
Extra large	–	$8/16$
Large	$8/16$	$5/16$
Medium	$5/16$	$4/16$
Small	$4/16$	$3/16$
Midget	$3/16$	$2/16$
Meal	$2/16$	$1/16$
Regular Amber	–	$4/16$
Small Amber	$4/16$	$2/16$

SHELLING PECANS

Pecan processing began in the early 1920s with the development of mechanical equipment for sizing, separation of faulty nuts, cracking, separation of meats and shells, sizing and grading of meats, drying and packaging. The utilization of pecans was increased by extending the storage life which was made possible by control of temperatures, relative humidities, air circulation, storage atmospheres, and packaging.

With these improvements the list of food products containing pecans has steadily increased (Woodroof and Heaton 1961).

Shelling reduces the weight of pecans by about 64%, and the volume by 50%. At the same time, shelling reduces the storage life of pecans by 75%, by making them more susceptible to insects, mold, staleness, and rancidity. However, the sensitivity of shelled pecans to deterioration has been more than overcome by improvements in packaging and storage methods.

The shelling of pecans has progressed far beyond the hammer and flat iron stage which existed before 1900. Lacking commercial shelling equipment, most pecans were then sold whole and shelled in the home. This resulted in the development of a wide variety of "parlor nut crackers" as shown in Fig. 12.20. Many principles of applying pressure

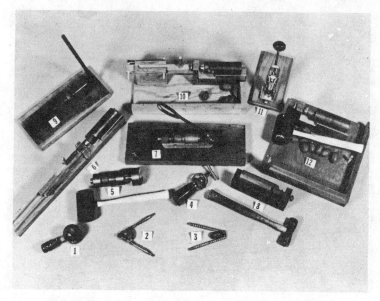

FIG. 12.20. TWELVE MODELS OF HOME NUT CRACKERS

(1) Wood screw to apply pressure on side of nut.
(2) & (3) Metal pincer to crack nut by pressure on side or end.
(4) Metal screw to apply pressure sidewise.
(5), (8), & (12) Horizontal plunger with impact applied to end of nut by one stroke of mallet.
(6) & (10) Same as above with force furnished by tension of large rubber band.
(7) Horizontal plunger activated by lever to apply pressure on end of nut; adjusted to size of nuts by screw-cylinder.
(9) Same as (7) except home-made.
(11) Vertical plunger activated by lever to apply pressure at end of nut; adjsuted to nut size by notches in upright staff.

were utilized in the crackers. Some used gentle pressure on the sides or ends of the nuts, others used a stroke on the tip or on the "shoulder" of the nut. They were made of wood, metal or a combination. Most of them resulted in crushing the meat along with the shells, and most of them were adjustable to nuts of different sizes.

The first successful automatic pecan cracker was designed by Lee J. Meyer of San Antonio, Texas, in 1918. It revolutionized the pecan industry and became the standard item in the nut processing business. The immediate advantage was the production of a higher volume of halves, as distinct from broken bits and pieces.

Courtesy of Meyer Machine Co.

FIG. 12.21. BATTERY OF 10 HIGH SPEED PECAN
CRACKING MACHINES

Included in a pecan shelling production line today are "tote boxes," elevators, separators, sizing and grading units, dryers, coolers, hoppers and conveyors. The capacity of pecan shelling plants is unlimited in that double lines and multiple units may be used. For example, most cracking machines are built in multiples of ten.

Several modern pecan shelling plants have been built since 1960. Two of these were by the Gold Kist Pecan Company at Canton, Mississippi,

Courtesy of Meyer Machine Co.

FIG. 12.22. BATTERY OF FIVE AUTOMATIC DRYING PANS FOR
PECAN MEATS

and Waycross, Georgia. Another is the Nut Tree Pecan Company, Albany, Georgia. One of the largest plants is the Sunshine Pecan Company of San Antonio, Texas. This is a seven-story structure located adjacent to a 5,000,000 lb cold storage plant. Pecans are conveyed by air to the top level and flow by gravity to various processing stations to packaging (Kennerly 1966). The plant operates year-round with a capacity of 7,000,000 lb of pecan meats annually. The majority of the nuts used are from Texas, Oklahoma and New Mexico.

A systematic sample of about 0.3% of the load is taken from every truck, cracked and tested. The sample tests are comprehensive enough to predict within 1% what the quality and quantity of the total pecans will be when processed. From the receiving hoppers the pecans are transported by bucket elevators to be air-cleaned using a dust cyclone. Following cleaning, the pecans are moved by air conduction to the air fountain atop the building where bubbler action slows the pecans and drops them into one of 36 bins each 10 × 10 × 50 ft. They are held at 0° to 1.1°C (32° to 34°F) with 60 to 70% relative humidity (Kennerly 1966).

PROCESSING WHOLE PECANS

Possibly the first pecans to be commercially polished and covered with paraffin were exhibited at the National Pecan Association in

Albany, Georgia, in 1924. They were prepared by Bob's Candy Company (Anon. 1924). Soon afterwards the National Pecan Growers Exchange of Albany marketed polished, bleached and dyed whole pecans with a phenomenal increase in sales due to improved appearance. The processing was said to last only about 2 min (Bullard 1934).

Processing in-shell pecans consists of grading for size and shape, bleaching by washing in wet sand to remove the black streaks and spots, polishing and waxing, and sometimes dyeing the shells.

Polishing in-shell pecans is a part of the processing industry separate from any other. It involves automatic grading, blowing, washing, sanding, drying, polishing and inspection. An antioxidant and dye may be applied to the shells just before waxing and polishing.

The demand for polished pecans reached a height about 1940 and has since been declining in favor of shelled meats. However, pecans polished, dyed and packed in windowed cartons have remained popular for export. This is a favorite nut in England and Europe for Thanksgiving and Christmas holidays. To supply this seasonal demand, polishing plants operate continuously during October, November and December and remain almost idle the remainder of the year.

Only certain cultivars, carefully graded for uniformity of size and shape, are polished in-shell. Stuart is by far the most popular cultivar for this.

PECAN SHELLING INDUSTRY

Since 1930, pecan production has increased greatly. The increased use of pecans by food manufacturers and consumers has resulted in increased demand for shelled pecans. The number of firms which shell the nuts and sell graded and sized kernels in bulk and retail packages has expanded.

By 1960, there were approximately 80 pecan-shelling firms in the United States, and they handled most of the pecans produced. During that year, the crop was 187.5 tons and more than 90% were shelled before marketing. Both the production and processing of pecans were operations carried on in conjunction with other farming and processing operations. For example, the shelling industry operated at only about 35% capacity. The low level of performance was due partly to small, part-time firms who operated only for the holiday season. The small firms operated at only about 10% of capacity, while the larger plants operated at 60% capacity. The large shellers became larger and the small plants quit shelling. In 1960, 8 firms sold over 5 million pounds each and accounted for 84% of the industry sales (Powell 1963).

Since 1960, pecan shelling plants have become larger and fewer operate practically year-round. This has been due to (a) refrigerated storage that provides a supply of good quality nuts year-round; (b) more mechanization that enables the operation to be done cheaper per man and per ton; (c) the demand for pecans for domestic use and export has been constant throughout the year and has increased annually since 1960; (d) spreading the shelling operation out over the year more efficiently utilizes the labor, transportation and shelling facilities; (e) storing pecans and shelling as needed enables the industry to operate smoothly over years of light and bumper crops (Woodroof and Heaton 1961).

Procuring a Supply of Pecans

Regardless of size, all shelling plants have the common problem of procuring an adequate supply of in-shell pecans each year. Even though pecans are produced in more than eleven states, the every-other-year production pattern of pecan trees increases the difficulty of maintaining a supply. Not all producing areas have a crop of pecans each year.

Thus, the larger pecan shelling firms have been forced to set up far-flung buying organizations to purchase their supply of nuts during the short harvest season in the fall. The farmers deliver the nuts to accumulators, who grade, bag and sell them at auction sales or directly to shellers.

Because a large portion of the total pecan crop is produced on wild trees, forecasting the size of the crop is difficult. Since the size of the crop is unknown, and there is sharp competition among buyers in short crop years to obtain an adequate supply, the price for in-shell pecans is often forced up to unrealistic levels. Buying and selling in-shell pecans is highly speculative, and in years of a heavy crop the price to the farmer is low and many low quality nuts remain unharvested.

High prices for in-shell pecans increase the kernel cost to the sheller. For example, a one cent increase in the cost of in-shell pecans increases the cost of pecan meats about three cents. The meat costs are also affected by the quality of the pecans. For instance, if the sheller pays 30 cents per pound for in-shell pecans, his meat cost is 85 cents per pound when the nuts yield 35% meat, but only 75 cents per pound if 40% is obtained.

Thus, pecan shellers operate under a great deal of uncertainty concerning the amount and average quality of pecans to be marketed each year (Powell 1963).

Equipment for Shelling Pecans

The capacity of a shelling plant is determined by the number of cracking machines used. Large plants operate as many as 100 cracking machines with a daily capacity of 60,000 lb, and a seasonal capacity of 8,000,000 lb.

Equipment necessary for operating a pecan shelling plant (see Figs. 12.23 and 12.24) consists of:

(1) Grading and sizing machinery equipped with screens and blowers for removing faulty nuts and foreign materials, and for segregating the nuts into 9 sizes with screen openings as follows: smaller than $\frac{9}{16}$, $\frac{9}{16}$, $\frac{10}{16}$, $\frac{12}{16}$, $\frac{13}{16}$, $\frac{14}{16}$, $\frac{15}{16}$ in. and larger;

(2) Machines with vats or tanks for dipping and "conditioning" pecans for shelling;

(3) Cracking machines, with a capacity of about 1000 lb of nuts per day each, which may be adjusted for different sized nuts and installed in series;

(4) Shellers for separating the shells and meats;

(5) Screens for separating halves and broken pieces of various sizes;

(6) Dryers for removing excess moisture from meats;

(7) Grading belts or tables for hand-picking the dried meats;

(8) Electric eyes for grading the meats; and

(9) Refrigerated rooms for storing unshelled and shelled pecans.

Courtesy of Minehan Pecan Co.

FIG. 12.23. BATTERY OF EIGHT MACHINES THAT CRACK MOISTENED PECANS LENGTHWISE, INDIVIDUALLY, AT A HIGH RATE OF SPEED

The nuts are then carried, automatically, by conveyor belt to shakers and screens for removal of the shells.

Courtesy of Gold Kist Pecans

FIG 12.24. A BATTERY OF 15 PECAN CRACKERS

All of the nuts of this lot are of the same size and after being
cracked are discharged on a single belt to the shellers.

Conditioning Pecans for Shelling

To prevent shattering of the meats, pecans should be moistened or
"conditioned" before cracking. This may be accomplished by one of the
following methods:

(1) The cold water method, which is generally used, in which the pecans
are soaked for 20 to 30 min in water containing 1000 ppm chlorine,
then drained and held 16 to 24 hours in sacks, vats, or barrels for
cracking at any time within the next 24 hours.

(2) The steam pressure method, by which the pecans are subjected to 5
lb steam pressure for 6 to 8 min, then cooled and held for 30 to 60 min.
This method is fast, but is less effective in controlling mold than the
cold water method. Further, it may cause slight darkening and a faint
cooked flavor.

(3) The hot water method, by which pecans are immersed for 20 min in
water heated to 62.8° (145°F), followed immediately by shelling, is fast
and yields meats of excellent quality.

Wetting agents—sodium tetraphosphate, santomerse, or polyoxy-
ethylene sorbitan triolate (Tween 85)—or vacuum, used in conjunction
with the cold or hot water treatments, improve penetration of the
shells and reduce the time the meats are wet.

TABLE 12.13

21 METHODS OF "CONDITIONING" STUART PECANS FOR SHELLING, BASED ON PERCENT OF PERFECT HALVES, AND RATED IN ORDER OF PREFERENCE, BASED ON QUALITY (COLORS, TEXTURE AND FLAVOR) OF MEATS

Treatment	Time of Treatment (min)	Time from Treatment to Cracking (hours)	Ease of Shelling	Structure of		Unbroken Halves (%)	Quality Score (%)	Order of Preference Based on Quality of Nuts
				Shells	Meats			
Live steam	10	¼	very easy	very brittle	very limp	90	75.6	19
Steam pressure, 5 lb	6	¼	very easy	very brittle	very limp	89	77.0	18
Live steam	15	¼	very easy	brittle	limp	86	72.9	21
Steam pressure, 5 lb	12	¼	very easy	brittle	very limp	85	74.4	20
Steam pressure, 5 lb	4	¼	easy	slightly tough	limp	83	86.7	16
Steam pressure, 5 lb	8	¼	easy	brittle	very limp	81	81.1	17
Water, 21.1°C (70°F)	20	16	easy	brittle	slightly brittle	79	94.8	2
Water, 21.1°C (70°F)	30	16	very easy	brittle	slightly brittle	79	90.0	6
Air, 90% RH	1440	0	easy	brittle	slightly brittle	78	88.9	8
Live steam	5	¼	easy	brittle	limp	77	82.2	15
Steam pressure, 5 lb	12	16	easy	brittle	slightly brittle	75	92.9	3
Water, 98.9°C (210°F)	5	¼	easy	brittle	slightly brittle	75	88.9	9
Water, 87.8°C (190°F)	20	¼	easy	brittle	slightly brittle	74	88.1	10
Water, 98.9°C (210°F)	5	¼	easy	brittle	slightly brittle	70	85.6	14
Water, 21.1°C (70°F), 0 to 1% wetting agent	20	16	fairly easy	tough	brittle	65	91.9	5
Water, 62.8°C (145°F)	20	15	hard	tough	brittle	62	92.8	4
Water, 62.8°C (145°F), wetting agent	20	¼	hard	tough	very brittle	62	95.8	1
Water, 62.8°C (145°F), wetting agent	20	16	hard	tough	brittle	60	87.4	12
Water, 62.8°C (145°F) vacuum	20	¼	hard to wet	tough	brittle	52	86.7	13
Water, 62.8°C (145°F) vacuum	20	16	hard	tough	brittle	52	88.1	11
Water, 62.8°C (145°F) vacuum, wetting agent	20	¼	hard	very tough	brittle	52	89.6	7
None	–	–	very hard	tough	very brittle	51	94.4	–

During conditioning, moisture enters the shell through the vascular system at the base and passes to the apex through the middle partition. The moisture content of the meats is raised from about 4 to 8%, and there is an increase in weight of the nuts of about 4%. For most satisfactory cracking and shelling, the pecan shells should be dry, brittle and easily shattered, while the kernels should be limp and pliable.

An experiment was conducted to determine the effect of conditioning pecans before shelling on the stability of the meats. Nuts of the Stuart cultivar and a seedling were (a) soaked in water for 20 min and drained overnight and (b) shelled without conditioning. After shelling the pecan meats were sealed in tin cans and stored at -28.9°, 0°, and 21.1°C (-20°, 32°, and 70°F), respectively, for examination after 5, 10, and 13 months.

Results showed that conditioning was very beneficial: (a) by greatly reducing the amount of bruising and breakage of the meats during cracking and shelling; (b) by improving the appearance, resulting in a lighter color, and (c) by extending the stability of the nuts by about 6%.

The pecans soaked before shelling were consistently rated higher in color, texture, and flavor than similar nuts shelled without soaking. The conditioned meats had a brighter color, more tender texture and better nut flavor. The results in favor of the conditioned nuts were statistically significant.

In comparison with water-soak processes currently used in industry, a 3 min live steam process developed by Forbus and Senter (1976) proved superior both for shelling and storage stability. The treatment consists of subjecting the pecans to live steam in a retort for 3 min, and holding them 20 min at 2l°C (70°F) at 65% RH before cracking.

The steam-treated pecans yielded 12 to 17% more halves than pecans soaked 1 hour in a 20°C (90°F) water bath with 1000 ppm chlorine, and held 20 min before cracking. During accelerated storage (21°C [95.4°F] 65% RH) the nutmeats steam-heated in the shell deteriorated at a slower rate than those of the commercial-type treatments. Besides improving efficiency and retarding rancidity, steam conditioning reduced total process time from 13 to 24 hours for the chlorine soak process to only several minutes (Anon. 1976).

Cracking and Shelling Pecans

Cracking is accomplished by applying force to the ends of the nuts individually. Tests have shown that pecans of average shell thickness (Stuart) require more than 200 lb of pressure on the ends to crush. Some cultivars require as much as 600 lb of gently applied pressure to crush.

The mechanical crackers are plungers operated by levers and gears, and are amazingly efficient and fast when arranged in series or batteries as shown in Fig. 12.24. The pecans are cracked individually after they are oriented and struck by a plunger on the end. The plunger and anvil are hollowed so that the concussion (about ⅛ in.) causes the sides of the shell to crack longitudinally into about 8 "barrel stave" pieces, each of which breaks in the middle. Thus, the shell of each nut is broken into about 16 pieces without crushing or breaking the meats. The blow from the plunger exerts pressure, not on the tip of the nut, but on a circular area around the tip about ½ in. in diameter. The halves are broken apart by shakers liberating the middle partition.

Crackers shown in Fig. 12.23 have a plunger with about ⅛ in. play. When placed firmly against a nut before being struck, this is sufficient distance to crack the nut. At the same time it protects the nut from being crushed irrespective of the weight of the blow.

Commercial shelling plants have batteries of crackers, each adjusted to nuts of specific sizes. A battery of 15 crackers as shown in Fig. 12.24 will crack 10,000 lb of small seedlings and 15,000 lb of large nuts per day. By passing the cracked nuts over a labyrinth of conveyors to shellers, blowers, reels, fans, graders and pickers, the meats and shells are separated. The shelled pecans are separated into grades based on the size of halves or pieces as shown in Figs. 12.25 and 12.26. Sizing is accomplished by passing the meats over a series of rapidly vibrating screens with holes of progressively larger diameter.

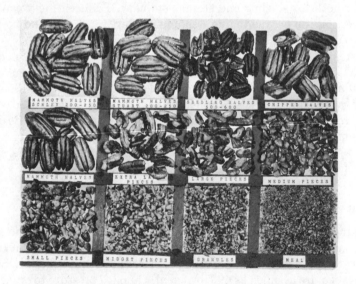

FIG. 12.25. SHOWING TWELVE GRADES OF PECAN MEATS

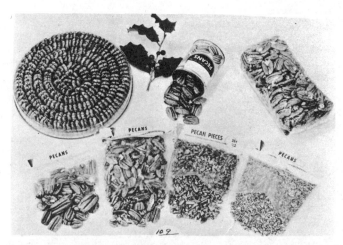

FIG. 12.26.   SEVEN METHODS OF GRADING AND PACKAGING
PECAN MEATS FOR RETAIL TRADE

When 38 lb of Stuart pecans were shelled, 49% by weight were meats and 51% shells. The meats occupied 61% as much space as the unshelled nuts, and the shells occupied 72% as much space. The space required for the meats and shells was 40% greater than that for the unshelled nuts.

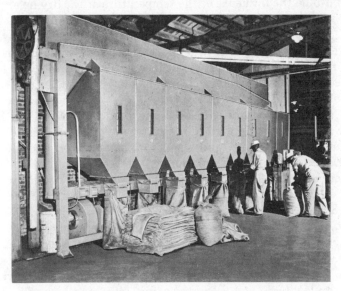

FIG. 12.27.   UNIT FOR SEPARATING FRESHLY HARVESTED
PECANS INTO NINE GRADES, ACCORDING TO SIZE;
AND FOR REMOVING "POPS" BY AIR BLAST

FIG. 12.28. PECAN SHELLS HAVE 56% OF THE WEIGHT AND
71% OF THE VOLUME OF THE NUTS; THE MEATS HAVE 44%
OF THE WEIGHT AND 50% OF THE VOLUME OF THE
UNSHELLED NUTS

Drying Pecan Meats

Pecan meats when shelled contain from 7 to 9% moisture. To maintain quality in the meats this must be reduced to 4% or lower. Experience has shown that this may be done by rapidly circulating dry air through the meats.

To determine the influence of the temperature of the drying air on the quality and shelf-life of pecans, 22 lb of freshly shelled, graded, and undried Stuart halves were obtained from a commercial shelling plant. They were separated into 2 lb lots and dried to a moderate moisture level in rapidly circulating air, as outlined in Table 12.14. Each lot was evaluated for moisture and quality immediately after drying, and for quality after 6 months storage at 0°C (32°F).

When drying temperatures of 48.9° to 60.0°C (120° to 140°F) and higher were used, oil migrated to the surface of the meats resulting in a greasy appearance, a dry and slightly tough texture, and a slightly cooked flavor which became stale during storage.

The rate of moisture loss from pecan meats during drying at 93.3°C (200°F) was approximately 1.5, 2.0, 2.75, 4.3, 10.4, and 35.0 times faster than at 82.2°, 71.1°, 60.0°, 48.9°, 37.8° and 26.7°C, (180°, 160°, 140°, 120°, 100° and 80°F), respectively.

Another experiment was set up to determine the equilibrium moisture content of pecan halves at various storage temperatures and air humidities. Before storage the moisture content of pecan halves was adjusted to low (1.6% and 2.18%), medium (4%), and high (6.7%) moisture levels. These pecan halves were placed in wire baskets (in duplicate), stored at each of the temperature and relative humidity conditions, and weighed at weekly intervals until they reached a constant

TABLE 12.14

EFFECT OF TEMPERATURE OF DRYING PECAN MEATS, FROM 7.49 to 4.06%
MOISTURE OR LOWER, ON THE QUALITY OF MEATS BEFORE AND AFTER STORAGE
FOR SIX MONTHS AT 0°C (32°F)

Drying				Quality	
Temperature (C)	(F)	Time (Hours)	Moisture (%)	Before Storage (Score of 100)	After Storage (Score of 100)
76.7°	170°	48	4.06	88.9	88.9
- 6.7°	20°	168	3.78	88.9	88.9
-17.8°	0°	168	3.83	88.9	88.9
26.7°	80°	15	3.56	88.9	88.9
37.8°	100°	2¾	4.16	86.7	85.6
48.9°	120°	1¾	3.59	85.6	86.7
60.0°	140°	1¼	3.44	83.3	82.2
71.1°	160°	1	3.14	84.4	81.1
82.2°	180°	¾	2.65	83.3	76.7
93.2°	200°	½	2.76	84.4	71.1

figure. The final moisture content of the meats was determined as
shown in Table 12.15.

Data showed that pecan halves with high moisture content dried to a
safe moisture level of 4% or lower during storage at -28.9°, -17.8°, -9.4°,

TABLE 12.15

THE INFLUENCE OF TEMPERATURE AND RELATIVE HUMIDITY ON EQUILIBRIUM
MOISTURE CONTENT OF STUART PECAN HALVES

Storage			Pecan Meats	
Temperature (C)	(F)	Relative Humidity (%)	Initial Moisture Content (%)	Equilibrium Moisture Content (%)
- 6.7°	20°	45–50	2.58 medium	3.78
-17.8°	0°	55–60	2.58 medium	3.61
-17.8°	0°	65–70	1.67 low	4.46
-17.8°	0°	65–70	2.18 low	4.57
-17.8°	0°	65–70	6.37 high	4.76
- 9.4°	15°	55–60	7.45 high	3.71
- 6.7°	20°	60–65	2.58 medium	3.50
- 6.7°	20°	75–80	1.67 low	6.34
- 6.7°	20°	75–80	2.18 low	6.77
- 6.7°	20°	75–80	6.37 high	6.18
- 3.9°	25°	70–75	1.67 low	3.90
- 3.9°	25°	70–75	2.18 low	3.87
- 3.9°	25°	70–75	2.58 medium	3.90
- 3.9°	25°	70–75	6.37 high	3.92
0°	32°	35–40	3.41 medium	2.34
0°	32°	65–70	3.41 medium	4.94
0°	32°	75–80	1.67 low	4.75
0°	32°	75–80	2.18 low	4.91
0°	32°	75–80	2.58 medium	4.51
0°	32°	75–80	6.37 high	5.07
10.0°	50°	50–65	7.20 high	3.00
21.1°	70°	50–65	7.20 high	2.80

-6.7°, -6.7°, 0°, 2.2°, 2.2°, and 21.1°C (-20°,0°, 15°, 20°, 32°, 36°, 36° and 70°F) when the relative humidity was 45 to 50, 60, 60, 75, 75, and 75%, respectively, and forced air circulation was maintained throughout the storage rooms. The data also showed that dry pecan halves increased in moisture to a desirable level when stored under these conditions.

In a third experiment, the rate of drying pecan meats while in freezing storage was studied by placing 30-lb cases of meats in storage at -9.4°C (15°F) with 45% relative humidity. Halves of Curtis pecans were reduced from 7.45% moisture to 3.85% in 15 days; halves of Van Deman nuts were similarly reduced to 3.81%; and pecan pieces were reduced from 9 to 2.5% moisture. It was found that pecan halves held at 45% relative humidity for more than two weeks and pieces held at this humidity for more than one week became excessively brittle, and complaints of breakage of meats during shipping came from customers. It was concluded that refrigerated drying should be done at 9.4° to -3.9°C (15° to 25°F) with 45% relative humidity for one to two weeks, and storage should be at -2.2° to 0°C (28° to 32°F) with 60 to 65% relative humidity for below freezing temperatures and 70% relative humidity for above freezing temperatures.

From these experiments on drying pecan meats it was concluded that:

(a) Moisture content of pecan meats may be increased or decreased by subjecting them to blasts of air with high or low humidity.

(b) Optimum relative humidity was 60 to 70%, causing the moisture content of the meats to equalize at 3.5 to 4.0%.

(c) Drying meats with hot air was fast, but the quality of the meats was adversely affected when the meats were dried at temperatures of 48.9°C (120°F).

(d) Drying meats with refrigerated air was slow, but those dried at 0°C (32°F) or lower retained natural appearance, aroma, color, and flavor in storage much longer than did those dried at 12.1°C (70°F) or higher.

STORING PECANS

Pecans are semiperishable, and unless properly stored, may become inedible due to mold, souring, insects, staleness, discoloration, or rancidity. Pecans are normally held for a period between harvesting and consumption, and experience has shown adequate drying, good packaging, and refrigeration to be most important. Storage is to be reckoned with by all who process pecans or pecan products. Paramount questions are how, where, when and with what they will be stored. Adequate storage is the solution to the problem of carry-over of pecans from a heavy crop to light crops ahead, and is a necessity for a sound export market.

Storage of pecans during the winter months requires little attention except that the nuts be kept dry and away from rodents, insects and products that would contaminate them flavorwise. But on the approach of warm weather in the spring, the nuts may become stale, insect infested and rancid within a few weeks, unless refrigerated or protected otherwise. Pecans placed in refrigerated storage as soon as properly cured are more suitable for long-term storage than those held at variable temperature and humidity conditions during the winter and placed in refrigerated warehouses in the spring. Most deteriorative processes in pecans are progressive and accumulative, and low-temperature storage is largely a preventive measure (Blackmon 1932; Brison 1945; Godkin et al. 1951; Switzler 1931; Wells 1951; Woodroof and Heaton 1949, 1953A, B, 1958, 1961, 1968).

Before about 1930, very few pecans were cold stored, they were not considered a year-round commodity, there was little or no export market, and most of the domestic markets were "seasonal." As the advantages of refrigeration were demonstrated and as refrigerated space became available to more rural areas, more of the space was allocated to pecans.

It was found that pecans could be held in good condition at 2.8°C (37°F) to 4.4°C (40°F), with 85% relative humidity for several months, and that they could be held from one season to the next at 0°C (32°F). However, there was still the problem of extending a crop 2 or 3 years to provide a supply over a short crop year. A large crop in 1961 encouraged pecan processors to store the nuts in freezer storage. It was estimated that more than 32,000,000 lb of unshelled pecans were stored under refrigeration that year; about 4% of them were shelled. It was significant that 2,180,000 lb or 6.4% of the pecans stored were held at -17.8°C (0°F) or lower, while only a few decades previously freezing was considered both detrimental and impractical for pecans. It was also significant that only 9.3% of the total quantity of stored pecans were shelled; 9.2% of those held in cold storage and 10.4% of the frozen nuts were shelled. The procedure was to store pecans under refrigeration directly from the grading shed and to shell and deliver to end-users as needed.

Experiments conducted by the Georgia Experiment Station have shown that controlled refrigerated storage (a) arrests insects, (b) prevents molding, (c) retards development of staleness and rancidity, and (d) preserves the natural color, flavor, and texture of shelled pecans for as long as eight years. Furthermore, refrigerated storage does not damage pecans even at temperatures as low as -76°C (-170°F), nor does it increase the rate of deterioration of nuts after removal from storage.

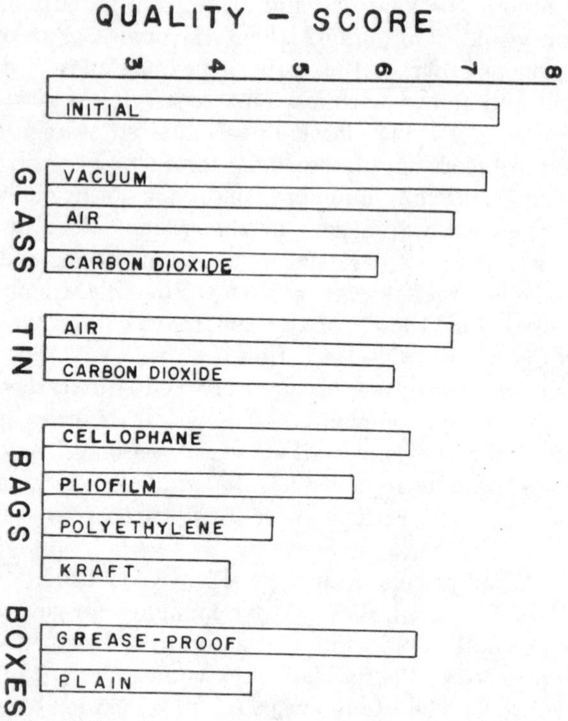

QUALITY − SCORE

FIG. 12.29. QUALITY SCORE OF STUART PECAN HALVES
INITIALLY AND AFTER BEING PACKAGED 11 WAYS
AND STORED AT 0°C(32°F) FOR 10 MONTHS. SCORES WERE:
8-VERY GOOD, 7-GOOD, 6-GOOD TO FAIR, 5-FAIR, 4-FAIR
TO POOR, AND 3-POOR

This is due to the fact that the carbohydrate content is low, the moisture content is only 4%, and the oil content is about 70%.

High Initial Quality

There is a tendency for pecans to deteriorate from the time they drop from the trees. The first requirement for successful storage is to check early stages of deterioration by prompt harvesting, drying and storage. Tests have shown that pecans should be harvested, dried, graded, and stored under refrigeration within a month after harvest. Grading consists of removing all hulls, trash and all faulty nuts. They may or may not be shelled before storage, though shelling has been found to reduce the storage life by one-half. Shelling also reduces the volume and weight to about one-half, and offers an excellent means of grading out faulty nuts.

Since cultivars such as Van Deman, Schley, Stuart and others that are well-filled have a longer shelf-life than Tesche, Frotcher, and other poorly filled cultivars, it is recommended that only those with good color, texture, flavor, and high oil content be stored at -17.8°C (0°F) for holding more than one year. Only pecans with high quality should be refrigerated, and only the best of these should be held from one year to the next.

Color, taste and smell are the best tests for good quality in pecans, though free fatty acids and the peroxide number, as expressed as aldehyde substances, are of some help. After the optimum flavor is developed in fresh pecans a short time after harvesting, there is a gradual loss of practically all desirable qualities—flavor, aroma, color and texture.

The sequence of changes are about as follows: (a) loss of readily volatile substances which tends toward blandness; (b) onset of oxidation causing the color to darken and a stale aroma and flavor; and (c) hydrolysis of fats resulting in increase of free fatty acids and acrid flavor.

In addition to the benefits of low temperature storage, it is advantageous to have a low moisture content. Brison (1945) dried pecan meats in an oven at 107.5°C (225°F) from 3.4% moisture to a moisture percentage of 2.9, 1.6, 1.0 and 0.7. The samples were packed in glass jars by the "hot-pack" process and closed hot, producing a vacuum of 5 to 7 in. All of the vacuum packed oven-dried samples were good in flavor after two years at room temperature; and those dried to 1.6% moisture or lower were edible after seven years. The samples with 3.4% moisture without vacuum were rancid in less than a year; while those packed under vacuum were still good.

Low Relative Humidity

High moisture in nuts when stored is the cause of more deterioration than any other single factor, and this may result in nuts becoming inedible within as short a time as two weeks. It is reported that at least 50% of shelled pecans in the channels of trade are darker than desired. This is due to too high moisture content at some time between maturity and end use. Most of this is due to (a) delayed harvesting from damp soil, (b) excessive moisture immediately before or after cracking, or (c) storing under conditions of too high relative humidity. Any of these conditions allows the tannin in the lining of the shell to dissolve

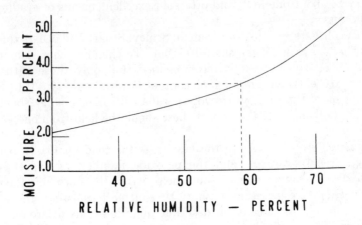

FIG. 12.30. SHOWING THE MOISTURE CONTENT OF PECAN
MEATS IN EQUILIBRIUM WITH CONTROLLED
RELATIVE HUMIDITY

A relative humidity of 50% equalized with a recommended moisture
content of 3.5% in stored meats.

and stain the seed coats. Once stained, the seed coats gradually become
darker due to oxidation in the air. This discoloration has some similarity to the "amber" color due to high temperature storage.

Relative humidity in the air below 0°C (32°F) is not a problem; but
above this temperature, high humidity may be very damaging to the
nuts. Shelled pecans, for storage of more than 3 months, require a
relative humidity of 65 to 70% in order for the moisture content to
equalize at the desired 3.5 to 4.0%. Unshelled pecans require a relative
humidity from 75 to 80% to avoid excessive drying of the nuts on one
hand and molding due to too high moisture on the other.

Low Constant Temperature

In general, the lower the temperature the longer will be the expected
storage life of the nuts, though there is no critical temperature at which
pecans must be held. The greatest benefit due to storage at low temperature is in retention of fresh flavor; the next is in color, followed
closely by aroma, with slight benefit in texture.

At 21.1°C (70°F) unshelled pecans may be expected to retain edible
quality for 6 months; with shelled halves 3 to 4 months. Pecans at this
temperature are subject to molding, insect infestation, development of
"amber" color, staling, and rancidity.

FIG. 12.31. TWO OF THE CHIEF WAYS THAT SHELLED PECANS WERE DAMAGED DURING STORAGE

(1) Holding due to too high relative humidity; (2) and blanching due to ammonia in the atmosphere; (3) normal pecans of five cultivars—(top to bottom) Farley, Mahan, Desirable, Stuart, Schley.

At 8.3°C (47°F) unshelled pecans may be held for 9 months and shelled halves for 6 months. The same types of deterioration as listed at 21.1°C (70°F) may develop, except that insects are "arrested."

At 0° to 2.2°C (32° to 36°F) the storage life of unshelled nuts may be extended to 18 months and that of shelled halves to one year. Staling and rancidity develop gradually.

At -6.7° to -3.3°C (20° to 25°F) unshelled pecans may be held for 30 months and shelled halves for 1½ to 2 years without molding, insect damage, discoloration, or rancidity. There may be slight staling and loss of flavor.

At -17.8°C (0°F) and below, either shelled or unshelled pecans, may be held for 6 to 10 years without appreciable loss of quality.

It was found that pecan pieces—large, medium, small, midget, meal— had a shorter storage life than pecan halves. The reduction in time was in proportion to the surface of the pieces. In general, storage of pecan pieces should be limited to a few weeks or months at temperatures above 0°C (32°F).

Because of the low moisture content of pecans, no permanent damage due to freezing to temperatures as low as -76°C (-170°F) has been found. It was found, however, that the temperature of storage should be free of wide fluctuations.

Courtesy of Gold Kist Pecans

FIG. 12.32.   SHELLED PECANS IN COLD STORAGE

Each case contains 30 lb of pecan meats.

Proper Packaging

The unbroken shell of pecans provides abundant protection to the meats in preventing bruising and partial protection against oxidation, insects, molding, and discoloration. For this reason fiber bags or cartons are adequate for storage of whole pecans.

Shelling bruises pecans, which causes the oil to "crawl" over the entire surface of the meats and onto the containers. The amount of crawling and "wicking" of the oil is in proportion to the amount of bruising caused by breaking and cutting. This greasy film becomes stale and rancid much more rapidly than the interior of the meats. For protection of pecan meats the container should have a barrier that is impermeable to air, moisture, and oil. Metal, foil, glass, or flexible films have been found adequate and practical. An antioxidant applied to the inner surface of the container has been found highly effective, while a wax

Courtesy of The Atlantic Company

FIG. 12.33. IN-SHELL PECANS IN COLD STORAGE

The bags contain about 120 lb, are stacked four high on pallets, and the pallets are stacked three high. The pallets are handled by forklift.

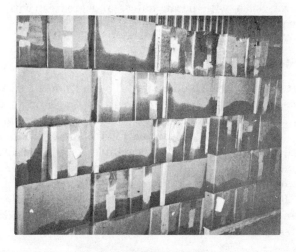

FIG. 12.34. 30-LB CASES OF PECAN MEATS THROUGH WHICH PECAL OIL HAS PENETRATED

This may be prevented by using oil-impermeable cases or storing at 10°C (50°F) or lower.

FIG. 12.35. CARTONS OF PECAN MEATS BADLY STAINED BY
OIL THAT "CRAWLED" FROM THE BROKEN PIECES

Rancidity was greatly accelerated by the added exposure to air.
Refrigeration caused the oil to solidify and practically eliminated staining of the cartons.

coating on the interior of corrugated boards is of less value. Crawling of
the free oil was least with pecan halves and greatest with the most
finely broken pieces.

Odor-Free Storage Room

Pecan meats readily absorb odors and flavors from the surroundings.
Imperfections in packages permit odors from the storage room, the
atmosphere, and other products to be absorbed, resulting in a foreign
flavor, odor, or color in the nuts. Even faint odors of wood, ammonia,
paint, asphalt, and most fruits and vegetables may accumulate in the
nuts and appear stronger than in the surroundings. While aeration or
the use of carbon filters are of some benefit, no practical means has
been found for restoring such nuts to their original state. For this
reason, pecans should be stored in a separate odor-free room or only
with products free of objectionable odors.

Removal From Freezing Storage

Frozen pecans are very brittle and excessive handling by stacking or
hauling may result in considerable breaking of halves. For this reason

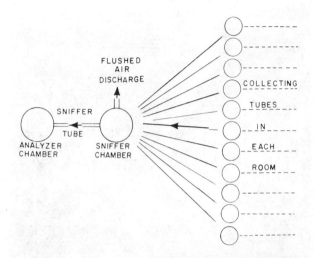

FIG. 12.36. DIAGRAM SHOWING METHOD OF COLLECTING
AND ANALYZING GAS IN STORAGE ROOMS WITHOUT
OPENING THE DOOR

Gas (ammonia, smoke or other) is collected from any room through
perforated tubes, by vacuum pump, into a sniffer chamber. From
here it is collected in analyzer chamber for bubbling through water
to be titrated with Nessler reagent or to activate color/electric
signal or alarm.

they should be allowed to thaw for a few hours after removal from the
freezer and before being shipped. Removal of pecans from refrigerated
storage should be gradual or in steps of about 10°C (15°F) each. "Tempering" in this manner reduces moisture condensation and the possibility of subsequent molding and eliminates the likelihood of breakage because of handling while frozen.

An excellent procedure in removing carloads or trailer loads of pecans
from refrigerated storage is to (a) use an insulated car or trailer with
closely fitted doors, (b) place the conveyor directly in front of the
refrigerated warehouse door, (c) transfer the nuts from the warehouse
to the conveyor as quickly as possible, (d) close all doors quickly and
securely, and (e) keep doors closed during transit, which may be from 3
to 5 days. During transit the nuts will "temper" gradually without the
atmosphere on the inside reaching the dew point. Tests showed no
advantage in using refrigerated trucks or cars for conditioning nuts in
transit.

Tempering pecans going into refrigerated storage is not necessary, but
a "certificate of condition" at the time they are received for storage, as
well as when they are removed, is highly important.

Courtesy of U.S. Cold Storage Corp.

FIG. 12.37. REFRIGERATED LOADING DOCK AT COLD
STORAGE WAREHOUSE

Nuts can be loaded in refrigerated railway cars or trucks
without moisture condensation.

STORAGE INSECTS

Insects are a major problem in nuts and nut products stored at temperatures above 9°C (48°F), especially if they are shelled; and prevention of insect infestation was the outstanding reason given by end-users for refrigerated storage of nuts.

Nuts, nutmeats or nut products may be protected from insects (a) by storing at temperatures below 9°C (48°F); (b) by fumigating for 24 hours at 21.1°C (70°F) with 9:1 mixture of carbon dioxide and ethylene oxide at the rate of 20 lb per 1000 cu ft or with 7:3 mixture of ethylene dichloride and carbon tetrachloride at the rate of 1.5 oz per 120 lb bag in insect-proof bags; or (c) by repeated fumigation.

Following are brief descriptions of insects which were found in stored nuts in the laboratory, in bakeries and candy plants, and in barns with various feedstuffs, and in commercial storage warehouses (Cotton 1947). (See description of insects p. 679 under Candy Storage.)

Confused Flour Beetle or Red Flour Beetle.—This is a very common insect in nuts and nut products, as well as in most cereals. When the temperature is high a complete generation is passed in three to four months.

Indian Meal Moth.—This is probably the most common insect in nut products. The infested material is webbed together and often fouled with dirty silken masses containing the excreta of the larvae. Under conditions usually encountered in heated buildings their life cycle is four to six weeks.

Cadelle.—This insect is less common than the two described above, but the damage is severe since it penetrates many boards, papers and other materials which are impervious to other insects. Once this insect enters, others will follow. Adult beetle is black or nearly black, ⅓ to ½ in. in length, with the head and prothorax distinctly separated from the rest of the body, to which it is attached by a rather loose, prominent joint.

Saw-Toothed Grain Beetle.—These are small dark-red beetles of flattened shape, which are able to work into food packages that are apparently tightly sealed. This insect winters in the adult stage and may complete a life cycle in as little as 24 to 30 days. The adult has been known to live over three years.

Carpet Beetles.—The larvae are short, rarely over ¼ in. long, chubby, and covered with erect brown or black bristles all over the body. The adult is a small, blackish hard-shelled beetle, sometimes flecked with white or reddish scales. The larvae attack such food as they can find and avoid the light. Even though present, they do not damage at temperatures below 4.4°C (40°F). They molt 5 to 11 times in the course of growth and the cast skins closely resemble living larvae.

Fumigation

Unrefrigerated shelled and unshelled nuts should be protected by fumigation during warm or hot weather. The first requirement for fumigation is to provide an airtight room or building made of concrete, metal or very closely fitting boards. In some cases nuts are fumigated in railroad cars after they are loaded for shipment. The temperature should be uniform throughout the space and satisfactory means must be provided for uniform distribution of the fumigant. Also, some fumigants must be removed after the treatment period.

There is no standard method for fumigating nuts. Several materials and uses are listed.

Chlorinated Hydrocarbon.—This is a 7:3 mixture of ethylene dichloride and carbon tetrachloride that may be used as a spray or placed on absorbent material in various locations through the pile of nuts. Since the fumes are heavier than air, the fumigant should be placed near the top of the pile. It should be used at the rate of 1.5 oz per 120-lb bag of nuts. The time of treatment should be 24 hours at 21.7°C (70°F). Over-doses or prolonged treatments may result in an off-flavor in the nuts.

Carboxide.—Carboxide is a 9:1 mixture of carbon dioxide and ethylene oxide, compressed in cylinders and used as a gas. After the nuts are placed in a tightly closed room the gas is admitted near the top of the room at the rate of 20 to 25 lb per 1000 cu ft of space. The room should remain at 21.7°C (70°F) for 24 hours. This fumigant has the advantage of being relatively non-toxic to warm-blooded animals, and has no residual odor or taste.

Methyl Bromide.—This is a common fumigant for nuts, and gives good results when the manufacturer's directions are followed. The bromine is believed to chemically alter the oil in nuts and is therefore not favored by some.

Cyanide.—Cyanide is a very powerful and dangerous poison that should be used for killing insects in nuts only under rigidly controlled conditions.

Storage Diseases of Pecans

Two storage diseases may cause serious damage in pecan storage. They are molds and pink rot.

Molding is the most serious storage disease of unshelled and shelled pecans, and is aggravated by high humidity in the air and high moisture in the pecans. There are many kinds of mold but the general causes and effects are similar. The best control is to keep the nuts dry at all times. The following procedure is used to separate mold from the nuts or meats and remove moldy odor and flavor: Immerse moldy pecan meats in solution of ammonium chloride, with 156 ppm chlorine (1 oz) Terramine per 5 gal. of water, rinse, dry immediately, and grade. The mold separates from the meats, rises to the surface of the solution and may be removed by flotation.

Many efforts have been made to control mold in pecan meats by (a) treating with ultraviolet light or ozone immediately before packaging, (b) the use of dips containing chlorine, sodium sorbate, peracetic acid or (c) other mold inhibitors. But the most satisfactory means is to dry the meats to 4.5% moisture or lower and store in an atmosphere of 65% relative humidity or lower. Refrigeration is a mold inhibitor in that temperatures above freezing greatly retard mold growth, and below 0°C (32°F) molding is stopped.

Pink rot is one of the serious after-harvest diseases of pecans before or after shelling. It produces a translucent, waterlogged appearance, which causes the meats to soften and darken. In severe cases the seed coat blackens due to ammonia developed from the fungus. It is always associated with high moisture and is worse (a) in some seasons than others; (b) on Schley and other thin-shelled, well-filled cultivars; and (c) on other cultivars attacked by scab in the orchard. The disease is contracted in the orchard and continues to worsen during storage, even after shelling. The best control is to keep the meats below 4% moisture.

Control of Rats in Storage

Rats are among the pests of stored pecans. They not only eat the nuts, whether shelled or unshelled, but spread filth, eat holes in containers, and cause bad odors.

In order to get rid of rats, five basic steps must be taken:

(1) A survey must be made of the area to determine the degree of infestation.

(2) Rodent parasites such as fleas, lice, mites, and ticks should be destroyed by spraying or dusting with approved insecticides.

(3) Sanitary measures must be taken around the premises. This means the use of sanitary containers, getting rid of breeding and hiding places, and destroying other sources of food.

(4) The use of anticoagulant poisons, for a period of 14 days, is one of the most potent ways of killing rats. These poisons, mixed with corn meal or rolled oats, are tasteless and odorless to the rodents and kill them without pain. Warfarin, fumarin, and similar rodenticides thin the blood and cause fatal hemorrhage inside the animals' body. Unlike most rat poisons, the anticoagulants do not arouse the rats' suspicion.

(5) Continue all of the above steps until the rats have been effectively controlled or exterminated.

Ammonia Damage to Pecans in Storage

Many shellers and warehousemen have experienced ammonia damage to pecans when stored in houses that were refrigerated by ammonia. The damage is not common, but may be disastrous in some cases. The symptoms are blackening of the seed coat, with little change in the flavor, nutritive value or texture of the nuts. There are many factors that influence the rate and degree of blackening of pecan meats by ammonia (Woodroof and Heaton 1966).

Ammonia in the Soil.—Ammonia from decaying manure or other organic matter in the soil, from the application of liquid ammonia

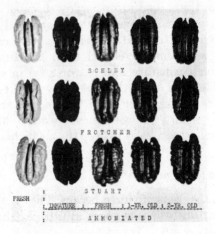

FRESH

: IMMATURE : FRESH : 1-YR. OLD : 2-YR. OLD

AMMONIATED

FIG. 12.38. VARYING DEGREES OF AMMONIA DAMAGE DUE TO CULTIVAR MATURITY AND AGE OF NUTS

FIG. 12.39. AMMONIA DAMAGED PECANS

1, 2, and 3 were taken from commercial plants in Kentucky, Texas, and Georgia, respectively; 4, undamaged.

fertilizer to the land, or from rapid developing mold, may cause pecans to show symptoms of ammonia damage even before they are harvested. In many such cases one side of an individual nut (the side that laid on the damp ground for several days) is damaged much more than the other.

Experimental samples of nutmeats suspended in jars above chicken manure, cow manure or rapidly disintegrating green manure were discolored by ammonia developed in the jars. In the case of the chicken manure, damage was severe within 24 hours, while discoloration was slower with cow manure and still slower with green manure.

Ammonia in Storage Rooms.—The damage may be due to traces of ammonia too low to smell, if the exposure is prolonged as in storage. The more concentrated the gas, the more rapid and intense the damage. In the presence of high ammonia concentrations, as with a broken pipe, blackening occurs within an hour or less, while in very low concentrations several months may be required for it to be detected. Damage is approximately four times worse in shelled than unshelled pecans.

Ammonia is 82.5% nitrogen and 17.75% hydrogen, and is 0.59 times as heavy as air. It is doubtful that it stratifies in a room, but rather tends to diffuse equally to all parts of the room. The lower limit of human perception is about 53 ppm, which will discolor pecan meats in less than an hour.

Effect of Temperatures.—There is a difference in the amount of damage to nuts and nutmeats caused by ammonia at different temperatures. In fact, the reaction of the ammonia with the tannin in the seed coats apparently follows the rule that the activity is doubled by each rise in temperature of 10°C (18°F). Following this rule, a given amount of damage occurring at 0°C (34°F) would be reduced to half by lowering the temperature to -10°C (16°F), and to one-fourth by lowering the temperature to -20°C (-2°F), and to one-eighth by lowering the temperature to -30°C (-20°F). Likewise, the reaction would be doubled by raising the temperature to 10°C (52°F), and quadrupled at 20°C (70°F).

An examination of more than 300,000 lb of four lots of in-shell pecans which had been exposed to ammonia gas for several months revealed only slight to moderate damage because the temperature had been held at -18.9°C (-2°F). Had the temperature been higher, the damage would have been much worse.

Age of Nuts.—Another factor affecting the degree of damage from ammonia is the age of the nuts. Freshly cured nuts are least affected; and as the nuts get "older" or the seed coat begins to "age" in color they become more sensitive to darkening by ammonia. Furthermore, poorly filled, damaged, or shriveled nuts are more sensitive to ammonia damage than well-filled, plump fresh nuts.

Influence of Packaging.—Stored pecans have been examined in many refrigerated warehouses throughout the United States. These have included in-shell nuts in 100 to 200-lb burlap bags and in 1500 lb tote boxes. Pecan meats have been stored in 1-lb, 5-lb, 30-lb and 60-lb corrugated boxes, with and without wax coating, and with and without cellophane or polyethylene bags. The relative amount of damage from ammonia when it was known to be present, as influenced by packaging, is shown in Table 12.16.

TABLE 12.16

THE RELATIVE AMOUNT OF DARKENING OF PECANS WHEN EXPOSED TO AMMONIA GAS IN COMMERCIAL REFRIGERATED WAREHOUSES, AS INFLUENCED BY PACKAGING

Package		Relative Degree of Blackening
	In-shell Pecans	
Burlap bags (100 to 120 lb)		+++++++++
Tote-boxes (1500 lb)		+++++++
	Shelled Pecans	
	(lb test)	
Kraft, plain corrugated boxes	200 test board	++++++
Kraft, plain corrugated boxes	275 test board	+++++
Kraft, plain corrugated boxes	250 test board	+++
Kraft, waxed corrugated boxes	275 test board	+
Polyethylene bag in box	275 test board	0
Cellophane bags in box	275 test board	0
Saran, any form	275 test board	0
Aluminum foil, laminated		0
Nylon film		0

In-shell pecans were damaged almost equally in burlap bags as in tote boxes, the damage always being less to nuts on the interior than near the outside of the package.

Pecan meats in boxes of light weight board were more severely damaged than those in boxes of heavier weight. Meats in boxes sealed with gum tape were less damaged than those in boxes that were stapled only, and damage was worse near the corners and edges than on the interior of the boxes. Lining boxes with wax was beneficial, but not so much as using polyethylene or cellophane bags. There was darkening of meats immediately beneath breaks or open seams of polyethylene bags.

Piling of Nuts.—In cases of ammonia leaks in rooms without circulating air, damage is worse: (a) in bags or loose nuts on top of the pile, and least near the floor; (b) in bags adjacent to the aisles and least in bags or loose nuts near the center of the pile; (c) in nuts near the outside of the bags or piles and least in the center of the bags.

FIG. 12.40. A 30-LB CASE OF PECANS THAT WAS DAMAGED
BY AMMONIA

Damage was worse around the edges of the carton and
decreased toward the center. Note greasy spots on lid
resulting from failure to line the carton with a protective
material.

Blackening Caused by Other Alkali

While ammonia, either in the soil or storage room, is almost always
the cause of blackening of seed coats of pecans, other alkalis may
produce similar discoloration, should they come in contact with the
nuts either as a liquid or gas.

Restoring Color to Nuts Not Feasible

No practical way was found for restoring normal color to pecans
blackened by ammonia. However, it was found that the color could be
partially restored by agitating the meats in a suspension of 6 oz (two
cups) of activated decolorizing carbon in 25 gal. of water for 20 min at
43.3°C (110°F); rinsing and dipping the meats in a solution of 8 tsp of
citric:ascorbic acids (94:6) in 8 gal. of water; and drying the meats to 4%
moisture in a current of air at 43.3°C (110°F).

Ammonia could be eliminated from a storage room by ventilation, or
by neutralizing with sulfur dioxide gas or muriatic acid fumes. The
longer the gas remains the harder it is to remove.

Means of eliminating ammonia damage to stored pecans were: preventing ammonia leaks in the pecan storage rooms, avoiding the entrance of escaping ammonia through the door, or using a refrigerant other than ammonia.

Assessing Ammonia Damage to Pecans

There are two methods of evaluating the damage to nuts by ammonia. The first is to measure the amount of discoloration as blackening. Since the action of ammonia on the tannins or anthocyanins in the seed coat is positive, it can be used as a color indicator. The blackening caused by ammonia is distinct from the reddish amber color of the seed coat, resulting in normal aging of pecans.

The second method of determining the extent of ammonia absorption is to chemically analyze the nuts for amino nitrogen. It has been determined that nitrogen content of pecans is about as follows: freshly harvested from the tree, 0.004%; detectable discoloration, 0.01%; definite blackening, 0.03%; and severe damage, 0.05%.

Susceptibility of Other Nutmeats to Darkening by Ammonia

The seed coats of most nuts are darkened by exposure to ammonia gas. Data in Table 12.17 show the relative susceptibility of the most common unblanched nutmeats to darkening by a concentration of ammonia gas that could be readily detected by smell (Woodroof and Heaton 1966).

TABLE 12.17

THE RELATIVE AMOUNT OF DARKENING OF UNBLANCHED NUTMEATS WHEN EXPOSED TO AMMONIA GAS, THAT COULD BE READILY DETECTED BY SMELL, FOR 48 HOURS

Nuts	Relative Degree of Blackening
Chestnuts	+++++++++
Pecans	+++++++
Filberts	+++++++
Brazil nuts	+++++++
Almonds	+++++
Black walnuts	++++
Apricot nuts	++++
Peanuts	+++

Sterilizing Refrigerated Rooms

The diethyl ester of pyrocarbonic acid is an effective nonpersistent chemical germicidal agent for refrigerated storage rooms. Diethylpyrocarbonate (DEPC) 1000 g in 1000 g of ethanol applied to the walls, ceiling, pallets, shelves and cases as a fine mist, effectively controls microorganisms for more than 5 days. The compound then breaks down by hydrolysis, $C_2H_5O \cdot CO \cdot O \cdot CO \cdot OC_2H_5 \cdot + H_2O \rightarrow 2C_2H_5 \cdot OH + 2CO_2$, without residues or undue side reactions. It is approved by the U.S. Food and Drug Administration, provided that sufficient pure material (at least 98%) is used and that it is prepared by a controlled reaction of sodium ethylate and carbon dioxide to form sodium ethyl carbonate which subsequently reacts with ethyl chloroformate.

The compound is toxic to humans. However, its lachrymatory and irritant activity are built-in safety precautions; and handling by moderately trained personnel under routine safety precautions (self-contained respirator, protective clothing and spark-proof prime movers) is feasible. Heavily mold infested rooms may be fumigated without loss of refrigeration, and safely reentered as long as no irritating effect is felt in the nose and when no fruity odor of the ester is noticed. No undue quality changes should occur in stored nuts (Popper and Nury 1966).

Moisture Determinations

This is a laboratory procedure in which the oven method is most accurate. Other Association of Official Agricultural Methods (Anon. 1965) may be used also.

The moisture determination balance is a magnetically adapted precision balance combined with a drying unit for automatic measurement of the moisture content of solid and liquid materials. Loss of moisture and weight of nuts and nut products may be read at all times throughout the drying cycle on a full-range optical scale, calibrated in percentage moisture lost. Drying is effected by a swiveling infrared heater lamp, infinitely variable from 0 to 250 watt. Automatic shutoff timer provides a setting up to 60 min, and the bell signals operator after elapse of present time.

Refrigerated Storage Rates

Refrigerated storage rates vary with (a) the temperature designated, (b) whether the nuts are shelled or unshelled, (c) the quantity stored, (d) the length of time in storage, and (e) in warehouses in different locations of the country. The handling charges (in and out) are practically "fixed," while the other rates vary as shown in Table 12.18 (Orahood 1964).

PROCESSING PECANS

The first step in processing is drying the nuts. This is done by the grower on the farm or by accumulators at assembly points throughout the growing areas. Since about 1950 more pecans are mechanically

TABLE 12.18

SCHEDULE OF STORAGE RATES, PER HUNDRED POUNDS OF NUTS, IN
REFRIGERATED WAREHOUSES

Product	Handling In and Out (dollars)	Storage Per Month (dollars)
Pecans, in-shell		
0° to 1.7°C (32° to 35°F)		
25,000 lb or more	0.11-0.15	0.12
Less than 25,000 lb	0.11-0.17	0.15
-6.7° to -4.4°C (20° to 24°F)		
25,000 lb or more	0.11	0.15
-17.8°C (0°F)	0.11	0.18
Pecans, shelled		
0° to 1.7°C (32° to 35°F)		
15,000 lb or more	0.18	0.17-0.22
5,000 lb to 15,000 lb	0.20	0.20-0.25
2,000 lb to 5,000 lb	0.22	0.27
Less than 2,000 lb	0.25	0.30
-6.7° to -4.4°C (20° to 25°F)	0.19	0.19
-17.8°C (0°F)	0.19	0.22
Almonds, shelled		
0° to 1.7°C (32° to 35°F)		
15,000 lb or more	0.17	0.15
5,000 to 15,000 lb	0.19	0.17
2,000 to 5,000 lb	0.22	0.20
Less than 2,000 lb	0.25	0.22
Other nuts, shelled		
0° to 1.7°C (32° to 35°F)		
15,000 lb or more	0.19	0.25
10,000 to 15,000 lb	0.21	0.28
5,000 to 10,000 lb	0.22	0.32
1,000 to 5,000 lb	0.23	0.40
Less than 1,000 lb	0.28	0.45
-17.8°C (0°F)		
15,000 lb or more	0.19	0.30
10,000 lb to 15,000 lb	0.21	0.33
5,000 to 10,000 lb	0.22	0.37
1,000 to 5,000 lb	0.23	0.45
Less than 1,000 lb	0.28	0.50

Source: Atlantic Co. and U.S. Storage Corp.

dried in progressively fewer but larger operations. A few major companies now dominate pecan drying operations.

Those that are to be processed are moved as quickly as possible to shelling plants, where they are stored and processed year-round. During processing, they are passed through a series of highly mechanized operations. These include conditioning, cracking, shelling, picking, grading, drying, packaging, and sometimes restoring.

From the sheller or refrigerated storage warehouse the nuts move continuously to the end users—ice cream manufacturers, bakeries, confectioners, salters and retailers.

Processing pecans after shelling consists essentially of subjecting them to conditions that would preserve all the good qualities and prevent deterioration until they reach the end-user or consumers. It includes treatments for protecting the meats from rancidity, insects, mold and chemical degradation. Much of this was discussed under "storing pecans" and will be dealt with in more detail under "salting pecans."

As the pecan industry increases in size, as the export market grows, and as more food products are made from pecans on a year-round schedule, pecan processing will become more important.

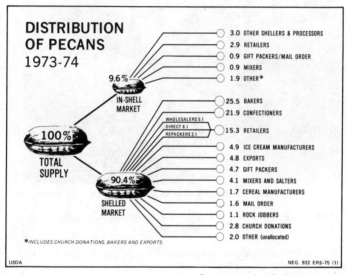

Courtesy of U.S. Dept. Agric.

FIG.12.41. DISTRIBUTION OF PECANS, 1973–74

Rancidity in Pecans

The high oil content of pecans (65 to 75%) renders them susceptible to rancidity. This limits the number of products made from them as well as the length of time they may be held. Development of rancidity is the most common cause of degrading pecans. Rancidity is accompanied by staleness and loss of fresh aroma and flavor. It is a gradual and continuous process first noticed in unshelled pecans held at 21.1°C (70°F) for about 4 months, and held at 1.1°C (34°F) for about 2 years. Along with rancidity there is reddening or browning of the seed coats.

A very mild, but detectable, rancid odor or flavor may not be objectionable in products that have flavors or odors which tend to mask rancidity. This is especially true with pecans in fruit cakes, spiced pecans or chocolate coated pecans.

Excessive drying seems to accelerate rancidity, possibly by replacing oxygen for water in the tissue. Pecans seem to be more stable at relative humidities from 75 to 80% and at moistures of about 4½%, or just short of molding.

Courtesy of A. B. Kinnerly, Canner/Packer

FIG. 12.42.   PECAN BREADED SHRIMP BEING PREPARED FOR
FREEZING

Fish and chicken are breaded in a similar manner.

Rancidity is used to describe many undesirable aromas and flavors developed in fats and oils, whether extracted or still contained in the nuts. It includes rank or tainted smells or tastes that are associated with oxidation or hydrolysis, and is usually accompanied by partial decomposition and formation of free fatty acids.

Three classes of rancidity are (a) hydrolysis of component glycerides of fat into free fatty acids and glycerol or mono- and diglycerides, (b) oxidation of double bonds of unsaturated glycerides to form peroxides and then decompose to aldehydes of objectionable odors and flavors, and (c) β-oxidation of free saturated fatty acids.

There is no single method for determining rancidity in nuts and nut products. In most cases smell and taste are sufficient. Chemical tests include the Kreis method, determination of 2-thiobarbutric acid, peroxide values, photochemical methods, determining total carbonyl compounds. These methods are described in proceedings of Association of Official Agricultural Chemists (1960). A more recent procedure is the use of gas chromatography.

Retarding Rancidity in Pecans

One of the most effective ways of retarding rancidity in pecans is by refrigeration. (See section on pecan storage.) They can be held from one season to the next by storing at 0°C (32°F) with 70 to 75% relative humidity (Blackmon 1932; Brison 1945; Wright 1941; Woodroof and Heaton 1961). At 10°C (50°F) they remain good for six months, and at 21.1°C (70°F) for about four months. The nuts must be harvested in the fall and stored before oil begins to leak out of the kernels or staleness begins.

A second method of retarding rancidity is by excluding air. This may be done by (a) the use of hermetically sealed containers; (b) packing under 25 in. or more of vacuum; (c) replacing the air in the containers with 97% inert gas such as nitrogen or hydrogen; or (d) coating the nuts with collodion or water glass. By excluding a high percentage of the air from the nuts the storage life may be extended two or three times, depending upon the amount of air excluded. Syrups and sugar coatings are fairly effective in excluding oxygen.

A third method of retarding rancidity in pecans is by the use of antioxidants as described in Table 12.19. Fresh pecans contain about

TABLE 12.19

ANTIOXIDANT FORMULAS

Antioxidant I

Butylated hydroxyanisole	20%
Butylated hydroxytoluene	20%
Vegetable oil	60%

Antioxidant II

Component	Solution	% of Total Solids
Dipotassium salt of ethylenediamine tetraacetic acid	0.024	0.20
Citric acid	0.048	0.40
Butylated hydroxyanisole (BHA)	0.24	2.0
Butylated hydroxytoluene (BHT)	0.24	2.0
Propyl gallate	0.24	2.0
Sorbitan monostearate (Span 60)	0.52	4.4
Polyoxyethylene stearate (G-2147)	5.12	43.0
Polyoxyethylene sorbitan tristearate (Tween 65)	5.47	46.0
Isopropyl alcohol (91%)	88.1	–

0.45% tocopherol, a naturally occurring antioxidant, which renders pecans quite stable for a while, depending largely on the temperature. Added antioxidants (0.1% of NDGA or BHA) are of more value in slightly aged pecans after the natural antioxidants have partially disappeared. Godkin *et al.* (1951) reported that the bitterness contributed by NDGA is undesirable and nullifies the efficiency of its rancidity delaying properties as an antioxidant.

Heating Pecan Meats.—Woodroof and Heaton (1961) and McGlammery and Hood (1951) reported that pecan meats heated to an internal temperature of 80°C (176°F) in dry air or in oil doubled the shelf-life by inactivating oxidative enzymes. Heating to higher temperatures produced a partially cooked flavor.

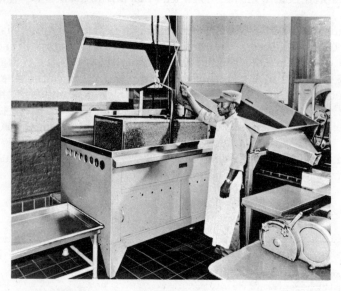

FIG. 12.43.   BATCH, OIL ROASTING PECAN MEATS

Heating pecan meats to 185°C (365°F) for 15 min by dry roasting or with infrared heat rays, destroys natural antioxidants but increases the aroma and flavor many times. Roasting in oil is slightly less satisfactory for flavor development.

Finely grinding roasted pecan meats and packing in jars to exclude air increased the storage life by more than 20 times, without refrigeration. Freshness was extended much longer when an antioxidant was added and refrigeration was used.

Other methods of retarding rancidity in pecan meats are by storing in the dark, and by the use of containers coated on the inside with an antioxidant.

It has been established that storage life of nuts and oils can be extended if antioxidants are added. BHA, BHT, and propyl gallate are among the chemicals now being used for this purpose. These antioxidants, used with nuts and oils or fat containing foods, present problems such as partial effectiveness with highly unsaturated oils, discoloration with metals, odors (particularly associated with phenolic-type antioxidants), and poor solubility.

FIG. 12.44.   PECAN HALVES AND PIECES; RAW, DRY ROASTED AND OIL ROASTED

Samples are spread on absorbent paper to show how roasting and chopping increases the "crawling" of the oil.

Sherwin and Thompson of Eastman Chemical Products, Kingsport, Tennessee, proceeded to develop what they report as a more effective antioxidant primarily for polyunsaturated oils. This product is tertiarybutylhydroquinone (TBHQ).

A rapid and efficient method of stabilizing pecan nutmeats with antioxidants—primarily for bakeries—was worked out (Anon. 1958). It was determined that nutmeats treated with Tenox BHA and Tenox BHT and used in bakery products had about twice the shelf-life of nuts not treated. Since the cost of adding the antioxidant at the shelling plant was light, the added shelf-life tended to increase the use of pecans in cookies, fruitcakes and other bakery items.

For complete control of rancidity in pecans and pecan meats several of the following procedures should be followed:

(1) Dry kernels to 4½% moisture as soon after maturity as possible using circulated air not higher than 38°C (100°F).

(2) Store at 3°C (38°F) or lower, with 65% relative humidity for pecan meats and 75% relative humidity for in-shell pecans.

(3) Heat to 80°C (176°F) for 2 min to inactivate oxidative enzymes.

(4) Reduce oxygen in the atmosphere by placing under vacuum, or in 98% nitrogen or carbon dioxide.

(5) Treat nuts or nutmeats with 0.1% BHA, BHT, or NDGA antioxidant.

(6) Coat nutmeats with sugar glaze, heavy syrup, zein, dextrins or collodion to exclude air.

(7) Pack in containers coated on inside with BHA, BHT or NDGA antioxidant.

(8) Keep in the dark or in amber colored containers.

Recovery of Pecan Oil

Pecans and other tree nuts, although rich sources of oil, must be considered primarily as luxury food items, and edible grades cannot therefore be pressed economically except to fill small demands for specialty oils. Shelling plants, however, reject large amounts of moldy and otherwise inedible meats which are entirely suitable for oil recovery. The shells contain a considerable percentage of unseparated meats, which are reclaimed by reducing the shells in a hammer mill, screening and pressing (Kester 1949).

Pecan oil is a by-product of several operations in pecan processing. It is recovered from pecans and most tree nuts for limited use in cooking, cosmetics and other special preparations. The quantity of nut oil is small as compared to that of cottonseed, soybeans, corn and peanuts, and its recovery is justified on the basis of special flavor, chemical and physical qualities.

The sources of nuts for oil recovery are (a) "meal" resulting from chopping or breaking the meats; (b) "screenings" from shelling operations containing a mixture of shells and meat particles; (c) nuts rejected from grading operations because of shape, size or defects. Clean pecan meats or meal run as high as 76% oil as shown in Tables 3.13 and 3.17.

The method of treatment and recovery varies with the kind of nuts but all follow the same general procedure for all tree nuts: (1) hulling or shelling the nuts; (2) removal of foreign materials, as shells, stones, pieces of wood or metal, from the meats; (3) rolling, crushing or chopping the material; (4) heating in moist air or steam; (5) removal of oil by hydraulic pressing, screw pressing, cage pressing or solvent extraction, or a combination of two or more of these; (6) removing foreign material by filtering; (7) refining by removal of free fatty acid with alkali and foreign odors with steam.

Costa and Mota (1942) indicated that, for the extraction of Brazil nut oil, screw pressing was very efficient and more practical than solvent extraction because with the latter the oil retains traces of the solvent and the fat-soluble vitamins are completely removed from the meal.

Pecan meal resulting from shelling amounts to about 3% of the pecans shelled. It is a mixture of fine particles of meats and shells and is inedible. It contains about 30% oil which may be recovered by grinding and pressing or solvent extracting. The oil is of excellent quality.

The meal is collected from shelling plants throughout the industry and shipped to one or more central points for processing. Due to the large surface exposure the meal may become stale within a few weeks at room temperature. While the quantity of pecans shelled increases almost annually, the percentage of meal decreases constantly due to improvements in pecan processing equipment. For this reason the production of oil from pecans or most tree nuts is not increasing.

Kester (1949) reported about 300 tons of pecan oil produced annually. This quantity has increased little if any in 20 years. The refined oil sold for 40 to 50 cents per pound. He reported the composition of the oil as follows: iodine value, 100 to 106; oleic acid, 70.9 to 77.8%; linoleic acid, 15.8 to 25.2%; saturated acids, 4.0 to 5.1%; and unsaponifiables, 0.4% (see Table 3.13).

Whitehead and Warshaw (1938) extracted and refined pecan oil which was transparent, bland, odorless, and comparable to olive and other high grade oils. There was no rancidity development in the oil after 12 months storage in glass bottles exposed to sunlight at room temperature. They found that the oil could be used to make excellent French dressing, mayonnaise, and cold cream, and could be substituted for other cooking fats. The meal left after oil extraction could be made into tasty muffins, biscuits, bread, and cookies, as well as blended with common flavors. The oil contained the following by percent: oleic acid, 77.8; linoleic acid, 15.8; myristic acid, 0.04; arachidic acid, 0.09; palmitic acid, 3.14; stearic, 1.82; cholesterol, 0.28; and lecithin, 0.5.

A ton of high quality pecans will yield approximately 400 lb of a clear high quality golden oil when subjected to 12 tons of pressure. When a good grade of pecans is used the press cake or pomace left after the oil is pressed or extracted, may be ground into a good flavored meal. This meal is used in candies, cakes, breads and possibly to produce breakfast foods and other products lower in calories than when regular pecan meats are used. Also, the pomace or unpressed pecans may be finely ground into a pecan butter (Blackmon 1937).

Another source of pecan meal from which oil may be recovered is from cutting and breaking operations when pecan meats are converted into smaller sizes. This meal is sieved from the pecan pieces and marketed for use in ice cream, cookies, candies and other recipes. It contains a higher percentage of torn seed coats and consequently is slightly bitter due to the tannin. The oil content runs about 60%.

The yield of edible meal from cutting operations varies from 2 to 5% depending upon the quality and condition of the meats and the fineness to which they are cut.

Solvent Extraction of Oil

Solvent extraction of oil from pecans and other nuts has the advantage that oil removal is more complete, and has the disadvantage that solvent soluble vitamins and other materials are removed from the meal. Solvent extraction is desirable when good quality nuts are used for making edible nut meal or flour.

Solvent extraction includes the steps of leaching the oil from the solid residue and subsequent recovery of solvent-free oil and meal. A good extractor must meet the following specifications: (1) it should extract substantially all the oil from the prepared seed, using an economical solvent:seed ratio; (2) it must be mechanically strong, and capable of continuous operation for many months without maintenance; (3) it must operate simply and automatically; (4) it should cause a minimum of particle size reduction in the solids; and (5) it should produce a miscellanea of maximum clarity possible.

There are two types of solvent extractors, the immersion-type and the percolation-type. In the immersion-type the solids are agitated in the solvent while in the percolation-type the solvent is run through fixed beds of solids. In each of these the contact between solvent and solids may be either continuous or stage-wise, with partial draining of the solvent from meats between stages. In all cases the flow of solvent and solids is made as countercurrent as possible.

Each type has application where it has peculiar advantage. The percolation requires that the solids form a porous bed through which the solvent can flow. This limits its application to well-prepared flakes or sized particles whereas the application of the immersion type is not limited. However, where the percolation-type can be used, it has the advantage of producing clear miscellanea by the filtration through the bed characteristic of its operation; of permitting adequate drainage by gravity, within the extractor, of the solvent in the extracted flakes; and of causing little reduction of particle size. The immersion-type generally requires auxiliary miscellanea clarification and auxiliary means of draining the solvent from extracted solids, such as drain boards, squeezers and centrifuges.

In practice, the distinction between the two types of extractors is not sharp since an effort is made in the design of several of the immersion extractors to establish a bed and to gain the advantages of percolation.

There are many extractors described in patent literature; among which are the following:

> The Centrifuge Extraction System
> Horizontal Cell Extraction
> The Screw Conveyor
> Verticle Column Tray Extractors System —
>   Allis-Chalmers, Anderson and Bonotto
>   The Basket Extractor
> The Rotocel Extractor

Each of these has special advantages for certain oily seeds and size of operation (Karnofsky 1949).

Improved Oilseed Extractor.—An efficient, vapor-tight, flake-feeding device for nut oil extraction was developed and may replace conventional equipment (Patton 1958). The design provides improvement over conventional screw-conveyor feeders by using an anti-bridging distributor conveyor in the hopper, and by using the material being fed to form a plug-type positive vapor seal at the discharge end of the feeder. The unit is self-contained and consists of a hopper, a distributor screw, a main feed screw, a variable speed mechanism and an electric motor. A desirable feature is that the unit eliminates bridging of the flakes above the feed screws and consequently ensures a continuous flow of material.

A short tubular extension is used at the discharge end of the screw through which the ground nuts can be forced, allowing them to compact gently and form a plug. This plug of nutmeats serves as a seal against the leakage of solvent out of the system, and also prevents the passage of air into the system.

Refining Pecan Oil

In the refining process the crude pecan oil is treated with a solution of caustic soda (sodium hydroxide) to neutralize the free fatty acids and precipitate much of the undesirable coloring matter. The alkali combines with the free fatty acids and with part of the oil to form a stock called "foots" which is removed by centrifuge.

The hot refined oil is mixed with a small quantity of bleaching clay and run through a filter press to decolorize it. It is deodorized by heating under vacuum and then steam distilled. The resulting product is bland, tasteless, almost colorless and much more stable than crude oil. The time before staleness and rancidity begins can be extended by as much as five times by adding an antioxidant; it can again be doubled by packing under vacuum, and doubled again by keeping in the dark; and extended almost indefinitely by a combination of all of these with storage at 0°C (32°F) or lower.

Uses for Pecan Oil

Pecan oil is competitive with most vegetable oils—peanut, corn, safflower, cotton and soybean—for uses in the diet. These include deep fat frying, hydrogenation, use in shortening, oleomargarine and others. However, pecan oil along with oil from other tree nuts—almond, Persian walnut, filbert, black walnut, cashew, macadamia, pine, and hickory—cannot compete pricewise with oil from the above named sources. There are a few chemical, physical and flavor properties in crude pecan oil that may give it an advantage in cosmetics, pharmaceuticals, and other specialty uses; but many of these characteristics are lost during the various steps in refining.

FIG. 12.45. ONE TEASPOON OF PECAN BUTTER ADDS
EXCELLENT FLAVOR, SMOOTH TEXTURE AND A "NUTMEG"
APPEARANCE TO MILKSHAKES

While pecan oil may be used in diets specifying a high degree of unsaturation, there are other, and cheaper, oils with the same properties.

Color Measurement of Nuts

Color is light energy that is reflected from the object being viewed; or, the color of the object is the color reflected from the object. The control of color quality in fresh, stored or processed nuts is very important.

Color measurements of nuts and nut products are made by one or more of four methods: (a) purely subjective, (b) comparatively subjective, (c) comparatively objective and (d) purely objective.

Courtesy of Tracy-Luckey Co.

FIG. 12.46. ELECTRIC EYE MACHINES SEPARATE PECAN PIECES ACCORDING TO COLOR

The two units shown may replace 10 people grading by hand.

Purely Subjective Color Measurements.—These are made by individuals using sensory facilities in conjunction with memory data to form a qualitative conclusion. Even with a wide array of instruments available, color measurements of nuts, and nut products are often made through the sensory instruments of recognized color inspection experts who have "an eye for color."

Comparatively Subjective Measurements.—These are made through visual comparison of samples with accepted standards. The standards may be in the form of color charts, colored papers or colored models of the products to be graded. U.S. Standards for Grades of pecans and other nuts are available. While these methods are effective for routine inspection and grading, gross differences of opinion do occur as a result of subjective factors such as the spectral response of the individual's optical mechanisms, or because of physical factors such as fading or discoloration of the standard, or differences in ambient lighting conditions. Nonetheless, subjective comparison is an obvious improvement over purely subjective methods because the standard provides a reasonably stable reference.

Comparative Objective Measurements.—Such measurements are made by an instrument which is designed to compare the spectral reflectance or transmittance of the sample with that of a standard. In general, the only errors in this type of system are those caused by individual inaccuracies of the optically active components and by spectral differences between similar standards. Unfortunately, the inaccuracies of the individual optical components are not necessarily minor. Very large spectral response differences have been noted between light sources, phototubes, and filters bearing the same model number and ostensibly conforming to the same general characteristic curves. Some spectrophotometers have a month-to-month reproducibility which is poorer than its short term duplication.

Purely Objective Measurements.—Objective measurements pertain to instrumentation which does not rely on comparison with a colored sample and in which sources of error have either been obviated or substantially minimized. Ideally such an instrument should be electronically rather than optically calibrated, and be designed such that the individual differences between similar components do not have an effect on the readout. In short, all instruments of a given type or model should read alike.

While the color measurement of homogeneous materials is relatively easy, when attempts are made to control objectively or define the color of nonhomogeneous and parti-colored product, several problems are encountered. Practically every tree nut, either raw or processed, has a statistical conglomerate of colors. The "nonhomogeneous" nature is even more inclusive when extended to include such physical properties as size, geometry, and surface irregularities.

Few colorimeters and spectrophotometers are designed for quality control, and to be suitable as such, they must meet the following criteria: (a) all similar instruments should read alike without need for constant calibration or mathematical correlation; (b) the instrument must be direct-reading in easily understood terms; (c) the instrument must withstand production area environments; (d) it must be easy to operate by semiskilled and even unskilled workers; and (e) the instrument must be reliable, requiring only infrequent cleaning and maintenance.

The Agtron instrument is suited to control color for raw materials or finished products—granules, paste, powder or liquid. Minute color variations are detected and color changes over a 100-point spread on a direct reading meter are projected. Thus, constant numerical values can be assigned to colors. The instrument is suitable for grading products of many consistencies such as kernels, pastes, crystals, purées and creams (Simmons 1966).

Automatic Filling Equipment

Much of the improvement in pecan processing has been in mechanical handling of the graded meats without hand labor. Following is a description of one type of filling machine. The twin discharge filler enables two operators to work filling two bags or containers simultaneously. The discharge spout and frame are designed for operation over and alongside conveyors, giving advantage of two fillers. The filler handles all semi- or free-flowing dry products.

The automatic rigid container filler with table top chain conveyor fills cans, bottles, tubes, jars, canisters, and other rigid containers with dry products such as nuts, candies or small bakery goods.

Food and Drug Administration officials keep a close watch on short weight packages. On the other hand food processors are concerned with overweight packages as this represents an almost imperceptible loss of great sums of money. The American Sanitation Institute performs short weight checks either as part of their regular sanitation audits or on separate assignment. It recognizes the need in the food processing industry to protect the consumer from short weight and the processors themselves from overweight.

The Institute follows Food and Drug Administration procedures and uses the same Gurley balance. Fifty packages are weighed and the average weight is taken and compared with the label statement. In the event a package is short weight, the American Sanitation Institute's "unofficial" weight check allows the packer to correct the infraction before it is encountered and acted upon "officially." The short weight check program has three prime objectives: (1) to help the client comply with the government's emphasis on full weight packages; (2) to help save clients the considerable amount of money that might be slipping out in overweight packages; and (3) to alert the client to any practices of "hidden" labeling of which they may be unwittingly guilty.

Vacuum Gassing Nutmeats

The equipment and process of packing nutmeats under inert gas may

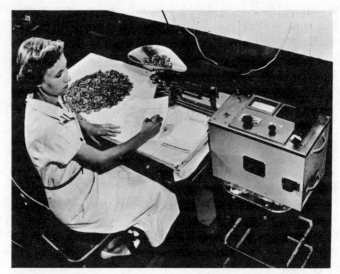

Courtesy of Tracy-Luckey Co.

FIG. 12.47. QUALITY IS CONTROLLED IN SHELLING PLANT AS
THE WEIGHTS, GRADES AND MOISTURE CONTENT
ARE RECORDED

be described as follows (Jerissa Nut Company 1962).

The vacuum gassing process of canning has been developed to eliminate the action of oxygen on the product packed. Air, due to its oxygen
content, is one of the most powerful agencies in the deterioration of
food products. In as much as air contains oxygen, it is necessary to
exhaust the air from the cans by means of a vacuum and then admit an
inert gas, such as carbon dioxide or nitrogen. The use of gas, in addition
to other benefits relieves the pressure on the can and prevents panels in
the larger cans.

Two kinds of gases many be used—carbon dioxide and nitrogen.
These are tasteless, odorless, and inert gases. Nuts have a tendency to
absorb carbon dioxide, and through this absorption a vacuum is created—strong enough to panel cans. Therefore, a high purity nitrogen is
used for the packaging of nuts. To accomplish this method of packing,
the air is withdrawn from the container by creating a vacuum in the
chamber of the machine and subsequently filling the chamber with the
high purity nitrogen at atmospheric pressure, or slightly above it, to
prevent the infusion of air before the container is permanently sealed.

The machine consists of a 15 pocket rotary valve with a timed chain.
On the chain are mounted doors with can carriers spaced in sequence to
fit in the valve pockets. The chain and doors are operated by six

stations of sprockets with an upper and lower sprocket at each station.

The cans are fed into a clinching machine, which feeds the covers automatically and clinches them to the can. The clinched cans are fed onto a transfer table, where the feed fingers transfer the can onto a can carrier. The can carrier, which is attached to the pivoted door, is now cammed to operate a little faster than the feedfinger, so that the finger does not hit the carrier. As the carrier takes control of the can, an outer guide centralizes the can on the carrier.

The can and carrier now enter the valve pocket, and at a predetermined point, the valve pocket is sealed by a spring operated finger until the vacuum seals the door to the valve.

The can is vacuumized in stages during the rotation of the valve to a point where the gassing cycle starts. At the end of the gassing cycle, the valve pocket is opened to the atmosphere. After the carrier leaves the valve pocket, the can is transferred to the closing machine infeed disc. The closing machine then permanently seals the cover. The vacuumizing and gassing valve government specifications require not more than 2% residual oxygen. The reason for this is that it is extremely difficult and costly to go below. With this new machine it is now possible to run at a constant of less than 1%.

A few of the benefits of this type pack are that the nuts (1) have a much longer shelf-life, (2) retain their original color and flavor, and (3) have better stability after exposure to elements.

A vacuum bag-in-box gives shelf-life of 18 months to nutmeats as compared to 6 months for canned nuts. The protection is in the bag that provides the vacuum. Its two layers of "alathon" polyethylene, one of polymercoated "mylar" film and another of Alcoa's aluminum foil, hold a vacuum with less than 1% residual oxygen. Mylar, as the outer ply, provides the bag's strength. Joined to the 35-mil foil by a ½ mil laminate of alathon, it also completes a formidable gas barrier. A 2½-mil extrusion coating of alathon serves to guard the foil liner from nut oils, acids or salts that might weaken it, and provides a "weld" when the vacuum is sealed.

Heat and pressure along the top edges of the filled and vacuumized pouch produce a solid seam of polyethylene. The vacuum immobilizes the nuts until the shield is broken, and in this way splits are reduced.

The carton is strong and rigid for easy stacking, storing or shipping. A tear tape makes opening quick and easy. Since the packages do not rust, dent or shatter, are easily disposed of, and the nuts stay fresh longer, this package is especially suitable for export items. Furthermore, there is a saving on packaging cost of about five cents per consumer unit, as compared to tin or glass (Anon. 1966).

Home Canning Nutmeats

Shelled nuts may be packed in tin cans and sterilized, in an effort to prolong the keeping qualities of the nuts. In the home, nutmeats may be heat processed in two ways. (1) They may be stored in sterilized jars from which the air has been exhausted. The jars are sterilized in boiling water, dried and filled with nutmeats of high quality. The lid is placed on the jar and it is partially sealed. It is then set in a container of hot water which comes to about 2 in. on the sides of the jar. After standing in boiling water for 30 min the jars are sealed, cooled, and stored in a cool, dry dark place. (2) The jars of nutmeats may be sterilized with steam pressure.

The most satisfactory way to hold nutmeats is to dry to a normal temperature, pack in moisture proof containers and freeze. They may be held in this manner for more than three years.

Sanitation in Processing Plant (see Chapter 18, p. 678)

Processing plants are faced with the ever-present problem of initiating economical sanitation programs. The sanitary supervisor must have no other job priorities to prevent his carrying out essential functions. Insects present real problems in processing pecans.

A gas sterilizing facility for treating nutmeats with 100% propylene oxide or 100% ethylene oxide, at Union City, California, was completed in 1966 by Griffith Laboratories. A similar plant is in operation in Los Angeles and four are in foreign lands.

Fungus-resistant papers for packaging nuts (Mosinee Paper Mills) are designed to meet definite conditions of exposure to specific fungi. The papers are of various colors as well as white, and may be impregnated with different fungus-proofing materials. Some of them have odors which should be avoided for packing nuts. One paper is resistant to soil molds and another is resistant to cultures of *Aspergillus niger, Chaetomium globosum,* and *Aspergillus terreus.*

Use of Insect-Free Raw Pecans[1].—Nuts to be stored for a long period must be insect-free initially. (See section on storing pecans.) The most common method of introducing an insect infestation into processed food is by using infested raw commodities. Although the processing will undoubtedly kill most of the insects present in the raw stock, a few may survive. One or two insects in a few packages is all that is needed to

---

[1]This section on "Protection of Nuts From Insect Damage" was prepared by H. Laudani, Entomologist, Stored-Product Insects Laboratory, U.S. Dept. of Agriculture, Savannah, Georgia (Laudani 1963).

develop into a major insect problem. In addition, insects present in the raw stock spread through the plant and form a source for infesting the food as it goes through the plant. Therefore, use only insect-free stock. If there is any indication that an insect infestation might be present, reject the commodity. If it must be accepted, fumigate it before it is brought into the plant. Use only approved fumigants, at the recommended doses.

Adequate Insect Control in Processing Plants.—Insects can be introduced into the plant in many ways other than in the primary raw material. They may be present in blending stocks, in condiments, and in various supplies and packaging materials; or they may enter the plant from nearby sources. Constant vigilance for insect infestation in the plant and in the materials brought into the plant is a must. It is important, therefore, to have effective surveillance and sanitation programs to prevent insects from entering the plants, becoming established, and serving as a source for infesting the food during processing. Frequent inspection and cleaning of every part of the plant and every piece of machinery and equipment in the plant is important. Fumigate difficult-to-clean machinery and enclosed spaces. Use residual insecticides and space treatment where and when possible. Always strive to prevent an insect infestation from becoming established in the plant, and if one is discovered, clean it up immediately.

Use of Insect-Resistant Packages.—Proper packaging is the most positive way of protecting processed foods against insect damage during shipment and storage. Pennies spent on insect-resistant packages pay larger dividends than dollars spent on insect control during shipment and storage.

The packaging material used greatly influences the protective value of a container by its natural resistance to insect penetration and its inherent suitability for forming an insect-tight container. Glass and sheet metal are the only food-packaging materials completely resistant to insect penetration. All others, such as paper, fiberboard, and foil, are subject to penetration by the cadelle, the lesser grain borer, and possibly by other stored-product insects. The comparative resistance of the more commonly used pliable packaging materials, in order of decreasing resistance, are polyester film, aluminum foil, polyethylene film, cellophane, kraft paper, rayon sheeting, cotton sheeting, and burlap. The last three materials offer little or no resistance to insects. Within each of the other types of material, the resistance increases in proportion to the thickness of the film.

To overcome the inherent susceptibility of pliable packaging materials to insect penetration, a chemical treatment has been developed

(Laudani and Davis 1955). A combination of pyrethrum and piperonyl butoxide applied at the rate of 5 mg and 50 mg/sq ft, respectively, will prevent insect penetration of multiwall paper bags for about 9 months. The Food and Drug Administration has approved this treatment and has established a temporary tolerance of 1 ppm for pyrethrins and 10 ppm for piperonyl butoxide in all foods packaged in treated multiwall paper bags.

The structural tightness of the package is as important as the packaging material used. The most resistant packaging material, whether natural or treated, is worthless if the container is not structurally insect-tight. The end closure of single-ply and multiwall paper bags should have pasted or heat-sealed tape-over-stitch closures. The insect-tightness of shell cartons is significantly improved by the use of well-sealed overwraps. Until better designed fiberboard shipping cases are made, complete taping of all joints is necessary (Laudani et al. 1958).

Of several hundred single and laminated films used for resistance to penetration by insects the most resistant is a single-ply polycarbonate type Lexan, supplied by General Electric Co. (Highland and Jay 1965).

Pyrethrum-piperonyl butoxide treatment on food packages has been accepted by U.S. Food and Drug Administration when used on the outside layer of multiwall paper bags (Lehman 1956). In addition to synergized pyrethrum, methoxychlor, lindane, and synergized allethrin have been found promising. Pyrethrum, in combination with piperonyl butoxide applied as a clay coating at the rate of 5 and 50 mg/sq ft on the outer ply of multi-walled paper bags, has been found effective in preventing insect infestation for 9 to 12 months (Laudani and Davis 1955).

Insect Prevention in Transport Facilities.—Transport facilities are a common source of insect infestations. Freight cars are notoriously bad because of their construction and their multiple use. Surveys have shown that, during the summer season, as high as 96% of the freight cars are insect-infested (Wagner 1956). Grains and cereal products lodge in the walls of the car and become excellent breeding places for stored-product insects. Thorough cleaning of the cars eliminates some of the infestation, but insects in the walls are almost impossible to kill off, even with fumigation. Residual sprays help to kill the insects as they emerge, but care must be taken that these treatments do not contaminate the food. The walls and floor of the cars should be lined with heavy kraft paper after the residual spray has dried. Similar precautions should be taken with motor transport facilities. Clean them out thoroughly, spray all inside surfaces with a good residual insecticide, and then line the floor and walls with heavy kraft paper before the food is loaded.

Physical Requirements of the Warehouse.—Successful protection of food against insect damage during storage requires a well-located, well-constructed storage facility, good warehouse practices, and the creation of an unfavorable environment for the insects.

Serious consideration should be given to locating the warehouse that is to be used for long-term storage of food. It should be as far away as possible from storage, handling, and processing facilities that deal with insect-infested material. The surrounding area should be free of any potential insect source.

The warehouse should be well constructed. The building should be tight to keep out insects, rodents, and birds, and to keep in fumigant gases if such a treatment becomes necessary. The floors and walls should be solid and should have smooth surfaces. There should be no cracks, crevices, or dead-air spaces, which are difficult to clean and are excellent breeding places for insects.

Most stored-product insects prefer darkness or semi-darkness. A well-lighted warehouse will help discourage some insect activities. Good lighting is also essential for proper inspection of the premises and the stock.

Warehousing Practices.—To protect nuts properly during long-term storage, good warehousing practices are essential. The warehousing practices used will have a direct influence on the effectiveness of the surveillance, sanitation, and insect-preventive programs. The nuts should be thoroughly inspected when they arrive at the warehouse. If infested, they should be rejected. If they must be accepted, then they should be fumigated before they are brought into the warehouse.

Stacking.—All food should be on pallets and arranged in neat stacks. Each stack should have a floor clearance of at least 8 in., cover no more than 1000 sq ft of floor space, and be completely surrounded with aisles at least 3 ft wide. Food should never be stacked up against a wall. The four sides of every stack should be exposed and accessible at all times. Arrangement of the food in this manner (a) permits close inspection of a large percentage of the packages, (b) facilitates the repair or removal of the broken packages, (c) permits more efficient rotation of the stock, (d) makes it easier to clean the premises, (e) increases the effectiveness of the insect-preventive program by better isolating small infestations, and (f) exposes the maximum number of packages to the insect-preventive treatments.

Sanitation.—Insects can develop, multiply, and survive on a relatively small amount of food. Spilled food and accumulated food dusts or sweepings can support heavy populations of stored-product insects. Good sanitation is, therefore, very important in preventing insect infestations in food warehouses. All surfaces should be kept clean at all times. This includes the open floor space as well as that under the pallets, on window sills, wall plates and girders, etc. A heavy-duty industrial vacuum cleaner should be used for this purpose to keep the dust to a minimum.

Broken packages are an invitation to insects. Insects find such packages very readily. Once an infestation gets established, it spreads to other packages. Broken packages or spillings should never be allowed to remain on the premises. The packages should be repaired or removed immediately, and the spillings cleaned up.

Frequent inspections should be made of the food in storage to determine whether an insect infestation exists. This should involve a very careful inspection of the surface of the stacks and between the packages. The older stock should be sampled periodically. If an infestation is found, its seriousness and extent should be determined. If the insects are in only one bag or one lot, remove the infested stock immediately, and watch the remaining stock closely to see whether the infestation has spread. If the infestation extends over a large part of the stock, either fumigate the entire area or get rid of the stock as soon as possible. If fumigation is not possible, more frequent space treatments may be administered to keep the infestation from getting out of hand. No new shipments should be placed in a warehouse where a general insect infestation exists.

Insect Preventive Measures.—In spite of every precaution, some insects will show up in warehouses where nuts are stored. It is necessary, therefore, to employ some means of preventing insects from reaching and infesting the foods. This can be accomplished by using pesticides or by creating unsuitable climatic or atmospheric conditions.

Protection With Pesticides.— There are three distinct uses of pesticides for protecting stored foods against insect infestations: (a) the treatment of floor and wall surfaces with residual-type insecticides to kill crawling insects; (b) periodic treatment of the airspace with aerosol or mist formulations to kill flying and possibly some crawling insects; and (c) the fumigation of foods suspected of being infested.

Residual Treatments.—The ideal residual treatment is toxic to a wide range of insects, is long-lasting, is compatible with the surface to which it is applied, and produces no undesirable effects on the food in storage or on the people working in the warehouse. No residual insecticide, whether of high or low toxicity, should be applied directly to stored food. Contamination of the food from "bounce-off" or drifting spray mist while floor and wall surfaces are treated should also be avoided. Equipment should be used that will produce a wet or coarse spray with a minimum of mist or "bounce-off." As a group, the chlorinated hydrocarbon insecticides have a longer residual life than the organic phosphates or carbomates. Residues of insecticides formulated as wettable powders generally last longer and resist chemical breakdown from contact with alkaline or moist surfaces better than those applied as emulsions or oil solutions. Translocation of the insecticide from a treated surface to nearby food is a serious problem, which should be considered in selecting the insecticide to be used. Before using any insecticide or fungicide, check with the Environmental Protection Agency, and read the label on the container.

Space Treatments.—Space treatments are used to kill any insect that may be flying or crawling on an exposed surface. Such a treatment kills insects only while the insecticide is suspended in the air—and perhaps for a very short time on the horizontal surface on which the insecticide has settled. To be effective in insect prevention, therefore, space treatments must be repeated frequently. Because such a treatment comes in contact with the food or containers, the possibilities of contamination are great. The only pesticides approved and recommended for this use at present are the insecticide pyrethrum and the synergist piperonyl butoxide. Pyrethrins are used with peperonyl butoxide at the ratio of 1 to 10. The established tolerances on processed foods are 3 ppm of pyrethrins and 20 ppm of piperonyl butoxide. DDVP and other organic phosphate insecticides that have a very short life when exposed to the air look very promising for space treatment in food warehouses. DDVP must not be used for this purpose until the residue and tolerance status are established.

Fumigation.—Residual and space treatments are effective against insects that fly or crawl in exposed places. They have little or no value for controlling insects that are inside or between packages or in protected locations within the structure of the warehouse. If such an infestation then develops in a food warehouse, either the infested food should be removed immediately from the warehouse, and the premises given a series of frequent space treatments, or the stacks of infested food and the surrounding areas should be fumigated.

Fumigants are dangerous to humans in the concentrations required to kill insects, and therefore, for the sake of effectiveness as well as safety, they should be applied only by experienced personnel. The fumigant should be selected carefully. It should be one that has been approved for, and is compatible with, all of the food and other materials present in the area under fumigation. The dose used and the number of times a single item is fumigated should be carefully controlled so that residue in the food will not exceed the established tolerance. A single fumigation with methyl bromide will leave on many nut products an inorganic bromide residue that is close to the allowable tolerance. Foods should not be subjected to repeated fumigation unless chemical analyses show that the accumulated residue will not exceed the tolerance. Methyl bromide and hydrogen cyanide have been approved for fumigating food, and tolerances have been established under the Food Additives Amendment.

Use of Unfavorable Environmental Conditions.—Insects require specific ranges of temperature, humidity, and air composition for development and survival. The creation of an unfavorable environment can be used very effectively for controlling or preventing insect infestations.

Cold storage.—Cold storage is an excellent example of the use of this principle. Generally speaking, temperatures of 21° to 32°C (70° to 90°F) are optimum for stored-product insects (Cotton 1960). Temperatures below or above this range have an adverse effect on the insects. At 15° to 21°C (60° to 70°F), the insects become sluggish and their development is very slow. Below 15°C (60°F), development practically stops. Freezing temperatures, if maintained long enough, will kill the insects. Although low temperatures can be used very effectively in protecting food against insects, temperatures in the range of 7° to 15°C (45° to 60°F) are ideal for many species of mites. These arthropods are smaller than insects, but they can be very damaging to many foods, such as cereals, dairy products, and dried fruits.

Most stored-product insects prefer high humidity and moisture, but they can get along very well at fairly low humidity, and many can feed on foods having a moisture content as low as 6 to 8%. Some can go even lower and provide their own moisture requirements by metabolic processes. The humidity-moisture factor, therefore, cannot be used as effectively as the temperature factor for control or prevention of stored-product insects, though it may be effective in preventing mite infestations. (See section on retarding rancidity in pecans.)

Controlled atmosphere.—Stored-product insects cannot survive in an atmosphere that contains less than 2% oxygen (Bailey 1955). By creating an atmosphere deficient in oxygen, food can be protected against insects. This principle has been used for many years in the storage of grain in airtight bins (Hyde and Oxley 1960). The respiration of the grain, insects, and fungi use up the oxygen, producing carbon dioxide. When the oxygen falls below the 2% level, the insects are killed off. A more recent use of this principle has been the exclusion of oxygen by drawing a vacuum or by flushing out the air with nitrogen as the food is packaged. Rather extensive use is also being made of controlled-atmosphere storage for the quality maintenance of certain fruit (Schomer and Sainsbury 1957).

As nitrogen becomes more abundant commercially and cheaper to produce, it may find extensive use for protecting bulk and packaged food against insects. Equipment has been developed that is capable of supplying large quantities of nitrogen and carbon dioxide from butane gas. It may be possible that the use of controlled atmosphere will be more economical than cold storage, and safer and more effective than pesticides.

Chlorinated and brominated wash waters (50 to 100 ppm) are ineffective when treating a high bacterial count on belts and elevators. Quaternary ammonium salts could be helpful in cleaning washers and other equipment.

Methyl bromide treatment of stored nuts is effective. But its use is limited because of the 50 ppm tolerance on inorganic bromide allowed. Propylene oxide treatment is effective but expensive. The use of propionates and sorbates, as biostatic agents, are being used.

Hydrogen cyanide has about 100 ppm residue tolerance, when used as a fumigant.

Malathion and piperonyl butoxide with pyrethrins are permitted for use as "protectants." Tolerances are 3 ppm and 1 ppm, respectively, for grains. Allethin has 2 ppm tolerance on grains, and methoxychlor has 2 ppm tolerance.

From an economic viewpoint insect infestation results in weight loss and reduces the grade. One processor "picked up" $16,000 worth of wormy cashew nuts which had escaped detection in the plant. It is desirable for nut handlers and processors to aim at complete insect eradication. Techniques have been developed for detecting internal insect infestation. Commonly employed are X-ray and flotation methods, both of which require laboratory facilities. The X-ray method is faster, more objective and quite accurate. While less accurate, sieving and flotation methods are simple to use. They can be used in the shelling plant level to provide "yes or no" evaluation of infestation.

PECANS IN BAKERY PRODUCTS

More than 26,000,000 lb of pecan meats are used in over 400 bakery products (Woodroof and Heaton 1961). The leading bakery products containing pecans are fruitcakes, custard pies, cookies, nut bread and cake fillings. Pecan halves are used for decorating cookies, cakes, and pies; pecan pieces are mixed into batters; and pecan granules, meal and butter are used to add flavor, consistency, and pleasing color to many products.

The number of pounds of pecans used by bakeries ranges from 150 to 1,000,000 lb annually with the greatest percentage being in the 2500 to 1,000,000 lb category. Sweet rolls and fruitcakes are the main bakery products involved, with coffee cakes and regular cakes also ranking high.

What bakers want from shellers and processors is a universal grading system with standard names, sizes, colors and quality for pecans. Some bakers want pecan shipping containers labeled with the crop date and shelling date.

Fruitcakes

Pecans are one of the major ingredients of fruitcakes. It is estimated that about 25% of the pecan crop is used in bakery products and that one-half of this quantity, or about 10,000,000 lb of pecan meats, is used in fruitcakes.

Most bakeries make fruitcakes on a seasonal basis for Thanksgiving and Christmas holidays, but others make them year-round. One bakery in Georgia uses from 3000 to 7000 lb of pecan meats per day for 4 or 5 months of the year and a smaller amount during the remaining months. This bakery has used as much as 1,000,000 lb of shelled pecans in one year.

Bakeries purchase shelled pecans by grades—large, medium and small halves, or medium, small or midget pieces. Pieces are cut from good grade pecan halves.

While most fruitcakes contain nuts, some do not. Fruitcakes with nuts vary from fairly light, low-spiced "nut bread," which requires as little as 1 oz of nuts per pound of cake to very dark, dense, heavily spiced cakes which contain as high as 4 oz of nuts per pound. Usually the highest quality fruitcakes contain the most nuts.

FIG. 12.48. FRUITCAKE WITH 20% PECANS, AND OLD FASHION
PECAN PIE WITH 25% PECANS

Pecans have been found to be excellent for use in fruitcakes to impart a crunchy texture, golden brown color, and nutty flavor. To accomplish this, halves or pieces are mixed into the dough, and halves may be placed on the sides or top for decoration. Pecans tended to offset the gummy texture, dark color, and molasses-like flavor imparted by many soft fruits.

Precoating Pecans for Fruitcakes.—Experiments showed that precoating pecan halves or pieces, prior to use in fruitcakes, improved the color, texture, and stability. A modified protein-starch (zeinacetoglyceride or Cozeen) coating, containing an antioxidant, reduced sogginess due to absorption of moisture, and reduced staleness by excluding contact with oxygen. Good results were obtained by warming the pecan meats to 37.8°C (100°F) and mixing 33 lb of meats and 1 pint (16 fl oz) of coating in a revolving pan or round bottom bowl for 15 min, then spreading the meats in thin layers to dry for 12 to 24 hours. Coated nutmeats (a) were brighter and more uniform in color, (b) were slightly firmer, (c) absorbed moisture from the cake batter more slowly, and (d) remained slightly crunchier. The treatment was equally effective with raw or toasted pecan meats.

Fruitcakes studied were of two types. One type was the light, low-nut, high-dough and high-fruit cake with a light wrapper, for seasonal trade (Thanksgiving and Christmas). These cakes contained a large portion of white raisins, preserved citron, preserved pineapple, glacé cherries, orange and lemon peel, orange juice, and about 10% pecan meats. Due to the formulation and method of packaging, light fruitcakes reached the peak of flavor within a month and became noticeably stale in two months.

Canned fruitcakes were similar to the above with the exception that they contained more spices and water and 20% pecans. The finished product was packed under vacuum in tin cans and processed at 149°C (300°F) for 2½ hours. Storage tests were conducted on canned fruitcakes.

Storage of Fruitcakes.—Canned fruitcakes were found to be quite stable for a bakery product. The storage life depended upon (a) ingredients used, (b) method of processing and packaging, and (c) storage temperature. Pecans were found to be more stable than the fruit ingredients. During long storage of fruitcakes, the pecans lost their characteristic taste and gradually took on the blended flavor of the cake. The major changes in the pecan meats, on and in the fruitcakes, were due to increase in moisture and absorption of flavors.

During storage fruitcakes undergo the following changes:

Moisture Equalization.—Individual fruit and nut ingredients vary in moisture in freshly made fruitcakes. During "aging" the moisture becomes fairly evenly distributed at about 18 to 20%, depending on the portion of ingredients, and the palatability and smoothness are improved. The moisture equalizes to some extent among the ingredients. High-nut, high-fruit cakes stored for 6 months had moisture content as follows: pecans, 4.8%; crumb, 14.7%; and fruit, 20.0%.

pH (Active Acidity) Equalization.—Fruit ingredients cause the product to be slightly acid. After equalizing, the pH was between 4.4 and 5.0.

Blend of Flavors.—Fruitcakes were at their best immediately after the flavors of the different ingredients became blended. During the 2 to 4 weeks required for the flavors to equalize, the quality of the cake improved.

Staling.—The first indication of loss of quality in fruitcakes was staling, as indicated by changes in the form of starch, drying of the crumb, and loss of fresh aroma and flavor. The chief means of retarding staling were reduction of air in the package and lowering of the storage temperature. Tests showed that there was practically no staling at -29°C (-20°F) during 5 years of storage. The same amount of staling that occurred in vacuum-packed, canned fruitcake in 3 months at 38°C (100°F) required 18 months at 21°C (70°F), 30 months at 8.3°C (47°F), and 60 months at 0°C (32).

Rancidity.—Rancidity occurred in the fats, usually after staling was well advanced. Rancidity was controlled in the batter by the use of hydrogenated fats, and in the pecans by precoating the nuts.

Rancidity in nuts was an indication that the nuts were of poor quality when added to the fruitcake or that the quality of the fruitcake had deteriorated. Slight traces of rancidity in nuts were frequently masked by sugars and flavors of other ingredients. Numerous tests have shown that pecans were more stable in fruitcakes than the fruit ingredients.

Darkening.—Darkening (browning) was one of the first evidences of over-aging in fruitcakes. It was first evident in the fruits such as raisins, prunes, and currants, and was caused in part by reaction of the sugars and amino acids to develop caramel-like aromas and flavors. Darkening later occurred throughout the crumb and other fruits. The same conditions which produced darkening also caused fading of added colors as well as the loss of natural colors of most of the fruits. Pecans in fruitcakes were affected very little by darkening (Heaton and Woodroof 1961).

Fruitcakes were made according to the following formula and stored under widely different conditions.

Canned Fruitcake

Batter	Lb
Flour	8.4
Shortening	6.3
Whole eggs (fresh shell, or frozen whole)	7.0
Sugar (baker's special)	9.5
Salt (not iodized)	0.2
Vanilla	as required
Water 38° to 60°C (100° to 140°F)	3.5

Fruit and Nut Blend

Raisins (seedless, unbleached)	8.1
Raisins (seedless, bleached)	8.1
Cherries (sweet, pitted, maraschino flavored, red colored)	16.3
Pecans (U.S. No. 1, small pieces)	13.0
Pineapple (processed with sugar and corn syrup)	9.8
Citron (processed with sugar and corn syrup)	4.6
Orange peel (processed with sugar and corn syrup)	2.6
Lemon peel (processed with sugar and corn syrup)	2.6
	100.0

Cream flour and shortening, blend sugar, salt, and whole eggs, then add to the creamed flour and shortening and mix evenly; add vanilla and hot water and mix thoroughly. Blend the fruit and nuts until evenly mixed, combine with batter, and mix thoroughly. Bake in slow oven 149° to 163°C (300° to 325°F) until done, or bake in cans and seal with 25 in. of vacuum when done.

A study was made of the stability of canned fruitcake made according to the formula. The cake was processed in 5-oz cans, and stored at −29°, 0°, 8.3°, 21.1°, and 38°C (−20°, 32°, 47°, 70°, and 100°F) for a maximum of 5 years. Evaluations were made at intervals of six months and consisted of sensory scores of appearance, aroma, color, texture and flavor. Chemical determinations of peroxide values and free fatty acids were also made at six-month intervals.

The fruitcake had an initial rating of 89% (very good), a peroxide value of 3.56 me-O_2 per kg oil, and free fatty acids, as oleic, of 2.26%. It was described by the taste panel as normal, except "slightly too dry and crumbly with mild oxidized flavor."

When stored at −29°C (−20°F) the canned fruitcake improved in texture and smoothness for 12 to 18 months, and remained practically unchanged for 36 months, with a rating of 84%. After 60 months the rating was 79%, the nuts being slightly soggy and the fruit somewhat faded. The peroxide value dropped to 1.60 in 18 months and to 1.10 in 36 months. The free fatty acids decreased to 1.10% in 36 months.

At 0°C (32°F) storage the fruitcake remained unchanged for 30 months, at which time it was scored 88%; at 42 months it was scored 80%, and at 60 months 72%. On examination after 60 months of storage the product was described as "pecans being slightly soggy and stale, the batter having a dry crumbly texture, and the fruit being slightly faded and tough with strong aroma and flavor." The peroxide values decreased to 1.58 in 36 months. Free fatty acids also decreased to 1.58% in 36 months.

At 8.3°C (47°F) storage canned fruitcake remained almost unchanged in eating qualities for 24 months, at which time it was scored 86%, but at 30 months it was scored 79%. Peroxide values decreased to 1.18 and the free fatty acids decreased to 1.68% in 36 months. The taste panel described the product as "nuts old and stale, fruit faded with strong molasses-like aroma and flavor."

At 21°C (70°F) storage canned fruitcake decreased significantly in eating qualities in 6 months at which time it was scored 78% and described as "pecans slightly soggy and stale, fruit darkened with a strong molasses-like flavor, and batter dark and crumbly." This product was unacceptable after storage for 12 months and after 30 months it was scored on 45%. Peroxide values decreased to 1.43 at 24 months.

At 38°C (100°F) storage this fruitcake was scored 61, 53, and 32% at the 6, 12, and 18 months examinations, respectively. The comments by the taste panel were, "pecans soggy and very strong and stale, fruit faded, with strong molasses-like flavor, and the batter dark, dry and crumbly."

The results from storing fruitcakes showed:

(a) That pecans in fruitcake were more stable than raisins, cherries and fruits, since the fruit were largely responsible for darkening of color and development of a strong burned-molasses flavor;

(b) In general the shelf-life of canned fruitcake stored at −29°, 0°, 8.3°, 21.1°, and 38°C (−20°, 32°, 47°, 70°, and 100°F) was 5 to 10 years, 5 to 7 years, 3 years, 2 years and 3 months, respectively; and

(c) The shelf-life of uncanned fruitcake held at these temperatures was 5 to 7 years, 9 to 12 months, 4 to 5 months, 2 to 3 months, and 2 to 3 weeks, respectively.

All of the chain grocery stores in the South, and hundreds of local bakeries have special recipes for fruitcakes containing a substantial quantity of pecans.

White Fruitcake

5 large eggs	1 lb glazed pineapple
½ lb butter	4 cups shelled pecans
1 cup white sugar	½ oz vanilla extract
1¾ cups plain flour	½ oz lemon extract
½ tsp baking powder	¾ lb glazed cherries

Cream butter. Add sugar gradually, creaming well until fluffy. Add eggs which have been well beaten with rotary beater. Chop nuts and fruit, and mix with part of the flour. Sift the remaining flour with baking powder. Fold into eggs and butter mixture. Add flavoring. Mix well. Fold in fruit and nuts. Pour into greased paper-lined tube pan or into small loaf pans. Place in cold oven and bake at 121°C (250°F) for 3 hours. Cool in pans or on cake rack. Keep well wrapped and in a cannister for at least 2 months.

Refrigerator Fruitcake

½ lb graham crackers, crushed
½ lb dates, cut fine
1 cup coffee cream
½ lb marshmallows, cut fine
½ cup chopped pecans, broken
10 maraschino cherries, chopped

Mix thoroughly all the ingredients. Press mix firmly into a pan which has been lined with oiled, heavy waxed paper. Let stand overnight or longer in the refrigerator, as it will keep moist if well covered. It may be served plain or with whipped cream.

Old-fashioned Fruitcake

⅔ cups plain flour	⅓ tsp cloves
⁵⁄₆ cup sugar	1 tsp vanilla
⅓ lb butter	1 tsp soda in cold water
5 eggs	⅓ cup wine
¼ cup cane sugar	1 lb crystallized citron
1 tbsp cinnamon	1 lb cherries
3 tbsp lemon and	1 lb pineapple
orange peel	1 lb package dates
½ lb currants	1 lb raisins
1 tbsp allspice	5 cups nuts
1 tsp mace and nutmeg	

Prepare fruit and dredge with extra flour. Cream sugar and butter. Add eggs, one at a time. Stir spices in with flour. Add flour alternately with wine. Add soda and water to syrup and stir into batter. Add vanilla, fruits and nuts. Place in well-greased pan and bake slowly at 149°C (300°F) about 5 hours. Makes 10 lb.

Dark Fruitcake

2 lb raisins or currants
½ lb candied cherries
½ lb candied pineapple
½ lb citron
1 lb figs
1 lb dark brown sugar
  (light brown or granu-
  lated may be used)
1 cup molasses

4 cups flour
6 eggs
⅓ cup sherry or brandy
1½ tsp nutmeg
3 tsp cloves
3 tsp cinnamon
3 tsp baking powder
1½ lb nutmeats

Cream butter and sugar. Add beaten eggs. Sift flour and measure, then take out 1 cup of flour for dusting the cut-up fruit. Sift remainder of flour with the other ingredients and spices. Add the flour mixture, and the fruits and nuts alternately with the molasses and wine to the egg and butter mixture. Mix well. Use a large pan, and grease and paper line tube cake pan. Bake in slow oven 135°C (275°F) for approximately 5 hours, or until done. Makes about 6½ lb.

Japanese Fruitcake

1 cup butter or margarine
2 cups sugar
4 eggs
1 cup buttermilk
1 cup chopped raisins
1 cup chopped nutmeats
3 cups flour

½ tsp salt
1 tsp cinnamon
1 tsp allspice
1 tsp cloves
1 tsp nutmeg
1 tsp soda

Cream butter and sugar together, add eggs one at a time, beating well after each addition. Sift dry ingredients together and combine the two mixtures. Flour raisins and nutmeats and add to above mixture. Pour into layers pans and bake in slow oven 149°C (300°F) about 1 hour, or until cake leaves sides of pan.

Japanese Fruitcake Filling

2 boxes of coconut
2½ cups sugar
2 tbsp flour

2 lemons grated rind and juice
1½ cups hot water

Combine all ingredients and cook until thick. Cool slightly. Spread between layers.

Famous Funsten Fruitcake[1]

15-oz package raisins	3 cups sifted, all-purpose flour
2 8-oz pkgs. red or green	1 tsp baking powder
candied cherries	½ tsp salt
2 3½-oz cans flaked coconut	1½ cups sugar
2 8-oz pkgs. candied mixed fruit	1½ cups shortening
2 cups pecans	8 eggs
8-oz pkg. candied pineapple tidbits	1 cup orange juice

Set oven at 135°C (274°F). Line two 9 × 5 × 3 in. pans with wax paper. Mix raisins, cherries, coconut, mixed fruit, pecans and pineapple in a very large pan. Sift flour, baking powder and salt onto wax paper. Mix sugar and shortening in a 3-qt bowl of electric mixer at medium speed until light and fluffy. Beat in eggs well, two at a time, scraping sides of bowl often. Beat in flour mixture alternately with orange juice at low speed, scraping sides of bowl often. Add batter to fruit-nut mixture. Mix well. Pour batter into pans. Bake near center of oven 2½ to 3 hours, or until toothpick inserted in center of cake comes out clean. Take from pan. Cool. remove paper. Makes 2 loaves, about 7½ lb.

Pecan Pies

The second most popular pecan bakery item is pecan custard pie. There are many recipes, but they are all very rich in sugar, fat and protein. They are very "filling" to eat and approach a soft candy in consistency and flavor. The moisture content is so low that they do not spoil readily. Pecan pies are made in 8, 6, and 4-in. sizes and are sold fresh, frozen, in vending machines, and as snacks.

Following are representative recipes for old-fashioned pecan pies. All of them are modifications of formulas that have been used for over a century.

Pecan Pie No. 1

1 cup white corn syrup	1 tsp vanilla
½ cup light brown sugar	¼ tsp salt
packed	1 cup chopped pecans
3 eggs unbeaten	

Combine syrup, sugar, eggs, vanilla and salt. Mix well; add pecans. Pour into an unbaked 8-in. pie shell. Bake in a moderate oven of 120°C (350°F) for 50 min or until done.

---

[1]Funsten Pecan Company.

Peach Pecan Pie

¼ cup butter	¼ tsp salt
¼ cup sugar	3 eggs
2 tbsp flour	1½ cups sliced peaches
½ cup light corn syrup	

Cream butter, sugar, flour. Stir in syrup and salt. Beat in eggs one at a time until blended. Add peaches. Pour into 9-in. unbaked pie shell.

Nut Crumb Topping

¼ cup flour	2 tbsp butter
¼ cup brown sugar	½ cup chopped pecans

Combine ingredients and sprinkle over filling. Bake at 204°C (400°F) about 35 min, or until knife inserted in center comes out clean. Serve chilled.

Miniature Pecan Pies

Cream Cheese Pastry

1 3-oz pkg. cream cheese
1 cup sifted flour
¼ lb softened butter

Blend thoroughly; chill dough. Pinch off 24 balls of dough and press into tiny muffin cups to form shells.

Filling

¾ cup brown sugar	¼ tsp salt
1 tbsp melted butter	½ tsp vanilla
1 egg	

Blend and beat all ingredients. Now spoon filling into unbaked shells, filling each not quite ¾ full. Sprinkle chopped pecans generously on top or use coconut. Bake 25 min at 175°C (350°F). Cool on rack and serve on tiny paper cupcake shells.

Pecan Pie No. 2[1]

¼ cup butter	4 eggs
1 cup sugar	1 cup broken pecans
1 tbsp flour	1 tsp vanilla
1½ cups white corn syrup	1 unbaked pastry shell
⅛ tsp salt	

---

[1]Pecan Shell & Proc. Assoc.

Cream butter. Add sugar and flour gradually and cream until fluffy. Add syrup. Beat well. Add salt and eggs, one at a time. Beat thoroughly. Add broken pecans and vanilla. Pour into unbaked pastry shell. Bake at 232°C (450°F) for 10 min, lower heat to 175°C (350°F) and bake for 50 min or until set. Yields one 9-in. pie.

V.I.P. Pecan Pie

1 cup clear corn syrup	1 cup sugar
3 eggs, slightly beaten	2 tbsp margarine, melted
⅛ tsp salt	1 cup pecans, halves or chopped
1 tsp vanilla	1 unbaked 9-in. pie shell

Mix all ingredients for filling together, adding pecans last. Pour into pastry shell. Bake in 205°C (400°F) oven for 15 min; reduce heat to 175°C (350°F) and bake 30 to 35 min longer. When pecan pie is done, outer edges of filling should be set, center slightly soft.

Pecan Sour Cream Pie

1 cup broken pecans	1 cup sour cream
2 tsp flour	2 eggs
¼ tsp cinnamon	1 cup sugar
¼ tsp cloves	½ tsp grated lemon rind

Line a pie plate with pastry and sprinkle it with pecans. Make custard by mixing flour, cinnamon, cloves and a little sour cream, gradually adding balance of sour cream. Stir in eggs—well beaten—sugar and lemon rind. Pour mixture into pie shell and place in hot oven of 230°C (450°F) lowering temperature control immediately to 165°C (325°F). Bake until filling is firm, about 40 min. Serves either warm or cold, with whipped cream. Yields one 9-in. pie.

Honey Pecan Pie

3 eggs	½ cup honey
⅓ cup granulated sugar	½ cup white corn syrup
⅓ cup light brown sugar	1 tsp vanilla
¼ tsp salt	1 cup pecan halves
¼ cup butter, melted	

Beat eggs. Mix in all other ingredients except pecan halves and pour into pastry lined 9-in. pie pan. Arrange pecan halves on filling in desired pattern. Bake 40 to 50 min at 185°C (375°F) until set and pastry is golden brown. Cool. Serve cold or slighty warm. Yields one 9-in. pie.

Chiffon pecan pies are not as rich as the traditional pecan pie. They are made in the home or in the bakeries for quick sale, and are too fragile for rough handling, even when frozen. Pecan chiffon pies are a delicacy for serving in public eating places, at outings or in the home.

Mocha Pecan Chiffon Pie

1 envelope unflavored gelatin	½ tsp imitation rum extract
¼ cup cold water	¼ tsp salt
3 tbsp cocoa	¼ cup sugar
¾ cup sugar	¾ cup finely chopped pecans
¾ cup water	1 baked 9-in. pie shell
2 tsp instant coffee powder	Pecan halves
3 eggs, separated	Whipping cream
1 tsp vanilla	

Soften gelatin in cold water. Combine in heavy saucepan the cocoa, ¾ cup sugar, water, and instant coffee powder; stir to dissolve sugar. Bring to boil, and let cook gently for 4 to 5 min. stirring constantly. Beat egg yolks slightly. Pour hot mixture on top slowly, stirring constantly. Return to saucepan. Stir over heat until mixture thickens. Remove from heat. Add gelatin, vanilla and rum extracts; stir until gelatin dissolves. Chill until mixture mounds slightly when dropped from a spoon. Beat egg whites and salt until foamy. Beat in ¼ cup sugar by single teaspoonfuls, beating constantly; beat until whites stand in stiff peaks. Fold with pecans into gelatin mixture. Turn into baked pie shell. Chill until set. Garnish with pecan halves and whipped cream. Yields one 9-in. pie.

Pecan Chiffon Pie

¾ cup milk	1 tbsp gelatin
¾ cup sugar	½ cup toasted pecans
3 eggs	½ tsp vanilla

Make custard of one-half of the sugar, milk, salt and egg yolks; add gelatin which has been dissolved in 1 tbsp cold water; add toasted chopped nuts. Cool.
Beat egg whites until stiff, add other half of sugar. Fold into cooled custard; add vanilla. Pour into baked pie shell and place in refrigerator. Serve cold with whipped cream.

Other Pecan Bakery Items

Butterscotch Pecan Meringue Pudding[1]

2 egg whites	2¼ cups milk
4 tbsp brown sugar	3 tbsp minute tapioca
¼ cup butter	⅛ tsp salt
⅓ cup firmly packed brown sugar	½ tsp vanilla
2 egg yolks	⅓ cup pecans, cut lengthwise

---

[1]General Foods Kitchens

Beat egg whites until foamy. Add 4 tbsp brown sugar and cook until sugar is dissolved. Mix egg yolks with small amount of the milk in saucepan. Add minute tapioca, salt, and remaining milk. Cook and stir over medium heat until mixture comes to a boil. Remove from heat and add brown sugar mixture and vanilla. Turn into casserole. Pile meringue lightly on top of tapioca mixture. Sprinkle with pecans. Bake at 185°C (375°F) for 15 min or until golden brown.

Coffee Toffee Bars

2⅔ cups flour
1 tsp baking powder
¼ tsp salt
2 sticks butter or margarine
1 cup light brown sugar,
    firmly packed

1 tsp almond extract
1½ tsp instant coffee
1 package chocolate chips
½ cup chopped nuts

Stir all ingredients together and press in pan (15 × 10 in.). Bake at 176°C (350°F) for 20 min.

Cinnamon Nut Sticks

2 sticks butter or margarine
1 cup sugar
2 cups flour
1 egg yolk

1 tbsp cinnamon
1½ cups chopped nuts
1 egg white

Cream butter and sugar; stir in other ingredients except egg white. Roll out on greased cookie sheet. Brush top with egg white; spread 1 cup finely chopped pecans over top. Bake at 165°C (325°F) for 35 to 40 min. Cut into sticks while warm.

Orange–Date Bread

3 cups sifted all-purpose flour
2 tsp baking powder
½ tsp baking soda
1 tsp salt
1 cup sugar
4 tbsp frozen orange juice
    concentrate, thawed

Water
3 tbsp corn oil or melted
    butter
2 eggs
1 cup chopped walnuts or
    pecans
¾ cup pitted,
    dates

Sift flour with baking powder, baking soda, salt and sugar. To orange juice concentrate, add enough water to make ¾ cup. Add juice, corn oil or butter, eggs, nuts and dates to dry ingredients. Stir until all dry particles are moistened and well blended. Pour mixture into a well-greased and floured 9 × 5 × 3 in. loaf pan. Bake in a preheated moderate oven of 175°C (350°F) for 1 to 1½ hours, or until top is well browned. Unmold and cool on a rack. Cool thoroughly before slicing. Makes one loaf.

Applesauce Cookies

¼ cup soft shortening	¼ tsp baking soda
½ cup granulated sugar	2 tsp double-acting baking
¼ cup canned applesauce	powder
1 tsp vanilla extract	½ cup light or dark raisins
1 cup unsifted potato	½ cup chopped pecans
flour	Confectioner's sugar

Heat oven to 175°C (350°F). Cream together shortening and sugar; blend in applesauce and vanilla extract; blend in the potato flour, baking soda and baking powder; then stir in raisins and pecans. Drop scant tablespoonfuls of batter onto lightly greased cookie sheet and bake for 15 to 20 min. Let cool slightly before removing from pan, then sprinkle with confectioner's sugar. Makes 24 to 27 cookies.

Courtesy of Kitchens of Sara Lee

FIG. 12.49. CARAMEL PECAN ROLLS

Butter-rich Danish pastry with a topping of honey–caramel and pecans. These rolls are swirled throughout with cinnamon. Caramel pecan rolls are baked upside down with the caramel and pecans on the bottom, and must be heated in the oven for a short time so they can be removed from the pan. As they heat, the topping spreads evenly across the rolls. This brief warming time in the oven also brings out all the full freshness. The foil pans should be turned upside down immediately on a serving plate, and the rolls separated into individual servings.

Wedding Cookies

1 cup flour	½ tsp vanilla
½ cup pecans, chopped	Dash of salt
1 stick margarine	Confectioner's sugar

Combine margarine, flour and pecans. Leave in refrigerator to chill. Shape into balls and place on cookie sheet. Bake at 175°C (350°F) until done, about 12 min. Roll in confectioner's sugar.

Choc-o-Pecan Cookies

2¼ cups sifted, all-purpose
  flour
½ tsp baking soda
¼ tsp salt
¾ cup sugar
1½ cups cut-up pecans
¾ cup shortening

2 eggs
2 tbsp water
2 tsp vanilla
2 cups semi-sweet chocolate pieces
¾ cup firmly packed brown
  sugar

Preheat oven to 175°C (350°F). Sift flour, baking soda and salt onto wax paper. Beat sugar, brown sugar, shortening, eggs, water and vanilla in a 3-qt bowl until fluffy. Mix in dry ingredients. Stir in chocolate pieces and pecans. Drop with two teaspoons onto greased cookie sheet. Bake near center of oven 10 to 12 min, or until light brown. Makes 5 dozen.

Sour Cream Drop Cookies

6 tbsp shortening
1 cup firmly packed dark brown
  sugar
1 egg
½ cup dairy-made sour cream
2 cups sifted all-purpose flour

½ tsp soda
2 tsp baking powder
¼ tsp salt
⅛ tsp nutmeg
½ cup raisins
½ cup chopped pecans

Cream together shortening, brown sugar and egg. Stir in sour cream. Sift together flour, soda, baking powder, salt and nutmeg. Stir into batter. Add raisins and nuts. Chill at least one hour. Drop rounded teaspoonfuls about 2 in. apart on lightly greased cookie sheet. Bake in hot oven of 205°C (400°F) 8 to 10 min or until delicately browned. Makes 3 dozen.

Ice Box Cookies

2 cups brown sugar
1 tbsp soda
1 tsp vanilla
½ tsp salt

3½ cups flour
1⅓ sticks butter
2 cups broken pecan
  meats

Cream butter and sugar, add eggs and remaining ingredients. Mix well. Form into rolls and roll in waxed paper. Refrigerate overnight. Slice and bake at 205°C (400°F) for 10 min.

Apricot Gold Bricks

1 cup chopped dried apricots
½ cup water

1 tsp baking powder
1 tsp soda

½ cup margarine
1 cup granulated sugar
½ cup firmly packed dark
  brown sugar
2 eggs
1½ cups sifted all-purpose flour

¼ tsp salt
½ cup buttermilk
1 cup chopped pecans
1 tbsp grated orange peel
Confectioners' sugar

Simmer apricots in water until tender; cool. Cream margarine with sugars until light and fluffy. Add eggs and beat well. Sift together flour, baking powder, soda and salt. Add to creamed mixture alternately with buttermilk. Mix until smooth after each addition. Stir in apricots, nuts and orange peel. Spread in 2 greased 9-in. square pans. Bake in moderate oven of 175°C (350°F) 25 min. Cool, cut into bars. Sprinkle with confectioners' sugar or roll bars in it. Makes 24 bars.

Pecan Honey Buns

1 package compressed or dry
  yeast
½ cup milk
¼ cup sugar
½ tsp salt
¼ cup shortening

1 egg
1¾ cups sifted enriched
  flour
1 cup currants
¼ cup chopped pecans
2 tsp caramel syrup

Soften yeast in lukewarm water. Scald milk. Add sugar, salt, and shortening. Cool to lukewarm. Add 1 cup enriched flour and beat well. Add softened yeast and egg, and beat well. Cover. Add ¾ cup flour to make a thick batter. Beat thoroughly until smooth. Let rise until double (about 1 hour). Stir down and add currants and pecans.

Into greased, fluted muffin pans place caramel syrup; sprinkle chopped pecans on glaze. Drop batter by spoonfuls into pans, filling ½ full. Let rise until double (about 45 min). Bake in moderate oven of 185°C (375°F) 24 to 30 min. Makes 8 buns.

Pecan Fingers

2¼ cups sifted all-purpose
  flour
½ tsp double-acting baking
  powder
Dash of salt
1 cup soft butter or margarine

¾ cup granulated sugar
1 egg
1 tsp almond extract
1 egg white
1½ cups chopped pecans

Prepare at least a day ahead:

Heat oven to 205°C (400°F). Sift together flour, baking powder, and salt. In bowl, with mixer at medium speed, beat butter or margarine with sugar until light and fluffy. Now beat in egg and almond extract. Then gradually add flour mixture while beating, until well blended.

Fill cookie press with dough, having spritz disk in place. Make 3-in. strips on ungreased cookie sheets; brush with slightly beaten egg white; sprinkle with pecans. Repeat till all dough is used. Bake 9 to 11 min, or until lightly browned at edges. With broad spatula, remove to cake rack to cool. Store in covered container. Makes 5 dozen.

Pecans Scandia

1 cup sugar
2 egg whites, stiffly beaten
1 lb pecan halves
Salt

Fold sugar into egg whites; mix in pecans. Melt butter in a jelly-roll pan in a 165°C (325°F) oven. Spoon nut mixture over butter. Bake at 165°C (325°F) for 30 min, stirring every 10 min. Sprinkle with salt as nuts bake. Cool. Makes about 4 cups.

New Orleans Pecan Squares

1 lb margarine	¾ oz vanilla
2 lb sugar, granulated	½ oz salt
1 lb eggs, beaten	8 oz egg whites
⅔ oz baking powder	1 lb 14 oz brown sugar
1 lb 8 oz flour	1 lb pecans, chopped

Cream margarine and white sugar together. Add beaten eggs, then flour, baking powder, salt and vanilla. Spread mixture in greased sheet pan (18 × 26 in.). Beat egg whites until stiff. Add brown sugar. Spread on top of cookie dough. Sprinkle with chopped pecans. Bake at 175°C (350°F) for 30 min. Cut into diamonds while still slightly warm.

Butterscotch Pecan Bars

4 lb, 11 oz. flour, all purpose	6 lb 13 oz brown sugar
2⅓ oz baking powder	2 lb 5 oz, whole eggs
1 oz salt	2¾ oz vanilla
2 lb 5 oz butter, margarine or shortening, melted	2 lb 5 oz pecans, broken

Combine flour, baking powder and salt; sift. Combine melted butter, margarine or shortening, sugar, eggs and vanilla in mixer. Beat until frothy. Stir in dry ingredients and pecans. Scale approximately 4 lb 10 oz each into well-greased and floured baking sheet, 19½ × 15½ × 1¼ in. Spread evenly. Bake in moderate oven of 175°C (350°F) until done, about 30 min. While warm, trim crusts and cut into bars approximately 3 in. long, 1 in. wide.

Pumpkin Nut Waffles

2½ cups sifted cake flour	3 eggs, separated
4 tsp baking powder	1¾ cups milk
1 tsp salt	½ cup melted shortening
¾ tsp cinnamon	½ cup canned pumpkin
¼ tsp nutmeg	¾ cup chopped pecans

Sift together dry ingredients. Beat egg yolks. Combine with milk, shortening and pumpkin. Add to dry ingredients. Beat egg whites stiff. Fold into batter.

Pour onto hot waffle iron. Sprinkle with a few chopped nuts and bake. Makes about 8 waffles.

Nut Muffins

2 cups sifted plain flour	1 cup finely chopped nuts
2 tbsp sugar	1 egg
3 tsp baking powder	¼ cup soft-type margarine
½ tsp salt	1 cup milk

Sift flour, sugar, baking powder and salt into mixing bowl. Stir in nuts. Beat together egg and margarine; add milk and mix well. Mix thoroughly; add milk mixture and stir just until dry ingredients are moistened (batter will be lumpy). Spoon into 12 muffin pans that have been coated with margarine (pans should be ⅔ full). Bake in 225°C (425°F) oven 20 to 25 min, until muffins are lightly browned and pull away from pan. Makes 12 muffins.

Orange Pecan Bread

1 egg	2 cups sifted all-purpose flour
1 cup orange juice	1 tsp baking powder
1 cup raisins,finely cut	½ tsp baking soda
1 tbsp grated orange rind	¼ tsp salt
2 tbsp shortening, melted	1 cup chopped pecans
and cooled slightly	1 tsp vanilla

Beat egg. Stir in orange juice, raisins, orange rind, shortening and vanilla. Sift flour, baking powder, soda, salt and sugar into liquid mixture. Mix well. Stir in pecans. Pour into well-greased 5 × 9 × 2½ in. loaf pan. Bake in a moderate oven of 175°C (350°F) for 1 hour.

Chocolate Pecan Bread Pudding

3 1-oz packets unsweetened product for chocolate baking	¼ tsp salt
	2 tsp vanilla
	15 slices white bread cut into cubes
½ cup sugar	
3 eggs, separated	¾ cup pecans
Pecan halves	3 cups milk

In top of a double-boiler, heat chocolate and milk; beat to blend. Combine sugar, egg yolks, salt and vanilla; gradually add milk. Stir in bread cubes and pecans. Beat egg whites until stiff, not dry, peaks form; gently fold whites into bread mixture. Pour mixture into a well-greased baking dish. Set dish on a cookie sheet in oven. Bake at 175°C (350°F) for 45 min. Garnish with pecan halves; serve hot or cold.

Pecan Chocolate Torte

6 eggs, separated	1 cup sifted all-purpose flour
½ tsp salt	1 cup finely chopped pecans
1 tsp vanilla	Chopped pecans for topping
¾ cup sugar	

Separate eggs; combine egg yolks, salt and vanilla. Beat until very light and lemon-colored. Beat in ½ cup sugar gradually; continue beating until very light and fluffy (about 5 min at medium speed). Stir in flour and 1 cup of finely chopped nuts.

Beat egg whites until they form peaks. Beat in remaining ¼ cup sugar gradually and continue beating until glossy. Fold into egg yolk mixture. Divide batter equally between 3 greased and floured 8-in. layer pans. Spread just enough to level. Bake in a slow oven of 150°C (300°F) until done, 20 to 25 min.

Cool in pans on rack 10 min; remove from pans and cool thoroughly on racks. Put layers together with chocolate cream filling using ⅓ of filling on each layer. Sprinkle with chopped pecans.

Chill in refrigerator until filling is firm. Scrape excess filling off of torte. Cover sides of torte with chocolate satin frosting. Chill and serve. Makes 8 to 10 servings.

Sour Cream Nut Bread

2 cups sifted flour	¼ tsp nutmeg
1 tsp baking powder	1 egg, beaten
1 tsp baking soda	1 cup brown sugar, firmly
1 tsp salt	packed
1 cup dairy sour cream	¼ tsp cinnamon
1 cup broken pecan meats	¼ tsp cloves

Sift flour, baking powder, soda and spices together. Beat egg. Add sugar and mix well. Stir in sour cream carefully. Add dry ingredients, stirring only enough to moisten them. Add the nutmeats. Pour into a well-buttered loaf pan (2½ × and 3½ × 7¾ in.) and bake in a preheated oven at 175°C (350°F) for 1 hour.

Cranberry Bread

1 cup sugar	¼ cup shortening
2 cups all-purpose flour	¾ cup orange juices
1½ tsp double-acting	1 tbsp grated orange rind
baking powder	1 egg well beaten
1 tsp salt	1 cup chopped nuts
½ tsp soda	1 cup fresh cranberries, chopped

Sift together flour, baking powder, soda and salt. Cut in shortening until mixture resembles corn meal. Combine orange juice and grated rind with beaten egg. Pour all at once into dry ingredients, mixing just enough to dampen. Bake as nut bread.

FIG. 12.50. SIX BAKERY PRODUCTS MADE FROM PECAN
PIECES—PECAN PIE, PECAN SQUARES, AND FOUR KINDS
OF COOKIES

Lemon Prune Bread

2 cups sifted flour	⅔ cup sugar
1 tsp baking powder	2 eggs
½ tsp soda	¾ cup prune juice
½ tsp salt	1 cup cooked cut up prunes,
⅓ cup shortening	well drained
2 tsp grated lemon peel	½ cup coarsely chopped
	pecans

Sift together flour, baking powder, soda and salt. Cream shortening with sugar. Add eggs and beat well. Add dry ingredients alternately with prune juice, stirring only enough to blend. Stir in prunes, lemon peel and nuts. Pour into greased and floured 8½ × 4½ ×2½-in. loaf pan. Bake at 175°C (350°F) 1¼ hours. Cool before removing from pan. Let stand overnight for easier slicing. Makes 1 loaf.

Pecan Vienna Dream Coffee Cake

Cake	*Topping*
4 cups sifted all-purpose flour	1 cup sifted all-purpose flour
4 tsp baking powder	¾ cup (firmly packed) light
1 tsp salt	brown sugar
1 cup butter or margarine	4 tsp cinnamon
1¾ cups granulated sugar	½ cup butter or margarine
3 eggs	2 cups chopped pecans
1 cup milk	
1 tsp vanilla or lemon extract	

Make topping. Combine flour, sugar, cinnamon and butter or margarine; blend until mixture is crumbly. Add pecans; mix well. Make cake. Sift together flour, baking powder and salt. Cream butter or margarine and sugar. Add eggs, one at a time, and beat until light and creamy after each addition. Add dry ingredients alternately with milk and flavoring, blending well after each addition.

Divide batter equally between 3 greased 9-in. aluminum foil or round cake pans. Cover each evenly with an equal amount of topping. Bake at 175°C (350°F) until done and browned, 30 to 35 min.

Pecan Cake

1¾ cups butter or margarine	4 cups flour
2 cups sugar	6 eggs
4 cups shelled pecans	4 tbsp lemon extract
1 tsp baking powder	4 oz candied cherries
2 cups white raisins	4 oz candied pineapple

Cream butter or margarine with sugar until smooth and fluffy. Sift dry ingredients together and mix with fruit and nuts. Add well-beaten eggs to creamed mixture. Add flour mixture. Mix well until fruits and nuts are coated with batter. Line bottom of pans with greased waxed paper. Grease sides of pans. Bake in 10-in. tube pan at 165°C (325°F) 2 to 2½ hours. The cake may be baked in 1-lb bread pans at 150°C (300°F) for about 2 hours.

Banana Pecan Cake

½ cup shortening	¾ tsp baking soda
1½ cups sugar	½ tsp salt
2 eggs	1 tsp vanilla
¾ cup mashed bananas	¼ cup buttermilk
2 cups sifted cake flour	¾ cup chopped pecans
¼ tsp baking powder	

Cream shortening. Add sugar gradually; cream well. Add eggs one at a time, beating thoroughly after each addition. Add bananas. Sift together flour, baking powder, soda and salt. Add alternately with buttermilk to which vanilla has been added. Stir in pecans. Pour into 2 greased 9-in. cake pans and bake for 30 to 35 min in a moderate oven of 175°C (350°F). Remove from pans and cool. Spread whipped cream between layers and on top and sides of cake, or frost with 7-min frosting.

Applesauce Date and Pecan Cake

2 cups unsifted plain flour	1 cup light brown sugar
2 tsp baking soda	(lightly packed)
1 tsp cinnamon	½ cup margarine
½ tsp allspice	2 cups hot applesauce
¼ tsp salt	1 cup chopped dates
2 eggs	¾ cup chopped pecans

Sift together in a large bowl, flour, soda, cinnamon, allspice and salt. Add eggs, brown sugar, softened margarine and 1 cup of the hot applesauce. Beat until just mixed at low speed, then at medium speed beat 2 min longer. Add remaining applesauce, dates and pecans. Beat 1 min. Pour into 9 × 9 × 2 in. pan. Bake for 50 min at 175°C S(350°F).

Butter Pecan Cake

2 cups pecans, chopped	2 cups sugar
1¼ cups butter	4 eggs
3 cups sifted plain flour	1 cup milk
2 tsp baking powder	2 tsp vanilla
½ tsp salt	

Toast pecans in ¼ cup butter at 175°C (350°F) for 20 to 25 min. Stir frequently. Sift flour with baking powder and salt. Cream 1 cup butter; gradually add sugar, creaming well. Blend in eggs one at a time; beat well after each addition. Add dry ingredients alternately with milk, beginning and ending with dry ingredients. Blend well after each addition. Stir in vanilla and 1⅓ cups pecans. Turn into three 8- or 9-in. round layer pans, greased and floured on the bottom. Bake at 175°C (350°f) for 25 to 30 min. Cool; spread frosting between layers and on top.

Butter Pecan Frosting.—Cream ¼ cup butter. Add 1 lb sifted confectioners' sugar, 1 tsp vanilla and 4 to 6 tbsp evaporated milk or cream until it reaches spreading consistency. Stir in remaining pecans.

NOTE: This cake can be made with a cake mix, with toasted pecans added.

Butter Pecan Torte

1½ sticks (¾ cup) butter	3 tsp baking powder
2 cups sugar	¼ tsp salt
4 eggs	1 cup milk
1 tsp vanilla	3 cups sifted cake flour

Cream butter and sugar. Add eggs and vanilla. Beat until well combined. Sift together flour, baking powder and salt. Add alternately with milk. Blend thoroughly. Pour equal amounts of batter into three 8-in. cake pans which have been lined with 2 layers of waxed paper. Bake at 185°C (375°F) for about 30 min.

Filling

2 sticks (1 cup) butter	2 cups finely chopped pecans
1 cup sifted powdered sugar	4 tsp grated lemon rind

Cream together butter and sugar. Blend in nuts and lemon rind.

Frosting

1 cup whipping cream
1 tbsp lemon juice
Few drops yellow food coloring

Whip cream, blending in lemon juice and food coloring. To assemble torte: Split each cake layer in half horizontally. Stack layers, spreading filling between. Frost. Garnish with whole pecans if desired.

PECAN CANDIES

It is estimated that 20% of the total production of pecans is used in confections, of which there are more than 100 varieties. The tree nut industry of the world owes its growth in large part to the confectionery industry which, in the case of almonds, takes more than 50% of domestic production. The candy manufacturers in the United States use about 10% of the walnut crop, 65% of the almond crop (62.6% of California's production), 20% of the pecan crop, and 25% of the filberts.

Of added importance is the fact that most manufacturers buy nutmeats rather than nuts in the shell. The main method of using nutmeats in candies is to add them (raw, blanched or toasted) to the finished batches just prior to molding or forming the desired pieces.

The "body" of candy is texture, and the "soul" is flavor; nuts impart both of these (Gott and van Houten 1958).

There are at least five variations in the formula for pecan pralines, one of which is chocolate coated. There are an equal number of formulas for pecan brittle, some of which use small amounts of coconut and other nuts as "stretchers." Pecan nut rolls are made with several formulations for the centers and coating.

FIG. 12.51. JARS OF PECAN BUTTER, AND PRALINES, PECAN FUDGE AND CHOCOLATE NUT FUDGE MADE FROM PECAN BUTTER

The most popular commercially made pecan candy is pralines. This is because they are (a) simple to make in a production line; (b) made in many sizes and shapes to sell at different outlets; (c) stable under a wide range of temperature and humidity conditions; and (d) "convenient" to package, carry and eat.

Pecan brittle is a favorite candy because it has the most toasted pecan flavor. Pecan divinity is the most commonly made candy in the home. Since it dries out readily, it should be eaten freshly made.

In Fig. 12.52 are shown 15 kinds of pecan candies made by one manufacturer. These are packed in a variety box or separately as shown in Figs. 12.53 and 12.54.

FIG. 12.52.   FIFTEEN KINDS OF PECAN CANDIES

Top row: pecan brittle, stuffed dates w/pecan halves, chocolate covered nougat, chocolate pecan cluster and sugared and spiced pecans. Middle row: chocolate covered pecan halves, maple pralines w/pecans, chocolate pralines w/pecans, and coconut pralines w/pecans. Bottom row: pecan glace, pecan nougat roll, pecan puffettes, maple fudge w/pecans, chocolate fudge w/pecans, and divinity w/pecans.

Courtesy of Stuckey's Inc.

FIG. 12.53.   SALTED PECANS, PECAN NUT BUTTER CRUNCH
AND SPICED PECANS ARE VACUUM PACKED IN 1–LB TINS,
FOR DOMESTIC AND FOREIGN SALES

Stuckey's Pecan Candies

Stuckey's, Inc. distributes 80 pecan products in 329 stores nationwide. Beginning with a roadside stand in 1936, in Eastman, Georgia, W.S.

Courtesy of Stuckey's, Inc.

FIG. 12.54. ONE-, TWO-, AND THREE-POUND PECAN
ROLLS ARE ONE OF THE MOST FAVORITE KINDS
OF PECAN CANDIES

Stuckey developed a national sales organization using 80,000 lb of pecans for in-shell and shelled packaged items. Stuckey's became a division of Pet, Inc., in 1964. As of 1977 this company has done most of the research/development work on pecan candies.

Pecans are used in 30 varieties of candies and scores of multipackaged items, and the company is continuously looking for new and interesting ways of using pecans. Biggest sellers are pecan log rolls, pralines, brittle, pecan divinity, fudge, pecan clusters and chocolate enrobed pieces. Only fancy nuts of top quality and color are used and product formulas are closely guarded.

Five elements of quality are maturity, texture, color, flavor and oil content. Even before the nuts are harvested the anticipated crop is analyzed with these qualities in mind. High quality pecans require suitable cultivars, good soil, ample moisture, proper fertilization, and insect and disease control. To maintain quality the following rules must be followed: (a) harvest when mature; (b) pick up often; (c) have proper curing and storage; (d) refrigerate if held over 3 months; (e) freeze and hold at -17.8°C (0°F) if held for over 10 months; and (f) store nuts separately because pecans absorb odors easily from other products.

Supplies of pecans are arranged for more than a year in advance to ensure against light crops. Production in all of the leading producing areas are watched closely at all times. Candies are made only on order at Eastman, and shipments of fresh candies are made weekly across the country (Anon. 1976). Stuckey's stores are located at strategic sites only after careful traffic surveys have been made.

American Association of Candy Technologists

This is a viable organization with more than 500 members that have contributed heavily to nut candy technology. The AACT was organized in 1948 and now has six active regional sections throughout the country. About half of the members are candy plant representatives, and about half consists of suppliers. They are all technically and professionally oriented, without revelation of trade secrets.

The AACT group works closely with the National Confectioners Association and the Retail Confectioners International in sponsoring training courses and Trade Expositions.

Stability of Pecan Candies

The following factors affect the stability and quality of pecan candies.

Moisture Content.—Changes in moisture content of pecan candies during storage accounted for more loss of quality than any other single factor. Each kind of candy has an optimum moisture content, and changes as small as 1% resulted in a measurable loss of quality. Decreases in moisture caused pecan candies to become dry, shrunken, grained, tough, and stale; increases in moisture caused them to become increasingly soft, moist, runny, and finally, moldy. Data in Table 12.20 show the optimum (initial) moisture content and changes during 10 weeks storage of 14 kinds of pecan candies.

Some pecan candies, such as log rolls, puffettes, and others, were made with all of the nutmeats on the surface where they were unprotected by coatings of chocolate, sugar, starch, or "glaze." These candies were particularly susceptible to changes in moisture content. Significant moisture changes are prevented by (a) wrapping individual pieces, (b) lining the boxes, or (c) overwrapping boxes (containing only one kind of candy or candies having similar moisture content) with cellophane, aluminum foil, or other moistureproof material.

Time, Temperature, and Relative Humidity.—Of 29 candies stored at 21°C (70°F) and 50% relative humidity, 14 remained acceptable for longer than 10 weeks, 18 for longer than 6 weeks, 27 for longer than 4 weeks, and all for longer than 2 weeks. At 21°C (70°F) and 90% relative humidity only 13 of the candies remained acceptable for longer than 2 weeks, and by 10 weeks all the candies had molded and were unacceptable. When well packaged, all of these remained in excellent condition for one year at -17°C (0°F).

Packaging.—The storage life of pecan candies is directly related to the method of packaging. Candies packed alone retain fresh quality longer than similar candies packed as part of an assorted box. When two or more candies with different flavors and different moisture contents are stored in boxes together, there is migration of flavors and

TABLE 12.20

CHEMICAL AND SENSORY VALUES OF 14 KINDS OF PECAN CANDIES INITIALLY AND AFTER STORAGE AT 21°C (70°F) WITH 50% RH

Candy	Moisture		Titratable Acidity 0.1N NaOH Per 100 g		Free Fatty Acids as Oleic		Peroxide Values Per kg of Oil		Quality		
	Initial (%)	After 10 Weeks (%)	Initial (ml)	After 10 Weeks (ml)	Initial (%)	After 10 Weeks (%)	Initial (mM)	After 10 Weeks (mM)	Initial Score (100)	Score After 10 Weeks (100)	Comments
Pecans, chocolate coated	1.15	1.31	62.7	76.6	–	0.81	–	1.40	100	86.4	very good
Dates, pecan stuffed	16.69	15.93	71.7	104.4	–	–	–	–	100	84.4	very good
Glace, pecan	3.00	3.19	31.6	36.1	0.25	0.36	1.10	1.29	100	82.2	dull, slightly stale
Sugared-spiced pecans	3.07	2.26	45.2	61.8	0.37	0.86	1.24	1.86	95.6	80.0	lost some spice flavor
Puffettes, pecan	7.54	7.23	19.8	46.0	–	0.79	0.97	0.86	100	75.6	dried around edges, flavor bland
Fudge, chocolate pecans	9.32	8.28	26.5	44.6	0.54	0.54	1.30	1.68	100	75.6	grained, slightly stale
Clusters, chocolate pecan	7.01	6.92	47.4	59.7	0.54	0.62	1.59	1.34	100	66.4	stale
Brittle, pecan	3.14	3.49	13.0	25.8	0.63	0.72	2.80	1.59	100	66.4	stale
Nougat, chocolate pecan	–	4.12	46.3	46.5	0.44	0.64	0.78	1.42	100	66.4	dry, grained, lost flavor
Pralines, maple pecan	9.17	7.55	22.0	23.8	0.31	0.95	1.32	2.36	100	66.4	dried out, stale
Roll, pecan log	8.67	7.25	26.5	38.4	0.50	0.59	1.20	1.17	100	64.4	dry, tough, stale
Pralines, chocolate pecan	8.94	8.21	29.9	37.7	–	–	–	–	97.8	64.4	dried out, stale
Divinity, pecan	7.95	6.69	15.2	21.2	–	–	–	–	100	55.6	"chalky", burny aftertaste
Fudge, maple pecan	8.22	7.03	21.5	34.4	0.36	0.42	2.18	8.07	95.6	53.3	grained, stale

Courtesy of Stuckey's Inc.

FIG. 12.55. INTERIOR OF CANDY PLANT SHOWING PECAN
FUDGE ON COOLING TABLES

Note clean equipment, and well lighted plant.

moisture from one piece of candy to another. This was eliminated by individually wrapping the pieces of candy with foil or other moistureproof material. Results show that set-up boxes with full telescoping lids and smooth edges are superior to similar boxes with extended edges, since the latter often puncture the overwrap during handling.

Location of Nuts.—Chocolate or sugar coated pecans, glacé and brittle retain higher quality than pecan halves, or candies with the nuts on the surface. In general, there are less changes in moisture and eating qualities of candies with nuts completely coated, as compared with pieces where nuts are partially coated. Data indicate that the shelf-life of partially coated candies would be lengthened if such pieces were completely coated. There is an increase in free fatty acid values of all candies high in nuts and other fats. Pieces high in fat or with embedded nuts, such as fudge, accumulate more peroxides than pieces with nuts exposed; however, rancidity does not build up sufficiently to be detected by taste. The total titratable acidity increases about twice as much in pieces with the nuts on the surface as in pieces with nuts embedded. The centers of candies with exposed nuts dry out, become tough, and lose eating qualities faster than the nuts.

Due to the high fat content of pecan candies, they have a comparatively short shelf-life. For this reason they should be manufactured at regular intervals, "dated," and sold as quickly thereafter as is practical.

Courtesy Rose Confections

FIG. 12.56. CHOCOLATE COATED MIXED NUTS

Chocolate coating assorted nuts extends the shelf–life and provides a variety of flavors and textures.

Storage of Nut Candies

The storage conditions for candies and nuts are similar in that all are more stable at low temperatures, low humidities and in odor-free atmospheres. Practically all nut candies are held for a period between manufacture and consumption. This may be in the plant where made, in warehouses, during transit, or in retail outlets. The period of holding may vary from one week to more than a year. It is very important that the candy not lose quality during this time.

Proper use of refrigeration in prolonging the shelf-life of candies is becoming increasingly important. The combined effects of refrigeration, antioxidants, humectants, emulsifiers, better packaging and improved formulas are resulting in more and better candies throughout the world. Only in recent years has low temperature been recommended as a means of maintaining candy quality, as it was generally believed that refrigeration was unnecessary, if not detrimental, to the finish of candies, particularly chocolates.

A surprisingly large proportion of candy manufacturers, salesmen, wholesalers, and warehousemen believe that refrigeration, below what is generally considered good air conditioning, is detrimental to candies. The belief has been substantiated by a few observations of poorly packaged candies that were placed in relatively humid cold rooms, and later removed directly to room temperatures and humidities. Within an hour or two, most candies under these conditions appear moist, sticky and without finish.

However, recent experiments and commercial practice have shown that low temperature storage does not produce these undesirable results if (a) the candy is properly packaged, (b) the storage room is sufficiently dry, and (c) the candy is brought to room temperature before opening. The storage period depends upon (a) the marketing season of the particular candy, (b) the stability of the candy, (c) the storage temperature, and (d) humidity.

The shelf-life of a particular kind of candy is determined by the stability of its individual ingredients. Common candy ingredients are sugars, including sucrose, dextrose, corn syrups, corn syrup solids and invert syrup; dark and milk chocolates; nuts, including coconut, peanuts, pecans, almonds, walnuts, and others; fruits, including cherries, dates, raisins, figs, apricots and strawberries; dried milk and milk products, butter, dried eggs, cream of tartar, gelatin, soybean flour, wheat flour, and starch; and artificial colors.

Refrigerated storage of candy ingredients is especially advantageous for seasonal products, such as peanuts, pecans, almonds, cherries, coconut and chocolate. Ingredients with delicate flavors and colors such as butter, dried eggs and dried milk retain quality more evenly year-round if kept refrigerated as directed for these products. Unless properly refrigerated, ingredients containing fats or proteins may lose considerable flavor or develop off-flavors before being used.

Candies are semi-perishable, and experience has shown that the finest candies or candy ingredients may be ruined by a few weeks of improper storage. This includes many candy bars, packaged candies, and some choice bulk candies, especially those with chocolate coating. Unless refrigeration is provided, from the time of manufacture through the retail outlet, the types of candies offered for sale must be greatly reduced in the summer.

Benefits from refrigerated storage of candies, especially during the summer, are: (a) insects are rendered inactive at temperatures below 9°C (48°F); (b) the tendency to become stale or rancid is reduced as the temperature is reduced; (c) candies remain firm as an insurance against sticking to the wrapper or becoming mashed; (d) loss of colors, aromas and flavors is reduced as the temperature is reduced; and (e) candies can be manufactured year-round, and stockpiled for periods of heavy sales, such as Easter, Mother's Day, Valentine's Day, Halloween, Thanksgiving and Christmas.

Flavor.—Retention of the original freshness of candies is one of the chief reasons for refrigerated storage. Most flavors added to candies are strong, such as peppermint, lemon, orange, cherry or grape, and are stable during storage. Less pronounced flavors of candy ingredients, such as butter, milk, eggs, nuts and fruits are more sensitive to high temperatures.

Low temperatures retard the development of staleness and rancidity in fats and fatty materials, preserve flavors in fruit ingredients, and prevent staleness and other off-flavors of candies containing milk, eggs, gelatin, nuts and coconut. While stored at room temperature or higher for more than a few weeks, candies containing fruits become strong in flavor and those containing nuts become rancid. While there are no known critical temperatures at which undesirable changes occur, the lower the temperature the more slowly they take place, and candies containing appreciable quantities of these semiperishable ingredients can be stored for only short periods without refrigeration.

Insects.—Candies containing fruits, chocolate, or nuts, including coconut, are favorite hosts for insects. Since fumigation and insect repellants are seldom permissible with candies, the use of temperatures below 9°C (48°F) as a means of inactivating insects in candy and candy ingredients is essential.

Common insects become active at about 10°C (50°F) and activity increases as the temperature is raised to 38°C (100°F). While common cold storage temperatures do not kill many insects, they are inactivated at temperatures below 10°C (50°F). Both adults and eggs may exist for months at above freezing temperatures without feeding or propagating. Candies with insect eggs, either on the product or on the wrappers, may be held under refrigeration for long periods with no apparent damage, but when brought back to warm rooms, a serious insect infestation may develop.

There is actual killing of both adults and eggs when infested materials are stored at or near −18°C (0°F). Lower temperatures and long storage periods are lethal to insects. It is very difficult to set a temperature or time at which all insect life in a given lot of candies ceases. However, storing candies at −18°C (0°F) for a few weeks usually destroys insect life. (See Chapter 18, p. 677.)

Storage Temperature.—As to their effect on candies, it is difficult to separate storage temperature from humidity, and of the two, the latter is more important. There are no critical refrigerated temperatures at which a certain type of candy must or must not be held. In general, the lower the temperature the longer the storage life, but the greater the problem of moisture condensation upon removal. Temperatures for candy storage will be considered under four practical conditions.

Air Conditioning at 20° to 21°C (68° to 70°F).—Since the storage of candies begins in the tempering room of the manufacturing plant, maintenance at 20°C (68°F) and 50% RH seems desirable to prevent soft, sticky pieces from being packaged. At this temperature all candies will remain firm, and the original luster can be held. Those containing nuts or chocolate become musty or rancid on prolonged storage and the colors and flavors may fade. Only *summer candies* should be held for more than a few weeks at 20° to 21.1°C (68° to 70°F) or higher. An air temperature of 20° to 21.1°C (68° to 70°F) is the maximum at which chocolate coated bars and packaged candies can be transported to advantage. Unless precautions are taken, the temperature of truck or rail shipments may rise to the melting point of semisoft candies or to the graying point of chocolates. Candies temporarily stored in the sunshine or in warm places in buildings may suffer severely in loss of shape, luster, and color. As portable refrigerators become more generally available, their use for candies should increase and thereby supply the missing links of "conditioned storage" for candies from manufacturer to consumer.

Cold Storage at 8° to 10°C (48° to 50°F).—Experiments have shown that candies stored at this temperature remain firm, and of good texture and color, and only those containing nuts, butter, cream or other fats became stale or rancid within four months. Candies which remained practically fresh for four months were fudge, caramels, sugar bonbons, marshmallows, hard creams and semisweet chocolates. Candies which became stale at this temperature were nut rolls and nougat bars. It appears that 10°C (50°F) would be better than higher temperatures for transporting candies or for temporary stockpiling. Since there was a detectable loss in flavor in 4 months with most candies at 10°C (50°F), a lower temperature should be used for prolonged storage.

Cold storage at 0° to 2°C (32° to 34°F).—Most candies can be successfully held in cold storage for one-half year at this temperature, and many can be held for much longer. Maintaining sufficiently low humidity in the cold storage room requires special effort and may not be easy to obtain. Experience has shown that no condensation of moisture occurred on candies on removal from refrigeration when they were adequately packaged and left unopened until the product reached room temperature.

Freezer Storage at -17°C (0°F) or Below.—The need and economic justification for freezing nut candies are similar to those for freezing other foods—better preservation for a longer time. This method of preservation is suitable for those candies (a) in which very high quality standards must be maintained; (b) in which a longer shelf-life is desired than is accomplished from other methods of storage; (c) which are normally manufactured from six to nine months in advance of consumption; and (d) which are especially suitable for retailing as frozen items.

One of the chief reasons for freezing nut candies is to hold them in an unchanged condition for as long as nine months, then thaw and sell them as fresh candies. Experience shows that this is not only possible but practical. The conditions that render such a procedure economical are as follows: (a) freeze only those candies that would lose quality when held at a higher temperature; (b) eliminate the few kinds that crack during freezing; (c) package the candies in moistureproof containers similarly as other frozen foods; (d) thaw the candies in the unopened packages to avoid condensation of moisture on the surface.

Frozen Candies Require Moisture-Proof Packages.—Candies for freezing require more protection than those for common storage, because the storage period is usually longer and there is a greater tendency for condensation upon removal. A single layer of moisture-proof material—aluminum foil, polyethylene, cellophane, glassine or laminations including one of these—affords adequate protection. Candies not fully protected from desiccation "grain", become hard and lose flavor. Most protection is provided when the moisture barrier is in contact with the candy in the form of a sealed, individual wrapper. Inner liners for the boxes protect candy, provided they are sealed (which was difficult and seldom accomplished). The usual manner of applying moisture barriers is as overwraps for the boxes chiefly because these are easiest to apply and seal by machines. Overwraps for boxes provide less protection than wraps for individual pieces of candy because of the relatively large amount of air enclosed within the former. For the same reason, boxes with extended edges offer less protection than do those without extended edges.

Frozen Candies Should be Thawed in the Unopened Packages.— While freezing, *per se,* affected only a few candies, the manner of removal from storage affected all of them, especially the candies unprotected by special coatings or individual wraps.

A Few Candies are Improved by Freezing.—Candies which are improved in freshness or mellowness or rendered smoother in texture by freezing include those with high moisture content and without protective coatings or individual wrapping. Usually these are candies which are ordinarily subject to surface drying. Caramels, fudges, divinities, coconut macaroons, nut loaves, coconut bonbons, panned nuts, and malted milk balls are in this group.

Pan Coating Pecans

Chocolate spraying speeds pan coating of nuts by a usual application of compressed air being made by a British confectioner. The new method for chocolate coating nuts reportedly increases production considerably.

In the system, chocolate is heated to a liquid state. Molten chocolate is pumped in pipe enclosed with a hot-water-jacketed pipe to maintain temperature necessary to keep it liquid. This chocolate terminates in 16 nozzles, each directed into a revolving pan containing the nuts to be coated.

The compressed air line is connected to the back of each nozzle so chocolate is sprayed on the nuts through the nozzle in atomized form. As the nuts are constantly tumbled, an even coating of chocolate is received by each nut. Simultaneously, each nut is hardened by a steady blast of cooled air from downpipes located at the opposite of the pan.

When the required buildup of chocolate has been achieved, the air is cut off, the nuts are transferred to polishing pans and from there to the packaging department (Anon. 1966).

Pecan Candy Formulas

The following are representative formulas for pecan candies from the National Pecan Shellers and Processors Association, Chicago.

Pralines

3 cups light brown sugar   1½ cups chopped pecans
¼ cup butter   ⅛ tsp ground cinnamon
1 cup cream

Mix the sugar, butter, and cream and cook until a small quantity dropped in cold water forms a soft ball. Add the chopped pecans and cinnamon. Beat until cool, then drop by spoonfuls onto waxed paper.

Spiced Nuts

1 cup sugar   ½ tsp nutmeg
½ cup water   ½ tsp cloves
1 tsp cinnamon   1 lb nuts (pecans or peanuts)

Boil sugar, water and spices until syrup threads from spoon. Drop 1 lb blanched nuts into syrup. Stir until nuts look dry. Pour out on waxed paper and let stand until cold and dry.

The following are formulas for large and small batches of pecan candies from Nulomoline of SuCrest Corporation (Anon. 1959).

Caramel Coating for Nougat Rolls

	Small Batch	Large Batch
Corn syrup	6 lb	30 lb
Sweetened condensed whole milk	6 lb	30 lb
Hardened edible oil	1 lb	4 lb
Nulomoline invert syrup	2 lb	10 lb
Salt	1 oz	4 oz

Granulated sugar	4 lb	20 lb
Water	2 lb	52 lb
Nutmeats	10 lb	50 lb
Vanilla and butter flavorings		

Place all the ingredients, except the flavorings, into a double-action mixing kettle and mix well. Cook the batch to a medium soft ball; then add the flavorings. This caramel may be used also for spreading to form a layer over nougat, coconut, etc., or nut meats may be mixed into the batch to form a caramel chew.

Rich Fondant Fudge

	Small Batch	Large Batch
Granulated sugar	10 lb	100 lb
Corn syrup	21½ lb	115 lb
Nulomoline	11½ lb	115 lb
Old fashioned molasses	½ lb	5 lb
Cream (18 to 26% butterfat)	12½ lb	125 lb
Coconut oil	½ lb	5 lb
Unsweetened evaporated milk	11½ lb	115 lb
Salt	to taste	6 oz
Pecans, walnuts, Brazil nuts	11½ lb	115 lb
Maple, vanilla, egg nog, or rum flavoring		

Place the sugar, corn syrup, Nulomoline, molasses, cream and coconut oil into a fudge cooking kettle and mix well. Stirring constantly, apply heat until the batch boils. Continue to stir. Gradually add the evaporated milk, about 1 pint at a time, and when all of the milk has been added, cook the batch to 114° to 117°C (238° to 242°F). Pour the batch on an open type beater to cool to approximately 49°C (120°F); add the salt and flavoring and beat until the batch becomes plastic; then add the nuts. Remove the batch from the beater, forming it into large mounds, or place it into large waxed-paper-lined baking pans.

The cooked batch may be placed into the hopper of an instantaneous continuous fondant beater and beaten at once. Add the flavoring, nuts, etc, to the beaten fondant fudge.

Special Chewing Nougat
Part 1

	Small Batch	Large Batch
Egg albumen—dissolved in	11 lb	22 lb
water	12 lb	24 lb
Old-fashioned molasses	10 lb	20 lb

Place the albumen solution into a beater, add the molasses and beat together until light. Meanwhile, prepare Part 2 as follows:

Part 2

	Small Batch	Large Batch
Granulated sugar	17½ lb	35 lb
Water	4 lb	8 lb
Invert syrup (Nulomoline)	7½ lb	15 lb
Corn syrup	25 lb	50 lb
Coconut oil	1½ lb	3 lb
Salt	2 oz	4 oz
Orange oil	½ oz	1 oz
Filberts, almonds, pecans, or		
roasted peanuts	7½ lb	15 lb

Cook the sugar, water, Nulomoline, and corn syrup to 135° to 138°C (275° to 280°F). Gradually add this to the beaten batch (Part 1), beating until light. Add the coconut oil, salt, orange oil and nutmeats, and mix just enough to distribute the oils.

Spread the batch on an oiled slab, leveling to the required height. As soon as the batch is cool, it should be cut into pieces of the desired size, then wrapped or coated.

Cut Grained Nougat
Part 1—Frappe

	Small Batch	Large Batch
Corn syrup	15 lb	25 lb
Invert syrup (Nulomoline)	15 lb	25 lb
Egg albumen, dissolved in	16 oz	21 ¾ lb
water	12 oz	24 lb

Cook the corn syrup to 119°C (245°F). Turn off the heat and add the Nulomoline, mixing until melted. Place the batch into a marshmallow beater, start the beater, then gradually add the albumen solution and beat until light.

Part 2

	Small Batch	Large Batch
Granulated sugar	12 lb	60 lb
Corn syrup	6 lb	30 lb
Water	3 lb	15 lb
Basic Fondant (formula p. 538)	2 lb	10 lb
Salt	1 oz	½ lb
Hardened edible oil (melting		
point 30° to 36°C [86° to 96°F])	½ lb	63 lb
Flavoring		
Nutmeats		

Cook the sugar, corn syrup, and water to 129° to 132°C (265° to 270°F). Pour this into the frappe (Part 1), beating continuously; add the fondant, mixing until the fondant is melted, then add the salt, and beat until the batch shows evidence of graining. Now add the edible oil (which has been cut into small pieces) and the flavoring and mix well; add the nutmeats and mix to thoroughly distribute. Spread the batch to form sheets.

Divinity Kisses
Part 1

	Small Batch	Large Batch
Invert sugar (Nulomoline)	2 lb	10 lb
Soy or vegetable albumen (no water)	3½ oz	1 lb

Heat the Nulomoline until melted (approximately 65°C [150°F]). Place this in a beater, add the albumen and beat until quite light.

Part 2

	Small Batch	Large Batch
Granulated sugar	7 lb	35 lb
Corn syrup	3 lb	15 lb
Water	2 lb	10 lb
Basic fondant (formula p. 538)	2 lb	50 lb
Salt	to taste	1 oz
Convertit	1 tsp	1 oz
Coloring and flavoring		
Nutmeats		

Place the sugar, corn syrup, and water into a kettle and stir occasionally until the batch boils. Wash down all sugar crystals that adhere to the kettle and cook the batch to 119° to 121°C (245° to 250°F).

Pour this into the whipped portion (Part 1), beating continuously. Add the fondant and salt and continue to beat until the batch becomes quite short; then add the Convertit, coloring, and flavoring, and mix well. Now add the nutmeats and mix to distribute. Spread the batch to form sheets or spoon into the shape of kisses.

For batches to be formed into kisses, cook to 119°C (246°F).

For forming into sheets, cook the batch to 121°C (250°F).

Sea Foam Sheets or Kisses
Part 1

	Small Batch	Large Batch
Egg albumen	3 oz	1 lb
Water	6 oz	2 lb
Invert sugar (Nulomoline)	2 lb	10 lb

Dissolve the albumen in the water and place into a beater. Add the Nulomoline (cold) and beat the batch until quite light.

Part 2

	Small Batch	Large Batch
Granulated sugar	7 lb	35 lb
Water	2 lb	10 lb
Corn syrup	4 lb	20 lb
Basic fondant (see below)	2 lb	10 lb
Convertit	1 tsp	1 oz
Flavoring and coloring		
Nutmeats		

Place the sugar, water, and corn syrup into a kettle and mix well. Apply heat and occasionally stir the batch until it boils. Cook to 118° to 121°C (245° to 250°F) and then pour this, in a fine stream, into the whipped portion (Part 1), beating at second speed.

After all of the cooked syrup has been added, beat for 1 or 2 min; then add the fondant, beating until the batch becomes plastic. Now add the Convertit, flavoring, and coloring, mixing well; then add the nutmeats, distributing well through the batch.

If the batch is to be formed into sheets or layers, cook to approximately 124°C (255°F).

For kisses, cook the batch to approximately 121°C (250°F).

Basic Fondant

	Small Batch	Large Batch
Granulated sugar	8 lb	80 lb
Corn syrup	2 lb	20 lb
Nulomoline	1 lb	10 lb
Water	2 lb	20 lb

Heat all ingredients together, stirring the batch occasionally until it boils. Wash down all grains of sugar that adhere to the kettle and cook the batch rapidly to 114° to 119°C (238° to 248°F). Cool the resulting syrup to 52° to 43°C (125° to 110°F); then beat into fondant.

Frappe No. 1

	Small Batch	Large Batch
Corn syrup	10 lb	50 lb
Nulomoline	10 lb	50 lb
Albumen (dissolved in	3 oz	1 lb
cold water)	6 oz	2 lb

Cook the corn syrup to 118.5°C (245°F). Turn off the heat, add the Nulomoline and stir until it is melted. Place the batch into a marshmallow beater, and start the beater; then gradually add the albumen solution and beat the batch until light.

Rolled Fruit and Nut Cream Bars

	Small Batch	Large Batch
Granulated sugar	10 lb	100 lb
Water	2½ lb	25 lb
Invert syrup (Nulomoline)	1 lb	10 lb
Corn syrup	½ lb	5 lb
Convertit	2 tsp	1½ oz
Salt	½ oz	4 oz
Vanilla flavoring (see above)		
Frappe No. 1	1½ lb	15 lb
Preserved (glacé) cherries	½ lb	5 lb
Preserved (glacé) pineapples	½ lb	5 lb
Preserved (glacé) citron	½ lb	5 lb
Pecans, walnuts, or Brazils	½ lb	5 lb

Condition the glacé fruits and nuts by boiling in Nulomoline for 2 or 3 min. Drain off the Nulomoline and permit the conditioned fruit and nuts to cool.

Meanwhile, heat the sugar, water, Nulomoline and corn syrup to the boiling point. Wash down all sugar crystals that adhere to the kettle and cook the batch to 121°C (250°F). Pour the batch on an open-type cream beater and when it has cooled to 43.3°C (110°F), start the beater. Now add the Convertit, salt, and flavoring and when the batch becomes opaque, add the frappe and beat until the batch becomes plastic. Add the conditioned fruits and nuts and mix well.

Take the batch from the beater and form it into egg shapes or bars before the batch cools to room temperature, using powdered sugar as a dusting medium.

Temper the eggs to approximately 24°C (75°F), then double-coat with chocolate. Adjust the consistency of the batch by increasing or decreasing the cooking temperature.

Spiced Sugared Pecans

2½ cups pecans halves
1 cup sugar
½ cup water

1 tsp cinnamon
½ tsp salt
1 tsp vanilla

Place pecans in shallow pan. Heat in 190°C (375°F) oven about 15 min. Remove from oven.

Cook together sugar, water, cinnamon and salt to soft ball stage. Remove from heat, add vanilla and nuts. Stir gently until nuts are well coated and mixture becomes creamy. Turn out on greased pan. Separate halves as they cool.

Quick Nut Fudge

1 lb. confectioners' sugar
¼ cup cocoa
¼ tsp salt
6 tbsp butter or margarine

4 tbsp milk
1 tbsp vanilla extract
1 cup chopped nuts

Combine all ingredients except nuts in top of double boiler. Place over hot water and stir until smooth. Add nuts and mix. Spread candy in buttered 9-in pan. Cool and cut in squares.

The following are pecan candy recipes from anonymous sources:

Pecan Roll

2 cups granulated sugar   1 cup evaporated milk
1 cup brown sugar   1½ cup chopped pecans
½ cup light corn syrup

Combine sugars, corn syrup, and milk; cook, stirring only until sugar dissolves, to soft ball stage of 113°C (236°F). Cool at room temperature, without stirring, until lukewarm, about 43°C (110°F); beat until mixture holds its shape. Cool and knead until firm. Shape in two 1½ in. rolls; roll in nuts; press nuts firmly into candy. Chill and slice ½ in. thick. Makes 30 slices.

Glace' Pecans

1½ cups nuts, salted or unsalted   ¼ tsp cream of tartar
2 cups sugar   1 cup hot water
                                          ⅛ tsp salt

Mix the sugar, cream of tartar, hot water and salt in a small saucepan and place over a hot fire. Stir until the sugar has dissolved. Let the syrup boil until it reaches a temperature of 144°C (293°F), or the hard-crack stage. Remove from the fire at once and place in a pan of hot water while dipping the nuts. Hold nuts separately with tweezers or on a long pin, and dip-in the syrup to cover. Place dipped nuts on waxed paper to dry. Reheat the syrup carefully if it becomes too thick.

Uncooked Candy

2 sticks of butter or margarine   2 cups coconut
2 lb confectioners' sugar   1 can sweetened condensed milk
2 cups ground pecans

Melt butter. Combine all ingredients and add to butter. Form into small balls by hand. Set on waxed paper on cookie sheet to harden.

12-oz pkg chocolate bits   ⅛ lb paraffin

Melt the chocolate and paraffin over hot water. Dip the candy balls into the chocolate mixture and then place on waxed paper to set.

Fruit Roll

½ lb raisins	½ lb prunes
1 small pkg dates	1 pkg dry coconut
½ lb pecans	1 tbsp orange juice

Grind all the ingredients together and add the orange juice. Shape into balls and roll in confectioners' sugar, or in cocoa and sugar mixture.

Chocolate-Drizzled Pecan Penuche

2 cups granulated sugar	1½ tsp vanilla extract
2 cups light brown sugar, packed	1 cup coarsely chopped pecans
½ cup light cream	½ 6-oz pkg semisweet
½ cup milk	chocolate pieces
3 tbsp butter or margarine	24 pecan halves

Make 2 or 3 days before serving:

(1) Butter bottom and sides of an 8 × 8 × 2 in. baking dish.

(2) Butter sides only of a heavy 2 ½ qt saucepan. In it combine sugars, cream, milk and butter or margarine. Stir, with wooden spoon, over medium heat, only until sugars dissolve and mixture boils. (Do not let candy coat sides of saucepan— it may become granular.) Then boil mixture, without stirring, until candy thermometer reads 114°C (238°F), or until a little of mixture, dropped in cold water, makes a soft ball. Immediately remove from heat, then allow it to cool to 43°C (110°F), without stirring.

(3) Now add vanilla and chopped pecans, then beat penuche vigorously with clean wooden spoon until it becomes thick and starts to lose its gloss. Quickly pour into baking dish, distributing evenly across bottom and into corners. While still warm, but firm, cut into 24 pieces with sharp knife. Set aside to cool.

(4) When penuche is cool, melt semisweet chocolate pieces in double boiler over hot, not boiling, water. Then, with a teaspoon, drizzle chocolate over top of cooled candy. Place a pecan half on top of each piece of candy.

(5) Cover penuche tightly with saran or foil; store at room temperature until serving time. Makes 24 squares.

ICE CREAM, SALTED PECANS, PECAN BUTTER, SHELLS AND TIMBER

Pecan Ice Cream

There are many uses for pecans which fluctuate with supply and price of the nuts. When the supply is short and the price is high other nuts or other flavors are used for ice cream or salted nuts. Ice cream is the third largest use for pecans, with about 5% of the meats going for this purpose. Pecan ice cream is a top selling nut flavor in most of the country, and ranking just behind vanilla and chocolate. With such popularity ice cream manufacturers regard the fortunes of the pecan industry as having a direct and vital influence upon their operations (Leeder 1964). Toasted pecan meats add flavor, texture and color to ice cream, and buttered pecan ice cream is one of the favorite ice cream flavors.

The sale of pecan ice cream fluctuates, depending upon whether there is an adequate supply of pecans, and whether pecans are available at a reasonably steady and competitive price. Both of these situations are being improved. Pecan pieces are the most expensive ingredient in pecan ice cream. Since pecan meal is a by-product of the cutting operations, it is the cheapest pecan product for ice cream.

Pecans may be added to ice cream mix as small pieces, granules, meal or as pecan paste or butter, depending on the texture and flavor desired. The smaller the particles used the more the flavor that is added, but the less the crunchiness. For maximum flavor, up to 6% pecan butter may be added to the ice cream batch, and for crunchiness up to 2% small pieces no larger than ⅛ in. are needed. Another way is to add a 5% mixture of 10 parts meal, 15 parts granules, and 75 parts small pieces.

For maximum flavor, pecans for ice cream are dry roasted at 185°C (375°F) for 15 min (2% butter and 1% salt may be added as optional ingredients), chopped to small size pieces, and added to the ice cream mix while hot.

Pecan Ice Cream

12% fat	6% pecan butter or meal
12% nonfat mild solids	2% small pecan pieces
14% sugar	0.35% stabilizer

In the above formula the fat (70%) in the pecan butter or meal is included in the total of 12% fat content, and about half as much pecan butter is used as would have been required if all chopped nuts had been used. The procedure is to freeze the mixture to 100% over-run, then add the pecan butter or meal, and continue to freeze until the temperature drops to -5°C (23°F). After freezing the ice cream is hardened to -29°C (-20°F) for 24 hours.

Buttered Pecan Ice Cream (Leeder 1964)

18½ qt standard white ice cream mix (12%)
2¼ lb buttered pecan halves
1 lb buttered pecans chopped

When continuous freezer is used, add the roasted nutmeats by means of a fruit feeder. In using a batch freezer, add the nuts to the ice cream as the refrigerant is turned off.

Cherry-Pecan Ice Cream (Leeder 1964)

16½ qt standard white ice cream mix (12½%)
1 ½ qt dry Maraschino cherries
1 ½ qt Maraschino cherry juice
1 ½ lb pecan halves or pieces
Red coloring to suit

Drain the juice from the cherries and add with the color directly to the mix. Add the nuts with a fruit feeder or directly into the batch freezer.

Varieties of Nutmeats in Ice Cream

There are many varieties of nutmeats used in ice cream and each has a different characteristic. Among those used (listed alphabetically) are almonds, Brazils, cashews, filberts, macadamias, mixed nuts, peanuts, pecans, pistachios and walnuts. In the past pecans, walnuts and almonds accounted for approximately 75% of all nut-flavored ice cream sales.

To buy quality nutmeats, careful attention must be given to purchasing, cleaning, storage and roasting techniques. Buying a grade of nutmeats that passes government standards is not enough because these standards permit tolerances up to $\frac{2}{10}$ of 1% by weight of foreign material. Most ice cream manufacturers, therefore, make arrangements to pick out shell fragments prior to roasting, or pay the sheller a premium for nutmeats guaranteed free from shells.

Nutmeats may be a very serious source of bacterial contamination when added to ice cream. The sanitary requirements for low tolerances of bacteria, mold and yeast organisms on nutmeats for ice cream are more strict than those for nutmeats for candies or bakery products. Due to microbial contamination during shelling (particularly nutmeats from foreign countries) raw nutmeats are seldom used in ice cream. Almonds, for example, are heated to 150°C (310°F) to destroy coliform and other types of bacteria. The requirements for well developed nut flavors, and lack of foreign flavors, are higher for nutmeats for ice cream than for other uses.

Roasting nutmeats for ice cream should be done immediately before use, and may be done by the ice cream manufacturer, or by someone who specializes in the operation. Nutmeats are heated to specific temperatures for an exact period of time to improve flavor characteristics of the respective nuts. The temperature and time vary according to the cultivar, grade and size of the nutmeat. Some nutmeats are dry-roasted but most are oil-roasted.

Gas-fired, automatically-controlled equipment is usually used for large scale roasting. On a small scale, it is possible to oil-roast nutmeats to a brown inside color in a steam-jacket kettle, using a perforated basket to hold nutmeats in a bath of frying oil. At the end of the roasting period, the nutmeats are air-cooled on a perforated stainless steel drying rack. Melted butter may be poured over them and mixed at the rate of 1 lb of butter to 8 lb of nutmeats. Light salting at the rate of ¾ oz per pound to develop the flavor is usually done at this stage. Whole nutmeats or large pieces roast better than small pieces because of size uniformity. In this case chopping after roasting is sometimes required.

While roasted nutmeats graded out to a uniform size look attractive in ice cream, a range of sizes from granules to large pieces is not objectionable, because the flavor is thereby enhanced and one gets wider distribution of the pieces in the mix. An essential characteristic of a good nutmeat in ice cream is crispness. While pecans and walnuts hold up extremely well, such nutmeats as cashews and peanuts get soggy very quickly in ice cream. Recently, edible protective coatings have been used to retain crispness and prolong shelf-life.

One of the protective coatings is an edible form of distilled acetylated monoglyceride. The film can be applied by a hot dip. Roasted nutmeats at 37.8° to 46°C (100° to 115°F) are dipped in a 104°C (220°F) bath of the coating and then allowed to drain free of excess coating material while the film sets. Coating weights of 1.6 to 2% are generally obtained. Such a coating retards the transfer of moisture from the ice cream into the nuts and the migration of the nut oil into the ice cream. The use of coatings on nutmeats is new and will no doubt increase due to the success it has already attained.

With few exceptions, nut-flavored ice cream requires a background flavoring agent to complement the delicate flavor of the nuts. Some flavors are combinations such as chocolate-almond, maple-almond, banana-nut, cherry-nut, caramel-almond, almond-toffee, almond-mocha, and maple-walnut; others are definite nut flavors such as butter-pecan, butter-almond, pistachio, pecan, cashew, black walnut or Persian walnut. For each there is a traditional coloring and flavoring agent, and much care must be used in the choice of background flavor.

A well-rounded ice cream flavor program should include one nut ice cream at all times. Additional nut flavors are frequently used as specials. As a group, nut ice creams rank high in consumer acceptance and from a marketing standpoint they command higher prices because they are accepted as quality flavors (Jacobsen 1964).

Salted Pecans

It is estimated that 15 million pounds of pecans are toasted and salted annually. These are (a) packed in flexible bags and consumed as snacks,

(b) packed under vacuum and used with cocktails or with meals, or (c) used in mixed nuts. Pecans are higher in price than, but are considered superior in quality to, most other nuts. Due to the short cooking time and high oil content, pecan meats are generally dry toasted. However, some processors prefer to cook pecan meats in oil because of the more uniform product, the ease of mechanical handling, and less loss in weight. During oil toasting there is a gain in oil content which compensates for the loss of about 4% moisture. The toasted nuts are coated with butter or other fat and thoroughly mixed with 1% of finely ground salt.

Experiments showed that pecan meats for salting should be toasted to a medium degree of doneness—185°C (375°F) for 12 to 15 min. When nuts were light toasted, either at a lower temperature or for a shorter time, they lacked aroma and flavor. On the other hand when the nuts were dark toasted, the product was objectionably brown and had a bitter over-cooked flavor. The time of toasting varies with the grade or size of meats used.

For salting, the toasted pecan kernels should be cooled quickly and uniformly to stop the cooking process and to remove traces of undesirable odors and flavors that develop during toasting. Cooling tunnels or perforated bins with forced air are preferred, although the nuts may be cooled in cylinders or spread thinly on tables in front of fans. Tests show that when hot toasted pecans were sealed in glass jars or tins stale odors and flavors developed within one week, while those that were properly cooled before being packaged remained stable for many weeks.

The cooled nuts should be screened to remove bits of shell, packing tissue, seed coat fragments, and other foreign matter, then graded to remove scorched or discolored kernels. The latter step is performed by an "electric eye," by hand on a conveyor belt, or by spreading the nuts thinly on a table.

Salted pecans are packaged in many ways—in vacuum cans, in vacuum jars, in flexible bags of different sizes, or sold in bulk. They are also sold as whole, halves or pieces, alone, or in "mixed nuts." The price of mixed salted nuts frequently is determined by the amount of pecans included.

Due to the relatively high cost and limited stability of salted pecans, as compared with other nuts, there is little likelihood that this outlet for pecans will greatly expand.

Formula for Salted Pecans

100 lb pecans, halves or large pieces
1 lb salt, powdered
0.01 oz antioxidant, butylated hydroxyanisole

Toast pecans in high grade vegetable oil at 185°C (375°F) for 6 min. Cool and coat with salt to which BHA has been added.

Attempts to impregnate raw unshelled and shelled pecans with salt were not successful. The method developed for salting raw peanuts in the shells consisted of immersing the nuts in saturated brine, subjecting them to vacuum and suddenly releasing it, then reducing the moisture by evaporation. When this method was tried for salting pecans, sufficient brine to adequately salt kernels did not penetrate the pecan shells. When shelled nuts were used, the salted product toasted unevenly, was too brittle and crisp, and developed an unnatural flavor. Salting greatly accelerated rancidification (Woodroof and Heaton 1961).

Salted Roasted Pecans

1 qt pecan halves
1 tsp salt
½ stick margarine

Melt margarine in shallow pan; add pecans and salt and stir. Roast at 107.5°C (225°F) for 1 hour; stir often.

Nuts and Bolts

6 tbsp butter or margarine
4 tsp Worcestershire sauce
1 tsp seasoned salt
1 tbsp salt

6 cups crisp whole cereal, any kind
1 cup salted pecans, or mixed nuts
2 tbsp garlic salt

Heat oven to 121°C (250°F). Slowly melt butter in shallow pan. Stir in Worcestershire and salt. Add cereal and pecans. Mix until all pieces are lightly coated. Heat in oven 45 min. Stir every 15 min. Spread on absorbent paper to cool.

Pecan Butter

Possibly the first pecan butter to be marketed commercially was packed in 3-oz and 6-oz glass containers by Nutsbert Packing Company, Albany, Georgia, in 1923. A similar product was Pe-Kons packed in 14-oz tin containers by Bob's Candy Company, Albany. It consisted of ground pecan kernels with concentrated pecan oil and sugar (Anon. 1924).

Blackmon (1937A, B) made pecan butter by: (a) grinding the raw meats into a fine, smooth paste; (b) grinding the pomace of cold pressed raw kernels; and (c) thoroughly heating, but not browning, the pomace in pecan oil and grinding. He found pecan butter to be "a delicious product with an excellent nutty flavor and a pleasing and appealing taste." He believed that it would find a ready outlet through industries which desired the rich nutty pecan flavor in foods and would be of most value in the confection, baking and ice cream industries. Numerous uses for it in the home were suggested. These included cake icings, sandwich spread, homemade candies, and other products.

According to Heaton and Woodroof (1960) pecan butter is made by finely grinding toasted pecans, to pass through a 200-mesh screen, and mixing with 1% salt, 2½% hydrogenated fat, ½% dextrose and an antioxidant. The fine grinding accentuates the flavor, the dextrose gives it a sweetish taste, and the stabilizer prevents the oil from rising to the surface.

Pecan Butter

Pecan meats, toasted at 185°C (375°F) 12 min	100 lb
Salt, powdered	11 lb
Hydrogenated fat, melted (melting point 63°C [145°F])	12½ lb
Dextrose, powder	2½ lb
Antioxidant, butylated hydroxyanisole	0.01 oz

Grind all ingredients together to a smooth, fine texture. The yield is approximately 210 8-oz jars.

Pecans for butter should be shelled, dried, graded, toasted, cooled and hand-picked. Additional equipment includes: (a) mill, either burr or stone, for very smooth grinding; (b) kettle with controlled steam or electric heat with mechanical stirrer for blending ingredients; and (c) filling, closing and labeling machines. The most desirable pecans for making butter are well filled, with plump, bright colored kernels, having pronounced aroma and flavor. Pecan meats lacking in these qualities produce inferior butter. The cultivar, oil content, degree of filling of pecans, and fineness of grinding influence the consistency and texture of the butter. Pecans with high oil content, such as the Schley, produce thin butter; those with medium oil content, as Stuart, yield butter with medium consistency; while Moneymaker and other low oil content cultivars produce rather heavy butter. Since the oil tends to "crawl" and become rancid, pecan butter must be packed in greaseproof, air-tight containers.

Pecan butter is reasonably stable against development of rancidity. Maximum shelf-life is about 4 months at 21°C (70°F), 9 months at 0°C (32°F), and several years at 18°C (0°F). Due to the low (about 1%) moisture content of pecan butter, there is no need for heat processing to prevent microbial spoilage.

Pecan butter is highly suitable for use in milkshakes. The natural stabilizer and antioxidants improve the foaming characteristics and stability. The creamy texture, nutmeg appearance and pecan flavor are well liked. Milkshakes should be mixed immediately before serving, using ½ cup vanilla ice cream, ⅓ cup whole milk, and 1 tbsp pecan butter. The ingredients should be vigorously mixed for 40 seconds.

Experimental results showed pecan butter, as a flavoring ingredient for milkshakes, was placed fourth among other popular flavors. It was surpassed by chocolate, vanilla and strawberry, and in turn was found more popular than cherry, raspberry, butter/pecan, walnut, butterscotch and pineapple.

Pecan butter is very suitable for use in bakery goods. Among these are butter cream icing, sugar cookies, angel food cake with butter cream icing, sweet loaf bread, butter cream pie, sweet dough bread, custard pie, butter cookies, syrup pie and chiffon pie.

Other uses for pecan butter are in ice cream, salads, toppings and many kinds of candies.

Since pecan butter has a very pronounced flavor that tends to be bitter when too much is used, care should be taken to avoid using too much. For this reason, it is not suitable for use on sandwiches alone.

The following are representative recipes for using pecan butter:

Pecan Butter Milkshakes
Using Regular (Hard) Ice Cream

1 tbsp pecan butter
7 oz ice cream
¾ cup milk

Combine ingredients, mix thoroughly, and serve immediately. The stability of the over-run is excellent.

Pecan Butter Milkshakes
Using Soft Ice Cream

1 tbsp pecan butter   ½ cup whole milk
7½ oz soft ice cream   ½ oz maple syrup

Combine ingredients, mix thoroughly, and serve immediately.

Commercial Pecan Butter Ice Cream

12% fat   6% pecan butter (72% fat in pecan
12% nonfat milk solids   butter included in the 12% fat
14% sugar   content)
                           0.35% stabilizer

Freeze according to standard procedure. The over-run was slightly less when the full amount of pecan butter was added to ice cream. For crunchiness a small quantity of pecan pieces may be added.

Pecan Butter "Foam"

¼ cup pecan butter
2 cups milk
1 tbsp honey

Mix in a rotary beater or electric blender until smooth and foamy.

Pecan Butter Fudge

3 tbsp pecan butter
2 cups sugar
¾ cup milk

1 tsp vanilla
Few grains salt

Boil sugar and milk without stirring until mixture forms soft ball when dropped into cold water. Remove from heat, let stand undisturbed until cool. Add salt, pecan butter and vanilla. Beat with wooden spoon or work with spatula on marble slab. Pour ¾ in. thick in buttered pan and mark in squares. Add a few pecan pieces for crunchiness and decoration.

Pecan Butter Cream Frosting

½ cup pecan butter
⅓ tsp salt
About ¼ cup milk or light cream

1½ tsp vanilla extract
3 cups sifted confectioners' sugar

Beat with electric mixer at medium speed, or "cream" with spoon. Thoroughly mix butter with salt and one cup confectioners' sugar until light and fluffy. Add rest of sugar and milk alternately, beating until very smooth and of spreading consistency. Add vanilla. Fill and frost two 8- or 9- in. layers, or frost 9 × 9× 2 in. cake.

Pecan Butter Chiffon Pie

4 tbsp pecan butter
1 cup water
1 pack plain gelatin

¼ cup sugar
1 cup evaporated milk, undiluted
1 baked pie shell

Bring water to a boil, add gelatin and stir until dissolved, mix in the sugar and cool until almost stiff, then stir in pecan butter. To whip the evaporated milk, chill in ice cube trays until soft ice crystals form around outside edges (15 to 20 minutes). Whip the evaporated milk until it stands in stiff peaks, pour on top of the gelatin mixture, and beat in slowly with rotary beater or electric mixer at low speed. Pour into baked pie shell. Chill at least one hour. Garnish with chopped pecans, if desired.

Pecan Butter Cookies

½ cup pecan butter	1 tsp vanilla
½ cup granulated sugar	1½ cups flour
½ cup dark brown sugar	¼ tsp salt
1 egg	Pinch salt

Cream sugar with pecan butter. Beat in egg. Add sifted dry ingredients and vanilla. Mix well. Shape in 1 in. balls. Preheat oven to 185°C (375°F). Place cookies on baking sheet and flatten with fork. Bake 11 to 12 min. Yield about 2 dozen cookies.

Pecan Shells

Pecan shells are a by-product of the shelling operations. They occupy about 80% as much space, and weigh about 60% as much as the unshelled nuts. Mixed with the shells are "pops," wormy, moldy and other defective nuts, which accumulate at shelling plants in huge quantities. They are blown outside the shelling plant, similar to sawdust, into a pile under a temporary shed. Here they are kept dry until they are disposed of.

Pecan shells are used in many ways, some of them as a profit, others as a means of disposing of the shells. Pecan shells are used for (1) "gravel" for walks and driveways; (2) fuel for heating the plant or operating a steam boiler; (3) mulch for ornamental plants; (4) soil conditioner in the fields; (5) stock bedding and poultry litters; (6) fillers for feeds, insecticides and fertilizers; (7) manufacture of tannin, charcoal and abrasives in hand soap; and (8) flour as a filler for plastic wood and veneer wood. In addition, pecan shells along with walnut shells are reduced to flours of various screen sizes and used as soft grit in non-skid paints, adhesives, dynamite and polishing of metals (Kester 1949). It is estimated that 22 million pounds of pecan shell flour are processed for polyester fillers annually.

Production and maintenance schedules set up during World War II resulted in development and expansion of uses for ground nut shell materials. Fine flours from walnut and pecan shells were needed as extenders in plywood adhesives. Soft grits from various nut shells were used by the Army Air Force in the air-blasting method for cleaning airplane parts and engines. Oil, dirt, corrosion products, stain, paint and grease are removed from metal surfaces by this method. The process is inexpensive and foolproof because the surfaces are cleaned without pitting or abrasion, such as occur with sand blasting.

Ground-up shells of walnuts, pecans, or apricots will "clean" jet engines of unwanted grease, bird feathers, or newspapers in a few seconds, a job requiring hours if the engines are dismantled. Feeding shells through the air intake provides just the right amount of abrasiveness. Furriers have found that shell flours are effective for cleaning furs and rugs. The small amount of oil present in shell flour is advantageous for this and many other applications (Anon. 1965).

Consisting of 38% lignin, 15% cellulose, 18% hemicellulose, and 24% pentosans, the shells contain 1.3% ash and 1.6% protein. They have 0.5% pectic substances, 0.14% total sugars, and are very low in reducing sugars. The tannin content of the outer pecan shells is 1%, and the lining material is 26.4% tannin. The composition of pecan shells eliminates use as animal feed (Averts and Pressey 1972).

Timber From Pecan Trees

Pecan now ranks third among fine hardwoods on the timber market, surpassed only by black walnut and wild cherry, numbers one and two, respectively. Pecan veneer and lumber are in great demand for use in decorative paneling and fine furniture. Depending upon grade, pecan lumber also may be used in flooring, implement handles, and in pallet manufacture. The increasing popularity of fireplaces in American homes now makes it possible to sell even the tops of felled pecan trees for firewood.

There are more than 600,000 acres of native pecan timber in Texas which can be utilized for pecan production. Thousands of pecan trees are removed each year because of crowding or unproductivity.

A rule of thumb in thinning a native pecan stand is to have 50% of the orchard floor under sunshine and 50% under shade at 12 noon in August. This promotes development of foliage essential to increased nut yields. The ideal stand requires continuous judicious thinning to maintain the correct sun/shade ratio.

All non-pecan species should be removed in the initial thinning operation. Removal of pecan trees should be based on productivity and nut quality. Locate and mark trees only after performance is known. The first pecan trees thinned should include low yielding trees or trees that produce low quality nuts. Where stands are very dense, thinning should be done over a period of two to five years to lessen the danger of sunscald on the trunks of remaining trees. Small trees that are not crowded should be saved for grafting to improved cultivars.

Unwanted trees and brush may be killed by bulldozing, cutting of trees at groundline, by frilling, and by girdling. The last three methods may require considerable dozer work and burning to complete the operation.

When timber values are considered, merchantable pecan trees and other species of trees to be removed in thinning are marked and a volume estimate made for "on the stump" sales to veneer companies and sawmills. After logging operations are complete, the tops may be removed for fuel wood (Shreve 1976).

PECAN ORGANIZATIONS

Growers Associations

The following are active, domestic organizations for the production and processing of pecans. Current addresses may be obtained from the Cooperative Extension Service in the respective states.

Alabama Pecan Growers Assoc.
Arizona Pecan Growers Assoc.
Arkansas Pecan Growers Assoc.
Albany (Ga.) Pecan Growers Assoc.
California Pecan Growers Assoc.
Federal Pecan Growers Assoc.
  of the United States
Florida Pecan Growers Assoc.
Georgia Pecan Growers Assoc.
Louisiana Pecan Growers Assoc.
Mississippi Pecan Growers Assoc.
New Mexico Pecan Growers Assoc.
Oklahoma Pecan Growers Assoc.

S. Carolina Pecan Growers Assoc.
Southeastern Pecan Growers Assoc.
Southern Oklahoma Pecan Growers
  Assoc.
Travis County (Texas) Pecan
  Growers Assoc.
Texas Pecan Growers Assoc.
  (since 1921)
West Texas Pecan Growers Assoc.
Western Irrigated Pecan Growers
  Assoc.
National Pecan Assoc.

Research

Agricultural Research Center, Monticello, Fla.
Alabama Experiment Station, Auburn, Ala.
Arkansas University, Fayetteville, Ark.
Coastal Plain Experiment Station, Tifton, Ga.
Florida Experiment Station, Gainesville, Fla.
Georgia Experiment Station, Experiment, Ga.
Georgia University, Athens, Ga.
New Mexico State University, Las Cruces, N.M.
Pecan Field Station, Shreveport, La.
Pecan Research and Extension Station, Robson, La.
South Carolina Experiment Station, Clemson, S.C.
University of California, Davis, CA

Southeastern Fruit and Nut Research Station, Byron, Ga.
Texas A&M University, Uvalde, Tex.
USDA Pecan Field Station, Brownwood, Tex.

Publications

All pecan research stations and most pecan associations have means of publishing their data and recommendations; the following publications are official organs of one or more associations.

Northern Nut Growers Association, Inc., Annu. Proc.
N.Y.S. Exp. Stn. Geneva, N.Y.
Pecan South, Inc., P.O. Box 13449, Atlanta, Ga.
The Pecan Quarterly, 1104 Winding Road, College Station, Tex.
Ontario Nut Growers Assoc. Proc.
RR #1, Niagara-on-the-Lake, Ontario, IOS IJO

REFERENCES

History
BLACKMON, G.H. 1927. Pecan growing in Florida. Fla. Agric. Exp. Stn. Bull. *191*.
BRISON, F.R. 1964. The pecan in Texas. Peanut J. and Nut World, *43*, 8, 30.
CAMPBELL, R.D. 1975. The noblest nut tree of them all. Newsletter of the Society of Ontario Nut Growers. No. 7, Niagara-on-the-Lake, Ontario.
FAIRCHILD, D. 1930. Exploring for Plants. Macmillan Co., New York.
HOMASKY, S. 1977. The pecan growing industry in Israel. Pecan South *4*, 4, 178-181, 185.
MCHATTON, T.H. 1957. History and distribution of the pecan. Southeast. Pecan Growers Assoc., *50*, 10-34.
PEARSON, R.A. 1977. Pecans grow in Africa. The Pecan Q. *11*, 2, 23-24.
REED, C.A. 1912. The pecan. Bureau Plant Industry, Bull. *251*.
REED, C.A. 1916. Pecan culture. U.S. Dep. Agric. Farmers Bull. *700*.
REED, C.A. 1925. Status of the pecan. Gainesville, Fla. Pecan Assoc. Proc. Annu.
STUCKEY, H.P., and KYLE, E.J. 1925. Pecan Production. Macmillan Co., New York.
TRUE, R.H. 1917. Notes on the early history of the pecan in America. Smithson. Inst., Annu. Rep., 2509.

Cultivars
ANON. 1970. This is centennial year for the Stuart. The Pecan Q. *4*, 4, 8-9.
BAGBY, J. 1964. Pecan production. Ala. Coop. Ext. Serv. Circ. *28*.

BEST, R.B. 1956. Pecans for northern areas. Northern Nut Growers Assoc., 47th Annu. Rep.

BLACKMON, G.H. 1927. Pecan growing in Florida. Fla. Agric. Exp. Stn. Bull. *191.*

HARDY, M.B. 1938. Top-working pecan trees. Proc. Southeast. Pecan Growers Assoc. *32,* 49-55.

LAWRENCE, F.P. 1965. Pecan production guide for Florida. Fla. Agric. Ext. Serv. Circ. *280.*

LIVINGSTON, R.L. 1963. Pecans in Georgia. Ga. Coop. Ext. Serv. Bull. *609.*

LIVINGSTON, R.L. 1975. Pecan varieties for Georgia. Pecan South 2, 6, 231.

MADDEN, G.D. 1972. High density planting. The Pecan Q. *6,* 3, 10.

POWELL, J.V. 1963. The pecan nursery industry. U.S. Dep. Agric., Agric. Econ. Rep. *44.*

SHARPE, R.H., and GAMMON, N., JR. 1958. Pecan growing in Florida. Fla. Agric. Exp. Stn. Bull. *601.*

WOODRUFF, A.W. 1923. Straightening out an important Texas record. Am. Nut J. *19,* 5, 88-89.

WOODWARD, O.J. 1942. Promising varieties of pecans. Proc. Southeast. Pecan Growers Assoc. *36,* 21-26.

Orchards

ALBEN, A.O., COLE, J.R., and LEWIS, R.D. 1932. New development in treating pecan rosette with chemicals. Phytopathology *22,* 979-981.

ALBEN, A.O. 1958. Irrigating Stuart pecans in Texas. Proc. Southeast. Pecan Growers Assoc. *51,* 61-68.

ANON. 1973. Plantation Services has main goal: Production. The Pecan Q. 7, 4, 8-10.

ANON. 1976. The world's largest pecan operation. Pecan South *3,* 2, 318-319.

BLACKMON, G.H., and BARNETT, R.M. 1936. A cover crop program for Florida pecan orchards. Fla. Agric. Exp. Stn. Bull. *297.*

CRAFTS, A.S. 1975. Modern Weed Control. Univ. Calif. Press, Berkeley

CROLL, D. 1973. Israeli pecan production. The Pecan Q. 7, 1, 5.

DANIELL, J.W. 1974. Herbicide tests in pecans. Pecan South *1,* 3, 6-7.

DANIELL, J.W. 1975. The use of herbicides in the pecan orchard to save fuel. Proc. 9th Annu. Conf. Georgia Pecan Growers Assoc. *5,* 43-46.

DANIELL, J.W. 1976A. Control of problem weeds in pecans. Pecan South *3,* 2, 332-334.

DANIELL, J.W. 1976B. Weed control in pecan row middles with roundup: Part I. Pecan South *3,* 3, 356-358.

DANIELL, J.W. 1976C. Effects of irrigating pecans (Abstr.) Proc. 36th Annu. Meeting Sou. Region Am. Soc. Hort. Sci. HortScience *11,* 3.

DENMAN, T.E., KENKNIGHT, G., and STOREY, J.B. 1966. Minutes of 1965 Pecan Res. Conf. Mimeo Report, March.

FIROR, G.H. 1930. Rejuvenation of old pecan orchards. Proc. Nat. Pecan Assoc. *29*, 83-85.

GARDNER, P. 1976. Australia adopts pecans. The Pecan Q. *10*, 1, 14-15.

GILLIN, E.F. 1973. Australians develop 1,850 acre project. The Pecan Q. *7*, 4, 5.

HAGLER, T.B., and JOHNSON, W.A. 1955. Relation of nutrient-element content of pecan leaves to yield of nuts. Proc. Southeast. Pecan Growers Assoc. *48*, 77.

HAMMAR, H.E., and HUNTER, J.H. 1948. The time of pecan tree fertilizer applications. Proc. Southeast. Pecan Growers Assoc. *41*, 36-43.

HARDY, M.B. 1939. Cultural practices for pecan orchards. Proc. Southeast. Pecan Growers Assoc. *33*, 58-64.

HARDY, M.B., and LUTZ, H. 1940. Factors associated with pecan drop. Proc. Southeast. Pecan Growers Assoc. *34*, 77-81.

HUNTER, J.H. 1952. Effect of minor elements on pecan production. Proc. Southeast. Pecan Growers Assoc. *45*, 69-75.

HUNTER, J.H., and HAMMAR, H.F. 1948. Nutritional deficiencies and filling of pecans. Proc. Southeast. Pecan Growers Assoc. *41*, 16-33.

ISBELL, C.L. 1928. Growth studies of the pecan. Ala. Agric. Exp. Stn. Bull. *226*.

ISRAELSEN, O.W., and HANSEN, V.E. 1962. Irrigation principles and practices. John Wiley and Sons, New York.

JOHNSON, W.A., and HAGLER, T.B. 1955. Response of pecans to applications of lime and zinc. Proc. Southeast. Pecan Growers Assoc. *48*, 78-79.

KENWORTHY, A.L. 1974. Trickle irrigation—simplified guidelines for orchard installation and use. Mich. State Univ. Agric. Exp. Stn. Res. Rep. *248*.

KLINGMAN, G.C., ASHTON, F.M., and NOORDHOFF, L.J. 1975. Weed Science: Principles and Practices. John Wiley and Sons, New York.

PAIR, C.H., HINZ, W.W., REID, C., and FROST, K.R. 1969. Sprinkler Irrigation. Sprinkler Irrig. Assoc., Washington, D.C.

ROMBERG, L.D. 1960. Irrigation of pecan orchards. Proc. Southeast. Pecan Growers Assoc. *53*, 20-25.

SARIG, Y. 1973. Israel: mechanized harvesting a must. The Pecan Q. *7*, 4, 12-13.

SHARPE, R.H., and GAMMON, N. 1958. Pecan growing in Florida. Fla. Agric. Exp. Stn. Bull. *601*.

SHUHART, D.V. 1927. Morphological differentiation of the pistillate flowers of the pecan. J. Agric. Res. *43*, 7, 687-696.

SMITH, C.L., and HARRIS, O.W. 1957. Chemical thinning of pecan crops. Proc. Southeast. Pecan Growers Assoc. *50*, 60-63.

SPARKS, D. 1974. The alternate fruit bearing problem in pecans. North. Nut Growers Assoc. 65th Annu. Rept. 145-158.

WELCHEL, D. 1964. Pecan irrigation demonstration. Proc. Southeast. Pecan Growers Assoc. *57*, 46-48.

WESLEY, W.K. 1975. Legumes in pecan orchards. Pecan South 2, 5, 192-193.

WOODWARD, O. 1949. Pecan culture and grove management. Georgia Agric. Exp. Stn. Circ. 15.

WOODROOF, J.G., and WOODROOF, N.C. 1929. Flowering and fruiting habit of the pecan. Proc. Nat. Pecan Growers Convention 28, 128-136.

WOODROOF, N.C. 1926. Fruit bud differentiation and subsequent development of flowers in Hicoria pecan. J. Agric. Res. 33, 677-685.

Orchard Diseases and Insects

ANON. 1965. USDA develops ground equipment for low-volume spraying. Peanut J. and Nut World 45, 1, 31.

COLE, J.R. 1961. Grower tests airplane to control pecan scab in Georgia. Proc. Southeast. Pecan Growers Assoc. 54, 120-121.

COLE, J.R. 1964. Past, present and future pecan disease control in the Southeast. Proc. Southeast. Pecan Growers Assoc. 57, 88-89.

COLE, J.R. 1965. Chemical control of pecan scab in areas of high rainfall. Proc. Southeast. Pecan Growers Assoc. 58, 60-71.

DENMAN, T.E., KENKNIGHT, G., and STOREY, J.B. 1966. Minutes of 1965 Annual Pecan Research Conference. Tex. Pecan Growers Assoc. College Station., Tx, Mimeo Rep. March.

DIENER, U.L., and GARRET, F. 1965. Control of pecan scab in Southeast Alabama. Proc. Southeast. Pecan Growers Assoc. 58, 73-74.

EMERY, C. 1963. Aerial application and need. Proc. Southeast. Pecan Growers Assoc. 56, 71-75.

GOSSARD, A.C. 1961. Some causes and effects of pecan leaf scorch. Proc. Southeast. Pecan Growers Assoc. 54, 43-46.

GRAVES, C.H., JR. 1961. Pecan disease experiments for 1960 in Mississippi. Proc. Southeast. Pecan Growers assoc. 54, 103.

GRAVES, C.H., JR. 1962. Aerial and mist blown fungicide application techniques for pecan disease control. Proc. Southeast. Pecan Growers Assoc. 55, 109.

GRAVES, C.H., JR. 1964. Aerial fungicidal applications for the control of plant diseases. Proc. Southeast. Pecan Growers Assoc. 57, 81-83.

GRAVES, C.H., JR. 1966. Application of Cyprex by low-volume aerial techniques. Proc. Southeast. Pecan Growers Assoc. 59.

HARDY, M.B., LUTZ, H., and MERRILL, S., JR. 1939. A preliminary report of pecan leaf scorch studies. Proc. Am. Soc. Hort. Sci. 37, 489-492.

HARRIS, E.D., JR., and MCGLOHON, N.E. 1966. Pecan insects and diseases and their control. Univ. of Ga., Coll. of Agric. Ext. Serv. Bull. 644.

HARRIS, E.D., ARNET, J.D., and ELLIS, H.C. 1976. Pecan Insects and Diseases and Their Control. Univ. of Ga., Coll. of Agric. Ext. Bull. 644.

HINES, C. 1967. Custom spraying and tree shaking service in Mississippi. Proc. Southeast. Pecan Growers Assoc. 59.

HOWITT, A.J., and PSHEA, A. 1965. The development and use of ultra low-volume ground sprayer for pests attacking fruit. Mich. State Univ. Q. Bull. 48, 144-160.

KENKNIGHT, G. 1965. Research on bunch diseases of pecans. Proc. Southeast. Pecan Growers Assoc. 58, 81-87.

KENKNIGHT, G. 1967. Research development on bunch disease. Proc. Southeast. Pecan Growers Assoc. 59.

LARGE, J.R. 1953. Airplane spraying to control pecan scab in 1952. Proc. Southeast. Pecan Growers Assoc. 46, 71-75.

LARGE, J.R. 1954. Summary of two years airplane spraying experiments to control pecan scab. Proc. Southeast. Pecan Growers Assoc. 47, 55-64.

LARGE, J.R. 1956. Airplane spraying to control pecan scab in 1955. Proc. Southeast. Pecan Growers Assoc. 49, 12-16.

LARGE, J.R. 1961. Concentrated chemicals applied from a helicopter for control of pecan scab. Proc. Southeast. Pecan Growers Assoc. 54, 95-101.

LARGE, J.R. 1967. Da-Ter (triphenyl tin hydroxide) provided excellent control of pecan scab during the wet summer of 1965 in north Florida. Proc. Southeast. Pecan Growers Assoc. 59.

LARGE, J.R., and COLE, J.R. 1964. Karathane-controlled powdery mildew on the Curtis and Pabst varieties of pecan in Florida and Georgia. Phytopathology 54, 9, 1174.

LATHAM, A.J. 1969. Zonate leafspot of pecan caused by Cristulariella pyramidalis. Phytopathology 59, 103-107.

LITTRELL, R.H. 1974. Foliar disorders that can be mistaken for fungal leaf scorch. Proc. Southeast. Pecan Growers Assoc. 67, 127.

LITTRELL, R.H., and LINDSEY, J.B. 1976. Detection of benomyl-tolerant and pecan scab isolates in production groves. Proc. Southeast. Pecan Growers Assoc. 69, 77.

OSBURN, M.R. 1962. Pecan insects and their control. Proc. Southeast. Pecan Growers Assoc. 55, 109-127.

OSBURN, J.R. 1964. Low-volume sprays for pecan weevil control. Proc. Southeast. Pecan Growers Assoc. 57, 59-60.

OSBURN, M.R. et al. 1963. Controlling insects and diseases of the pecan. U.S. Dep. Agric., Farmers Handb. 240.

PAPE, H.C. 1960. Methods and results in controlling caterpillars. Proc. Southeast. Pecan Growers Assoc. 53, 54.

PHILLIPS, A.M. 1945. An unusual habit of the pecan bud moth in Florida. Science Note, J. Econ. Entomol. 38, 5, 620.

PHILLIPS, A.M. 1963. Aerial applications of parathion with micronair rotary atomizers for control of the pecan bud moth. Proc. Southeast. Pecan Growers Assoc. 56, 86-91.

PHILLIPS, A.M. 1965A. Observations on Cambium Curculio and Lepidopterous larvae damage in pecan propagation. Proc. Southeast. Pecan Growers Assoc. 58, 37-41.

PHILLIPS, A.M. 1965B. Preliminary tests for control of hickory shoot curculio on pecan. Proc. Southeast. Pecan Growers Assoc. *58*, 42-44.

PHILLIPS, A.M., LARGE, J.R., and COLE, J.R. 1964. Insects and diseases of the pecan in Florida. Fla. Agric. Exp. Stn. Bull. *619A*.

PIERCE, W.C. 1960. Status of the work on methods of applying insecticides for control of pecan insects. Proc. Southeast. Pecan Growers Assoc. *53*, 42-44.

PIERCE, W.C. 1963. Aerial application of insecticides for control of pecan insect pests. Proc. Southeast. Pecan Growers Assoc. *56*, 60-66.

POTTS, S.F. 1962. Potts mist blower method for spraying pecans. Proc. Southeast. Pecan Growers Assoc. *55*, 105-108.

TAYLOR, J. 1975. Zonate leafspot control. Proc. Ga. Pecan Growers Assoc. *68*, 39.

TEDDERS, W.L., JR., and OSBURN, M. 1966. Blacklight traps for timing insecticide control of pecan insects. Proc. Southeast. Pecan Growers Assoc. *59*, 102-106.

WELLS, J.M., PAYNE, J.A., and MCGLOHON, N.E. 1976. Chemical control of pecan scab and scorch in a year of severe disease incidence. Proc. Southeast. Pecan Growers Assoc. *69*, 59-62.

Harvesting, Drying and Grading

ANON. 1965. Speed harvesting nut crops. Eng. Wis. Motor Corp., Milwaukee, Wis.

ANON. 1976. New tree shaker by FMC. Pecan South *3*, 4, 451.

BRISON, F.R. 1956. Mechanical huller and separator for pecans. Peanut J. and Nut World *35*, 4, 37.

CARLTON, R.L. 1975. Birds and animal damage control in pecans. Pecan South 2, 5, 214-216.

GAMMON, N., JR. 1976. Mechanical harvesting of pecans. Pecan South *3*, 5, 214-216.

HAMMAR, H.E., and HUNTER, J.H. 1946. Some physical changes in the composition of pecan nuts during kernel filling. Plant Physiol. *21*, 476-491.

HEATON, E.K., and WOODROOF, J.G. 1965. Importance of proper drying of pecans. Proc. Southeast. Pecan Growers Assoc. *58*, 119-127.

HEATON, E.K., SHEWFELT, A.L., BADENHOP, A.E., and BEUCHAT, L.R. 1977. Pecans: handling, storage, processing & utilization. Ga. Exp. Stn. Res. Bull. *197*.

KAYS, S.J., and WILSON, D.M. 1976. Pecan kernel color. Pecan South *3*, 5, 471-473.

KAYS, S.J., and WILSON, D.M. 1977. Altering pecan kernel colors. J. Food Sci. *42*, 4, 982-984.

KENNEMAR, E.F. 1959. Controlling crows and other orchard pests. Proc. Southeast. Pecan Growers Assoc. *52*, 32-34.

MALSTROM, H.L. 1975. New variety performance in the Southeast. Pecan South 2, 3, 100-101.

MCCRORY, S.H. 1929. Pecan drying. Proc. Nat. Pecan Assoc. 28, 96-98.

MCGLAMMERY, J.B., and HOOD, M.P. 1951. Effect of two heat treatments on rancidity in unshelled pecans. Food Technol. 16, 80-84.

MCNAIR, J.B. 1945. Plant fats in relation to environment and evolution. Bot. Rev. 11, 1, 1-59.

SCOTT, L. 1957. Pecan inspection. Proc. Southeast. Pecan Growers Assoc. 50, 72-73.

SCOTT, L. 1960. Inspection and specifications for U.S. Grades. Proc. Southeast. Pecan Growers Assoc. 53, 74-81.

SENTER, S.D. 1976. Phlobaphene and anthocyanidin formation in stored pecans (Carya illinoensis). Ph.D. Dissertation, Univ. Ga. Athens.

SENTER, S.D., FORBUS, W.R., JR., and SMIT, C.J.B. 1977. Leucoanthocyanidin oxidation in pecan kernels: relation to discoloration and kernel quality. J. Food Sci.

SMITH, C.L., and LOUITALOT, A.J. 1944. Effects of harvest date and curing on the composition and palatability of pecan meats. J. Agric. Res. 68, 395-403.

THOR, C.J.B., and SMITH, C.L. 1935. A physiological study of seasonal changes in the composition of the pecan during fruit development. J. Agric. Res. 50, 97-121.

WOODROOF, J.G., and HEATON, E.K. 1958. Maintaining quality of pecans. Proc. Southeast. Pecan Growers Assoc. 51, 25-29.

WOODROOF, J.G., and HEATON, E.K. 1961. Pecans for processing. Ga. Agric. Exp. Stn. Bull. N.S. 80.

WOODROOF, J.G., and WOODROOF, N.C. 1927. The development of the pecan, nut (Hicoria pecan) from flower to maturity. J. Agric. Res. 34, 1049-1063.

WRIGHT, J.S. 1929. Sheet method of harvesting pecans. Proc. Nat. Pecan Growers Assoc. 28, 145-147.

Shelling and Grading

ANON. 1924. Exhibits. Proc. Nat. Pecan Growers Assoc. 23, 79.

ANON. 1961. Edible nut processing machinery. Peanut J. and Nut World 40, 11, 11-14.

ANON. 1976. A sauna bath for pecans. Pecan South 3, 5, 484-485.

BULLARD, W.P. 1934. The effect of bleaching and coloring on the demand for pecans. Proc. Pecan Growers Assoc. 28, 61-64.

CRANE, H.L., and HARDY, M.B. 1934. Interrelation between cultural treatment of pecan trees, the size and degree of filling of the nuts and the composition of kernels. J. Agric. Res. 49, 643-661.

FORBUS, W.R., JR., and SENTER, S.D. 1976. Conditioning pecans to improve shelling efficiency and storage stability. J. Food Sci. 41, 4, 794-798.

KENNERLY, A.B. 1966. Gravity flow plant cuts handling cost for Texas pecan packer. Canner/Packer 135, 8, 33-34.

MCGLAMMERY, J.B., and HOOD, M.P. 1951. Effect of two heat treatments on rancidity in unshelled pecans. Food Technol. *16*, 80-84.

POWELL, J.V. 1963. The pecan shelling industry. Peanut J. and Nut World *42*, 6, 34-35.

SANLILIPPO, J.B., GRAZIANO, N., and GRAZIANO, J.C. 1966. Separation of nutmeat fragments from shell fragments. U.S. Pat. 3,249,219. May 3.

WOODROOF, J.B., and HEATON, E.K. 1961. Pecans for processing. Ga. Agric. Exp. Stn. Bull. N.S. *80*.

Storing

ANON. 1965. Official and Tentative Methods of Analysis, 87th Edition. Assoc. Off. Agric. Chem., Washington, D.C.

BLACKMON, G.H. 1932. Cold storage of pecans. Fla. Exp. Stn. Annu. Rep. 102-106.

BLACKMON, G.H. 1933. Pecan cold storage experiments. Gainesville, Fla. Pecan Growers Assoc. Proc. 6-11.

BRISON, F.R. 1945. The storage of shelled pecans. Tex. Agric. Exp. Stn. Bull. *667.*

COTTON, R.T. 1947. Insect Pests of Stored Grains and Grain Products. Burgess Publishing Co., Minneapolis, Minn.

GODKIN, W.J., BEATTIE, H.G., and CATHCART, W.H. 1951. Retardation of rancidity in pecans. Food Technol. *5*, 442-447.

HARRIS, H. 1959. Storing pecans. Proc. 52nd Annu. Conv. Southeast. Pecan Growers Assoc. 17-22.

HEATON, E.K., and WOODROOF, J.G. 1955. Effect of varieties and other factors on extending the shelf-life of pecans. Proc. 48th Annu. Conv. Southeast. Pecan Growers Assoc. 47-49.

HEATON, E.K., and WOODROOF, J.G. 1956. Storing pecans for home use. Ga. Exp. Stn. Leaflet *11*.

HEATON, E.K., and WOODROOF, J.G. 1968 Storage of nuts for food. 59th Annu. Rep. Northern Nut Growers Assoc. 72-77.

ISBELL, C.L. 1928. Cold storage of pecans. Ala. Exp. Stn. Annu. Rep. *39*, 24-26.

MEDLOCK, O.C. 1931. Pecan Storage. Ala. Exp. Stn. Annu. Rep. *42*, 50-51.

ORAHOOD, E.G. 1964. Storage of pecans. Proc. 57th Annu. Conv. Southeast. Pecan Growers Assoc. 103-104.

POPPER, K., and NURY, F. 1966. DEPC sterilization of cold storage rooms. ASHRAE J. *8*, 8, 80-81.

SWITZLER, R.H. 1931. Cold storage warehousing with reference to pecans. Proc. Nat. Pecan Growers Assoc. 30th Annu. Conv. 83-86.

WELLS, A.W. 1951. Storage of edible nuts. U.S. Dep. Agric. Transportation and Storage Off. Rep. *240*.

WOODROOF, J.G., and HEATON, E.K. 1952. Storing and processing pecans. Proc. Assoc. South Agric. Workers, 112-113.

WOODROOF, J.G., and HEATON, E.K. 1953A. Keeping pecans in refrigerated storage. Ga. Exp. Stn. J.S. *241*.

WOODROOF, J.G., and HEATON, E.K. 1953B. Year-round on pecans by refrigerated storage. Food Eng. *25*, 5, 83-85.

WOODROOF, J.G., and HEATON, E.K. 1958. Maintaining quality of pecans for year-round use. Proc. 51st Annu. Conv. Southeast. Pecan Growers Assoc., 25-29.

WOODROOF, J.G., and HEATON, E.K. 1961. Pecans for processing. Ga. Agric. Exp. Stn. Bull. N.S. *80*.

WOODROOF, J.G., and HEATON, E.K. 1966. Ammonia damage to pecans. Proc. 59th Annu. Conv. Southeast. Pecan Growers Assoc., 128-135, 146, 147.

Processing

ABBOTT, O.D. 1932. Preventing rancidity in pecans. Fla. Agric. Exp. Stn. Annu. Rep. *94*.

ANON. 1958. Flavor preservation of pecans can be a factor in bigger market. Peanut J. and Nut World *37*, 7, 34-35.

ANON. 1960. Official and Tentative Methods of Analysis, 6th Edition. Assoc. Off. Agric. Chemists, Washington, D.C.

ANON. 1966. The box that goes "whoosh." Dupont Magazine *60*, 5, 7-9.

BAILEY, S.W. 1955. Air-tight storage of grain: its effects on insect pests. J. Agric. Res. *6*, 33.

BLACKMON, G.H. 1932A. Cold storage experiments with pecans. Proc. Nat. Pecan Assoc. Rep. *31*.

BLACKMON, G.H. 1932B. Cold storage of pecans. Fla. Exp. Stn. Annu. Rep. 102-106.

BLACKMON, G.H. 1937. Some new pecan products. Proc. Southeast. Pecan Growers Assoc. *31*, 55-58.

BRISON, F.R. 1945. The storage of shelled pecans. Tex. Agric. Exp. Stn. Bull. *667*.

COSTA, D., and MOTA, D. 1942. Improvement of Brazil nut for food purposes. Chemical Abstracts. Cult. Med., 3e 4, IX, 35, 1942. (*Cited by* Costa, D., O. Hospital, 3a. Edicao, July 1945).

COTTON, R.T. 1960. Insect Pests of Stored Grain and Grain Products. Burgess Publishing Co., Minneapolis, Minn.

CRUESS, W.V., and ARMSTRONG, M. 1947. Experiments with antioxidants for walnuts. Fruit Prod. J. *26*, 327.

DUSTMAN, R.B. 1936. The storage of black walnut kernels. Food Res. *1*, 247.

GODKIN, W.J., BEATTIE, H.G., and CATHCART, W.H. 1951. Retardation of rancidity in pecans. Food Technol. *5*, 442-447.

HEATON, E.K. and WOODROOF, J.G. 1955. Effect of varieties and other factors on extending the shelf life of pecans. Proc. Pecan Growers Assoc. *48*, 47-49.

HEATON, E.K., and WOODROOF, J.G. 1960. Pecan butter. Ga. Agric. Exp. Stn. Circ. *19.*

HESS, E.G. 1925. 800 proven pecan recipes. Keystone Pecan Res. Lab., Lancaster, Pa.

HIGHLAND, H.A., and JAY, E.G. 1965. An insect-resistant film. Mod. Packag. *38*, 7, 205-207.

HYDE, M.B., and OXLEY, T.A. 1960. Experiments on the airtight storage of damp grain. Ann. Appl. Biol. *48*, 687.

JERISSA NUT COMPANY. 1962. Vacuum-gassing equipment. Peanut J. and Nut World *41*, 6, 20.

KARNOFSKY, G. 1949. The mechanics of solvent extraction. J. Am. Oil Chem. Soc. *26*, 570-574.

KESTER, E.B. 1949. Minor oil producing crops of the United States. J. Am. Oil Chem. Soc. *26*, 65.

LAUDANI, H. 1963. Protection of food from insect damage during long-term storage. Food Technol. *17*, 12, 50-53.

LEHMAN, A.J. 1956. Food packaging. Assoc. Food and Drug Officials of U.S., *20*, 4, 159-168.

LUNDBERG, W.O., HALVERSON, H.O., and BURR, G.O. 1944. The antioxidant properties of NDGA. Oil and Soap *2*, 33.

MCGLAMMERY, J.B., and HOOD, M.P. 1951. Effect of two heat treatments on rancidity development in unshelled pecans. Food Res. *16*, 80.

PATTON, E.L. 1958. Vapor-tight feeder for oilseed extractors. Peanut J. and Nut World *37*, 8, 34-35.

ROCKLAND, L.B., SWARTHOUT, D.M., and JOHNSON, R.A. 1961. Studies on English (Persian) walnuts, *Juglans regia.* III. Food Technol. *15*, 3, 112-116.

SCHOMER, H.A., and SAINSBURY, G.F. 1957. Controlled-atmosphere storage of Starking delicious apples in the Pacific Northwest. U.S. Dep. Agric. Circ. *AMS-178.*

SIMMONS, P.M. 1966. Objective color measurements. (unpublished manuscript) Magnuson Engineers, San Jose, Calif.

WAGNER, G.B. 1956. Stored-product insect losses can be reduced. Proc. Chem. Specialties Mfg. Assoc. *42*, 116.

WELLS, A.W. 1951. The storage of edible nuts. U.S. Dep. Agric., Agric. Res. Adm. Bull. Plant Ind., Soils and Agr. Eng. H.T. and S. Rep. *240.*

WHITEHEAD, T.H., and WARSHAW, H. 1938. Studies in the utilization of Georgia Pecans. I. Composition, properties, and uses of hulls, oils, and meats. Ga. State Eng. Exp. Stn. Bull. *4, 1,* 5, 3-11.

WOODROOF, J.G., and HEATON, E.K. 1958. Maintaining quality for year-round care of pecans. Proc. Pecan Growers Assoc. *51*, 25-29.

WOODROOF, J.G., and HEATON, E.K. 1961. Pecans for processing. Ga. Agric. Exp. Stn. Bull. N.S. *80.*

WRIGHT, R.C. 1941. Investigations on the storage of nuts. U.S. Dep. Agric. Tech. Bull. *770.*

Pecans in Bakery Products

ANON. (undated) Newsletters. Nat. Pecan Shellers and Processors Assoç., Chicago.

ANON. 1959. Basic candy formulas. Nulomoline Div. SuCrest Corp., New York.

ANON. 1966A. Chocolate spraying speeds coating. Food Eng. *38,* 6, 75.

ANON. 1966B. Redbook's Time Saver Cookbook. Redbook *127,* 3, 40-42.

BLACKMON, G.H. 1932. Cold storage of pecans. Fla. Exp. Stn. Annu. Rep. 102-106.

BLACKMON, G.H. 1937. Pecan products. Fla. Agric. Exp. Stn. Annu. Rep. *80.*

BLACKMON, G.H. 1937. Some new pecan products. Proc. Southeast. Pecan Growers Assoc. *31,* 55-58.

BUCKLIN, H.A. 1966. What the pecan industry is learning from the bakery industry. Peanut J. and Nut World *45,* 5, 34.

HEATON, E.K., and WOODROOF, J.G. 1960. Pecan butter. Ga. Agric. Exp. Stn. Circ. N.S. *19.*

HEATON, E.K., and WOODROOF, J.G. 1960. Pecans for fruitcakes. Ga. Agric. Res. *2,* 2, 11-12.

KESTER, E.B. 1949. Minor oil producing crops of the United States. J. Am. Oil Chem. Soc. *26,* 65.

PATTON, E.L. 1958. Vapor-tight feeder for oilseed extractors. Peanut J. and Nut World *37,* 8, 34-35.

WHITEHEAD, T.H., and WARSHAW, H. 1938. Studies in the utilization of Georgia pecans. 1. Composition, properties, and uses of hulls, oils, and meats. Ga. St. Eng. Exp. Stn. Bull. *4, 1,* 5, 3-11.

WOOD, N. 1948. 1,000 Recipe Cook Book. Dell Publishing Co., New York.

WOODROOF, J.G. 1966. Storage of candies, nuts, dried fruits and vegetables. ASHRAE Data Book, Refrigeration Applications, New York.

WOODROOF, J.G., and HEATON, E.K. 1961. Pecans for processing. Ga. Agric. Exp. Stn. Bull. N.S. *80.*

Candies

ANON. 1959. Basic candy formulas. Nulomoline Division, SuCrest Corp., New York.

ANON. 1966. Chocolate spraying speeds coating. Food Eng. *38,* 6, 75.

ANON. 1976. Stuckey's and Pecans. Pecan South *3,* 2, 326-328.

GOTT, P.P., and VAN HOUTEN, L.F. 1958. All about candy and chocolate. Nat. Confectioners Assoc. of U.S., Chicago.

HESS, E.G. 1925. 800 proved pecan recipes. Keystone Pecan Res. Lab., Philadelphia.

U.S. DEP. OF COMM. 1965. Confectionery sales and distribution. Government Printing Office, Washington, D. C.

WOOD, D. 1948. 1000 Recipe Cook Book. Dell Publishing Co., New York.

WOODROOF, J.G. 1966. Storing candies, nuts, dried fruits and vegetables. ASHRAE Guide and Data Book, 675-680, New York.

WOODROOF, J.G. and CECIL, S.R. 1951. Nuts: better kept, better candy. Food Eng. *33*, 11, 129-131, 148, 150.

WOODROOF, J.G., and HEATON, E.K. 1961. Pecans for processing. Ga. Agric. Exp. Stn. Bull., N.S. *80*.

Ice Cream

ANON. 1924. Exhibits. Proc. Nat. Pecan Growers Assoc. *23*, 79.

ANON. 1965. Many uses for nut shells. Peanut J. and Nut World *45*, No. 2, 10-11.

AVERTS, J.K., and PRESSEY, R. 1972. Uses of pecan shells. The Pecan Q. *6*, 4, 19.

BLACKMON, G.H. 1937A. Pecan products. Fla. Agric. Exp. Stn. Annu. Rep. *80*.

BLACKMON, G.H. 1937B. Some new pecan products. Proc. Southeast. Pecan Growers Assoc. *31*, 55-58.

HEATON, E.K., and WOODROOF, J.G. 1960. Pecan butter. Ga. Agric. Exp. Stn. Circ. N.S. *19*.

JACOBSEN, W.B. 1964. Nuts and candy in ice cream. Ice Cream Rev. *47*, No. 12, 26-27, 51.

KESTER, E.B. 1949. Minor oil-producing crops of the United States. J. Am. Oil Chem. Soc. *26*, 65-68.

LEEDER, J.G. 1964. Nuts and ice cream. Ice Cream Rev. *47*, No. 6, 22-23, 29.

SHREVE, L.W. 1976. Timber production potential of native pecan stands. Pecan South *3*, 6, 520-521.

WOODROOF, J.G., and HEATON, E.K. 1961. Pecans for processing. Ga. Agric. Exp. Stn. Bull. N.S. *80*.

13

Pine Nuts

Pine nuts, piñon nuts, or pignolias (*Alpinus pinea*) have a long history over much of both hemispheres. They are referred to in the Bible (Hosea 14:8) as coming from the "green fir tree." In southern Europe, especially in Italy and the southern part of France, and in the southeastern United States, the name is applied indiscriminately to at least five species of pine trees bearing seed large enough for food. *Pinus edulis* is the most important species and is found on mountain slopes in New Mexico, eastern Arizona, southern Colorado and some parts of western Texas. *Pinus monophylla* grows in Utah, Nevada and California. Scattered stands of *Pinus flexilis* are found from Texas to California and north to Canada. *Pinus cembroides* is limited to southwestern New Mexico, southern Arizona, and the northern half of Mexico. This species is second to *Pinus edulis* in importance. Another edible species, *Pinus quadrifolia*, is found in extreme southern California, but is not commercially important (Bryant 1967).

In southern Europe the tree attains a height of 30 to 60 ft, with a hemispheric top. The cones are solitary or paired, and practically terminal on the branches. The seeds are wingless, sweet, and nut-like, and resemble almonds somewhat.

The Araucarias with their large starchy pine nuts furnish carbohydrate food for the peoples of the southern hemisphere of both continents and Australia. Nuts of the Bunya pine vary from the size of Persian walnuts, down to the size of buckwheat. Many of the imported pine nuts come from the southern hemisphere because the trees are not hardy to cold climates.

The seed of the Cembra pine constitutes an important food to the Siberian taiga, which is the swampy, coniferous forests of Siberia. They are regularly collected each fall as a winter source of fat and protein. It is estimated that two million tons of kernels are produced from the Cembra pine.

Pine nuts are grown in a limited way in Italy, Spain, Portugal and the United States. They are imported, both shelled and unshelled, by European countries, Latin America and North America. World production has steadily declined from about 525 tons in 1935 to about 130 tons in 1975.

Pine nuts, one of the most delicate and choice of all tree nuts (the supply of which has never been able to meet the demand), cannot be grown under modern horticultural conditions. The small scrubby pines grow only on mountainsides at elevations of 5000 to 7000 ft, under conditions that defy cultivation, fertilization, irrigation, and all kinds of mechanical spraying, harvesting and shelling. All operations are done by hand under pre-modern conditions, in competition with rats, birds and insects. Furthermore, the wood of the trees has very low value for fuel or other uses.

TABLE 13.1

PIGNOLIAS: IMPORTS INTO UNITED STATES
(IN METRIC TONS)

Country of Origin	Year Beginning September 1					
	1968-69	1969-70	1970-71	1971-72	1972-73	1973-74
	In-shell					
Italy	7	213	—	—	—	—
Mexico	—	1	—	—	220	123
Spain	—	2	—	2	7	5
Other	—	—	3	—	8	2
Grand Total	7	216	3	2	235	130
	Shelled					
Europe						
Italy	318	5	8	7	—	—
Portugal	324	245	167	199	155	195
Spain	261	236	186	126	233	138
Other	—	—	312	—	—	—
Total	303	286	373	332	188	133
Other Countries	—	8	—	—	220	124
Grand Total	303	294	373	332	208	157

Source: Anon. (1976).

The various species of the pine family of nuts differ greatly in their composition. The oil content usually exceeds that of all other constituents and is often several times the protein content. Starch is a minor constituent, at least in the species growing in Europe and the United

States. The European and Brazilian nuts are longer than those growing in the United States, which have the further disadvantage of being thick-shelled. The European cultivars are, therefore, more popular and are used in this country, where they are known as pignolia. Italy and Spain are the chief sources of supply (Blumenthal 1947).

PINE NUTS IN NEW MEXICO

The pine nut tree is the official state tree of New Mexico, where it has grown for centuries. The piñon tree and its distinctive seed, or nuts, were mentioned in the records of the 16th Century explorers of the Southwest "Land of Enchantment." Coronado and Cabeza de Vaca described it and archaeologists found evidence of the nuts in excavations of cliff dwellers and ancient Pueblos.

The nuts have always been an important food crop for the Indians. As more Americans have become familiar with the unusual flavor of the nut, the piñon harvest has attained importance as a source of revenue on the Navajo reservation. Indian children gather piñon nuts for food from native pine trees on the slope of Mt. Blaca.

Three successive growing seasons are needed to produce mature piñon cones in New Mexico. The trees grow slowly and do not bear until they are 25 years old and from 5 to 10 ft tall. At 75 years of age the trees begin to produce enough nuts for commercial harvesting. Native trees continue growing and bearing for hundreds of years.

The piñon tree is well adapted to a dry climate, since it does well with 12 to 14 in. of rainfall a year. Although it is known in southern Colorado and eastern Arizona, it is also found in Utah, Nevada and California and is most abundant in New Mexico and Mexico, being widely distributed over elevations of 5000 to 7000 ft.

Although the tree is drought resistant, moisture is essential to the production of the nut-bearing cones. Forest Service men have reported a distinct correlation between the amount of harvest and the summer rainfall. Popular belief held that the piñon produces an abundant harvest every seven years. More scientific observations indicate that a good harvest comes three years (the time needed for the cones to mature) after a season of good rainfall (Anon. 1962).

Harvesting Pine Nuts

Each year in August or September, the Forestry Service estimates the acreage and prospective crop, and issues information telling where the prospects are good, fair and poor-to-failure. This information aids pickers and buyers in locating and harvesting the crop.

FIG. 13.1. PINE NUTS
1—In the cones.   2—Nuts in the shells.
3—Empty shells.   4—Shelled (blanched) nuts.

After the frosts come in the fall, the mature cones open and the nuts fall to the ground. The oldest and most common method of harvesting is to pick them off the ground by hand. A fast picker can gather 20 lb a day. The nuts are so small that pine nuts often average 1500 per lb, which means picking up 30,000 nuts in a day. Most of the harvesting in the United States is done by Indian children and by weekend travellers. For this reason it is difficult to estimate the amount of the total harvest. The crop is of considerable economic importance to Navajos living on reservations in New Mexico and Arizona. The Bureau of Indian Affairs estimates that 2,500,000 lb were harvested in 1960.

Improvements in methods of harvesting include the use of suction machines similar to a vacuum cleaner, and tree shakers which shake the cones and loose nuts onto a canvas spread beneath the trees. In either case there are pine needles, cones and other litter to contend with. Most of this can be removed by successive screening through hardware cloth. The seeds are practically wingless.

Piñons usually lose 7 to 15% of moisture within 30 days after they are harvested. Drying loss is most rapid at the beginning of the drying period when it may be 0.5 to 1.0% per day. Losses are greater and more rapid with nuts picked from the tree or from damp or shaded ground, and there may be moisture gains during damp weather.

In curing, the nuts require dry air. Storing rooms should be closed on damp days, and the nuts should not be shipped to a humid climate more than a few months before they are to be consumed, unless kept in rooms conditioned for 50% relative humidity or lower.

Piñon nuts have excellent keeping quality. They can be marketed after as much as three years of common storage, if unshelled. However, when shelled they become rancid in 3 to 6 months. Long storage is due in part to the very low moisture in the nuts and surrounding air.

Pine nuts contain 42% shells. The kernels contain 3.1 to 4.9% moisture, 12.5 to 31.2% protein, 48.4 to 60.6% oil, and 2745 to 3080 calories per lb. The carbohydrates contain 4.3% ash, 1.0% fiber, 4.3% sugars with no starch. Characteristics of the oil are iodine value 102.1, oleic acid 56.7%, linoleic acid 31.6%, and saturated acids 8.5% (Kester 1949).

Processing and Using Pine Nuts

The majority of pine nuts belong to the sweet, highly flavored and oily group with high protein content. European nut pines, "pinochi" of Italy, are used in cakes and puddings, or as delicacies, but have a strong flavor resembling turpentine.

The nuts of most species are not good raw, but *P. pinea* or piñon nuts may be eaten raw. They are also delicious when roasted.

Work at the New Mexico Experiment Station confirms that the Indians were wise in extensively using piñon nuts of that region for food. The tiny nuts contain protein with a high rate of digestibility. They contain supplies of vitamin B-1, vitamin C, and iron.

Another way of preparing pine nuts of the oily group consists in covering them with a little water and squeezing out the contents with a press. The thick milky residue—pine milk—being subjected to partial evaporation, will keep for a long time and may partially take the place of meat in the diet. The cake residue is valuable for stock and fowl feed.

Pine Nut Cookies

4 eggs	2½ cups sifted flour
1½ cups granulated sugar	¼ tsp salt
½ tsp grated lemon rind	¼ cup confectioners' sugar
Few drops oil of anise	1 cup pine nuts

Put eggs and granulated sugar in the top of double boiler over hot water. Beat with rotary beater until mixture is lukewarm. Remove from water; beat until foaming and cool. Add flavorings, and fold in flour and salt. Drop by teaspoons onto greased and floured cookie sheets. Sprinkle with confectioners' sugar and nuts. Let stand for 10 min; bake in moderate oven of 185°C (375°F) for about 10 min. Makes 5 dozen cookies.

Halibut Baked in Salsa Gaditana

2 lb halibut, preferably in one piece	¼ cup pine nuts
4 tbsp Spanish olive oil	¼ cup minced parsley
1 large or 2 small garlic cloves	2 cups (1-lb can) canned tomatoes
	Salt, pepper to taste

Sprinkle all surfaces of fish with salt; place fish in shallow baking dish which has been lightly rubbed with olive oil. Pour remaining olive oil in heavy skillet, add the whole garlic cloves and the nuts, fry until golden, then remove with slotted spoon to mortar or wooden bowl.

Place the chopped onions in the olive oil; simmer over moderate heat until soft and golden. As onions cook, mash both garlic and nuts, using a pestle or back of wooden spoon.

When garlic and nuts are mashed to a paste, work in a little of the parsley at a time along with 1 tsp of the oil from the skillet, until you have a smooth green paste.

When onions are soft, add the canned tomatoes, simmer 5 min, stir in the green garlic-parsley paste, then season to taste with salt and pepper. Pour this sauce over the fish so that fish is completely covered. Bake at 176.6°C (350°F) for 30 min.

Serve from the dish, or, if preferred, turn out upside down on platter so that fish is over sauce. Garnish with croutons, if desired. Serves 6.

Since pine trees propagate by seed by the millions on land that is too steep and sometimes too poor for agriculture, foresters and food scientists have been neglectful in selecting and cultivating trees which produce large crops of high quality pine nuts.

REFERENCES

ANON. 1962. The piñon, our State tree. Extension News, N.M. State Univ., Las Cruces, N.M.

ANON. 1965. Foreign Agriculture. Foreign Agric. Serv. Rept., U.S. Dep. Agric.

ANON. 1976. Foreign Agric. Serv. January. U.S. Dep. Agric.

BAILEY, L.H. 1935. Cyclopedia of Horticulture, Vol. 3. Macmillan Co., New York.

BLUMENTHAL, S. 1947. Food Products. Chemical Publishing Co., Brooklyn, N.Y.

BODKIN, C.W., and SHIRES, L.B. 1948. The composition and value of piñon nuts. N.M. Agric. Exp. Stn. Bull. *344.*

BRYANT, D. 1967. Production of piñon nuts in New Mexico. Northern Nuts Grow. Assoc., 58th Ann. Rept., 116-118. Knoxville, Tenn.

DUTTON, T. 1966. Colorado's undiscovered mountains. Ford Times *59* (8) 4-6.

FULLER, A.S. 1904. The Nut Culturist. Orange Judd Co., New York.

KESTER, E.B. 1949. Minor oil-producing crops of the United States. J. Am. Oil Chem. Soc. *26*, 65-77.

MOLDENKE, H.N., and MOLDENKE, A.L. 1952. Plants of the Bible. Chronica Botanica Co., Waltham, Mass.

MORRIS, R.T. 1921. Nut Growing. Macmillan Co., New York.

SMITH, J.R. 1929. Tree Crops. Harcourt, Brace and Co., New York.

14

Pistachio Nuts[1]

The pistachio tree (*Pistacia vera* L.) is native to western Asia and Asia Minor, and was introduced into Mediterranean Europe at approximately the beginning of the Christian era. It is found growing in areas with a hot dry climate, such as Lebanon, Palestine, Syria, Iran, India, southern Europe, the desert countries of Asia and Africa, and California.

This tree is one of eleven species in the genus *Pistacia*, most of which exude turpentine or mastic (Zohary 1952). Some of its relatives in the family Anacardiaceae include such well-known plants as cashew, mango, poison ivy, poison oak, pepper tree and sumac. Several species of the genus *Pistacia* are referred to as pistachio, but that name correctly applies only to the tree and the nut of commerce that it produces. The fruits of all *Pistacia* species are classified as drupes, a type of fruit that also characterizes the almond, apricot, cherry, plum and peach. The edible portion of the pistachio and almond, however, is the seed. There is considerable variation in size of fruits from one species of *Pistacia* to another and in development of the various parts composing the fruits. Only the fruits of *P. vera* attain sufficient size to satisfy consumer requirements for an edible nut. The small kernels of *P. atlantica* Desf. and *P. terebinthus* L. are eaten in their native habitat but are considered more useful as a source of oil. Also, only the shells (endocarp) of *P. vera* fruits split along their sutures, a highly desirable trait because pistachios are usually marketed in-shell, to be opened by hand.

The pistachio tree is both deciduous and dioecious (Fig. 14.1). Shoot extension begins the last of March and terminates in late April to

---

[1]This chapter was prepared originally from material furnished by Whitehouse (1957) and Bloch and Brekke (1960). It was revised by Julian C. Crane, Professor of Pomology, University of California, Davis (1977).

Courtesy of Julian C. Crane

FIG. 14.1. INFLORESCENSES OF TWO PISTACHIO CULTIVARS
Left, male inflorescenses of the "Peters" cultivar; right, female
inflorescenses of the "Kerman" cultivar. Photographed on April
15 a few days past full bloom and before shoot growth and leaf
expansion were complete

mid-May. A pinnately compound leaf at each node subtends one axillary bud. Most of the buds differentiate into inflorescence primordia (staminate or pistillate, depending upon the sex of the tree) during April and May and grow to their ultimate size for the season by about June 1. Generally, one or two axillary buds located near the tips of the shoots remain vegetative. These are considerably smaller than the inflorescence buds, and may give rise to lateral branches the following year or they may remain dormant. The inflorescence buds expand the last of the following March and wind pollination of the 100 to 300 flowers per panicle occurs during the first 2 weeks of April. Thus, the pistachio bears its fruits laterally on wood produced the previous season (Fig. 14.2).

Pistachio trees, after an indefinite number of years, ultimately produce a heavy crop one year followed by little or none the next. The mechanism involved is unique in comparison with that of other biennial bearing fruit and nut trees. Biennial bearing in other species is usually the result of greatly reduced flower bud formation during the year of a heavy crop. In contrast, it is brought about in pistachio by inflorescence bud abscission during the summer that a heavy crop of

Courtesy of Julian C. Crane

FIG. 14.2. RELATIONSHIP BETWEEN PISTACHIO NUT
PRODUCTION AND ABSCISSION OF INFLORESCENCE
The nut–bearing branch (left) abcised most of its inflorescence
buds on the new growth, whereas the nonbearing branch (right)
retained all of its inflorescence buds

nuts is being produced (Fig. 14.2). Crane and Nelson (1971) reported
that bud abscission generally begins in late June and is most intense
during July and August when seed growth and development are most
rapid. Degree of bud abscission, in some instances almost 100%, increases as the number of nuts per branch increases. This suggested to
Crane *et al.* (1972, 1973) that competition between developing nuts and
buds for nutrients might be responsible for abscission of the buds. In a
subsequent study, however, Crane *et al.* (1976) found sugar and starch
levels in nut-bearing branches not to be appreciably different prior to
and during the period of bud-drop from levels in nonbearing branches.
They concluded that the inflorescence bud-drop phenomenon is not the
result of carbohydrate deficiency and suggested that a hormone(s) may
be involved.

Following pollination and fertilization of the flowers in April, the ovary walls (pericarp) expand very rapidly in length and diameter and attain practically ultimate size by the middle of May (Fig. 14.3). There is little or no growth, both externally and internally, for the next five or six weeks when the seed (kernel) begins rapid expansion the last of June. By the first of August, the seed has filled the ovarian cavity and

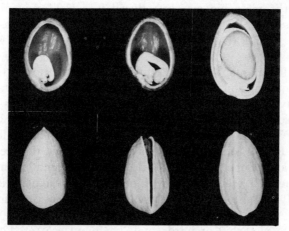

Courtesy of Julian C. Crane

FIG. 14.3. INTERNAL DEVELOPMENT OF THE
"KERMAN" PISTACHIO NUT
TOP, left, pericarp attains about ultimate size by mid May and encloses a curved funiculus supporting a single young seed at its apex; center, lengthened funiculus supporting an expanding seed. (June 26); right, seed that has about filled the locule (July 22). BOTTOM, left, mature fruit before removal of the hull (exocarp and mecocarp); center, after hull removal and drying, showing dehisced shell (endocarp) enclosing seed; right, undehisced shell which may or may not contain a seed

dehiscence of the shell, but not of the hull, occurs soon thereafter (Crane *et al.* 1971). Sugars reach a peak of over 40% of the dry weight early in development of the kernel, but then decrease to about 7% at nut maturity. Concomitantly, crude fat increases from a low of 3% early in kernel development to a maximum of 40% at maturity (Crane and Al-Shalan 1974).

The production of blank (empty) pistachio nuts is an important problem wherever the crop is produced. The seriousness of the problem is indicated by the fact that an experimental 'Kerman' orchard in California produced an average of 26% (by count) blanks for the first 4 years of nut production. Blank production has been shown to result from parthenocarpy (Crane 1973) and from seed abortion (Crane 1975), the latter being responsible for the major portion. Various abnormalities in seed development that lead to abortion have been described by Grundwag and Fahn (1969) and by Bradley and Crane (1975).

U.S. PRODUCTION

Although the pistachio was introduced into California about 1890, little interest was generated in its commercial possibilities until the past decade. During that period approximately 30,000 acres were planted, over 8500 acres in 1972 alone. The development of new cultivars by the U.S. Department of Agriculture, the accumulation of tree growth and yield information under California conditions, and the development and availability of mechanical harvesting and processing equipment were some of the factors responsible for the rapid growth of this new industry. While the United States has imported annually an average of over 11,000 tons of pistachios during the past decade, primarily from Iran and Turkey (Table 14.1), domestic production will soon fulfill this need. Presently, however, only a small quantity is produced commercially in California, as the newly planted trees came into bearing in 1977.

While some pistachio orchards may be found scattered throughout the Sacramento and San Joaquin Valleys of California, the major portion of the acreage is located in the hot and dry southern San Joaquin Valley near Bakersfield. Climatic conditions in this area are very similar to those in the pistachio producing areas of Iran.

PISTACHIO NUTS IN ASIA

In central Asia (Turkestan), *P. vera* is found growing wild with a few exceptions. It is rather widespread over southern central Asia in the low mountains and foothills in what is considered a semi-desert zone along all mountain chains of the south of central Asia, beginning with the Caspian Sea (Kopet-Dagh mountains) up to Fergana, the region of Tashkent and the mountains of Karatan. East of Karatan in central Tian-Shan, the wild pistachio is found in only three separate small areas. It is not found in the deserts of the Aral-Caspian lowland. Only two small stands are found on the western end of the Kopet-Dagh mountains near the Caspian Sea and near the Iranian frontier. One of the largest in Central Asia is the so-called Badkhyz pistachio stand, near Kushka, in the extreme south of Turkmenistan, near the Afghan frontier.

These wild pistachio groves extend into northern Afghanistan. Be-

TABLE 14.1
IMPORTS OF PISTACHIOS INTO UNITED STATES
(METRIC TONS)

Country of Origin	Year Beginning September 1					
	1968−69	1969−70	1970−71	1971−72	1972−73	1973−74
IN-SHELL						
Europe						
Turkey	3,065	926	5,811	1,763	4,792	1,698
Other	15	−	65	−	−	−
Total	3,080	926	5,876	1,763	4,792	1,698
Other Countries						
Afghanistan	763	16	43	−	−	−
India	33	−	30	−	−	−
Iran	6,927	6,877	7,939	4,701	10,416	11,129
Other	71	−	32	−	42	2
Total	7,794	6,893	8,044	4,701	10,458	11,131
Grand total	10,874	7,819	13,920	6,464	15,250	12,829
SHELLED						
Europe						
Italy	14	−	−	7	22	32
Turkey	71	12	70	48	168	21
Other	−	8	−	−	−	1
Total	85	20	70	55	190	54
Other Countries						
Afghanistan	147	44	214	29	−	−
Iran	89	102	93	43	24	−
Other	−	−	4	−	2	−
Total	236	146	311	72	26	−
Grand total	321	166	381	127	216	54

Source: Foreign Agric. Serv., U.S. Dep. Agric.

yond the river Amu-Daria, in the low mountains of the Pamir-Alai, the pistachio is seen everywhere from mountainous Bokhara through the region of Samarkand and the whole of Fergana up to the western Tian-Shan. Large stands are found only in the region adjoining the Amu-Daria, the lower course of the rivers, Kafirnahan, Vakhsha and Kizil-Zu. The distribution of the wild pistachio is sporadic even in its principal area. Historical records tell of pistachios growing in many places where none exist today. The distribution of pistachios has been determined largely by the needs of the local populations who in some instances use the trees as a source of fuel, thus eventually killing them; in addition, heavy pasturing of cattle in some areas has prevented a natural renewal. The age of the trees ranges from 6 to 240 years.

WORLD PRODUCTION OF PISTACHIO NUTS

The majority, if not all, of the "Pista" nuts consumed in Afghanistan or exported by that country are harvested from the wild pistachio forests. In India, the crop for the most part is obtained from the wild trees in the hilly tracts of the Northwest Frontier Province and Baluchistan.

In Iran, the pistachio tree has been planted commercially for hundreds of years, but only in the last 60 years has there been a recognition of the value of the nut as an agricultural crop for export, the rate of new plantings keeping pace with the rapid increase in American consumption.

The principal producing area in Iran is Kerman, which is located in the arid southeast. Extensive plantings are located also in the vicinity of Rafsenjan, Sirjan and Ghazvin.

Syria and the Palestinian area have long been famous for their pistachio trees and the town of Tavna in the Aleppo region is thought to have its name derived from the abundance of pistachio nuts grown there. Damascus is noted for the quality of its pistachio nuts.

Pistachio culture in Turkey is centered in the dry, barren foothills and lower ranges of southeastern and western Turkey. The principal producers are the valeyets of Gaziantep and Urfa.

Sicily produces pistachios of good quality and high commercial value. The pistachio nuts of Tunisia are smaller than those of Sicily and have less commercial value, but are equally appreciated. Their lack of uniformity in shape, flavor, and size, in contrast to those harvested from known cultivars in Sicily, is attributed to their seedling origin. Pistachios require long, hot, dry summers to properly mature the nuts, and winters sufficiently cold to satisfy the chilling requirement of the buds. Insufficient winter chilling causes delayed foliation and seriously reduces growth and nut production. Late spring frosts also limit the areas in which this crop may be produced successfully. Summer rains and high humidity, particularly during the period of harvest, are detrimental. Generally, areas suitable to commercial olive production are satisfactory for pistachios.

CULTIVARS OF PISTACHIO NUTS

Pistachio nuts are classified in the trade according to the country of origin, i.e., Afghan, Iranian, Sicilian, Syrian and Turkish. The Iranian pistachios are considered dry and have a light yellow kernel. The larger sizes lack somewhat the rich, oily nut-like flavor of the Sicilian, Syrian and Turkish nuts, which are preferred because, on the whole, they are considered better tasting and the kernels are more uniformly green. Italian nuts sell at a premium because of the dark green color of the kernels; the smaller Afghanistan nuts, also preferred for the deep green color of their kernels, are in demand by the ice cream and pastry industries.

Importers purchase their nuts in the "natural state," grading, processing and selling them under their own brand names. Iranian 8 Star Colossal, Iranian 7 Star Giants, Italian 5 Star Extra Jumbo, Turkish 4 Star Jumbo, and Afghan 3 Star Buds are the brand names of one New York firm; Iranian Giants (Monarch), Iranian Midgets (Tulip), Sicilian (Royal) and Syrian (Crown) are the brands of another.

Iranian growers in the Rafsenjan area under the leadership of the Agah family have been selecting and naming some of the best of their seedlings. The following are some of the best cultivars grown in Iran today: Momtaz, which bears large clusters of nuts with light shells; Owhadi, the old standard cultivar that bears large clusters of nuts smaller than Momtaz but of good quality; Agah, which combines the good qualities of Momtaz and Owhadi; and Kalehghouchi, the largest and highest priced nut, but lowest in yield.

TABLE 14.2
COMPOSITION (%) AND SHAPES OF PISTACHIO KERNELS OF VARIOUS ORIGINS

No.	Local Name	Shape	Origin	Moisture	Ash	Oil	Fiber	Protein	Carbohydrate
1	Badami	almond	Rafsanjan	3.9	2.5	55.8	2.0	19.3	16.7
2	Ohadi	hazelnut	Rafsanjan	3.1	2.3	58.4	2.0	17.8	16.4
3	Momtaz	almond	Rafsanjan	2.7	2.2	60.5	1.9	15.0	17.7
4	Badami riz	almond	Rafsanjan	2.5	2.2	60.4	1.9	17.6	15.4
5	Shah-passand	almond	Damghan	3.3	2.2	57.6	1.8	18.4	16.7
6	Jowzi	hazelnut	Damghan	4.1	2.2	56.0	2.0	20.8	14.9
7	Khanjari	almond	Damghan	3.9	2.2	58.0	2.0	17.6	16.3
8	Noghli	hazelnut	Damghan	3.1	2.5	58.0	1.8	17.6	17.0
9	Kallehpazi	almond	Ghazvin	4.0	2.4	55.2	1.7	21.2	15.5
Mean				3.4	2.5	57.7	1.9	18.3	16.1

Source: Kamangar and Farsam (1977).

Turkey has a number of named cultivars, the two most commonly planted being the Uzun and Kirmizi. Nearly half of the crop harvested in some areas consists of nuts of these two cultivars. Uzun nuts are long (24 to 26 mm) and plump, some being half as wide as they are long. The Kirmizi is a red-hulled, thin-shelled, free-splitting, green-kerneled nut of medium size, containing 10% more protein than the Turkish Red Aleppo cultivar. Kernels of the latter cultivar were found to contain 20.3% protein and 65.47% oil. The origin of the 'Red Aleppo' in California is not clear. In 1906, it was presented to the Office of Seed and Plant Introduction by Rev. A. Fuller, under the name 'Large Red Aleppo', for trial at Chico. Presumably, it is a seedling of the Turkish 'Red Aleppo', the hulls of which are so characteristically red.

In Syria, there are distinct cultivars: Alemi, Obiad, Mirhavy, Achoury, Ayimi, El Bataury, Aintab, Ashoori, for example.

The Trabonella and Bronte cultivars introduced into California from Sicily in the early 1900s came from the Duke of Bronte's estate. Sanguigna, Girasola, Girasola Cappuecia, Bianca Giardino, Bianca Regina, Rappa di Sessa, Minnullina, and the three Gialla strains are also well-known Sicilian cultivars.

The first cultivars tested at the USDA Plant Introduction Station in Chico, California, included Bronte, Red Aleppo, Sfax and Trabonella. Sfax was introduced from Algeria although it was formerly grown in the area of Sfax, Tunisia. It produces dense clusters of good quality nuts with a high percentage of split shells. Bronte and Trabonella are similar in appearance and quality. Kernel quality of all five cultivars was acceptable but size and yield were not adequate to recommend their commercial production.

An intensified program by the U.S. Department of Agriculture for the development of better cultivars was begun in 1929 by the importation of promising seeds selected from various sources in Iran and Turkestan. Three trees produced from these seeds were selected for their outstanding nut qualities and were named Damghan, Kerman, and Lassen. Damghan proved to be a shy bearer and was not made available for general distribution. Because Lassen was found later to be incompatible with *P. atlantica* rootstock, it also was not distributed for commercial production. Kerman was the choice for commercial production because of its high yielding capacity of large nuts of superior quality (Fig. 14.4). It alone makes up all commercial acreage in California.

Kerman is not without fault, however, and a search is being made by The Pistachio Association and the University of California for additional cultivars. As pointed out above, the pistachio has a biennial bearing habit and Kerman appears to have a stronger tendency in that respect than some other cultivars. Another serious fault of Kerman is the high percentage of blanks that it produces. There is considerable variation in blank production from year to year which suggests that temperature must be associated with this phenomenon (Crane 1976). Kerman also develops dark canker-like areas in the hulls and shells which also adversely affects kernel development. Affected nuts may drop from the trees or they may remain and develop abnormally, depending upon the stage of nut growth and development when the cankers appear. The extent of this problem also varies considerably from year to year and appears to be controlled genetically.

Sfax is the first to mature its crop, but Bronte, Red Aleppo and Trabonella follow closely. They may be harvested in late August to the middle of September, while Kerman normally matures about the middle of September.

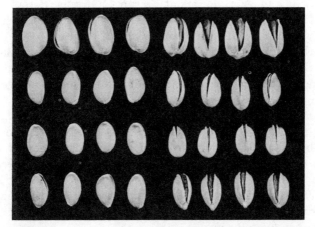

Courtesy of Julian C. Crane

FIG. 14.4. "KERMAN," "RED ALEPPE," "SFAX" AND
"TRABONELLA" PISTACHIO NUTS (TOP TO BOTTOM). ACTUAL SIZE

TABLE 14.3
MINERAL CONTENT (% × 0.001) OF PISTACHIO KERNELS OF VARIOUS ORIGINS

No.	Local Name	Na	K	Ca	Minerals P	Fe	Cu	Mg
1	Badami	6.5	1116	135	509.5	6.0	1.1	160.5
2	Ohadi	6.7	1060	120	504.2	5.8	1.3	165.0
3	Momtaz	5.9	1142	135	506.7	6.2	1.1	157.5
4	Badamiriz	4.7	1120	125	505.1	6.3	1.4	162.5
5	Shah-passand	4.0	1056	142	496.5	5.9	1.0	162.0
6	Jowzi	4.3	1078	132	494.0	6.0	1.4	158.0
7	Khanjari	4.0	1048	138	499.0	6.2	1.1	160.0
8	Noghli	4.2	1050	140	500.0	5.8	1.2	163.5
9	Kallehpazi	7.0	1120	150	514.5	11.4	1.4	165.0
Mean		5.2	1087	135	503.3	6.6	1.2	161.6

Source: Kamangar and Farsam (1977).

Bronte and Trabonella produce about the greenest kernels, Sfax and Red Aleppo are intermediate, and Kerman is lightest, varying from straw-yellow to light greenish yellow.

The male cultivar Peters sheds its pollen during a period that corresponds, at least in part, to the period of receptivity of most female cultivars. Peters, therefore, is probably the closest of all males to being a universal pollinator. Some years, however, it may be somewhat late for early blooming cultivars such as Red Aleppo and Trabonella or somewhat early for complete overlapping of Kerman. It was selected in the early 1900s by A. B. Peters at Fresno, California. Peters trees vary greatly in vigor, depending upon the seedling stocks on which they are growing. The trees produce pollen abundantly.

Chico, selected from seedlings grown from seed imported from Aleppo, Syria, is a vigorous growing cultivar and a prolific pollen producer. It is earlier than Peters and particularly suitable for pollinating early types such as Sfax or Red Aleppo, but it is too early for Kerman.

To ensure good pollination of Kerman at all times, a male with a blooming period slightly later than Peters is desirable. Two seedlings selected by USDA personnel at Chico from seed imported from the Azsheron Peninsula in the USSR appear to meet this need. These seedlings, 02—16 and 02—18, are more vigorous and later blooming than Peters, and are prolific pollen producers. Some of the newly planted orchards in California contain both Peters and 02—16 or 02—18 as pollinators for Kerman.

Since pistachio is wind pollinated, the degree to which pollination occurs is dependent upon prevailing weather conditions. To be independent of this potentially disastrous situation, research is being conducted by the University of California towards collecting and storing pollen for use later in supplementing natural pollination. In tests with several species and cultivars of *Pistacia*, the viability of fresh pollen held at room temperature 22° to 24°C (72° to 75°F) rapidly deteriorated in 3 to 4 days to zero (Crane *et al.* 1974).

PROPAGATING PISTACHIO NUT TREES

Because cuttings taken from *P. Vera* trees do not produce roots, the pistachio is propagated by budding or grafting it on seedling rootstocks. Seedlings of several *Pistacia* species have been used successfully in different parts of the world where pistachios are grown (Whitehouse 1957). Because of their growth characteristics and resistance to nematodes (Joley and Whitehouse 1953), seedlings of *P. atlantica* and *P. terebinthus* are used in California. Seedlings of both species grow more slowly the first year or two than those of *P. vera*; but, according to Joley (1969), cultivars budded on them shortly outgrow and outyield those on *P. vera* roots. Crane and Forde (1976) reported that during the first five years of production, significantly greater yields of nuts were obtained with Kerman growing on *P. atlantica* than on three other rootstocks.

Fruits of *P. atlantica* and *P. terebinthus* mature in September and October. When harvested, the hulls are removed and the seeds dried. The seed is surrounded by a bony, indehiscent endocarp which is extremely hard and somewhat resistant to the passage of water. With prolonged exposure to moisture, the layer cementing the two halves of the shell softens, permitting their separation. This, in turn, permits the embryo to grow and develop. However, such exposure frequently brings about deterioration and rotting of the seed, which results in a disappointingly low germination percentage and seedling survival rate from a given lot of seed. However, reducing the thickness of the shells by acid scarification speeds germination and increases the percentage of seeds that germinate (Crane and Forde 1974).

Courtesy of Julian C. Crane

FIG. 14.5. *PISTACIA ATLANTICA* SEEDLINGS GROWING IN PAPIER-MACHE POTS BEFORE TRANSPLANTING TO PERMANENT ORCHARD SITE

As *Pistacia* seedlings do not withstand transplanting in the bare root condition, they are grown in containers, not in nursery rows. After soaking the seed in water overnight, most nurserymen plant the seeds in Jiffy-7 peat pellets (JPA Company, West Chicago, Ill.), one seed per pellet. In three to four weeks, roots of the seedlings will have grown out of the peat pellets. These are rubbed off to stimulate lateral branching and the pellets containing the seedlings are placed in papier-maché pots about 18 in. tall and 7 in. in diameter containing sterilized loamy soil mixed with peat and sand (Fig. 14.5). Seeds planted in January or February in the greenhouse may be transplanted into containers in March and grown outside in full sunlight until planting in the orchard in mid-June. Under ideal conditions, the seedlings are large enough for budding in September.

T-budding is the most satisfactory method of propagating the pistachio. The diameter of the rootstock should be at least ⅜ to ½ in. at the point of bud insertion because the buds of pistachio are larger than those of most fruit trees. Although budding may be done anytime when the bark of the rootstock is slipping, best results are generally obtained with buds set in September or early October.

Planting distance in the orchard varies from 12 to 15 ft in the row with 24 to 30 ft between rows. When the trees start crowding within the row, every other one may be removed. Mature trees growing in rich soils will require at least 30 ft between trees. Male trees are spaced throughout the orchard to take advantage of prevailing winds. Usually one male tree is adequate to pollinate 10 to 12 female trees.

Training and Pruning

In California, the shoot from the bud inserted on the stock is trained up and tied to a stake. A modified leader system of training with 3 or more primary scaffold branches at 1-ft intervals on the trunk is the ideal framework structure. The height of the bottom-most branch is 3 to 4 ft above ground, depending upon the harvesting machine used. In establishing the framework of the young tree, summer pinching of new shoots 30 in. or longer is desirable in order to prevent their bending down from the desired 45° angle. This also forces lateral branching and speeds framework development. The centers of the trees must be kept open to admit sunlight in order for flower bud formation and subsequent fruiting to occur. After the basic framework of the tree has been established, only light pruning is necessary. As the pistachio produces its flower buds laterally on shoots, new length growth must be stimulated each year for maximum nut production. This results in a continual spreading of the tree and in the bearing area becoming further and further away from the center. Pruning to prevent or correct this situation is difficult because of the limited number of lateral vegetative buds to cut back to. It is desirable to avoid making large cuts because the pruning wounds heal very slowly.

Soil and Water Requirements

The wild pistachio tree has been found growing on the rocky soils of Lebanon, Palestine and the Isle of Cyprus. At Kushka and in the areas adjoining the lower course of the rivers Kafirnahan, Wakhsha and Kizel-Zu, the soil is composed of varicolored loose gypsoferous rocks of the Cretaceous and Tertiary period, as well as products of their disintegration, the loams and sandy loams rich in gypsum and carbonates. It is also found growing to a lesser extent on the loess-like loams of the foothills, the grey-colored, crystalline calcareous rocks and stony slopes lacking in gypsum, and on the sandstone rocks without gypsum, such as those in the mountains of Kopet-Dagh.

The pistachio is thus a gypso-calciphilous plant, putting up with stony substratum, but always found growing on slopes with perfectly drained soil and unable to stand excess water in the soil. Although apparently adapted to all kinds of soil, it prefers relatively deep, light or dry sandy loams with high lime content. In Syria, it grows well on chalky clay soil, well drained, but retentive of sufficient moisture for good growth. On rocky sites it prefers 25 to 30 in. of top soil, the roots extending into the rocky subsoil to get moisture. A southern exposure and a well-drained soil make a good combination. In Greece, pistachio trees on *P. terebinthus* rootstocks make good growth on the lime soils along the seashore of Phaleron and Aigina, which are poor and dry, and their growth response to applications of hard or salty water is excellent. It is evident that the pistachio will tolerate a wide range of soil types. For superior growth and production, however, it requires a deep, fertile, well-drained soil.

In Turkey, which has an average rainfall of about 16 to 18 in., irrigation is not practiced, but care is taken to maintain a good dust mulch. In India, there is sufficient retention of the large quantities of water supplied by winter rains to enable the pistachio tree to make a good growth without summer irrigation. In Iran, where the average rainfall runs about 6 to 7 in., land which cannot be irrigated is valueless for pistachio orchards.

Although pistachio trees appear to tolerate drought, successful commercial nut production in California necessitates the existence of adequate soil moisture particularly during the summer months. Under the usual summer drought conditions in the Sacramento Valley where the winter rainfall is 16 to 20 in., leaves on unirrigated pistachio trees turn yellow and drop in August before the crop is mature. When the soil is irrigated in July to a depth of 6 ft, the leaves usually remain green on the trees until normal leaf fall in November. In an area of 16 to 18 in. of winter rainfall, at least 2 irrigations are necessary to maintain good tree performance. In drier areas, such as the San Joaquin Valley, additional irrigations are necessary. The root systems of pistachio trees do not tolerate prolonged wet conditions that may exist in poorly drained soils. Sites subject to high water tables should also be avoided. Pistachio orchards in California are irrigated primarily by the furrow or drag-line sprinkler system. Many orchards are also being irrigated by the low pressure drip system.

Nutritional Requirements

Uriu and Crane (1976) reported the seasonal mineral element changes that occur in pistachio leaves which may serve as guidelines for leaf sampling and interpretation of chemical analysis data. Their study indicated that there were no significant differences in concentration of mineral elements in leaflets as compared to one another and to the whole leaf. Thus, by sampling individual leaflets rather than whole leaves, many more leaves may be represented in a sample for chemical analysis. They recommended that, if leaf sampling is to be done but once a year, the best time is during the one-month period preceding harvest. To eliminate variable effects of cropping on mineral element composition, leaflets only from shoots on nonbearing branches should be sampled. The concentration range in mineral elements over which normal growth with healthy leaves occurred was as follows:

Element	Range (dry wt basis)
Na	2.5−2.9%
Pa	0.14−0.17%
Ka	1.0−2.0%
Ca	1.3−4.0%
Mg	0.6−1.2%
Na	0.002−0.007%
Cl	0.1−0.3%
Mn	30−80 ppm
Ba	55−230 ppm
Zn	7−14 ppm

Climatic Requirements

It has been pointed out that the pistachio is a very xerophilous plant, able to withstand great dryness of soil and air; humidity is unfavorable to its development. The pistachio tree thrives best in areas having cool enough winters for properly breaking bud dormancy and long, hot, dry summers for maturing the nuts. In Iran, for example, the best pistachio nut orchards are grown at an elevation of 4000 ft on the extensive plateau which makes up the heart of that country and which is reputed to be one of the worst deserts in the world. Rainfall averages 10 to 15 in. per year, and in the south and east is less than 5 in. Summer temperatures reach 37.5°C (100°F) in the northern portion of this plateau.

The Badkhys region of U.S.S.R., where wild forests of pistachios are growing, is a semi-desert zone characterized by dryness of air, very significant cloudiness, low precipitation, hot summers, and relatively cold winters. The pistachio tree flowers and produces fruit freely in England, but the summers are not warm enough for the nuts to ripen.

In Syria, it is found inland at an altitude up to 1200 meters where the air is dry.

Under the dry, arid climate of Arizona pistachio trees have survived a winter temperature of -14°C (6°F) without injury. They flourish in eastern Iran where temperatures vary from -9.4°C (15°F) in the winter to 42.2°C (108°F) in the summer, and grow well in the interior San Joaquin and Sacramento valleys of California, where somewhat the same temperatures are experienced. The wild trees of the Kuska, U.S.S.R. region withstand winter temperatures below -17.8°C (0°F).

The pistachio grows and fruits well as far south as Bakersfield, California, but beyond there, particularly around Los Angeles, production is irregular, the trees bearing good crops of nuts only after fairly cold winters or at altitudes sufficiently high to provide winter temperatures similar to those of the San Joaquin Valley. At Indio, California, where a thriving date industry exists, the pistachio nut cannot be successfully grown. *P. atlantica* of North Africa thrives here as would be expected. At Sacaton, Arizona, a crop of pistachio nuts is borne only one year out of five on the average, for in most years there is not quite enough cold weather to break bud dormancy and delayed foliation occurs. Little is known of the northern limits of pistachio growing although it is believed that in areas with a shorter growing season than that of the Sacramento Valley, it might be difficult to mature and harvest the crop, especially when the fall rains and cool weather start in September. In general, areas adapted to almonds and olives are suitable.

Diseases and Insects

Experience in the San Joaquin Valley, California, indicates that the most serious disease of the pistachio is verticillium wilt (*Verticillium albo-atrum*). Considerable tree mortality has occurred from infection by this soil-borne fungus in many areas where plantings have been made, particularly on land that had been planted previously to cotton. The mortality rate has been highest with newly planted trees, but 10-and 12-year-old trees have been killed by this disease. Pre-plant fumigation with a 1:1 mixture of chloropicrin-methyl bromide reduces the inoculum of verticillium in soils previously cropped with cotton to about the level observed in virgin soils. In established orchards, verticillium damage is minimized by growing a grass cover crop. As noted above, however, many pistachio orchards are drip irrigated, a system that does not lend itself to grass culture.

Crown rot (*Phytophthora parasitica*) is reported by Kouyeas (1952) to attack pistachio trees in Greece. *P. terebinthus*, the popular rootstock for the pistachio in Greece, he states, is immune to the fungus. In

California, trees in poorly drained areas have been attacked most often by this disease.

Septoria spp., which cause leaf spotting and consequent defoliation, have been reported to occur in Greece (Anagnostopoulos 1938) and in the United States (Maas *et al.* 1971). Fortunately, they are easily controlled through the use of copper sulphate spray. Anagnostopoulos (1938) states that in Greece the pistachio is subject to severe injuries by fungus parasites in all stages of its development. Of these, the most serious is a fungal parasite of the genus *Phomopsis* which attacks the female flowers in the spring, starting at the tips and extending over all or part of the cluster. It becomes inactive in the summer and resumes its activity in the early fall, when it frequently destroys entire clusters of fruits as well as the midribs and petioles of the leaves. The fungus gains its entrance through insect punctures, principally those of the lepidopterous insect, *Tinea pistaciae* Anagnos. Control programs consist of burning infested plant parts and the application of oil sprays in January to destroy the overwintering stage of the insect. Some assistance is obtained from its natural enemies, the animal parasites.

Similar damage may be done by a *Fusarium* sp., which is also a causal agent of the drying of the fruit. *Fusarium* and other secondary fungi follow *Phomopsis* in its work of destruction; therefore, insect control measures that check the spread of *Phomopsis* serve also to check the others. Additional control is obtained by the application of three Bordeaux mixture sprays at specified intervals. Fall applications of this spray are used to control the leaf spot. In countries other than the United States, a rust fungus, *Uromyces terebinthi,* occurs on *P. vera* and practically all of the species of *Pistacia*. Fortunately, this disease does not cause serious injury.

Kreutzberg (1940) discovered a new virus disease on a wild pistachio tree in the Badkhyz Mountains, Turkmenia, U.S.S.R., in 1935. Later it was also observed in Uzbekistan and Tadzhikistan. When attacked, the pistachio tree forms rosettes of varying size presenting a dense interlacement of short, thin branching twigs. Growth of the tree is seriously checked.

Currently, the pistachio seed chalcid (*Megastigmus pistaciae*) is the only serious insect that threatens the pistachio in California. It is confined to a small area in the northern Sacramento Valley but may spread to the San Joaquin Valley unless a control measure is quickly found.

Brown scale (*Coccus hesperidum*) has been observed from time to time and it is generally controlled by parasitism. Larvae of the Indianmeal moth (*Plodia interpunctella*) can do severe damage to stored nuts not refrigerated.

Nematode infestation of pistachio roots has been observed by Joley and Whitehouse (1953). Loss due to the presence of nematodes is difficult to assess, but it is assumed that heavily infested roots will seriously restrict tree growth and production.

Yield and Harvest

As mentioned above, the pistachio tree is a biennial bearer in that a heavy crop one year is followed by a light one the next. It is evident from the data in Table 14.4 that production in Iran and Turkey may vary as much as 600% from one year to the next.

Based on yields from small experimental plantings maintained by the U.S. Department of Agriculture and the University of California, it is estimated that production will average about 50 lb of marketable nuts per mature tree annually. This is equivalent to approximately 1 to 2 tons per acre, depending upon planting distance.

TABLE 14.4
COMMERCIAL PRODUCTION OF IN-SHELL PISTACHIOS IN SPECIFIC COUNTRIES
(1000 METRIC TONS)

Year	Iran	Turkey
1965	7.5	5.0
1966	15.0	4.8
1967	4.0	5.0
1968	15.5	12.0
1969	7.5	2.0
1970	16.0	12.0
1971	7.5	2.0
1972	20.0	14.0
1973	20.0	6.5
1974	28.0	23.0

Source: Foreign Agric. Serv.,U.S. Dep. Agric.

Under normal conditions the nuts hang well, so that, if the crop is left on the tree until most of the nuts are ripe, all that are well filled are harvested in one picking. In Iran, most growers spread burlap or cloth under the tree to catch the clusters which, after being picked by hand, are thrown to the ground. Some throw the clusters on the dry soil. After harvest, the nuts are placed in bags and carried to a central location where mature nuts are removed from the stems and the outer husks are removed by hand. The husks of a small percentage of the nuts, which are overmature or immature, adhere to the shell but are readily removed after a short period of soaking in water. Nuts which, for one reason or another, lack fully developed kernels float on the surface of water and are easily removed. The nuts are dried in the sun on stone,

TABLE 14.5
PISTACHIOS: IN-SHELL EXPORTS FROM IRAN
(METRIC TONS)

Country of Destination	Year Beginning March 21					
	1968-69	1969-70	1970-71	1971-72	1972-73	1973-74
United States	2,210	5,466	6,603	5,143	8,505	9,670
Europe						
Belgium-Luxembourg	48	57	13	14	53	27
Cyprus	6	11	18	97	165	109
Czechoslovakia	–	15	225	178	318	345
France	232	347	127	166	191	202
Germany, West	22	46	73	57	41	211
Hungary	–	–	60	91	47	44
Netherlands	9	3	22	46	14	38
Romania	–	–	–	164	80	47
Switzerland	1	15	19	16	39	49
United Kingdom	20	25	43	108	108	137
Other	2	20	149[1]	18	45	36
Total	340	539	749	955	1,101	1,245
Other Countries						
Australia	3	7	19	29	106	92
Bahrain	–	–	5	93	87	72
Doby	42	196	31	1,527	99	201
Iraq	118	21	7	58	10	146
Israel	359	377	522	454	395	499
Japan	15	94	44	136	445	1,301
Kuwait	289	431	411	313	422	382
Lebanon	404	394	553	770	878	816
Mexico	2,293	1,185	203	90	161	21
Oman	76	114	142	70	97	48
Saudi Arabia	42	6	27	52	62	120
Syria	64	86	64	12	84	150
Other	133	372	182	172	316	307
Total	3,838	3,283	2,210	3,776	3,162	4,155
Grand Total	6,388	9,288	9,562	9,874	12,768	15,070

SHELLED

	1968-69	1969-70	1970-71	1971-72	1972-73	1973-74
Europe						
Czechoslovakia	–	1	8	3	30	138
Germany, West	28	39	70	61	107	164
United Kingdom	1	5	24	10	17	118
Other	15	1	7	14	38	112[2]
Total	44	46	109	88	192	232
Other countries (total)	76	7	43	14	37	239[3]
Grand Total	120	53	152	102	229	471

Source: Foreign Agric. Serv. FN 1-76, U.S. Dep. Agric.
[1]Includes 130 M.T. from Poland
[2]Includes 39 m.t. from Denmark, 19 m.t. from France and 20 m.t. from Romania.
[3]Includes 53 m.t. from U.S.A., 53 m.t. from Lebanon and 36 m.t. from Kuwait.

concrete or dry earthen floors. After drying they are put in bags and placed in storage rooms for curing. Grading is done in the villages by shaking the nuts through coarse sieves or by hand. Additional grading is usually required before sale to dealers.

In Turkey, the freshly harvested nuts are pulled from the clusters, thoroughly dried, and then stored with the hulls intact in heavy gunny sacks. Storage insects do more damage to hulled nuts than to unhulled ones. The nuts are processed as orders for them are received. After the dried nuts are soaked in water, revolving stone rollers are run over them until the hulls are loosened from the shell. A fanning mill, which separates chaff from grain, is used to separate the nuts from the moist pulp. Hand labor is required to remove the unhulled nuts for recrushing and also to separate those with split shells from the unsplit. Empty nuts are removed by screening, and unsplit nuts after washing are cracked by hand. Most of the nuts are sold through marketing cooperatives, which have been in existence for many years.

TABLE 14.6
PISTACHIOS: EXPORTS FROM ITALY
(METRIC TONS)

County of Destination	Year Beginning October 1					
	1968-69	1969-70	1970-71	1971-72	1972-73	1973-74
	IN-SHELL AND SHELLED					
United States	–	–	–	–	22	31
France	41	78	63	84	106	141
Germany, West	85	138	40	209	75	311
Other	20	33	22	43	30	53
Grand Total	146	249	125	336	233	536

Source: Foreign Agric. Serv. FN 1-76, U.S. Dep. Agric.

Although in California some pistachios are harvested by shaking the nuts from the trees onto canvas (Fig.14.6), most are harvested mechanically with conventional prune harvesting equipment consisting of a tree shaker or vibrator and a catching frame with a conveyor belt. The harvesters are in two separate units; one is the shaker, the other is the catching frame. Both are self-propelled and are positioned simultaneously on either side of the tree. Canvas shrouds deflect the nuts falling from the tree so that they are not lost or damaged in the shaker mechanism. The nuts roll down the canvas apron of the catching frame to a collector belt which conveys them past a primary cleaner and deleafer before they are dumped into bins for transportation to the processing plant. Two men operating these machines harvest about one acre of trees per hour.

Courtesy of Julian C. Crane

FIG. 14.6. HARVESTING PISTACHIO NUTS FROM
10-YEAR-OLD "KERMAN" TREES, BY SHAKING NUTS WITH
BOOM ONTO CANVAS

A preliminary study by Crane and Dunning (1975) indicated that mechanical harvesting has the potential for aid in the separation of blanks from good nuts and consequently eliminates needless handling. A force sufficient to remove the good nuts from the trees leaves most of the blanks attached.

DEHULLING PISTACHIO NUTS

The hulls of the freshly harvested pistachio nuts slip off fairly easily. In Iran the hulls are manually removed at this stage. If the nuts have been dried in-hull for storage, they are soaked in water for a short time to ease removal of the hulls. In Turkey, removal of hulls is accomplished by rubbing the nuts with stone rollers, followed by separation of the nuts from the loose hulls by means of a kind of fanning mill. Occasionally, the hulls are removed by a man wearing rubber boots treading the nuts in a tank of water, followed by manually transferring and washing from one pail to another and back, until the nuts are free from hulls.

Early attempts in the United States to mechanize the hulling process by using unmodified almond or walnut hulling machines were not successful because of breakage of shells, failure to dehull a large percentage of the nuts, and excessive losses otherwise. Subsequent experimentation indicated that abrasive vegetable peeling machines were suitable for dehulling the nuts both in the fresh state immediately after

TABLE 14.7
PISTACHIOS: EXPORTS FROM TURKEY
(METRIC TONS)

Country of Destination	Calendar Year					
	1969	1970	1971	1972	1973	1974
IN-SHELL						
United States	1,630	3,034	3,280	3,112	4,212	1,049
Europe (total)	6	39	21	48	81	88
Other Countries	10	6	1	38	98	14
Grand total	1,646	3,079	3,302	3,198	4,391	1,151
SHELLED						
United States	80	37	590	207	158	16
Europe						
France	14	23	21	17	24	7
Germany, West	101	62	113	67	106	24
Switzerland	18	11	22	70	29	11
Other	21	9	8	8	16	3
Total	154	105	164	162	175	45
Other Countries						
Lebanon	–	98	6	5	72	12
Syria	–	–	–	–	92	101
Other	2	12	3	81	11	11
Total	2	110	9	86	175	124
Grand total	236	252	763	455	508	185

Source: Foreign Agric. Serv. FN 1-76, U.S. Dep. Agric.

harvest, or after drying in the hull (Bloch and Brekke 1960). The machine, a basic potato peeler, consists of an upright cylinder coated on the inside with an abrasive; the bottom of the cylinder is a rapidly revolving, undulated disc, also coated with an abrasive. The nuts to be dehulled are thrown by centrifugal force of the rotating disc against the abrasive wall surface, while a stream of water introduced from the top washes the nuts and flushes the disintegrated hulls through an outlet of the machine. This type of machine produces an attractive product, particularly when freshly harvested nuts are dehulled in it; nuts that have been dried in the hull before dehulling have shells that are stained and unattractive. They are dyed to hide discoloration.

The abrasive vegetable peelers are limited to dehulling a batch of nuts at a time and are not adaptable to dehulling the large volumes of pistachios that will be forthcoming in the near future. For that reason and for greater efficiency, attention has been focused on the development of machines that produce large volumes of dehulled nuts continuously. Walnut dehulling machines employing revolving discs and designed for continuous operation have been modified and now work satisfactorily on pistachios. Another type of machine consists of two

Courtesy of U.S. Dept. Agric.

FIG. 14.7. COMMERCIAL SIZE ABRASIVE MACHINE FOR
DEHULLING PISTACHIO NUTS

Courtesy of U.S. Dept. Agric.

FIG. 14.8. SMALL ABRASIVE PEELING MACHINE FOR
DEHULLING PISTACHIO NUTS

parallel rubberized belts rotating in the same direction, one faster than the other. The nuts are fed in between the belts, which are adjustable, and emerge dehulled at the opposite end into a tank containing water where they are washed and those with split shells separated from the unsplits.

SEPARATING SPLIT AND UNSPLIT NUTS

At the time of harvest, the shells of a large proportion of pistachio nuts are split at the suture at the apical end. The demand is for split pistachios and much time and labor are spent in the middle eastern countries to separate manually the split from the unsplit nuts.

The kernels of unsplit pistachio nuts are usually not fully developed; a high percentage are shriveled or empty. The ratio of meat to shells and the 100-kernel weight is, therefore, lower than split pistachios.

When immersed in water, most of the dehulled, dried pistachio nuts in-shell floated, regardless of whether they were split or unsplit. If, however, immediately after the abrasive dehulling operation, the wet nuts were discharged into water, all unsplit nuts floated and 60 to 80% of the split nuts sank. Determination of the apparent specific gravity of sinkers and floaters indicated a sufficient difference in the specific gravities of split and unsplit pistachio nuts to make a separation procedure possible:

Pistachio Nuts In-Shell, Dried to 4% Moisture

	Sinkers (All Split)	Floaters Split	Floaters Unsplit
Specific gravity	1.09	1.09	0.625
Weight of 100 nuts (g)	125	120	90
% Meat	55.7	55.2	37.5

The specific gravity is determined by means of a 100-ml glass cylinder as pycnometer and toluene as displacement liquid. A small copper screen, tared with the cylinder, keeps floating nuts submerged. The specific gravities of pistachio nutmeat and of the shells were as follows:

	Specific Gravity
Nutmeat (3.1% moisture)	0.97
Shells (6.8% moisture)	1.22

Calculation of the specific gravity of split nuts from the proportions and specific gravities of the components (meat and shells) gave a value of 1.09, the same as determined; however, for the unsplit nuts, the specific gravity calculated from the components figured 1.13, compared to the determined specific gravity of 0.625. It is only the enclosed air that makes pistachio nuts float on water. This is indeed shown when, by application of a vacuum under water, the air is drawn out from the unsplit nuts through the shells; after the vacuum is broken, both the unsplit and split nuts sink. When pistachio nuts dried in-hull are allowed to absorb moisture during the abrasive dehulling, the apparent specific gravity is again found to be 1.09 for the split nuts and 0.63 for unsplit; thus a separation based on the difference in apparent specific gravities is not dependent on the moisture content of the nuts at levels reached during abrasive dehulling of nuts dried in-hull after the harvest. However, when freshly harvested pistachio nuts, which as a rule show a moisture content of 35 to 45%, are subjected to abrasive dehulling, and subsequently are discharged into water, a different kind of separation takes place; a portion of the unsplit nuts sinks with the split nuts. This behavior is discussed below.

The expulsion of air from split pistachio nuts immersed in water was accomplished by application of centrifugal force. Pistachio nuts were immersed in water and centrifuged on a laboratory centrifuge in 200-ml cups for 2 min at 1000 rpm; the split nuts sank while the unsplit nuts floated. Similar results with 94 to 96% separation efficiencies were realized with a 17-in. basket centrifuge equipped with 1500 rpm drive.

A high-speed stirrer removed the air entrapped in the split pistachio nuts as effectively as a centrifuge, provided the nuts were protected by a screen from being broken by the impact of the propeller.

The separation of split from unsplit nuts is done preferably following the dehulling process; the separation works in different ways, depending on whether the nuts are dehulled immediately after harvest or after drying in-hull.

Freshly harvested pistachio nuts, dehulled in the abrasive machine, are discharged through the discharge gate of the peeling machine into the tank with stirrer described above. All split nuts and the full unsplit nuts sink. The floaters are unsplits only, with less than 15% meat content. The floaters are scooped off, and the sinkers are removed by lifting the basket. The two fractions were dried on trays at 35° to 37.5°C (95° to 100°F).

In order to separate the sinkers into split and unsplit nuts, the dried sinkers are subjected to a re-separation with the same equipment by agitation in water for about 6 min. After the agitation is discontinued, the nuts are allowed to separate into floaters and sinkers. The floaters are practically 100% unsplits, the sinkers, practically 100% splits.

DRYING THE NUTS

In order to prevent spoiling, the pistachio nuts must be dried immediately after harvest. The dehulling (and separation of split pistachio nuts from unsplit nuts) may precede the drying, or the dried pistachio nuts may be stored in-hull until processed further. The advantage of drying and storing in-hull is the lessened possibility of insect damage and relief of the work load at harvest time. On the other hand, one drying operation is omitted when dehulling takes place immediately after harvest, and there is no staining of the shells.

Pistachio nuts are dried, with forced air at 35° to 37.5°C (95° to 100°F). The moisture content of freshly harvested nuts, with up to 45%, was reduced to 5% in about 18 hours.

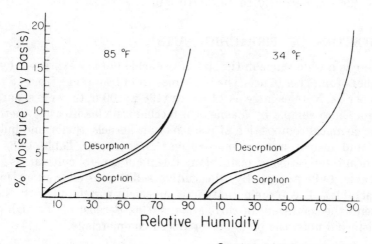

Courtesy of U.S. Dept. Agric.

FIG. 14.9. MOISTURE EQUILIBRIUM CURVES OF PISTACHIO
NUTMEATS

GRADING THE NUTS

Improvements in grading technology for the nut industry as a whole have taken place in the last few years. Several equipment companies manufacture electric-eye sorters that have the capability of removing pistachio nuts with blemishes and of color sorting them as well. The walnut and pecan industries have used these machines successfully for several years with excellent performance characteristics and efficiency of operation. After the nuts are sorted they are graded into four sizes in a squirrel cage sizer. Until salted, roasted and packaged, the nuts are held in cold storage.

SALTING AND ROASTING IN-SHELL NUTS

About 90% of all pistachios reach the consumer salted and roasted in-shell for "snack" consumption. The balance is nutmeats sold for commercial uses such as flavoring, confectionery and ice cream. The nuts are salted by passing them rapidly through a saturated brine solution. Roasting temperatures above 121°C (250°F) bring about darkening of the kernels; for this reason it is advisable not to expose the nuts to roasting temperatures when the moisture content is high. Bloch and Brekke (1960) obtained good results with the following roasting schedule: the salted nuts were dried in a rotary-screen drier at 71.1°C (160°F) for 30 min, until the moisture taken up by the salting was removed. Then the temperature was raised during a 30-min period to 120°C (248°F) and held there for 10 min.

PROPERTIES OF PISTACHIO NUTS

There is a wide range in the size of pistachio nuts as expressed by the number of nuts per ounce. The pistachios from Iran range from 18 to 40 nuts per oz. Nuts as large as 14 per oz (198 g/100 nuts) were separated from a Chico sample by means of a mechanical classification method.

The chemical composition of pistachio nut kernels, shells, and hulls of split and unsplit nuts of one cultivar is shown in Table 14.8. The chemical composition of pistachio nutmeats of several cultivars is given in Table 14.9. Apparently, the cultivars differ in oil content (ether extractable). The protein content is inversely correlated with the oil content; the coefficient of correlation is 0.96. Because of the high price of pistachio nuts, the oil is not produced commercially.

TABLE 14.8
COMPOSITION OF PISTACHIO NUT KERNELS, SHELLS, AND HULLS
RED ALEPPO CULTIVAR, 1957 CROP (%, DRY BASIS)

	Kernels		Shells		Hulls	
	Split Nuts	Unsplit Nuts	Split Nuts	Unsplit Nuts	Split Nuts	Unsplit Nuts
Protein N × 6.25	19.41	19.58	0.42	1.06	7.66	9.35
Oil, ether extractable	58.3	54.7	0.56	0.58	7.82	8.27
Crude fiber	1.74	2.19	54.0	53.4	14.1	17.4
Ash	2.95	3.55	0.42	1.06	15.56	13.30
Calcium	0.13	0.13	0.06	0.06	0.07	0.25
Potassium	1.04	1.22	0.22	0.49	6.71	5.88
Phosphorus	0.54	0.64	0.02	0.04	0.12	0.24

Source: Bloch and Brekke (1960).

Courtesy of Calif. Assoc. of Pistachio Producers

FIG. 14.10. GROVE OF PISTACHIO NUTS IN CALIFORNIA

TABLE 14.9
COMPOSITION OF PISTACHIO NUTMEAT FROM SPLIT NUTS (%, DRY BASIS)

	Red Aleppo			Kerman		Trabonella		Bronte
	1956	1957	1958	1956	1958	1956	1958	1956
Protein (N × 6.25)	23.00	19.41	21.56	26.75	28.88	24.25	24.13	24.81
Oil, ether extractable	54.4	58.3	58.0	50.6	48.3	54.6	55.7	53.2
Crude fiber	1.81	1.74	1.65	2.11	1.93	1.74	1.97	2.11
Ash	3.34	2.95	3.18	2.95	3.50	2.90	2.85	3.03
Phosphorus	0.57	0.54	0.56	0.54	0.64	0.50	0.49	0.55
Calcium	0.14	0.13	0.16	0.11	0.10	0.18	0.11	0.18
Magnesium	0.17	–	–	0.15	–	0.17	–	0.18
Potassium	1.07	1.04	1.17	0.93	1.18	0.86	1.06	0.92
Total sugar (as sucrose)[1]	7.2	–	7.5	8.4	7.9	6.1	6.2	6.4

Source: Bloch and Brekke (1960).
[1] Paper chromatography showed sucrose and raffinose present in about equal proportion.

USES OF PISTACHIO NUTS

The most popular form of pistachio nuts is roasted and salted in the shell. These are often colored red, or white. Some are shelled, roasted and salted. Products containing pistachios include ice cream, confections, bakery goods and meat dishes.

Mandarin Chocolate Tarts

1 roll refrigerated cookies	1½ tsp orange extract
1 pkg chocolate frost and	1 cup chopped pistachio
fill frosting mix	nuts
3 tbsp brandy flavoring	Mandarin orange segments

Slice cookie dough ⅛ in. thick. Place paper baking cups over back of muffin cups or custard cups. Arrange three cookie slices on each cup with edges overlapping and about half of the round extending beyond the bottom edge of the cup. Let stand at room temperature about 15 min or until cookies soften. Press to seal where cookies overlap and mold down over sides of cup slightly. Bake at 176.6°C (350°F) for 10 to 12 min until golden brown. Cool. Remove paper liners. Prepare frost and fill as directed on package. Fold in brandy flavoring and orange extract. Spoon into cookie shells. Garnish with garland of pistachio nuts around an orange segment. Chill 1 to 3 hours before serving. Yields 20 to 24 tarts.

Holiday Salad with Pistachios

2 cups fresh cranberries	2 tbsp cold water
1 orange, sliced	½ cup seedless grapes
1 cup water	1 cup diced celery
¾ cup sugar	¼ cup chopped pistachio nuts
1 tbsp gelatin	

Cook cranberries, orange, water and sugar together until cranberry skins open. Put through fine sieve. Soften gelatin in cold water and dissolve in hot cranberry mixture. Chill until slightly thickened. Pour a thin layer of mixture into bottom of ring mold and arrange grapes in circle to form topping. Fold celery and nuts into remaining mixture and add to ring mold. Surround ring with cream cheese balls rolled in parsley; sprinkle with paprika. Serve with mayonnaise or French dressing. Serves 6.

Imperial Pistachio Gourmet Pie

2 pkg (1 lb) brown-and-serve sausage links
4 leeks or 8 green onions
Boiling salt water
Pastry for 2 crust 9 in. pie
2 tbsp butter
2 tbsp flour
Salt to taste
Dash freshly ground white pepper
½ cup heavy cream or evaporated milk
1 tbsp horseradish
½ cup pine nuts or pistachio nuts, chopped
Nutmeg

Cut sausage in ½ in. slices, and sauté until brown. Put aside. Cut leeks in 1 in.

lengths and split. Cover with water and cook until tender. Drain, reserving 1 cup liquid. Line 9-in. pie pan with crust. Make sauce using butter, flour, liquid, seasonings and cream. Add leeks, horseradish and nuts with sausage. Pour into shell, adjust top crust, prick; sprinkle with nutmeg. Bake in hot oven of 217°C (425° F) for ½ hour, or until golden brown. Serves 6 to 8.

Almond-Pistachio Nougat

1 cup sugar	2 egg whites
½ cup water	2½ cups almonds
½ cup strained honey	½ cup pistachio nuts
3 tbsp light corn syrup	1 tsp vanilla

Blanch almonds and pistachio nuts and shred them coarsely. Brown almonds slightly in oven. Cook sugar, water and one-half of corn syrup together, stirring until sugar is dissolved. Continue cooking to the temperature 198°C (290°F). Remove from fire. Add the syrup gradually to the egg whites which have been beaten stiff, continuing the beating during the addition.

While adding the syrup to the eggs, begin cooking honey and remainder of corn syrup together, and cook until temperature of 198°C (290°F) is reached. Remove from heat and add to egg white mixture, pouring gradually and beating while adding. Add nuts and cook over hot water until mixture dries, stirring while cooking. To test candy take small amount on spoon. If it holds its shape when cold and is not sticky to the touch, it is done. Add vanilla; pour into pans which have been lined with nougat wafers, and cover with nougat wafers. Place a board or pan over the top of the candy and press with a heavy weight for 12 hours. Remove candy from pan and cut into pieces. Wrap in waxed paper. Yield, 48 pieces.

Pistachio Frosting

½ cup butter or margarine
5 cups confectioners' sugar
4 to 5 tsp milk
¼ tsp almond flavoring
Pistachio nuts
Green food coloring

Cream butter or margarine. Add sugar gradually, while creaming. Add just enough milk to make frosting easy to spread. Add almond flavoring. Tint pale green with food coloring. Yield: enough to fill and frost top and sides of 10-in., 2-layer cake. Fill in pattern with pistachio nuts.

Rice With Fennel

½ cup rice	¼ cup raisins
½ tsp fennel seed	¼ cup orange flower water
3 cups light cream	3 tbsp chopped pistachio nuts
1 cup sugar	

Put rice and fennel seed in container of electric blender and blend until rice is consistency of coarse salt. In a heavy, deep sauce pan, bring cream to a boil. Add rice and fennel seed and cook, stirring constantly, for 3 to 4 min. Add sugar and raisins and continue cooking and stirring until mixture is consistency of custard. Add orange flower water and cook another 2 min. Pour into a 1-qt casserole and sprinkle with pistachios. Refrigerate before serving. Yields 6 to 8 servings.

REFERENCES

ANAGNOSTOPOULOS, P.T. 1938. The enemies of hazelnut, chestnut and pistachio nut trees. Hort. Res. (Greece) *4*, 499-558.

ANON. 1976. Tree Nuts. Foreign Agric. Serv. TN 1-76, U.S. Dep. Agric.

BLOCH, F., and BREKKE, J.E. 1960. Processing of pistachio nuts. Econ. Bot. *14*, 129-144.

BRADLEY, M.V., and CRANE, J.C. 1975. Abnormalities in seed development in *Pistacia vera* L. J. Amer. Soc. Hort. Sci. *100*, 461-464.

CRANE, J.C., and NELSON, M.M. 1971. The unusual mechanism of alternate bearing in the pistachio. HortScience *6*, 489-490.

CRANE, J.C., BRADLEY, M.V., and NELSON, M.M. 1971. Growth of seeded and seedless pistachio nuts. J. Amer. Soc. Hort. Sci. *96*, 78-80.

CRANE, J.C., and NELSON, M.M. 1972. Effects of crop load, girdling, and auxin application on alternate bearing of the pistachio. J. Amer. Soc. Hort. Sci. *97*, 337-339.

CRANE, J.C. 1973. Parthenocarpy—a factor contributing to the production of blank pistachios. HortScience *8*, 388-390.

CRANE, J.C., AL-SHALAN, I., and CARLSON, R.M. 1973. Abscission of pistachio inflorescence buds as affected by leaf area and number of nuts. J. Amer. Soc. Hort. Sci. *98*, 591-592.

CRANE, J.C., and AL-SHALAN, I. M. 1974. Physical and chemical changes associated with growth of the pistachio nut. J. Amer. Soc. Hort. Sci. *99*, 87-89.

CRANE, J.C., and FORDE, H.I., 1974. Improved *Pistacia* seed germination. Calif. Agric. *28*, 8-9.

CRANE, J.C., FORDE, H.I. and DANIEL, C. 1974. Pollen longevity in *Pistacia*. Calif. Agric. *28*, 8-9.

CRANE, J.C. 1975. The role of seed abortion and parthenocarpy in the production of blank pistachio nuts as affected by rootstock. J. Amer. Soc. Hort. Sci. *100*, 267-270.

CRANE, J.C., and DUNNING, J.J. 1975. Separation of blank pistachio nuts by mechanical harvesting. Calif. Agric. *29*, 6-7.

CRANE, J.C., and FORDE, H.I. 1976. Effects of four rootstocks on yield and quality of pistachio nuts. J. Amer. Soc. Hort. Sci. *101*, 604-606.

CRANE, J.C., CATLIN, P.B., and AL-SHALAN, I. 1976. Carbohydrate levels in the pistachio as related to alternate bearing. J. Amer. Soc. Hort. Sci. *101*, 371-374.

GRUNDWAG, J., and FAHN, A. 1969. The relation of embryology to the low seed set in *Pistacia vera* (Anacardiaceae). Phytomorphology *19*, 225-235.

JOLEY, L.E., and WHITEHOUSE, W.E. 1953. Root knott nematode susceptibility—a factor in the selection of pistachio nut rootstocks. Proc. Amer. Soc. Hort. Sci. *61*, 99-102.

JOLEY, L.E. 1969. Pistachio. *In* Handbook of North American Nut Trees. R.A. Jaynes (Editor).The W.F. Humphrey Press, Geneva, N. Y.

KAMANGAR, T., and FARSAM, H. 1977. Composition of pistachio kernels of various Iranian origins. J. Food Sci. *42*, 4, 1135-1136.

KOUYEAS, V. 1952. The footrot of pistachio tree *(Pistachia vera)*. Ann. Inst. Phytopath., Benaki *6*, 81-87.

KREUTZBERG, V.E. 1940. A new virus disease of *Pistacia vera*. USSR, C.R. Acad. Sci. *27*, 614-615.

MAAS, J.L., VAN DER ZWET, T., and MADDEN, G. 1971. A severe septoria leaf spot of pistachio nut trees new to the United States. Plant Disease Reporter *55*, 72-76.

URIU, K., and CRANE, J. C. 1976. Mineral element changes in pistachio leaves. J. Amer. Soc. Hort. Sci. 102, 155-158.

WHITEHOUSE, W. E. 1957. The pistachio nut—a new crop for the Western United States. Econ. Bot. *11*, 281-321.

ZOHARY, M. 1952. A monographical study of the genus *Pistacia*. Palestine J. Bot., Jerusalem Ser. *5*, 187-228.

15

Black Walnuts

The genus *Juglans,* including about 15 native species, comprises woody plants with handsome foliage and mostly edible nuts. The four species in order of importance for edible nuts are: *J. regia,* Persian, English, or California walnut; *J. nigra,* American black walnut; *J. sieboldiana,* Japanese walnut and heartnut; *J. cinera,* butternut or American white walnut. None of the cultivars requires cross-pollination.

Black walnut trees (*J. nigra*), among the noblest of the American forests, are grown for the handsome foliage, superior quality wood, and edible nuts. They are grown from Massachusetts to Florida, and west to Minnesota and Texas.

HISTORY

Black walnuts were an important food item to the American Indians, colonial Americans, and countless frontier herds of swine. Black walnut kernels contributed considerably to the making of candy, ice cream and breads by early Americans. Harvesting and cracking the walnuts provided food, employment and income for hundreds of families throughout the eastern half of the United States, particularly Tennessee, Kentucky and other states of the Appalachian region. Millions of wild trees produced nuts which, when stored properly, could be used for food practically year-round.

The Northern Nut Growers Association has been instrumental for more than 66 years in (a) encouraging farmers and research workers to locate and propagate superior black walnut seedlings; (b) establishing walnut shelling plants throughout the area where they are grown; and (c) utilizing the nuts in foods.

One of the cultivars best known is the Stabler. The kernels come out of the shell easily, usually in unbroken halves. Some of the kernels come out

FIG. 15.1. NATIVE RANGE OF BLACK WALNUTS

in one piece whole. The parent tree, located about 20 miles north of Washington, D.C., was 12 ft in circumference, had a limb spread of 75 ft (in 1915 when it was 60 years old), and bore as many as 16 bu of nuts in one year. Other famous, old black walnut trees may be found throughout the Appalachian area.

CULTURE

Black walnut trees are very sensitive to soil conditions, requiring a deep, well-drained, nearly neutral soil with a generous supply of moisture and nutrient material for best growth. Trees make poor growth on wet bottomlands, or on sandy, dry ridges and slopes. Walnut trees are common on limestone soils and do especially well on deep loams, loess soils, and fertile alluvial deposits. Most good agricultural soils in the eastern United States are favorable sites for walnut planting.

Abundant crops are produced irregularly, perhaps twice in five years. Well-spaced trees produce a crop in 8 years, and continue for more than 100 years. About 15 cultivars having outstanding qualities are propagated by budding and grafting. Most of the selections were from seedlings that originated from nuts buried by squirrels in the fall. The preferred burying and storage spots appear to be the places where walnut seedlings have the best chance to survive. These are in natural openings in the forest or grassy areas on the forest fringe. Normal freezing and thawing usually cause the seed to break dormancy the following spring, but germination is often delayed.

Under nursery conditions the nuts may be stratified (buried in a layer of nuts and a layer of sand or peat moss) in the fall and planted in the early spring. If the seeds are never allowed to dry out they will germinate within two months after planting, or as soon as the soil becomes warm. If they are allowed to dry, they may not germinate for another year; in the meantime many will rot.

Seedlings emerge in April or May, and may grow 3 ft the first year, and double this in the second growing season. On deep, rich loamy soil walnut trees may grow 2 or 3 ft each succeeding year. Height growth begins rather slowly in the spring, reaches a peak in May, and is essentially complete by July. In general, the trees lose the leaves early in the fall, before the nuts drop. The trees mature in about 100 years, but may live and produce nuts for 250 years. By this time, they may have a height of 150 ft and a diameter of 6 ft. Most walnut trees are cut for lumber before they reach full size.

Regardless of the season or method of planting used, careful choice of planting site is imperative. The most suitable places for planting walnuts is along streams, at the base of slopes, or in coves.

Walnuts seldom grow well in pure stands. There seems to be an antagonism between walnuts and many other plants which excludes some species from the root zone of walnuts. This has been attributed to a toxic substance, possibly juglone, which is present in the roots and other parts of the plant.

Actual contact with the walnut roots apparently is necessary before the associated plants are harmed. Most tree species appear to be immune, yet walnut seedlings do not persist under or adjacent to established trees. In many cases, this condition cannot be explained satisfactorily by competition for light and moisture. It is quite possible that walnut seedlings also are affected by the toxic substance (Brinkman 1957). See Walnut Toxicity, p. 625.

Disease and Pests

Black walnuts have few important insect enemies. The most serious is the walnut caterpillar (*Datana intergerrima*) which is distributed over much of the United States. Heavily infested trees may suffer some loss of current growth by defoliation, but trees seldom are killed by defoliation alone.

Damaged or weakened trees or trees on poor sites are particularly susceptible to European canker, caused by *Nectria galligena*. Although infected trees eventually die, the rate of spread is quite slow. Apparently the disease is less important on exposed sites than in moist locations.

The trees are quite wind-firm and not easily damaged by ice or windstorms. The thick bark and naturally durable heartwood make walnut trees resistant to damage and decay following fires.

Cultivars

More than 100 cultivars of black walnuts have been selected through the years. The Thomas, Ohio and Stabler cultivars were thought worthy of recommendation for general planting by the Northern Nut Growers Association in 1926. Several thousand grafted trees were planted in widely scattered locations east of the Mississippi River, and a few west of it.

The Thomas is a vigorous grower, sometimes growing 7 ft per year. Ten pounds of meats of unusual excellence may be cracked from a bushel of nuts, with 90% of them unbroken quarters.

FIG. 15.2 STAMBAUGH BLACK WALNUT—A GOOD CRACKING
CULTIVAR BUT NOT VERY HARDY TO COLD

Cultivars grown in specific states are: Pennsylvania—Ohio, Stabler, Ten Eyck, Thomas; Missouri—Stabler, Bowser, Peanuts, Thorp, Seward Berhow, Hines, Mintle, Scringer, Vanderstoot; Michigan—Somers, NCI, Fately, Harrison, McDermid, Breslan, Jacobs, Watts (Zarger 1956).

HARVESTING AND SHELLING

The large, distinctly flavored nuts ripen in September and October, and are much sought after in southern markets. The wild nuts furnish food for red squirrels, eastern gray squirrels, eastern fox squirrels, red-bellied woodpeckers and white-tailed deer. Cows will eat the green hulls and crack many of them for the meats. Pigs relish walnuts. The distinctive flavor of black walnuts is not impaired by cooking. This renders them especially suitable for bakery items, confections, salting and use in salads and desserts.

Harvesting wild nuts is done by allowing them to drop to the ground and gathering by hand. Where the trees are planted in rows and the topography of the land and condition of the soil is suitable, they may be harvested mechanically, like Persian walnuts. This consists of shaking the trees, windrowing the nuts, and harvesting by sweeping them onto large "dust pans." (See Figs. 15.3–15.8.)

Courtesy of Gould Bros., Inc.

FIG. 15.3.   SHAKER HEADS FOR MEDIUM SIZE AND
VERY LARGE NUT TREES

Courtesy of Gould Bros., Inc.

FIG. 15.4.   CLOSE-UP OF THE "BEAN BAG" CUSHION ON THE
JAWS OF THE SHAKER TO PREVENT BRUISING OF THE TREES

Courtesy of Gould Bros., Inc.

FIG. 15.5 SHAKER FOR VERY LARGE NUT TREES

Shown here is a native pecan tree 4 ft in diameter.

Courtesy of Gotcher Engineering and Machine Co.

FIG. 15.6 SWEEPER FOR WINDROWING NUTS

The 6 ft wide unit utilizes rubber fingers rotating on angled auger. A sensitive hydraulic control and adustable gage wheels provide finger-tip control.

FIG. 15.7. NUT SWEEPER FOR WINDROWING FALLEN
WALNUTS IN PREPARATION FOR MECHANICAL HARVESTER

FIG. 15.8. SWEEP-TYPE MACHINE SWEEPING WALNUTS
INTO WINDROWS

Shelling

Before about 1945, when the mechanical sheller made mass processing economically practical, most farmers gathered a few bushels of walnuts for their own use and left the rest for squirrels. Tedious hand labor in removing the hulls, cracking the shells, and picking out the meats was not worth the bother commercially.

One of the country's biggest black walnut processors operating today (there are only six large ones) is the Hammons Products Company of Stockton, Missouri. The company shells more than 15,000,000 lb in good crop years. Walnuts from Missouri, Arkansas, Tennessee, Kentucky, Ohio and West Virginia are shelled here.

Courtesy of American Plywood Association

FIG. 15.9. FORKLIFT, TOTE-BOXES HOLDING 1500 LB
OF IN-SHELL NUTS ARE RAPIDLY REPLACING BAGS

The boxes are made of plywood, fiberwood or steel wire mesh

The company's chief concern is to recover and market the kernels (10% of the hulled nuts). The kernels are graded for size, stored in 15 refrigerated warehouses across the nation, and handled by 75 food brokers.

Black walnut meats are shipped in bulk throughout the country to ice cream plants, bakeries, confectioners, wholesale grocers, packagers and brokers. Bad kernels are fed to hogs and the shells are pulverized and sold for a variety of industrial uses (Hammons 1954).

Black walnut kernels are sold in four sizes: large fancy, in cellophane bags, glass or vacuum tins; large medium, for candy and topping; regular medium, for cookies; and small, for ice cream and bakery products.

To maintain natural color and flavor, black walnuts should be shelled within two weeks after harvest. The following are desirable characteristics: plump kernels, light colored kernels (dark kernels are thrown out); thin shells; large nuts; and dryness (less than 3% moisture).

About three-fourths of black walnut kernels are sold for Thanksgiving and Christmas holidays. The remainder are cold-stored for distribution to bakers and confectioners throughout the year.

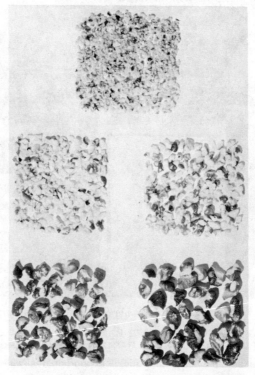

Courtesy of Hammons Products Co.

FIG. 15.10. BLACK WALNUT KERNELS, ACTUAL SIZE

(a) Fancy large; (b) large medium for candy and topping; (c) regular medium for bakery goods; (d) ice cream size and for bakers.

Use of Shells.—Since a black walnut is 90% shell, accumulation at cracking plants creates a disposal problem for shellers. Of this waste the shells can be ground into flour with commercial possibilities. The process includes preliminary reduction in size by hammermilling, then grinding by attrition milling, and finally fractionation by air separation. A satisfactory flour is produced, but tailings from the operation are difficult to convert to flour economically.

Walnut shell flour is successfully used in plastic moulding powder. It compares favorably with wood flour as a filler for certain mixes, and excels in resistance to moisture absorption and flow properties. The flour may be used as a glue extender. Coarsely ground shell waste has certain other industrial applications (Zarger 1956).

A wide range of industrial applications has been found. The shells are reduced to three sizes by hammermill. The finest is face powder texture; one size is granular—like salt; and the third is like small grain. Shell added to drilling mud seals off underground cavities and prevents loss of mud used to keep the drill from overheating. The cracks are sealed off by virtue of the sharp edges retained by walnut shell particles through grinding, causing them to build up. Rounded particles of the coarser sizes are used as a propping agent in fracturing oil wells.

FIG. 15.11. LEFT, BOWL MADE OF BLACK WALNUT WOOD;
REAR, BASKET MADE OF WALNUT SHELLS; RIGHT,
"SQUIRREL" MADE OF WALNUTS; FOREGROUND, BLACK
WALNUTS

Ground walnut shells are used to sand blast jet engines. They clean away carbon and other residue, but unlike sand, they do not cut the metal. Motor car manufacturers use powdered shells for polishing, burnishing, and deburring metal parts and for cleaning foundry molds. They are also used for polishing and finishing a variety of products ranging from fountain pen parts to typewriter parts.

Another use is to spray ground shells and other ingredients on car or truck tires to provide traction on muddy or icy surfaces. The substance is said to cling to the tires briefly, just long enough to overcome the impasse (Anon. 1962).

USES OF BLACK WALNUTS

Black walnuts are considered superior to most nuts for candies, ice cream and some cakes. Because of the characteristic flavor, texture and color added to these products by black walnuts, the demand for the kernels exceeds the supply.

Most of the recipes for pecan meats and Persian walnut kernels work equally well for black walnuts. However, the black walnut flavor is more distinctive.

When black walnut meats are as cheap as those of other nutmeats, their use in ice cream increases. They are used not only in regular black walnut ice cream, but in other flavors as well, such as banana nut, caramel nut, date nut and combinations.

From 220 lb of black walnuts a commercial sheller may expect slightly more than 15 lb of salable, top grade kernels. The other 205 lb is made up of about 1 lb of salable ambers, 132 lb of finished shells, and the other 72 lb of water, waste and nonusable kernels.

The biggest need in the industry is a steady supply of nuts, most of which are from unplanted and uncultivated trees. There is a tremendous potential export market if an annual supply were available.

Until about 1930, sale of black walnut kernels was almost strictly a pre-Christmas luxury to be used in cakes, cookies and holiday candies. The main reason for this was lack of a suitable method, other than heat, to sterilize, or otherwise kill the yeast, mold, *E. coli* and other bacteria on the kernels. With the discovery of suitable sterilization methods, and the availability of refrigerated storage, ice cream plants, bakers and confectioners found that they could make black walnut ice cream year-round; and consumer packages became generally available on the market (Hammond 1971).

Black Walnut Recipes

Black Walnut Cake

	Home	Commercial
Sugar	1½ cups	9 lb
Butter	½ cup	3 lb
Flour	2 cups	6 lb
Baking powder	1 tsp	¼ cup
Small black walnut pieces	1 cup	3 lb
Egg whites	4	48

Cream butter and gradually add the sugar, creaming until light and fluffy. Sift together the baking powder and flour. Add it alternately with the water to the creamed mixture. Carefully fold in the nuts and then the beaten egg whites. Bake in layer pans for 30 to 35 min in a 176°C (350°F) oven.

Elegant Black Walnut Pound Cake

1 cup butter	1 tbsp baking powder
2 cups sugar	1 cup milk or cream
4 eggs	1 tsp vanilla
3 cups sifted flour	1 cup finely chopped black walnuts

Grease 9-in. tube pan, line bottom with foil. Cream butter, gradually add sugar, and cream until light and fluffy. Add eggs, one at a time, beating well after each addition. Sift together dry ingredients and fold in alternately with milk and vanilla. Fold in nuts. Spoon into pan. Bake in moderate oven, 176°C (350°F), 1¼ hours, or until done. Cool in pan; remove and sieve confectioners' sugar over the top. This cake does not need an icing. However, a thin buttercream icing may be used. Makes 12 to 16 servings. The cake improves in flavor and is more moist if stored several days in a tightly covered container.

Source: Nancy Carter's Cook Book, C.B.S. Homemaker Series.

Chewy Brown Sugar Cakes

2 cups brown sugar	½ lb butter
2 cups flour	1 tsp vanilla
2 cups black walnuts	Pinch of salt

Cream butter and sugar. Add other ingredients and blend well. Pour into a buttered and floured cake pan. Allow space for rising. Bake in a 176°C (350°F) oven until golden brown—about 30 min. Cut into squares and place on wax paper until cold.

REFERENCES

ANON. 1962. Hammond turns walnuts into dollars. Peanut J. and Nut World *42* (1) 40-42.

BAILEY, L.H. 1935. The Standard Cyclopedia of Horticulture: Macmillan, New York.

BRINKMAN, K.A. 1957. Silvical characteristics of black walnut. Forest. Serv. Cen. States For. Exp. Stn. Miscel. Release *22*. U.S. Dep. Agric.

HAMMOND, D. 1971. Problems in commercial processing of black walnuts. Nor. Nut Growers Assoc. 62nd Annu. Rep. 58-62. Knoxville, Tenn.

HAMMONS, R.E. 1954. Machine shelling walnuts. Peanut J. and Nut World *33*, 4, 44-45.

ZARGER, T.G. 1956. Tree crop investigations in the Tennessee Valley. Northern Nut Grow. Assoc. 47th Annu. Rep. 57-68.

16

Persian Walnuts[1]

In the time of Solomon the Persian walnut (*Juglans regia*) was widely cultivated for its fruit in the Orient. It was called "one of the noblest of trees," and is now cultivated everywhere in the higher parts of the region, usually in woods, near watercourses, and by the village fountains and wells, for its delicious nuts and valuable timber. Native seedlings grow extensively in the Himalayan Mountains of India.

Although not introduced into England until about 360 years ago, the walnut is now popular there and is commonly known as the "English" walnut. However, the name Persian is preferred because it indicates the area in which the species originated. It is widely cultivated in middle and southern Europe today, as well as in India and California. Its fruit is one of the most important of all present-day commercial nuts, world production being about 200,000 metric tons (in-shell basis) annually (Anon. 1976).

PRODUCTION IN AMERICA

Originally walnuts were planted mainly in the southern counties of California. Only 35% of all the bearing acreage was found in the areas north of the Tehachapi Mountains. Then the picture began to change and one of the most dramatic horticultural moves in history took place. Since that time the center of walnut production has shifted from the south central area to near Stockton.

Today less than 3% of the bearing acreage lies in the southern counties while more than 97% lies in the central and northern areas. There are less than 400 acres of walnuts in Los Angeles County now, and less than 10 acres in Orange County. Ventura County, which used to be the largest producer with 25,000 bearing acres in 1942, now has less than 1300.

---

[1]Revised by Julian C. Crane, Professor of Pomology, University of California, Davis (1977).

Reasons for the shift were many. Some southern California orchards became decadent and others were of low yielding cultivars; subdivisions moved rapidly into walnut-growing areas. Better growing sections, improved irrigation and pest control methods plus better cultivars were helping the spread to the north where greater yields were evident.

While over 95% of commercially grown walnut trees are in California, the neighboring states of Oregon and Washington also contribute somewhat less than 5% of the commercial walnut crop each year, the amount depending upon growing conditions and the resulting crop in each particular year. Plantings are concentrated in the Willamette Valley in Oregon and in southern Washington. Walnuts are grown in other states of the nation but are not of commercial importance.

Walnut production in Oregon reached a peak in 1949 when there were 30,000 acres (Lagerstedt 1974). A combination of factors since then, such as adverse weather conditions, blackline, poor crops, poor nut quality and low prices paid to growers, has brought about large reductions in acreage. A severe freeze in 1972 further reduced the acreage so that now it is estimated to be between 3000 and 5000 acres.

Carpathian Walnuts

Possiblilities for growing Persian walnuts in the northern United States have greatly improved since the introduction of hardy trees growing in the Carpathian Mountains of Poland. The trees will survive and produce good crops where winter temperatures dip to -35°C (-30°F). A suggested northern limit for growing Carpathians is a line running across New Hampshire, perhaps one-third the way up bending slightly south as it crosses Vermont, north across Maine.

Carpathians require cross-pollination, good air and water drainage, and a light, well-nourished, and nearly neutral soil (O'Rourke 1969).

WALNUT CULTURE

Soil Requirements

Walnuts do best on soils where roots can develop evenly to a depth of 9 to 12 ft. In addition to good topsoil, this means that subsoil must be free of rock, impervious clay, or layers of gravel.

Soil type alone is not sufficient to determine a satisfactory site for a walnut orchard. An auger, soil tube, or posthole digger should be used to check to a depth of 10 ft or so. A few feet beneath the surface may be found solid rock or compact subsoils with a mottled color indicating poor aeration and drainage. Besides affording few or no pores large enough for roots to enter, this kind of subsoil layer often supports a water layer that further restricts root growth. Some excellent surface soils are underlain by loose gravel and coarse sand with such large pore spaces that excessive aeration and drainage permit little or no root growth.

Unfortunately, not much can be done to improve unfavorable soil conditions. Blasting has not been effective. Often it merely increases the trouble by compacting the soil further. In a few cases "subsoiling" has helped where the impervious layer is not thick and is close to the surface, but generally this practice can not be recommended. If the orchard is already established and is declining because of subsoil problems, thinning the trees is about the only helpful practice.

Temperature Requirements

Walnut trees are sensitive to both low and high temperatures. High summer temperatures result in sunburning of the hulls and shriveled kernels. Some damage occurs at 38°C (100°F) and severe damage at 40° to 43°C (105° to 110°F) or higher. Considerable difference in tolerance to high temperatures exists among cultivars.

Low Temperatures

Walnut cultivars grown in California are not resistant to extremely low winter temperatures. When dormant they can tolerate -11° to -9°C (12° to 16°F) without serious injury. Thus, the California cultivars generally are not adapted to eastern United States or to mountain climates. They generally are restricted by winter temperatures to the coastal area, interior valley and foothill areas west of the Sierra Nevada and Cascade Mountain ranges in central and northern California and Oregon, and to parts of southern California and southwestern Arizona. Small acreages of Carpathian cultivars are growing in eastern Washington, eastern Oregon and Idaho.

Young Persian walnut trees which continue to grow into late fall, because of unseasonably warm temperatures, are subject to killing of the wood by frosts. A temperature of -9°C (16°F) on November 15, 1959, caused severe injury in most interior valley areas of California. Cultivars of the Eureka group were damaged most severely.

The amount of winter chilling needed to break the rest or dormant period is an important climatic factor that determines where walnuts may be grown satisfactorily. Cultivars of the Payne and Franquette types require 700 and 1500 hours, respectively, at or below 7°C (45°F). Unless these conditions are met, the results are seriously delayed bud opening, poor crops and dieback of branches. Franquette and other cultivars of the French race are so severely delayed that it is not practical to grow them in the coastal section of southern California.

Cultivars of Walnuts

After having determined that a site is satisfactory for growing walnuts, the next step is to decide what cultivars to plant. This is not an easy decision.

During the past 15 years the proportion of total sales of Persian walnuts as kernels has steadily increased to where the major portion of total production is shelled. As a result, more emphasis is now placed on yield and quality of the kernels. The appearance of the shell is not the important factor it used to be in choosing a cultivar to plant, although it is important for that portion marketed in-shell. Well-sealed shells strong enough to withstand machine pick-up, hulling and handling and to protect the kernels from injury, dirt or contamination until the nuts are cracked are desired.

The data indicate that some of the old popular cultivars are not being planted now (Table 16.1). Placentia, for example, was a popular southern California coastal cultivar but its young trees are not very productive and kernel quality is poor when grown in the hot interior valleys. Since the industry has been moving out from southern California, the total acreage of Placentia has markedly declined and none has been planted for several years. Similarly, Concord and Mayette are not being planted in central and northern California because of low yields and quality defects.

TABLE 16.1
PERSIAN WALNUT ACREAGE IN CALIFORNIA BY CULTIVARS AS OF JUNE 1976

Cultivar	Bearing	Nonbearing	Total
Ashley	9,836	4,521	14,357
Blackmer	1,504	31	1,535
Concord	1,042	0	1,042
Eureka	19,498	829	20,327
Franquette	33,977	1,124	35,101
Hartley	49,857	9,482	59,339
Mayette	3,735	24	3,759
Nugget	1,833	54	1,887
Payne	31,511	4,088	35,599
Placentia and Similar	1,041	0	1,041
Serr	2,080	11,927	14,007
Tehama	1,890	4,029	5,919
Trinta	1,079	1,087	2,166
Vina	875	1,232	2,107
Waterloo	1,294	29	1,323
Others	5,591	3,669	9,260
All walnuts	166,643	42,126	208,769

Source: California Crop and Livestock Reporting Service.

The old French cultivar Franquette is still popular in California and also Oregon mainly because of its high quality kernels and late leafing. It still is being planted in mountain districts of California and Oregon where late leafing is desirable to escape spring frosts and early spring blight attack. Yields, however, are not satisfactory and growers have turned to Hartley, a more consistent producer and currently the leading cultivar. Payne and Eureka constitute more than 25% of the total walnut area in California. Payne trees begin bearing relatively early; they produce heavy crops consistently, especially in semi-coastal districts where summer temperatures are not excessively high. Eureka is not as productive as Payne and is injured by high summer temperatures but its nuts are large and the kernels are of high quality in semi-coastal areas. It is a parent of several cultivars in commercial production, including Marchetti and Waterloo. The latter crossed with Payne gave rise to the highly fruitful cultivars Gustine, Lompos and Tehama.

In situations where early leafing is not accompanied by frost injury, Ashley and Serr are being planted. The latter is one of ten new cultivars released by the University of California in 1968. Its popularity is indicated by the fact that it already ranks sixth in total area. The Serr is a large Payne-type nut with exceptionally high kernel percentage (59%). The kernels are of light color and high quality. Because the nuts are resistant to sunburn damage, the cultivar is especially well adapted to the hotter areas of the San Joaquin and Sacramento valleys, wherever late spring frosts are not a hazard.

Flowering and Fruiting

The walnut is monoecious; the male flowers, or catkins, develop on the previous year's growth, and the female flowers are borne on the tips of the spring flush of new shoots. Pollen is produced in the catkins, which are 4 to 6 in. long, and is distributed to the female flowers by wind, not insects. In most of the older cultivars, only the terminal and one subterminal bud on the previous season's growth give rise to shoots bearing nuts. In the Payne cultivar, as well as Serr, Tehama and others introduced by the University of California, a large portion of the lateral buds on previous season's growth gives rise to female flowers. This results in greatly increased bearing potential of young trees and enables them to produce worthwhile crops at an early age. Since they often tend to overbear and restrict vegetative growth, it is usually necessary to prune them more severely than the less fruitful cultivars.

Although all walnut cultivars are self- and cross-fertile, most have some degree of self-unfruitfulness because of dichogamy; that is, the male and female flowers do not mature simultaneously and the pollen is shed either before or after the female flowers are receptive. This reduces the proportion of female flowers that are self-pollinated and lowers the yield potential. Generally, most of the cultivars now being grown commercially in California shed pollen too early. Some of the most fruitful cultivars, however, have so many female flowers that they produce good crops consistently in single cultivar plantings, even though pollen shedding does not entirely overlap the female receptivity period.

The best way of ensuring adequate pollination for maximum production is to provide for cross-pollination by planting two or more cultivars. By planting a cultivar that sheds its pollen early with one that sheds late, there will be pollen available during the entire female receptive period for both cultivars. Observations have indicated that in young orchards with considerable space among the trees pollination can be effective from a good source of pollen for 500 to 600 ft or more. As the trees grow and become dense, the pollen is not carried as freely through the orchard and 200 to 300 ft is a better maximum distance. Most growers favor having every tenth crosswind row a pollinizer row.

Rootstocks

J. hindsii, the northern California Black Walnut, is the most commonly used rootstock in California even though it is susceptible to crown rot (*Phytophora cactorum*) and root lesion nematode (*Pratylenchus vulnus*) and exhibits delayed incompatibility or blackline (Serr 1969). Blackline is most serious in the San Francisco Bay area and in the Willamette Valley in Oregon. New plantings in Oregon are made on Manregian rootstocks, *J. regia* stocks of the Manchurian race. Carpathian seedlings are also used there. In California areas where blackline is serious, vigorous *J. regia* seedlings are used if the land is free of oak root fungus (*Armillaria mellea*). *J. regia* is very susceptible to injury by this fungus, whereas *J. hindsii* is resistant. This is one of the reasons why *J. hindsii* is being used in most of the Sacramento and San Joaquin valley areas where most of the new plantings are being made. Also, blackline has not yet become severe in these valleys.

Paradox hybrid is the rootstock of second-most importance in California. It is resistant to crown rot and somewhat resistant to the root lesion nematode. Paradox seedlings generally grow much faster than those of *J. hindsii.*

Planting the Orchard

Most new walnut orchards are quadruple-or at least double-planted in order that they may begin heavy production and make financial returns to the grower as quickly as possible. University of California trials showed that per tree yields of young walnuts were practically the same for the first 10 years with 48 trees per acre planted 30 by 30 ft, as with 17 trees per acre planted 50 by 50 ft. By close planting the early and heavy bearing new cultivars mentioned above, yields sufficient to cover all cash expenses in the fifth or sixth year may be realized and over a ton of nuts may be produced per acre during the seventh or eighth year. High yields per unit of land may be maintained by the gradual removal of excess trees over a period of five to six years. The initial step in tree removal in a quadruple square planting may begin the 10th or 11th year after planting, when the tips of branches on adjacent trees come within 3 ft of each other.

Alternate diagonal rows are selected at that time to be temporary rows and the lower limbs on the trees are cut back severely. Severe cutting back of higher framework branches on these trees is done before they begin to crowd the trees in adjacent rows. The permanent trees are allowed to grow and fill in the space formerly occupied by the temporary trees. The severe cutting back of the temporary trees year after year results in their assuming a fan and ultimately columnar shape. Complete removal of the temporary trees should be done prior to the time at which they shade the lower limbs of the adjacent trees.

Gradual removal of one-half of the remaining trees is begun when their lower branches grow within 3 ft of branches on adjacent trees. Where vigorous trees are planted 25 by 25 ft or 30 by 30 ft on good soils, the second removal process generally begins when the trees are 18 to 20 years old. The alternate rows selected for gradual removal will be parallel with the margin of planting, rather than on the diagonal.

Cultural Practices

Cultivation.—Walnut trees are deep-rooted and the type of cultivation employed is of minor importance. Subsoiling or deep tillage in established orchards is never justified as it may result in severe root damage. Cultivation by plowing, disking, harrowing or any other method is a means to an end. In itself, cultivation is not a practice essential to the well-being of the orchard. Cultivation, however, is practiced for one or more of the following reasons: to incorporate covercrops or fertilizers into the surface soil; to eliminate competition for water and mineral elements by weeds; to construct and subsequently remove irrigation furrows, dikes, or basins; to prepare the soil surface for mechanical harvesting; and to prepare a seed bed for planting a covercrop.

Covercropping.—Covercrops may be grown to improve the physical and chemical condition of the soil. They are important in preventing soil erosion in orchards planted on sloping land and in increasing the rate of water penetration. Legume covercrops may add nitrogen to a soil but generally not in sufficient quantity to obviate the necessity for applying additional amounts.

The water-holding capacity of a soil is at best only temporarily affected by the incorporation of a covercrop. The amount of material actually incorporated is small in proportion to the weight of an acre-foot of soil, and the rapid loss by decomposition constantly reduces the amount present.

Immature plants contain a larger percentage of nitrogen than plants which are mature. The more mature a covercrop is before being incorporated in the soil, the longer the period necessary for it to decompose because of its relatively low nitrogen content.

Plants suitable for covercropping are clover, vetch, mustard, rape, rye and barley. Legume crops such as vetch and clover grow relatively slowly and should be planted as soon after walnut harvesting as possible. Crops like mustard and rape grow more rapidly in the winter and may produce relatively heavy tonnages in 90 to 100 days. Nitrogenous fertilizer application in most situations will greatly benefit the growth of the covercrop. In districts of low rainfall, one or more irrigations may be necessary to replace the water used by the covercrop (Aldrich et al. 1976C).

Irrigation.—In interior California valleys where most of the walnuts are grown, an irrigation water supply to provide for a total of 2½ to 5 ft of water (including rainfall) throughout the year is usually needed. The period of irrigation in most districts is from June to October but early spring, late fall or winter irrigation may be necessary in areas of low average rainfall or in very dry years. Approximately one-half of the total seasonal water requirement occurs in the months of June, July and August.

The distribution of walnut roots under various soil conditions has been determined by irrigation studies which have traced the loss of soil moisture at different depths. These studies indicated that soil-moisture control to a depth of 9 ft is sufficient to maintain a mature walnut orchard in good condition. Approximately 80% of the soil moisture used by the tree to a depth of 9 ft during the growing season is taken from the upper 6 ft of soil.

In heavy soils a greater proportion of the water withdrawal from the upper 6 ft is concentrated in the top 3 ft; in light soils it may be more nearly equal in the 0 to 3 and 3 to 6 ft depths. The variations in soil of the top 6 ft do not, however, seem to affect the water withdrawal from the 6 to 9 ft depths; regardless of the nature of the surface soils, the 6 to 9 ft depths seem to account for only about 20%. A sharply stratified surface soil and subsoil, or impervious layers of hardpan or rock, or a shallow water table will limit root activity to less than normal depths.

Under interior valley conditions the soil dries out during the harvest period. Unless fall rains are unusually early and heavy, the trees may suffer from water shortage during fall months and fail to mature their wood properly. The wood is then subject to killing back by winter frosts. Therefore, an irrigation immediately after harvest is desirable.

When winter rainfall is not sufficient to wet the soil to field capacity to a depth of at least 6 ft, irrigation water should be applied during late winter to make up the deficiency. Winter irrigation, when rainfall is insufficient, supplies moisture for the spring growth of the trees. The most rapid growth of the nuts takes place during the five or six weeks immediately after the blossoming period. A shortage of soil moisture in a walnut orchard during the early part of the growing period will result in the production of a large percentage of small nuts. No amount of mid-summer or late irrigation water will increase the size after the walnut shell hardens (Aldrich *et al.* 1976A).

Pruning.—The modified central leader system of training young walnut trees is used in most western orchards (Serr 1969). With this system a fully developed tree usually has a minimum of four to five primary scaffold branches spaced both vertically and horizontally on the trunk. The lowermost should not be less than 6 ft from the ground to enable shaking with a trunk shaker for many years. The other primary scaffolds are spaced horizontally about 120 degrees and vertically about 2 ft between each other. After the primary scaffolds are established dominance of the leader is no longer maintained.

With the very fruitful new cultivars, heavy pruning is necessary to prevent the weight of the crop from bending the scaffolds out of the desired position. The framework branches, which grow from 4 to 10 ft in length in one season, are therefore cut back in dormant pruning as much as 50%.

Tree Fertilization.—There are few commercial walnut orchards in California over five years of age that are not given annual applications of nitrogen. Zinc deficiency is second to nitrogen in frequency and has been found to occur in practically all walnut-producing areas of the state, though most commonly where sandy soils prevail.

Deficiencies of boron, iron, manganese and potassium are not widespread, but occur in a few districts on certain soils. Boron deficiency is encountered in Oregon and in the Sierra Nevada mountain foothills of California, although boron excess is a much more important problem in California valley and Coast Range orchards. Iron and manganese deficiencies are most common in southern coastal counties of California, and sometimes also occur in the southern parts of the Sacramento and San Joaquin valleys. Potassium deficiency is most serious in the Chico area. Copper and phosphorus deficiencies are less common and are seriously limiting in only a few of the walnut areas of California.

An annual minimum of 100 to 150 lb of actual nitrogen per acre is applied after harvest to bearing orchards. Many high-yielding orchards receive 200 to 250 lb. Ammonium sulfate is generally preferred in California where sulfur is considered beneficial in counteracting soil alkalinity.

The procedures for treating zinc, manganese and copper deficiencies are outlined in Table 16.2.

Boron deficiency is eliminated for 2 to 4 years by surface soil treatment of about 50 lb of borax per acre. Excessive applications cause burning of leaf tips in moderate cases and entire leaf margins in severe cases.

Iron deficiency or lime-induced chlorosis is difficult and expensive to correct. Trees on Paradox hybrid rootstock are generally not affected. Application of 50 lb of sulfur per tree has greatly improved the chlorotic condition but has not completely eliminated it. Iron chelate application has also been fairly effective for a short time.

Where potassium deficiency has appeared, soil application of 1300 lb of potassium sulfate per acre has been effective. The material is applied in furrows 6 in. deep and 3 ft apart, or drilled into the soil to a similar depth. Noticeable improvement in leaf appearance occurs the second year following treatment.

In the few cases where phosphorus deficiency has occurred, 60 lb of triple superphosphate applied in a circular trench in late fall or early winter has been effective for 8 to 10 years. Improved growth and yield occurred the second year after treatment (Aldrich 1976B).

Walnut Toxicity

Walnut toxicity is a part of a new branch of science termed allelopathy, concerned with the interaction between plants and their environment. MacDaniels and Pinnow (1976) summarized the status of the problem as follows.

(1) In 1943 Gries stated that Pliny had reported the toxic relation of walnut (presumably *Juglans regia*) to other plants in the first century A.D. Since that time there have been many citaions of damage to plants growing near walnut trees, though the evidence has been inconclusive.

(2) A toxic substance, a napthaquinone called juglone, has been isolated from many plants in the walnut family including Persian walnut, *J. regia;* black walnut, *J. nigra;* butternut, *J. cinerea; J. sieboldiana;* and *J. mandshurica.* The hickories, *Carya ovata, C. alba, C. olivaeformis* and *Pterocarya caucasica* have also yielded juglone. See p. 606.

(3) Tomato plants showing wilting on contact with walnut roots exhibit

browning of vascular tissues resembling and resulting from fungus or bacterial diseases but no pathogen has been found in the wilted plants. Some confusion arises from the difficulty of identifying the symptoms of wilting caused by walnut toxicity and those caused by water deficiency. The area occupied by the roots of walnut may be five or six times the area of the crown of the tree and the toxic effect extends over the entire area occupied by the roots. Wilting caused by walnut toxicity occurs suddenly even when there is plenty of water in the soil. It may also occur only in part of the plant. The wilting can be partially overcome by applications of nitrogen and irrigation. This behavior of affected plants suggests a reduction of the absorbing function by injury to root hairs and other root absorbing surfaces.

(4) The symptoms and effects of walnut toxicity are found only when the roots of affected plants are in contact with, or very close to, live walnut roots in the soil or when exposed to live root bark in solutions or in direct contact.

Leachate from walnut husks poured on the soil will quickly bring earthworms to the surface where they die within a short time, indicating the presence of an active poison in the leachate.

(5) In most soils, roots do not occupy the surface layers. Thus, many shallow-rooted plants growing under walnut trees may not come into contact with walnut roots, and are not affected by them. This is why many grain crop plants appear not to be affected by walnut toxin.

(6) Tomatoes and alfalfa have been found growing normally under small walnut trees, which suggests that the toxic substance may not be formed by young trees, or that the roots of young trees are too small to be toxic. Maybe walnut trees do not form toxic materials under all growing conditions.

(7) Evidence indicates that the toxic effect does not remain in the soil for more than one year after removal of the walnut tree.

(8) Walnuts apparently tolerate a wider pH range than many plants which may explain why some plants become injured more than others. Injury is apparently due to toxicity rather than to difference in acidity.

(9) Plants may be grouped according to their sensitivity to juglone in the following ways: (a) very sensitive—alfalfa, tomatoes, potatoes, blackberry, rhododendron, mountain laurel, blueberry and heaths; also some pines, apple and others; (b) moderately sensitive—sweet pepper, lilac, red pine, peony, crabapple, crocus and others; and (c) plants improved by growing under walnut trees such as—bluegrass, clovers, timothy, red top, beets, snapbeans, lima beans, and many others.

Much has been learned concerning walnut toxicity during the past 40 years, but there are also many unsolved problems.

Lee and Campbell (1969) reported juglone (5-hydroxyl-1, 4-naphtho-quinone) occurring in the leaves, hulls and roots of black walnut trees in 1.23, 6.71 and 7.73 mg/g, respectively.

Controlling Pests in Orchard

The pest control program in Table 16.2 is based upon research investigations carried out by the University of California Agricultural Experiment Station and Agricultural Extension Service, in cooperation with the State Departments of Agriculture and Public Health, Fish and Game, the U.S. Department of Agriculture, and the agricultural and chemical industries.

WALNUT MATURITY

Walnut kernels are mature, lightest in color, and of highest value when the packing tissue between the kernel halves has just turned brown. Practical harvest, however, can begin only when the hulls dehisce and about 80% of the nuts can be removed from the trees by shaking. The interval between the time at which the packing tissue turns brown and when the nuts are harvestable varies with climate. These events often coincide in cool coastal areas, but in hot interior valleys as much as three weeks difference may occur. During the three-week interval the kernels become darker and insect damage may also increase, particularly from the navel orangeworm. Thus, nut quality seriously deteriorates.

The use of ethephon, a growth regulator, reduces deterioration in quality by shortening the interval between kernel maturity and time at which harvesting can be done. Applied as a spray to the trees when the kernels become mature, this material advances harvest 7 to 10 days and generally brings about 100% nut removal from a single shake. The growth regulator also promotes hull splitting.

The orchard floor must be prepared for harvesting, whether nuts are handpicked or machine-harvested. For machine picking a smooth orchard floor is required.

Preparation of the orchard floor for harvesting usually consists of a thorough cultivation about mid-September. This cultivation is followed by rolling or dragging. All walnuts do not mature and fall at the same time, so either shaking or several pickings are required. Sometimes a second harvesting is necessary even when tree-shakers are used.

HARVESTING WALNUTS

Walnut harvesting in California begins in mid-September and con-

TABLE 16.2
SPRAY SCHEDULE FOR PERSIAN WALNUTS

Time of application	Purpose of application	Spray material and AMOUNT PER ACRE except Where otherwise stated. THESE DOSAGES FOR USE IN AIR BLAST SPRAYERS	Remarks
I. Dormant			CAUTION: Oil sprays should not be used in the dormant period on trees that have suffered from a lack of adequate soil moisture, high scale populations, or other stressing factors at any time during the growing season or during the period of dormancy. If these conditions exist, do not apply oils to walnut trees during the dormant period. If frosted, European fruit lecanium, calico, Putnam or San Jose scale needs controlling during the dormant period and trees may be susceptible to oil injury, use diazinon, ethion, parathion, or Trithion without the oil as listed in Sections A and B below. The use of these materials without oil will suppress scale insects, but treatments may be needed again during late spring or early summer (see Section IV).
	A. Frosted, European Fruit, Lecanium, and Calico Scale	1) 2½ lb 50% diazinon wettable or 5 lb 25% parathion wettable plus 2 to 4 gal. dormant oil emulsion in 200 gal. of water 2) 2 qt Trithion emulsifiable (carbonphenothion) (4 lb per gal.) plus 2 to 4 gal. dormant oil emulsion in 200 gal. of water. 3) 8 lb 25% ethion wettable plus 2 to 4 gal. dormant oil emulsion in 200 gal. of water 4) 18 gal. dormant oil emulsion in 100 to 200 gal. of water	Treatments for these scale insects should be applied between January 1 and March 1. The later oil treatments are applied between these dates, the less phytotoxicity will occur. All of these treatments are effective in killing the overwintering eggs of the the walnut aphid and aid in the control of Putnam and San Jose scale. If these scales are the major problem, use the rates below in Section 1B. Trithion or ethion plus oil will also control overwintering eggs of European red mite. Be certain to read the CAUTION section above.
	B. Putnam and San Jose Scale	2½ lb 50% dianzinon wettable or 2½ lb 50% dianzinon wettable or 5 lb 25% parathion wettable, plus 8 gal. dormant oil emulsion, in 200-400 gal.	Treatment applied January 1 to February 15. This treatment is effective against the above soft scales and overwintering eggs of the walnut aphid.

C. Italian Pear Scale	10 to 15 hydrated lime plus 1 gal. dormant oil emulsion in 100 gal. water applied by hand sprayer.	This treatment is for control of moss and lichens which will aid in control of Italian pear scale.
D. Zinc Deficiency (Little Leaf)	Soil treatment	Soil treatments for zinc deficiency have worked in some areas. See your University of California Farm Advisor for suggestions or local recommendations.
E. Sunburn Protection	White interior water-base paint	Prior to any bud swelling or growth paint trunks of young trees to at least 1 in. below the soil line. If soil settles around tree or orchard operations expose unpainted trunks, these areas should be painted. This treatment also should reduce flat-headed borer infestations.
II. Prebloom and Bloom		
A. Walnut Blight	Fixed copper	Two treatments are suggested for the bloom period: the first in early prebloom (1% pistillate blooms showing), and the second when 10 to 20% pistillate* blooms are showing. When rain threatens, additional applications made before or immediately after the rain are important. In a few Sacramento Valley counties Bordeaux mixture at 16-10-100 plus ½ gal. 80% summer oil emulsion used as a safener has been used without injury in the early prebloom stage before foliage develops. In other areas of the state injury to the trees has been reported from Bordeaux applications (*NOT the catkins).
		Use according to manufacturer's directions. When organic phosphates are added to copper sprays for control of aphids, they tend to reduce the beneficial effect of the copper in blight control. Such mixtures must be used promptly following their addition to the spray tank.
III. Postbloom		
A. Walnut Blight	Same as under II-A above.	One application at this time except in areas where copper injuries occur.
B. Zinc Deficiency (Little Leaf)	1) 1 lb of zinc sulfate (36% zinc) per 100 gal. of water	Two to three applications per season using the same concentration are suggested. Full coverage is necessary for best results. The first application should be made closely following full bloom when the "feathers" on pistillate flowers have turned.

TABLE 16.2 (Continued)

Time of application	Purpose of application	Spray material and AMOUNT PER ACRE except where otherwise stated. THESE DOSAGES FOR USE IN AIR BLAST SPRAYERS	Remarks
		2) 2 lb of zinc EDTA per 100 gal. of water	brown. In most areas and during most seasons, this will coincide with the time when terminal shoot growth is from 6 to 10 in. long and most of the leaves have lost their reddish color. The second and third applications should be made at two to three weeks following the previous application. Single material applications are recommended unless local experience has shown that the zinc compounds can be used in combination with other spray chemicals. See your local University of California Farm Advisor for additional information. WARNING: Leaf symptoms can occur if the recommended rates are exceeded.
	C. Manganese Deficiency	5 lb manganese sulfate per 100 gal. of water	Apply when most of the young leaves of the spring flush of growth are fully expanded but not quite mature, usually mid-April to late May or early June, depending on cultivar and location.
	D. Copper Deficiency	Bordeaux Mixture 10-10-100	Apply in spring at end of pollination period, usually in late April, May or early June, depending on cultivar and location. Spray trees showing copper deficiency symptoms only.
	E. Walnut Aphid	The walnut aphid has been greatly suppressed by introduction of a parasitic wasp. Treatments for this aphid were seldom required during the past season. Treatment for aphid control should be considered if the average number of aphids per leaflet reaches 10-20. Use 50-150 gal. of water per acre, or if treatment combined with the codling moth spray increase to 200 gal. per acre.	
		1) 1 pt Phosphamidon (8 lb/gal.) (dimcron)	Will also aid in control of codling moth. When this material is applied early in the foliage season some marginal leaf burn and leaf spotting may occur.

2) Zolone, 3E, 3-6 pt

Use lower dosage for walnut aphid only. Use higher dosage if mites are also a problem. If 6 pt dosage is applied at correct timing for codling moth control, codling moth will also be controlled.

3) 3 lb 50% Thiodan wettable or 3 qt Thiodan emulsifiable (endosulfan)

4) Optional materials: 1½ pt Systox (demeton) (2 lb/gal.) 1 qt Trithion (carbophenothion) (4 lb/gal.), 4 lb 25% ethion wettable, 1 qt OMPA (4 lb/gal.), 1½ lb 25% parathion wettable, 4 lb 25% malathion wettable, 2 lb 50% diazinon wettable

Do not apply Systox until leaves are fully expanded. Further applications should not exceed a total of 3 pt in a single treatment or during a season and no treatment should be made less than 3 weeks before harvest. Systox tends to induce an increase in soft scale population. Walnut aphid has shown resistance in some areas to Trithion, Ethion, Systox, parathion, OMPA, diazinon, malathion and Thiodan.

F. Codling Moth and Navel Orangeworm

Timing:

Two options are possible: a) an integrated pest management program or b) a standard chemical control program. Where there is a history of satisfactory control on Payne and other cultivars, one properly timed and applied treatment has maintained adequate control. Timing for an integrated pest management program may be followed as in a) below. This timing is also customary is there is a "worm" problem on late cultivars. Where codling moth and navel orangeworm infestations are excessive, a chemical control program is suggested as in b) below.

a) **Integrated pest management program:** In order to minimize interference with the aphid parasite and in most cases avoid necessity for aphid treatments, apply the codling moth treatment against second brood. Accurate timing is essential. Synthetic pheromone trapping can detect emergence of moths of first brood which lay eggs of the second brood. Treatment should be applied within 7 days of beginning of this emergence. Follow farm advisors newsletters. Treatment usually falls during last two weeks of June. Include a material for mite control (see IV. B below) if European red mite is a problem or if the other species of mites are a chronic problem.

b) **Chemical control program:** Time the codling moth treatment against first brood. Apply treatment at the first evidence of increase in moth flight as determined by synthetic pheromone traps. Install traps when Payne nuts are ¼ in. in diameter. An alternate method of timing is to treat when Payne walnuts reach ⅜–½ in. in diameter. In severe infestations, a second treatment may be required during the last two weeks of June. Time this treatment as in a) above.

TABLE 16.2 *(Continued)*

Time of application	Purpose of application	Spray material and AMOUNT PER ACRE except where otherwise stated. THESE DOSAGES FOR USE IN AIR BLAST SPRAYERS	Remarks
		1) 3 lb 50% Guthion wettable or 3 qt Guthion 2E (azinphosmethyl) in 200 gal. water	The incorporation of an aphicide with this treatment is frequently advisable if applied against first brood codling moth. In some locations Guthion will provide aphid control. Sevin may increase spider mite problem.
		2) 8 to 10 lb 50% Sevin wettable (carbaryl) in 200 gal. water	
IV. Late Spring and Early Summer	A. Aphids	Where necessary apply one of the aphicides listed under Postbloom III-E.	
	B. Spider Mites	In areas where spider mites are a chronic problem incorporate one of these materials with the codling moth treatment. If resistance develops, change from one type of acaricide to another, i.e., change from one of the following groups to another: 1) chlorinated hydrocarbons-Kelthane, Chlorobenzilate or Tedion, 2) organophosphates-Ethion, Zolone, Trithion or Delnav or 3) Omite.	
		1) 4 lb 30% Omite wettable or 1.6 pt Omite 6E	No more than 2 applications per season. Do not graze cover crop under trees. When European red mite is the major problem, 6 lb 30% Omite wettable or 2.4 pt Omite 6E may be used. If no treatments have been applied for codling moth, mite predators may be active and Omite is the material of choice as it is selective and favors survival of mite predators.
		2) 6 pt Zolone 3E	
		3) 2¼ to 3 qt 35% Kelthane emulsifiable (dicofol) or 5 to 6 lb 35% Kelthane wettable (dicofol) in 200 gal. water	
		4) 1½ qt Chlorobenzilate EC (4 lb per gal.)	Chlorobenzilate may cause yellow spotting of leaves.

5) 1 qt Trithion (carbophenothian) (4 lb per gal.) in 100 to 200 gal. water

6) 2 qt Delnav emulsifiable (dioxathion) (4 lb per gal.) in 200 gal. water

7) 8 lb 25% Ethion wettable

8) 4 to 6 gal. Supreme or Superior oil*

Apply in late May or early June as soon as the eggs have hatched. If only a single branch is involved, it should be cut out.

C. Oyster Shell Scale

5 lb 25% parathion wettable in 200 gal. water

D. Frosted, European Fruit Lecanium, and Calico Scale

3 qt summer oil emulsion
plus either
2 to 3 lb 25% parathion wettable
or
6 lb 25% malathion wettable

These pests can be controlled from June 25 through August 15. Trithion, parathion, ethion, and malathion used for aphid control exert a suppressing action on these scales.

E. San Jose Scale

4 gal. Supreme or Superior oil*
plus either
8 lb 25% parathion wettable
or
4 lb 50% diazinon wettable
or
4 lb 50% diazinon wettable (carbophenothion)
or
8 lb 25% Ethion wettable in 400 gal. water per acre

Apply in 400 gal. of water per acre. Apply spring treatments in late May or early June when scale crawlers are moving.
These treatments will also control walnut aphids, mites and other scale insects.
For walnut scale use either the parathion oil or diazinon-oil treatment.

V. Mid to Late Summer   A. Walnut Husk Fly

Husk fly treatments are timed by use of Frick traps (ice cream cartons charged with ammonium carbonate) or bait pans. Place traps or bait pans in the orchard by July 1 and inspect them three times a week. Catches of adult husk flies during early July are scattered and fluctuating. Later a sharp or steady increase in catches occurs. Apply the first treatment within 10 days after catches begin to show this increase. This usually occurs in early August but may be earlier or later on some cultivars and/or in certain areas.

Bait Pans

See Walnut Husk Fly IV-D in Southern California section of this leaflet.

TABLE 16.2 (Continued)

Time of application	Purpose of application	Spray material and AMOUNT PER ACRE except where otherwise stated. THESE DOSAGES FOR USE IN AIR BLAST SPRAYERS	Remarks
		Frick Trap	Use at least 5 traps in the orchard. Hang traps on the north side of each tree in dense foliage 8 to 15 ft above the ground. Traps should hang free and be able to rotate. Replenish the ammonium carbonate every 14 days. For further details on Frick traps, see your University of California Farm Advisor.
		1) 1 pt Phosphamidon (dimecron) (8 lb per gal.)	Use in 200 gal. water per acre. This material can be used to control larvae in the husks. It may be applied after the eggs have been laid but before larval feeding causes the husk to darken. Phosphamidon will also control aphid and aid in control of codling moth.
		2) 6 lb 25% Trithion wettable (carbophenothion)	Use in 200–300 gal. water per acre. Trithion will also control European red mites, two spotted mites and aphids. Ethion will also control European red mites and aphids. Malathion and parathion will also control aphids in some areas. These materials are for control of adult flies.
		3) 6 lb 25% Ethion wettable	
		4) 8 lb 25% malathion wettable	
		5) 8 lb parathion wettable	
		6) 3 lb 25% Trithion wettable (carbophenothion) plus 2 qt corn protein hydrolysate (Staleys Protein Bait No. 7)	These materials may be applied in 100 gal. of water per acre by air blast sprayer or in 10 gal. of water by aircraft. Trithion plus bait applied by air blast sprayer will also control mites. Malathion plus bait may cause severe mite and aphid buildup. These materials are for control of adult flies.
		7) 4 lb 25% malathion wettable plus 2 qt corn protein hydrolysate (Staleys Protein Bait No. 7)	
	B. Red Humped Caterpillar	1) lb 50% diazinon wettable	For spot treatments use hand sprayer. The dosages for these chemicals are per 100 gal. water.
		2) 1 lb 50% Thiodan wettable	
		3) 2 lb 25% malathion wettable	
		4) ¾ lb 50% Guthion wettable	

VI. Late Summer	A. False Spider Mite	An important pest in parts of San Joaquin County. The use of OMPA for aphid and spider mite control exerts a suppressing action on population of false spider mites.	
		2½ qt 35% Kelthane emulsifiable (dicofol) or 5 lb 35% Kelthane wettable (dicofol) in 200 gal. water	Apply when leaves first show bronzing.
	B. Navel Orange-worm	1) Obtain complete control of the codling moth. 2) Practice plant and orchard sanitation. 3) Follow practices that discourage walnut blight. 4) Harvest crop as soon as nuts are hullable. 5) Dry nuts immediately 6) Fumigate nuts immediately after harvest. 7) Place in dry clean storage.	

SOIL FUMIGATION

	C. Armillaria Root Rot (Oak-Root Fungus Disease)	Soil fumigation with carbon bisulfide prior to planting is the accepted method of soil treatment. However, complete eradication is not always achieved. Re-treatment may be necessary in localized areas. The fungus may survive on dead roots. Therefore remove from the soil as many roots as possible and burn on the infected site before treating the soil. If infected roots are removed for burning elsewhere some of the roots may be dropped and new sites of infection established. Warm, dry well-worked soil is essential for effective treatment. Application is often made in September. In making the carbon bisulfide application, sprinkle lightly to moisten the upper 3 in. of soil to confine the gas. Next, lay off area to be treated in 18-in spacings on the diamond and open holes to a depth of 5 to 6 in. Pour 2 oz of carbon bisulfide into each hole and close immediately by tamping with the heel. Special manually or mechanically operated injectors can also be used for applying the chemical. Remember, this chemical is very toxic and will kill plants. Applications should not be made closer than the edge of the tree drip. Do not plant in treated soil for 6 to 8 weeks after treatment. CAUTION: Carbon bisulfide is a heavy, volatile, highly explosive liquid. Do not permit smoking or any open flame in the area where it is being handled.	
VII. Before fall rains	Deep and shallow canker	Bordeaux 10-10-100	Cover trunks and scaffold branches. This is a suggested program based on limited data.

TABLE 16.2 (Continued)

Time of application	Purpose of application	Spray material and AMOUNT PER ACRE except where otherwise stated. THESE DOSAGES FOR USE IN AIR BLAST SPRAYERS	Remarks
VIII. Post Leafroll	Crown gall	Bacticin (full strength)	Remove soil from the crown area of the tree. Remove as much of the crown gall tissue as possible with a hatchet or chisel. Apply bacticin with a paint brush to the wounded area. Do not treat more than ½ of the circumference of the tree at one time.
IX. Pre-plant only	Root-lesion Nematodes a. Replanting old orchard or vine yardland	1) DD at 60-170 gal. per acre 2) Telone at 60-137.5 gal. per acre 3) Vapam at 50-75 gal. per acre	Use higher rates for heavy soils. Apply DD and Telone by chisel injection at 10-12 in. depth on 12 in. spacing. Seal soil soon after treatment with ring roller or drag. Meter Vapam into 6-8 acre in. of water in flood irrigation in basins (checks). Soil should be warm (50°-85°F at 6 in. depth), moist and cultivated thoroughly before application. Remove roots and other plant debris. Fall application usually is best because of warm soils. Pre-irrigation may be necessary to provide sufficient moisture.
	b. Land used previously for annual crops	1) DD or Telone at 40-60 gal. per acre 2) Vapam at 50-75 gal. per acre	Do not plant until period of time equivalent to at least one week for each 10 gal. of DD or Telone. In heavy soils, and when soils are cold and/or wet after treatment, this period should be extended. When Vapam has been used, wait 14-21 days if soil is of a light to medium texture, well drained and warm; when soil is cold (below 60°F), wet, fine textured or high in organic matter, a waiting period of 30-60 days may be necessary. A two-year fallow period is suggested before treatment following removal of old trees to allow decay of roots. A period of one to several months of fallow also may be necessary after removal of annuals, especially deep-rooted crops such as cotton. All rootstocks are more or less susceptible to root-lesion nematodes; some Paradox hybrids tolerate infestation when well established. All rootstocks will benefit from preplanting soil treatment.

*SUPREME AND SUPERIOR SPRAY OILS

The oils under these definitions are highly refined petroleum products. They are clear to lightly colored, odorless, stable and formulated as emulsifiable. They are unclassified within the California petroleum oil classification and are exempt of a Federal Food and Drug residue tolerance. The active ingredient is referred to as 98% or higher petroleum or mineral oil. They are generally safe to use throughout the dormant and growing season on deciduous fruit and nut crops. These oils are recommended to be used at the rates of 1 to 1½ gal. oil per 100 gal. of water in dilute sprays and 4 to 6 gal. of oil per acre in concentrate sprays.

The Supreme and Superior base stock oils for which there is California pest control information and referred to in this program have the following specifications:

	Distillation 50% point	10 mm Hg °F 10–90% range	Viscosity (SSU 100°F)	Gravity (API 60°F)	UR (Vol.%–ASTM)
Orchex 796	443	70	73	35.3	96
PGSO-2	439	50	90	31.8	94
Volck Supreme	490	107	145	31.0	94

CAUTIONS: These oils, although safe to use under most conditions, may cause plant or fruit injury under certain conditions. Follow spray recommendations, compatibility charts and label instructions closely for incompatible combinations with other materials. Oil applications made to trees that are weak or suffering from a moisture stress or when slow drying of spray occurs may cause bud, twig or leaf injury. Phytoxicity studies have not been made on all fruit and nut cultivars or in all the growing areas of California.

Source: California Agricultural Experiment Station Extension Service

TO CONVERT	INTO	MULTIPLY BY
acres	hectares	.4047
gallons	liters	3.785
pounds	kilograms	.4536
quarts	liters	.9463
inches	centimeters	2.540
°F	°C	(°F 32) 5⁄9

tinues into late November. Methods used depend upon the size of the particular orchard, and upon the equipment and crew a grower has available to him. The cultivar, size of trees and yield per acre also influence the harvesting method.

Mechanical shaking has replaced hand shaking and the boom type of shaker is generally used, it being a one-man operation. Skilled operators are required so as to prevent excessive bruising or injury of the tree limbs.

Both handpicking and mechanical picking are done in California walnut orchards, the method depending upon the size of the orchard, labor available, equipment available, yield per acre, and proportion of crop being harvested in going over the orchard one time. Because of shortages of labor, improvements in mechanical pickers, and increasing wage rates, the majority of walnuts are harvested mechanically.

Courtesy of Julian C. Crane

FIG. 16.1. WINDROWING WALNUTS. AFTER THE NUTS ARE "SHAKEN" TO THE GROUND THEY ARE WINDROWED TO ALLOW MECHANICAL HARVESTERS TO PICK THEM UP FOR CLEANING AND HULLING

The rate at which a mechanical picker works depends upon the type of machine, the condition of the ground and how the walnuts were positioned by raking for the mechanical operation, the amount of foreign material on the ground and the number of men required in a crew for optimum operation of the whole process. If the loosened green hull has not fallen off the walnut, hulling is required. Many years ago it was done by hand, but today's mechanical machines both hull and wash the walnuts as they are brought in from the orchards.

Courtesy of Julian C. Crane

FIG. 16.2. SELF-PROPELLED OR TRACTOR-PULLED
HARVESTERS ELEVATE THE WINDROWED NUTS INTO LARGE
BINS THAT ARE DELIVERED TO THE HULLING MACHINE

Courtesy of Julian C. Crane

FIG. 16.3. THE NUTS ARE ELEVATED TO THE TRASH
REMOVER, LEFT; PASSED THROUGH THE HULLER AND
WASHER, CENTER; ELEVATED INTO LARGE BINS (NOT
SHOWN), RIGHT; AND SUBSEQUENTLY DEHYDRATED

After hulling and washing, the grower must thoroughly dry the walnuts
to prevent deterioration. Most growers dry by mechanical dehydration,
and even those who have only a few walnut trees and who do not own a
dehydrator usually share a neighbor's rather than practicing the old-time

sun-drying method which depends upon the weather. The walnuts are then well started on the first part of their journey to the consumer.

Harvesting walnuts in Oregon is more complicated than in California. In Oregon, fall rains usually begin before harvesting is completed. Mud, fallen wet leaves, and fragments of split hulls all increase the harvesting problem. Machine harvesting in Oregon has not been practiced to any appreciable extent because of the difficulty of getting machinery through wet orchards. Wet leaves are difficult to remove by present field-cleaners or harvesting machines. Most walnuts in Oregon are still hand-harvested.

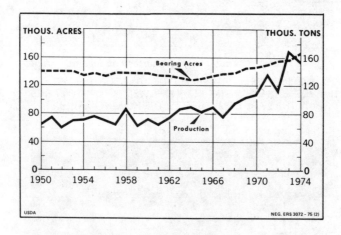

FIG. 16.4. ACREAGE AND PRODUCTION OF WALNUTS
IN OREGON AND CALIFORNIA

DRYING

Many methods of drying are in use, but the underlying principle usually is the same. Warm air, at a temperature not higher than 32° to 38°C (90° to 100°F) is circulated around the individual nuts. Walnuts have a critical temperature of 43°C (110°F). If heated higher the oil in the kernels will become rancid and make them inedible. Rancidity is not apparent immediately after overheating but requires from a few weeks to several months to develop. Commercial driers finish to a moisture content of about 8%. Walnut kernels containing this moisture or less will snap when broken.

PROCESSING AND PRODUCTS

Shellers, processors and end-users of walnuts must plan their production and advertising programs two or more years in advance.

Rising costs of materials, labor and the consumers' demand for stricter sanitation and better quality of walnuts is resulting in larger outlay for money, machinery and equipment. Examples are the necessity of better refrigeration for shelled and unshelled nuts and use of electric sorting equipment for color grading, more controlled dryers, better packaging, and larger operations.

Walnuts for sale are "in-shell" or shelled "kernels." The trend has been moving from the in-shell to shelled form since the development of automatic shelling equipment. Now about 90% of all nuts are marketed as kernels or meats. Most of the in-shell walnuts are of the large, improved cultivars, featured as holiday or gift specialties, or are exported for home consumption. They are usually sold in 1-lb bags or boxes, may be polished and waxed, and are sometimes dyed.

Courtesy of Diamond/Sunsweet

FIG. 16.5. HAYES CRACKING MACHINES CRACK 5000 WALNUTS PER MINUTE

TABLE 16.3
INDUSTRY WALNUT SUPPLY

Year	Carry In	Crop	Total Supply
1970	34,740	111,800	146,540
1971	36,300	137,000	173,300
1972	38,400	116,800	155,200
1973	25,360	174,000	199,360
1974	62,875	156,000	218,875
1975	57,000	199,300	256,300
1976	47,000	183,300	230,300

Source: Kuzio (1977).

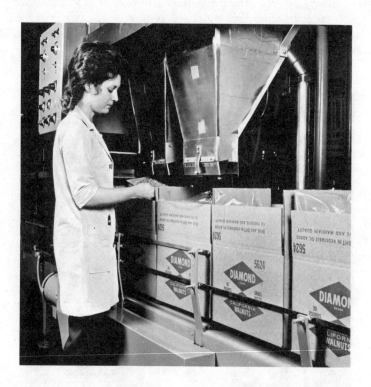

FIG. 16.6. AUTOMATIC EQUIPMENT FILLS CASES WITH THE
CORRECT AMOUNT OF WALNUTS

DIAMOND WALNUT GROWERS

Over 80% of the walnut crop is handled by Diamond Walnut Growers, Inc., with about 11,000 members. The Walnut Control Board sets the percentage of the crop that can be sold in the shell, and the percentage that must be shelled. The return for better quality walnuts in the shell has been good in recent years, but there is a limit to the tonnage that can be marketed at good prices.

Plant Facilities

Facilities of the Diamond Walnut Growers Associated are located on a 50-acre tract, at Stockton, California. The plant has four 700 ft long rail spurs through the entire structure, and dock accommodations for 10 trailer trucks. Storage bays measure 80 × 60 ft, with a clear stacking height of 20 ft from floor to roof, and are maintained at 1.1°C (34°F) with 60% relative humidity.

The floor of the 13-acre plant is on one level, and there are no interfering columns to restrict fork-truck movement. Large doors permit rail car movement in the refrigerated areas. The handling system employs railcar bulk transport and in-plant conveyor systems to replace lift trucks. This eliminates costly handling and maintenance of millions of bags. The conveyor system for handling shelling stock is rather complex and entirely mechanized.

Product Handling

About 60 to 65% of more than one million bags (100-lb size) are used for in-shell packaging. The stock is received in bulk by rail car or trucks. Rail shipments are scooped from cars onto conveyors which feed into conveyors supplying storage bins. Truck deliveries are weighed, then the entire loads are dumped into a hopper from which the nuts are moved to storage bins. Here the nuts are size graded.

The nuts are conveyed from storage as needed to the shelling department, where they are cracked and conveyed further to air-separators, where meats are sorted from shells and fiber. By bucket elevator and conveyor systems, the meats are moved to electronic color graders, manual inspection tables, and the station for final packaging in tins or in bulk cartons.

Quality control of walnuts begins in the field, where a crew of inspectors sees that every lot of walnuts is checked before shipping to the plant. The main concern is to evaluate the percentage of sound, edible, light-colored kernels. To do this, field men first take samples of nuts from a lot, crack them, and grade the kernels, counting the number of blanks, splits and defective nuts.

Having removed culls, the lot is then graded into three sizes (large, medium and baby), which are stored separately. Each of these fractions is graded for quality, and tagged for in-plant indentification. The grower is paid on the basis of the last evaluation.

At the main plant, a 1-lb sample is taken every 3 or 4 min, from secondary storage bins as they are filled. Results of this grading determines fitness for packaging or the need for regrading in the electronic sorter.

A battery of 50 electronic sorters handle from 4500 to 8750 lb of nutmeats per hour—a job that would take 250 to 400 manual workers. Each color-sorter handles nutmeats at 90 to 175 lb per hour. Each unit accepts products within a narrow, fixed color range, and rejects all others. Thus, if the unit is set for selecting top-quality meats, the photoelectric device accepts meats of this color and chutes them straight-through to conveyors and elevators. Nutmeats of other shades are chuted to conveyors and elevators that whisk them into seconday storage bins.

In the final processing step, nutmeats pass through a bank of air separators, then are chuted to can or bulk packaging bins.

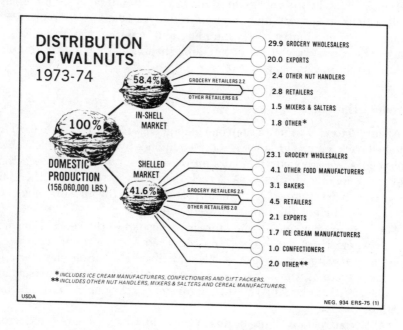

FIG. 16.7. DISTRIBUTION OF U.S. GROWN WALNUTS

BY-PRODUCT PROCESSES

While most of the shells are used for boiler fuel, part of them are sold for "sand-blasting" uses. Also, two processing techniques recover other products.

Even with efficient air separation, the shells still retain about 5% of the nutmeats. Thus, a wet-separation technique—the Armstrong Process—is used to recover some 4000 lb of these remaining good-quality edible meats per 8-hour shift.

After air separation, the material is batched into tanks. A 28½ in. vacuum is drawn and held for one hour to remove air from shell cells. Next the vacuum is broken and fresh water is introduced under 5 lb per square in. for ½ hour to soak shells. Contents of the tank are then dropped into a sluice that carries the waterlogged shells to a brine separation tank.

Here, the meats—being lighter than the water-soaked shells—are separated by flotation, spray washed in a bucket elevator, and centrifuged. Meats are then surface-dried to 4% moisture in a dehydrator and conveyed to inspection tables. This product is 99.9% shell free.

The shells are air conveyed to storage bins for further processing into by-products.

Walnut hulls are used to dye fabric for rugs and dresses (Anon. 1966).

There still remains a potential of ¼ to 1% nutmeats in the shells. Therefore, further extracton is economically feasible. The material is moved from shell storage bins to a disk mill and shaker. The resultant meal, called "concentrate" is mixed with inedible meats (discarded from grading operations) and pressed in a French oil mill of the expeller type.

The walnut oil, which has rapid drying characteristics, is used in paints, after being filtered. It is pumped into rail tank cars for shipment. The expeller cake, which is high in protein, is ground, screened and bagged for stock feed (Buffington and Havighorst 1957).

Walnut Oil

The amount of walnut oil produced in the United States is about 600 tons annually. Raw material for oil pressing is divided between inedible meats rejected during shelling and meat fragments recovered from shells. The former have a slightly lower oil content (55.6%) than edible meats. One plant produces most of the walnut oil from the shelling plant of a large California cooperative. Screw press equipment is used. There have been years when the supply of walnuts exceeded the demand and edible-grade nuts were pressed for oil, but current production is entirely from rejected meats.

Walnut oil is similar to linseed oil and when the supply is plentiful may be used for the coating industry. But usually it is consumed as a specialty food oil (Kester 1949).

RETARDING RANCIDITY IN WALNUTS

Shelled walnuts are highly susceptible to darkening and development of rancidity. Moisture, heat, light and air are primary factors in their deterioration. Maximum flavor and color stability is at about 3.1% moisture, and with an antioxidant kernels at 2.8 to 4.0% moisture and 4.4°C (40°F) may be held for 18 months within acceptable limits. At temperatures below 3.3°C (38°F) walnut meats are stable over a moisture range from 1.5 to 6.0%, and the optimum moisture varies nearly linearly with the temperature between 3.3° and 60°C (38° and 140°F). At 22.5°C (72.5°F) it lies between 3.0 and 3.8%.

Enhanced stability of kernels occurs when they are adjusted to the optimum moisture and treated with various antioxidants. Oxygen absorption is minimized in both treated kernels when held at moisture levels of 3.0 to 3.5% in sealed jars. Free fatty acids in untreated kernels increase about 100% faster when stored in ambient light than in the dark.

Oxygen absorption by walnut meats, from the air in the headspace of containers, is a measure of oxidative rancidity and formation of free fatty acids. It is also useful in comparing the effectiveness of antioxidants applied to the meats. BHA (butylated hydroxyanisole) and BHT (butylated hydroxytoluene) in vegetable oil, when applied to shelled walnuts, reduce the oxygen absorbed by approximately two-thirds. BHA-PG formulation reduces the oxygen absorption by about one-half. Oxygen absorption increases as moisture content increases (Swarthout *et al.* 1958).

Uncooked and unsalted walnut meats are not prone to pick up moisture, as indicated by the fact that under tropical conditions of 37.8°C (100°F) with 80% relative humidity, weight gain is less than 1%. The most meaningful indications of walnut meat shelf-life are free fatty acids, color and taste. Other indicators such as crispness, peroxide numbers and change in weight are less significant.

WORLD WALNUT CROP

The United States is by far the leading walnut producing country in the world, followed by France, Italy, India, Turkey and Iran (Table 16.4). World production has steadily increased during the past ten years with all of the increase coming from the United States. This trend is likely to continue for the next several years as there are 42,126 acres of walnuts in California that are not yet of bearing age (Table 16.1).

Total world exports of walnuts has steadily increased during the past five to six years, due mainly to the steady increase in exports from the United States (Table 16.5). Exports from the United States have increased almost 900% in the past six years, West Germany being the biggest buyer, followed by Spain and Canada.

TABLE 16.4
COMMERCIAL WALNUT PRODUCTION IN SPECIFIED COUNTRIES
IN-SHELL BASIS (1000 MT)

Year	France	India	Iran	Italy	Turkey	Total Foreign	United States	Grand Total
1965	16.0	14.0	6.0	24.5	7.3	67.8	72.8	140.6
1966	30.0	16.0	3.0	17.0	6.4	72.4	87.1	159.5
1967	25.0	11.0	3.5	23.0	7.3	69.8	69.3	139.1
1968	27.5	14.0	4.0	16.0	9.0	70.5	86.7	157.2
1969	23.0	10.0	5.0	18.0	8.4	64.4	95.7	160.1
1970	36.3	14.0	4.0	20.0	9.0	83.3	101.4	184.7
1971	22.5	11.0	3.5	21.0	7.5	65.5	123.7	189.2
1972	26.0	14.0	3.2	15.0	8.0	66.2	106.0	172.2
1973	29.3	13.5	3.0	20.0	8.5	74.3	157.9	232.2
1974	18.6	9.5	3.3	13.0	9.0	53.4	142.0	195.4

TABLE 16.5
WALNUT EXPORTS FROM SPECIFIED COUNTRIES, IN-SHELL BASIS (MT)

Country	1968-69	1969-70	1970-71	1971-72	1972-73	1973-74
France	9,300	10,889	13,171	8,314	10,139	12,278
India	9,471	4,462	5,366	5,121	8,080	7,385
Iran	830	657	463	712	921	498
Italy	6,465	7,020	7,317	9,421	3,587	6,012
Turkey	7,449	5,476	4,621	4,236	7,733	4,704
China, People's Republic	17,459	13,489	12,356	18,938	19,763	13,735
Total Foreign	50,974	41,993	43,294	46,742	50,223	44,612
United States	2,923	6,461	9,446	17,068	15,157	26,254
Grand Total	53,897	48,454	52,740	63,810	65,380	70,866

Source: Foreign Agric. Serv., U.S. Dep. Agric.

WALNUT PRODUCTION AND PROCESSING IN INDIA

Juglans regia is native to the foothills of the Himalayan mountains, in the Jammu and Kashmir states of northern India. There are an estimated 584,000 bearing seedling trees and 538,960 trees coming into bearing in a 54,600 sq mi area in the valleys. More than 80% of India's 14,000 tons of walnuts produced, and all of her 7000 tons of exported walnuts, come from this area.

Due to the density of population and small size of farms, there are few laid-out orchards. Plantings consist of a few dozen seedlings on farms consisting of three to six acres where everything is done by hand. The climate and thick alluvial soil are well suited to walnuts.

The flat land of the numerous valleys is devoted to intensive rice culture; around the edges on the slopes are apple orchards; higher up the slopes at an elevation of about 6000 ft are walnut orchards; and above these are forest trees. There are many thousands of walnut trees planted in the forests for timber and wild nuts. A thriving walnut wood carving industry exists in the area.

FIG. 16.8. A TYPICAL BEARING SEEDLING WALNUT TREE
GROWING ON THE FOOTHILLS OF THE HIMALAYAN
MOUNTAINS IN NORTHERN INDIA

During the centuries that walnuts have been grown in the Himalayas, trees that could not survive the cold, heat, soil and competition from other plants and animals have died, and those that survived are extreme-ely hardy. While moderate fertilization, pruning, watering and spraying occurs, it is difficult to show an economic feasibility of these practices. This is due largely to the fact that walnut trees are grown on hilly, rocky and margin land that cannot be easily reached with any equipment except a hoe. The deep and spreading root system of the trees allows them to thrive under the adverse conditions of the Kashmir area.

Expansion in Walnut Quantity and Quality

With the help of national and international funds, the walnut industry in India is rapidly expanding in every dimension. The first move is to gradually replace seedling trees, which come into commercial production in about 17 years, with earlier bearing, more productive selections that come into bearing in half the time. Nuts currently produced range from very hard to very soft shells; from dark shells and kernels to very bright; from small to large, poorly filled shells; and with a wide variety of flavors. About 1965 a program of selecting and propagating superior type trees was begun. Thirty-two selections of early bearing, heavy producing trees of exceptional vigor, that produce medium size, well-filled, bright color shells and kernels are being planted. Six nurseries are propagating 10,000 trees per year for additional plantings.

Projections are that by 1980 there will be 799,584 trees producing 20,396 tons, and by 1990 there will be 1,818,544 trees producing 40,480 tons—or an increase in production of 264% in 13 years.

A program of top-working vigorous trees that produce poor nuts with scions from selected trees is underway. This is the quickest way to upgrade the quantity of good nuts on the same land. There is also a movement to extend walnut orchards further up the mountains at higher elevations.

The second move is to improve the quality of the nuts. The nuts normally fall to the ground as the hulls loosen. But, in order to get walnuts on the early market, harvesting is generally done by shaking the branches by hand or striking them with bamboo poles which often have hooks attached to the ends. This is repeated two or three times at intervals to collect the whole crop.

The nuts are collected by trees, with hand labor. They are cleaned of leaves and trash, and placed in heaps covered with wet leaves where the hulls ferment or "rot" for 9 to 15 days, depending upon the maturity and characteristics of the particular tree and nuts.

Plans are underway to build 15 Grading-Processing Centers, with a capacity of 5 tons per day for 100 days. The freshly harvested walnuts will be sold in the hulls to the co-op on a per tree basis. A sample will be drawn to determine the shelling percentage and quality grade: (a) well-filled, bright, smooth large nuts; (b) culls that are poorly filled, dark, heavily ridged or small; (c) inedible nuts for oil stock. About half of the hulls will come off easily.

FIG. 16.9. WALNUTS DRYING ON THE GROUND IN THE SUN IN INDIA. THEY ARE FIRST HARVESTED, HULLED AND WASHED BY HAND

The nuts with hulls still on will be dipped in a solution of 1500 ppm Ethrel (2-Chloro-ethyl phosponic acid) and piled on the ground 10" deep for 3 to 4 days for the hulls to loosen. The hulls will be removed by motor-driven, abrasion hullers and the nuts spread on the ground to dry. After drying they will be bleached by dipping in 26 to 28% calcium hypochlorite, followed by dipping in a 1% sulfurous acid and thorough rinsing. Following redrying in the sun and with artificial heat, the nuts are size-graded. The small, dark-colored, deeply furrowed or off-type nuts are shelled by hand with a smooth rock.

The shelled nuts will be quality and color-graded by "electronic eye," and packed in 12.5-kg and 25-kg wood boxes, with ends reinforced with metal straps. Most of these will be consumed in India by the Thanksgiving and Christmas trade.

About half of the total production will be packed in-shell in 25-kg boxes, or 100-kg gunny bags, and shipped to Bombay where they will be fumigated and exported to the United Kingdom, Canada, Australia, New Zealand and Western Europe. Fumigation is carried out with methyl bromide using either the vacuum process or the atmospheric pressure tent method.

A small amount of walnuts are exported throughout the year. Shelled walnuts are exported according to the export demand.

USES OF WALNUTS

Walnuts are used in hundreds of ways—raw, salted, in confections, ice cream, bakery goods and others. In popularity and in numbers of ways of serving, walnuts are exceeded only by almonds. Dozens of the recipes for using almonds, Brazil nuts, filberts and pecans are equally suitable for walnuts.

FIG. 16.10.   CHOCOLATE BROWNIES THAT ARE "CHUCK FULL OF WALNUTS"

The Diamond Walnut Growers regularly develop and publish ways of using walnuts. The Walnut Cook Book contains a few dozen top favorite walnut recipes, including cookies, cakes and frostings, pies, desserts, salads, gourmet main dishes, breads, and candies. A similar booklet on Walnut Candy Formulas may be obtained from the Diamond Walnut Growers Incorporated.

Free leaflets may be obtained from the University of California Cooperative Extension Service on: "Some Uses for Edible Nuts," "Preparing and Storing Edible Nuts," "Home Preservation of Shelled Walnuts," and "Walnut Bleaching."

Following are a few useful recipes for using walnuts.

Walnut Chess Pie

1½ tbsp all purpose flour	1 cup heavy cream
½ cup packed brown sugar	½ cup seedless raisins
½ tsp salt	1 cup cut-up pitted dates
1 tsp vanilla extract	1 cup broken walnut meats
2 eggs	Unbaked 9-in. pie shell

Beat eggs until thick and lemon colored. Mix flour, sugar and salt. Add to eggs and beat well. Stir in remaining ingredients, except pie shell. Spoon into shell. Bake in moderate oven 176.6°C (350°F) for 50 min, or until a silver knife inserted in center comes out clean. Cool and serve.

Jellied Walnut Strawberry Cream Pie

3 pkg (9 oz) strawberry flavored gelatin dessert	1 cup chopped walnuts
1½ cups boiling water	1 cup dairy sour cream
1 pkg (10 oz) frozen strawberries	Baked deep 9-in. pie shell
1 can (15¾ oz) crushed pineapple, drained	½ cup heavy cream, whipped
	Fresh strawberries

Dissolve gelatin in boiling water. Add frozen strawberries (undrained). Chill until thickened. Add pineapple and nuts; fold in sour cream. Pour into pie shell and chill until firm. Decorate with whipped cream and fresh berries.

Layer Walnut Fruit Cake

2 cups sugar	1½ cups fresh or frozen coconut
1 cup margarine	1 cup buttermilk
3 eggs	1 tsp soda
3 cups flour	1 cup chopped walnuts
1 tbsp allspice	
1 cup seedless blackberry jam	

Cream sugar and margarine. Add eggs one at a time. Beat after each. Add soda to buttermilk. Add flour and allspice alternately with milk. Add jam and coconut, then nuts. Bake in 3 greased and floured 9-in. layer pans, at 176.6°C (350°F) for 30 to 35 min.

Frosting

2 cups sugar
1 cup evaporated milk
½ cup margarine

1 cup chopped walnuts
1 cup chopped dates
1 tsp vanilla

In sauce pan, combine sugar, milk and margarine. Cook to soft ball stage. Remove from heat and beat until creamy. Stir in nuts, dates and vanilla, until dates are soft. Spread between layers and on top of cake, let run down sides.

Walnut Freezer Roll

1 cup butter or margarine
2 cups brown sugar, packed
½ tsp salt
1½ cups coarsely chopped
   walnuts

3 tsp double-acting baking powder
2 eggs
1 tsp vanilla extract
3 cups sifted all-purpose
   flour

Make, then freeze ahead, as follows:
(1) With mixer at medium speed beat butter with sugar until light and fluffy; beat in eggs and vanilla.
(2) Sift flour with baking powder and salt; beat into butter mixture. Stir in coarsely-chopped walnuts. Wrap in foil, then refrigerate several hours or until firm.
(3) Divide dough in half; shape into two long rolls about 2 in. in diameter; freezer-wrap, then freeze.
To serve: Start heating oven to 190°C (375°F). Unwrap a cookie roll, slice off as many cookies as desired, about ⅛ to ¼ in. thick; freezer-wrap and return unused portion to freezer. Place sliced cookies on greased cookie sheet. Bake about 8 min or until light brown. Cool on wire racks. Makes about 7 dozen.

Walnut-Raisin Bread

1 tbsp vinegar
1 cup milk
1½ cups sifted all-purpose flour
¾ tsp salt
½ tsp double-acting baking
   powder
1 tsp baking soda
Whipped cream cheese, softened

½ cup granulated sugar
1 egg, beaten
⅓ cup molasses
¾ cup uncooked rolled oats
¾ cup seedless raisins
¼ cup chopped California
   walnuts

On the day before: (1) Add vinegar to milk; let stand. (2) Start heating oven to 176°C (350°F). Grease well and lightly flour 9 × 5 × 3 in. loaf pan. (3) Sift together flour, salt, baking powder, baking soda and sugar. Then stir in egg, molasses and milk mixture all at once. Fold in oats, raisins and walnuts. Turn at once into prepared pan. Bake 60 to 70 min or until cake tester, inserted in center, comes out clean. (4) Cool on wire rack, wrap in Saran or foil, store overnight. Serve, sliced, with cheese. Makes one loaf. Nice in lunch boxes.

For 2 loaves: Double ingredients above; proceed as directed.

Walnut Party Bread

2 cups sifted all-purpose flour
4 tsp double-acting baking powder
1 tsp salt
⅔ cup granulated sugar
½ cup coarsely broken California
    walnuts
1 egg, well beaten

½ cup finely snipped pitted
    dates
1 6-oz pkg semisweet
    chocolate pieces
1 cup strong coffee
⅛ tsp baking soda
2 tbsp salad oil

One day or several days ahead:
(1) Grease well and flour 9 × 5 × 3 in. loaf pan. Into large bowl sift flour, baking powder, salt and sugar. Add walnuts, dates and chocolate pieces; then stir with spoon, until all are well coated with flour mixture. (2) Now stir in coffee beverage, soda, egg and salad oil. Pour into baking dish and let stand 20 min. Meanwhile, start heating oven to 190°C (375°F). Bake bread 60 min or until cake tester, inserted in center, comes out clean. (3) Cool 20 min in pan, then remove to wire rack to finish cooling. When cool, wrap in foil or Saran and refrigerate until ready to slice and serve.

Crunchy Walnut Fudge Bar

¾ cup sifted flour
½ tsp baking soda
½ tsp salt
1 cup firmly packed brown sugar
½ cup vegetable shortening

1 egg
½ tsp vanilla
1 cup crushed corn flakes
1 cup quick uncooked oatmeal
⅓ cup chopped nuts

Sift together flour, soda, salt and set aside. Combine sugar, shortening and egg. Add vanilla. Beat until creamy. Blend in gradually the flour mixture; stir in cornflakes, oats and nuts. Reserve 1 cup dough firmly packed. Press into a greased 9 in. square pan the remaining dough and set aside. Prepare filling.

Walnut Applesauce Cake Bars

½ cup margarine
1 cup granulated sugar
1 egg
1 tsp vanilla
1 cup finely sliced dates
1 cup coarsely chopped walnuts

1 can (1 lb 1 oz) applesauce
2¼ cups sifted cake flour
½ tsp cinnamon
¼ tsp cloves
½ tsp soda

Cream margarine and sugar, add egg and vanilla and beat. Add remaining ingredients, mixing well. Turn into well-greased 13 × 9½ × 2 in. pan. Bake in moderate oven, 176.6°C (350°F) 35 min. Cut into bars and dust with confectioners' sugar. Makes 24 bars.

REFERENCES

ALDRICH, T.M. *et al.* 1976A. Soil Management. Part I. Irrigation. Diamond Walnut News *58* (2) 6-7, 33-34.

ALDRICH, T.M. *et al.* 1976B. Soil Management. Part II. Fertilization. Diamond Walnut News *58* (3) 8-9, 25.

ALDRICH, T.M. *et al.* 1976C. Soil Management. Part III. Cultivation. Diamond Walnut News *58* (4) 32-34.

ANON. 1966. The old crafts find new hands. Life Magazine *61* (5) 29, 34.

ANON. 1967. Commercial walnut crop estimated. Peanut J. and Nut World *46* (3) 30-31.

ANON. 1976. Tree nuts, world production, and trade statistics. Foreign Agric. Circ. FN1-76, U.S. Dep. Agric., Foreign Agric. Serv., Wash., D.C.

BATCHELOR, L.D., BRAUCHER, O.L., and SERR, E.F. 1945. Walnut Production in California. Calif. Agric. Exp. Sta. Circ. 364.

BUFFINGTON, A. L., and HAVIGHORST, C. R. 1957. Streamlined processing of nut meats. Food Eng. *29* (6) 64-74, 120-123.

CANNON, P. 1966. Line a day. Ladies Home Journal *83* (8) 90.

DIAMOND WALNUT GROWERS. 1966. Walnut Cook Book. Diamond Walnut Growers, Inc., Stockton, Calif.

FORDE, H.I. 1976. Varieties, old and new. Diamond Walnut News *58*, 8-11, 15.

GRIES, G.A. 1943. Juglone, the active agent in walnut toxicity. Northern Nut Growers Assoc. 34 Annu. Rpt. *42*, 52-55.

JURD, L. 1956. The sterol and carbohydrate constituents of the walnut *Juglans regia.* J. Org. Chem. *21*, 759.

JURD, L. 1956. Plant polyphenols I. The polyphenolic constituents of the pellicle of the walnut, *Juglans regia.* J. Am. Chem. Soc. *78*, 3449.

JURD, L. 1957. Plant polyphenols II. The benzylatin of ellagic acid. J. Am. Chem. Soc *79*, 6043.

KESTER, E.B. 1949. Minor oil-producing crops of the United States. J. Am. Oil Chemists Soc. *26*, 65-83.

KING, J.A. 1961. Diamond Walnut candy formulas. Diamond Walnut Growers, Inc., Stockton, Calif.

KUZIO, W. 1977. Nutmeat Roundup. Candy Ind. *142*, 6, 25-42.

LAGERSTEDT, H.B. 1974. The Oregon walnut industry: A history of its struggle for survival. Proc. Nut Growers Soc. Oreg. & Wash. *59*, 59-63.

LEE, K.C., and CAMPBELL, R.W. 1969. Nature and occurrence of juglone in *Juglans nigra*. Hortscience *4*, 4, 297-298.

LOWE, E., ROCKLAND, L.B., and YANASE, K. 1961. Studies in English (Persian) walnuts, *Juglans regia* IV Food Technol. *15*, 116-117.

MACDANIELS, L.H., and PINNOW, D.L. 1976. Walnut toxicity, an unsolved problem. Northern Nut Growers Assoc. 67th Annu. Rpt. 114-122.

MOHUN, D.T. 1967. Export market for walnuts. Peanut J. and Nut World *46*, *(3)*, 31-32.

O'ROURKE, F.L.S. 1969. The Carpathian (Persian) walnut. *In* Handbook of North American Nut Trees. R.A. Jaynes (Editor). The W.F. Humphrey Press Inc., Geneva, N. Y.

PETERSON, J.K. 1958. Packaging of walnut parts and halves. Research Rept. LMR 58-18. Reynolds Metals Co., Richmond, Va.

ROCKLAND, L.B. 1962. Studies on the processing of shelled walnuts. Calif. Macadamia Soc. Yearb. *8*, 30-34.

ROCKLAND, L.B., LOWE, E., SWARTHOUT, D.M., and JOHNSON, R.A. 1960. Dehydration of kernels of English walnuts with the belt-through drier. Food Technol. *14*, 615-618.

ROCKLAND, L.B., LOWE, E., SWARTHOUT, D.M., and JOHNSON, R.A. 1960. Studies in English (Persian) walnuts, *Juglans regia* II. Food Technol. *14*, 615-618.

ROCKLAND, L.B., and NOBE, B. 1964. Free amino acids in English walnut kernels. J. Agr. and Food Chem. *12*, 528.

ROCKLAND, L.B., SLODOWSKI, P.C., and LUCHSINGER, E.B. 1956. Evaluation of skin color in shelled walnuts. Food Technol. *10*, 113-116.

ROCKLAND, L.B., SWARTHOUT, D.M., and JOHNSON, R.A. 1961. Stabilization of English walnut kernels. Food Technol. *15*, 112-116.

ROMBERG, F.B. 1940. Process and apparatus for separating nut meats and shells. U.S. Patent No. 2,216,050. Sept. 24.

ROMBERG, F.B. 1941. Method and apparatus for detaching and separating nut meats from shells. U.S. Patent No. 2,241,737. May 13.

SERR, E.F. 1969. Persian walnuts in the western states. 240-263. *In* Handbook of North American Nut Trees. R.A. Jaynes (Editor.) The W. F. Humphrey Press Inc., Geneva, N. Y.

SIBBETT, G.S. *et al.* 1974. Walnut kernel quality. Part I. Diamond Walnut News *56* (3) 10, 27.

SIBBETT, G.S. *et al.* 1974. Walnut kernel quality. Part II. Diamond Walnut News *56* (4) 9, 21-23.

STEBBINS, R.L. and GRODER, R.H. 1975. Producing walnuts in Oregon. Oreg. Ext. Bul. 795.

SWARTHOUT, D. M., JOHNSON, R. A., and DE WITTE, S. 1958. Effect of moisture and antioxidant treatment on shelled English walnuts. Food Technol. *12*, 599-601.

17

Tree Nuts of Less Importance

APRICOT NUT

The apricot (*Prunus armeniaca*) is a stone fruit native to the Orient. The kernels of apricots are much like almonds or peaches. Some are sweet, but most are bitter (Bailey 1935).

The kernels are by-products of certain cultivars of apricots grown in the northwestern United States. The "nuts" are roasted, salted and used in confections and cookery. The flavor is mild, and the texture is a little harder and more brittle than that of almonds. The nuts are extremely stable, and have been held edible in dry storage without refrigeration, for more than ten years. The nuts can be blanched, ground or made into paste, and used in many dishes calling for almonds.

The kernels of most apricots are bitter due to the presence of a glycoside compound called amygdalin. Amygdalin, which is a cyanogenic, releases hydrocyanic (prussic) acid in the presence of appropriate enzymes (emulsin). Sweet apricot meats contain only the enzyme but not the amygdalin, hence no bitterness.

A few cultivars or individual trees of sweet apricots are grown in California, Oregon and Idaho. About 1950 a breeding program was embarked on at the Vineland Horticultural Research Institute at Vineland, Ontario, to develop sweet apricot seeds. Of many cultivars and selections tested, four—Reliable, Montgamet, 510915 and 60031—proved to contain sweet kernels.

In all four cultivars, kernels cracked out whole with hand nut crackers. The pits averaged 5.6% of the fruit, with 20 to 25% kernels. Sweet apricot kernels were about one-third the size of almonds, yielding about 90 per oz.

In almonds a single dominant gene controls the sweet-bitter characteristic of the kernel. Single gene dominance is probably not so with apricots, since different degrees of bitterness occur among seedlings.

It has been reported that most of the apricots of central Asia have sweet kernels (Grimo 1972).

BEECHNUT

The beeches (*Fagaceae*) include at least eight species in the northern hemisphere. The trees are tall, deciduous, of noble symmetrical habit, with smooth light gray bark and clean dark green foliage, which is rarely attacked by insects and diseases. They are the most ornamental and beautiful trees for park planting and are attractive at every season. All of the eight species, save one, are cultivated and differ comparatively little from each other.

Courtesy of Diamond/Sunsweet

FIG. 17.1. BEECHNUT FRUIT AND SEED

FIG. 17.2. WILD BEECHNUT TREES IN MIDDLE TENNESSEE

The common beeches of both Europe and North America are closely related. The former is associated with ancient myths and stories of love and war, and celebrated in poetry and song. The beech in Europe is found in the forests of Great Britain, Norway, Sweden, France, and Germany, and southward to Constantinople, Palestine, Asia Minor and Armenia. It was well known and highly appreciated by all the early inhabitants of these countries. As a monumental tree the beech has no rival, for it has a smooth gray bark, is perennial, and remains almost unchangeable.

American Beech

The American beech (*Fagus grandifolia*) thrives in valleys of the Appalachian Mountains, and extends from New Jersey and southern Illinois to Florida and Texas. The trees thrive in a cool climate at higher elevations, and tolerate considerable shade and competition from other trees. The bark is lighter in color, the head is broader and more roundish, and the leaves are less shiny than the European beech.

European Beech

The European beech (*Fagus sylvatica*) has an oval head and shining foliage, which turns reddish brown in the fall and remains on the branches through almost the whole winter. It is the common hardwood tree of central Europe, particularly Denmark and Germany (Bailey 1935). This tree is sometimes used for hedges.

Uses of Beechnuts

Beechnuts are triangular in shape and are born in small burrs, which shed naturally in late summer. They fall over a period of several weeks and deteriorate within two weeks unless harvested and dried. The kernels are born in shells, which comprise of about 46% of the nuts. The composition of the edible portion is 6.6% water, 21.8% protein, 49.9% fat, 18% carbohydrates, 3.7% ash, and contains 2740 calories per pound. The well-ripened nuts yield 17 to 20% of a nondrying oil suitable for illumination and cooking (Smith 1928; Buszewicz 1962).

In Europe, the nuts have been esteemed as food for man as well as for wild and domestic animals. They have been found to be eaten by 15 species of birds, as well as wild turkeys, foxes, squirrels, bears and deer. Swine fattened on beechnuts have for ages been noted for their excellent flesh. Beechnuts have long been important in Europe as food for the wild boar of the forest and for the semi-wild hog of Europe.

American-grown beechnuts are seldom collected for food because of the small size, often poor filling qualities, and the difficulty of harvesting. The black beech grown in Kentucky has nuts that are black and about twice the size of ordinary beechnuts. While the oil roasted or dry roasted nuts have excellent quality, and there are many ways to use them in the diet, a search of published recipes reveals practically none that use beechnuts.

Even when the nuts are small they may be collected in quantities and the oil expressed, as has been done in European countries. Beechnut oil is valuable for cooking purposes and as a salad oil. In some parts of Europe it is used in place of butter. The cakes which remain after the oil is pressed out serve as food for stock and fowls.

The best uses of beechnuts in America seem to be for the beauty of the trees and for the abundant supply of nuts for wild and domestic animals.

Betel Nut

The Betel nut (*Areca catechu*) is the fruit of a palm grown on the South Sea islands. Chewing the nut as a stimulant is a part of life in Palau and Yap islands in the Carolinas. The seed contains a red dye which stains the teeth and lips, and may produce oral cancer. Early in 1876 the FDA banned selling the nuts in the United States, importing them, or carrying them across state lines. The nuts grow on palm trees in bunches and are as large as prunes.

BUTTERNUT

Few persons of the present generation are acquainted with the butternut (*Juglans cinerea*), sometimes called the white walnut. Nonetheless, among nut enthusiasts the quality of this nut rates at or close to the top for quality. From a nutritive standpoint it leads all others, with 3370 calories per pound to the 3300 calories of its closest competitor, the pecan. In protein content, the butternut also tops the list, as it is made up of 27.9% of this important ingredient.

The wood is highly prized for cabinet making, which explains the rapid disappearance of this fine tree from native stands. Were it not for a limited number of nurserymen propagating some of the named cultivars and others selling seedlings, this species could follow the path of the native American chestnut, *Castanea dentata*, and disappear.

The butternut has much to commend itself, both as a bearer of tasty nuts and as a specimen tree. It is the hardiest of all nut species and is most likely to succeed in poor soil. In general, the trees are not difficult to transplant on their own roots, are early bearing, and are relatively easy to grow. The bark is lighter and grayer than that of black walnut and much smoother.

Courtesy of D.F. Millikan

FIG. 17.3.   YOUNG BUTTERNUT TREE SHOWING CLOSE
SIMILARITY WITH BLACK WALNUT TREE

Additional Characteristics

The heartwood is light chestnut brown, and a fine, hairy fuzz covers the young twigs, petioles, leaves, buds and fruit. These tiny hairs exude a sticky substance containing a dye, once used in the mountains of West Virginia, Kentucky and Tennessee prior to the days of the chemical dyes. The leaf is compound, similar to that of the black walnut, having 11 to 19 leaflets which are serrated and pointed at their tips.

The nut is pointed and oblong, with deep ridges running the length of the shell. Except for selected cultivars, the kernel is thin and somewhat difficult to remove from the shell. This kernel is sweet, oily and fragrant, with a taste like no other nut, although it is approached in flavor by the Japanese butternut, *J. sieboldiana*, a close relative.

Unfortunately, butternuts have the reputation of being susceptible to disease and therefore short-lived. Location may be a prime factor in their survival, since trees in favorable situations of soil and moisture live to be of large size and an old age.

Two diseases commonly affect the butternut. One of these is a leaf spot caused by the fungus responsible for the anthracnose disease of black walnut. Defoliation resulting from this disease probably predisposes the tree to injury by other pathogens, including the other disease, melanconis blight. Normally, this disease is of little consequence, since the causative fungus, *Melaconis juglandis*, is a weak pathogen and attacks only trees already weakened by other difficulties.

The earliest cultivar selected for propagation was the Aiken. Since that time over 30 cultivars have been described, but only a few remain in the trade. Presently, Buckley, Love, Craxezy, Kenworthy and Weschecke are sold. Buckley originated in Iowa; Craxezy and Love were discovered in Michigan; and Kenworthy and Weschecke are natives of Wisconsin.

Butternuts, like other nut trees, are difficult to propagate by budding or grafting. The species has a more fibrous root system than that of black walnut and will graft most easily to its own seedlings. However, since the trees are longer-lived on black walnut roots and these seedlings are readily available, the better cultivars are generally worked on black walnut roots.

The rich flavor of the nut combined with the precocious bearing habit (two to three years) of the species makes butternuts an attractive addition to the family of edible nut crops. Early maturity into interesting tree forms with appealing gray bark suggests that this species deserves much more attention from the suburban landscaper.

Butternuts are harvested, shelled, stored and used similarly to black walnuts. They are especially useful in candy, ice cream and bakery products (Millikan 1966).

CHINQUAPINS

Chinquapins (*Castinea pumila*) are widespread throughout the area west of the Cascade Mountains of Oregon and Washington. They are common in the foothills or lower mountains where they are very abundant at times. The trees recover from forest fires ahead of most forest trees. The evergreen trees reach a height of 50 to 100 ft.

Chinquapins, known as bushy chestnuts, are also grown as small trees in the Appalachian areas, extending south to middle Georgia. The trees are relatively resistant to chestnut blight; hybrids between chestnuts and chinquapins may solve the blight problem. No efforts have been made in the United States to cultivate chinquapins, though they are useful for planting on slopes and roadsides.

The nuts are small, resembling chestnuts or beechnuts, and are relatively hard to shell from the spiny burs. Chinquapin nuts are sweet and more palatable than chestnuts, and were prized as food by the Indians and early Americans. They have been traded or marketed for more than two centuries. The numerous burs are an 1½ in. in diameter, and commonly arranged in a spike-like cluster. The plant blooms in June and the brown nuts ripen in September. The burs contain one or two nuts. The nuts are round, somewhat pointed at the top, and about half as large as the American chestnut. They have much the same appearance of small acorns.

They may be badly infested with nut weevils while on the tree, and are a favorite host for squirrels, worms and mold after being harvested.

Chinquapins contain about 5% fat, 5% protein, 40% starch, and 1800 calories per pound. They are eaten raw, roasted in the shell, and used like chestnuts.

Corozo Nut

The corozo palm (*Carnauba cerifera*) of Brazil is one of the world's most useful trees. It grows to a height of 35 to 40 ft. Lumber dealers refer to it as the "department store tree" for it gives everything from medicine to cattle feed. Its roots make a valuable drug that is used as a blood purifier. Its timber takes a high polish and is in demand among cabinet makers for fine work. The sap is made into wine or vinegar. Starch and sugar can also be obtained from the sap. The fruit of the tree is used as cattle food; the nut is a good coffee substitute; and the pitch makes cork.

Also, since 1846 it has produced the well-known carnauba wax. The leaves are cut from the trees during the dry season. They are then dried, shredded, and flailed to remove the wax which becomes a yellowish powder. The wax is used in various products, such as shoe polish, auto polish, carbon paper, lubricating grease, electric insulation, anti-fouling paints, lipstick and candles (Anon. 1976).

Heartnut

The heartnut or Japanese walnut (*Juglans sieboldiana*) is a native of Japan and was introduced into the United States along with the Japanese chestnuts about 1860. It resembles the American butternut in productivity, flavor and uses. The nut resembles a heart in shape, both before and after being hulled, and the kernel is heart-shaped.

Production of heartnuts in the United States is on the increase, especially in the areas adapted to black walnuts and Carpathian walnuts. This is the east central region from Missouri to the Atlantic coast. Heartnuts are equal to either of these in hardiness, but seem to be shorter lived. A bunch disease of the tree is one of the worst problems in production.

Though it was introduced in California first, it adapted better to more northern climates. It has been grown successfully in many southern

Ontario locations as well as in British Columbia. However, interest in it was only of a novelty nature, and serious considerations of its use as a commercial nut tree never materialized.

Many selections have been made of the heartnut, but few have been named or tested. There has been little organized interest in the heartnut in Canada, though, ironically enough, the Gellatly's, a Canadian family, have been responsible for the most named cultivars of heartnut of any one source in North America.

The tree nut grows rapidly on good loam soils and produces an apple tree sized, wide-spreading tree with large compound leaves that give it a lush tropical appearance. They begin to bear quite young. The green nuts hang down in clusters and ripen in September, when they drop to the ground. The thin husk can be tramped off and the nuts are then washed and dried for use.

Heartnut trees have been known to survive -40°F. The heartnut readily hybridizes with the butternut, the hardiest of the walnut species. Nut enthusiasts have long searched for a butternut in a heartnut shell with the butternut hardiness.

The nuts are produced in clusters of ten or more, are smaller than black walnuts, and have a rather thick shell. They are about the size of large hickory nuts. Cracking is easy and the kernels come out either whole or in halves. They may be mild to butternut-like in flavor.

The several steps in processing heartnuts, including harvesting, hulling, drying, storing and shelling, are similar to those of black walnuts. The uses are as a flavoring and texture-improving ingredient for confections, bakery goods and ice cream. Recipes using heartnut meats are similar to those for black walnuts. The chemical composition and nutritional values are similar to those of Persian walnuts.

Hickory Nut

Notwithstanding the high esteem in which several native species of hickory nuts have been held since the settlement of America by the white men, little progress has been made in their domestication and improvement, except with pecans. Of the ten or more species found, pecans have received more attention than all of the others combined.

Doubtless no other nut has a kernel with the aromatic properties of the hickory, and no other has as high flavor in cookery. In flavor and quality of kernel the shagbark hickory is esteemed by most Americans as the choicest of native hickories, along with the pecan and shellbark. The thinner shell and larger proportion of kernel have given the pecan first place, the shagbark hickory second, and the shellbark hickory third place. Hickory nutmeats are considered to be a specialty item.

FIG. 17.4.   COROZO NUTS

Description of Species

Of about a dozen native species of hickories, brief descriptions of six follow. The others are of minor importance.

Shagbark Hickory.—Shagbark hickory (*C. ovata*) is one of the most abundant hickories in the eastern and central states as shown in Fig. 17.11. It is the fastest growing of hickories and probably the most distinctive in appearance because of the long, loose plates of bark. Common names include scalybark, shellbark, upland and shagbark. It grows in humid climates, and is found on upland slopes and lowlands. They are often found on fertile soil, near streams and springs.

Courtesy of L.H. MacDaniels

FIG. 17.5.   HICKORY NUTS AND SHUCKS, *C. OVATA*, WILCOX
VARIETY

Native trees begin bearing in about 10 years, much later than when cultivated, and produce nuts for 300 years. The trees reach a height of 140 ft and are highly resistant to insects and diseases.

Courtesy of U.S. Forest Service

FIG. 17.6. SHAGBARK HICKORY TREE IN WEST VIRGINIA
MONONGAHELA NATIONAL FOREST

There are at least 15 cultivars of shagbark hickories grown and prop-
agated by nurseries. These are Curtis, Dover, Eliot, Hale, Papershell,
Jackson, Kentucky, Kirtland, Leaming, Meridian, Milford, Rice, Swain,
Vest and Woodbourne.

The nuts are moderate in size, and thin shelled, and are consumed as
food by both humans and wildlife, with a limited commercial market.
They are an important portion of the diet of red squirrel (*Sciurus
hudsonicus*), Eastern gray squirrel (*S. carolinunsis*), Eastern fox squirrel

Courtesy of U.S. Forest Service

FIG. 17.7. HULL AND NUT OF SHAGBARK HICKORY

(*S niger*), Eastern chipmunk (*Tamias striatur*), and raccoon (*Procyon lotor*) (Nelson 1961). Shagbark is a heavy-seeded species and averages 100 seeds per pound. Wide variations occur in size, shape and color of the nut, in the thickness of the shell, and in sweetness of the nutmeat.

The fruit ripens in September and October and the seeds are dispersed from September through December. The older trees are too large and tall

Courtesy of L.H. MacDaniels

FIG. 17.8. WILCOX SHAGBARK HICKORY

Very good shell structure with good cracking quality

to shake the nuts down, consequently some trees hold a large part of the crop until Christmas. The nuts fall out of the hulls while on the tree, so no hulling by hand is necessary.

Trees producing easy-to-shell nuts have been developed and are available from nurserymen. These are planted in areas too far north for the production of pecans.

Shellbark Hickory.—Shellbark hickory (*C. laciniosa*) is confused with the shagbark hickory, and is sometimes called by that name. These have somewhat shaggy bark with strips that are thicker and hang on longer. They are most abundant in the eastern Mississippi Valley.

The nuts are large, and very abundant, have a thick shell, and are good to eat. The kernels are sweet, difficult to crack out in large pieces but of excellent quality. At least three cultivars—Lefevre, Rieke and Weiker—are propagated.

Courtesy of L.H. MacDaniels

FIG. 17.9. UNNAMED SEEDLING SHAGBARK HICKORY
THICK SHELL KERNELS BOUND SO THAT KERNELS
CAN ONLY BE RECOVERED IN FRAGMENTS

Courtesy of U.S. Forest Service

FIG. 17.10. TRUNK AND BARK OF SHAGBARK HICKORY

Mocknut Hickory.—Mocknut hickory (*C. tomentosa*), big bud or white hickory (*C. alba*) has a wide range, but is most abundant in the southern United States. Though it grows in abundance in southern uplands, it extends north into Canada.

SHAGBARK
HICKORY

Courtesy of U.S. Forest Service

FIG. 17.11. NATURAL RANGE OF SHAGBARK HICKORY

The range of mocknut hickories is similar to that of pignut hickories, but not quite so extensive in the south, west and north.

These are among the largest hickory trees, which produce the largest nuts with the thickest shells. Though the quality of the meats is excellent, they are seldom marketed due to the difficulty of extraction and low cracking percentage. There are a lot of poorly filled and otherwise faulty nuts.

Pignut Hickory.—Pignut hickory is an ambiguous term. No less than five presently recognized species of hickory are called by this name. The most widely recognized pignut hickory is *C. glabra*. Other common names for this cultivar include oval pignut hickory, red hickory, redheart hickory, small-fruited hickory and sweet pignut.

Pignut hickory is distributed from southern Maine to southern Ontario and southern Michigan south to the Atlantic Coastal plains (Fig 17.16), and reaches its greatest height of 90 ft in the basin of the lower Ohio River. It is the hickory most commonly found in the Appalachian forest and grows at higher elevations in this area (Nelson 1961).

The nuts mature from September through October. It is one of the lighter-seeded hickories, averaging 200 seed per pound. Although the kernels are sweet and eaten by animals (hence the name pignut), they are too small and tedious to hull and shell for extensive collection as human food. The hulls do not normally split separate from the nut; therefore, dehulling is a separate operation not common with most hickories. The

Courtesy of U.S. Forest Service

FIG. 17.12.   PIGNUT HICKORY TREE IN GREEN COUNTY,
GEORGIA

trees are extremely prolific producers and large quantities of the nuts can
be raked up and cracked for oil extraction. The adhering hulls give the
nuts added protection after they fall to the ground, and are a favorite
food for squirrels, raccoons, chipmunks and some birds during the winter
months.

Courtesy of U.S. Forest Service

FIG. 17.13.   HULL AND NUT OF PIGNUT HICKORY

Courtesy of U.S. Forest Service

FIG. 17.14. TRUNK AND BARK OF PIGNUT HICKORY,
DISTRICT OF COLUMBIA

The pignut which is similar to shagbark in area of distribution is much inferior to the other species in quality, but shows wider variations than either the shagbark, shellbark or mocknut hickory.

Bitternut Hickory.—Bitternut hickory (*C. cordiformis*), sometimes called swamp hickory pignut, is the only member of the hickory group common to the northeastern United States, and is probably the most

Courtesy of U.S. Forest Service

FIG. 17.15. LEAF AND FRUIT OF PIGNUT HICKORY

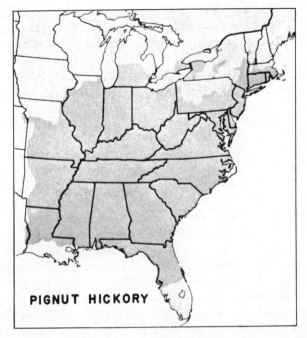

PIGNUT HICKORY

Courtesy of U.S. Forest Service

FIG. 17.16. NATURAL RANGE OF PIGNUT HICKORY

abundant and uniformly distributed. It is common from southern New England west to Iowa and from southern Michigan south to Kentucky.

Production begins when the trees are about 30 years old and continues until they are 175 years old. A heavy drop is produced only about every three to five years. While relished by wild animals and useful for oil, they are not processed into foods because of the bitter flavor.

Hybrids.—Hybrid species of hickories are known to cross and produce hybrids. This is why many trees or types do not fit the description of any species. While this is confusing to the botanist, it is no deterrent to one seeking to find a superior cultivar. In fact, hybridizing may be a short cut to improving the eating qualities.

Hundreds of trees with superior qualities, and supposed to be hybrids, have been found and propagated. The most valuable of these are known as hicans, and are presumed to be hybrids. A few of these are identified as Hinke, McCallister, Burton (shagbark X *C. illinoiensis*), Burlington (shellbark X *C. illinoiensis*), Pleas (bitternut X *C. illinoiensis*), and Berger (shellbark X mocknut.).

Superior Cultivars.—More than 50 cultivars of hickories have been propagated in various sections of the country. The Fox is the best known and most consistent bearer in Minnesota. The Kirtland is an old, but less dependable cultivar.

Qualities demanded in hickory nuts are good yield, large nutmeats, well-filled shells, high kernel content, ease in shelling, and agreeable flavor.

Because hickory nuts have not been planted or grown commercially to any great extent in the United States, little effort has been made to accumulate systematic information on their production, processing and products. Hickory nutmeats are available from specialized markets.

Of 38 cultivars planted at Beltsville, Maryland, all were poor bearers as compared with other tree nuts. Lingerfelter, Schinnerling and Shaul cultivars have been found to be outstanding in yield and leaf spot resistance, and are recommended for planting in spite of only average cracking qualities. Standard cultivars as Romig, Hagen, Kirtland and Kentucky have good cracking qualities but are susceptible to leaf spot. While trees of the shellbark and shagbark hickories are similar, the nuts of the former are much larger (McKay and Crane 1957).

Many cultivars for one defect or another, such as poor cracking qualities, inferior kernels and others, have been abandoned over the years, even though they bore generously. Among these are Abscoda, Davis, Gohun, Honeybrooke, Lingerfelter, Mefford and Stratford. All points weighed, the most promising cultivars of shagbark hickories for the South are Fox, Wilcox, Romig, Whitney, Shaul, Manahan, Weschoke, Mann, Joliffee and Grainger (Dunstan 1960).

For northern states, Wilcox and Davis are first choice; in the second choice come Bauer, Clark, Berger and Bridgewater; and in the third place are Cedar Rapids, Fox, Minnie, Neilson and Triplett. The Anthony cultivar is promising (Smith 1960).

Harvesting Hickory Nuts

Most hickory nuts mature and fall to the ground in October or early November. Different species or individual trees mature at different times, but generally the nuts fall about two weeks ahead of the leaves, and the leaves fall following the first frost. Hickories do not need to be shaken or knocked from the trees.

When mature, the hulls of hickories, of all species except the pignuts, split into four or five sections and loosen from the nut. The nuts, hulls, leaves, sticks and other debris collect on the ground and present problems in harvesting. Since hickory nut trees are almost always in the woods and on uncultivated land, the soil cannot be mechanically cleared of trash.

The most feasible and economical way to harvest hickory nuts is to allow the nuts to fall to the ground and pick them up by hand. In the woods there is the ever present competition with squirrels, chipmunks, racoons, crows, wild turkeys and human "nut hunters."

The following cultivars in New York state ripen their nuts in a season of 150 days from the time the buds first burst into leaf: Anthony (130 days), Weschoke (133 days), Bauer (140 days), Cedar Rapids (140 days), Fox (143 days), Clark (145 days), Wilcox (148 days), Minnie (148 days), and Davis (150 days) (Smith 1960).

Care After Harvesting

Most hickory nuts contain about 10% moisture when harvested, and will mold if not dried to about 5% moisture. Drying and curing should be done with circulated dry air without heat. The nuts may be placed on racks, either loose or in half-filled mesh bags, and dried in the sun or shade. About two weeks are required for full flavor development.

After drying, the nuts may be placed in mesh bags containing about 100 lb each and held in a cool dry place until they are shelled. Common storage will hold hickory nuts through the winter and until warm weather in spring. Nuts stored under ordinary atmospheric conditions will be of about the right degree of dryness. Those held for longer periods should be stored at 0° to 1.1°C (32° to 34° F) with 65% relative humidity. They may be held for two years.

Shelling Hickory Nuts

Hickory nuts are difficult to shell, and at best the yield of meats seldom runs above 25%, with 15% being more common. Three steps are involved. First, the nuts are moistened about 12 hours in advance, which prevents the meats from becoming excessively brittle. Second, the nuts are cracked by striking or applying pressure at several points on the shoulder of either end of each nut. The plunger crushes the nut for about 1/16 in. which shatters the shells but leaves the meats whole. Third, the shells and meats are separated by a series of shaker screens. The meats are not only separated but are graded into halves, large pieces, medium pieces, small pieces and meal.

The meats become stale or rancid with one month unless refrigerated, but may be held for 6 months at 0° to 1.1°C (32° to 34°F), and for 2 years at 17.8°C (0°F).

Future of Hickory Nuts

The production of hickory nuts has been declining for several decades and will continue to for the following reasons: (a) while many cultivars have been developed, the nuts have not been "domesticated," and the supply is largely from wild trees; (b) under the conditions they are grown, mechanized harvesting is impossible and harvesting by hand is prohibitive cost-wise; (c) the shelling percentage is as low as 20% which further increases the cost of the meats; (d) the yield per tree or per acre is low as compared with other nuts; and (e) the inroads of highways, parks, industries and shopping centers are cutting out native hickory trees faster than they are allowed to reproduce. It is regrettable that horticulturists, foresters and food scientists have not done more to provide products with possibly the most delicious of all nuts.

Saving the better hickory trees has been a major concern of the Northern Nut Growers Association. Over a period of 50 years many trees have been selected for their superior cracking quality and given clonal names. The best of these have kernels that can be recovered as whole halves but they do not approach the better pecan cultivars in percentage of kernels, weight of kernel, or ease of cracking.

The greatest obstacles to the culture and improvements of the hickories are the difficulty of producing nursery trees, problems of transplanting, and their delayed bearing. Shagbark seedling stocks are of slow growth and during the first seedling years form an unbranched taproot that is larger than the above-ground parts. Producing an acceptable nursery tree of a shagbark may take six to seven years, and then transplanting failure may occur unless special care is used.

Uses of Hickory Nuts

The limited supply of hickory nutmeats restricts the use to a few special recipes. Where available they may be substituted for pecan meats in most of the recipes on pp 507 to 522. Due to the high flavor and delicate texture only about half the quantity of hickory nuts is used in ice cream, cookies and candies as is indicated for pecan meats.

Since hickory nut meats seldom appear as halves, and are more expensive than most other nuts, they are practically never salted, used in fruitcakes, or for topping pies.

Hickory Nut Custard

Home	Commercial
1 cup hickory nut kernels, rolled	1½ lb
3 tbsp cornstarch	1 cup
1 egg	6
1 cup molasses	3 pints
1 cup water	3 pints

¼ tsp salt
1 cup whipping cream
2 baked pie crusts

1½ tsp
3 pints
12 pie crusts

Combine the kernels, sugar and cornstarch. To beaten eggs, add the molasses, water and salt. Pour slowly into the sugar-nut mixture, blending thoroughly. Boil until thick, cool, pour into pie crusts, and top with sweetened whipped cream. Chill for several hours before serving.

Hickory Nut Soup

When hickory nuts are dry, crack between rocks or by other means. Sieve out the large hulls, place the kernels and small hulls in a beater, and pound until a paste is formed. Roll in balls and keep until needed. For serving, place several balls in hot water with constant stirring. When made into a thick soup it may be served with any type of bread or dumpling. If made into a thin soup it may be used as a drink, as soon as the first soup has been poured off more water may be added. Do not drink the very last of the mixture because it contains bits of hulls (Beck 1966).

REFERENCES

ANON. 1965. Foreign Agriculture. Foreign Agric. Serv., October. U.S. Dep. Agric.

ANON. 1976. Your questions answered. The Nutshell. Northern Nut Growers Assoc. *30*, 1, 2. Knoxville, Tenn.

BAILEY, L.B. 1935. The Standard Cyclopedia of Horticulture, Vols. 2 and 3. Macmillan, New York.

BECK, M.U., and BECK, S.E. 1966. The Cherokee Cooklore. The Stephens Press, Asheville, N. C.

BRYANT, D. 1967. Production of piñon nuts in New Mexico. Northern Nut Growers Assoc. 58th Annu. Rep. 116-118.

BUSZEWICZ, G.M. 1962. The longevity of beechnuts in relation to storage conditions. Great Brit. Forest Comm. Rep. Forest Res. *196.* 117-126.

CLARK W.S. 1966. Edible nut production correspondence course in Agriculture. Circ. *153*, Pa. State Univ.

DUNSTAN, R.T. 1960. Hickories for the upper south. Northern Nut Growers Assoc. 51st Annu. Rep. 74-76.

FULLER, A.S. 1904. The Nut Culturist. Orange Judd Co., New York.

GELLATLY, J.U. 1966. Heartnuts—outstanding selections and hybrids. Northern Nut Growers Assoc. 57th Annu. Rep. 103-110.

GRIMO, E. 1972. Dual purpose apricots. Northern Nut Growers Assoc. 63rd Annu. Rep. 105-107.

HOOKER, W.V. 1967. Chinquapins in Oklahoma. Northern Nut Growers Assoc. 58th Annu. Rep. 118-120.

MACDANIELS, L.H., and PINNOW, D.L. 1976. Walnut toxicity. Northern Nut Growers Assoc. 67th Annu. Rep. 114-121.

MCKAY, J.W., and CRANE, H.L. 1957. Yield and leaf spot ratings for hickories. Northern Nut Growers Assoc. 48th Annu. Rep. 61-65.

MILLIKAN, D.F. 1966. The butternut. American Nurseryman *123*, 8, 15.

MILLIKAN, D.F., and HIBBARD, A.D. 1967. Butternuts, an overlooked tree crop. Northern Nut Growers Assoc. 58th Annu. Rep. 120-122.

NELSON, T.C. 1961. Silvical characteristics of shagbark hickory. U.S. Agric. Forest Serv., Southeast Forest Exp. Stn. No. 135, Asheville, N.C.

18

Candy Plant Sanitation

INSECT PESTS[1]

The hardy pioneer in traveling through the wilds of North America was little concerned about sanitation as we know it today. Drinking water was as close as the nearest stream. Food depended on a steady aim with a rifle. Bathing was viewed as inimical to health and total immersion only occurred when someone fell into a stream.

Man, being gregarious, began to live in groups, usually near water for mutual protection against hostile Indians and other environmental hazards. Exchange of labor and goods became easier.

With this developing society, problems of sanitation began to develop such as contaminated food and polluted air and water. People were in closer contact and the transmission of contagious diseases became easier.

Typhoid fever has been traced to carriers of typhoid bacteria. Contaminated water suppliers have also caused cholera epidemics; plague-infected rats are reservoirs of this disease which is transmitted by the bite of the rat fleas to human contacts, and malaria is still a world health problem. The list is long. As man's knowledge has developed, the causes of those things harmful and beneficial to man have become more and more evident. Disease-producing bacteria have been traced to nuts. Filth in storage rooms is spread by insects and rodents.

Catastrophe often precedes and brings into focus the necessity for social change. As urban communities developed, sanitation did not develop accordingly. Hence, during the nineteeth century the outbreaks of epidemics of yellow fever, smallpox, typhoid fever, typhus, etc., occurred. In our modern society, indoor plumbing is usual rather than unusual.

---

[1] By Gerald S. Doolin, former Director of Research and Sanitation, National Confectioners Association, Chicago, Illinois.

Our modern society also has developed the techniques of mass food production. This highly developed technology created problems of food sanitation. These sanitation problems were reflected usually in a quality of candies and other food unacceptable to the consumer. The consumer is not concerned with the sanitation problems of the food manufacturer. He expects clean, wholesome palatable foods. Prevention is the key to good sanitation. Basically, people are the cause of good or poor sanitation in candy plants, and insects follow closely as main causes.

Insect Control

The continued increase in the number of candy and other food manufacturing establishments and distribution patterns led to the development of guides for the safe handling of nuts, sugar and the like, so that the consumer would be protected against health hazards.

The basic provisions of the Federal Food and Drug Acts are concerned with:

(1) Harmful adulterations that are of immediate danger to health. An example is poisons accidentally mixed with food such as insecticides in flour or sugar, insecticides mistaken for food, etc.

(2) Esthetic requirements such as preventing filth in foods or foods manufactured in filthy environments. Examples are live or dead insects, insect fragments, or rodent hair in foods, indicating rodent filth.

(3) Economic requirements directed toward protecting the consumer's pocketbook. Examples are "fill of container," labeling misrepresentation as to the true nature of the food, etc.

The Federal Food and Drug Act also regulates, through the courts, the consignment of foods in interstate commerce as well as those foods that have moved in interstate commerce. The special problems in confectionery manufacture concern the storage and handling of nuts so they do not become stale, rancid or infested with insects. The insects attacking nutmeats are pests at the agricultural level. Their small size makes it easy for them to pass through the shellers, cleaners, graders and other equipment used to process nuts. One or two of these insects can be easily missed by visual inspection—for example, in a case of nutmeats. In the absence of adult insects, there might be present microscopic eggs which will hatch and eventually become adult insects.

It is a questionable practice to destroy insects after the infestation has become obvious. While insects may be killed by heat, cold, fumigants, or rays, the dead insects and insect fragments remain. These insects and fragments can be detected by appropriate analytical methods, and the courts have not made a legal distinction between dead or live insects in foods.

Control begins with preventing insects from multiplying in foods. It is important to recognize the insects to be controlled. It is also important to know their appearance, habitat, breeding habits, size, etc. A basic knowledge of these insects often reveals a weak spot in their ecology, making control procedures more efficient. The insects that attack confectionery ingredients, other than sugar and corn syrup, are referred to as the "stored grain insects" or the "stored product insects." These insects fall into two groups—those that attack whole or intact grains, and those that attack broken grains or feed on grain fragments. There are many publications by the U.S. Department of Agriculture, State University Experiment Stations, private agencies and corporations describing these insects and their habits in detail.

Common Insects

The two orders of insects that are of prime importance as pests of stored foods are: Coleoptera—this order includes the confused flour beetles, saw tooth grain beetle, cadelle beetle and dermestid beetles; and Lepidoptera—this includes the chocolate moth, Mediterranean flour moth, the Indian meal moth and others.

Females lay from 40 to 350 eggs near the food. The eggs hatch in from 2 days to 2 weeks into whitish caterpillars. They may require 2 weeks to 2 years to reach full growth, reaching a length of about ⅓ to ½ in. It is this stage in the life cycle of the representative Coleoptera and Lepidoptera larvae that causes the damage to food ingredients. The adult Coleoptera also cause damage by feeding. The adult Lepidoptera usually do not cause damage by feeding.

See p. 468 for description of insects in stored nuts.

Confused Flour Beetles (*Tribolium confusum*) and Red Flour Beetles (*Tribolium castaneum*).—These insects (Figs. 18.1 and 18.2) are similar in their feeding habits. They are also very similar in appearance, so similar, in fact, that the two species were confused for a number of years. It should be pointed out that the observers and not the insects were confused. The difference is only of taxonomic interest. Both species feed on nuts, legumes, flour, starchy products, cereals, ginger, dried fruits, chocolate, drugs, cayenne pepper, snuff and many compound foods.

They are very active when disturbed, and may live two years in a favorable environment. During this time the female may lay 1000 eggs. These eggs hatch in 5 to 12 days into small worms or larvae and grow to about ⅐ in. in length. They form a pupa or inactive feeding stage for

Courtesy of U.S. Dept. Agric.

FIG. 18.1.   ADULT CONFUSED FLOUR BEETLE

about two weeks. This stage is similar to the cocoon formed by moths. A complete generation may occur about every three to five months, depending on temperature and food.

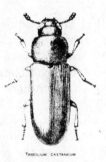

Courtesy of U.S. Dept. Agric.

FIG. 18.2.   RED FLOUR BEETLE

These two species of beetles feed on broken and particulate materials. There are a number of other beetles belonging to this group that are collectively referred to as "bran bugs." The adults vary in length from $\frac{1}{16}$ to $\frac{1}{17}$ in.

Saw-Toothed Grain Beetle (*Orzaephilus surinamensis L.*).—It is somewhat compressed dorso-ventrally, enabling this species (Fig. 18.3) to penetrate between seams of apparently tightly packaged food. Its food preference is similar to the confused flour beetle. The adults can survive throughout the winter in unheated buildings. When examined under a lens, six tooth-like projections will be noted on each side of the thorax. This is the area where the legs are attached, immediately behind the head. This characteristic makes it easy to identify the insect.

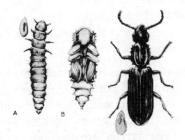

Courtesy of U.S. Dept. Agric.

FIG. 18.3. SAW-TOOTHED GRAIN BEETLE

(a) Larva, (b) pupa and adult.

The female lays eggs that hatch in 3 to 18 days into a white 6-legged larva with a brown head. The larva becomes full grown in 2 to 10 weeks and measures about ⅛ in. in length. The full grown larva forms a protective covering from bits of food material. It remains inactive in this pupal stage from one to three weeks and emerges as an adult insect. Reports indicate that four to six generations occur yearly in the United States. Under favorable conditions the entire life cycle may be completed in 24 to 30 days.

Cadelle Beetles (*Tenebroides mauritanicus L.*).—This beetle may become a pest where bulk nuts and grains are stored, particularly if the storage equipment is constructed of wood. This black beetle is one of the largest beetles attacking grains. The adult measures ⅓ to ½ in. in length. Eggs are laid in groups of 10 to 60. A single female beetle has been reported to lay 1300 eggs. The eggs hatch in one or two weeks into larvae having black heads, and black spots on the first three thoracic segments. The larvae are about ⅔ in. when fully grown (Fig. 18.4).

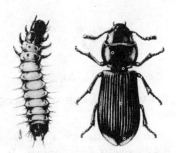

Courtesy of U.S. Dept. Agric.

FIG. 18.4. CADELLE BEETLE, LARVA AND ADULT

Depending on environmental conditions the larvae may complete their development from 70 days to 14 months. Full grown larvae and adults may bore into wood adjoining their food source and cut into many varieties of packaged goods.

Dermestidae (*Attagenus picus* [*Oliv.*] **and** *Trogoderma sp.*).—The dermestid beetles are mentioned because they are occasionally found in dried animal or vegetable products. They are primarily scavengers. They feed on dried meat, milk feathers, bristles, grains, fur, flour and many other products. The larvae are covered usually with hairs or bristles. These hairs are arranged in definite patterns according to the species. An example of this family is the black carpet beetle, *Attagenus picus Oliv.* (Fig. 18.5). Another example is *Trogoderma sp.* (Fig. 18.6). The damage caused by these beetles is due to the feeding by adults and larvae.

Courtesy of U.S. Dept. Agric.

FIG. 18.5.   ADULT BLACK CARPET BEETLE (A DERMISTID)

Courtesy of U.S. Dept. Agric.

FIG. 18.6.   TROGODERMA, LARVA AND ADULT (A DERMESTID)

Indian Meal Moth (*Plodia interpunctella* [*Hubner*]).—This insect is a representative of the insect order *Lepidoptera*. It is a pest of stored grain, dried fruits, nuts, dried milk, etc. The adult moth is about ½ to ¾ in. from wing tip to wing tip and is active in dark places. When at rest the wings are folded. The front of the base of the forewings is whitish in color and the other two-thirds of the wings are reddish brown.

Courtesy of U.S. Dept. Agric.

FIG. 18.7. WEBBING, FRASS, AND FEEDING DAMAGE IN NUTS, CAUSED BY INDIAN MEAL MOTH. ENLARGEMENT AT BOTTOM

Ephestia Species.—These moths have similar development characteristics and food preferences, as noted in the Indian meal moth. They are not very striking in appearance, the adults measuring from ¼ to ½ in. long. The eggs are laid on or near food in cracks and crevices. They hatch in 3 to 6 days depending on temperature. When full grown the larva may measure ⅝ in. On hatching, the larva immediately begins to spin silken threads. These threads bind particulate matter together. A pencil or probe drawn through accumulation of nut and other residues where an infestation has been or is present will pick up chunks of material bound together by the webbing.

The caterpillars, when fully grown, are about ⅜ in. The life cycle may be completed in 9 to 10 weeks at room temperature. The larva pupate requires from 7 to 19 days. The damage done by these insects is mechanical obstruction from the webbing masses in equipment and the feeding by the larvae on food stuffs. These moth larvae often form cocoons where two plane surfaces join, such as in the corners of a room. These cocoons have the appearance of dusty bits of cotton. These cocoons should be removed as they may contain a live insect.

SANITATION PROGRAM

Every candy plant should have a sanitation and insect control program, and a competent person in charge. No possible insect harborage should be overlooked in a preventive control program. The following areas are illustrative of possible insect harborages.

Physical Plant

Floors, Walls and Ceilings.—Generally, the floors of candy plants are constructed of masonry or wood. Contraction or expansion of the floor along the walls may result in cracks. During the routine floor cleaning operation, nuts, chocolate and other spillage will be swept into these cracks. The situation then becomes ideal for all insects.

Masonry cracks can be sealed with lead wool, or tar, or caulking compounds. To repair wood floor separations along the wall, remove the quarter round, clean and caulk the crack, and reset the round. This will prevent further accumulation of nut and cocoa dust and also will eliminate the insects that breed in this dust. The removal of dust is also important because, if insects and rodents are present, characteristic trails can be detected. Moth cocoons, if present, may be found by examining the point of contact between two plane surfaces such as the corner of a room.

Windows, Doors, and Ventilators.—These are usually found in all departments. Windows used for ventilation should be screened. Generally, all openings leading to the outside and from one department to another should be screened to keep out insects, rodents and birds.

Exhaust fans should be equipped with louvers that close when the fans are shut off. Doors that cannot be screened should be equipped with fans blowing through the open doorway to the outside. This procedure will discourage flying insects. This is particularly important for doorways where shipping and receiving is handled. Ventilators that run to the roof should also be screened. Birds have been known to seek refuge from the elements and enter the plant through unscreened ventilators.

Surfaces.—Paint protects surfaces and gives eye appeal to the plant. Smooth, painted surfaces are easier to keep clean.

Electrical Equipment.—Fuse boxes with sloping tops are easier to clean and prevent employees from storing on top of them small items such as nuts and bolts for nearby machinery. Electricians often install fuse boxes, switch panels and other equipment against an uneven wall. The crack behind this box may become infested with stored grain beetles, roaches and other insects. Switch panels and boxes that are not absolutely flush with the walls should be caulked. New installations should be set out from the wall far enough so that they can be easily inspected.

Conduits running horizontally along a wall will collect dust between the "v" formed by the conduit and the wall. If this is nut dust, flour, dried milk or cocoa dust, it will support insect growth. These conduits should be set out from the wall at least ½ in.

Candy Manufacture

Trash Containers.—Everything that falls on the floor should be placed in the trash barrel immediately. Keep the barrels covered and label the barrels "Trash." Scald these barrels weekly to eliminate odors and residues in which insects breed. Cherry barrels should be kept covered and scalded when empty. This will prevent fruit flies (*Drosophila*) from developing.

Candy Trimmings.—Candy trimmings should be kept in clean non-corrosive containers with tight fitting lids to prevent contamination with dust, insects and rodents. If there is the possibility of fermentation, trimmings should be kept in the refrigerator. The use of corrugated paper and wooden containers for moist trimmings should be avoided.

Stock Racks.—Any candy spillage falling behind tiers of stock boxes should be removed routinely. If this candy remains undisturbed, moths and beetles may breed in this spillage. These stock racks should be constructed preferably without backs and the bottom shelf should be high enough above the floor to permit easy cleaning. Heavy wire mesh shelves have proven helpful in determining whether candy spillage has occurred. Frequent inspections and removal of spillage will be more effective than dependence entirely on insecticides.

Cooking Department.—The chief production and sanitation problem here is the removal of steam, water of condensation, and spillage. In the manufacture of candy, water is added to dissolve the ingredients. The removal of this water is then necessary to produce candy with the desired consistency. It has been our recommendation that all kettles be equipped with individual motor powered exhaust systems to aid in the removal of steam and to prevent steam from condensing and running back into the batch. These exhaust conduits should be constructed of metal that will not corrode. This will do much to eliminate colored iron and other metallic salts, etc., and scale from falling into the batch causing off-colors in the goods. Also, the action of steam against painted ceilings and walls is very corrosive and causes flaking. The paint flakes may fall into exposed batches of candy. Hoods equipped with exhaust fans are often installed over multiple processing kettles.

Equipment.—Machines used in candy production should be cared for as follows.

Nutmeat Granulators and Pulverizers.—Some of the granulators have liners and flow directors in the hoppers made of wood. Oil and nut fragments will pack behind these liners and will eventually become rancid. This rancid oil in contact with fresh nuts will hasten the development of undesirable flavors in these nuts. The area behind the wooden blocks and liners are excellent harborages for weevils.

These machines should be cleaned daily, or weekly, without fail. A weekly cleaning will destroy the life cycle of weevils. These liners and flow directors should be replaced with stainless steel.

Conveyors for Nutmeats.—Nut fragments may pack in corners, cracks and boots of conveyor systems. Weekly removal of these fragments will do much to eliminate harborages where insects breed. The use of spot fumigants will also help in controlling these pests.

Crackers and Fanners.—These machines should be cleaned of shells daily. Some of the older equipment is constructed of tongue and groove wood. Infestation may occur at the junction of the tongue and groove. These cracks should be examined for webbing, moths and live weevils. The interiors of this equipment should be smooth metal without open seams.

Nutmeat Blanchers, Graders, Cooling Carts, etc.—These machines, including any exhaust system where skins and fragments accumulate, should be thoroughly cleaned at least weekly. The false bottom on peanut cooling carts should not be overlooked. These cooling carts should have easily removable screens so that the corners of the cart can be easily cleaned. Wooden cooling carts have been found infested and should be replaced with metal carts for easy cleaning.

Cooling Tunnels, Tempering Kettles and Tables.—Chocolate coating that has accumulated on equipment should be removed. Particular attention should be paid to the interiors of chocolate cooling tunnels. The interiors of these tunnels are dark and any stray moth will move toward these darkened areas. Stored product beetles will also breed in residues of chocolate and nut tailings. This will occur more often in enrobing tunnels that have been discontinued or have remained idle for some time. Enrobing tunnels should be so constructed that they can be easily opened for complete cleaning. Routine treatment with "spot fumigants" will also help. Whenever a tunnel is discontinued for any reason, it should be cleaned and the open ends sealed.

Chocolate tempering kettles with the hollow mushroom-shaped base should be raised or have an opening made in the base, level with the floor, so that the base may be easily washed out. The hollow base can also be filled with concrete, level with the opening. There are chocolate tempering kettles available that are equipped with pipe frame legs.

Nougat Cutters and Caramel Strippers.—Nougat cutters and caramel strippers should be kept free of flour and candy residues. Candy residues, particularly those containing nutmeats and chocolate, create an ideal situation in which weevils breed. The wooden board beneath the conveyor belt of the nougat cutters should be replaced with metal. Canvas belts have been replaced by stainless steel mesh belts that have proven satisfactory in many plants.

Flour used on these machines or any other machine increases the hazard of weevils. Starch has been used successfully instead of flour. Apparently weevils do not thrive in starch. However, starch containing nut or chocolate tailings may become infested.

Machinery Guards.—Solid machinery guards for these machines should be easily removable or constructed of wire mesh that is open at the bottom.

Nutmeat fragments and dust, chocolate residues, and flour that accumulate in these machine guards furnish an ideal harborage for moths and the stored grain insects. Weekly cleaning will break the life cycle of insects commonly found in candy plants.

Spillage from Conveyors.—In cases where conveyors penetrate double walls, spillage and dust may collect between the walls. These openings should be completely sealed with metal flashing. An alternate method is to cut the wall opening down to the floor, seal the cut edges and install a removable panel where temperature control is desired in adjacent rooms. The panel can be removed during cleaning procedures. Chocolate conveyor belts should not be overlooked.

Seal Openings.—Seal around the openings of all pipes and electrical conduits where they enter and leave a room. This will prevent the accumulation of dust and do much to eliminate insect harborages and the movement of insects from one location to another.

Intake Lines.—Intake lines and connections such as those leading to corn syrup, liquid sugar, and chocolate coating tanks should be capped when not in use. The line and connections up to the cut-off valve leading to the storage tanks and from the tank car should be scalded before the connections are made. Syrup drippings on the ground beneath the intake valve will create conditions favorable for fly breeding.

Pest Harborages and Sanitation Problems.—Avoid streamlining of equipment that creates pest harborages. Enclosing motors, water pipes, and steam pipes may create condensation problems and trash catchers. Conditions thus created are ideal for roaches, as they prefer dark humid areas. Make sure that such enclosures, frequently justified from a safety standpoint, are so constructed that enclosed areas can be easily and readily cleaned.

When wet cleaning is done, equipment should be raised off the floor. Otherwise spillage may be trapped in hard-to-clean pockets. This creates a condition favorable for insect harborages. This is particularly important in the chocolate and nut processing department. Equipment with skirts installed over the gears, pulleys, etc., extending to the floor should receive careful attention. Floor washing and/or spillage may collect behind the skirts creating conditions favorable to insect harborage. Some firms have removed the bottom 2 or 3 in. of the skirt and a similar amount from the channel iron supporting the pulleys. The engineer should be consulted before any changes in the equipment are made. When the floor is flushed any spillage is washed out or through the channels supports into the drains. Where dry cleaning is done, easy-to-move panels should be large enough so that when they are removed the entire interior of the equipment is readily visible to the naked eye. This is particularly important in the case of chocolate cooling tunnels. Streamlining may improve the appearance of equipment; however, it may also create sanitation problems.

Care should be exercised to see that pulleys, belts and bearings are not over open candy production lines. This includes open candy conveyors, slabs, exposed trays of candy, etc. Local health codes usually specify where sewer and water lines may be installed.

Angle iron, if used in construction of equipment, should be turned downward wherever possible. This will prevent trash from accumulating in the angles. The use of angle iron for equipment should be discouraged. Pipe frame construction is more sanitary and easier to keep clean.

Generally, when equipment is designed to handle nutmeats or chocolate, the several considerations should be taken into consideration. Wood or metal should be avoided if, in the construction of the equipment, it is necessary to fasten two or more pieces together. Nut and chocolate trash will pack in the cracks causing insect harborages. Wood is also porous and will absorb moisture. Metal construction without seams is the most desirable in preventing insect harborages.

Toilets.—The U.S. Public Health Service Bulletin No. 280 (1943), "Ordinance and Code Regulating Eating and Drinking Establishments," has a section in regard to toilet construction and hand washings. As candy is a food, this section is applicable to candy manufacturing plants also. This code states that satisfactory compliance is attained if:

(1) Adequate toilet facilities conveniently located and complying with the city plumbing code are provided for employees.

(2) In restaurants (or candy plants) there is an intervening room or vestibule between any toilet room and any room in which food and drink are prepared, served, or stored, or in which utensils are handled or stored.

(3) The toilet room doors are provided with springs or checks to make them self-closing.

(4) The toilet room and fixtures are kept clean, sanitary, in good repair, and free from flies.

(5) The toilet room is well lighted and ventilated to the outside air.

(6) Durable, legible signs directing employees to wash their hands before returning to work are posted conspicuously in each toilet room. Such signs may be stenciled on the wall to prevent removal.

A booth open at the top or bottom shall not qualify as a toilet room. Privies shall be constructed and operated in accordance with the standards of the State Board of Health. This code is a guide as to how to protect foods from flies and other insects, and also to minimize contamination of foods by human contacts. Flies develop in filth on their bodies and transmit filth to everything with which they come in contact.

Usually, hand washing facilities are located inside the toilet area. If these facilities were located outside the toilet rooms you could determine quickly if someone failed to wash his hands before returning to the candy production line.

Ingredient Storage.—Ingredients, especially those received in jute bags such as peanuts, filberts, almonds, cocoa beans, etc., are subject to attack by stored grain insects and contamination by rodents. Insects can crawl or fly from sack to sack. The open weave of a sack is such that the insects can crawl through the mesh. Ingredients subject to infestation should be fumigated before they are brought into the plant as a control of any residual infestation not visually apparent. Fumigated ingredients should not be stored with unfumigated ingredients. A point to remember is that the usual cold storage temperatures cannot be depended upon to kill insect infestation. Also, the fumigation of infested ingredients does not remove the insect fragments.

Ingredients should be placed on skids away from the wall. This permits easy inspection along the walls by inspection personnel and cleaning by the sanitation crews. The double-faced pallet placed on the floor serves as a general dirt catcher. Spillage from broken sacks and floor sweepings accumulate between the slats. Even when the pallet is moved, the chances are that the pallet will not be cleaned. An alternate method would be the use of skids on the floor and pallets for stacking.

The use of long, unwieldy storage platforms should be avoided. It is difficult to clean under them and the cleaning crew usually can't see what they are doing. We have suggested that storage platforms should be in sections that can easily be moved by one man.

For almonds The California Almond Grower's Exchange recommends the following storage conditions by the candy manufacturer:

(1) Temperature -1° to 3.3°C (30° to 38°F). Maximum prolonged temperature 4.4°C (40°F).

(2) Relative humidity 65 to 70% at above temperatures.

(3) Away from ammonia-type refrigeration.

(4) Do not store almonds in the same room with such odorous commodity items as apples, citrus, onions, paint or solvents.

(5) Containers that are odor-free will not impart a flavor and will not produce a moisture condensation on the inner walls of such, when drastic temperature changes are experienced.

(6) Any almonds left at room temperature for any period over a week should be in rigid or sealed containers which are considered to be insect-proof, or reasonably so.

(7) When stored in cardboard cartons or paper-lined burlap bags, the merchandise should be inspected carefully, weekly, for any sign of insect or rodent activity.

(8) Where dry, warm storage is mandatory, the time period should be kept at the very minimum, because of quality loss under less than cold storage conditions.

In such instances, a program of space fogging in the area should be followed weekly to prevent flying storage pests from starting a reproductive cycle on or near the almonds. The fogging material can be a pyrethrin-piperonyl butoxide formulation which can be furnished by local suppliers of insecticides.

The general area should be sprayed also with a premium grade malathion spray; this would include walls and floor perimeters up to 2 ft away from wall. This material should not be sprayed on the almonds or their containers.

Local suppliers can also furnish, or formulate, a spray containing premium grade malathion, either in a water base or in a deodorized petrolatum distillate.

Ingredients.—Stored ingredients should be visually inspected weekly and, most important, the older ingredients should be used first.

Bagged ingredients show surface infestation by the presence of insects and webbing which gives the exterior of the sack a waxed appearance. Raising the bag where it is in contact with another bag will often reveal live insects or moth cocoons. This is the beginning of a major infestation.

The beam of a flashlight directed between stacks or materials will disturb resting moths.

Employees.—The plant personnel can either make or break a sanitation program. There is more to sanitation than seeing that the floors are swept, the desks dusted, and trash barrels emptied.

Sanitation discussions should be part of every production conference held in the plant. Safety meetings are frequently held. The plant accident rate is reflected in the insurance rating. The cost of poor sanitation may not be apparent directly in dollars and cents unless sales fall off, due to unacceptable merchandise, or if regulatory action is initiated. Resulting publicity from such actions hurts every candy manufacturer. The pressure for sanitation consciousness must come from top management.

Clean clothing is one of the musts in the production of candy. Hair nets, caps, or the equivalent should be worn. Objections to head covering by the employees occur from time to time. Candy plant top management should set the example and always wear a head covering when visiting production areas of the plant. Regulatory inspectors include in their reports the appearance of employees' clothing and the absence or presence of head coverings.

Outside Sanitation Service.—There are many firms that deal in a variety of sanitation supplies and services. Some firms deal solely in cleaning compounds, insecticides, mops, brooms, and equipment which may be purchased. The "know-how" of properly applying these materials is very important. Pest control services are like a lot of other services. Generally, those firms supplying services are doing a good job. However, pest control services should include something more than pest executions. The pest control firms should make recommendations to candy plant management as to elimination of rodent and insect harborages. In the absence of specific knowledge concerning a pest control service the following questions should be answered and information obtained:

(1) Do they carry product and property liability insurance?

(2) What is the rating with Better Business Bureau or standing with the National Pest Control Asscociation?

(3) Require a report of each survey, indicating the pests, if any, that are found.

(4) Supply a list of active ingredients being used in the plant. Avoid secret preparations. Make sure the pesticides and rodenticides comply with Federal Food and Drug, State and local regulations.

(5) Make a complete report of what candy plant management should do to make a preventive program effective.

It is of utmost importance that close cooperation be maintained between candy plant management and the pest control service man. Often there must be a compromise in the application of pest control materials in regard to the kind of food manufactured.

Care should be taken that in controlling one pest, one does not create another pest. For example, cereals are frequently used in rodent baits. If these cereals are infested, a focus of infestation may be established that could spread throughout the entire plant.

Applications of rodenticides in the form of a tracking powder or powdered insecticides should not be placed in starch rooms or other dusty areas. A poison dust easily could be blown into the exposed food. Trapping is very effective if properly serviced.

It is erroneous to believe that unscreened windows will permit the flies to get out, and that flies do not occur above a certain floor, and also that rodent entries should not be stopped for the same reason. It is important to work with the pest control operator so that there is no misunderstanding as to what is expected of both parties in the contract.

The area surrounding the plant is very important. Spillage around the shipping and receiving platform arising from damaged sacks or cartons will attract birds and rodents. Stagnant water serves as a breeding area for mosquitos and flies. Trash should be stored in metal containers with tightly fitting lids. A plant may be located in an area where adjoining industries are creating undesirable conditions. Situations such as this should be referred to the Board of Health.

An effective plant sanitation program depends on active interest and cooperation by all administrative and production personnel. The impetus for an effective program must come from top management with sufficient impact to be felt throughout the entire plant. The assignment of definite responsibilities for plant sanitation to key personnel is a must for an effective program.

REFERENCES

ANON. 1943. Ordinance and Code Regulating Eating and Drinking Establishments. U.S. Public Health Serv. Bull. *280*.

BUCKLIN, H.A. 1966. What the pecan industry is learning from the bakery industry. Peanut J. and Nut World 45, 5, 34.

COTTON, R.T. 1960. Insect Pests of Stored Grain and Grain Products. Burgess Publishing Co., Minneapolis, Minn.

LAUDANI, H., and DAVIS, D.F. 1955. The status of federal research on the development of insect-resistant packages. Tappi 38, 6, 322.

LAUDANI, H., DAVIS, D.F., and SWANK, G.R. 1958. Improved packaging methods can cut insect infestation. Mod. Sanitation and Building Maintenance 10, 3, 17.

LEHMAN, A.J. 1956. Food packaging. Assoc. Food and Drug Officials of U.S. 20, 4, 159-168.

WAGNER, G.B. 1956. Stored-product insect losses can be reduced. Proc. Chem. Specialties Mfg. Assoc. 42, 116.

WOODROOF, J.G. 1966. Storage of candies, nuts, dried fruits and vegetables. ASHRAE Data Book, Refrigeration Applications, New York.

WOODROOF, J.G. 1966. Storing candies, nuts, dried fruits and vegetables. ASHRAE Guide and Data Book, 675-680, New York.

WOODROOF, J.G., and CECIL, S.R. 1951. Nuts: better kept, better candy. Food Eng. 33, 11, 129-131, 148, 150.

U. S. Standards for Grades of Shelled Almonds, August 15, 1960 [1]

GRADES

§51.2105   U.S. Fancy.

"U.S. Fancy" consists of shelled almonds of similar varietal characteristics which are whole, clean and well dried, and which are free from decay, rancidity, insect injury, foreign material, doubles, split or broken kernels, particles and dust, and free from injury caused by chipped and scratched kernels, and free from damage caused by mold, gum, shriveling, brown spot or other means. (See §§51.2114 and 51.2115.)

(a) In order to allow for variations incident to proper grading and handling, the following tolerances, by weight, shall be permitted:

(1) *For dissimilar varieties.* 5 per cent, including not more than one-fifth of this amount, or 1 per cent, for bitter almonds mixed with sweet almonds;

(2) *For doubles.* 3 per cent;

(3) *For kernels injured by chipping and/or scratching.* 5 per cent;

(4) *For foreign material.* Two-tenths of 1 per cent (0.20%);

(5) *For particles and dust.* One-tenth of 1 per cent (0.10%); and,

(6) *For other defects.* 2 per cent, including not more than one-half of this amount, or 1 per cent, for split or broken kernels, and including not more than one-half of the former amount, or 1 per cent, for seriously damaged kernels.

§51.2106   U.S. Extra No. 1.

"U.S. Extra No. 1" consists of shelled almonds of similar varietal characteristics which are whole, clean and well dried, and which are free from decay, rancidity, insect injury, foreign material, doubles, split or broken kernels, particles and dust, and free from damage caused by chipped and scratched kernels, mold, gum, shriveling, brown spot or other means. (See §§51.2114 and 51.2115.)

(a) In order to allow for variations incident to proper grading and handling, the following tolerances, by weight, shall be permitted:

(1) *For dissimilar varieties.* 5 per cent, including not more than one-fifth of this amount, or 1 per cent, for bitter almonds mixed with sweet almonds;

(2) *For doubles.* 5 per cent;

(3) *For kernels damaged by chipping and/or scratching.* 5 per cent;

(4) *For foreign material.* Two-tenths of 1 per cent (0.20%);

(5) *For particles and dust.* One-tenth of 1 per cent (0.10%); and,

(6) *For other defects.* 4 per cent, including not more than one-fourth of this amount, or 1 per cent, for split or broken kernels, and including not more than three-eighths of the former amount, or 1½ per cent, for seriously damaged kernels.

§51.2107   U.S. No. 1.

"U.S. No. 1" consists of shelled almonds of similar varietal characteristics which are whole, clean and well dried, and which are free from decay, rancidity, insect injury, foreign material, doubles, split or broken kernels, particles and dust, and free from damage caused by chipped and scratched kernels, mold, gum, shriveling, brown spot or other means. (See §§51.2114 and 51.2115.)

(a) In order to allow for variations incident to proper grading and handling, the following tolerances, by weight, shall be permitted:

(1) *For dissimilar varieties.* 5 per cent, including not more than one-fifth of this amount, or 1 per cent, for bitter almonds mixed with sweet almonds;

(2) *For doubles.* 15 per cent;

(3) *For kernels damaged by chipping and/or scratching.* 10 per cent;

(4) *For foreign material.* Two-tenths of 1 per cent (0.20%);

(5) *For particles and dust.* One-tenth of 1 per cent (0.10%); and,

(6) *For other defects.* 5 per cent, including not more than one-fifth of this amount, or 1 per cent, for split or broken kernels, and including not more than three-tenths of the former amount, or 1½ per cent, for seriously damaged kernels.

§51.2108   U.S. Select Sheller Run.

"U.S. Select Sheller Run" consists of shelled almonds of similar varietal characteristics which are whole, clean and well dried, and which are free from decay, rancidity, insect injury, foreign material, doubles, split or broken kernels, particles

---

[1]Packing of the product in conformity with the requirements of these standards shall not excuse failure to comply with the provisions of the Federal Food, Drug, and Cosmetic Act or with applicable State laws and regulations.
Source: United States Department of Agriculture, Agricultural Marketing Service.

and dust, and free from damage caused by chipped and scratched kernels, mold, gum, shriveling, brown spot or other means. (See §§51.2114 and 51.2115.)

(a) In order to allow for variations incident to proper grading and handling, the following tolerances, by weight, shall be permitted:

(1) *For dissimilar varieties.* 5 per cent, including not more than one-fifth of this amount, or 1 per cent. for bitter almonds mixed with sweet almonds;

(2) *For doubles.* 15 per cent;

(3) *For kernels damaged by chipping and/or scratching.* 20 per cent;

(4) *For foreign material.* Two-tenths of 1 per cent (0.20%);

(5) *For particles and dust.* One-tenth of 1 per cent (0.10%);

(6) *For split and broken kernels.* 5 per cent: *Provided,* That not more than two-fifths of this amount, or 2 per cent shall be allowed for pieces which will pass through a round opening ²⁰⁄₆₄ inch in diameter; and,

(7) *For other defects.* 3 per cent, including not more than two-thirds of this amount, or 2 per cent, for serious damage.

§51.2109   U.S. Standard Sheller Run.

"U.S. Standard Sheller Run" consists of shelled almonds of similar varietal characteristics which are whole, clean and well dried, and which are free from decay, rancidity, insect injury, foreign material, doubles, split or broken kernels, particles and dust, and free from damage caused by chipped and scratched kernels, mold, gum, shriveling, brown spot or other means. (See §§51.2114 and 51.2115.)

(a) In order to allow for variations incident to proper grading and handling, the following tolerances, by weight, shall be permitted:

(1) *For dissimilar varieties.* 5 per cent, including not more than one-fifth of this amount, or 1 per cent, for bitter almonds mixed with sweet almonds;

(2) *For doubles.* 25 per cent;

(3) *For kernels damaged by chipping and/or scratching.* 20 per cent;

(4) *For foreign material.* Two-tenths of 1 per cent (0.20%);

(5) *For particles and dust.* One-tenth of 1 per cent (0.10%);

(6) *For split and broken kernels.* 15 per cent: *Provided,* That not more than one-third of this amount, or 5 per cent, shall be allowed for pieces which will pass through a round opening ²⁰⁄₆₄ inch in diameter; and,

(7) *For other defects.* 3 per cent, including not more than two-thirds of this amount, or 2 per cent, for serious damage.

§51.2110   U.S. No. 1 Whole and Broken.

"U.S. No. 1 Whole and Broken" consists of shelled almonds of similar varietal characteristics which are clean and well dried, and which are free from decay, rancidity, insect injury, foreign material, doubles, particles and dust, and free from damage caused by mold, gum, shriveling, brown spot or other means.

(a) In this grade not less than 30 per cent, by weight, of the kernels shall be whole. Doubles shall not be considered as whole kernels in determining the percentage of whole kernels.

(b) Unless otherwise specified, the minimum diameter shall be not less than ²⁰⁄₆₄ of an inch. (See §§51.2114 and 51.2115.)

(c) In order to allow for variations incident to proper grading and handling, the following tolerances, by weight, shall be permitted:

(1) *For dissimilar varieties.* 5 per cent, including not more than one-fifth of this amount, or 1 per cent, for bitter almonds mixed with sweet almonds;

(2) *For doubles.* 35 per cent;

(3) *For foreign material.* Three-tenths of 1 per cent (0.30%);

(4) *For particles and dust.* One-tenth of 1 per cent (0.10%);

(5) *For undersize.* 5 per cent; and,

(6) *For other defects.* 5 per cent, including not more than three-fifths of this amount, or 3 per cent, for serious damage.

§51.2111   U.S. No. 1 Pieces.

"U.S. No. 1 Pieces" consists of shelled almonds which are not bitter, which are clean and well dried, and which are free from decay, rancidity, insect injury, foreign material, particles and dust, and free from damage caused by mold, gum, shriveling, brown spot or other means.

(a) Unless otherwise specified, the minimum diameter shall not be less than ⁵⁄₆₄ of an inch. (See §§51.2114 and 51.2115.)

(b) In order to allow for variations incident to proper grading and handling, the following tolerances, by weight, shall be permitted:

(1) *For bitter almonds mixed with sweet almonds.* 1 per cent;

(2) *For foreign material.* Three-tenths of 1 per cent (0.30%);

(3) *For particles and dust.* 1 per cent; and,

(4) *For other defects.* 5 per cent, including not more than three-fifths of this amount, or 3 per cent, for serious damage.

Mixed Varieties

§51.2112   Mixed varieties.

Any lot of shelled almonds consisting of a mixture of two or more dissimilar varieties which meet the other requirements of any of the grades of U.S. No. 1, U.S. Select Sheller Run, U.S. Standard Sheller Run, U.S. No. 1 Whole and Broken may be designated as: "U.S. No. 1 Mixed;" "U.S. Select Sheller Run Mixed;" "U.S. Standard Sheller Run Mixed;" or "U.S. No. 1 Whole and Broken Mixed," respectively; but no lot of any of these grades may include more than 1 per cent of bitter almonds mixed with sweet almonds.

§51.2113   Unclassified.

"Unclassified" consists of shelled almonds which have not been classified in accordance with any of the foregoing grades. The term "unclassified" is not a grade within the meaning of these standards but is provided as a designation to show that no definite grade has been applied to the lot.

§51.2114   Size requirements.

The size may be specified in terms of range in count of whole almond kernels per ounce or in terms of minimum, or minimum and maximum diameter. When a range in count is specified, the whole kernels shall be fairly uniform in size, and the average count per ounce shall be within the range specified. Doubles and broken kernels shall not be used in determining counts. Count ranges per ounce commonly used are shown below, but other ranges may be specified: *Provided, That the kernels are fairly uniform in size.*

Count Range per Ounce

16 to 18, inclusive.
18 to 20, inclusive.
20 to 22, inclusive.
22 to 24, inclusive.
23 to 25, inclusive.
24 to 26, inclusive.
26 to 28, inclusive.
27 to 30, inclusive.
30 to 34, inclusive.
34 to 40, inclusive.
40 to 50, inclusive.
50 and smaller.

§51.2115   Tolerances for size.

(a) When a range is specified as, for example, "18/20," no tolerance for counts above or below the range shall be allowed.

(1) When the minimum, or minimum and maximum diameters are specified, a total tolerance of not more than 10 per cent, by weight, may fail to meet the specified size requirements: *Provided,* That not more than one-half of this amount, or 5 per cent, may be below the minimum size specified.

§51.2116   Application of tolerances.

The tolerances for the grades are to be applied to the entire lot, and a composite sample shall be taken for determining the grade. However, any container or group of containers in which the almonds are found to be materially inferior to those in the majority of the containers shall be considered a separate lot.

§51.2117   Similar varietal characteristics.

"Similar varietal characteristics" means that the kernels are similar in shape and appearance. For example, long types shall not be mixed with short types, or broad types mixed with narrow types, and bitter almonds shall not be mixed with sweet almonds. Color of the kernels shall not be considered, since there is often a marked difference in skin color of kernels of the same variety.

§51.2118   Whole.

"Whole" means that there is less than one-eighth of the kernel chipped off or missing, and that the general contour of the kernel is not materially affected by the missing part.

§51.2119   Clean.

"Clean" means that the kernel is practically free from dirt and other foreign substance.

§51.2120   Well dried.

"Well dried" means that the kernel is firm and brittle, and not pliable or leathery.

§51.2121   Decay.

"Decay" means that the kernel is putrid or decomposed.

§51.2122   Rancidity.

"Rancidity" means that the kernel is noticeably rancid to the taste.

§51.2123   Insect injury.

"Insect injury" means that the insect, web, or frass is present or there is definite evidence of insect feeding.

§51.2124   Foreign material.

"Foreign material" means pieces of shell, hulls or other foreign matter which will not pass through a round opening $\frac{5}{64}$ of an inch in diameter.

§51.2125   Doubles.

"Doubles" means kernels that developed in shells containing two kernels. One side of a double kernel is flat or concave.

§51.2126   Split or broken kernels.

"Split or broken kernels" means seven-eighths or less of complete whole kernels but which will not pass through a round opening $\frac{5}{64}$ of an inch in diameter.

§51.2127   Particles and dust.

"Particles and dust" means fragments of almond kernels or other material which will pass through a round opening $\frac{5}{64}$ of an inch in diameter.

§51.2128   Injury.

"Injury" means any defect which more than slightly detracts from the appearance of the individual almond, or the general appearance of the lot. The following shall be considered as injury:

(a) Chipped and scratched kernels when the general appearance of the lot is more than slightly affected, or when the affected area on an individual kernel aggregates more than the equivalent of a circle one-eighth inch in diameter.

§51.2129   Damage.

"Damage" means any defect which materially detracts from the appearance of the individual kernel, or the general appearance of the lot, or the edible or shipping quality of the almonds. Any one of the following defects or combination thereof, the seriousness of which exceeds the maximum allowed for any one defect shall be considered as damage:

(a) Chipped and scratched kernels, when the general appearance of the lot is materially affected, or when the affected area on an individual kernel aggregates more than the equivalent of a circle one-quarter inch in diameter;

(b) Mold, when visible on the kernel, except when white or gray and easily rubbed off with the fingers;

(c) Gum, when a film of shiny, resinous appearing substance covers more than one-eighth of the surface of the kernel;

(d) Shriveling, when the kernel is excessively thin for its size, or when materially withered, shrunken, leathery, tough or only partially developed: *Provided*, That partially developed kernels are not considered damaged if more than three-fourths of the pellicle is filled with meat; and

(e) Brown spot on the kernel, either single or multiple, when the affected area aggregates more than the equivalent of a circle one-eighth inch in diameter.

§51.2130   Serious damage.

"Serious damage" means any defect which makes a kernel or piece of kernel unsuitable for human consumption, and includes decay, rancidity, insect injury and damage by mold.

§51.2131   Diameter.

"Diameter" means the greatest dimension of the kernel, or piece of kernel at right angles to the longitudinal axis. Diameter shall be determined by passing the kernel or piece of kernel through a round opening.

§51.2132   Fairly uniform in size.

"Fairly uniform in size" means that, in a representative sample, the weight of 10 per cent, by count, of the largest whole kernels shall not exceed 1.70 times the weight of 10 per cent, by count, of the smallest whole kernels.

U.S. Standards for Grades of Almonds in the Shell, July 15, 1964[1]

GRADES

§51.2075 U.S. No. 1.

"U.S. No. 1" consists of almonds in the shell which are of similar varietal characteristics and free from loose extraneous and foreign material. The shells are clean, fairly bright, fairly uniform in color, and free from damage caused by discoloration, adhering hulls, broken shells or other means. The kernels are well dried, free from decay, rancidity, and free from damage caused by insects, mold, gum, skin discoloration, shriveling, brown spot or other means.

(a) Unless otherwise specified, the almonds are of a size not less than ²⁹⁄₆₄ of an inch in thickness.

(b) In order to allow for variations incident to proper grading and handling, the following tolerances are provided as specified:

(1) *For external (shell) defects.* 10 per cent, by count, for almonds which fail to meet the requirements of this grade other than for variety and size;

(2) *For dissimilar varieties.* 5 per cent, by count, including therein not more than 1 per cent for bitter almonds mixed with sweet almonds;

(3) *For size.* 5 per cent, by count, for almonds which are smaller than the specified minimum thickness;

(4) *For loose extraneous and foreign material.* 2 per cent, by weight, including therein not more than 1 per cent which can pass through a round opening ²⁵⁄₆₄ inch in diameter: *Provided,* That such material is practically free from insect infestation; and,

(5) *For internal (kernel) defects.* 10 per cent, by count, for almonds with kernels failing to meet the requirements of this grade: *Provided,* That not more than one-half of this tolerance or 5 per cent shall be allowed for kernels affected by decay or rancidity, damaged by insects or mold or seriously damaged by shriveling, including not more than one-half of 1 per cent for almonds with live insects inside the shell.

§51.2076 U.S. No. 1 Mixed.

"U.S. No. 1 Mixed" consists of almonds in the shell which meet the requirements of U.S. No. 1 grade, except that two or more varieties of sweet almonds are mixed.

§51.2077 U.S. No. 2.

"U.S. No. 2" consists of almonds in the shell which meet the requirements of U.S. No. 1 grade, except that an additional tolerance of 20 per cent shall be allowed for almonds with shells damaged by discoloration.

§51.2078 U.S. No. 2 Mixed.

"U.S. No. 2 Mixed" consists of almonds in the shell which meet the requirements of U.S. No. 2 grade, except that two or more varieties of sweet almonds are mixed.

UNCLASSIFIED

§51.2079 Unclassified.

"Unclassified" consists of almonds in the shell which have not been classified in accordance with any of the foregoing grades. The term "unclassified" is not a grade within the meaning of these standards but is provided as a designation to show that no definite grade has been applied to the lot.

APPLICATION OF TOLERANCES

§51.2080 Application of tolerances.

The tolerances for the foregoing grades are applied to the entire lot of almonds, based upon a composite sample drawn from containers throughout the lot.

---

[1] Packing of the product in conformity with the requirements of these standards shall not excuse failure to comply with the provisions of the Federal Food, Drug, and Cosmetic Act or with applicable State laws and regulations.

Source: United States Department of Agriculture, Agricultural Marketing Service.

DETERMINATION OF GRADE

§51.2081   Determination of grade.

In grading the inspection sample, the percentage of loose hulls, pieces of shell, chaff and foreign material is determined on the basis of weight. Next, the percentages of nuts which are of dissimilar varieties, undersize or have adhering hulls or defective shells are determined by count, using an adequate portion of the total sample. Finally, the nuts in that portion of the sample are cracked, and the percentage having internal defects is determined on the basis of count.

DEFINITIONS

§51.2082   Similar varietal characteristics.

"Similar varietal characteristics" means that the almonds are similar in shape, and are reasonably uniform in degree of hardness of the shells, and that bitter almonds are not mixed with sweet almonds. For example, hard-shelled varieties, semisoft-shelled varieties, soft-shelled varieties and paper-shelled varieties are not mixed together, nor are any two of these types mixed under this definition.

§51.2083   Loose extraneous and foreign material.

"Loose extraneous and foreign material" means loose hulls, empty broken shells, pieces of shells, external insect infestation and any substance other than almonds in the shell or almond kernels.

§51.2084   Clean.

"Clean" means that the shell is practically free from dirt and other adhering foreign material.

§51.2085   Fairly bright.

"Fairly bright" means that the shells show good characteristic color.

§51.2086   Fairly uniform color.

"Fairly uniform color" means that the shells do not show excessive variation in color.

§51.2087   Well dried.

"Well dried" means that the kernel is firm and brittle, not pliable or leathery.

§51.2088   Decay.

"Decay" means that part or all of the kernel has become decomposed.

§51.2089   Rancidity.

"Rancidity" means that the kernel is noticeably rancid to the taste.

§51.2090   Damage.

"Damage" means any specific defect described in this section; or an equally objectionable variation of any one of these defects, or any other defect, or any combination of defects which materially detracts from the appearance or the edible or shipping quality of the almond or of the lot. The following defects shall be considered as damage:

(a) Discoloration of the shell which is medium gray to black and affects more than one-eighth of the surface in the aggregate. Normal variations of a reddish or brownish color shall not be considered discoloration;

(b) Adhering hulls which cover more than 5 per cent of the shell surface in the aggregate;

(c) Broken shells when a portion of the shell is missing, or the shell is broken or fractured to the extent that moderate pressure will permit the kernel to become dislodged;

(d) Insects when an insect or insect fragment, web or frass is present inside the shell, or the kernel shows distinct evidence of insect feeding;

(e) Mold when attached to the kernel and conspicuous; or when inconspicuous white or gray mold affects a total of more than one-eighth of the surface of the kernel;

(f) Gum which is shiny and resinous and covers more than one-eighth of the surface of the kernel;

(g) Skin discoloration when more than one-half of the surface of the kernel is affected by very dark or black stains contrasting with the natural color of the skin;

(h) Shriveling when the kernel is excessively thin or when less than three-fourths of the pellicle is filled with meat. An almond containing two kernels shall not be classed as damaged if either kernel has more than three-fourths of the pellicle filled with meat; and,

(i) Brown spot which affects an aggregate area on the kernel greater than the area of a circle one-eighth inch in diameter.

§51.2091   Serious damage.

"Serious damage" means the specific defect described in this section; or an equally objectionable variation of this defect, or any other defect, or any combination of defects which seriously detracts from the appearance or the edible or shipping quality of the almond. The following defect shall be considered as serious damage:

(a) Shriveling when less than one-fourth of the pellicle is filled with meat. An almond containing two kernels shall not be classed as seriously damaged if either kernel has more than one-fourth of the pellicle filled with meat.

§51.2092   Thickness.

"Thickness" means the greatest dimension between the two semi-flat surfaces of the shell measured at right angles to a plane extending between the seams of the shell.

U. S. Standards for Grades of Brazil Nuts in the Shell June 1, 1966

GRADE

§51.3500   U.S. No. 1.

"U.S. No. 1" consists of well cured whole Brazil nuts in the shell which are free from loose extraneous and foreign material and meet one of the size classifications in §51.3501. The shells are clean and free from damage caused by splits, breaks, punctures, oil stain, mold or other means, and contain kernels which are reasonably well developed, free from rancidity, mold, decay, and from damage caused by insects, discoloration or other means.

(a) In order to allow for variations incident to proper grading and handling, the following tolerances are provided:

(1) *For defects of the shell.* 10 per cent, by count, may fail to meet the requirements of the grade, including therein not more than 5 per cent for serious damage by split, broken or punctured shells, oil stains, mold or other means.

(2) *For defects of the kernel.* 10 per cent, by count, may fail to meet the requirements of the grade, including therein not more than 7 per cent for serious damage by any cause: *Provided,* That not more than five-sevenths of the latter amount, or 5 per cent, shall be allowed for damage by insects: *Provided further,* That included in this 5 per cent tolerance not more than one-half of 1 per cent shall be allowed for Brazil nuts with live insects inside the shell.

(3) *For loose extraneous and foreign material.* 1 per cent, by weight: *Provided,* That such material is practically free from insect infestation.

SIZE CLASSIFICATIONS

§51.3501   Size classifications.

(a) Extra large: Not more than 15 percent, by count, of the Brazil nuts pass through a round opening $^{79}\!/_{64}$ inches in diameter, including not more than 2 per cent which pass through a round opening $^{71}\!/_{64}$ inches in diameter; or count does not exceed 45 nuts per pound (see paragraph (d) of this section);

(b) Large: Not more than 15 per cent by count, of the Brazil nuts pass through a round opening $^{73}\!/_{64}$ inches in diameter, including not more than 2 per cent which pass through a round opening $^{60}\!/_{64}$ inch in diameter; or count does not exceed 50 nuts per pound (see paragraph (d) of this section);

(c) Medium: Not more than 15 per cent, by count, of the Brazil nuts pass through a round opening $^{59}\!/_{64}$ inch in diameter, including not more than 2 per cent which pass through a round opening $^{50}\!/_{64}$ inch in diameter; or count is not less than 51 nuts per pound but not more than 65 nuts per pound (see paragraph (d) of this section); and,

(d) When size is based on count per pound, the 10 smallest nuts per 100 weigh at least 6 per cent of the total weight of the 100 nut sample.

UNCLASSIFIED

§51.3502   Unclassified.

"Unclassified" consists of Brazil nuts in the shell which have not been classified in accordance with the foregoing grade. The term "unclassified" is not a grade within the meaning of these standards but is provided as a designation to show that no definite grade has been applied to the lot.

APPLICATION OF STANDARDS

§51.3503   Application of standards.

The grade of a lot of Brazil nuts shall be determined on the basis of a composite sample drawn at random from containers in various locations in the lot. However, any identifiable portion of the lot in which the Brazil nuts are obviously of a quality or size materially different from that in the majority of containers shall be considered as a separate lot, and shall be sampled and graded separately.

Source: United States Department of Agriculture, Agricultural Marketing Service.

U.S. Standards for Grades of Filberts in the Shell, September 1, 1970

GRADE

§51.1995   U.S. No. 1.

"U.S. No. 1" consists of filberts in the shell which are of similar type and dry. The shells shall be well formed, clean and bright, free from blanks, broken or split shells, and free from damage caused by stains, adhering husk or other means. The kernels shall be reasonably well developed, not badly misshapen, free from rancidity, decay, mold, insect injury and free from damage caused by shriveling, discoloration or other means.

(a) The filberts shall meet one of the following size classifications as specified for round type and for long type varieties:

SIZE REQUIREMENTS

Size classifications	Maximum size	Minimum size
	Will pass through a round opening of the following size.	Will not pass through a round opening of the following size.
Round type varieties:		
Jumbo	No maximum	$^{56}/_{64}$ inch.
Large	$^{56}/_{64}$ inch	$^{49}/_{64}$ inch.
Medium	$^{49}/_{64}$ inch	$^{45}/_{64}$ inch.
Small	$^{45}/_{64}$ inch	No minimum.
Long type varieties:		
Jumbo	No maximum	$^{47}/_{64}$ inch.
Large	$^{49}/_{64}$ inch	$^{41}/_{64}$ inch.
Medium	$^{45}/_{64}$ inch	$^{37}/_{64}$ inch.
Small	$^{35}/_{64}$ inch	No minimum.

(b) *Tolerances.* In order to allow for variations incident to proper grading and handling, the following tolerances, by count, are permitted as specified:

(1) *For mixed types.* 10 per cent for filberts which are of a different type.

(2) *For defects.* 10 per cent for filberts which are below the requirements of this grade: *Provided.* That not more than one-half of this amount or 5 per cent shall consist of blanks, and not more than 5 per cent shall consist of filberts with rancid, decayed, moldy or insect injured kernels, including not more than 3 per cent for insect injury.

(3) *For off-size.* 15 per cent for filberts which fail to meet the requirements for the size specified, but not more than five-sixths of this amount, or 10 per cent shall consist of undersize filberts.

UNCLASSIFIED

§51.1996   Unclassified.

"Unclassified" consists of filberts which have not been classified in accordance with the foregoing grade. The term "unclassified" is not a grade within the meaning of these standards but is provided as a designation to show that no grade has been applied to the lot.

DEFINITIONS

§51.1997   Similar type.

"Similar type" means that the filberts in each container are of the same general type and appearance. For example, nuts of the round type shall not be mixed with those of the long type in the same container.

Source: United States Department of Agriculture, Agricultural Marketing Service.

§51.1998   Dry.

"Dry" means that the shell is free from surface moisture, and that the shells and kernels combined do not contain more than 10 per cent moisture.

§51.1999   Well formed.

"Well formed" means that the filbert shell is not materially misshapen.

§51.2000   Clean and bright.

"Clean and bright" means that the individual filbert and the lot as a whole are practically free from adhering dirt and other foreign material, and that the shells have characteristic color.

§51.2001   Blank.

"Blank" means a filbert containing no kernel or a kernel filling less than one-fourth the capacity of the shell.

§51.2002   Split shell.

"Split shell" means a shell having any crack.

§51.2003   Damage.

"Damage" means any specific defect described in this section; or an equally objectionable variation of any one of these defects, any other defect, or any combination of defects which materially detracts from the appearance, or the edible or shipping quality of the filberts. The following specific defects shall be considered as damage:
(a) Stains which are dark and materially affect the appearance of the individual shell.
(b) Adhering husk when covering more than 5 per cent of the surface of the shell in the aggregate.
(c) Shriveling when the kernel is materially shrunken, wrinkled, leathery and tough.
(d) Discoloration when the appearance of the kernel is materially affected by black color.

§51.2004   Reasonably well developed.

"Reasonably well developed" means that the kernel fills one-half or more of the capacity of the shell.

§51.2005   Badly misshapen.

"Badly misshapen" means that the kernel is so malformed that the appearance is materially affected.

§51.2006   Rancidity.

"Rancidity" means that the kernel is noticeably rancid to the taste. An oily appearance of the flesh does not necessarily indicate a rancid condition.

§51.2007   Moldy.

"Moldy" means that there is a visible growth of mold either on the outside or the inside of the kernel.

§51.2008   Insect injury.

"Insect injury" means that the insect, frass or web is present inside the nut or the kernel shows definite evidence of insect feeding.

APPLICATION OF STANDARDS

§51.2009   Application of standards.

(a) The grade of a lot of filberts shall be determined on the basis of a composite sample drawn from containers in various locations in the lot. However, any container or group of containers in which the filberts are obviously of a quality, type or size materially different from that in the majority of containers shall be considered a separate lot, and shall be sampled separately.
(b) In grading the sample, each filbert shall be examined for defects of the shell before being cracked for kernel examination. The nut shall be classed as only one defective nut even though it may be defective externally and internally.

§51.2010 Metric conversion table.

Inches:	Millimeters (mm)
62/64	24.6
58/64	23.4
56/64	22.2
49/64	19.4
48/64	19.0
47/64	18.6
45/64	17.9
44/64	17.5
42/64	16.7
35/64	13.9
34/64	13.5

UNITED STATES STANDARDS FOR GRADES OF
SHELLED PECANS [1]
(34 F. R. 9377)
Effective July 15, 1969

AUTHORITY: The provisions of this subpart issued under secs. 203, 60 Stat. 1087, as amended; 1090 as amended; 7 U.S.C. 1622, 1624.

GRADES

§ 51.1430 U.S. No. 1 Halves.

"U.S. No. 1 Halves" consists of pecan half-kernels which meet the following requirements:
(a) For quality:
(1) Well dried;
(2) Fairly well developed;
(3) Fairly uniform in color.
(4) Not darker than "amber" skin color;

(5) Free from damage or serious damage by any cause;
(6) Free from pieces of shell, center wall and foreign material; and,
(7) Comply with tolerances for defects (see   51.1439); and
(b) For size:
(1) Halves are fairly uniform in size;
(2) Halves conform to size classification or count specified; and,
(3) Comply with tolerances for pieces, particles, and dust (see   51.1437).

§ 51.1431 U.S. No. 1 Halves and Pieces.

The requirements for this grade are the same as those for U.S. No. 1 Halves except:
(a) For size:
(1) At least 50 percent, by weight, are half-kernels;
(2) Both halves and pieces will not pass through a $5/16$-inch round opening; and,
(3) Comply with tolerances for undersize. (See Table III.)

§ 51.1432 U.S. No. 1 Pieces.

The requirements for this grade are the same as those for U.S. No. 1 Halves except:
(a) For quality:
(1) No requirement for uniformity of color; and
(b) For size:
(1) No requirement for percentage of half-kernels;
(2) Conform to any size classification or other size description specified; and,
(3) Comply with applicable tolerances for off-size. (See Table III.)

§ 51.1433 U.S. Commercial Halves.

The requirements for this grade are the same as those for U.S. No. 1 Halves except:
(a) For quality:
(1) No requirement for uniformity of color; and,
(2) Increased tolerances for defects (see § 51.1439); and
(b) For size:
(1) No requirement for uniformity of size.

[1] Packing of the product in conformity with the requirements of these standards shall not excuse failure to comply with the provisions of the Federal food, Drug, and Cosmetic Act or with applicable State laws and regulations.

§ 51.1434 U.S. Commercial Halves and Pieces.

The requirements for this grade are the same as those for U.S. No. 1 Halves and Pieces except:
(a) For quality:
(1) No requirement for uniformity of color; and,
(2) Increased tolerances for defects. (See § 51.1439.)

§ 51.1435 U.S. Commercial Pieces.

The requirements for this grade are the same as those for U.S. No. 1 Pieces except for:
(a) Increased tolerances for defects. (See § 51.1439.)

COLOR CLASSIFICATIONS

§ 51.1436 Color classifications.

(a) The skin color of pecan kernels may be described in terms of the color classifications provided in this section. When the color of kernels in a lot generally conforms to the "light" or "light amber" classification, that color classification may be used to describe the lot in connection with the grade.
(1) "Light" means that the kernel is mostly golden color or lighter, with not more than 25 percent of the surface darker than golden, and none of the surface darker than light brown.
(2) "Light amber" means that the kernel has more than 25 percent of its surface light brown, but not more than 25 percent of the surface darker than light brown, and none of the surface darker than medium brown.
(3) "Amber" means that the kernel has more than 25 percent of the surface medium brown, but not more than 25 percent of the surface darker than medium brown, and none of the surface darker than dark brown (very dark-brown or blackish-brown discoloration.).
(4) "Dark amber" means that the kernel has more than 25 percent of the surface dark brown, but not more than 25 percent of the surface darker than dark brown (very dark-brown or blackish-brown discoloration).
(b) U.S. Department of Agriculture kernel color standards, PEC-MC-1, consisting of plastic models of pecan kernels, illustrate the color intensities implied by the terms "golden," "light brown," "medium brown," and "dark brown" referred to in paragraph (a) of this section. These color standards may be examined in the Fruit and Vegetable Division, C&MS, U.S. Department of Agri-

culture, South Building, Washington, D.C. 20250; in any field office of the Fresh Fruit and Vegetable Inspection Service; or upon request of any authorized inspector of such Service. Duplicates of the color standards may be purchased from NASCO, Fort Atkinson, Wis. 53538.

SIZE CLASSIFICATIONS

§ 51.1437 Size classifications for halves.

The size of pecan halves in a lot may be specified in accordance with on the the the size classifications shown in Table I:

TABLE I

Size classifications for halves	Number of halves per pound
Mammoth	250 or less.
Junior mammoth	251–300.
Jumbo	301–350.
Extra large	351–450.
Large	451–550.
Medium	551–650.
Small (topper)	651–750.
Midget	751 or more.

(a) The number of halves per pound shall be based upon the weight of half-kernels after all pieces, particles and dust, shell, center wall, and foreign material have been removed.
(b) In lieu of the size classifications in Table I, the size of pecan halves in a lot may be specified in terms of the number of halves or a range of numbers of halves per pound. For example, "400" or "600-700".
(c) Tolerance for count per pound: In order to allow for variations incident to proper sizing, a tolerance shall be permitted as follows:
(1) When an exact number of halves per pound is specified, the actual count per pound may vary not more than 5 percent from the specified number; and
(2) When any size classification shown in Table I or a range in count per pound is specified, no tolerance shall be allowed for counts outside of the specified range.
(d) *Tolerances for pieces, particles, and dust.* In order to allow for variations incident to proper sizing and handling, not more than 15 percent, by weight, of any lot may consist of pieces, particles, and dust: *Provided,* That not more than one-third of this amount, or 5 percent, shall be allowed for portions less than

one-half of complete half-kernel, including not more than 1 percent for particles and dust.

§ 51.1438 Size classifications for pieces.

The size of pecan pieces in a lot may specified in accordance with one of the size classifications shown in Table II.

TABLE II

Size classification	Maximum diameter (will pass through round opening of following diameter)	Minimum diameter (will not pass through round opening of following diameter)
		Inch
Mammoth pieces ....No limitation		$8/16$
Extra large pieces ....$9/16$ inch		$7/16$
Halves and pieces ....No limitation		$5/16$
Large pieces ....$8/16$ inch		$5/16$
Medium pieces ......$6/16$ inch		$3/16$
Small pieces ....$4/16$ inch		$2/16$
Midget pieces ....$3/16$ inch		$1/16$
Granules ....$2/16$ inch		$1/16$

(a) In lieu of the size classifications in Table II, the size of pieces in a lot may be specified in terms of minumum diameter, or as a range described in terms of minimum and maximum diameters expressed in sixteenths or sixty-fourths of an inch.

(b) Tolerances for size of pieces: In order to allow for variations incident to proper sizing, tolerances are provided for pieces in a lot which fail to meet the requirements of any size specified. The tolerances, by weight, are shown in Table III.

TABLE III

Size classification	Total tolerance for offsize pieces	Tolerance (included in total tolerance) for pieces smaller than	
		$2/16$ inch	$1/16$ inch
	Percent	Percent	Percent
Mammoth pieces	15	1	.....
Extra large pieces	15	1	.....
Halves and pieces	15	1	.....
Large pieces	15	1	.....
Medium pieces	15	2	.....
Small pieces	15	2	.....
Midget pieces	15	2	
Granules	15	5	
Other specified size ..	15	1	

TOLERANCES FOR DEFECTS

§ 51.1439 Tolerances for defects.

In order to allow for variations incident to proper grading and handling in each of the foregoing grades, the following tolerances, by weight, are provided as specified:

(a) U.S. No. 1 Halves, U.S. No. 1 Halves and Pieces, and U.S. No. 1 Pieces grades:

(1) 0.05 percent for shell, center wall, and foreign material;

(2) 3 percent for portions of kernels which are "dark amber" or darker color, or darker than any specified lighter color classification but which are not otherwise defective; and

(3) 3 percent for portions of kernels which fail to meet the remaining requirements of the grade, including therein not more than 0.50 percent for defects causing serious damage: *Provided,* That any unused portion of this tolerance may be applied to increase the tolerance for kernels which are "dark amber" or darker color, or darker than any specified lighter color classification.

(b) U.S. Commercial Halves, U.S. Commercial Halves and Pieces, and U.S. Commercial Pieces grades:

(1) 0.15 percent for shell, center wall, and foreign material;

(2) 25 percent for portions of kernels which are "dark amber" or darker color, or darker thanny specified lighter color classification, but which are not otherwise defective; and,

(3) 8 percent for portions of kernels which fail to meet the remaining requirements of the grade, including therein not more than 1 percent for defects causing serious damage.

APPLICATION OF STANDARDS

§51.1440 Application of standards.

The grade of a lot of shelled pecans shall be determined on the basis of a composite sample drawn at random from containers in various locations in the lot. However, any identifiable container or number of containers in which the pecans are obviously of a quality or size materially different from that in the majority of containers, shall be considered as a separate lot, and shall be sampled and graded separately.

DEFINITIONS

§ 51.1441 Half-kernel.

"Half-kernel" means one of the separated halves of an entire pecan kernel with not more than one-eighth of its original volume missing, exclusive of the portion which formerly connected the two halves of the kernel.

§ 51.1442 Piece.

"Piece" means a portion of a kernel which is less than seven-eighths of a half-kernel, but which will not pass through a round opening two-sixteenths inch in diameter.

§ 51.1443 Particles and dust.

"Particles and dust" means, for all size designations except "midget pieces" and "granules," fragments of kernels which will pass through a round opening two-sixteenths inch in diameter.

§ 51.1444 Well dried.

"Well dried" means that the portion of kernel is firm and crisp, not pliable or leathery.

§ 51.1445 Fairly well developed.

"Fairly will developed" means that the kernel has at least a moderate amount of meat in proportion to its width and length. (See Figure I.)

Figure 1

CROSS SECTION ILLUSTRATION

1. WELL DEVELOPED

Lower limit. Kernels having less meat content than these are not considered well developed.

2. FAIRLY WELL DEVELOPED

Lower limit for U.S. No. 1 grade. Kernels having less meat content than these are not considered fairly well developed and are classed as damaged.

3. POORLY DEVELOPED

Lower limit, damaged but not seriously damaged. Kernels having less meat content than these are considered undeveloped and are classed as seriously damaged.

§ 51.1446 Poorly developed.

"Poorly developed" means that the kernel has small amount of meat in proportion to its width and length. (See Figure I.)

§ 51.1447 Fairly uniform in color.

"Fairly uniform in color" means that 90 percent or more of the kernels in the lot have skin color within the range of one or two color classifications.

§ 51.1448 Fairly uniform in size.

"Fairly uniform in size" means that, in a representative sample of 100 halves, the 10 smallest halves weigh not less than one-half as much as the 10 largest halves.

§ 51.1449 Damage.

"Damage" means any specific defect described in this section; or an equally objectionable variation of any one of these defects, or any other defect, or any combination of defects, which materially detracts from the appearance or the edible or marketing quality of the individual portion of the kernel or of the lot as a whole. The following defects should be considered as damage:

(a) Adhering material from inside the shell when attached to more than one-fourth of the surface on one side of the half-kernel or piece;

(b) Dust or dirt adhering to the kernel when conspicuous;

(c) Kernel which is not well dried;

(d) Kernel which is "dark amber" or darker color;

(e) Kernel having more than one dark kernel spot, or one dark kernel spot more than one-eighth inch in greatest dimension;

(f) Shriveling when the surface of the kernel is very conspicuously wrinkled;

(g) Internal flesh dicoloration of a medium shade of gray or brown extending more than one-fourth the length of the half-kernel or piece, or lesser areas of dark discoloration affecting the appearance to an equal or greater extent; and,

(h) Poorly developed kernel. (See Figure I.)

§ 51.1450 Serious damage.

"Serious damage" means any specific defect described in this section; or an equally objectionable variation of any one of these defects, or any other defect, or any combination of defects, which seriously detracts from the appearance or the edible or marketing quality of the individual portion of kernel or of the lot as a whole. The following defects shall be considered as serious damage:

(a) Any plainly visible mold;

(b) Rancidity when the kernel is distinctly rancid to the taste. Staleness of flavor shall not be classed as rancidity;

(c) Decay affecting any portion of the kernel;

(d) Insects, web, or frass or any distinct evidence of insect feeding on the kernel;

(e) Internal discoloration which is dark gray, dark brown, or black and extends more than one-third the length of the half-kernel or piece;

(f) Adhering material from inside the shell when attached to more than one-half of the surface on one side of the half-kernel or piece;

(g) Dark kernel spots when more than three are on the kernel, or when any dark kernel spot or the aggregate of two or more spots affect an area of more than 10 percent of the surface of the half-kernel or piece;

(h) Dark skin discoloration, darker than "dark brown," when covering more than one-fourth of the surface of the half-kernel or piece; and,

(i) Undeveloped kernel. (See Figure I.)

METRIC CONVERSION TABLE

§ 51.1451 Metric conversion table.

Inches	Millimeters (mm)
$8/16$	12.7
$7/16$	11.1
$6/16$	9.5
$5/16$	7.9
$4/16$	6.4
$3/16$	4.8
$2/16$	3.2
$6/64$	2.4
$5/64$	2.0
$1/16$	1.6

These standards shall become effective on July 15, 1969, and will thereupon supersede the U.S. Standards for Shelled Pecans which have been in effect since October 19, 1952 (7 CFR, § 51.1430–51.1453).

Dated: June 10, 1969.

JOHN E. TROMER,
Acting Deputy Administrator,
Marketing Services.

UNITED STATES STANDARDS FOR GRADES OF
PECANS IN THE SHELL[1]
(32 F.R. 15073)
Effective November 1, 1967

GRADES

Sec.
51.1400 U.S. No. 1.
51.1401 U.S. Commercial.

UNCLASSIFIED

51.1402 Unclassified.

SIZE CLASSIFICATION

51.1403 Size classification.

KERNEL COLOR CLASSIFICATION

51.1404 Kernel color classification.

TOLERANCES

51.1405 Tolerances.

APPLICATION OF STANDARDS

51.1406 Application of standards.

DEFINITIONS

51.1407 Fairly uniform in color.
51.1408 Loose extraneous or foreign material.
51.1409 Well developed.
51.1410 Fairly well developed.
51.1411 Poorly developed.
51.1412 Well cured.
51.1413 Light color.
51.1414 Light amber color.
51.1415 Amber color.
51.1416 Dark amber color.
51.1417 Damage.
51.1418 Serious damage.

AUTHORITY: The provisions of this subpart issued under secs. 203, 205, 60 Stat. 1087, as amended; 1090 as amended; 7 U.S.C. 1622, 1624.

GRADES

§ 51.1400 U.S. No. 1

"U.S. No. 1" consists of pecans in the shell which meet the following requirements:

(a) Free from loose extraneous or foreign material.

(b) Shells are:

(1) Fairly uniform in color; and,

(2) Free from damage by any cause.

(c) Kernels are:

(1) Free from damage by any cause.

(d) Comply with tolerances in　51.1405.

§ 51.1401 U.S. Commercial.

The requirements for this grade are the same as for U.S. No. 1 except for

(a) No requirement for uniformity of color of shells; and,

(b) Increased tolerances for defects (see 51.1405).

UNCLASSIFIED

§ 51.1402 Unclassified.

"Unclassified" consists of pecans in the shell which have not been classified in accordance with either of the foregoing grades. The term "unclassified" is not a grade within the meaning of these standards but is provided as a designation to show that no grade has been applied to the lot.

SIZE CLASSIFICATION

§ 51.1403 Size classification.

Size of pecans may be specified in connection with the grade in accordance with one of the following classifications. To meet the requirements for any one of these classifications, the lot must conform to both the specified number of nuts per pound and the weight of the 10 smallest nuts per 100-nut sample:

Size classification	Number of nuts per pound	Minimum weight of the 10 smallest nuts in a 100-nut sample
Oversize	55 or less	In each classification,
Extra large	56 to 63	the 10 smallest nuts
Large	64 to 77	per 100 *must* weigh at
Medium	78 to 95	least 7 percent of the
Small	96 to 120	total weight of the 100-nut sample.

KERNEL COLOR CLASSIFICATION

§ 51.1404 Kernel color classification.

(a) Color of a lot of pecans having kernels generally lighter than "amber color" may be specified in connection with the U.S. No. 1 grade in terms of one of the classifications as follows:

(1) Light color; or,

(2) Light amber color.

(b) For tolerances see § 51.1405.

TOLERANCES

§ 51.1405 Tolerances.

In order to allow for variations incident to proper grading and handling in each of the foregoing grades, the following tolerances are provided as specified:

(a) *U.S. No. 1*—(1) *For shell defects, by count.* (i) 5 percent for pecans with damaged shells, including therein not more than 2 percent for shells which are seriously damaged.

(2) *For kernel defects, by count.* (i) 12 percent for pecans with kernels which fail to meet the requirements for the grade or for any specified color classifications, including therein not more than 5 percent for kernels which are seriously damaged by any cause.

(ii) In addition, 8 percent for kernels which fail to meet the color requirements for the grade or for any specified color classification, but which are not seriously damaged by dark discoloration of the skin; *Provided,* That these kernels meet the requirements for the grade other than for skin color.

(3) *For loose extraneous or foreign material, by weight.* (i) 0.5 percent (one-half of 1 percent).

(b) *U.S. Commercial*—(1) *For shell defects, by count.* (i) 10 percent for pecans with damaged shells, including therein not more than 3 percent for shells which are seriously damaged.

(2) *For kernel defects, by count.* (i) 30 percent for pecans with kernels which fail to meet the requirements of the U.S. No. 1 grade, including therein not more than 10 percents for pecans with kernels which are seriously damaged: *Provided,* That not more than six-tenths of this amount, or 6 percent, shall be allowed for kernels which are rancid, moldy, decayed or injured by insects.

(3) *For loose extraneous or foreign material, by weight.* (i) 0.5 percent (one-half of 1 percent).

APPLICATION OF STANDARDS

§ 51.1406 Application of standards.

The grade of a lot of pecans shall be determined on the basis of a composite sample drawn at random from containers in various locations in the lot. However, any identifiable containers in which the pecans are obviously of a quality or size materially different from that in the majority of containers, shall be considered as a separate lot, and shall be sampled and graded separately.

DEFINITIONS

§ 51.1407 Fairly uniform in color.

"Fairly uniform in color" means that the shells do not show sufficient variation in color to materially detract from the general appearance of the lot.

§ 51.1498 Loose extraneous or foreign material.

"Loose extraneous or foreign material" means loose hulls, empty broken shells, or any substance other than pecans in the shell or pecan kernels.

§ 51.1409 Well developed.

"Well developed" means that the kernel has a large amount of meat in proportion to its width and length. (See Fig. 1.)

§ 51.1410 Fairly well developed.

"Fairly well developed" means that the kernel has at least a moderate amount of meat in proportions to its width and length. Shriveling and hollowness shall be considered only to the extent that they have reduced the meatiness of the kernel. (See Fig. 1.)

§ 51.1411 Poorly developed.

"Poorly developed" means that the kernels has a small amount of meat in proportion to its width and length. (See Fig. 1.)

§ 51.1412 Well cured.

"Well cured" means that the kernel separates freely from the shell, breaks cleanly when bent, without splintering, shattering, or loosening the skin; and the kernel appears to be in good shipping or storage condition as to moisture content.

§ 51.1413 Light color.

"Light color" means that the skin of the outer surface of the kernel is mostly golden color, or lighter, with not more than 25 percent of the outer surface darker than golden, and none of that 25 percent area darker than light brown.

§ 51.1414 Light amber color.

"Light amber color" means that more than 25 percent of the skin of the outer surface is light brown, with not more than 25 percent of the outer surface darker than light brown, and none of that 25 percent area darker than medium brown.

§ 51.1415 Amber color.

"Amber color" means that more than 25 percent of the skin of the outer surface of the kernel is medium brown, with not more than 25 percent of the outer surface darker than medium brown, and none of that 25 percent area darker than dark brown.

§ 51.1416 Dark amber color.

"Dark amber color" means that more than 25 percent of the skin of the outer surface of the kernel is dark brown, with not more than 25 percent of the outer surface very dark or blackish-brown (dark discoloration).

§ 51.1417 Damage.

"Damage" means any specific defect described in this section; or an equally objectionable variation of any one of these defects, or any other defect, or any combination of defects, which materially detracts from the appearance or the edible or marketing quality of the individual pecan or the general appearance of the pecans in the lot. The following defects shall be considered as damage:

(a) Adhering hull material or dark stains affecting an aggregate of more than 5 percent of the surface of the individual shell;

(b) Split or cracked shells when the shell is spread apart or will spread upon application of slight pressure;

(c) Broken shells when any portion of the shell is missing;

(d) Kernels which are not well cured;

(e) Poorly developed kernels;

(f) Kernels which are dark amber in color;

(g) Kernel spots when more than one dark spot is present on either half of the kernel, or when any such spot is more than one-eighth inch in greatest dimension;

(h) Adhering material from the inside of the shell when firmly attached to more than one-third on the outer surface of the kernels and contrasting in color with the skin of the kernel; and,

(i) Internal flesh discoloration of a medium shade of gray or brown extending more than one-fourth inch lengthwise beneath the center ridge, or an equally objectionable amuount in other portions of the kernel; or lesser areas of dark discoloration affecting the appearance to an equal or greater extent.

§ 51.1418 Serious damage.

"Serious damage" means any specific defect described in this section; or an equally objectionable variation of any one of these defects, or any other defect, or any combination of defects, which seriously detracts from the appearance or the edible or marketing quality of the individual pecan. The following defects shall be considered as serious damage:

(a) Adhering hull material or dark stains affecting an aggregate of more than 20 percent of the surface of the individual shell;

(b) Broken shells when the missing portion of shell is greater in area than a circle one-fourth inch in diameter;

(c) Worm holes when penetrating the shell;

(d) Rancidity when the kernel is distinctly rancid to the taste. Staleness of flavor shall not be classed as rancidity;

(e) Mold, on the surface or inside the kernel, which is plainly visible without magnification;

(f) Decay affecting any portion of the kernel;

(g) Insect injury when the insect, web or frass is present inside the shell, or the kernel shows distinct evidence of insect feeding;

(h) Kernel spots when more than three dark spots are on either half of the kernel, or when any spot or the aggregate of two or more spots on one of the halves of the kernel affects more than 10 percent of the surface;

(i) Dark discoloration of the skin which is darker than dark amber over more than 25 percent of the outer surface of the kernel;

(j) Internal flesh discoloration of a dark shade extending more than one-third the length of the kernel beneath the ridge, or an equally objectionable amount of dark discoloration in other portions of the kernel; and

(k) Undeveloped kernels having practically no food value, or which are blank (complete shell containing no kernel)

The U.S. Standards for Grades of Pecans in the Shell contained in this subpart shall become effective November 1, 1967, and will thereupon supersede the U.S. Standards for Pecans in the Shell which have been in effect since October 1, 1951 (7 CFR 51.1400-51.1416).

Dated: October 27, 1967.

G. R. Grange
Deputy Administrator,
Marketing Services.

Figure 1

CROSS SECTION ILLUSTRATION

1. WELL DEVELOPED

Lower limit. Kernels having less meat content than these are not considered well developed.

2. FAIRLY WELL DEVELOPED

Lower limit for U. S. No. 1 grade. Kernels having less meat content than these are not considered fairly well developed and are classed as damaged.

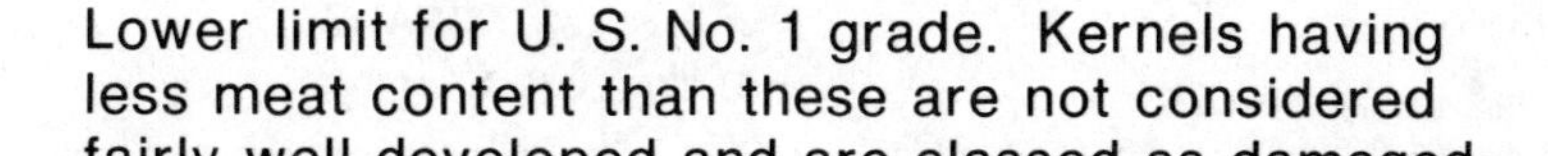

3. POORLY DEVELOPED

Lower limit, damaged but not seriously damaged. Kernels having less meat content than these are considered undeveloped and are classed as seriously damaged.

UNITED STATES STANDARDS FOR
SHELLED WALNUTS (Juglans regia)[1]
Effective January 25, 1959 (23 F.R. 10354)
As Amended September 1, 1968 (22 F.R. 10840)

GENERAL

Sec.
51.2275 Application.
51.2276 Color chart.

GRADES

51.2277 U.S. No. 1.
51.2278 U.S. Commercial.

UNCLASSIFIED

51.2279 Unclassified.

TOLERANCES FOR GRADE DEFECTS

51.2280 Tolerances for grade defects.

COLOR REQUIREMENTS

51.2281 Color classifications.
51.2282 Tolerances for color.
51.2283 Off color.

SIZE REQUIREMENTS

51.2284 Size classifications.
51.2285 Tolerances for size.

APPLICATION OF TOLERANCES

51.2286 Application of tolerances.

DEFINITIONS

51.2287 Well dried.
51.2288 Clean.
51.2289 Shell.
51.8890 Insect injury.
51.8891 Rancidity.
51.8892 Damage.
51.8893 Serious damage.
51.8894 Very serious damage.
51.8895 Half kernel.
51.8896 Three-fourths half kernel.

AUTHORITY: §§ 51.2275 to 51.2296 issued under sec. 205, 60 Stat. 1090, as amended; 7 U.S.C. 1624.

GENERAL

§ 51.2275 Application.

The standards contained in this subpart apply only to walnuts commonly known as English or Persian walnuts (Juglans regia). They do not apply to walnuts commonly known as black walnuts (Juglans nigra).

§ 51.2276 Color chart.

The color chart (USDA Walnut Color Chart) to which reference in made in §§ 51.2281 and 51.2282 illustrates the four shades of walnut skin color listed as color classifications.

(a) *Availability of color chart.* The USDA Walnut Color Chart cited in this subpart has been filed with the original document and is available for inspection in the Office of the Federal Register. The color chart is also available for inspection in the Fruit and Vegetable Division, C&MS, U.S. Department of Agriculture, South Building, Washington, D.C. 20250, in any field office of the Fresh Fruit and Vegetable Inspection Service of the Fruit and Vegetable Division, or upon request of any authorized inspector of such Service. Copies of the color chart may be purchased from Munsell Color Co., Inc., 2441 North Calvert Street, Baltimore, Md. 21218.

GRADES

§ 51 2277 U.S. No. 1

"U.S. No. 1" consists of portions of walnut kernels which are well dried, clean, free from shell, foreign material, insect injury, decay, rancidity, and free from damage caused by shriveling, mold, discoloration of the meat or other means. (See § 51.2280.)

(a) Color shall be specified in connection with this grade in terms of one of the color classifications. (See §§ 51.2276, 51.2281 and 51.2282.)

(b) Size shall be specified in connection with this grade in terms of one of the size classifications. (See §§ 51.2284 and 51.2285.)

§ 51.2278 U.S. Commercial.

"U.S. Commercial" consists of portions of walnut kernels which meet the requirements of U.S. No. 1 grade, except for increased tolerances. (See § 51.2280.)

[1] Packing of the product in conformity with the requirements of these standards shall not excuse failure to comply with the provisions of the Federal Food, Drug and Cosmetic Act or with applicable State laws and regulations.

(a) Color of walnuts in this grade shall be not darker than "amber" classification, and color need not be specified. However, color may be specified in connection with the grade in terms of one of the color classifications. (See §§ 51.2276, 51.2281 and 51.2282.)

(b) Size shall be specified in connection with this grade in terms of one of the size classifications. (See §§ 51.2284 and 51.2285.)

UNCLASSIFIED

§ 51.2279   Unclassified.

"Unclassified" consists of portions of walnut kernels which have not been classified in accordance with either of the foregoing grades. The term "unclassified" is not a grade within the meaning of these standards, but is provided as a designation to show that no grade has been applied to the lot.

TOLERANCES FOR GRADE DEFECTS

§ 51.2280   Tolerances for grade defects.

(a) All percentages shall be calculated on the basis of weight.

(b) In order to allow for variations, other than for color and size, incident to proper grading and handling, tolerances shall be permitted for the respective grades as indicated in Table I:

TABLE I

Grade	Tolerances for grade defects			
	Total defects	Serious damage	Very serious damage	Shell and foreign material
	Percent	*Percent*	*Percent*	*Percent*
U. S. No. 1	5	2 (included in 5 percent total defects).	1 (included in 2 percent serious damage).	0.05 (included in 1 percent very serious damage).
U. S. Commercial	8	4 (included in 8 percent total defects).	2 (included in 4 percent serious damage).	0.05 (included in 2 percent very serious damage).

COLOR REQUIREMENTS

§ 51.2281   Color classifications.

The following classifications are provided to describe the color of any lot: "Extra Light", "Light", "Light Amber" or "Amber". The portions of kernels in the lot shall not be darker than the darkest color permitted in the specified classification as shown on the color chart.

§ 51.2282   Tolerances for color.

(a) All percentages shall be calculated on the basis of weight.

(b) In order to allow for variations incident to proper grading and handling, tolerances shall be permitted for the respective color classifications as indicated in Table II:

TABLE II

Color classification	Tolerances for color			
	Darker than extra light [1]	Darker than light [1]	Darker than light amber [1]	Darker than amber [1]
Extra light	15 percent	2 percent (included in 15 percent darker than extra light).		
Light		15 percent	2 percent (included in 15 percent darker than light).	
Light amber			15 percent	2 percent (included in 15 percent darker than light amber).
Amber				10 percent.

[1] See illustration of this term on color chart.

§ 51.2283   Off color.

The term "off color" is not a color classification, but shall be applied to any lot which fails to meet the requirements of the "Amber" classification.

SIZE REQUIREMENTS

§ 51.2284   Size classification.

The following classifications are provided to describe the size of any lot: "Halves", "Pieces and Halves", "Pieces" or "Small Pieces". The size of portions of kernels in the lot shall conform to the requirements of the specified classification as defined below:

(a) *Halves.* Lot consists of 85 percent or more, by weight, half kernels, and the remainder three-fourths half kernels. (See § 51.2285.)

(b) *Pieces and halves.* Lot consists of 20 percent or more, by weight, half kernels, and the remainder portions of kernels that cannot pass through a sieve with 24/64 inch round openings. When a lot exceeds this minimum requirement, the actual percentage of halves may be specified. (See § 51.2285.)

(c) *Pieces.* Lot consists of portions of kernels that cannot pass through a sieve with 24/64 inch round openings. (See § 51.2285.)

(d) *Small pieces.* Lot consists of portions of kernels that pass through a sieve with 24/64 inch round openings, but that cannot pass through a sieve with 8/64 inch round openings. When desired, the actual size ranges within such size ranges may be specified. (See § 51.2285.)

§ 51.2285   Tolerances for size.

(a) All percentages shall be calculated on the basis of weight.

(b) In order to allow for variations incident to proper sizing and handling, tolerances shall be permitted for the respective size classifications as indicated in Table III:

TABLE III

Size classification	Tolerances for size				
	Smaller than three-fourths halves	Will not pass through 24/64 inch round hole	Pass through 24/64 inch round hole	Pass through 19/64 inch round hole	Pass through 8/64 inch round hole
	Percent	*Percent*	*Percent*	*Percent*	*Percent*
Halves_____	5			1 (included in 5 percent).	
Pieces and halves ¹___			18	3 (included in 18 percent).	1 (included in 3 percent).
Pieces_____			25	5 (included in 25 percent)	1 (included in 5 percent).
Small pieces ²_____		10			2.

¹ No part of any tolerance shall be used to reduce the percentage of halves required or specified in a lot of "pieces and halves".

² The tolerances of 10 percent and 2 percent for "small pieces" classification shall apply, respectively, to any smaller maximum or any larger minimum sizes specified.

APPLICATION OF TOLERANCES

§ 51.2286   Application of tolerances.

The tolerances provided in these standards are on a lot basis, and they shall be applied to a composite sample representative of the lot. However, any container or group of containers in which the walnuts are obviously of a quality materially different from that in the majority of containers shall be considered a separate lot, and shall be sampled separately.

DEFINITIONS

§ 51.2287   Well dried.

"Well dried" means that the portion of kernel is firm and crisp, not pliable or leathery.

§ 51.2288   Clean.

"Clean" means that the appearance of the individual portion of kernel, or of the lot as a whole, is not materially affected by adhering dust, dirt or other foreign material.

§ 51.2289   Shell.

"Shell" means the outer shell and/or the woody partition from between the halves of the kernel, and any fragments of either.

§ 51.2290   Insect injury.

"Insect injury" means that the insect, web, frass or other evidence of insects is present on the portion of kernel.

§ 51.2291   Rancidity.

"Rancidity" means that the portion of kernel is noticeably rancid to the taste. Rancidity should not be confused with a slightly astringent flavor of the pellicle (skin) or with staleness (the stage at which the flavor is flat but not objectionable).

§ 51.2292   Damage.

"Damage" means any defect, other than color, which materially affects the appearance, or the edible or shipping quality of the individual portion of kernel, or of the lot as a whole. Any one of the following defects or any combination of defects the seriousness of which exceeds the maximum allowed for any one defect shall be considered as damage:

(a) Shriveling when more than one-eighth of the portion of kernel is severely shriveled, or a greater area is affected by lesser degrees of shriveling producing an equally objectionable appearance, except that kernels which are thin in cross-section but which are otherwise normally developed shall not be considered as damaged;

(b) Mold when plainly visible;

(c) Discoloration of the meat when more than one-eighth the volume of the portion of kernel is severely discolored, or a greater volume is affected by lesser degrees of discoloration producing an equally objectionable appearance;

(d) Not well dried; and,

(e) Not clean.

§ 51.2293   Serious damage.

"Serious damage" means any defect, other than color, which seriously affects the appearance, or the edible or shipping quality of the individual portion of kernel or of the lot as a whole. Any one of the following defects or any combination of defects the seriousness of which exceeds the maximum allowed for any one defect shall be considered as serious damage:

(a) Shriveling when more than one-fourth of the kernel is severely shriveled, or a greater area is affected by lesser degrees of shriveling producing an equally objectionable appearance;

(b) Mold when plainly visible on more than one-eighth of the surface of the kernel in the aggregate; and,

(c) Discoloration of the meat when more than one-fourth the volume of the portion of kernel is severely discolored, or a greater volume is affected by lesser degrees of discoloration producing an equally objectionable appearance.

§ 51.2294   Very serious damage.

"Very serious damage" means any defect, other than color, which very seriously affects the appearance, or the edible or shipping quality of the individual portion of kernel or of the lot as a whole. Any one of the following defects or any combination of defects the seriousness of which exceeds the maximum allowed for any one defect shall be considered as very serious damage:

(a) Shriveling when more than 50 percent of the portion of kernel is severely shriveled;

(b) Mold when plainly visible on more than one-fourth of the surface of the portion of kernel in the aggregate;

(c) Discoloration of the meat when more than one-half the volume of the portion of kernel is severely discolored;

(d) Insect injury;

(e) Rancidity or decay; and,

(f) Shell, or any foreign material.

§ 51.2295   Half kernel.

"Half kernel" means the separated half of a kernel with not more than one-eighth broken off.

§ 51.2296   Three-fourths half kernel.

"Three-fourths half kernel" means a portion of a half of a kernel which has more than one-eighth but not more than one-fourth broken off.

This printing of these standards incorporates amended Section 51.2276, effective September 1, 1968.

U.S. Standards for Grades of Walnuts (*Juglans regia*) in the Shell, Effective September 12, 1964 As Amended September 1, 1968

GENERAL

§51.2945   Application.

The standards contained in this subpart apply only to walnuts commonly known as English or Persian walnuts (*Juglans regia*). They do not apply to the walnuts commonly known as black walnuts (*Juglans nigra*).

§51.2946   Color chart.

The walnut color chart[2] to which reference is made in §§51.2948, 51.2949, 51.2950, 51.2954 and 51.2963 has been prepared by the United States Department of Agriculture as a part of this subpart.

§51.2947   Method of inspection.

In determining the grade of a lot of walnuts, all of the nuts in the sample first should be graded for size and then examined for external defects. The same nuts then should be cracked and examined for internal defects. The nuts must meet the requirements for both external and internal quality in order to meet a designated grade.

GRADES

§51.2948   U. S. No. 1.

"U. S. No. 1" consists of walnuts in shells which are dry, practically clean, bright and free from splits, injury by discoloration, and free from damage caused by broken shells, perforated shells, adhering hulls or other means. The kernels are well dried, free from decay, dark discoloration, rancidity, and free from damage caused by mold, shriveling, insects or other means. (See §51.2954.)

(a) At least 70 per cent, by count, of the walnuts have kernels which are not darker than "light amber" (see color chart), and which are free from grade defects: *Provided,* That at least four-sevenths of the above amount, or 40 per cent of the walnuts have kernels which are not darker than "light" (see color chart[2]). Higher percentages of nuts with kernels not darker than "light amber" which are free from grade defects and/or higher percentages with kernels not darker than "light" which are free from grade defects, may be specified in accordance with the facts. (See §51.2954.)

(b) Size shall be specified in connection with the grade. (See §51.2952.)

§51.2949   U. S. No. 2.

"U. S. No. 2" consists of walnuts in shells which are dry, practically clean and free from splits, and free from damage caused by broken shells, perforated shells, adhering hulls, discoloration or other means. The kernels are well dried, free from decay, dark discoloration, rancidity, and free from damage caused by mold, shriveling, insects or other means. (See §51.2954.)

(a) At least 60 per cent, by count, of the walnuts have kernels which are not darker than "light amber" (see color chart[2]), and which are free from grade defects. Higher percentages of nuts with kernels not darker than "light amber" which are free from grade defects, and/or percentages with kernels not darker than "light" (see color chart[2]) which are free from grade defects, may be specified in accordance with the facts. (See §51.2954.)

(b) Size shall be specified in connection with the grade. (See §51.2952.)

§51.2950   U. S. No. 3.

"U. S. No. 3" consists of walnuts in shells which are dry, fairly clean, free from splits, and free from damage caused by broken shells, and free from serious damage caused by discoloration, perforated shells, adhering hulls or other means.

---

[1] Source: United States Department of Agriculture, Agricultural Marketing Service.
    Packing of the product in conformity with the requirements of these standards shall not excuse failure to comply with the provisions of the Federal Food, Drug, and Cosmetic Act or with applicable State laws and regulations.
[2] The Walnut color chart has been filed with the original document and is available for inspection in the Office of the Federal Register or in the Fruit and Vegetable Division, United States Department of Agriculture, South Building, Washington 25, D.C. A printed copy of this color chart may be obtained from the Agricultural Marketing Service, United States Department of Agriculture, Washington, D.C.

The kernels are well dried, free from decay, dark discoloration, rancidity, and free from damage caused by mold, shriveling, insects or other means. (See §51.2954.)

(a) There is no requirement in this grade for the percentage of walnuts having kernels which are "light amber" or "light." However, the percentage, by count, of nuts with kernels not darker than "light amber" (see color chart) which are free from grade defects and/or the percentage with kernels not darker than "light" (see color chart) which are free from grade defects, may be specified in accordance with the facts. (See §51.2954.)

(b) Size shall be specified in connection with the grade. (See §51.2952.)

<h2 style="text-align:center">UNCLASSIFIED</h2>

§51.2951   Unclassified.

"Unclassified" consists of walnuts in the shell which have not been classified in accordance with any of the foregoing grades. The term "unclassified" is not a grade within the meaning of these standards but is provided as a designation to show that no grade has been applied to the lot.

<h2 style="text-align:center">SIZE SPECIFICATIONS</h2>

§51.2952   Size specifications.

Size shall be specified in accordance with the facts in terms of one of the following classifications:

(a) *Mammoth size.* Mammoth size means walnuts of which not over 12 per cent, by count, pass through a round opening $^{96}/_{64}$ inches in diameter;

(b) *Jumbo size.* Jumbo size means walnuts of which not over 12 per cent, by count, pass through a round opening $^{80}/_{64}$ inches in diameter;

(c) *Large size.* Large size means walnuts of which not over 12 per cent, by count, pass through a round opening $^{77}/_{64}$ inches in diameter; except that for walnuts of the Eureka variety and type, such limiting dimension as to diameter shall be $^{76}/_{64}$ inches;

(d) *Medium size.* Medium size means walnuts of which at least 88 per cent, by count, pass through a round opening $^{77}/_{64}$ inches in diameter, and of which not over 12 per cent, by count, pass through a round opening $^{73}/_{64}$ inches in diameter;

(e) *Standard size.* Standard size means walnuts of which not over 12 per cent, by count, pass through a round opening $^{73}/_{64}$ inches in diameter;

(f) *Baby size.* Baby size means walnuts of which at least 88 per cent, by count, pass through a round opening $^{74}/_{64}$ inches in diameter, and of which not over 10 per cent, by count, pass through a round opening $^{60}/_{64}$ inch in diameter; and,

(g) *Minimum diameter, or minimum and maximum diameter.* In lieu of one of the foregoing classifications, size of walnuts may be specified in terms of minimum diameter, or minimum and maximum diameter: *Provided,* That not more than 12 per cent, by count, pass through a round hole of the specified minimum diameter, and at least 88 per cent, by count, pass through a round hole of any specified maximum diameter.

<h2 style="text-align:center">VARIETY OR TYPE SPECIFICATIONS</h2>

§51.2953   Variety or type specifications.

The variety of type of any lot of walnuts in the shell may be specified in accordance with the facts as follows:

(a) If the lot is of one named variety, that variety name may be specified, *Provided,* That not over 10 per cent, by count, of the walnuts in the lot are of another variety or type than that specified; and,

(b) If the lot is a mixture of two or more distinct varieties or types it may be specified as "Mixed Varieties."

<h2 style="text-align:center">TOLERANCES FOR GRADE DEFECTS</h2>

§51.2954   Tolerances for grade defects.

In order to allow for variations incident to proper grading and handling, the following tolerances shall be permitted for nuts which fail to meet the requirements of the respective grades as indicated. Terms in quotation marks refer to color classification illustrated on the color chart.

§51.2955   Application of tolerances.

The tolerances provided in these standards are on a lot basis, and they shall be applied to a composite sample representative of the lot. However, any identifiable container or group of containers in which the walnuts are obviously of a quality materially different from that in the majority of the containers shall be considered as a separate lot, and shall be sampled separately.

Grade	External (shell) defects	Internal (kernel) defects	Color of kernel
U.S. No. 1	10 pct. by count for splits. 5 pct, by count, for other shell defects, including not more than 3 pct seriously damaged.	10-pct total by count, including not more than 6 pct which are damaged by mold or insects or seriously damaged by other means, of which not more than ⅝ or 5 pct may be damaged by insects, but no part of any tolerance shall be allowed for walnuts containing live insects.	No tolerance to reduce the required 70 pct of "light amber" kernels or the required 40 pct of "light" kernels or any larger percentage of "light amber" or "light" kernels specified.
U.S. No. 2	10 pct, by count, for splits. 10 pct, by count, for other shell defects, including not more than 5 pct serious damage by adhering hulls.	15 pct total, by count, including not more than 8 pct which are damaged by mold or insects or seriously damaged by other means, of which not more than ⅝ or 5 pct may be damaged by insects, but no part of any tolerance shall be allowed for walnuts containing live insects.	No tolerance to reduce the required 60 pct or any specified larger percentage of "light amber" kernels, or any specified percentage of "light" kernels.
U.S. No. 3	Same as above tolerance for U.S. No. 2.	Same as above tolerance for U.S. No. 2.	No tolerance to reduce any percentage of "light amber" or "light" kernel specified.

DEFINITIONS

§51.2956   Practically clean.

"Practically clean" means that, from the viewpoint of general appearance, the walnuts are practically free from adhering dirt or other foreign matter, and that individual walnuts are not damaged by such means. A slightly chalky deposit on the shell is characteristic of many bleached nuts and shall not be considered as dirt or foreign matter.

§51.2957   Bright.

"Bright" means a fairly light, attractive appearance. A slight chalky deposit on the shell shall not be considered as affecting brightness.

§51.2958   Splits.

"Splits" means walnuts with the seam opened completely around the nut so that the two halves of the shell are held together only by the kernel.

§51.2959   Injury by discoloration.

"Injury by discoloration" means that the color of the affected portion of the shell objectionably contrasts with the color of the rest of the shell of the individual nut.

§51.2960   Damage.

"Damage" means any specific defect mentioned in this section; or an equally objectionable variation of any one of these defects, any other defect, or any combination of defects which materially detracts from the appearance or the edible or shipping quality of the individual walnut or the lot as a whole. The following specific defects shall be considered as damage:

(a) Broken shells when the area from which a portion of the shell is missing is greater than the area of a circle one-fourth inch in diameter; or when the two halves of the shell have become completely broken apart and separated from each other;

(b) Perforated shells when the area affected aggregates more than that of a circle one-fourth inch in diameter. The term "perforated shells" means imperfectly developed areas on the shell resembling abrasions and usually including small holes penetrating the shell wall;

(c) Adhering hulls when affecting more than 5 per cent of the shell surface;

(d) Discoloration (or stain) which covers, in the aggregate, one-fifth or more of the surface of the shell of an individual nut, and which is brown, reddish brown, gray, or other color in pronounced contrast with the color of the rest of the shell or the majority of shells in the lot, or darker discoloration covering a smaller area if the appearance is equally objectionable;

(e) Mold when attached to the kernel and conspicuous; or when inconspicuous white or gray mold affects an aggregate area larger than one square centimeter or one-eighth of the entire surface of the kernel, whichever is the lesser area;

(f) Shriveling when more than 5 per cent of the surface of the kernel, including both halves, is severely shriveled, or a greater area is affected by lesser degrees of shriveling producing an equally objectionable appearance. Kernels which are thin in cross section but which are otherwise normally developed shall not be considered as damaged; and,

(g) Insects when an insect or insect fragment, web or frass is present inside the shell, or the kernel shows distinct evidence of insect feeding.

§51.2961   Well dried.

"Well dried" means that the kernel is firm and crisp, not pliable or leathery.

§51.2962   Decay.

"Decay" means that any portion of the kernel is decomposed.

§51.2963   Dark discoloration.

"Dark discoloration" means that the color of the skin of the kernel is darker than "amber." (See Color Chart.)

§51.2964   Rancidity.

"Rancidity" means the stage of deterioration in which the kernel has developed a rancid flavor. Rancidity should not be confused with a slightly astringent flavor of the pellicle (skin) or with staleness, the stage at which the flavor is flat but not distasteful.

§51.2965   Fairly clean.

"Fairly clean" means that, from the viewpoint of general appearance, the lot is not seriously damaged by adhering dirt or other foreign matter, and that individual walnuts are not coated or caked with dirt or foreign matter. Both the amount of surface affected and the color of the dirt shall be taken into consideration.

§51.2966   Serious damage.

"Serious damage" means any specific defect mentioned in this section; or an equally objectionable variation of any one of these defects, any other defect, or any combination of defects which seriously detracts from the appearance or the edible or shipping quality of the walnut. The following specific defects shall be considered as serious damage;

(a) Discoloration (or stain) which covers, in the aggregate, one-third or more of the surface of the shell of an individual nut and which is brown, reddish brown, gray, or other color in pronounced contrast with the color of the rest of the shell or the majority of shells in the lot, or darker discoloration covering a smaller area if the appearance is equally objectionable;

(b) Perforated shells when the area affected aggregates more than that of a circle three-eighths of an inch in diameter. The term "perforated shells" means imperfectly developed areas on the shell resembling abrasions and usually including small holes penetrating the shell wall;

(c) Adhering hulls when affecting more than one-eighth of the shell surface in the aggregate;

(d) Shriveling when both halves of the kernel are affected by severe shriveling over an area totaling more than one-eighth of the surface; or when both halves are affected over a greater area by lesser degrees of shriveling producing an equally objectionable appearance. When one of the halves of the kernel shows no shriveling, the kernel shall not be considered seriously damaged unless the other half shows shriveling to the extent that over 50 per cent of its surface is severely shriveled, or a greater area is affected by lesser degrees of shriveling producing an equally objectionable appearance. Kernels which are thin in cross section, but which are otherwise normally developed shall not be considered as damaged;

(e) Rancidity or decay; and,

(f) Uncured kernels which are wet, rubbery and "green."

English/Metric Equivalents

LONG MEASURES

Inches	Centimeters	Feet	Meters	Miles	Kilometers
1	2.54	1	0.3048	1	1.6093
2	5.08	2	0.6096	2	3.2186
3	7.62	3	0.9144	3	4.8279
4	10.16	4	1.2192	4	6.4372
5	12.70	5	1.5240	5	8.0465
6	15.24	6	1.8288	6	9.6558
7	17.78	7	2.1336	7	11.2651
8	20.32	8	2.4384	8	12.8744
9	22.86	9	2.7433	9	14.4833
10	25.40	10	2.0480	10	16.0936
11	27.94	11	3.3528	11	17.7023
12	30.48	12	3.6575	12	19.3116
24	60.96	14	4.2672	13	20.9209
36	91.44	15	4.5720	14	22.5300
48	121.92	20	6.096	15	24.1395
60	152.40	30	9.444	16	25.7488
		40	12.192	17	27.3581
		50	15.240	18	28.9674
		60	18.288	19	30.5767
		70	21.336	20	32.1850
		80	24.384	30	48.2790
		90	27.432	40	64.3720
		100	30.480	50	80.4650
		200	60.960	100	160.9300
		500	152.400		
		1000	304.800		

LIQUID MEASURES

Quarts	Liters	Gallons	Liters
1/2	0.47	1	3.76
1	0.94	2	7.52
2	1.88	3	11.28
3	2.82	4	15.04
4	3.76	5	18.80
5	4.70	6	22.56
6	5.64	7	26.32
7	6.58	8	30.08
8	7.52	9	33.84
9	8.46	10	37.60
10	9.40	20	75.20
11	10.34	30	112.80
12	11.28	40	150.40
24	22.56	50	188.00
36	33.84	100	376.00
48	45.12	500	1880.00
60	56.40	1000	3760.00

WEIGHTS

Ounces	Grams	Pounds	Kilograms
1	28.37	1	0.453
2	56.74	2	0.907
3	85.11	3	1.377
4	113.48	4	1.816
5	141.85	5	2.270
6	170.22	6	2.724
7	198.59	7	3.178
8	226.96	8	3.632
9	255.33	9	4.086
10	283.70	10	4.538
11	312.07	11	4.994
12	340.44	12	5.448
13	368.81	13	5.902
14	397.18	14	6.356
15	425.55	15	6.810
16	453.92	16	7.264
		17	7.718
		18	8.172
		19	8.626
		20	9.078
		40	18.16
		60	27.24
		80	36.32
		100	45.30
		200	90.78
		300	135.90
		400	181.60
		500	226.50
		1000	453.00
		2000	907.80

SQUARE MEASURES

Acres	Hectares
1	0.4047
2	0.8094
3	1.2141
4	1.6188
5	2.0235
6	2.4282
7	2.8329
8	3.2376
9	3.6423
10	4.0470
11	4.4517
12	4.8564
13	5.2611
14	5.6658
15	6.0705
20	8.0940
30	12.1410
40	16.1880
50	20.2350
100	40.470

SMALL MEASURES

Utensil	Capacity (ml)
1 cup	236.6
½ cup	118.3
⅓ cup	78.9
¼ cup	59.2
1 tablespoon	14.79
½ tablespoon	7.39
1 teaspoon	4.93
½ teaspoon	2.46
¼ teaspoon	1.23

MISCELLANEOUS CONVERSIONS

Temperature Conversion Formulas:
  °F equals ⁹⁄₅ (T °C plus 32)
  °C equals ⁵⁄₉ (T °F minus 32)

1 milligram	0.001 gram
1 centigram	0.01 gram; 0.0035 ounce
1 gram	0.035 ounce; 15.432 grain
1 hectogram	100 grams
1 kilogram	1000 grams; 2.205 pound
1 metric ton	0.98421 English ton
1 milliliter	0.001 liter; 1 cubic centimeter; 0.034 ounce
1 centiliter	0.01 liter; 100 cubic centimeter; 0.1057 liquid quart
1 liter	1000 cubic centimeters; 908 dry quart; 1.057
1 hectoliter	100 liters; 2.838 bushel
1 kiloliter	1000 liters; 1057 quart
1 millimeter	0.001 meter
1 centimeter	0.01 meter; 3.937 inch
1 meter	39.37 inch; 3.27 feet; 1.09 yards
1 hectometer	100 meters
1 kilometer	1000 meters; 3270 feet; 0.62127 mile
1 hectare	2.47 acres

Index

Other AVI Books

CHOCOLATE, COCOA AND CONFECTIONERY:
SCIENCE AND TECHNOLOGY   *Minifie*

COCONUTS, 2nd Edition
Woodroof

COOKIE AND CRACKER TECHNOLOGY
2nd Edition   *Matz and Matz*

FOOD AND THE CONSUMER
Kramer

FOOD COLORIMETRY: THEORY AND APPLICATIONS
Francis and Clydesdale

FOOD PRODUCTS FORMULARY
Vol. 1   *Tressler and Woodroof*

FOOD SCIENCE
3rd Edition   *Potter*

HANDBOOK OF PACKAGE MATERIALS
Sacharow

MODERN PASTRY CHEF
Vol. 2   *Sultan*

PACKAGING REGULATIONS
Sacharow

PEANUTS: PRODUCTION, PROCESSING PRODUCTS
2nd Edition   *Woodroof*

RHEOLOGY AND TEXTURE IN FOOD QUALITY
deMan, Voisey, Rasper and Stanley

SNACK FOOD TECHNOLOGY
Matz

SOURCE BOOK FOR FOOD SCIENTISTS
Ockerman

SUGAR CHEMISTRY
Shallenberger and Birch

SYMPOSIUM: SWEETENERS
Inglett

TWENTY YEARS OF CONFECTIONERY AND CHOCOLATE PROGRESS
Gress Pratt